Project Management

[3, 7, 8, 13]

The Managerial Process

Fourth Edition

About the Authors

Clifford F. Gray

CLIFFORD F. GRAY is professor emeritus of management at the College of Business, Oregon State University. He continues to teach undergraduate and graduate project management courses overseas and in the United States; he has personally taught more than 100 executive development seminars and workshops. His research and consulting interests have been divided equally between operations management and project management; he has published numerous articles in these areas, plus a text on project management. He has also conducted research with colleagues in the International Project Management Association. Cliff has been a member of the Project Management Institute since 1976 and was one of the founders of the Portland, Oregon, chapter. He was a visiting professor at Kasetsart University in Bangkok, Thailand in 2005. He has been the president of Project Management International, Inc. (a training and consulting firm specializing in project management) since 1977. He received his B.A. in economics and management from Millikin University, M.B.A. from Indiana University, and doctorate in operations management from the College of Business, University of Oregon.

Erik W. Larson

ERIK W. LARSON is professor of project management in the department of management, marketing, and international business at the College of Business, Oregon State University. He teaches executive, graduate, and undergraduate courses on project management, organizational behavior, and leadership. His research and consulting activities focus on project management. He has published numerous articles on matrix management, product development, and project partnering. He has been a member of the Portland, Oregon, chapter of the Project Management Institute since 1984. In 1995 he worked as a Fulbright scholar with faculty at the Krakow Academy of Economics on modernizing Polish business education. In 2005 he was a visiting professor at Chulalongkorn University in Bangkok, Thailand. He received a B.A. in psychology from Claremont McKenna College and a Ph.D. in management from State University of New York at Buffalo. He is a certified project management professional (PMP).

Gautam V. Desai

GAUTAM V. DESAI is a professor of project management at S. P. Jain Institute of Management and Research, Mumbai, one of the top business schools in India. He has had a brilliant academic record and has Fellowship from the University of Illinois, Urbana. He has had extensive industrial experience of over 40 years in general management and project management. His project management experience covers practically all phases of managing a project—from conceptualization, feasibility studies and project financing to engineering design, procurement and project construction. He has published a number of articles and cases on project management in several Indian magazines.

SPECIAL INDIAN EDITION

Project Management

The Managerial Process

Fourth Edition

Clifford F. Gray
Oregon State University

Erik W. Larson
Oregon State University

Gautam V. Desai
S. P. Jain Institute of Management and Research, Mumbai

goldplating: Attempting to deliver a high grade product than the customer needs.

"better- is worse than good enough"

"exceeding scope"

Functional

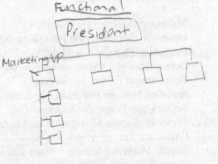

Projectized

Matrix

Tata McGraw Hill Education Private Limited

NEW DELHI

McGraw-Hill Offices
New Delhi   New York   St Louis   San Francisco   Auckland   Bogotá   Caracas
Kuala Lumpur   Lisbon   London   Madrid   Mexico City   Milan   Montreal
San Juan   Santiago   Singapore   Sydney   Tokyo   Toronto

 **Tata McGraw-Hill**

Project Management, 4/e (SIE)

Indian Adaptation done by arrangement with The McGraw-Hill Companies, Inc., New York

Sales Territories: India, Pakistan, Nepal, Bangladesh, Sri Lanka and Bhutan

First reprint 2010
RAZYCRYZRBLLC

Tata McGraw Hill Edition 2010

ISBN (13): 978-0-07-070085-7
ISBN (10): 0-07-070085-0

Managing Director: *Ajay Shukla*
Head—Higher Education Publishing & Marketing: *Vibha Mahajan*
Publishing Manager—B&E/HSSL: *Tapas K Maji*
Deputy Manager—Sponsoring *Surabhi Khare*
Development Editor: *Shalini Negi*
Assistant Manager (Editorial Services): *Anubha Srivastava*
Senior Copy Editor: *Sneha Kumari*
Senior Production Manager: *Manohar Lal*
Production Executive: *Atul Gupta*
Deputy Marketing Manager: *Vijay S Jagannathan*
Senior Product Specialist: *Daisy Sachdeva*
General Manager—Production: *Rajender P Ghansela*
Assistant General Manager—Production: *B L Dogra*

Published by the Tata McGraw Hill Education Private Limited, 7 West Patel Nagar, New Delhi 110 008, typeset at The Composers, 260, C.A. Apt., Paschim Vihar, New Delhi 110 063 and printed at Krishna Offset, 10/122, Vishnu Gali, Vishwas Nagar, Delhi 110 032

Cover Design: K Anoop

Cover Printer: Rashtriya Printers

The McGraw·Hill Companies

To Mary, Kevin, and Robert

C.F.G.

To Ann, Mary, Rachel, and Victoria

E.W.L.

To Pauravi, Gauravi, Priyadarshi, and Shambhavi

G.V.D.

Preface

Our motivation for writing this text was to provide students with a holistic, integrative view of project management. A holistic view focuses on how projects contribute to the strategic goals of the organization. The linkages for integration include the process of selecting projects that best support the strategy of a particular organization and that in turn can be supported by the technical and managerial processes made available by the organization to bring projects to completion. The goals for prospective project managers are to understand the role of a project in their organizations and to master the project management tools, techniques, and interpersonal skills necessary to orchestrate projects from start to finish.

The role of projects in organizations is receiving increasing attention. Projects are the major tool for implementing and achieving the strategic goals of the organization. In the face of intense, worldwide competition, many organizations have reorganized around a philosophy of innovation, renewal, and organizational learning to survive. This philosophy suggests an organization that is flexible and project driven. Project management has developed to the point where it is a professional discipline having its own body of knowledge and skills. Today it is nearly impossible to imagine anyone at any level in the organization who would not benefit from some degree of expertise in the process of managing projects.

Audience

This text is written for a wide audience. It covers concepts and skills that are used by managers to propose, plan, secure resources, budget, and lead project teams to successful completions of their projects. The text should prove useful to students and prospective project managers in helping them understand why organizations have developed a formal project management process to gain a competitive advantage. Readers will find the concepts and techniques discussed in enough detail to be immediately useful in new-project situations. Practicing project managers will find the text to be a valuable guide and reference when dealing with typical problems that arise in the course of a project. Managers will also find the text useful in understanding the role of projects in the missions of their organizations. Analysts will find the text useful in helping to explain the data needed for project implementation as well as the operations of inherited or purchased software. Members of the Project Management Institute will find the text is well structured to meet the needs of those wishing to prepare for PMP® (Project Management Professional) or CAPM® (Certified Associate in Project Management) certification exams. The text has in-depth coverage of the most critical topics found in PMI®'s *Project Management Body of Knowledge* (PMBOK® GUIDE, Fourth Edition). People at all levels in the organization assigned to work on projects will find the text useful not only in providing them with a rationale for the use of project management tools and techniques but also because of the insights they will gain on how to enhance their contributions to project success.

Our emphasis is not only on how the management process works, but more importantly, on *why* it works. The concepts, principles, and techniques are universally applicable. That is, the text does not specialize by industry type or project scope. Instead, the text is written for the individual who will be required to manage a variety of projects in a variety of different organizational settings. In the case of some small projects, a few of the steps of the techniques can be omitted, but the conceptual framework applies to all organizations in which projects are important to survival. The approach can be used in pure project organizations such as construction, research organizations, and engineering consultancy firms. At the same time, this approach will benefit organizations that carry out many small projects while the daily effort of delivering products or services continues.

Content

In this latest edition of the book, we have responded to feedback received from both students and teachers, which is deeply appreciated. As a result of the this feedback, the following changes have been made to the fourth edition:

- Expanded discussions of managing virtual teams, communication plans, critical chain project management, phase gating, balanced scorecard, and risk assessment.
- Revised Chapter 12 to focus on the important trend toward outsourcing project work. Chapters 3, 4, 5, and 7 have been restructured and updated. Chapter 8 now includes both resource and cost scheduling and concludes with the establishment of a time-phased baseline budget. Chapter 16 has been revised to focus on project oversight—methods organizations use to improve their project management systems.
- New student exercises and cases have been added to most chapters. Several computer exercises have been revised.
- The "Snapshot from Practice" boxes feature a number of new examples of project management in action as well as new research highlights that continue to promote practical application of project management.

Overall the text addresses the major questions and issues the authors have encountered over their 60 combined years of teaching project management and consulting with practicing project managers in domestic and foreign environments. The following questions represent the issues and problems practicing project managers find consuming most of their effort: What is the strategic role of projects in contemporary organizations? How are projects prioritized? What organizational and managerial styles will improve chances of project success? How do project managers orchestrate the complex network of relationships involving vendors, subcontractors, project team members, senior management, functional managers, and customers that affect project success? What factors contribute to the development of a high-performance project team? What project management system can be set up to gain some measure of control? How do managers prepare for a new international project in a foreign culture? How does one pursue a career in project management?

Project managers must deal with all these concerns to be effective. All of these issues and problems represent linkages to an integrative project management view. The chapter content of the text has been placed within an overall framework that integrates these topics in a holistic manner. Cases and snapshots are included from the experiences of practicing managers.

One important feature we introduced for this special Indian edition is case studies with Indian socio-economic, business and industrial conditions as a backdrop. We hope that the eleven additional cases, based on Indian industrial and social background introduced in this edition, would be of some help to the Indian reader to relate the learning from the book on a more personal level and apply it for the job in hand.

Another important feature we have introduced in this special Indian edition is the appendices integrating the subject topics with the way they have been treated in the PMBOK® GUIDE, Fourth Edition. An important group of Indian students of project management also looks forward to securing Project

Management Professional (PMP®) certification from the Project Management Institution, U.S.A. (PMI). In India also, the PMI membership has shown a very significant growth in the past decade—India has the third largest PMI membership (after the United States and Canada). An increasing number of students are looking for learning material for the purpose. It was felt that a single resource book should also cater to the need of these aspirants of PMP certification and hence this approach of adding appendices for integration.

The international edition of the book covers project management subjects holistically, comprehensively and in a step-wise guiding mode with a view that a project management professional can apply that knowledge in his work. On the other hand, the PMBOK® GUIDE, Fourth Edition takes a system approach to the subject and classifies good project management' practices into distinct and discrete 42 project management processes, each with the necessary inputs or information inflows, the tools and techniques for processing them, and creating outputs useful for project management work. Thinking that an integration of the theoretical concepts with the framework presented in PMBOK® GUIDE, Fourth Edition would add considerable value to this special Indian adaptation, we have added eleven appendices to the book. These appendices, attached to different chapters, include the approach used in PMBOK® GUIDE, Fourth Edition for treating the subject matter covered by those relevant chapters. Also, student can visit the book's website (www.mhhe.com/sie-gray) to have access to a wealth of resources on these appendices, such as Power Point slides, multiple choice questions and two additional Indian cases.

The appendices and cases added in this Special Indian Edition (SIE) are listed separately after this preface.

The future for project managers appears to be promising. Careers will be determined by success in managing projects.

Clifford F. Gray

Erik W. Larson

Gautam V. Desai

Acknowledgments

Clifford F. Gray and Erik W. Larson

We want first to acknowledge with special thanks and appreciation the contribution of Diane Parente–who prepared the SimProject extended case in the appendix. This case consists of a series of exercises tied to the chapters of this book that coordinate with and make use of SimProject, a project management simulation developed by Diane and her colleague at Penn State–Erie, Jeffrey Pinto. SimProject adds a hands-on, experiential dimension to this course.

In addition, we would like to thank Ed Blevins, DeVry University–Irving, for updating the Test Bank; Charlie Cook, University of West Alabama, for creating PowerPoint slides; and Julie Mehra for accuracy checking the text and Instructor's Resource Manual content.

Next, it is important to note that the text includes contributions from numerous students, colleagues, friends, and managers gleaned from professional conversations. We want them to know we sincerely appreciate their counsel and suggestions. Almost every exercise, case, and example in the text is drawn from a real-world project. Special thanks to managers who graciously shared their current project as ideas for exercises, subjects for cases, and examples for the text. Shlomo Cohen, John A. Drexler, Jim Moran, John Sloan, Pat Taylor, and John Wold, whose work is printed, are gratefully acknowledged. Special gratitude is due Robert Breitbarth of Interact Management, who shared invaluable insights on prioritizing projects. University students and managers deserve special accolades for identifying problems with earlier drafts of the text and exercises.

We are indebted to the reviewers of the first and second editions who shared our commitment to elevating the instruction of project management. The reviewers include Paul S. Allen, Rice University; Denis F. Cioffi, George Washington University; Joseph D. DeVoss, DeVry University; Edward J. Glantz, Pennsylvania State University; Michael Godfrey, University of Wisconsin–Oshkosh; Robert Key, University of Phoenix; Dennis Krumwiede, Idaho State University; Nicholas C. Petruzzi, University of Illinois– Urbana/Champaign; William R. Sherrard, San Diego State University; S. Narayan Bodapati, Southern Illinois University at Edwardsville; Warren J. Boe, University of Iowa; Burton Dean, San Jose State University; Kwasi Amoako-Gyampah, University of North Carolina– Greensboro; Owen P. Hall, Pepperdine University; Bruce C. Hartman, University of Arizona; Richard Irving, York University; Robert T. Jones, DePaul University; Richard L. Luebbe, Miami University of Ohio; William Moylan, Lawrence Technological College of Business; Edward Pascal, University of Ottawa; James H. Patterson, Indiana University; Art Rogers, City University; Christy Strbiak, U.S. Air Force Academy; David A. Vaughan, City University; and Ronald W. Witzel, Keller Graduate School of Management.

In the fourth edition we continue to commit to improving the text content and improving instruction of project management. We are grateful to those reviewers who provided helpful critiques and insights on the third edition, which helped us prepare this revision. The reviewers for the fourth edition include Nabil Bedewi, Georgetown University; Scott Bailey, Troy University; Michael Ensby, Clarkson University; Eldon Larsen, Marshall University; Steve Machon, DeVry University–Tinley Park; William Matthews, William Patterson University; Erin Sims, DeVry University– Pomona; Kenneth Solheim, DeVry University–Federal

Way; and Oya Tukel, Cleveland State University. We thank you for your many thoughtful suggestions and for making our book better. Of course we accept responsibility for the final version of the text.

In addition, we would like to thank our colleagues in the College of Business at Oregon State University for their support and help in completing this project. In particular, we recognize Mark Pagell, Prem Mathew, and Ping-Hung Hsieh for their helpful advice and suggestions. We also wish to thank the many students who helped us at different stages of this project, most notably Neil Young, Rebecca Keepers, Katherine Knox, and Amanda Bosworth. Mary Gray deserves special credit for editing and working under tight deadlines on earlier editions. Special thanks go to Pinyarat Sirisomboonsuk for her help in preparing this edition.

Finally, we want to extend our thanks to all the people at McGraw-Hill/Irwin for their efforts and support. First, we would like to thank Scott Isenberg for continuing to champion and provide editorial direction and guidance through all four editions of the book, and Cynthia Douglas, who took over management of the book's development from Wanda Zeman for the fourth edition. And we would also like to thank Jim Labeots, Gina Hangos, Jeremy Cheshareck, Jillian Lindner, Brian Nacik, and Elizabeth Mavetz for managing the final production, design, supplement, and media phases of the fourth edition.

Gautam V. Desai

I wish to express with deep gratitude my appreciation to the S.P. Jain Institute of Management and Research for providing me with the opportunity of teaching project management and for the ambience of free inquiry and knowledge promotion which pervades the institution. I am especially thankful to the Dean Dr. Manesh L. Shrikant and the Director Dr. Sesha Aiyer for taking personal interest in my work and giving encouragement. Among other senior professors and colleagues, who extended valuable support over the years, I am especially thankful to Prof. S.D. Kshirsagar, Prof. Suresh Mony, Prof. Dr. Tapan Bagchi and Prof. Ajay Parasrampuria.

I am also thankful to The ICFAI University Press for publishing a number of my cases in their prestigious magazine, 'Projects and Profits'.

I also thank my wife Pauravi for her active collaboration by reviewing and discussing the cases while I was writing them and making valuable suggestions. I am also thankful to my children Gauravi, Priyadarshi and Shambhavi for their encouragement and support all along.

Along with the publishers, I acknowledge the following reviewers for their invaluable feedback without which this book would have not come out in its present shape:

Rajeev Mishra, Xavier Labour Relations Institute, Jamshedpur
Bodhibrata Nag, Indian Institute of Management Calcutta, Kolkata
Vidhu Shekhar Jha, Goa Institute of Management, Goa
Sunil Sharma, Faculty of Management Studies, University of Delhi, Delhi
Nitin Seth, Indian Institute of Foreign Trade, New Delhi

In the end, I sincerely thank all the people at Tata McGraw-Hill for their efforts and support and I would like to make here a special mention of Ms Surabhi Khare and Mr Tapas Maji for their very helpful and patient coordination without which this work would not have been possible.

Note to Student

You will find the content of this text highly practical, relevant, and current. The concepts discussed are relatively simple and intuitive. As you study each chapter we suggest you try to grasp not only how things work, but why things work. You are encouraged to use the text as a handbook as you move through the three levels of competency:

I know.

I can do.

I can adapt to new situations.

Project management is both people and technical oriented. Project management involves understanding the cause-effect relationships and interactions among the sociotechnical dimensions of projects. Improved competency in these dimensions will greatly enhance your competitive edge as a project manager.

The field of project management is growing in importance and at an exponential rate. It is nearly impossible to imagine a future management career that does not include management of projects. Résumés of managers will soon be primarily a description of the individual's participation in and contributions to projects.

Good luck on your journey through the text and on your future projects.

Brief Contents

Contents

List of Special Appendices In this SIE
(for integration with PMBOK® Guide, Fourth Edition)

List of Indian Cases in this SIE

CHAPTER 1

Modern Project Management

All of mankind's greatest accomplishments—from building the great pyramids to discovering a cure for polio to putting a man on the moon—began as a project.

This is a good time to be reading a book about project management. Business leaders and experts have proclaimed that project management is a strategic imperative. Project management provides people with a powerful set of tools that improves their ability to plan, implement, and manage activities to accomplish specific organizational objectives. But project management is more than just a set of tools; it is a results-oriented management style that places a premium on building collaborative relationships among a diverse cast of characters. Exciting opportunities await people skilled in project management.

The project approach has long been the style of doing business in the construction industry, U.S. Department of Defense contracts, and Hollywood as well as at big consulting firms. Now project management has spread to all avenues of work. Today, project teams carry out everything from port expansions to hospital restructuring to upgrading information systems. Automakers such as Toyota, Nissan, and BMW credit their ability to capture a significant share of the auto market to the use of project management teams, which quickly develop new cars that incorporate the latest automotive technology. The impact of project management is most profound in the area of information technology, where the new folk heroes are young professionals whose Herculean efforts lead to the constant flow of new hardware and software products.

Project management is not limited to the private sector. Project management is also a vehicle for doing good deeds and solving social problems. Endeavors such as providing emergency aid to the Gulf Coast devastated by hurricane Katrina, devising a strategy for reducing crime and drug abuse within a city, or organizing a community effort to renovate a public playground would and do benefit from the application of modern project management skills and techniques.

Perhaps the best indicator of demand for project management can be seen in the rapid expansion of the Project Management Institute (PMI), a professional organization for project managers. PMI membership has grown from 93,000 in 2002 to more than 230,000 currently. See the PMI Snapshot from Practice for information regarding professional certification in project management.

It's nearly impossible to pick up a newspaper or business periodical and not find something about projects. This is no surprise! Approximately $2.5 trillion (about 25 percent of the U.S. gross national product) are spent on projects each year in the United States alone. Other countries are increasingly spending more on projects. Millions of people around the world consider project management the major task in their profession.

Project management is not without problems. The Standish Group has tracked the management of information technology (IT) projects over the years. This firm's periodic landmark reports summarize the

Snapshot from Practice   The Project Management Institute

The Project Management Institute (PMI) was founded in 1969 as an international society for project managers. Today PMI has members from more than 125 countries and more than 230,00 members. PMI professionals come from virtually every major industry, including aerospace, automotive, business management, construction, engineering, financial services, information technology, pharmaceuticals, health care, and telecommunications.

PMI provides certification as a *Project Management Professional (PMP)*—someone who has documented sufficient project experience, agreed to follow the PMI code of professional conduct, and demonstrated mastery of the field of project management by passing a comprehensive examination. The number of people earning PMP status has grown dramatically in recent years. In 1996 there were fewer than 3,000 certified project management professionals. By the end of 2005 there were more than 200,000 PMPs! Figure 1.1 shows the rapid growth in the number of people earning project management professional certification from 1995 to 2005.

Just as the CPA exam is a standard for accountants, passing the PMP exam may become the standard for project managers. Some companies are requiring that all their project managers be PMP certified. Moreover, many job postings are restricted to PMPs. Job seekers, in general, are finding that being PMP certified is an advantage in the marketplace.

PMI recently added a certification as a *Certified Associate in Project Management (CAPM)*. CAPM is designed for project team members and entry-level project managers, as well as qualified undergraduate and graduate students who want a credential to recognize their mastery of the project management body of knowledge. CAPM does not require the extensive project management experience associated with the PMP. For more details on PMP and CAPM, "google" PMI to find the current Web site for the Project Management Institute.

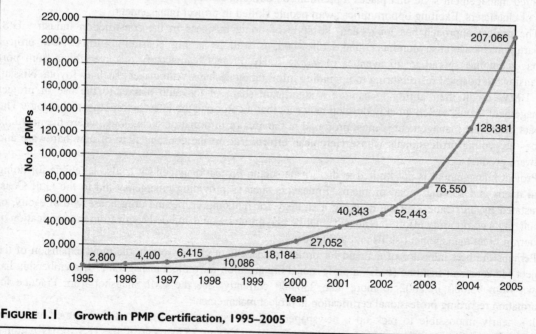

FIGURE 1.1   Growth in PMP Certification, 1995–2005

continued need for improved project management. In 1994 approximately 16 percent of IT projects were completed on time, on budget; in 2004 the success rate moved up to 29 percent. Failed projects also declined from 31 percent in 1994 to 18 percent in 2004. However, the number of projects late or over budget has not changed; these "seriously challenged projects" remain at 53 percent.

The trend of improvement is clear, but there is an urgent need for elevating performance! The waste on failed projects and cost overruns is estimated in the neighborhood of $150 billion!

These statistics are limited to information technology projects. Discussions with project managers in other industries suggest application to other industries may be a stretch, but the seriousness of the problems is just as great.

Project management is not restricted to specialists. Managing projects is often a vital part of everyone's job. For example, Brian Vannoni, formerly of General Electric Plastics, states:

> We have very few dedicated project managers. Our project managers might be process engineers, they might be scientists, they might be process control technicians, maintenance mechanics, degreed and nondegreed people. A short answer for GE Plastics is that anyone, any level, any function could be a project manager.[*]

Companies recognize that their entire organizational staff can benefit from being trained in project management, not just project management wannabes.

The growth of project management can also be seen in the classroom. Ten years ago major universities offered one or two classes in project management, primarily for engineers. Today, many universities offer multiple sections of project management classes, with the core group of engineers being supplemented by business students majoring in marketing, management information systems (MIS), and finance, as well as students from other disciplines such as oceanography, health sciences, computer sciences, and liberal arts. These students are finding that their exposure to project management is providing them with distinct advantages when it comes time to look for jobs. More and more employers are looking for graduates with project management skills. The logical starting point for developing these skills is understanding the uniqueness of a project and of project managers.

What Is a Project?

What do the following headlines have in common?

New Web Video Phone Is Here to Stay
Farm Aid concert raises millions for family farmers
New Zealand BritoMart Transportation System opens ahead of schedule
Contract for building citywide WiFi site awarded
Optical Security System on Line

All these events resulted from the management of projects. A project can be defined as follows:

> A project is a complex, nonroutine, one-time effort limited by time, budget, resources, and performance specifications designed to meet customer needs.

Like most organizational effort, the major goal of a project is to satisfy a customer's need. Beyond this fundamental similarity, the characteristics of a project help differentiate it from other endeavors of the organization. The major characteristics of a project are as follows:

1. An established objective.
2. A defined life span with a beginning and an end.
3. Usually, the involvement of several departments and professionals.
4. Typically, doing something that has never been done before.
5. Specific time, cost, and performance requirements.

---

[*] Harold Kerzner, *Applied Project Management* (New York: John Wiley & Sons, 2000), p. 221.

First, projects have a defined objective—whether it is constructing a 12-story apartment complex by January 1 or releasing version 2.0 of a specific software package as quickly as possible. This singular purpose is often lacking in daily organizational life in which workers perform repetitive operations each day.

Second, because there is a specified objective, projects have a defined endpoint, which is contrary to the ongoing duties and responsibilities of traditional jobs. In many cases, individuals move from one project to the next as opposed to staying in one job. After helping to install a security system, an IT engineer may be assigned to develop a database for a different client.

Third, unlike much organizational work that is segmented according to functional specialty, projects typically require the combined efforts of a variety of specialists. Instead of working in separate offices under separate managers, project participants, whether they be engineers, financial analysts, marketing professionals, or quality control specialists, work closely together under the guidance of a project manager to complete a project.

The fourth characteristic of a project is that it is nonroutine and has some unique elements. This is not an either/or issue but a matter of degree. Obviously, accomplishing something that has never been done before, such as building a hybrid (electric/gas) automobile or landing two mechanical rovers on Mars, requires solving previously unsolved problems and breakthrough technology. On the other hand, even basic construction projects that involve established sets of routines and procedures require some degree of customization that makes them unique.

Finally, specific time, cost, and performance requirements bind projects. Projects are evaluated according to accomplishment, cost, and time spent. These triple constraints impose a higher degree of accountability than you typically find in most jobs. These three also highlight one of the primary functions of project management, which is balancing the trade-offs between time, cost, and performance while ultimately satisfying the customer.

What a Project Is Not   Projects should not be confused with everyday work. A project is not routine, repetitive work! Ordinary daily work typically requires doing the same or similar work over and over, while a project is done only once; a new product or service exists when the project is completed. Examine the list in Table 1.1 that compares routine, repetitive work and projects. Recognizing the difference is important because too often resources can be used up on daily operations which may not contribute to longer range organization strategies that require innovative new products.

The terms *program* and *project* are often used interchangeably in practice, which sometimes causes confusion. Programs and projects are similar in the sense that they both are directed toward goals and require plans and resources to reach their goals. Both use similar tools, methods, and policies. The differences lie

TABLE 1.1   Comparison of Routine Work with Projects

Routine, Repetitive Work	Projects
Taking class notes	Writing a term paper
Daily entering sales receipts into the accounting ledger	Setting up a sales kiosk for a professional accounting meeting
Responding to a supply-chain request	Developing a supply-chain information system
Practicing scales on the piano	Writing a new piano piece
Routine manufacture of an Apple iPod	Designing an iPod that is approximately 2 × 4 inches, interfaces with PC, and stores 10,000 songs
Attaching tags on a manufactured product	Wire-tag projects for GE and Wal-Mart

primarily in scope and time horizon. *A program is a series of coordinated, related, multiple projects that continue over extended time intended to achieve a goal.* A program is a higher level **group** of projects targeted at a common goal. The classic example is the U.S. space program to place a space station on the moon to serve as a springboard to other space explorations.

Each project within a program has a project manager. A major difference between a program and project lies in scale and time span. Examples of programs and their goals are a set of projects that aim to increase computer chip speed each year; several new pharmaceutical products for arthritis; and Denver's 12-year, $4.7 billion urban transportation system that will extend 120 miles on six new rail lines.

The Project Life Cycle

Another way of illustrating the unique nature of project work is in terms of the project life cycle. Some project managers find it useful to use the project life cycle as the cornerstone for managing projects. The life cycle recognizes that projects have a limited life span and that there are predictable changes in level of effort and focus over the life of the project. There are a number of different life-cycle models in project management literature. Many are unique to a specific industry or type of project. For example, a new software development project may consist of five phases: definition, design, code, integration/test, and maintenance. A generic cycle is depicted in Figure 1.2.

The project life cycle typically passes sequentially through four stages: defining, planning, executing, and delivering. The starting point begins the moment the project is given the go-ahead. Project effort starts slowly, builds to a peak, and then declines to delivery of the project to the customer.

1. **Defining stage:** Specifications of the project are defined; project objectives are established; teams are formed; major responsibilities are assigned.

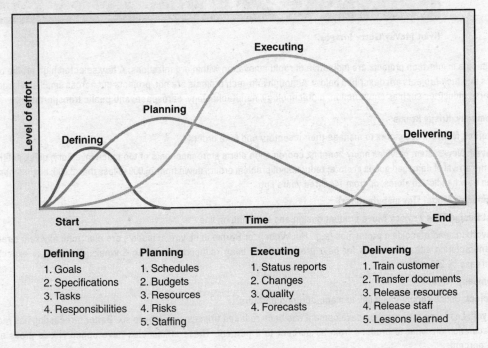

FIGURE 1.2   Project Life Cycle

Snapshot from Practice   Project Management at Work*

Ryan McVay/Getty Images.

Investments in info-tech projects are indicative of rapid innovation within organizations. A few selected high profile organizations and their projects are described below. Although info-tech projects are hot, projects cut across small and large firms in diverse industries such as construction, biotechnology, nanotechnology, aerospace, and public transportation.

1. **Company: Krispy Kreme**

   Project: Network 320 stores to manage their inventory and take orders

   Payoff: New system provides many benefits: coordination alerts store managers of too much inventory; quick notification of the arrival of damaged goods at store; reduction of problem orders down from 26,000 to less than 3,000; district managers can now handle 320 stores, up from 144 three years ago.

2. **Company: Mattel (Toy manufacturer)**

   Cut Design Time Project: Move product design and licensing on line

   Payoff: Instead of molding prototypes (e.g., Hot Wheels or Barbie doll), virtual models are electronically sent directly to manufacturing sites. Approvals for new products have been reduced from 14 to 5 weeks. Revenue is expected to increase by 200 million.

3. **Company: Nike**

   Project: Online supply-chain link to manufacturing partners

   Payoff: Lead time for new shoe development has been reduced from nine months to six. Better forecasting has reduced speculation on what to produce from 30 percent to 3 percent. These efficiencies have upped Nike's gross margin 2.1 percent.

4. **Company: FBI**

   Project: Digitizing millions of fingerprint cards and connecting law enforcement agencies to the data base

   Payoff: Local law enforcement departments can have the FBI check against 46 million sets of fingerprints and respond within two hours. In addition, the FBI conducts background checks for private enterprises (e.g., schools, insurance and securities industry, private security agencies). This latter service resulted in revenue of 152 million for one year.

5. **Company: Kinko's**

   Project: Replace 51 training sites with e-learning network

   Payoff: E-courses online are available to 20,000 employees. Courses range from products, to policies, to new product rollouts. Kinko's expects to save around $10 million a year on employee training. Kinko's is now moving into training for customers—such as making banners, holiday cards, and jazzy transparencies. Stores offering online customer training saw revenues rise 27 percent versus 11 percent in non-online stores.

6. **Company: BMW**

   Project: Build cars to specific customer orders

   Payoff: Updating supply chain from suppliers to customer allows customer (or salesperson) to use the Internet to order cars without altering production-line efficiency; delivery date is delivered in five seconds. Suppliers are notified when order is confirmed so parts arrive just-in-time for production. Cars are off the production line in 11 to 12 days and can be in the United States in 12 additional days. Eighty percent of European buyers design their own custom Beemer. Thirty percent of U.S. buyers access the custom service with the number increasing each year.

7. **Company: Sony**

   Project: Produce and use a secure website to rescue *Lord of the Rings* schedule

   Payoff: Important special effects for the film *Two Towers* fell behind schedule. Coordination between New Zealand, London, and the U.S. became a nightmare. A secure website using special custom software allowed all sites to download and edit over 100 scenes. Simultaneously, each site could use a digital pointer to discuss specific details or pull up specific footage. The one million dollar cost was small relative to the potential wasted cost of missing the promotions and ads deadlines.

   *Adapted from Heather Green, "The Web," *BusinessWeek,* November 24, 2003, pp. 82–104.

2. **Planning stage:** The level of effort increases, and plans are developed to determine what the project will entail, when it will be scheduled, whom it will benefit, what quality level should be maintained, and what the budget will be.

3. **Executing stage:** A major portion of the project work takes place—both physical and mental. The physical product is produced (a bridge, a report, a software program). Time, cost, and specification measures are used for control. Is the project on schedule, on budget, and meeting specifications? What are the forecasts of each of these measures? What revisions/changes are necessary?

4. **Delivering stage:** Includes the two activities: delivering the project product to the customer and redeploying project resources. Delivery of the project might include customer training and transferring documents. Redeployment usually involves releasing project equipment/materials to other projects and finding new assignments for team members.

In practice, the project life cycle is used by some project groups to depict the timing of major tasks over the life of the project. For example, the design team might plan a major commitment of resources in the defining stage, while the quality team would expect their major effort to increase in the latter stages of the project life cycle. Because most organizations have a portfolio of projects going on concurrently, each at a different stage of each project's life cycle, careful planning and management at the organization and project levels are imperative.

The Project Manager

In a small sense project managers perform the same functions as other managers. That is, they plan, schedule, motivate, and control. However, what makes them unique is that they manage temporary, nonrepetitive activities, to complete a fixed life project. Unlike functional managers, who take over existing operations, project managers create a project team and organization where none existed before. They must decide what and how things should be done instead of simply managing set processes. They must meet the challenges of each phase of the project life cycle, and even oversee the dissolution of their operation when the project is completed.

Project managers must work with a diverse troupe of characters to complete projects. They are typically the direct link to the customer and must manage the tension between customer expectations and what is feasible and reasonable. Project managers provide direction, coordination, and integration to the project team, which is often made up of part-time participants loyal to their functional departments. They often must work with a cadre of outsiders—vendors, suppliers, subcontractors—who do not necessarily share their project allegience.

Project managers are ultimately responsible for performance (frequently with too little authority). They must ensure that appropriate trade-offs are made between the time, cost, and performance requirements of the project. At the same time, unlike their functional counterparts, project managers generally possess only rudimentary technical knowledge to make such decisions. Instead, they must orchestrate the completion of the project by inducing the right people, at the right time, to address the right issues and make the right decisions.

While project management is not for the timid, working on projects can be an extremely rewarding experience. Life on projects is rarely boring; each day is different from the last. Since most projects are directed at solving some tangible problem or pursuing some useful opportunity, project managers find their work personally meaningful and satisfying. They enjoy the act of creating something new and innovative. Project managers and team members can feel immense pride in their accomplishment, whether it is a new bridge, a new product, or needed service. Project managers are often stars in their organization and well compensated.

Good project managers are always in demand. Every industry is looking for effective people who can get the right things done on time. Clearly, project management is a challenging and exciting profession. This text is intended to provide the necessary knowledge, perspective, and tools to enable students to accept the challenge.

The Importance of Project Management

Project management is no longer a special-need management. It is rapidly becoming a standard way of doing business. See Snapshot from Practice: Project Management at Work. An increasing percentage of the typical firm's effort is being devoted to projects. The future promises an increase in the importance and the role of projects in contributing to the strategic direction of organizations. Several reasons why this is the case are briefly discussed below.

Compression of the Product Life Cycle

One of the most significant driving forces behind the demand for project management is the shortening of the product life cycle. For example, today in high-tech industries the product life cycle is averaging 1 to 3 years. Only 30 years ago, life cycles of 10 to 15 years were not uncommon. *Time to market* for new products with short life cycles has become increasingly important. A common rule of thumb in the world of high-tech product development is that a six-month project delay can result in a 33 percent loss in product revenue share. Speed, therefore, becomes a competitive advantage; more and more organizations are relying on cross-functional project teams to get new products and services to the market as quickly as possible.

Global Competition

Today's open market demands not only *cheaper* products and services but also *better* products and services. This has led to the emergence of the quality movement across the world with ISO 9000 certification a requirement for doing business. ISO 9000 is a family of international standards for quality management and assurance. These standards cover design, procurement, quality assurance, and delivery processes for everything from banking to manufacturing. Quality management and improvement invariably involve project management. For many, their first exposure to project management techniques has been in quality workshops.

Increased pressures to reduce costs have not only led to the migration of U.S. manufacturing operations to Mexico and Asia, which by itself is a significant project, but also a transformation in how organizations try to achieve results. More and more work is being classified as projects. Individuals are being assigned responsibility to achieve a specific objective within a given budget and by a specified deadline. Project management, with its triple focus on time, cost, and performance, is proving to be an efficient, flexible way to get things done.

Knowledge Explosion

The growth in new knowledge has increased the complexity of projects because projects encompass the latest advances. For example, building a road 30 years ago was a somewhat simple process. Today, each area has increased in complexity, including materials, specifications, codes, aesthetics, equipment, and required specialists. Similarly, in today's digital, electronic age it is becoming hard to find a new product that does not contain at least one microchip. Product complexity has increased the need to integrate divergent technologies. Project management has emerged as an important discipline for achieving this task.

Corporate Downsizing

The last decade has seen a dramatic restructuring of organizational life. Downsizing (or rightsizing if you are still employed) and sticking to core competencies have become necessary for survival for many firms. Middle management is a mere skeleton of the past. In today's flatter and leaner organizations, where change is a constant, project management is replacing middle management as a way of ensuring that things get done. Corporate downsizing has also led to a change in the way organizations approach projects. Companies outsource significant segments of project work, and project managers have to manage not only their own people but also their counterparts in different organizations.

Increased Customer Focus

Increased competition has placed a premium on customer satisfaction. Customers no longer simply settle for generic products and services. They want customized products and services that cater to their specific needs. This mandate requires a much closer working relationship between the provider and the receiver. Account executives and sales representatives are assuming more of a project manager's role as they work with their organization to satisfy the unique needs and requests of clients.

Increased customer attention has also prompted the development of customized products and services. For example, 10 years ago buying a set of golf clubs was a relatively simple process: You picked out a set based on price and feel. Today, there are golf clubs for tall players and short players, clubs for players who tend to slice the ball and clubs for those who hook the ball, high-tech clubs with the latest metallurgic discovery guaranteed to add distance, and so forth. Project management is critical both to development of customized products and services and to sustaining lucrative relationships with customers.

Small Projects Represent Big Problems

The velocity of change required to remain competitive or simply keep up has created an organizational climate in which hundreds of projects are implemented concurrently. This climate has created a multiproject environment and a plethora of new problems. Sharing and prioritizing resources across a portfolio of projects is a major challenge for senior management. Many firms have no idea of the problems involved with inefficient management of small projects. Small projects typically carry the same or more risk as do large projects. Small projects are perceived as having little impact on the bottom line because they do not demand large amounts of scarce resources and/or money. Because so many small projects are going on concurrently and because the perception of the inefficiency impact is small, measuring inefficiency is usually nonexistent. Unfortunately, many small projects soon add up to large sums of money. Many customers and millions of dollars are lost each year on small projects in product and service organizations.

Many small projects can eat up the people resources of a firm and represent hidden costs not measured in the accounting system. Organizations with many small projects going on concurrently face the most difficult project management problems. A key question becomes one of how to create an organizational environment that supports multiproject management. A process is needed to prioritize and develop a portfolio of small projects that supports the mission of the organization.

In summary, there are a variety of environmental forces interacting in today's business world that contribute to the increased demand for good project management across all industries and sectors. Project management appears to be ideally suited for a business environment requiring accountability, flexibility, innovation, speed, and continuous improvement.

Project Management Today—An Integrative Approach

Some project managers have used different tools that are useful for managing projects. For example, networks, bar charts, job costing, task forces, partnering, and scheduling all have been used—sometimes very successfully and other times with poor results. As the world becomes more competitive, the importance of managing the process of project management and "getting it right the first time" takes on new meaning. Piecemeal systems fail to tie to the overall strategies of the firm. Piecemeal project priority systems fail to connect the selected projects to resources. Piecemeal tools and techniques fail to be integrated throughout the project life cycle. Piecemeal approaches fail to balance the application of project planning and control methods with appropriate adjustments in the organization's culture to support project endeavors.

Today, emphasis is on development of an integrated project management process that focuses all project effort toward the strategic plan of the organization and reinforces mastery of both the project management tools/techniques and the interpersonal skills necessary to orchestrate successful project completion. For some organizations, integrating projects with strategy will require reengineering the entire business management process. For others, integration will mean carefully establishing linkages among the piecemeal systems already in place and altering the focus to one of a total system. At the individual level, for some professionals to become effective project managers will require augmenting their leadership and team-building skills with modern project planning and control methods. For others it will require complementing their administrative skills with the capacity to inspire and lead a divergent cast of professionals to project completion.

Integration in project management directs attention to two key areas. The first area is integration of projects with the strategic plan of the organization. The second area is integration within the process of managing actual projects. Each of these areas is examined next.

Integration of Projects with the Strategic Plan

In some organizations, selection and management of projects often fail to support the strategic plan of the organization. Strategic plans are written by one group of managers, projects selected by another group, and projects implemented by another. These independent decisions by different groups of managers create a set of conditions leading to conflict, confusion, and—frequently—an unsatisfied customer. Under these conditions, resources of the organization are wasted in non-value-added activities/projects.

An integrated project management system is one in which all of the parts are interrelated. A change in any one of the parts will influence the whole. Every organization has a customer it is seeking to satisfy. The customer sets the raison d'être for the organization. Mission, objectives, and strategies are set to meet the needs of customer(s). Development of a mission, objectives, and organization strategies depend on the external and internal environmental factors. External environmental factors are usually classified as political, social, economic, and technological; they signal opportunities or threats in setting the direction for the organization. Internal environmental factors are frequently classified as strengths and weaknesses such as management, facilities, core competencies, and financial condition. The outcome of the analysis of all these environmental factors is a set of strategies designed to best meet the needs of customers. But this is only the first step (see Figure 1.3).

Implementing strategies is the most difficult step. Strategies are typically implemented through projects. Creative minds always propose more projects than there are resources. The key is selecting from the many proposals those projects that make the largest and most balanced contribution to the objectives and strategies (and thus, customers) of the organization. This means prioritizing projects so that scarce resources are allocated to the right projects. Once a project has been selected for implementation, the focus switches to the project management process that sets the stage for how the project will be implemented or delivered.

Integration within the Process of Managing Actual Projects

There are two dimensions within the project management process (see Figure 1.4). The first dimension is the technical side of the management process, which consists of the formal, disciplined, pure logic parts of the process. The technical side relies on the formal information system available.

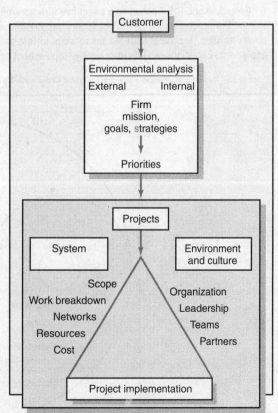

FIGURE 1.3   Integrated Management of Projects

Research Highlight

Works Well with Others*

The phrase "works well with others" has long been a staple on grade school report cards; now, in the IT world, it's the No. 1 criterion for management candidates. In a nationwide survey conducted in 1999, 27 percent of chief information officers (CIOs) cited strong interpersonal skills as the single most important quality for reaching management levels. Advanced technical skills came in second, receiving 23 percent of the response.

The project was sponsored by RHI Consulting, which provides information technology professionals on a project basis. An independent research firm was hired to administer the survey. Over 1,400 CIOs responded to the questionnaire.

Survey respondents were also asked:

In 2005, how frequently will employees in your IT department work on project-based teams with members of other departments throughout the company?

Their responses:	Very frequently	57%
	Somewhat frequently	26%
	Somewhat infrequently	10%
	Very infrequently	6%
	Never	1%

Greg Scileppi, RHI Consulting's executive director, recommends that IT professionals develop their interpersonal skills. "The predominance of project teams has created a corresponding need for strong communication and team-player abilities. Technical staff put these skills to test daily as they work with employees at all levels to create and implement IT solutions ranging from simple troubleshooting to corporate web initiatives and system wide upgrades."

*Joanita M. Nellenbach, "People Skills Top Technical Knowledge, CIOs Insist," PMNetwork (August 1999), pp. 7–8.

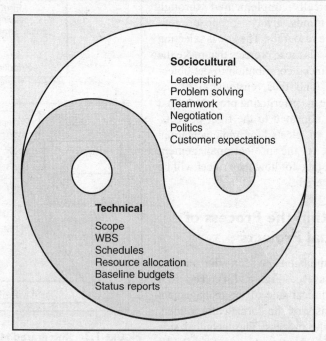

FIGURE 1.4   The Technical and Sociocultural Dimensions of the Project Management Process

This dimension includes planning, scheduling, and controlling projects. Clear project scope statements are written to link the project and customer and to facilitate planning and control. Creation of the deliverables and work breakdown structures facilitate planning and monitoring the progress of the project. The work breakdown structure serves as a database that links all levels in the organization, major deliverables, and all work—right down to the tasks in a work package. Effects of project changes are documented and traceable. Thus, any change in one part of the project is traceable to the source by the integrated linkages of the system. This integrated information approach can provide all project managers and the customer with decision information appropriate to their level and needs. A successful project manager will be well trained in the technical side of managing projects.

The second dimension is the sociocultural side of the project management process. In contrast with the orderly world of project planning, this dimension involves the much messier, often contradictory and paradoxical world of implementation. It centers on creating a temporary social system within a larger organizational environment that combines the talents of a divergent set of professionals working to complete the project. See Research Highlight: Works Well with Others. Project managers must shape a project culture that stimulates teamwork and high levels of personal motivation as well as a capacity to quickly identify and resolve problems that threaten project work. This dimension also involves managing the interface between the project and external environment. Project managers have to assuage and shape expectations of customers, sustain the political support of top management, negotiate with their functional counterparts, monitor subcontractors, and so on. Overall, the manager must build a cooperative social network among a divergent set of allies with different standards, commitments, and perspectives.

Some suggest that the technical dimension represents the "science" of project management while the sociocultural dimension represents the "art" of managing a project. To be successful, a manager must be a master of both. Unfortunately, some project managers become preoccupied with the planning and technical dimension of project management. Often their first real exposure to project management is through project management software, and they become infatuated with network charts, Gantt diagrams, and performance variances and attempt to manage a project from a distance. Conversely, there are other managers who manage projects by the "seat of their pants," relying heavily on team dynamics and organizational politics to complete a project. Good project managers balance their attention to both the technical and sociocultural dimensions of project management.

Summary

There are powerful environmental forces contributing to the rapid expansion of project management approaches to business problems and opportunities. A project is defined as a nonroutine, one-time effort limited by time, resources, and performance specifications designed to meet customer needs. One of the distinguishing characteristics of project management is that it has both a beginning and an end and typically consists of four phases: defining, planning, executing, and delivering. Effective project management begins with selecting and prioritizing projects that support the firm's mission and strategy. Successful implementation requires both technical and social skills. Project managers have to plan and budget projects as well as orchestrate the contributions of others.

Text Overview

This text is written to provide the reader with a comprehensive, integrative understanding of the project management process. The text focuses both on the science of project management and the art of managing projects. Following this introductory chapter, Chapter 2 focuses on how organizations go about evaluating and selecting projects. Special attention is devoted to the importance of linking project selection to the mission and strategy of the firm. The organizational environment in which projects are implemented is the focus of Chapter 3. The discussion of matrix management and other organizational forms is augmented by a discussion of the role the culture of an organization plays in the implementation of projects.

The next six chapters focus on developing a plan for the project; after all, project success begins with a good plan. Chapter 4 deals with defining the scope of the project and developing a work breakdown structure (WBS). The challenge of formulating cost and time estimates is the subject of Chapter 5. Chapter 6 focuses on utilizing the information from the WBS to create a project plan in the form of a timed and sequenced network of activities.

Risks are a potential threat to project management, and Chapter 7 examines how organizations and managers identify and manage risks associated with project work. Resource allocation is added to the plan in Chapter 8 with special attention devoted to how resource limitations impact the project schedule. After a resource schedule is established, a project time-phased budget is developed. Finally, Chapter 9 examines strategies for reducing ("crashing") project time either prior to the initiation of the project or in response to problems or new demands placed on the project.

Chapters 10 through 12 focus on project implementation and the sociocultural side of project management, beginning with Chapter 10, which focuses on the role of the project manager as a leader and stresses the importance of managing project stakeholders within the organization. Chapter 11 focuses on the core project team; it combines the latest information on team dynamics with leadership skills/techniques for developing a high-performance project team. Chapter 12 continues the theme of managing project stakeholders by discussing how to outsource project work and negotiate with contractors, customers, and suppliers.

Chapter 13 focuses on the kinds of information managers use to monitor project progress, with special attention devoted to the key concept of earned value. Issues surrounding the termination or completion of the project are dealt with in Chapter 14. Implementation of project management in multicultural, international environments is the subject of Chapter 15. Finally, Chapter 16 notes the need for organizational oversight and how it impacts the management of projects. A special segment on pursuing a career in project management is also included.

Throughout this text you will be exposed to the major aspects of the project management system. However, a true understanding of project management comes not from knowing what a scope statement is, or the critical path, or partnering with contractors, but from comprehending how the different elements of the project management system interact to determine the fate of a project. If, by the end of this text, you come to appreciate and begin to master both the technical and sociocultural dimensions of project management, you should have a distinct competitive advantage over others aspiring to work in the field of project management.

Key Terms

ISO 9000	Project	Project Management Professional (PMP)
Program	Project life cycle	Sociotechnical perspective

Review Questions

1. Define a project. What are five characteristics that help differentiate projects from other functions carried out in the daily operations of the organization?

2. What are some of the key environmental forces that have changed the way projects are managed? What has been the effect of these forces on the management of projects?

3. Why is the implementation of projects important to strategic planning and the project manager?

4. The technical and sociocultural dimensions of project management are two sides to the same coin. Explain.

5. What is meant by an integrative approach to project management? Why is this approach important in today's environment?

Exercises

1. Review the front page of your local newspaper, and try to identify all the projects contained in the articles. How many were you able to find?

2. Individually identify what you consider to be the greatest achievements accomplished by mankind in the last five decades. Now share your list with three to five other students in the class, and come up with an expanded list. Review these accomplishments in terms of the definition of a project. What does your review suggest about the importance of project management?

3. Individually identify projects assigned in previous terms. Were both sociocultural and technical elements factors in the success or difficulties in the projects?

4. Check out the Project Management Institute's home page at *www.pmi.org*.

   a. Review general information about PMI as well as membership information.

   b. See if there is a PMI chapter in your state. It not, where is the closest one?

   c. Use the search function at the PMI home page to find information on Project Management Body of Knowledge (PMBOK). What are the major knowledge areas of PMBOK?

   d. Explore other links that PMI provides. What do these links tell you about the nature and future of project management?

Note: If you have any difficulty accessing any of the Web addresses listed here or elsewhere in the text, you can find up-to-date addresses on the home page of Dr. Erik Larson, coauthor of this text: *http://www.bus.oregonstate.edu/faculty/bio.htm?UserName=Larson*

References

Benko, C. and F. W. McFarlan, *Connecting the Dots* (Boston: HBS Press, 2003).

Cohen, D. J. and R. J. Graham, *The Project Manager's MBA* (San Francisco: Jossey-Bass, 2001).

Kerzner, H. *Project Management: A Systems Approach to Planning, Scheduling, and Controlling* (New York: Wiley, 2003).

Larkowski, K. "Standish Group Report Shows Project Success Improves 50 Percent," *www.standishgroup.com*, 2004, Third Quarter.

Peters, T. *PM Network,* January 2004, Vol. 18, No. 1, p. 19.

Project Management Institute, *Leadership in Project Management Annual* (Newton Square, PA: PMI Publishing, 2006).

Stewart, T. A. "The Corporate Jungle Spawns a New Species: The Project Manager," *Fortune* (September 1996), pp. 14–15.

Wysocki, B. "Flying Solo: High-Tech Nomads Write New Program for Future of Work," *The Wall Street Journal* (August 19, 1996), p. 1.

APPENDIX 1.1

PART (A)

Definitions of Project, Program, Portfolio and Other Key Terms

One of the aims of the PMBOK® Guide is to promote the use of a common vocabulary within the project management profession for discussing and writing on the subject of project management. In project management literature and some corporate communications, the terms 'project' and program and 'program' and 'portfolio', are used somewhat interchangeably, which introduces ambiguity in the discussion across a much wider audience. Therefore, at the start, we shall take up some key definitions.

Project: *Project is defined as a temporary endeavor to create a unique product, service or result.*

Though the exact phrases used for this definition are not the same as the definition of project given in this chapter under the heading "What is a Project?", a very strong undercurrent of the same idea running through both definitions could be easily seen. The words 'non-routine and one-time effort" correspond to 'temporary endeavor' and 'performance specifications designed to meet customer needs' correspond to 'unique product, service or result" part of the definition.

The phrase, temporary emphasizes the specific start and end of the project—the start of the project to begin a specific set of activities to achieve some objectives and the end of the project when the objectives are achieved or the organization is convinced that achieving the objectives is either not possible or not in the interest of the organization in light of changed macro-economic or social factors.

Product created by the project is some form of a physical asset. Examples of the product of the project are a building, a road, a manufacturing facility, a refinery, a new motor cycle, etc.

Service created by the project is some form of capability to provide service; it might include some physical assets as well as some technology, trained service personnel, and procedures and methods to serve some specific business or social function. Setting up a telephone or electric power supply network in an area, setting up water and drainage systems, setting up colleges for education, hospitals for healthcare, setting up within a corporate a new IT system or new procurement system, and major modifications or enhancements of the governmental services like defense systems are examples of services created by the project.

Result created by the project is some specific outcome within an organization or impacting the environment. Within an organization, the outcome like reducing accident level, saving energy usage, developing a new drug or improving quality or productivity in manufacturing are instances of results within an organization. Extending the market share, providing the services to a new geographical area or another country, an election campaign, and a military campaign are examples of results of projects which also impact an environment external to the organization.

The term 'unique' in the definition lays emphasis on the non-routine nature of the project work and is meant to distinguish project from routine operation. The predominantly large part of the work performed in an organization is of operational nature. For manufacturing companies, manufacture of products or providing services are the organization's main business. For example, manufacture of computers for a computer manufacturer, petroleum and LPG for a petroleum refinery, mobile handsets for a handset manufacturer or cloth for a textile mill. Similarly the operations for banks would be to provide financial services, for colleges the education for specific programs, for hospitals medical services and electric power supply or communication network for electric power and telephone companies. In addition, the supporting activities for these main operational agendas (finance, materials procurement, human relations management, quality control, maintenance, etc.) are also parts of routine operations or activities. Both ongoing routine operations and projects require people to carry out work. Both are required to be completed within constraints of resources and require planning, effective execution of the plans, and a close monitoring and control to ensure the delivery of planned objectives. However, these activities are carried out repetitively day in and day out, year in and year out. The procedures, policies, the organization structure, physical assets, technology and materials—all are standardized and pre-set.

Some repetitive operations might be used for creating the product of the project—for example two projects at different sites and during different period may require use of the same building materials, building trade practices or even the construction teams for constructing a number of buildings. In such situations, under the broad overall similarities, an in-depth analysis would reveal a significant variation in details necessary for planning, execution and control for effectively and efficiently managing the projects.

As it so often happens with many words in general usage, the term project is often used loosely to designate anything important or special. So preparing for and going to an important meeting is called "a project". Negotiating a large sales order is called "a project". Manufacturing a standard production order, but with some minor variation in technical specifications is called "a project". The planned shutdown and repairs in a continuous operation-type manufacturing unit (e.g. a petroleum refinery or a blast furnace in a steel plant) is called "a project". This usage of the term "project" is a trivialization of the term in ordinary usage. Generally, these are instances of routine operations, but sometimes managed using the tools and techniques ordinarily employed for project management. At best, they are instances of "*management by project*".

Characteristics of a project: Taking into account the ideas underlying the definition of the project and the nature of the activities constituting the projects, the characteristics of the project can be summarized as follows:

- Temporary Endeavor
- Creation of a unique product, service or result
- Vehicle for change—implementing the strategic plans of the organization
- Progressive elaboration of the scope
- Time-bound completion of project work
- Constraints on resources—budget
- Special need for project risk analysis and management

We have already discussed the first two project characteristics while discussing the definition of the project. We shall take up discussion of other characteristics later after discussing programs and portfolios.

Program

The term program is applied to a group of related projects managed in a coordinated way to obtain benefits and control not available from managing them individually. Program may include elements of related work outside the scope of the discrete projects in a program.

Let us study the implications in this definition. The role played by the projects is as instruments of change and implementing the organization's strategic policy. The organization would formulate its strategic plan for long-term and short-term future operations and chalk out a program which would include a number of projects, each with a set of specific objectives to create a unique product, service or result envisioned in the strategic plan. There may also be some common work related to all projects but outside the scope of the individual projects. The program would be managed in such a manner that the quantum and timing of allocating the resources is optimized for most efficient use of resources. The program management also takes into account the interdependencies of the products of the projects for delivering the strategic thrust.

As illustrations of the program we can cite:

- Interconnected highways network—'golden quadrangle corridors' connecting four metros in India
- A nuclear powered submarine
- Defense Research Department Organization's Program for defensive missile systems
- Electric power supply network based on a hydroelectric power plant
- Setting up an on-line airlines or railway booking system

Each of these programs would need to set up a number of projects which would be managed in a coordinated way and which would share critical resources for optimized usage.

Portfolio

The term portfolio is applied to a collection of projects and programs that are grouped together for pursuing objectives focused on some specific business strategy.

This definition points out that the scope of portfolio is wider than projects and programs. Unlike the programs, which hold groups of interrelated projects managed in a coordinated way, the portfolio need not be limited to inter-relationship. The portfolio of diversified large companies may include projects and programs in the wide spectrum of commercial and industrial activities. For example, the portfolio may include the transportation, industrial equipment and large infrastructure civil construction, or, say, a petroleum refinery, petrochemicals complexes, textile mills and mobile telephone services. Portfolio management is handled at the highest managerial level, often the owners or entrepreneurs themselves or their close associates look after portfolio management. The focus of portfolio management is on the broad macro-economic and industrial conditions and trends in the nation; and how the organization's resources can be augmented and employed for optimum benefits to the organization.

Place of Projects for Implementing the Organization's Strategic Objectives

While discussing the characteristics of the project, a reference was made with regards to the place of projects as a vehicle or instrument for change in the organization and for implementing the organization's broad strategic vision. Let us look more closely at this aspect of the project: the very reason for existence— initiation and authorization—of the project

The Current Operations

All organizations—commercial organizations, not-for-profit social organizations and governmental institutions—are actively engaged in carrying out some function involving day-to-day routine operations in an on-going manner year-after-year.

- A company manufacturing electric motors or lap top computers would keep on producing in its plants electric motors or lap top computers.
- The company providing telecom or banking services would routinely keep providing telecom or banking services.
- Educational institutions would attend to the tasks of providing education, and
- Government departments concerned with defense or environmental administration would attend to tasks cut out for them.

A predominantly large part of the work force of an organization is, therefore, understandably busy with carrying out these routine activities and a predominantly large part of all resources are actively employed in the routine operations.

Need for creating a new product service or result

While doing these routine operations, from time to time the organizations find the need for some change in their operations for more effective, more efficient, larger scale or improved operation. While doing routine operations, the manufacturing organization may find the need to increase the capacity for manufacture, or to bring out a new product, or to improve the quality of the products, or to employ new technology for saving cost by more efficient use of materials or labour, or say setting up facilities for safer routine operations or for meeting the government's environmental regulations. The service organization may feel the need to extend the scope of services, or cover a larger geographical area, or supply a more satisfactory level of service or exploit a new technology to provide an altogether new service. In other words, the organization might feel *the need for creation of some product, service or result different from the current operations.*

These needs may fall into any of the following categories:

- Business need: Setting up a new business, starting a profitable venture for investment, entrepreneurial vision for developing new technology.
- Market need: Improving product mix, developing a new product, a customer's requests for some features and others
- Customer request for project management: For organizations performing projects on contract—like companies in civil, electrical, HVAC or mechanical and piping construction and project consultancies providing engineering-procurement construction services
- Technological push: developing new technology, making products compatible with new technology
- Organizational structure change, geographical expansion, recruitment & training campaigns
- Legal or social requirement, effluent treatment plant; employees welfare schemes, etc.

Initiating projects to provide these new capabilities to the organization

However, most operating organizations do not have the infrastructure, other resources or people to create new products, services or results, which they need. For managing these changes in the mode of ongoing operations, the organizations embark on projects and commit their resources with the objective of creating these products, services or results, which becomes the scope of the authorized project. The very reason for creation and existence of the project is to manage the project in such a manner that the full scope of the project is accomplished in a cost-effective and timely manner.

The projects are the bridges which take an organization from current activities (products and services) to new products and services. Project extends the capability of the organization from here-and-now to the visions of future. The projects are thus the vehicles for the changes, which routine operations do not cover. The projects are vehicles for implementing the organization's vision, short and long-term plans, and business strategy. Peter Drucker once wrote that the primary purpose of the management in an enlightened organization is to introduce innovation; the rest is just routine business. The projects are the instruments for these innovations and in this dynamic business scenario and global competitions era, it is the organizations that envision the right projects for innovation and implement them effectively that will survive and grow.

Progressive Elaboration of Project Scope

Another important characteristic of the project is the progressive elaboration. Projects are involved in activities, which the organization had not handled routinely before. Therefore, surprises are bound to come and the project planning must be altered to overcome any unexpected difficulty. This is obvious. Less obvious aspect for progressive elaboration springs from the fact that most projects are initiated to implement the vision or broad strategy of the organization. At the very start of the project, the detailed planning is not chalked out. As the project planning is started and pieces of jigsaw puzzle for project planning start falling in place, issues which had remained out of focus at the very initial authorization stage come to light. For meeting the basic objectives underlying the taking up of the project or for effective and efficient project management, some alterations in the project scope is often necessary. That is why, though project managers generally loathe changes and oppose them, all good project managers accept, even look for some minor changes which would optimize the project objectives.

Other Characteristics of the Project

We will briefly touch other characteristics of projects:

- *Time-bound completion of project work:*
  The very definition of the project as a temporary endeavor implies the time bound nature of the project—a definite start and a definite end to carry out the work for meeting the project objectives. But there is additional connotation here to the term 'time bound'. Projects are managed not just to start and complete as a whole according to some schedule, but milestones for end of important project deliverables or key activities are also planned and closely monitored and controlled.
- *Constraints on resources—budget*
  The projects are authorized with a specific quantum of resources—the total cost budgeted for the project or the resources in term of the manpower allocated or permitting the use of existing infrastructure for project work.
- *Special need for project risk analysis and management*
  Unexpected events—risk events or conditions—may occur during routine operations as well as during project work. However, project work might involve undertaking many activities with which the organization may not have prior experience. The need for risk analysis and proactively managing the risks is therefore somewhat greater in project work.

The above three characteristics, in a way, define the role of a successful project manger. He is supposed to achieve the project objectives with effective coordination of a number of activities making necessary trade-offs between cost and time and proactively managing the risks which could adversely impact the project.

PART (B)

Project Life Cycle
and the Characteristics of Project Phases

1. Nature of Project Life Cycle and Phases

Work to be carried out between the start of the project and the close of the project is called the project life cycle. This concept evolves from the fact that the projects have finite life and the level and nature of work to be carried out for project between the start and end of the project follows a certain pattern for most projects. All project phases have the following characteristics:

- *Project Phase:* Each phase consists of a set of inter-related activities generally carried out sequentially.
- *Pre-planned deliverables or technical hand-offs:* After carrying out the set of activities during a particular phase, the pre-planned deliverables or technical hand-offs are given by the preceding phase to the next phase. The deliverables of the previous phase are prerequisite for the start of the next phase and it is only after satisfactory hand-off that the next project phase starts. It is like a relay race. The first runner runs his lap and passes on the baton to the next runner. The second runner can start his race part only after receiving the baton in proper order from the first runner.
- *Decision making control gate for project:* The end of one phase and the start of another phase serves as a decision making control gate for project. At such gates, the project results up to that point are reviewed and given necessary directional inputs.
- *Project termination:* If at any decision making gate at the end of a phase, it becomes clear that the project in its present form cannot meet the desired objectives or that the need for the project objectives no longer exists, the project may be terminated at the gate.

2. Project Life Cycle Phases

Depending on the predominant nature of work to be carried out, the project life cycle may be divided into specific phases for good understanding and control of the project during the life cycle. The nomenclature of the phases given below is according to the 4th Edition of the PMBOK® Guide; this was given slightly differently in the 3rd Edition.

(i) **Starting the project (Defining Stage)**

In this phase, the project is conceived and the preliminary scope of the project, budget, schedule, etc. are estimated; necessary approval or permission from the authorities are obtained (customer, top management, government agencies controlling the industry, etc.) and the approved project is handed over for detailed planning to the project team for the next phase. The project charter or firm order from a client or approval, permission or license from the governing authority is the deliverable or hand-of from the stage.

(ii) **Organizing and preparing the project (Planning Stage)**

In this phase, planning is carried out in sufficient detail for all work required to be carried out for project activities. This would include preparing integrated detailed plans for project activities for proactively managing project scope, schedule, budget, quality, communications, project team, risk and procurement. The technical hand-offs from this phase are the detailed plans for project execution.

(iii) **Carrying out the project work (Executing Stage)**

In this phase, most of the actual project work planned during the development phase is carried out using the resources authorized for project work. Project manager and his team monitor and control the project quality, technical & performance specifications of work performed, completion of major activities as per milestones and within budgeted cost.

(iv) **Closing the project (Delivering Stage)**

In this phase, the project is systematically brought to a close. All deliverables are checked out to ensure that they meet the criteria for project success or agreed specifications. After the technical documentation is handed over and the procurement contracts are settled, the project is handed over to the client or the operating group.

3. Characteristics of Project Phases

There is considerable variation in the different project phases depending on the industry and nature of the project. However certain general trends do emerge:

- The work content, staffing and cost are small in the early life cycle of the project. They pick up and maximum staffing, work and cost expenditure occur during the middle phases and the work content, staffing and cost taper off to zero at the project close.
- The level of uncertainty or risk to the project success is the highest near the early phases of the project life cycle. It would gradually taper off as the jig-saw puzzle pieces start falling in place and reduces to a very low level near the close of the project.
- The ability of stakeholders to influence the project is the highest during the early phases and preliminary project planning. As the details of project start getting firmed up and executed, the influence of stakeholders decreases and it tapers off to practically no influence near the project close.
- On the other hand if any correction or change is required to be done, the maximum cost and difficulty occur near the project's later phases. It is relatively easy to take care of changes or modifications suggested by different stakeholders at the start of the project.

4. Product Life Cycle—How It Differs from Project Life Cycle

Project life covers the project time span, viz. time during which a specific product, result or service is created by the project. The project creates the product, result or service and hands it over to the operation. The operation then uses the project's product and maintains it till the product's utility is exhausted. At the end of that stage, some modifications or extensive remodeling would be planned and another project would be started for such work. Thus product life cycle is the whole life of the product: from its conception, creation and use till the end. Only a small part of the product life cycle, the part during which such product service or result is created, constitutes project life cycle. In other words, the project life cycle is a sub-set of the product life cycle. So there is life for a project's product after the project's death, i.e. the period during which the operation uses and maintains the project's product till its useful life.

PART (C)

Project Management Processes and Their Classification

1. Use of Project Management Processes as Framework for Project Management Discussion

Most discussion on project management topics in books and technical literature is generally presented as some specific topics of interest, techniques or managerial approaches recommended for efficient and effective project management.

PMBOK® Guide appears to make a radical departure in the framework used for discussion of project management by

1. introducing the concept of 'project management processes' (good management practices common to management of almost all projects),

2. their classification into discrete project management processes by life cycle and knowledge areas, and

3. systemic description of each of these processes in terms of the inputs, tools & techniques and outputs.

Some detailed discussion on this approach is presented below.

2. Project Management Processes

All work required to be performed in connection with the project is recognized as belonging to two classes or types.

Product-oriented processes

These processes are actually used in creating the product of the project and they are specific to different industries, technologies and application areas. For example, the product-oriented processes for civil construction would be the design of foundations or structure, preparing and placing reinforced concrete, structural steel fabrication and so forth.

Project management processes

From the analysis of the past experience of management of a very large number of projects related to a large variety of industrial and commercial activities, several practices in project management have been identified to be effective as well as efficient. The knowledge, skills and tools and techniques associated with these good project management practices, the desired results or outputs from them and the necessary data or other inputs for using these techniques are collectively identified as a project management process. These processes are common to almost all projects and they are concerned with the flow of information throughout the project life and some generally accepted tools and techniques for project initiating, planning, executing, monitoring and controlling or closing. The project manager performs his function by judicious application of the necessary project management processes to the project work and achieves the desired project objectives.

Project management is, accordingly, the application of the knowledge, skills and tools and techniques to project activities for successfully managing a project. The PMBOK® Guide, 4th Edition, recognizes such 42 discrete project management processes and classifies them into 5 process groups according to the project life cycle phase with they are associated and 9 knowledge areas according to the knowledge discipline involved with those processes.

3. Description of a Typical Project Management Process

Let us take the typical project management process: project cost estimation. Now, there could be inputs to the cost estimation from several different sources. The project scope will provide information for what needs to be accomplished, so the cost estimation has to take that into account. Similarly, the market—availability and prices of products and services required would be another input for cost estimation. There would be different tools and techniques for cost estimation using these inputs based on the purpose for which cost estimate is required: costs based on historical data (Analogous Cost Estimating Technique for preliminary evaluation), cost based on system analysis and parameters (Parametric Cost Estimating Technique for a closer look for project selection stage), cost built up from small project package elements (Bottom-up Cost Estimating Technique for detailed project planning and budgetary control), etc. Using the appropriate technique or tools and corresponding inputs of information, the cost of a project phase or entire project is estimated. The process thus can be visualized as a transforming apparatus, where the inputs are utilized to deliver the outputs using the tools and techniques specific to the process.

4. Classification of Project Management Processes According to Project Life Cycle

There are similarities between many project management processes and this similarity can be used as criteria for classifying the project management processes. These processes are common to almost all projects and they are concerned with the flow of information throughout the project life and some common generally accepted good tools and techniques. Analysis also shows that a number of project processes are closely inter-related and they are often carried out in close sequence during the specific phase of the project life cycle: PMBOK® Guide, 4th Edition, has identified such 42 project management processes and classified them into 5 major process groups according to the basic nature of the process and during which part of the life cycle of the project it is predominantly carried out.

1. *Initiating Process Group:* This group of processes defines and authorizes the project or project phase.
2. *Planning Process Group:* This group of processes defines and refines the project objectives and plans detailed course of action for the project activities to attain the project objectives.
3. *Executing Process Group:* This group of processes manages people (own and vendors') and other resources (materials, equipment and technology) to actually carry out the activities as envisaged in the project management plan.
4. *Monitoring & Controlling Process Group:* This group of processes continually measures the performance and monitors the progress against the standards and project objectives so that the corrective action can be taken to keep project on course.
5. *Closing Process Group:* This group of processes formalizes the acceptance of the product, service or result created by the project and brings all project activities to an orderly close.

5. Classification of Processes According to Knowledge Area

Another classification of the project management processes can be made on the basis of knowledge area with which the processes are primarily concerned. Cost estimating, Budgeting and Cost Control—all three processes are concerned with the cost of resources and their monetary value. So all these processes are grouped under the Project Cost Management as knowledge area. Similarly, Scope planning, Scope definition, Work Breakdown Structure, Scope Verification and Scope Control—all are concerned about how the project scope is to be managed, so they are grouped under Project Scope Management knowledge area. Total nine knowledge management areas that have been identified are listed as follows:

Project Scope Management takes care of the processes required to ensure that the project includes all the work required to complete the project successfully. Of total 5 processes, three processes belong to the planning group (Collect Requirements, Define Scope and Create Work Breakdown Structure) and two belong to monitoring and controlling process group (Verify Scope and Control Scope).

Project Time Management includes the processes required for timely completion of the project. Of total 6 time management processes, five processes belong to the planning group (Define Activities, Sequence Activities, Estimate Activity Resources, Estimate Activity Durations, and Develop Schedule) and one to monitoring and controlling process group (Control Schedule).

Project Cost Management includes the processes required for estimating the project cost, preparing the project budget and controlling the costs for completion of the project within the approved budget. Of total 3 cost management processes, two processes belong to the planning group (Estimate Cost and Determine

Budget) and one process is classified as belonging to monitoring and controlling process group (Control Cost)

Project Quality Management includes the processes required to ensure that all project work conforms to the accepted quality criteria for authorizing the project and all policies and procedures of the performing organization for quality are followed. Of total 3 quality management processes, one process each is classified as belonging to the planning group (Plan Quality), the executing process group (Perform Quality Assurance), and the monitoring and controlling process group (Perform Quality Control).

Project Human Resource Management includes the processes required to acquire, organize, train and manage the project team. Of total 4 human resources management processes, one processes is classified as belonging to the planning group (Develop Human Resource Plan), and the other three processes are classified as belonging to the executing process group (Acquire Project Team, Develop Project Team, and Manage Project Team).

Project Communication Management includes the processes required to ensure timely generation, collection, distribution and storage of all necessary project information to ensure its availability and satisfy the stakeholders. Of total 5 communications management processes, one process is classified as an initiating process (Identify Stakeholders), one process each is classified as belonging to the planning group (Plan Communications), and to monitoring and controlling process group (Report Performance), and two processes belong to the executing process group (Distribute Information and Manage Stakeholders' Expectations).

Project Risk Management includes the processes required to identify the project risks, prepare qualitative and quantitative analysis and prepare suitable risk mitigation plans to ensure that the project is completed successfully. Of total 6 risk management processes, five processes are classified as belonging to the planning group (Plan Risk Management, Identify Risks, Perform Qualitative Analysis, Perform Quantitative Analysis, and Plan Risk Response) and one process belongs to the monitoring and controlling process group (Monitor and Control Risks).

Project Procurement Management includes the processes required to acquire materials, products, technologies or services for carrying out the project activities from outsourcing. Of total 4 procurement management processes, one process is classified as belonging to the planning each group (Plan Procurements), the executing process group (Conduct Procurements), the monitoring and controlling process group (Administer Procurements) and the closing process group (Close Procurements).

Project Integration Management: These processes are concerned with proactively managing and integrating the project management processes related to the above eight knowledge areas by defining, unifying, coordinating, and making suitable trade-offs. Of total 5 integration management processes, one process is classified as an initiating process (Develop Project Charter), one process each is classified as belonging to the planning group (Develop Project Management Plan), and the executing process group (Direct and manage Project Execution), two processes are classified as belonging to monitoring and controlling process group (Monitor & Control Project Work and Perform Integrated Change Control) and one belongs to the closing process group (Close Project or Phase).

In the set of appendices to the relevant chapters in the book, these project management processes would be described in detail (the nature of the process, major inputs, outputs and tools and techniques) according to the knowledge area group they belong to—all cost management process together, all time management process together and so on. Along with the individual processes, common concepts and techniques would also be described.

APPENDIX 1.2

Project Integration Management

1. Nature of Project Integration Management

Being in overall charge of the project, the project manager is responsible for all project related decisions and all initiating, planning, executing, monitoring, controlling and closing activities for the project. While doing this, the project manager has to take a holistic view of the entire project and identify and define all project activities, combine and unify them for synergistic effect and coordinate them for effective and efficient outcomes. When there are conflicting requirements or objectives of different stakeholders, or when constraints force a choice between the one or the other of the project objectives, the project manager and his team would have to decide on the course of trade-offs and devise an optimum solution. The project manager and his team has to manage the stakeholders' expectations, to decide resources allocation, to perform integrated control on all project changes, and to orchestrate all project activities for project success. Resolving the conflicts between the component plans for managing project scope, time, cost, quality and risks and developing and executing a unified project plan is also a part of the project integration management.

PMBOK® Guide has classified these general management activities for project work in a group and labeled it a separate knowledge area: Project Integration Management.

One overarching process of the project integration nature is recognized in each project management process groups based on project life cycle and included in the project integration management knowledge area:

I. Develop Project Charter (Initiating Process Group)
II. Develop Project Management Plan (Planning Process Group)
III. Direct and Manage Project Execution (Executing Process Group)
IV. Monitor and Control Project Work (Monitoring and Controlling Process Group)
V. Close Project or Phase (Closing Process Group)

Monitoring and controlling process group includes an additional process in the project integration management knowledge area: Perform Integrated Change Control.

2. Project Integration Management Processes

A brief description of each process, its inputs, outputs and tools & techniques is given below.

2.1 Develop Project Charter (Initiating Process Group)

This process belongs to initiating process group whose output is Project Charter. PMBOK® Guide defines Project Charter as a document issued by the project initiator or sponsor that formally authorizes the existence of a project (or a project phase) and provides the project manager with the authority to apply organization's resources to project activities.

Project charter is a very important project document and it serves as a reference for making all major decisions during the entire project life cycle - for planning the project details or during the project execution phase. It would include a brief summary all important details considered while authorizing the project:

- The business case (justification of the project and the alignment of the project with the organization's business strategy)
- Major project objectives and measurable criteria for judging success
- High level description of the requirements and product of the project
- Overview of project risks
- Constraints and assumptions based on organizational, environmental and external factors.
- Major project activities completion milestones
- Project cost estimate and summary budget
- Nomination of project manager and key members of the project team; authority levels and responsibilities.
- Name, designation and authority of the person authorizing the project charter

Inputs

Developing the project charter involves the analysis based on strategic planning, the alignment of the project selected with this strategy and somewhat detailed definition of the project - the product or services proposed to be created by the project. The strategic planning, in turn, would start from SWOT analysis: the strengths and weaknesses of the organization and the threats and opportunities present in the macroeconomic and industrial environment. In this light, the important inputs for developing the project charter are:

The Business Case: For internal projects, the project is identified or selected to align with the strategic analysis and meet one of the business needs. The business need may fall into any of the following categories:

- Business need or opportunity for investment: Setting up a new business, Expanding production capacity, Backward or forward integration, starting a profitable venture for diversification of investment, entrepreneurial vision
- Market need: Offering a suitable product mix to different market segments, Developing a new product, Responding to customer requests for some features
- Technological push: Developing new technology, Making products compatible with new technology
- Organizational structure change, Geographical expansion, Recruitment & training campaigns
- Legal or social requirement: Effluent treatment plant; Employee welfare schemes

Project Statement of Work (SOW): SOW is the narrative description of the product or service to be created by the project and description of product scope. SOW is another important input for project charter.

Customer Request for Project Management: For organizations performing projects on contract, the project contract provides the main input.

Organizational Process Assets: The experience of the organization during earlier similar projects, the lessons learned, templates developed or successful measures used for project planning and execution are also very useful inputs.

Enterprise Environmental Factors: External constraints from organization's structure, industry practice and market place, legal and environmental standards also have to be taken into account for developing the project charter.

Tools & Techniques

Expert Judgment

Project Charter is almost like a blue print for the planning and execution of the project. Developing this document requires considerable knowledge, experience and managerial maturity to evaluate a number of factors and resolve conflicts among objectives for charting the course for successful future operations. Expert judgment is the only technique for this high level integrative process.

Output

Project Charter This is the sole output from this process.

2.2 Develop Project Management Plan (Planning Process Group)

As the name suggests, the process involves developing project management plan. PMBOK® Guide, 4th Edition, defines Project Management Plan as a formal, approved document that defines how project is executed, monitored and controlled; it would be summary or detailed and composed of one or more subsidiary management plans and other planning documents.

Project management plan, an integrated result of all project management planning, is meant to define and refine project objectives and work out, in sufficient details, the course for effective execution of all project activities. The project management plan takes holistic view of the whole project and integrates all subsidiary component plans (plans for managing scope, time, cost, quality, human resource, communication, procurement and risks) by unifying and combining the component plans, resolving conflicts and coordinating for efficient execution.

A brief description of the inputs, tools and techniques and outputs follows.

Inputs

Project Charter This is the starting point—what the project has been authorized to accomplish.

Outputs from other planning processes The purpose of this integration processes is to unify, combine and coordinate the planning requirements separately developed for addressing the issues related to management of scope, time, cost, quality, communication, human resources, risk and procurement. The outputs from these, other planning process become the inputs for development of an integrated plan.

Enterprise Environmental Factors (organization's infrastructure, existing policies and procedures, industry standards and government regulations) and Organization's Process Assets (earlier experience of the organization, lessons learned and the techniques developed for handling time, scope, risk or quality issues, etc.) are other inputs.

Tools and Techniques

Expert Judgment: Expert judgment developed from experience, knowledge, and managerial maturity is necessary to unify, combine and coordinate diverse project component plans, make proper trade-offs and develop a project management plan.

Outputs

Project Management Plan The output from the process is the document developed by integration of the planning outputs from other planning areas. It would include:

- Subsidiary Plans for management of scope, time, cost, quality, human resources, communication, risk and procurement,
- Project baselines for managing three core areas -project scope, time and cost
- Overall plan for managing the project through all phases of the project life cycle and change management plan

2.3 Direct and Manage Project Execution (Executing Process Group)

During the execution phase, all the work defined in the planning process for accomplishing the project objectives is completed to the required quality standard by application of the resources (human resources, project funds, infrastructure and technology) and all major stakeholders are kept informed of the project status and the forecasts for project schedule and budget. Direct and Manage Project Execution is the overarching execution process integrating the project management processes in the human resources, quality, procurement and communication areas.

Inputs

The inputs for this process are Project Management Plan, Approved Change Requests, the usual constraints from Organizational Environmental Factors and help from Organization Process Assets. The nature and underlying reasons for other inputs mentioned above is self-explanatory. A brief explanation of Approved Change Requests as an input would be in place here.

Approved Change Requests: The process of defining and refining the details of the activities usually continues throughout the entire project life cycle. This on-going change process is to some extent unavoidable since very often some refinements and necessary changes become apparent only after the project has progressed through some planning and execution. The Integrated Change Control process, described hereafter, ensures that the changes are approved only after going through a set of procedural reviews before their approval, so that project resources are not frittered away on changes concerned with outcomes of subsidiary importance. It is the task of the project manager and his team to integrate all such approved change requests and execute them.

Tools and Techniques

Expert Judgment: Effective project execution requires a project manager to be able to be work on diverse issues at the same time, manage the expectations of the stakeholders, and be a true leader of the project team. The constant attention to details while keeping the larger picture in view, resolving conflicts and making proper trade offs are other requirements for successful project execution. These traits and project management decisions based on them are summed up under the title 'Expert Judgment'.

Project Management Information Systems: These systems help in tracking the progress and communication the status and forecasts of project outcomes to the key stakeholders.

Output

Execution process completes the planned project work and produces the project *deliverable*—'a unique and verifiable product, service result or capability to perform' included as the one of the project objectives.

Other outputs of this execution process are the updates necessary as the ongoing work necessitates: *updates in project documents* (like project charter, scope statement, risk register, etc.), *updates in the component plans* (for management of scope, time, cost, quality, communication, human resources, risk and procurement) and *updates in project baselines* (for scope, time and cost areas).

2.4 Monitor and Control Project Work (Monitoring and Controlling Process Group)

PMBOK® Guide, 4th Edition, defines this process as the work necessary to track, review and regulate the process to meet the performance objectives defined in the project management plan.

The usual feed-back control loop employed for process control is also the basis for this process. It starts with the project plan and the details worked out for meeting the project objectives, which serves as the standard for comparison. By the inspection and testing of the deliverables, it is checked if the deliverables meet the objective measurable technical specifications and performance criteria, which the project was set to accomplish. If the deliverables pass the tests successfully, they are formally approved and handed over. If the deliverables fail to meet the tests, the necessary defect repair or correction is initiated.

With this overview of the nature of the process, brief explanation of the inputs, tools and techniques and outputs of this process should be self-explanatory.

Inputs

Project Management Plan,Performance Reports, Enterprise Environmental factors, and *Organizational Process Assets* are the inputs.

Tools and Techniques

Like for other project integrating processes, *Expert Judgment* (in this case, expertise in the industry practice or technology, which could assist the project manager in interpreting the results and evaluating the outcomes) is the main tool or technique.

Outputs

Change Requests As a part of the inspection and testing for monitoring and controlling the deliverables, the process would issue when necessary change requests for corrective actions for overall project direction and repair of specific defects of deliverables in progress.

Corresponding *Updates in Project Component Plans* and *Updates in Project Documents* are other outputs.

2.5 Perform Integrated Change Control (Monitoring and Controlling Process Group)

This is a very important process and it is at the heart of managing changes to projects –a very necessary and critical aspect of project management. On one hand, the project manager has to ensure that changes to the project are minimal and the resources of the project are not frittered away on peripheral objectives. On the other hand, the project manager must ensure that all changes, originating from thoughtful review of the project work planned or executed up to a point and considered desirable for meeting the basic objectives for which the project was authorized are accepted and implemented.

The change management activities carried out during the process include:

- Ensuring that only the approved changes get implemented and preventing the unapproved changes to slip through the change control process
- Setting up procedures for proposing changes and for evaluating their impact on project scope, quality, cost and schedule
- Setting up criteria and organization for acceptance of change (Change Control Board or Committee for a major infrastructure project)
- Approving the changes which meet the criteria for acceptance and reject the changes which do not meet the criteria for acceptance
- Incorporating the approved changes into the component plans, project baselines for scope, cost and schedule, and overall project management plan and ensure their execution

- Keeping a record of proposed changes and issues, the summary of evaluation and the acceptance or rejection record and formal acceptance of deliverable based on approved change

With this overview of the nature of the process, brief explanation of the inputs, tools and techniques and outputs of this process should be self-explanatory.

Inputs

The inputs for this process are *Project management Plan, Work Performance Information, Change Requests submitted for approval, Enterprise Environmental Factors* and *Organizational Project Assets.*

Tools and Techniques

Expert Judgment (value judgment in assessing proposed changes, guidance from consultants or other experts) is again the only technique for this integrative process.

Outputs

The decisions taken on the change requests are the main outputs from this essentially decision making process. The outputs are, therefore, *Change Request Status Updates* (whether a change request is accepted, rejected or under review), *Updates in the Project Management Plan* and *Updates in Project Documents* (to reflect the effect of approved changes on the activity list and sequence, project schedule, project quality and project cost).

2.6 Close Project or Phase (Closing Process Group)

PMBOK® Guide, 4th Edition, defines this process as finalizing all activities across all of the project management process groups to formally complete the project or phase. In case of projects completed and closed in a normal manner, the process would include the following activities:

- Reviewing information on all earlier project phases to ensure that all project work is completed to the scope and quality standards set at the project authorization stage
- Closing all project contracts, arranging for disbanding the project team by reassigning the project team to their new positions
- Getting formal acceptance of the deliverables from the operating department or project sponsor in case of internal projects and client in case of external project and handing over the product of the project
- Completing the minor left out items or taking corrective action and repair of the defects found during the formal acceptance check to facilitate formal acceptance of the project by the client or operating department
- Preparing a detailed review of the project (formal Project Audit in some case) and record lessons learned from the success and failures in project activities for the organization's knowledge and capability to manage similar projects in future
- Preparing a detailed status report of all the project work at the stage at which the project is terminated before its normal completion
- Analyzing the reasons for failure or termination prior to its normal completion and closing

The inputs, tools and techniques and outputs of the process as described in PMBOK® Guide are briefly listed below to make this summary of integration management processes comprehensive. A detailed and more complete account of the project closing is given in Chapter 14: Project Audit and Closure, under the heading' Project Closure'.

Inputs

Project management Plan (For reference of the original scope of project work)

Accepted Deliverables (For formal acceptance of deliverables prior to hand over—based on "Verify Scope" process).

Organizational Process Assets (Project closure guidelines of the organization and the procedures for archiving the lessons learnt).

Tools and Techniques

Expert Judgment (experience and proficiency in use of administrative procedures) is the only technique.

CASE 1.1

A Day in the Life

Rachel, the project manager of a large information systems project, arrives at her office early to get caught up with work before her co-workers and project team arrive. However, as she enters the office she meets Neil, one of her fellow project managers, who also wants to get an early start on the day. Neil has just completed a project overseas. They spend 10 minutes socializing and catching up on personal news.

It takes Rachel 10 minutes to get to her office and settle in. She then checks her voice mail and turns on her computer. She was at her client's site the day before until 7:30 P.M. and has not checked her e-mail or voice mail since 3:30 P.M. the previous day. There are 7 phone messages, 16 e-mails, and 4 notes left on her desk. She spends 15 minutes reviewing her schedule and "to do" lists for the day before responding to messages that require immediate attention.

Rachel spends the next 25 minutes going over project reports and preparing for the weekly status meeting. Her boss, who just arrived at the office, interrupts her. They spend 20 minutes discussing the project. He shares a rumor that a team member is using stimulants on the job. She tells him that she has not seen anything suspicious but will keep an eye on the team member.

The 9:00 A.M. project status meeting starts 15 minutes late because two of the team members have to finish a job for a client. Several people go to the cafeteria to get coffee and doughnuts while others discuss last night's baseball game. The team members arrive, and the remaining 45 minutes of the progress review meeting surface project issues that have to be addressed and assigned for action.

After the meeting Rachel goes down the hallway to meet with Victoria, another IS project manager. They spend 30 minutes reviewing project assignments since the two of them share personnel. Victoria's project is behind schedule and in need of help. They broker a deal that should get Victoria's project back on track.

She returns to her office and makes several phone calls and returns several e-mails before walking downstairs to visit with members of her project team. Her intent is to follow up on an issue that had surfaced in the status report meeting. However, her simple, "Hi guys, how are things going?" elicits a stream of disgruntled responses from the "troops." After listening patiently for over 20 minutes, she realizes that among other things several of the client's managers are beginning to request features that were not in the original project scope statement. She tells her people that she will get on this right away.

Returning to her office she tries to call her counterpart John at the client firm but is told that he is not expected back from lunch for another hour. At this time, Eddie drops by and says, "How about lunch?" Eddie works in the finance office and they spend the next half hour in the company cafeteria gossiping about internal politics. She is surprised to hear that Jonah Johnson, the director of systems projects, may join another firm. Jonah has always been a powerful ally.

She returns to her office, answers a few more e-mails, and finally gets through to John. They spend 30 minutes going over the problem. The conversation ends with John promising to do some investigating and to get back to her as soon as possible.

Rachel puts a "Do not disturb" sign on her door, and lies down in her office. She listens to the third and fourth movement of Ravel's string quartet in F on headphones.

Rachel then takes the elevator down to the third floor and talks to the purchasing agent assigned to her project. They spend the next 30 minutes exploring ways of getting necessary equipment to the project site earlier than planned. She finally authorizes express delivery.

When she returns to her office, her calendar reminds her that she is scheduled to participate in a conference call at 2:30. It takes 15 minutes for everyone to get online. During this time, Rachel catches up on some e-mail. The next hour is spent exchanging information about the technical requirements associated with a new version of a software package they are using on systems projects like hers.

Rachel decides to stretch her legs and goes on a walk down the hallway where she engages in brief conversations with various co-workers. She goes out of her way to thank Chandra for his thoughtful analysis at the status report meeting. She returns to find that John has left a message for her to call him back ASAP. She contacts John, who informs her that, according to his people, her firm's marketing rep had made certain promises about specific features her system would provide. He doesn't know how this communication breakdown occurred, but his people are pretty upset over the situation. Rachel thanks John for the information and immediately takes the stairs to where the marketing group resides.

She asks to see Mary, a senior marketing manager. She waits 10 minutes before being invited into her office. After a heated discussion, she leaves 40 minutes later with Mary agreeing to talk to her people about what was promised and what was not promised.

She goes downstairs to her people to give them an update on what is happening. They spend 30 minutes reviewing the impact the client's requests could have on the project schedule. She also shares with them the schedule changes she and Victoria had agreed to. After she says good night to her team, she heads upstairs to her boss's office and spends 20 minutes updating him on key events of the day. She returns to her office and spends 30 minutes reviewing e-mails and project documents. She logs on to the MS project schedule of her project and spends the next 30 minutes working with "what-if" scenarios. She reviews tomorrow's schedule and writes some personal reminders before starting off on her 30-minute commute home.

1. **How effectively do you think Rachel spent her day?**
2. **What does the case tell you about what it is like to be a project manager?**

CASE 1.2

Coal Fired Boilers Project
(A Case Focusing on Project Proposal & Overview)

The whole world is a unified place and the echoes of events in one country resound loudly in some distant lands. Altaf Hussein worked as an engineering and maintenance manager in National Mills, an old textile mill in the hinterlands of India. His daily work life was quite routine and hardly ever anything exciting new happened. All this changed suddenly in March of 1973, when in an OPEC meeting held in distant Riyadh, the decision was taken to raise the crude prices. The crude oil price has been observed to fluctuate or even gradually creep upwards over the years. But the price revision this time was an abrupt upward leap—from US $2.73 a barrel to US $9.82 a barrel.

The textile mills are heavy users of low pressure steam for their processing departments—dyeing, bleaching and finishing and the cost of steam accounts for a substantial portion of their processing costs. Use of coal as a fuel for raising low-pressure steam would reduce steam costs, but coal is a much dirtier and inconvenient fuel compared to oil and so switching over to coal-fired boilers was strongly resisted by the plant management all along. Some textile mills located near the metropolis areas and well-connected by rails had switched over to coal for steam generation, but the procurement and transportation of coal to the hinterland being cumbersome, National Mills had continued to depend on steam generated from oil fired boilers. But with this four fold increase in the price of oil derived from costly crude, the mill faced dire future. It must do something about the steam cost or face closure of the entire mill.

Altaf had all along hated the old oil fired boilers with frequent breakdowns and causing unexpected emergencies and work loads on him and his staff, but his proposals for replacing the old boilers with new ones had been rejected twice in the last four years with the argument, "New boilers and the trouble free continuity in the processing departments is fine, but the investment won't pay for itself." Projection of economic benefits is sometimes difficult to cast into hard cash numbers and Altaf had ultimately lost out on earlier occasions.

Altaf saw in the new situation one more opportunity to push his favourite boiler replacement project—this time with an added twist—new coal-fired boilers, which can be justified for economic benefits now hands down. He prepared a brief 3-pages proposal for the new coal fired boilers and sent it to Kamal Nayan Bajaj, Executive Vice-President on Friday morning. The proposal was so attractive that Mr.Bajaj summoned Altaf for further discussion that very afternoon. Altaf had projected Rs 35 millions as the project cost for 80 tonnes/hr capacity boilers and the cost of generated steam to drop from Rs 135 per tonne to Rs 105 per tonne.

Mr. Bajaj shot a number of questions: "Altaf, the idea is good, but unfortunately, may be, we are late for it.How fast can we execute the project? How sure are you of the viability of the project—the cost of project, saving in operating cost by its generation with coal as fuel? Of course, the most crucial question would be: can we get the boiler on line by February 1974, say latest by March 1974? If your answer to the last question is yes, we can announce in the next annual general meeting in May that the operation cost situation is under control. That would save the day."

"Sir, I am pretty sure of my cost of project and operational cost savings numbers. The project has become now not only just viable but a very attractive investment;" enthused Altaf.

"Well, if that is the case, I would be ready to authorize the project right away. You would be the Project Manager and if you deliver the goods, the next promotion to Assistant Vice President is yours! But, remember, you will have to prove your projections first to Mr. Patel, and as the Company Financial Controller, he is as hard nosed as seasoned accountants are. We don't have much time. For a starter, why don't you give me by Monday morning an executive summary of your project proposal, which should include brief project overview?"

Altaf had done his homework well before; so he prepared the executive summary (shown below as an exhibit to this case), which could reassure Mr. Bajaj on all issues raised by him. At Mr. Bajaj's suggestion, Altaf prepared the detailed project proposal, along with a number of documents supporting the figures and projections used in the executive summary:

- Project objectives and criteria for judging project success (particularly the project schedule)
- Financial justification for the project (economic feasibility of the proposal—backed by cash flows based on operating costs and savings, estimated return on investment using pay-back period and net present value methods for calculations)
- Scope of the overall work and technical and performance specifications of key deliverables
- Project time frame—milestones for major activities completion
- Preliminary project cost estimate (with breakdown showing major expense heads)

- Key project team members (to be released for working on this project)
- Plan for project communications

After a close scrutiny, Mr. Patel confirmed as realistic the projections in Altaf's proposal and the new Coal-based Steam Generation Project was soon authorized.

Coal Fired Boilers Project Proposal Executive Summary

1. Project Scope Statement

Design, procure, install and commission by February 28, 1974 a system for generating 80 tonnes per hour of steam using coal as fuel at a total project cost not exceeding Rs 35 millions. The minimum return on investment of Rs 35 millions should be 50 % per annum.

2. Project Objectives and Criteria for Project Success

No.	Project Objectives	Criteria for Success
1	To reduce the cost of production of steam by switching from furnace oil to coal as fuel	Reduce the cost from Rs 135/- per tonne to Rs 105/- per tonne
2.	To commission the project as early as possible latest by March 31, 1974 so that in the annual general meeting the prospects for improved profitability of the mill's operations could be announced and the market capitalization of the shares can be upgraded	Commission the project latest by March 31, 1974 Announce the results of improved profitability in annual general meeting in May, 1974
3	To complete the project within estimated budget	Complete the project within +/- 5 % of budgeted cost of Rs 35 millions
4.	To earn adequate return on investment (ROI)	Ensure capability for earning about 50 % ROI on investment of Rs 35 millions

3. Customer/ Project Sponsor

There is no external customer; the executive vice-president Kamal Nayan Bajaj is the project sponsor.

4. Summary of Economic Viability

Estimated Investment:	Rs 35 millions
Saving in cost of production of steam (Based on coal based steam cost of Rs 105/ tonne Compared to Rs 135/ tonne for furnace as fuel)	Rs 30/- per tonne
Annual savings in steam production cost (based on 85 % annual average use of the installed Capacity of 80 tonnes/hr at 90 % annual average operating time)	Rs 17.7 millions
Return on Investment	50.4 %

5. Preliminary Stakeholders Analysis

Project Sponsor: Kamal Nayan Bajaj, Executive Vice President

Senior Officers of National Mills:
Mr. Patel, Company Finance Controller
Heads of operating departments using low pressure steam:
Heads of Dyeing, Bleaching and Finishing Departments
Head of Materials Department for coal procurement, quality testing and storage
Head of Maintenance Department for maintenance and upkeep of the system

Project Team
Project Manager: Altaf Hussein
Key members of the project team: The members deputed to the cross-functional project team (material procurement assistant, senior engineers in charge of civl construction and mechanical and electrical installations

6. Fit with Current Operations/Similarities to Previous Projects

- The project has a very close fit to the current operations-generating process steam; only the fuel is planned to be switched. The project would have immediate impact on the entire operations of the mill.
- Some modifications were carried out from time to time in the mill's steam distribution system and piping, but no major installation of the size and scope of the proposed project was undertaken in the last seven years by the company.

7. Major Deliverables

Deliverable 1   *System Design:*
Study the plant's present steam distribution and steam requirements for overall system design
Equipment layouts in boiler/coal handling areas and piping layouts and detailed construction drawings

Deliverable 2   *Procurement:*
Procure system components
Coal-fired boiler and coal handling system
Structural components for pipe rack and
Piping, valves and other piping components

Deliverable 3   *Project Construction at the site:*
Civil construction for boiler control room, equipment foundations and pipe rack structure,
Mechanical installation of boiler, electrical & instrumentation for boiler, Mechanical installation of coal handling system
Installation of steam distribution piping

Deliverable 4   *System commissioning*

Deliverable 5   *Training & handing over the project to operating departments:*
Operation & maintenance manuals for boiler, coal handling equipment and special new instrumentation

Deliverable 6   *Project Management:*

Receiving statutory approvals from Boilers Inspector, Factory Inspector, etc. Effective project management to deliver the project on time and within budget.

8. Summary Budget (In Rs Millions)

Buildings and Structures	3.0
Machinery & Equipment	
Boiler	16.0
Coal handling equipment	6.0
Other equipment	3.0
Installation-materials & labour	3.5
SUB-TOTAL MACHINERY & EQUPMENT	28.5
Provision for contingency at approx 10 %	3.5
TOTAL ESTIMATED PROJECT COST	35.0

9. Summary Milestones

The installation of coal-handling system:	January 15, 1974
The installation of the boiler and all systems:	February 1, 1974
The Trial runs for statutory approvals:	February 15, 1974
The performance guarantee runs of entire system:	March 1, 1974
The steam headers and connections to users:	March 15, 1974

10. Assumptions, Risks, and Constraints

SCHEDULE ASSUMPTIONS AND RISKS:

(a) Authorized capital budget request is received latest by April1, 1973.

(b) Statutory approvals from The Boiler Inspectorate and Environment Protection Agency for the preliminary proposal for installation of coal fired boiler are approved latest by May15, 1973.

(c) Engineering consulting company is selected and awarded the contract by April30, 1973.

(d) All key project team members are released to work full time on this project latest by April 30,1973

(e) The deliveries at the site for the critical major equipment (coal fired boiler and coal handling equipment) are completed by December 31, 1973 under late delivery penalty purchase order.

SCHEDULE CONSTRAINTS:

(a) Two potential key members of the project team are presently working on other urgent projects and their release in the desirable time may be doubtful.

(b) The Boiler Inspectorate is notorious of delays in giving for approvals for proposals.

(c) Ordinarily boiler delivery period is of the order of 8-9 months minimum, while 6-7 months maximum delivery period is necessary to meet project schedule. (Special efforts to locate a suitable supplier, extra price premium over routine competitive prices and stiff late delivery penalty may be necessary to overcome this.)

(d) The foundation casting must be completed before expected onset of monsoon by June 15.

(e) A large number of holidays would be in August-November period—the expected peak activity period for project construction.

Discussion and Questions

Projects play a very important role as instruments of change and as instruments for implementing the organization's business strategy. Judicious selection is, therefore, as important as effective and efficient planning and execution of the projects. Most organizations follow a specific methodology for preparing proposals and decision making for major projects: the type of data to be collected, its presentation and scrutiny for decision making and the availability of necessary supporting details. The executive summary specimen of the case illustrates one such project proposal presentation. It would help to give the readers exposure to some aspects of the modern project planning and management techniques and also serve as a preview of the knowledge, approach and techniques for planning and managing projects presented in the subsequent sections of the book.

a. General: Study the proposal closely. Notice the issues which a major capital expenditure project should address. Compare them with the capital expenditure authorization practice in your organization.

b. Notice the critical role a major project would play in the organization. For this textile mill, the very existence of the organization depends on coming up with and efficiently managing this major project

c. Notice the nature of specificity and objective measurable standards included in describing the proposal.

- The inclusion of the technical specifications of the product of the project (Statement of Works or S.O.W.), budget and schedule in the opening project scope statement

- The project objectives and the objectively measurable criteria for judging the project success for each of those objectives

- Focus on sponsor or main customer and identifying all major stakeholders; managing the key stakeholders is a major contributor for project success

- Summary of economic viability analysis, project cost estimate and major milestones for schedule; these figures demarcate the boundaries for project cost and schedule

- Provision for contingency in project cost and schedule—it is one of the tools for managing project risks

- Major deliverables and including separately project management as a specific deliverable

- Analysis of Assumptions, Risks and Constraints.

- This list is very useful in focusing on major issues and at all later stage reviews of the project for giving it the right direction.

CHAPTER 2

Organization Strategy and Project Selection

Strategy is implemented through projects. Every project should have a clear link to the organization's strategy.

Project managers commonly complain that projects appear out of nowhere. Comments such as the following are samples of those heard in practice:

- Where did this project come from?
- Should I stop working on this project and start on the new one?
- Why are we doing this project?
- How can all these projects be first priority?
- Where are we going to get the resources to do this project?

There are too many organizations in which many managers cannot identify a project's priority and link it with the strategic plan. This is not good management! Every project should contribute value to the organization's strategic plan, which is designed to meet the future needs of its customers. Ensuring a strong linkage between the strategic plan and projects is a difficult task that demands constant attention from top and middle management. The larger and more diverse an organization, the more difficult it is to create and maintain this strong link. Ample evidence still suggests that many organizations have not developed a process that clearly aligns project selection to the strategic plan. The result is poor utilization of the organization's resources—people, money, equipment, and core competencies. Conversely, organizations that have a coherent link of projects to strategy have more cooperation across the organization, perform better on projects, and have fewer projects.

How can an organization ensure this link and alignment? The answer requires integration of projects with the strategic plan. Integration assumes the existence of a strategic plan and a process for prioritizing projects by their contribution to the plan. A crucial factor to ensure the success of integrating the plan with projects lies in the creation of a process that is open and published for all participants to review. This chapter presents an overview of the importance of strategic planning and the process for developing a strategic plan. Typical problems encountered when strategy and projects are not linked are noted. A generic methodology that ensures integration by creating very strong linkages of project selection and priority to the strategic plan is then discussed. The intended outcomes are clear organization focus, best use of scarce organization resources (people, equipment, capital), and improved communication across projects and departments.

Why Project Managers Need to Understand Strategy

Project management historically has been preoccupied solely with the planning and execution of projects. Strategy was considered to be under the purview of senior management. This is old-school thinking.

New-school thinking recognizes that project management is at the apex of strategy and operations. Aaron Shenhar speaks to this issue when he states, ". . . it is time to expand the traditional role of the project manager from an operational to a more strategic perspective. In the modern evolving organization, project managers will be focused on business aspects, and their role will expand from getting the job done to achieving the business results and winning in the market place."

There are two main reasons why project managers need to understand their organization's mission and strategy. The first reason is so they can make appropriate decisions and adjustments. For example, how a project manager would respond to a suggestion to modify the design of a product to enhance performance will vary depending upon whether his company strives to be a product leader through innovation or to achieve operational excellence through low cost solutions. Similarly, how a project manager would respond to delays may vary depending upon strategic concerns. A project manager will authorize overtime if her firm places a premium on getting to the market first. Another project manager will accept the delay if speed is not essential.

J. P. Descamps has observed that project managers who do not understand the role their project plays in accomplishing the strategy of their organization tend to make the following serious mistakes:

- Focusing on problems or solutions that have low priority strategically
- Focusing on the immediate customer rather than the whole market place and value chain
- Overemphasizing technology as an end in and of itself, resulting in projects that wander off pursuing exotic technology that does not fit the strategy or customer need
- Trying to solve every customer issue with a product or service rather than focusing on the 20 percent with 80 percent of the value (Pareto's Law)
- Engaging in a never-ending search for perfection that no one except the project team really cares about

The second reason project managers need to understand their organization's strategy is so that they can be effective project advocates. Project managers have to be able to demonstrate to senior management how their project contributes to their firm's mission. Protection and continued support come from being aligned with corporate objectives. Project managers also need to be able to explain to team members and other stakeholders why certain project objectives and priorities are critical. This is essential for getting buy-in on contentious trade-off decisions.

For these reasons project managers will find it valuable to have a keen understanding of strategic management and project selection processes, which are discussed next.

The Strategic Management Process: An Overview

Strategic management is the process of assessing "what we are" and deciding and implementing "what we intend to be and how we are going to get there." Strategy describes how an organization intends to compete with the resources available in the existing and perceived future environment.

Two major dimensions of strategic management are responding to changes in the external environment and allocating scarce resources of the firm to improve its competitive position. Constant scanning of the external environment for changes is a major requirement for survival in a dynamic competitive environment. The second dimension is the internal responses to new action programs aimed at enhancing the competitive position of the firm. The nature of the responses depends on the type of business, environment volatility, competition, and the organizational culture.

Strategic management provides the theme and focus of the future direction of the organization. It supports consistency of action at every level of the organization. It encourages integration because effort and resources are committed to common goals and strategies. See Snapshot from Practice: Move Beyond

Snapshot from Practice   Move Beyond Computers*

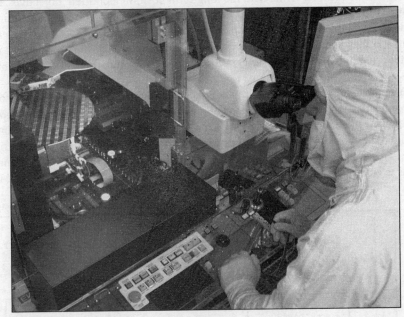

Courtesy Intel Corporation.

INTEL CEO Craig R. Barrett is planning his last hurrah only 15 months before his retirement to chairman of the board. His vision for INTEL is to move beyond computers: think INTEL everywhere. Barrett says, "Everything in the world is going digital." He wants INTEL chips to be the guts of every digital device on the planet—especially in the communications, consumer electronics, and entertainment industries. Think—cell phones, wireless home networks, video players, flat panel TVs—INTEL's expertise fits right in.

He is hitting the market today with a chip technology called WiMax "that can be used to deliver high speed Internet access throughout a small city (or 30 miles) for about $100,000, which is about one-tenth the cost of rolling out fiber optic lines today." (A competitor, WiFi, has a range of about 200 feet.) Cable and phone companies are very interested because of low entry costs.

Some critics believe Barrett's shotgun approach is too risky. He doesn't see it that way. Rather than following INTEL's past go-it-alone approach to new products, he wants INTEL to forge closer ties with customers by designing products they need rather than designing products no one asked for. He admits going into consumer markets will be a challenge and a half. He intends to provide financial support and cooperation for companies creating new products that will use INTEL chips. Barrett feels the risk of providing financial support for smaller companies creating new products is low, even if some go bust. If most of the new products take off, risk is minimized because their markets will lead to increasing demand for new, larger, and faster PCs where INTEL manufacturing dominates cost.

Implementing the new vision will not keep INTEL's manufacturing from remaining on the cutting edge. By 2005 five new factories will manufacture 12-inch wafers printed with 90-nanometer circuit lines, just 0.1 percent the width of a human hair. These plants are expected to slash chip costs in half.

The mission has been set: Create INTEL chips to meet the need of new digital products. Right or wrong, everyone in the organization knows the game plan and can focus their efforts in this new consumer-oriented direction. Projects related to digital products will be ranked high priority.

* Adapted from Cliff Edwards, "What Is CEO Craig Barrett Up To?" *Business Week,* March 8, 2004, pp. 56–64.

Computers. It is a continuous, iterative process aimed at developing an integrated and coordinated long-term plan of action. Strategic management positions the organization to meet the needs and requirements of its customers for the long term. With the long-term position identified, objectives are set, and strategies are developed to achieve objectives and then translated into actions by implementing projects. Strategy can decide the survival of an organization. Most organizations are successful in *formulating* strategies for what course(s) they should pursue. However, the problem in many organizations is *implementing* strategies—that is, making them happen. Integration of strategy formulation and implementation often does not exist.

The components of strategic management are closely linked, and all are directed toward the future success of the organization. Strategic management requires strong links among mission, goals, objectives, strategy, and implementation. The mission gives the general purpose of the organization. Goals give global targets within the mission. Objectives give specific targets to goals. Objectives give rise to formulation of strategies to reach objectives. Finally, strategies require actions and tasks to be implemented. In most cases the actions to be taken represent projects. Figure 2.1 shows a schematic of the strategic management process and major activities required.

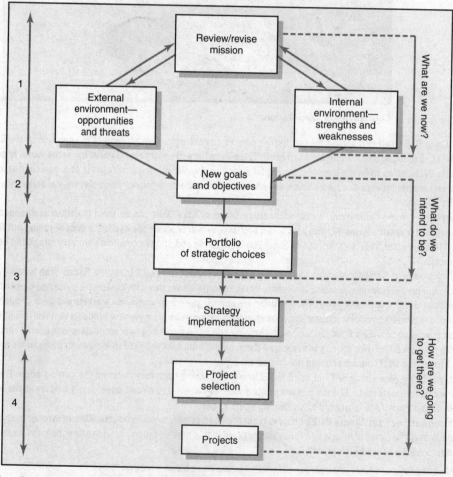

FIGURE 2.1   Strategic Management Process

Four Activities of the Strategic Management Process

The typical sequence of activities of the strategic management process is outlined here; a description of each activity then follows:

1. Review and define the organizational mission.
2. Set long-range goals and objectives.
3. Analyze and formulate strategies to reach objectives.
4. Implement strategies through projects.

Review and Define the Organizational Mission

The mission identifies "what we want to become," or the raison d'être. Mission statements identify the scope of the organization in terms of its product or service. A written mission statement provides focus for decision making when shared by organizational managers and employees. Everyone in the organization should be keenly aware of the organization's mission. For example, at one large consulting firm, partners who fail to recite the mission statement on demand are required to buy lunch. The mission statement communicates and identifies the purpose of the organization to all stakeholders. Mission statements can be used for evaluating organization performance.

Traditional components found in mission statements are major products and services, target customers and markets, and geographical domain. In addition, statements frequently include organizational philosophy, key technologies, public image, and contribution to society. Including such factors in mission statements relates directly to business success.

Mission statements change infrequently. However, when the nature of the business changes or shifts, a revised mission statement may be required. For example, Steve Jobs of Apple Computer envisioned the use of computer technology beyond the PC desktop. His mission was to look at computer technology as the vehicle for work and entertainment. As a result he developed the iPod for selling music and masterminded the development of animated movies such as *Finding Nemo* through the Pixar organization. See the adjacent Apple snapshot from practice to find out more about how Apple's mission shapes new product development projects.

More specific mission statements tend to give better results because of a tighter focus. Mission statements decrease the chance of false directions by stakeholders. For example, compare the phrasing of the following mission statements:

Provide hospital design services.
Provide voice/data design services.
Provide information technology services.
Increase shareholder value.
Provide high-value products to our customer.

Clearly, the first two statements leave less chance for misinterpretation than the others. A rule-of-thumb test for a mission statement is, if the statement can be anybody's mission statement, it will not provide the guidance and focus intended. The mission sets the parameters for developing objectives.

Long-Range Goals and Objectives

Objectives translate the organization mission into specific, concrete, measurable terms. Organizational objectives set targets for all levels of the organization. Objectives pinpoint the direction managers believe the organization should move toward. Objectives answer in detail *where* a firm is headed and *when* it is going to get there. Typically, objectives for the organization cover markets, products, innovation, productivity,

Snapshot from Practice   Apple's Strategy

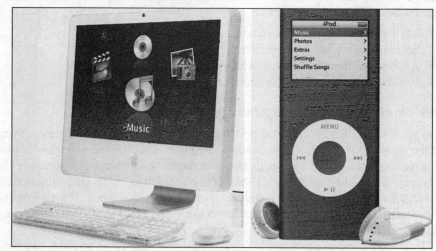

Courtesy of Apple Computer.

Since Steve Jobs returned to Apple Computers as CEO in 1997, he has been strikingly successful in developing a turnaround strategy that has developed new markets and increased market share. It all begins with strict adherence to the mission statement:

> Apple is committed to bringing the best personal computing experience to students, educators, creative professionals and consumers around the world through its innovative hardware, software and Internet offerings.

The thrust of the turnaround strategy includes mass customization and targeting market segments. Apple's primary competitive advantage is that it controls both the hardware and software aspects of most of its products. The vision, coupled with this strong strategic advantage, allows Apple to offer innovation in hardware, software, and Internet offerings. From the vision statement many product strategies have been forthcoming. For example, Jobs first segmented Apple's market into consumer and professional. This segmentation reduces the number of products and sharply targets products to specific end users.

Several specific strategies have developed for the consumer market. For example, Jobs believes users should be able to connect their MP3 players, iPods, DVD players, CD players, digital cameras, PDAs, DV camcorders, and other gadgets to a central computer, known as the digital hub. Development of iTunes allows users to mix and burn CDs from the comfort and ease of their computer. Along with burning CDs, users are able to use iTunes to sync their music files with MP3 players such as iPod.

Apple's competitive advantages provide strong support for its product strategies. Some of the more obvious are listed here:

- Control over both hardware and software—avoids compatibility problems
- High quality and innovation image
- Common Architecture fits most products and eases development time
- Free Software
- Ease of use
- Loyal customer base

For over ten years the string of innovative products from Apple has been spectacular. No end is in sight. Each new product endeavor closely aligns with the mission statement and current strategies. Launching new products in new markets requires executing projects within tight time, cost and scope constraints.

quality, finance, profitability, employees, and consumers. In every case, objectives should be as operational as possible. That is, objectives should include a time frame, be measurable, be an identifiable state, and be realistic. Doran created the memory device shown in Exhibit 2.1, which is useful when writing objectives.

Each level below the organizational objectives should support the higher-level objectives in more detail; this is frequently called cascading of objectives. For example, if a firm making leather luggage sets an objective of achieving a 40 percent increase in sales through a research and development strategy, this charge is passed to the marketing, production, and R&D departments. The R&D department accepts the firm's strategy as their objective, and their strategy becomes the design and development of a new "pull-type luggage with hidden retractable wheels." At this point the objective becomes a project to be implemented—to develop the retractable wheel luggage for market within six months within a budget of $200,000. In summary, organizational objectives drive your projects.

EXHIBIT 2.1   Characteristics of Objectives

S	Specific	Be specific in targeting an objective
M	Measurable	Establish a measurable indicator(s) of progress
A	Assignable	Make the objective assignable to one person for completion
R	Realistic	State what can realistically be done with available resources
T	Time related	State when the objective can be achieved, that is, duration

Analyze and Formulate Strategies to Reach Objectives

Formulating strategy answers the question of *what* needs to be done to reach objectives. Strategy formulation includes determining and evaluating alternatives that support the organization's objectives and selecting the best alternative. The first step is a realistic evaluation of the past and current position of the enterprise. This step typically includes an analysis of "who are the customers" and "what are their needs as they (the *customers*) see them."

The next step is an assessment of the internal and external environments. What are the internal strengths and weaknesses of the enterprise? Examples of internal strengths or weaknesses could be core competencies, such as technology, product quality, management talent, low debt, and dealer networks. Managers can alter internal strengths and weaknesses. Opportunities and threats usually represent external forces for change such as technology, industry structure, and competition. Competitive benchmarking tools are sometimes used here to assess current and future directions. Opportunities and threats are the flip sides of each other. That is, a threat can be perceived as an opportunity, or vice versa. Examples of perceived external threats could be a slowing of the economy, a maturing life cycle, exchange rates, or government regulation. Typical opportunities are increasing demand, emerging markets, and demographics. Managers or individual firms have limited opportunities to influence such external environmental factors; however, in recent years notable exceptions have been new technologies such as Apple using the iPod to create a market to sell music. The keys are to attempt to forecast fundamental industry changes and stay in a proactive mode rather than a reactive one. This assessment of the external and internal environments is known as the SWOT analysis (strengths, weaknesses, opportunities, and threats).

From this analysis, critical issues and a portfolio of strategic alternatives are identified. These alternatives are compared with the current portfolio and available resources; strategies are then selected that should support the basic mission and objectives of the organization. Critical analysis of the strategies includes asking questions: Does the strategy take advantage of our core competencies? Does the strategy exploit our competitive advantage? Does the strategy maximize meeting customers' needs? Does the strategy fit within our acceptable risk range?

Strategy formulation ends with cascading objectives or tasks assigned to lower divisions, departments, or individuals. Formulating strategy might range around 20 percent of management's effort, while determining *how* strategy will be implemented might consume 80 percent.

Implement Strategies through Projects

Implementation answers the question of *how* strategies will be realized, given available resources. The conceptual framework for strategy implementation lacks the structure and discipline found in strategy formulation. Implementation requires action and completing tasks; the latter frequently means mission-critical projects. Therefore, implementation must include attention to several key areas.

First, completing tasks requires allocation of resources. Resources typically represent funds, people, management talents, technological skills, and equipment. Frequently, implementation of projects is treated as an "addendum" rather than an integral part of the strategic management process. However, multiple objectives place conflicting demands on organizational resources. Second, implementation requires a formal and informal organization that complements and supports strategy and projects. Authority, responsibility, and performance all depend on organization structure and culture. Third, planning and control systems must be in place to be certain project activities necessary to ensure strategies are effectively performed. Fourth, motivating project contributors will be a major factor for achieving project success. Finally, an area receiving more attention in recent years is prioritizing projects. Although the strategy implementation process is not as clear as strategy formulation, all managers realize that, without implementation, success is impossible.

The Need for an Effective Project Portfolio Management System

Implementation of projects without a strong priority system linked to strategy creates problems. Three of the most obvious problems are discussed below. A project portfolio system can go a long way to reduce, or even eliminate, the impact of these problems.

Problem 1: The Implementation Gap

In organizations with short product life cycles, it is interesting to note that frequently participation in strategic planning and implementation includes participants from all levels within the organization. However, in perhaps 80 percent of the remaining product and service organizations, top management pretty much formulates strategy and leaves strategy implementation to functional managers. Within these broad constraints, more detailed strategies and objectives are developed by the functional managers. The fact that these objectives and strategies are made *independently* at different levels by functional groups within the organization hierarchy causes manifold problems.

Some symptoms of organizations struggling with strategy disconnect and unclear priorities are presented here.

- Conflicts frequently occur among functional managers and cause lack of trust.
- Frequent meetings are called to establish or renegotiate priorities.
- People frequently shift from one project to another, depending on current priority. Employees are confused about which projects are important.
- People are working on multiple projects and feel inefficient.
- Resources are not adequate.

Because clear linkages do not exist, the organizational environment becomes dysfunctional, confused, and ripe for ineffective implementation of organization strategy and, thus, of projects. The implementation gap refers to the lack of understanding and consensus of organization strategy among top and middle-level managers.

A scenario the authors have seen repeated several times follows. Top management picks their top 20 projects for the next planning period, without priorities. Each functional department—marketing, finance, operations, engineering, information technology, and human resources—selects projects from the list. Unfortunately independent department priorities across projects are not homogenous. A project that rates first in the IT department can rate 10th in the finance department. Implementation of the projects represents conflicts of interest with animosities developing over organization resources.

If this condition exists, how is it possible to effectively implement strategy? The problem is serious. One study found that only about 25 percent of *Fortune 500* executives believe there is a strong linkage, consistency, and/or agreement between the strategies they formulate and implementation. Middle managers considered organizational strategy to be under the purview of others or not in their realm of influence. It is the responsibility of senior management to set policies that show a distinct link between organizational strategy and objectives and projects that implement those strategies. The research of Fusco suggests the implementation gap and prioritizing projects are still overlooked by many organizations. He surveyed 280 project managers and found that 24 percent of their organizations did not even publish or circulate their objectives; in addition, 40 percent of the respondents reported that priorities among competing projects were not clear, while only 17 percent reported clear priorities.

Problem 2: Organization Politics

Politics exist in every organization and can have a significant influence on which projects receive funding and high priority. This is especially true when the criteria and process for selecting projects are ill-defined and not aligned with the mission of the firm. Project selection may be based not so much on facts and sound reasoning, but rather on the persuasiveness and power of people advocating projects.

The term "sacred cow" is often used to denote a project that a powerful, high-ranking official is advocating. Case in point, a marketing consultant confided that he was once hired by the marketing director of a large firm to conduct an independent, external market analysis for a new product the firm was interested in developing. His extensive research indicated that there was insufficient demand to warrant the financing of this new product. The marketing director chose to bury the report and made the consultant promise never to share this information with anyone. The director explained that this new product was the "pet idea" of the new CEO, who saw it as his legacy to the firm. He went on to describe the CEO's irrational obsession with the project and how he referred to it as his "new baby." Like a parent fiercely protecting his child, the marketing director believed that he would lose his job if such critical information ever became known.

Having a project sponsor can play a significant role in the selection and successful implementation of product innovation projects. Project sponsors are typically high-ranking managers who endorse and lend political support for the completion of a specific project. They are instrumental in winning approval of the project and in protecting the project during the critical development stage. Savvy project managers recognize the importance of having "friends in higher courts" who can advocate for their case and protect their interests.

The significance of corporate politics can be seen in the ill-fated ALTO computer project at Xerox during the mid-1970s. The project was a tremendous technological success; it developed the first workable mouse, the first laser printer, the first user-friendly software, and the first local area network. All of these developments were five years ahead of their nearest competitor. Over the next five years this opportunity to dominate the nascent personal computer market was squandered because of internal in-fighting at Xerox and the absence of a strong project sponsor.

Politics can play a role not only in project selection but also in the aspirations behind projects. Individuals can enhance their power within an organization by managing extraordinary and critical projects. Power and status naturally accrue to successful innovators and risk takers rather than to steady producers. Many ambitious managers pursue high-profile projects as a means for moving quickly up the corporate ladder. For example, Lee Iacocca's career was built on successfully leading the design and development of the highly successful Ford Mustang. Managers become heroes by leading projects that contribute significantly to an organization's mission or solve a pressing crisis.

Many would argue that politics and project management should not mix. A more proactive response is that projects and politics invariably mix and that effective project managers recognize that any significant project has political ramifications. Likewise, top management needs to develop a system for identifying and selecting projects that reduces the impact of internal politics and fosters the selection of the best projects for achieving the mission and strategy of the firm.

Problem 3: Resource Conflicts and Multitasking

Most project organizations exist in a multiproject environment. This environment creates the problems of project interdependency and the need to share resources. For example, what would be the impact on the labor resource pool of a construction company if it should win a contract it would like to bid on? Will existing labor be adequate to deal with the new project—given the completion date? Will current projects be delayed? Will subcontracting help? Which projects will have priority? Competition among project managers can be contentious. All project managers seek to have the best people for their projects. The problems of sharing resources and scheduling resources across projects grow exponentially as the number of projects rises. In multiproject environments the stakes are higher and the benefits or penalties for good or bad resource scheduling become even more significant than in most single projects.

Resource sharing also leads to multitasking. Multitasking involves starting and stopping work on one task to go and work on another project, and then returning to the work on the original task. People working on several tasks concurrently are far less efficient, especially where conceptual or physical shutdown and startup are significant. Multitasking adds to delays and costs. Changing priorities exacerbate the multitasking problems even more. Likewise, multitasking is more evident in organizations that have too many projects for the resources they command.

The number of small and large projects in a portfolio almost always exceeds the available resources (typically by a factor of three to four times the available resources). This capacity overload inevitably leads to confusion and inefficient use of scarce organizational resources. The presence of an implementation gap, of power politics, and of multitasking adds to the problem of which projects are allocated resources first. Employee morale and confidence suffer because it is difficult to make sense of an ambiguous system. A multiproject organization environment faces major problems without a priority system that is clearly linked to the strategic plan.

In essence, to this point we have suggested that many organizations have no meaningful process for addressing the problems we have described. The first and most important change that will go a long way in addressing these and other problems is the development and use of a meaningful project priority process for project selection.

How can the implementation gap be narrowed so that understanding and consensus of organizational strategies run through all levels of management? How can power politics be minimized? Can a process be developed in which projects are consistently prioritized to support organizational strategies? Can the prioritized projects be used to allocate scarce organizational resources—for example, people, equipment? Can the process encourage bottom-up initiation of projects that support clear organizational targets?

What is needed is a set of integrative criteria and a process for evaluating and selecting projects that support higher-level strategies and objectives. A single-project priority system that ranks projects by their contribution to the strategic plan would make life easier. Easily said, but difficult to accomplish in practice. Organizations that managed independent projects and allocated resources ad hoc have shifted focus to selecting the right portfolio of projects to achieve their strategic objectives. This is a quickening trend. The advantages of successful project portfolio systems are becoming well recognized in project-driven organizations. See Exhibit 2.2, which lists a few key benefits; the list could easily be extended.

A project portfolio system is discussed next with emphasis on selection criteria, which is where the power of the portfolio system is established.

EXHIBIT 2.2   Benefits of Project Portfolio Management

- Builds discipline into project selection process.
- Links project selection to strategic metrics.
- Prioritizes project proposals across a common set of criteria, rather than on politics or emotion.
- Allocates resources to projects that align with strategic direction.
- Balances risk across all projects.
- Justifies killing projects that do not support organization strategy.
- Improves communication and supports agreement on project goals.

A Portfolio Management System

Succinctly put, the aim of portfolio management is to ensure that projects are aligned with strategic goals and prioritized appropriately. As Foti points out, portfolio management asks "What is strategic to our organization?" Portfolio management provides information that allows people to make better business decisions. Since projects clamoring for funding and people usually outnumber available resources, it is important to follow a logical and defined process for selecting the projects to implement.

Design of a project portfolio system should include classification of a project, selection criteria depending upon classification, sources of proposals, evaluating proposals, and managing the portfolio of projects.

Classification of the Project

Many organizations find they have three different kinds of projects in their portfolio: *compliance* and emergency (must do), *operational,* and *strategic* projects. Compliance projects are typically those needed to meet regulatory conditions required to operate in a region; hence, they are called "must do" projects. Emergency projects, such as rebuilding a soybean factory destroyed by fire, meet the must do criterion. Compliance and emergency projects usually have penalties if they are not implemented. Operational projects are those that are needed to support current operations. These projects are designed to improve efficiency of delivery systems, reduce product costs, and improve performance. TQM projects are examples of operational projects. Finally, strategic projects are those that directly support the organization's long-run mission. They frequently are directed toward increasing revenue or market share. Examples of strategic projects are new products, research and development. (See Figure 2.2.) For a good, complete discussion on classification schemes found in practice, see Crawford, Hobbs, and Turne.

The strategic value of a proposed project must be determined before it can be placed in the project portfolio. Under rare circumstances, there are projects that "must" be selected. These compliance or emergency projects are those that must be implemented or the firm will fail or suffer dire penalties or consequences. For example, a manufacturing plant must install an electrostatic filter on top of a smokestack in six months or close down. EU courts are trying to force Microsoft to open their software architecture to allow competing software firms to be compatible and interact with Microsoft. This decision may become a compliance project for Microsoft. Any project placed in the "must" category ignores other selection criteria. A rule of thumb for placing a proposed project in this category is that 99 percent of the organization stakeholders would agree that the project must be implemented; there is no perceived choice but to implement the project. All other projects are selected using selection criteria linked to organization strategy.

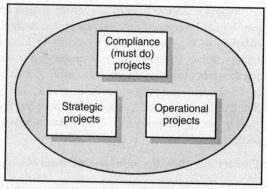

FIGURE 2.2   Portfolio of Projects by Type

Selection Criteria

Although there are many criteria for selecting projects, selection criteria are typically identified as *financial* and *nonfinancial*. A short description of each is given next, followed by a discussion of their use in practice.

Financial Models   For most managers financial criteria are the preferred method to evaluate projects. These models are appropriate when there is a high level of confidence associated with estimates of future cash flows. Two models and examples are demonstrated here—payback and net present value (NPV).

Project A has an initial investment of $700,000 and projected cash inflows of $225,000 for 5 years.
Project B has an initial investment of $400,000 and projected cash inflows of $110,00 for 5 years.

1. The payback model measures the time it will take to recover the project investment. Shorter paybacks are more desirable. Payback is the simplest and most widely used model. Payback emphasizes cash flows, a key factor in business. Some managers use the payback model to eliminate unusually risky projects (those with lengthy payback periods). The major limitations of payback are that it ignores the time value of money, assumes cash inflows for the investment period (and not beyond), and does not consider profitability. The payback formula is

$$\text{Payback period (yrs)} = \text{Estimated Project Cost/Annual Savings}$$

Exhibit 2.3 compares the payback for Project A and Project B. The payback for Project A is 3.1 years and for Project B is 3.6 years. Using the payback method both projects are acceptable since both return the initial investment in less than five years and have returns on the investment of 32.1 and 27.5 percent.

2. The net present value (NPV) model uses management's minimum desired rate-of-return (discount rate, for example, 20 percent) to compute the present value of all net cash inflows. If the result is positive (the project meets the minimum desired rate of return), it is eligible for further consideration. If the result is negative, the project is rejected. Thus, higher positive NPV's are desirable. Excel uses this formula

$$\text{Project NPV} = I_0 + \sum_{t=1}^{n} \frac{F_t}{(1 + k)^t} \qquad \text{where}$$

I_0 = Initial investment (since it is an outflow, the number will be negative)
F_t = Net cash inflow for period t
k = Required rate of return

Exhibit 2.3 presents the NPV model using Microsoft Excel software. The NPV model accepts project A, which has a *positive* NPV of $54,235. Project B is rejected since the NPV is *negative* $31,283. Compare the

EXHIBIT 2.3   Example Comparing Two Projects: Net Present Value (NPV) and Payback Method

	A	B	C	D	E	F	G	H	I	J
1										
2					Exhibit 2.3					
3										
4					Example Comparing Two Projects Using NPV					
5	Project A			Year 0	Year 1	Year 2	Year 3	Year 4	Year 5	Total	Formulas
6	Required rate of return	15%								
7	Outflows		−$700,000						−$700,000	
8	Inflows			$225,000	$225,000	$225,000	$225,000	$225,000	$1,125,000	
9	Net inflows			$225,000	$225,000	$225,000	$225,000	$225,000	$425,000	Project A: =C7+NPV(B6,D9:H9)
10	NPV	$54,235								
11										
12										
13	Project B									
14	Required rate of return	15%								
15	Outflows		−$400,000						−$400,000	
16	Inflows			$110,000	$110,000	$110,000	$110,000	$110,000	$550,000	
17	Net inflows			$110,000	$110,000	$110,000	$110,000	$110,000	$150,000	Project B: =C15+NPV(B14,D17:H17)
18	NPV	−$31,263								
19										
20										
21										
22	NPV comparison: Accept Project A---NPV is positive.									
23	Reject Project B---NPV is negative.									
24										
25										
26										
27					Example Comparing Two Projects Using the Payback Method					
28										
29					Project A		Project B			
30										
31										
32			Investment	$700,000		$400,000			Project A Payback: =(D32/D33)
33			Annual savings	$225,000		$110,000			Project B Payback: =(F32/F33)
34										
35			Payback period*	3.1 years		3.6 years			
36										
37			Rate of return**	32.1%		27.5%			Project A: =(D33/D32)
38									Project B: =(F33/F32)
39	Project A: Accept. Less than 5 years and exceeds 15% desired rate.								
40										
41	Project B: Accept. Less than 5 years.								
42										
43	* Note: Payback does not use the time value of money.								
44	** Note: Rate of return is reciprocal of Payback.								
45										

NPV results with the payback results. The NPV model is more realistic because it considers the time value of money, cash flows, and profitability.

When using the NPV model, the discount rate (return on investment hurdle rate) can differ for different projects. For example, the expected ROI on strategic projects is frequently set higher than operational projects. Similarly, ROI's can differ for riskier versus safer projects. The criteria for setting the ROI hurdle rate should be clear and applied consistently.

Unfortunately, pure financial models fail to include many projects where financial return is impossible to measure and/or other factors are vital to the accept or reject decision. One research study by Foti showed that companies using predominantly financial models to prioritize projects yielded unbalanced portfolios and projects that aren't strategically oriented. Other studies make similar claims.

Nonfinancial Criteria

Financial return, while important, does not always reflect strategic importance. The sixties and seventies saw firms become overextended by diversifying too much. Now the prevailing thinking is that long term survival is dependent upon developing and maintaining core competencies. Companies have to be disciplined in saying no to potentially profitable projects that are outside the realm of their core mission. This requires other criteria be considered beyond direct financial return. For example, a firm may support projects that do not have high profit margins for other strategic reasons including:

To capture larger market share
To make it difficult for competitors to enter the market
To develop an enabler product, which by its introduction will increase sales in more profitable products
To develop core technology that will be used in next-generation products
To reduce dependency on unreliable suppliers
To prevent government intervention and regulation

Less tangible criteria may also apply. Organizations may support projects to restore corporate image or enhance brand recognition. Many organizations are committed to corporate citizenship and support community development projects.

Since no single criterion can reflect strategic significance, portfolio management requires multi-criteria screening models. These models often weight individual criteria so those projects that contribute to the most important strategic objectives are given higher consideration.

Two Multi-Criteria Selection Models

Since no single criterion can reflect strategic significance, portfolio management requires multi-criteria screening models. Two models, the checklist and multi-weighted scoring models, are described next.

Checklist Models   The most frequently used method in selecting projects has been the checklist. This approach basically uses a list of questions to review potential projects and to determine their acceptance or rejection. Several of the the typical questions found in practice are listed in Exhibit 2.4. One large, multiproject organization has 250 different questions!

A justification of checklist models is that they allow great flexibility in selecting among many different types of projects and are easily used across different divisions and locations. Although many projects are selected using some variation of the checklist approach, this approach has serious shortcomings. Major shortcomings of this approach are that it fails to answer the relative importance or value of a potential project to the organization and fails to allow for comparison with other potential projects. Each potential project will have a different set of positive and negative answers. How do you compare? Ranking and prioritizing projects by their importance is difficult, if not impossible. This approach also leaves the door open to the potential opportunity for power plays, politics, and other forms of manipulation. To overcome these serious shortcomings experts recommend the use of a multi-weighted scoring model to select projects, which is examined next.

Multi-Weighted Scoring Models   A weighted scoring model typically uses several weighted selection criteria to evaluate project proposals. Weighted scoring models will generally include qualitative and/or quantitative criteria. Each selection criterion is asssigned a weight. Scores are assigned to each criterion for the project, based on its importance to the project being evaluated. The weights and scores are multiplied to get a total weighted score for the project. Using these multiple screening criteria, projects can then be compared using the weighted score. Projects with higher weighted scores are considered better.

Selection criteria need to mirror the critical success factors of an organization. For example, 3M set a target that 25 percent of the company's sales would come from products fewer than four years old versus the old target of 20 percent. Their priority system for project selection strongly reflects this new target. On the other hand, failure to pick the right factors will render the screening process "useless" in short order.

EXHIBIT 2.4 Sample Selection Questions Used in Practice

Topic	Question
Strategy/alignment	What specific organization strategy does this project align with?
Driver	What business problem does the project solve?
Success metrics	How will we measure success?
Sponsorship	Who is the project sponsor?
Risk	What is the impact of not doing this project?
Risk	What is the project risk to our organization?
Risk	Where does the proposed project fit in our risk profile?
Benefits, value, ROI	What is the value of the project to this organization?
Benefits, value, ROI	When will the project show results?
Objectives	What are the project objectives?
Organization culture	Is our organization culture right for this type of project?
Resources	Will internal resources be available for this project?
Approach	Will we build or buy?
Schedule	How long will this project take?
Schedule	Is the time line realistic?
Training/resources	Will staff training be required?
Finance/portfolio	What is the estimated cost of the project?
Portfolio	Is this a new initiative or part of an existing initiative?
Portfolio	How does this project interact with current projects?
Technology	Is the technology available or new?

Figure 2.3 represents a project scoring matrix using some of the factors found in practice. The screening criteria selected are shown across the top of the matrix (e.g., stay within core competencies . . . ROI of 18 percent plus). Management weights each criterion (a value of 0 to a high of, say, 3) by its relative importance to the organization's objectives and strategic plan. Project proposals are then submitted to a project priority team or project office.

Each project proposal is then evaluated by its relative contribution/value added to the selected criteria. Values of 0 to a high of 10 are assigned to each criterion for each project. This value represents the project's fit to the specific criterion. For example, project 1 appears to fit well with the strategy of the organization since it is given a value of 8. Conversely, project 1 does nothing to support reducing defects (its value is 0). Finally, this model applies the management weights to each criterion by importance using a value of 1 to 3. For example, ROI and strategic fit have a weight of 3, while urgency and core competencies have weights of 2. Applying the weight to each criterion, the priority team derives the weighted total points for each project. For example, project 5 has the highest value of 102 $[(2 \times 1) + (3 \times 10) + (2 \times 5) + (2.5 \times 10) + (1 \times 0) + (1 \times 8) + (3 \times 9) = 102]$ and project 2 a low value of 27. If the resources available create a cutoff threshold of 50 points, the priority team would eliminate projects 2 and 4. (Note: Project 4 appears to have some urgency, but it is not classified as a "must" project. Therefore, it is screened with all other proposals.) Project 5 would receive first priority, project *n* second, and so on. In rare cases where resources are severely limited and project proposals are similar in weighted rank, it is prudent to pick the project placing less demand on resources. Weighted multiple criteria models similar to this one are rapidly becoming the dominant choice for prioritizing projects.

At this point in the discussion it is wise to stop and put things into perspective. While selection models like the one above may yield numerical solutions to project selection decsions, models should not make the final decisions—the people using the models should. No model, no matter how sophisticated, can capture the total reality it is meant to represent. Models are tools for guiding the evaluation process so that the decision-makers will consider relevant issues and reach a meeting of the minds as to what projects should be supported and not supported. This is a much more subjective process than calculations suggest. See Snapshot from Practice: A Derailed Vision.

Criteria / Weight	Stay within core competencies	Strategic fit	Urgency	25% of sales from new products	Reduce defects to less than 1%	Improve customer loyalty	ROI of 18% plus	Weighted total
	2.0	3.0	2.0	2.5	1.0	1.0	3.0	
Project 1	1	8	2	6	0	6	5	66
Project 2	3	3	2	0	0	5	1	27
Project 3	9	5	2	0	2	2	5	56
Project 4	3	0	10	0	0	6	0	32
Project 5	1	10	5	10	0	8	9	102
Project 6	6	5	0	2	0	2	7	55
⋮								
Project *n*	5	5	7	0	10	10	8	83

FIGURE 2.3   Project Screening Matrix

Applying a Selection Model

Project Classification   It is not necessary to have exactly the same criteria for the different types of projects discussed above (strategic and operations). However, experience shows most organizations use similar criteria across all types of projects, with perhaps one or two criteria specific to the type of project—e.g., strategic breakthrough versus operational.

Regardless of criteria differences among different types of projects, the most important criterion for selection is the project's fit to the organization strategy. Therefore, this criterion should be consistent across all types of projects and carry a high priority relative to other criteria. This uniformity across all priority models used can keep departments from suboptimizing the use of organization resources. Anyone generating a project proposal should classify their proposal by type, so the appropriate criteria can be used to evaluate their proposal.

Selecting a Model   In the past, financial criteria were used almost to the exclusion of other criteria. However, in the last two decades we have witnessed a dramatic shift to include multiple criteria in project selection. Concisely put, profitability alone is simply not an adequate measure of contribution; however, it is still an important criterion, especially for projects that enhance revenue and market share such as breakthrough R&D projects.

Today, senior management is interested in identifying the potential mix of projects that will yield the best use of human and capital resources to maximize return on investment in the long run. Factors such as researching new technology, public image, ethical position, protection of the environment, core competencies, and strategic fit might be important criteria for selecting projects. Weighted scoring criteria seem the best alternative to meet this need.

Snapshot from Practice   A Derailed Vision*

AP/Wide World Photos.

The Transrapid Shanghai train is deemed a great engineering success. The magnetic levitation train travels at 267 miles per hour (430 kph) from the Pudong International Airport to close to Shanghai's business center in less than eight minutes.

Although the super fast train is deemed an engineering and technical success, it has not been a financial success. The train can carry 453 passengers on a trip, but the trains are riding virtually empty; a total of only 500 to 600 passengers ride the train in a day. The train now operates on a reduced schedule. Basically, the price per ride is well beyond what most Chinese families can afford. Second-class tickets are 75 yuan (US$9), and first-class tickets cost 150 yuan (US$18). The return on investment has been severely under expectations. The link between final customer needs and the financial case was not a top priority. Imposed project deadline (operate before 2003), scope reduction (shift to a station away from downtown), and apparent misconception of community needs all contribute to poor utilization of the train. The current model actually forces people to leave the train, wait, and then take public transportation to downtown Shanghai; time lost and cost have not convinced potential riders of the benefits of using the train.

The project demonstrates a classic error of not linking customer need with return on investment. The political strategy outweighed public needs.

*———, "Case Analysis: A Derailed Vision," *PM Network,* vol. 18, no. 4 (April 2004) p. 1.

Weighted scoring models result in bringing projects to closer alignment with strategic goals. If the scoring model is published and available to everyone in the organization, some discipline and credibility are attached to the selection of projects. The number of wasteful projects using resources is reduced. Politics and "sacred cow" projects are exposed. Project goals are more easily identified and communicated using the selection criteria as corroboration. Finally, using a weighted scoring approach helps project managers understand how their project was selected, how their project contributes to organization goals, and how it compares with other projects. Project selection is one of the most important decisions guiding the future success of an organization.

Criteria for project selection are the area where the power of your portfolio starts to manifest itself. New projects are aligned with the strategic goals of the organization. With a clear method for selecting projects in place, project proposals can be solicited.

Sources and Solicitation of Project Proposals

As you would guess, projects should come from anyone who believes his or her project will add value to the organization. However, many organizations restrict proposals from specific levels or groups within the organization. This could be an opportunity lost. Good ideas are not limited to certain types or classes of organization stakeholders. Encourage and keep solicitations open to all sources—internal and external sponsors.

Figures 2.4 A and B provide an example of a proposal form for major projects. Note that this form includes a preliminary risk assessment as well as problem definition and project objectives. Risk analysis is the subject of Chapter 7.

```
Date _____                                    Number _____

  Project Title _____

  Responsible Manager _____  Project Manager _____


  □ _____    □ General support    □ Quality          □ Legal          □ New product
  □ _____    □ _____            □ Cost reduction    □ Replacement     □ Capacity
  □ _____    □ _____            □ _____           □ _____        □ _____


  YES □  NO □    The project will take more than 500 labor hours?
  YES □  NO □    The project is a one-time effort? (will not occur on a regular basis)
  YES □  NO □    The project proposal was reviewed by the product manager?


                        Problem definition
  Describe the problem/opportunity.
  _____
  _____

                        Goal definition
  Describe the project goal.
  _____
  _____

                      Objective definition
  Performance: Quantify the savings/benefits you expect from the project.



  Cost: Labor hours, materials, methods, equipment.



  Schedule: Overall duration in months.
```

FIGURE 2.4A   Major Project Proposal

What are the three major risks for this project?		
1.		
2.		
3.		

What is the probability of the above risks occurring?	0 to 1.0 none high	Risk 1 above	
		Risk 2 above	
		Risk 3 above	
What is the impact on project success if these risks do occur?	0 to 10 none high	Risk 1 above	
		Risk 2 above	
		Risk 3 above	

Resources available? _____ Yes _____ No

Current project status

Start date _____ Estimated finish date _____

Status: ☐ Active   ☐ On hold

Update:

Priority team action: ☐ Accepted   ☐ Returned

☐ Discovery—project not defined   ☐ Duplicate to: _____

☐ Operational—proposal not a project   Project # _____

☐ Need more information—to prioritize project   ☐ Completed project

FIGURE 2.4B   Risk Analysis

In some cases organizations will solicit ideas for projects when the knowledge requirements for the project are not available in the organization. Typically, the organization will issue an RFP (Request for Proposal) to contractors/vendors with adequate experience to implement the project. In one example, a hospital published an RFP that asked for a bid to design and build a new operating room that uses the latest technology. Several architecture firms submitted bids to the hospital. The bids for the project were evaluated internally against other potential projects. When the project was accepted as a go, other criteria were used to select the best qualified bidder. See Appendix 2.1 of this chapter for a complete description of requests for proposal (RFP).

Ranking Proposals and Selection of Projects

Culling through so many proposals to identify those that add the most value requires a structured process. Figure 2.5 shows a flow chart of a screening process beginning with the creation of an idea for a project.

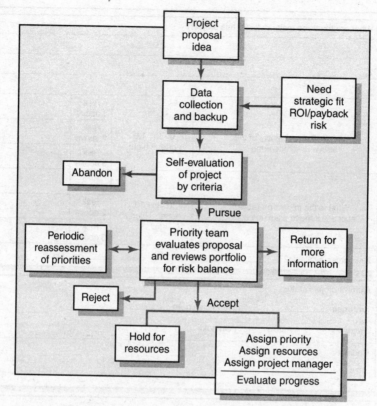

FIGURE 2.5   Project Screening Process

Data and information are collected to assess the value of the proposed project to the organization and for future backup. If the sponsor decides to pursue the project on the basis of the collected data, it is forwarded to the project priority team (or the project office). Note that the sponsor knows which criteria will be used to accept or reject the project. Given the selection criteria and current portfolio of projects, the priority team rejects or accepts the project. If the project is accepted, the priority team sets implementation in motion.

Figure 2.6 is a partial example of an evaluation form used by a large company to prioritize and select new projects. The form distinguishes between must and want objectives. If a project does not meet designated "must" objectives, it is not considered and removed from consideration. Organization (or division) objectives have been ranked and weighted by their relative importance—for example "Improve external customer service" carries a relative weight of 83 when compared to other want objectives. The want objectives are directly linked to objectives found in the strategic plan.

Impact definitions represent a further refinement to the screening system. They are developed to gauge the predicted impact a specific project would have on meeting a particular objective. A numeric scheme is created and anchored by defining criteria. To illustrate how this works, let's examine the $5 million in new sales objective. A "0" is assigned if the project will have no impact on sales or less than $100,000, a "1" is given if predicted sales are more than $100,000 but less than $500,000, a "2" if greater than $500,000. These impact assessments are combined with the relative importance of each objective to determine the predicted overall contribution of a project to strategic objectives. For example, project 26 creates an opportunity to fix

			Project number			
Must objectives	**Must meet if impacts**		**...26**	**27**	**28**	**29**
All activities meet current legal, safety, and environmental standards	Yes-Meets objective No-Does not meet obj N/A-No impact		n/a			
All new products will have a complete market analysis	Yes-Meets objective No-Does not meet obj N/A-No impact		yes			

Want objectives	**Relative Importance 1-100**	**Single project impact definitions**	**Weighted score**	**Weighted score**	**Weighted score**	**Weighted score**
Provides immediate response to field problems	99	0 ≤ Does not address ①= Opportunity to fix 2 ≥ Urgent problem	99			
Create $5 million in new sales by 20xx	88	⓪< $100,000 1 = $100,000–500,000 2 > $500,000	0			
Improve external customer service	83	0 ≤ Minor impact 1 = Significant impact ②≥ Major impact	166			
		↓				
	Total weighted score					
	Priority					

FIGURE 2.6 Priority Analysis

field problems, has no effect on sales, and will have major impact on customer service. On these three objectives, project 26 would receive a score of 265 [99 + 0 + (2 × 83)]. Individual weighted scores are totaled for each project and are used to prioritize projects.

Responsibility for Prioritizing

Prioritizing can be an uncomfortable exercise for managers. Prioritizing means discipline, accountability, responsibility, constraints, reduced flexibility, and loss of power. Top management commitment means more than giving a blessing to the priority system; it means management will have to rank and weigh, in concrete terms, the objectives and strategies they believe to be most critical to the organization. This public declaration of commitment can be risky if the ranked objectives later prove to be poor choices, but setting the course for the organization is top management's job. The good news is, if management is truly trying to direct the organization to a strong future position, a good project priority system supports their efforts and develops a culture in which everyone is contributing to the goals of the organization.

Managing the Portfolio System

Managing the portfolio takes the selection system one step higher in that the merits of a particular project are assessed within the context of existing projects. At the same time it involves monitoring and adjusting selection criteria to reflect the strategic focus of the organization. This requires constant effort. The priority system can be managed by a small group of key employees in a small organization. Or, in larger organizations, the priority system can be managed by the project office or the enterprise management group.

Senior Management Input

Management of a portfolio system requires two major inputs from senior management. First, senior management must provide guidance in establishing selection criteria that strongly align with the current organization strategies. Second, senior management must annually decide how they wish to balance the available organizational resources (people and capital) among the different types of projects. A preliminary decision of balance must be made by top management (e.g., 20 percent compliance, 50 percent strategic, and 30 percent operational) before project selection takes place, although the balance may be changed when the projects submitted are reviewed. Given these inputs the priority team or project office can carry out its many responsibilities, which include supporting project sponsors and representing the interests of the total organization.

The Priority Team Responsibilities

The priority team, or project office, is responsible for publishing the priority of every project and ensuring the process is open and free of power politics. For example, most organizations using a priority team or project office use an electronic bulletin board to disperse the current portfolio of projects, the current status of each project, and current issues. This open communication discourages power plays. Over time the priority team evaluates the progress of the projects in the portfolio. If this whole process is managed well, it can have a profound impact on the success of an organization.

Constant scanning of the external environment to determine if organizational focus and/or selection criteria need to be changed is imperative! Periodic priority review and changes need to keep current with the changing environment and keep a unified vision of organization focus. Regardless of the criteria used for selection, each project should be evaluated by the same criteria. If projects are classified by must do, operation, and strategic, each project in its class should be evaluated by the same criteria. Enforcing the project priority system is crucial. Keeping the whole system open and aboveboard is important to maintaining the integrity of the system and keeping new, young executives from going around the system. For example, communicating which projects are approved, project ranks, current status of in-process projects, and any changes in priority criteria will discourage people from bypassing the system.

Balancing the Portfolio for Risks and Types of Projects

A major responsibility of the priority team is to balance projects by type, risk, and resource demand. This requires a total organization perspective. Hence, a proposed project that ranks high on most criteria may not be selected because the organization portfolio already includes too many projects with the same characteristics—e.g., project risk level, use of key resources, high cost, nonrevenue producing, long durations. Balancing the portfolio of projects is as important as project selection. Organizations need to evaluate each new project in terms of what it adds to the project mix. Short-term needs need to be balanced with long-term potential. Resource usage needs to be optimized across all projects, not just the most important project.

Two types of risk are associated with projects. First are risks associated with the total portfolio of projects, which should reflect the organization's risk profile. Second are specific project risks that can inhibit the execution of a project, such as schedule, cost, and technical. In this chapter we look only to balancing the organizational risks inherent in the project portfolio, such as market risk, ability to execute, time to market, and technology advances. Project-specific risks will be covered in detail in Chapter 7.

David and Jim Matheson studied R&D organizations and developed a matrix that could be used for assessing a project portfolio (see Figure 2.7). The vertical axis reflects a project's probability of success. The horizontal axis reflects potential commercial value. The grid has four quadrants, each with different project dimensions.

Bread and butter projects typically involve evolutionary improvements to current products and services. Examples include software upgrades and manufacturing cost reduction efforts.

Pearls represent revolutionary commercial advances using proven technical advances. Examples include next-generation integrated circuit chip and subsurface imaging to locate oil and gas.

Oysters involve technological breakthroughs with high commercial payoffs. Examples include embryonic DNA treatments and new kinds of metal alloys.

White elephants are projects that at one time showed promise but are no longer viable. Examples include products for a saturated market or a potent energy source with toxic side effects.

The Mathesons report that organizations often have too many white elephants and too few pearls and oysters. To maintain strategic advantage they recommend that organizations capitalize on pearls, eliminate or reposition white elephants, and balance resources devoted to bread-and-butter and oyster projects to achieve alignment with overall strategy. Although their research centers on R&D organizations, their observations appear to hold true for all types of project organizations.

Summary

Multiple competing projects, limited skilled resources, dispersed virtual teams, time to market pressures, and limited capital serve as forces for the emergence of project portfolio management that provides the infrastructure for managing multiple projects and linking business strategy with project selection. The most important element of this system is the creation of a ranking system that utilizes multiple criteria that reflect the mission and strategy of the firm. It is critical to communicate priority criteria to all organizational stakeholders so that the criteria can be the source of inspiration for new project ideas.

Every significant project selected should be ranked and the results published. Senior management must take an active role in setting priorities and supporting the priority system. Going around the priority system will destroy its effectiveness. The project priority team needs to consist of seasoned managers who are capable of asking tough questions and distinguishing facts from fiction. Resources (people, equipment, and capital) for major projects must be clearly allocated and not conflict with daily operations or become an overload task.

The priority team needs to scrutinize significant projects in terms of not only their strategic value but also their fit with the portfolio of projects currently being implemented. Highly ranked projects may be deferred or even turned down if they upset the current balance among risks, resources, and strategic initiatives. Project selection must be based not only on the merits of the specific project but also on what it contributes to the current project portfolio mix. This requires a holistic approach to aligning projects with organizational strategy and resources.

The importance of aligning projects with organization strategy cannot be overstated. We have discussed two types of models found in practice. Checklist models are easy to develop and are justified primarily on the basis of flexibility across different divisions and locations. Unfortunately, questionnaire checklist models do not allow comparison of the relative value (rank) of alternative projects in contributing toward organization strategy. The latter is the major reason the authors prefer multi-weighted scoring models. These models keep project selection highly focused on alignment with organization strategy. Weighted scoring models require major effort in establishing the criteria and weights.

Key Terms

Implementation gap	Priority team	Strategic management
Net present value	Project portfolio	process
Organizational politics	Project screening	
Payback	matrix	
Priority system	Sacred cow	

Review Questions

1. Describe the major components of the strategic management process.
2. Explain the role projects play in the strategic management process.
3. How are projects linked to the strategic plan?
4. The portfolio of projects is typically represented by compliance, strategic, and operations projects. What impact can this classification have on project selection?
5. Why does the priority system described in this chapter require that it be open and published? Does the process encourage bottom-up initiation of projects? Does it discourage some projects? Why?
6. Why should an organization not rely only on ROI to select projects?
7. Discuss the pros and cons of the checklist versus the weighted factor method of selecting projects.

Exercises

1. You manage a hotel resort located on the South Beach on the Island of Kauai in Hawaii. You are shifting the focus of your resort from a traditional fun-in-the-sun destination to eco-tourism. (Eco-tourism focuses on environmental awareness and education.) How would you classify the following projects in terms of compliance, strategic, and operational?

   a. Convert the pool heating system from electrical to solar power.
   b. Build a 4-mile nature hiking trail.
   c. Renovate the horse barn.
   d. Replace the golf shop that accidentally burned down after being struck by lightning.

e. Launch a new promotional campaign with Hawaii Airlines.

f. Convert 12 adjacent acres into a wildlife preserve.

g. Update all the bathrooms in condos that are 10 years old or older.

h. Change hotel brochures to reflect eco-tourism image.

i. Test and revise disaster response plan.

j. Introduce wireless Internet service in café and lounge areas.

How easy was it to classify these projects? What made some projects more difficult than others? What do you think you now know that would be useful for managing projects at the hotel?

2. Two new software projects are proposed to a young, start-up company. The Alpha project will cost $150,000 to develop and is expected to have annual net cash flow of $40,000. The Beta project will cost $200,000 to develop and is expected to have annual net cash flow of $50,000. The company is very concerned about their cash flow. Using the payback period, which project is better from a cash flow standpoint? Why?

3. A five-year project has a projected net cash flow of $15,000, $25,000, $30,000, $20,000, and $15,000 in the next five years. It will cost $50,000 to implement the project. If the required rate of return is 20 percent, conduct a discounted cash flow calculation to determine the NPV.

4. You work for the 3T company, which expects to earn at least 18 percent on its investments. You have to choose between two similar projects. Below is the cash information for each project. Your analysts predict that inflation rate will be a stable 3 percent over the next 7 years. Which of the two projects would you fund if the decision is based only on financial information? Why?

Omega Year	Inflow	Outflow	Netflow	Alpha Year	Inflow	Outflow	Netflow
Y0	0	$225,000	−225,000	Y0	0	$300,000	−300,000
Y1	0	190,000	−190,000	Y1	$ 50,000	100,000	−50,000
Y2	$ 150,000	0	150,000	Y2	150,000	0	150,000
Y3	220,000	30,000	190,000	Y3	250,000	50,000	200,000
Y4	215,000	0	215,000	Y4	250,000	0	250,000
Y5	205,000	30,000	175,000	Y5	200,000	50,000	150,000
Y6	197,000	0	197,000	Y6	180,000	0	180,000
Y7	100,000	30,000	70,000	Y7	120,000	30,000	90,000
Total	1,087,000	505,000	582,000	Total	1,200,000	530,000	670,000

5. The Custom Bike Company has set up a weighted scoring matrix for evaluation of potential projects. Below are three projects under consideration.

a. Using the scoring matrix on the next page, which project would you rate highest? Lowest?

b. If the weight for "Strong Sponsor" is changed from 2.0 to 5.0, will the project selection change? What are the three highest weighted project scores with this new weight?

c. Why is it important that the weights mirror critical strategic factors?

Project Screening Matrix

Criteria / Weight	Strong sponsor	Supports business strategy	Urgency	10% of sales from new products	Competition	Fill market gap	Weighted total
	2.0	5.0	4.0	3.0	1.0	3.0	
Project 1	9	5	2	0	2	5	
Project 2	3	7	2	0	5	1	
Project 3	6	8	2	3	6	8	
Project 4	1	0	5	10	6	9	
Project 5	3	10	10	1	8	0	

References

Benko, C., and F. W. McFarlan, *Connecting the Dots: Aligning Projects With Objectives in Unpredictable Times* (Boston: Harvard Business School Press, 2003).

Bigelow, D., "Want to Ensure Quality? Think Project Portfolio Management," *PM Network,* vol. 16 (1) April 2002, pp. 16–17.

Boyer, C., "Make Profit Your Priority," *PM Nework,* vol. 15 (10) October 2003, pp. 37–42.

Cohen, D., and R. Graham, *The Project Manager's MBA* (San Francisco: Jossey-Bass, 2001), pp. 58–59.

Crawford, L., B. Hobbs, and J. R. Turne, "Aligning Capability with Strategy: Categorizing of Projects to Do the Right Projects and Do Them Right," *Project Management Journal,* vol. 37 (2) June 2006, pp. 38–50.

Descamps, J. P., "Mastering the Dance of Change: Innovation as a Way of Life," *Prism,* Second Quarter, 1999, pp. 61–67.

Doran, G. T., "There's a Smart Way to Write Management Goals and Objectives," *Management Review* (November 1981), pp. 35–36.

Floyd, S. W., and B. Woolridge, "Managing Strategic Consensus: The Foundation of Effectiveness Implementation," *Academy of Management Executives,* vol. 6 (4) 1992, pp. 27–39.

Foti, R., "Louder Than Words," *PM Network,* December 2002, pp. 22–29.

Frank, L., "On Demand," *PM Network,* vol. 18 (4) April 2004, pp. 58–62.

Fusco, J. C., "Better Policies Provide the Key to Implementing Project Management," *Project Management Journal,* vol. 28 (3) 1997, pp. 38–41.

Hutchens, G., "Doing the Numbers," *PM Network,* vol. 16 (4) March 2002, p. 20.

Johnson, R. E., "Scrap Capital Project Evaluations," *Chief Financial Officer,* May 1998, p. 14.

Kaplan, R. S., and D. P. Norton, "The Balanced Scorecard-Measures That Drive Performance," *Harvard Business Review,* January-February 1992, pp. 73–79.

Kenny, J., "Effective Project Management for Strategic Innovation and Change in an Organizational Context," *Project Management Journal,* vol. 34 (1) 2003, pp. 45–53.

Kharbanda, O. P., and J. K. Pinto, *What Made Gertie Gallop: Learning from Project Failures* (New York: Van Nostrand Reinhold, 1996), pp. 106–11, 263–283.

Leifer, R., C. M. McDermott, G. C. O'Connor, L. S. Peters, M. Price, and R. W. Veryzer, *Radical Innovation: How Mature Companies Can Outsmart Upstarts* (Boston: Harvard Business School Press, 2000).

Matheson, D., and J. Matheson, *The Smart Organization* (Boston: Harvard Business School Press, 1998), pp. 203–209.

Milosevic, D. Z., and S. Srivannaboon, "A Theoretical Framework for Aligning Project Management with Business Strategy," *Project Management Journal,* vol. 37 (3) August 2006, pp. 98–110.

Morris, P. W., and A. Jamieson, "Moving from Corporate Strategy to Project Strategy," *Project Management Journal,* vol. 36 (4) December 2005, pp. 5–18.

Shenhar, A., "Strategic Project Leadership: Focusing Your Project on Business Success," *Proceedings of the Project Management Institute Annual Seminars & Symposium,* San Antonio, Texas, October 3–10, 2002, CD.

Woodward, H., "Winning in a World of Limited Project Spending," *Proceedings of the Project Management Institute Global Congress North America,* Baltimore, Maryland, September 18–12, 2003, CD.

APPENDIX 2.1

Request for Proposal (RFP)

Once an organization selects a project, the customer or project manager is frequently responsible for developing a request for proposal (RFP) for the project or sections of the project.

The responsible project manager will require input data from all stakeholders connected to the activities covered in the RFP. The RFP will be announced to external contractors/ vendors with adequate experience to implement the project. For example, government projects frequently advertise with a "request for proposal" to outside contractors for roads, buildings, airports, military hardware, space vehicles. Similarly, businesses use RFPs to solicit bids for building a clean room, developing a new manufacturing process, delivering software for insurance billing, conducting a market survey. In all of these examples, requirements and features must be in enough detail that contractors have a clear description of the final deliverable that will meet the customer's needs. In most cases the RFP also specifies an expected format for the contractor's bid proposal so the responses of different contractors can be fairly evaluated. Although we typically think of RFPs for external contractors, in some organizations RFPs are used internally; that is, the organization sends out an RFP to different divisions or departments.

The content of the RFP is extremely important. In practice, the most common error is to offer an RFP that lacks sufficient detail. This lack of detail typically results in conflict issues, misunderstandings, often legal claims between the contractor and owner, and, in addition, an unsatisfied customer. All RFPs are different, but the outline in Figure A2.1 is a good starting point for the development of a detailed RFP. Each step is briefly described next.

---

1. Summary of needs and request for action
2. Statement of work (SOW) detailing the scope and major deliverables
3. Deliverable specifications/requirements, features, and tasks
4. Responsibilities–vendor and customer
5. Project schedule
6. Costs and payment schedule
7. Type of contract
8. Experience and staffing
9. Evaluation criteria

FIGURE A2.1   Request for Proposal

1. Summary of needs and request for action. The background and a simple description of the final project deliverable are given first. For example, through simulated war games, the U.S. Navy has found their giant warships of the past are too vulnerable against today's technology (an example is the Silkworm antiship missiles). In addition, the Navy's mission has shifted to supporting ground forces and peacekeeping missions, which require getting closer to shore. As a result, the Navy is revamping ships for near-shore duty. The Navy will select three designs for further refinement from the responses to its RFP. In general, it is expected that the new ship will be capable of at least 55 knots, measure between 80 and 250 feet in length, and be fitted with radar absorbing panels to thwart guided missiles.

2. Statement of work detailing the scope and major deliverables. For example, if the project involves a market research survey, the major deliverables could be design, data collection, data analysis, and providing recommendations by February 21, 2008, for a cost not to exceed $300,000.

3. Deliverable specifications/requirements, features, and tasks. This step should be very comprehensive so bid proposals from contractors can be validated and later used for control. Typical specifications cover physical features such as size, quantity, materials, speed, and color. For example, an IT project might specify requirements for hardware, software, and training in great detail. Tasks required to complete deliverables can be included if they are known.

4. Responsibilities—vendor and customer. Failing to spell out the responsibilities for both parties is notorious for leading to serious problems when the contractor implements the project. For example, who pays for what? (If the contractor is to be on site, will the contractor be required to pay for office space?) What are the limits and exclusions for the contractor? (For example, who will supply test equipment?) What communication plan will be used by the contractor and owner? If escalation of an issue becomes necessary, what process will be used? How will progress be evaluated? Well-defined responsibilities will avoid many unforeseen problems later.

5. Project schedule. This step is concerned with getting a "hard" schedule which can be used for control and evaluating progress. Owners are usually very demanding in meeting the project schedule. In today's business environment, time-to-market is a major "hot button" that influences market share, costs, and profits. The schedule should spell out what, who, and when.

6. Costs and payment schedule. The RFP needs to set out very clearly how, when, and the process for determining costs and conditions for progress payments.

7. Type of contract. Essentially there are two types of contracts—fixed-price and cost-plus. Fixed-price contracts agree on a price or lump sum in advance, and it remains as long as there are no changes to the scope provisions of the agreement. This type is preferred in projects that are well defined with predictable costs and minimal risks. The contractor must exercise care estimating cost because any underestimating of costs will cause the contractor's profit to be reduced. In cost-plus contracts the contractor is reimbursed for all or some of the expenses incurred during performance of the contract. This fee is negotiated in advance and usually involves a percent of total costs. "Time and materials" plus a profit factor are typical of cost-plus contracts. Both types of contracts can include incentive clauses for superior performance in time and cost, or in some cases, penalties—for example, missing the opening date of a new sports stadium.

8. Experience and staffing. The ability of the contractor to implement the project may depend on specific skills; this necessary experience should be specified, along with assurance such staff will be available for this project.

9. Evaluation criteria. The criteria for evaluating and awarding the project contract should be specified. For example, selection criteria frequently include methodology, price, schedule, and experience; in some cases these criteria are weighted. Use of the outline in Figure A2.1 will help to ensure key items in the proposal are not omitted. A well-prepared RFP will provide contractors with sufficient guidelines to prepare a proposal that clearly meets the project and customer's needs.

Selection of Contractor from Bid Proposals

Interested contractors respond to project RFPs with a written bid proposal. It is likely that several contractors will submit bid proposals to the customer.

The final step in the RFP process is to select the contractor who best meets the requirements requested in the RFP. The selection criteria given in the RFP are used to evaluate which contractor is awarded the contract to implement the project. Losing contractors should be given an explanation of the key factors that lead to the selection of the winning contractor/vendor; appreciation for their participation and effort should be acknowledged.

APPENDIX 2.2

Project Selection Methods Based on Financial Criteria for Selection

Introduction

Organizations embark on projects for a wide array of objectives and use project selection methods particularly suitable for evaluating the individual project or a program or portfolio of projects for achieving those objectives. For this purpose, a systematic procedure for evaluation of the individual project's contribution in achieving the objectives is developed and used for selecting a project. In this section, we would take a look at the methodology for use of financial criteria for selection of the projects.

Before starting discussion on that topic, we will make a brief review of the place of the projects in an organization, the strategic business analysis, the different types of organizational needs revealed by the strategic analysis, and non-financial criteria for selection of projects to fulfill such needs. This review would reveal the rationale behind methods of selection and bring out the role played and importance of using the financial criteria for project selection.

1. Place of Projects in an Organization

(a) The Current Operations
All organizations (commercial organizations, not-for-profit social organizations and governmental institutions) are actively engaged in carrying out some function involving day-to-day routine operations in an on-going manner year-after-year. A predominantly large part of the work force of an organization is, therefore,

understandably busy with carrying out these routine activities and a predominantly large part of all resources are actively employed in the routine operations.

(b) Strategic Analysis of Operations –
Identifying the need for creating a new product service or result

While doing these routine operations, from time to time the organizations find the need for some change in their operations for more effective, more efficient, larger scale or improved operation. While doing these routine operations, the manufacturing organization may find the need to increase the capacity for manufacture, or to bring out a new product, or improve the quality of the products, or employ new technology for saving cost by more efficient use of materials or labour or setting up facilities for safer routine operations or for meeting the government's environmental regulations. The service organization may feel the need to extend the scope of services, or cover a larger geographical area, or supply a more satisfactory level of service or exploit a new technology to provide an altogether new service. In other words, the organization might feel the need for creation of some product, service or result different from the current operations.

These needs may become apparent to the decision makers by intuitive vision, general observation and analysis of the changing external environment (macro-economic conditions, technology trends, industry trends, global influences, etc.) and the assessment of the organization's own innate strengths and resources – core competencies (proficiency in certain technology, expertise in manufacturing or marketing some products, strong brand images, networking and influencing capability, labour management capability, etc.).

Another way would be to carry out a formal strategic planning for identifying the needs for initiating a project. It would involve:

(i) SWOT analysis:
- Assessing the organization's present capabilities or core competencies (The "AS –IS" Scenario– an analysis of its strengths and weaknesses)
- Assessing the present state and directions of change in the macro-economic and industrial environment to perceive the opportunities and threats it would present to the organization for its future operations and growth.

(ii) Formulating the strategy to manage the future operating scenario:
Creating a vision of the way the organization should change to meet the challenges it is likely to face in the future ("SHOULD-BE" Scenario)

(iii) Developing the program to implement the strategy (Strategy-based Program for Identification of Project Objectives)
Developing the program to implement the strategy and include in the program specific projects; each with an objective to meet the need for creating a new product, service or result envisioned in the strategic program.

(iv) Initiate individual projects to meet the strategic needs:
Initiating and authorizing individual projects, each addressing a specific part of the organizational strategic program for creating a unique product, service or result

These needs identified by strategic analysis may fall into any of the following categories:

- Business need: Setting up a new business, starting a profitable venture for investment, entrepreneurial vision
- Market need: Product mix, new product, customer requests for some features
- Customer request for project management (for organizations performing on contract)
- Technological push: Developing new technology, making products compatible with new technology
- Organizational structure change, geographical expansion, recruitment and training campaigns
- Legal or social requirement: Effluent treatment plant; Employee welfare schemes

The projects can be visualized as the bridges, which take an organization from current activities (products and services) to new products and services. Project extends the capability of the organization from here-and-now to the visions of future. The projects are thus the vehicles for the changes, which routine operations do not cover. The projects are vehicles for implementing the organization's vision, short and long-term plans, and business strategy.

2. Project Selection Using Non-Numerical Methods
(Methods not based on financial criteria)

Based on the strategic needs of the organization the suitable methods for project selection are used, arrived at either by formal analysis or intuitive vision, non-numerical methods, essentially based on non-financial criteria, are used for the projects almost forced on the organization due to operating necessity (manufacturing), competitive necessity (market), legal or social requirements (business continuation) or for pet projects of the power centers in the organization. The projects may be authorized for manufacturing facilities for retaining the competitiveness of the manufacturing operations in the market place, absorbing new technology, saving raw material or energy cost, improving product quality or meeting a legal or social obligations (effluent treatment, operational safety and health of workers, etc.) fall in this operating necessity category. The projects for maintaining the product mix for meeting the changing market pattern, retaining the market share, increasing geographical coverage of services, making products compatible with new technology, meeting specific customer requests or developing a new product fall in competitive necessity category. The projects for reorganization and training of production or sales employees, necessary to remain competitive in the market place, are also the projects forced on the organization due to competitive necessity. The projects executed on behalf of clients by orders do not require any project selection criteria. Like it or not, the similar logic also applies to pet projects of high and mighty in the organization—particularly in entrepreneur-centered organizations.

3. Place for Project Selection Based on Financial Criteria

However, for a very large number of projects based on business needs, financial criteria for selection are very important and often casts the vote to settle the decision.

For setting up a manufacturing facility, the projects could be for

- Setting up a manufacturing unit of a new product (a new venture or diversification from existing business lines),
- Carrying out major expansions of existing manufacturing operations
- Carrying out a forward or backward integration of the product already being manufactured.

For marketing operations, the projects could be for

- Setting up new warehouses or distribution facilities
- Market expansion in new areas or countries
- Setting up new branch offices
- Setting up IT-based customer service facilities
- For marketing a new product

Large infrastructural projects for public welfare (like building roads and bridges, setting up network for supply of electric power. telephones, water or effluent disposal, etc.) are also often selected on the basis of financial criteria.

4. Importance of Rigour in Financial Criteria for Selection

The rigour in application of methods based on financial criteria is very necessary and important, even though it requires collection and analysis of a large amount of data and complex and time- consuming analytical methods. There are several reasons for such pain-staking data collection and analysis; some of them are listed as follows:

- The investments involved in many projects are large and improper selection of project would misdirect the flow of scarce resources from a critical and important project to a project of peripheral importance. The profitability and growth of the entire organization may be jeopardized with improper selection of the project.
- The investment decisions are irreversible. Most of the projects have a long term effect on the organization's operations and tend to commit the organization to a path of growth or stagnancy.
- The project decisions are for future operations and involve considerable risks. Inadequate financial analysis may expose the organization to large risks. There are instances of many successful organizations going bankrupt after embarking on an improperly selected project.

It must be emphasized here that the methods based on financial criteria (or for that matter any other criteria) only provide a basis for the decision maker. To start with, the numerical analysis carried out in the financial methods is based on the collected data and assumptions for future events. Any error or serious gaps in data for market, project cost or production costs would reflect in the financial analysis based on them. Secondly, no matter how sophisticated and carefully worked out the assumptions underlying the methods may be, they cannot reflect the reality and all the uncertainties associated with it. In the end, all analysis can take you only so far; it is the flesh and blood decision makers who have to take the decision.

5. Methods Based on Financial Projections and Analysis

The methods for financial analysis are based on making

- projections for operating results from the product of the project (surplus inward cash flows), and
- comparing the surplus inward cash flows from the project with the investment or outward cash flow using a specific criteria and calculation method to provide a basis for decision making.

The project selection methods based on financial criteria are of two types:

- *The methods based on the use of raw future cash flows in the decision making process:* Average Return on Investment (ROI), Payback Period for Investment, and Accounting Rate of Return (ARR) are such methods.
- *The methods, which discount the future cash flows according to some method and work out a parameter for assisting the investment decision:* Net Present Value (NPV), Internal Rate of Return (IRR) and Profitability Index are this type of methods.
  In the subsequent part of this chapter, we shall discuss each of these methods, calculation procedures, and the merits or limitations of the decisions based on the techniques. However, before doing that, we shall briefly discuss some basic concepts on
    (i) cash flows, procedures to calculate them and the assumptions for projections of future cash flows,
   (ii) principles underlying discounting of future cash flows
  (iii) the basis for selecting the factor to be used for discounting—Weighted Average Cost of Capital (WACC)

5.1 Calculation of Project Cash Flows

5.1.1 Principles for Estimating Project Cash Flows

All investment evaluation methods, which discount returns from the project's earnings in future, use project cash flows as their foundation. Therefore, cash flows should be estimated in confirmance with the theoretical construct of the evaluation methods. Without going into the complexities of theoretical basis for the rules, a brief summary of the rules to be used for estimating the cash flows is presented below.

- Interest charges on debt are taken into account in working out the factor used for discounting future cash flows (Average Weighted Cost of Capital AWCC). To avoid double accounting, the cash flows are estimated before interest charges.
- Only the incremental value of cash flows directly connected with the project under consideration should be used. In other words, the difference between the cash flows likely with and without the project under consideration should be used.
- There is common psychological block, which backs financing the project for which some costs have been already incurred. Investment evaluation is concerned with the future benefits or future costs, if the project is undertaken. So, the sunk costs should be ignored.
- Often, the project proposal involves use of resources, which might be available and lying idle. While evaluating the new project, the opportunity costs associated with the use of that resource (the benefits not available due to not being able to put that resource to some alternative use) should be considered.
- The investor is concerned with the net return he can earn from the project after payment of all taxes; if that return is acceptable, the project would be given a go-ahead. So, cash flows should be estimated after making provision for taxes.
- There is a tendency to allocate the overheads based on some factor like sales or occupied area or number of employees. While evaluating the new proposal also, the overheads would be automatically allocated using the same principle, which would give an unnecessary negative bias to the new project. The point likely to be missed out is that existing overheads cannot be wished away if the new project is not accepted. Only the incremental overheads connected with the new projects should be considered while evaluating the proposal for new project.
- Another common pitfall is not making adequate provision for the incremental working capital for the project. The incremental working capital, especially during the increased scale of operation in the later years, is usually not as apparent as the new fixed investment for the project. This pitfall should be avoided.
- Depreciation is a book entry (and not an actual expenditure in cash) permitted as an allowance in lowering the taxable income for calculation of tax liability. The cash flow should be before depreciation charges.
- It is a moot point how the effect of inflation on future costs and prices should be accounted while estimating cash flows. One alternative would be to work out the costs and sales at current prices and project the pro-rata amounts for working out the future cash flows only making the adjustments for operating capacity changes. This alternative assumes that the future sale prices and costs will attain a balance somewhat similar to what exists presently. This is a rational assumption and easier to use for calculations. The alternative would be to assume different inflationary trends for different cost inputs and prices and work out cash flow projections. Since the risks associated with all future events are difficult to project, usually the additional efforts and cost in the exercise are not worthwhile.

Using the above rules, the project operating cash flows, project investment and recovery of residual investment at the end of the economic life of the project are calculated as follows:

5.1.2 Project Operating Cash Flows

1. Estimate the operating capacity and corresponding sales for the future years from the project's operation.
2. Calculate the operating costs, which should include
   - Direct material cost per unit
   - Direct labour cost per unit
   - Direct fuel or energy cost per unit
   - Indirect material cost per period or year (spares and consumables for facilities)
   - Indirect labour cost per period (factory supervision, support functions like maintenance, quality control, warehouse or stores, etc.)
   - Other overheads (rents, taxes, general utilities, etc.)
   - Administrative costs (salary and facility operational costs in office)
   - Selling costs(packing, transportation and distribution charges, sales commissions, advertising, salary of sales and marketing personnel)
3. Calculate interest and depreciation charges
4. Deduct the total operating costs (item 2) and depreciation and interest charges (item 3) from estimated sales (item 1) to work out the taxable income.
5. Calculate tax on the taxable income (item 4) and deduct it from taxable income to work out profit after taxes (PAT).
6. Add back interest and depreciation (item 3) to the profit after tax (PAT, item 5) to arrive at the profit before interest and depreciation but after taxes. This figure is the project's operating cash flows for the year.

5.1.3 Initial Investment Cash Flow

This should include the investment in the new fixed assets and the incremental margins on working capital A brief explanation is in order for margin on working capital. Ordinarily, the organizations avail of the short term loans from the commercial banks against the raw material, goods in process and finished stocks. The banks advance a certain portion of the value of this stock and the organization has to provide finance for the balance or the margin on the working capital. As the operating capacity of the project increases, the working capital requirements also increase and the incremental margins on working capital should be provided in the initial and subsequent year investments.

5.1.4 Cash Flow for Recovery of Residual Investment

In case of cash flow for recovery of residual investment at the end of economic life of the project, the recovery of working capital should also be taken into account along with addition to the recovery from the fixed assets.

5.2 Principle underlying discounting of future cash flows

Among the methods based on financial criteria for investment, the methods which discount the future cash flows by some pre-determined rate are more authentic.

Why discount the future cash flows and if so in what manner?
'A bird in hand is worth two in the bush' is an age old wisdom. We all know that money in hand now is worth much more than money in future. Putting it the other way, the money expected to be received in future is much less than its face value; so, the value of future cash flow should be suitably reduced or discounted. There are good reasons rooted in human nature and economics for this. The human psychology is to use or

consume right away than defer or postpone it to future. The economic reasons are that the money as a resource can be invested to earn more money. On the other hand, in modern times, the inflation reduces the real value of money and the same amount of money, which we did not spend today to buy one kilogram of rice, would be able to buy less than a kilogram of rice after a year due to inflation and consequent erosion of the real value of money.

The correlation of a future cash receipt with its value now is based on the principle of compound interest. It rests on the idea that the principal amount P invested at an r % per annum interest rate will grow to a value $P(1 + r)$ at the end of one year. If the principal and interest are not returned to the lender, in effect the lender has advanced to the borrower an amount $P(1 + r)$. Using this new principal amount, the value at the end of the second year would be $P(1 + r)^2$. Using the same logic for the subsequent years, we get the general formula by expressing the relationship between the principal amount P and its future value Pf after the end of n years as follows:

$$P_f = P_{(1 + r)^n}$$

The factor $(1 + r)^n$ is the relationship between the present value or principal of a single amount and its future value after n years when compounded at r % per annum. Notice that the factor is always greater than 1; so when an amount is multiplied by it, it increases and when you divide by that factor, the value decreases. If we wish to find the value of the future cash flow from the present value, we should multiply by that factor and the amount would grow. If we want to find the present value of a future cash flow, we should divide the future cash flow by that factor and the amount would be reduced or discounted.

If Pv is the present value of future cash flow Pf in the nth year,

$$P_v = P_{f / (1 + r)^n} \quad \text{and} \quad P_f = P_{v \times (1 + r)^n}$$

5.3 The Rationale for selecting the factor to be used for discounting: Weighted Average Cost of Capital (WACC)

For investment decisions, it is quite common to take future cash flows from 5 to 15 years into account. Even relatively small changes in the rate r % per annum, the value of discounting factor, $(1 + r)^n$ becomes significantly different. For example for a 10 years period, the discounting factor for 8 % per annum rate would be 2.159, while for a 10 % per annum rate, it would be 2.594. The investment decision for comparing two projects with different pattern for future cash flows would depend on the discounting factor selected. So, what should be the rationale for selecting the discounting factor?

One approach would be to use the interest rate offered for bank deposits on long term fixed deposits or rates offered on similar safe investment outlets. However, most successful business earn more profit (their money grows at a higher rate) than the fixed deposit interest rate. That is precisely the reason that the companies borrow money from the banks and even after paying the principal and interest, they are in a position to retain some surplus. So the discounting rate should be higher than the fixed deposit interest rate.

A somewhat involved and complex finance theory derives this factor to equal the Weighted Average Cost of Capital (WACC). The companies finance a part of the project cost from equity or own funds and a part of the project cost from debts or long term loans from banks and other financial institutions. Depending on the return expected on equity and its proportion in overall project financing and the interest payable for the debt or long term loans and its corresponding proportion in financing the project, a composite weighted average can be worked out. This composite discount rate worked out from the ratio of debt to equity in project financing and the corresponding interest rate is called the Weighted Average Cost of Capital (WACC). It is given by the following simple formula to calculate the weighted average:

WACC = (The Proportion of Equity) $\times$ (Rate at which equity is expected to earn) +
(The proportion of debt) $\times$ (Interest agreed for debt service)

To illustrate the method of calculation, if a project is financed by equal proportion of equity and debt (i.e. the equity to debt ratio is 1: 1), the liability for debt servicing is 10 % annum and the expectation to earn from equity is 18 % per annum, then

$$WACC = (0.5 \times 18) + (0.5 \times 10) = 14 \% \text{ per annum.}$$

The calculations for rate of return expected from equity are based on market capitalization pattern for a stock of a publicly quoted company. The calculation of rate expected on equity from quoted market value is quite involved and access to that value or the overall equity to debt ratio is limited to the highest echelons in the organizations. For practical purpose, the top management promulgates a discount factor, which is uniformly used for all discounted cash flows calculations for project evaluations. The exact value of the discount rate may vary from organization to organization and from time to time. Most commonly used value of the discount factors range from 12% to 16 %. In absence of specific guidance or rule for evaluating projects, discount rate of 14 % or 15 % per annum discount rate would generally be a good choice.

6. 0 The Project Selection Methods Based on Financial Criteria

6.1 The Methods Based on the Use of Raw Future Cash Flows (without discounting)

There are two popular methods based on the use of undiscounted future cash flows:

  i. Average Return on Investment (ROI) and Accounting Rate of Return (ARR) Methods, and
  ii. Payback Period Method

We shall take a brief look at these methods in what follows.

6.1.1 Average Return on Investment (ROI) Method

Average rate of return on investment estimates undiscounted or raw values of the profits or returns from investment and expresses them as a ratio or percentage of the incremental investment for the project. Depending on the organizational practice, several variations are prevalent. The numerator, profits or returns from the project may be (a) an estimate of average profit after tax, (b) profits after tax but before interest, or (c) profits before interest and taxes. The denominator would usually be initial investment for new fixed assets and margin on incremental working capital. The higher the ROI of a project, the more attractive the project investment and hence greater preference for its selection.

To illustrate the concept, if the average profits before tax and interest for a project investment of Rs 1 millions are Rs 250,000, the average return on investment (ROI) is 25 % (using the convention mentioned in alternative (c) above). Often, the lower or middle operating levels of the organization do not have access to interest and tax positions of the company. For facilitating the decisions on smaller operating level investments, the conventions mentioned in alternatives (b) and (c) above are used.

The merits of the method are that:

- It is easy to understand and simple to apply even for those managers, who have no grounding in accounting.
- The information for calculating ROI would be available with an operating manager required to take a decision on a operational project

The main disadvantage is that it does not take into account the difference in values of the present and future cash flows. In doing so, it disregards an important basic tenet of economics, which introduces distortion in the realistic economic evaluation of the projects.

6.1.2 Accounting Rate of Return (ARR) Method

As the name suggests, this method follows the principles used in routine accounting reporting. For the future years under consideration, projections are worked out with appropriate assumptions and detailed working for the sales, operating costs, interest, depreciation and taxes and in effect to forecast the effect of project on the profit and loss account of the company. The investment decision is taken by considering in totality the effect of the investment on the organization's profitability.

The merits of the method, as in the earlier ROI case, are the simplicity in the use of the method and acceptance by businessmen and other managers as the method follows familiar accounting principles and helps in projecting the future profit and loss account. The information for calculation is readily available and easily verifiable from the organization's routine accounting system. The demerit of this method, like the ROI method, is the disregard of the basic economic principle by equating the future cash flows with present values.

6.1.3 Payback Period Method

This method also works out the future cash flows from the project and determines the time required for the project returns to recover the original investment. If a project with an investment of Rs 1 million earns cash flows of Rs 300,000 in the 1st year, Rs 400,000 in the 2nd year and Rs 500,000 in the third year, the pay-back period of the project is 2.6 years (Rs 700,000 are recovered in the first two years and the balance Rs 300,000 would be recovered in the 0.6 part of the third year).If the profitability of the project is high, the period required for recovery of the original project investment will be small and hence preferable to another project with a longer recovery or payback period. Ordinarily, organizations set a norm of certain maximum payback period and the projects which cannot meet this standard are automatically rejected.

The merits of the method are that it is easy to understand and simple to apply. One additional important advantage is that it would tend to select the projects with high profitability in the short term. In the times, when the macroeconomic conditions are fast changing and the industry is undergoing a major transformation, this method would screen out the more risky and late blooming projects. The demerits of the method, like the earlier two methods using undiscounted future cash flows, is not taking into account the time value of money. Another objection is that the method focuses on the project only until the investment is recovered. What happens after that is disregarded. This method would therefore tend to overlook the long term continued profitability of the project during the selection process.

6.2 The Methods Based on the Use of Discounted Cash Flows

In the recent times, a predominant majority of organizations have been using one of the methods based discounted cash flows for investment evaluation and project selection. Among the methods depending on financial criteria for project selection using discounted cash flows, two methods are more popular:

- Net Present Value (NPV) Method and its refined version using Benefit to Cost Ratio
- Internal Rate of Return (IRR) Method

We shall briefly discuss each method in what follows.

6.2.1 Net Present Value (NPV)

This is one of the most popular methods. It depends on calculating the net present value (NPV) of all the cash flows from the project. The method consists of summing up the present values of all the project cash flows for the economic life of the project or for a specified period [i.e. the raw estimate of cash flow for the nth year discounted by the corresponding discounting factor, viz. $1 / (1 + r)n$]. The investments are considered negative cash flows and the returns from the project are considered positive cash flows.

If the initial investment (for new fixed assets and margin on incremental working capital) is I, CF_1, CF_2, CF_3 ... and CF_n are the project cash flows respectively at the end of the 1st, 2nd, 3rd and nth year of project operation, and discount rate is r % per annum, then

$$\text{N.P.V. of project} = [\ CF_1/(1+r)\ ] + [CF_2/(1+r)^2] + [CF_3/(1+r)^3] \ldots [CF_n/(1+r)^n] - I$$

The NPV gives a measure of the benefits a company would get from undertaking a project after fully providing for the cost of capital and the involved time period for receiving the benefits. If this net present value is positive, the project is prima facie acceptable. If the NPV is negative, the project should be rejected. The larger the NPV value, the more profitable and preferable the investment in the project.

It can be seen from the formula above that if the discounting rate r % is increased, the NPV would decrease and if the discount rate r % is decreased, the NPV would increase. The impact of the small changes in the discount rate r is usually quite large on the NPV. The selection of the right discounting rate is, therefore, very important. The discount rate used for NPV calculations is based on the Average Weighted Cost of Capital (AWCC) discussed in 5.3 above. This is a very realistic assumption and since, NPV method is based on the assumption of discounting the future cash flows at that rate, the method is based on sound economic principles and realistic assumptions.

There are some objections against using the NPV method alone. NPV method only gives the value of the total surplus of discounted project cash flows, but it does not relate it to the original investment. Hence the efficiency of the capital for generating NPV is not taken into account. If two projects A and B give equal NPV values, but the investment for project A is much less than investment for project B, project A should be obviously favoured but NPV method as such does not help to distinguish between the two.

6.2.2 Refinement of NPV Method Using Benefits to Cost Ratio

This objection can be overcome by introducing the benefits to cost ratio concept. If the net present value of a project (Project Benefits) is P_B and the total incremental investment for the project (Project Cost) is I, then the ratio P_B/I is the benefit to cost ratio for a project. This ratio helps to distinguish between the projects with more efficient use of capital. The higher this benefits to cost ratio, the more efficient use of project investment and hence a preferable investment option.

6.2.3 Internal rate of Return (IRR) Method

In the NPV method, the discount rate appears to be chosen somewhat arbitrarily, though the choice of the factor rests on sound economic principles and realistic assumption (average weighted cost of capital). In the IRR method, this objection can also be overcome. IRR is defined as that value of discount rate, which would make the NPV of the project equal to zero. In other words, the NPV of the project cash flows, when discounted at IRR, equals the initial project investment.

If the initial investment (for new fixed assets and margin on incremental working capital) is I, CF_1, CF_2, CF_3 ... and CF_n are the project cash flows respectively at the end of the 1st, 2nd, 3rd and nth year of project operation, and discount rate is r % per annum, then IRR is found by trial and error solution of the following equation:

$$I = [\ CF_1/(1+r)\ ] + [CF_2/(1+r)^2] + [CF_3/(1+r)^3] \ldots [CF_n/(1+r)^n\}$$

If the value of IRR is higher than a certain rate specified by the organization (often called 'hurdle rate'), the project is accepted and if it lower, the project is rejected. If two projects have IRR values higher than the specified hurdle rate, the project with the higher value of IRR is preferred. The hurdle rate, or minimum acceptable IRR value specified by the organization, is usually based on the WACC – weighted average cost of capital. So, if IRR is higher than hurdle rate, a positive NPV would be assured when discount rate used for NPV calculations is WACC.

It would be noted that NPV and IRR methods are very close in basic principles – discounting the project cash flows and relating them with the initial investment. Both methods would give similar evaluation (for acceptance or rejection of a project and comparative evaluation of two projects) if the project cash flows follow the conventional pattern of investment in the initial period and positive returns in the subsequent years. If this condition is not satisfied, the IRR method would be subject to serious theoretical objections. There is also another objection based on the theoretical construct of IRR, which assumes that the project cash flows from future years are reinvested into projects which give IRR rate of return. This assumption may not often hold and it can introduce some distortion in the selection metric. Another set of difficulty with the IRR method is of mathematical nature. When the method is applied to projects which do not have steady conventional cash flows but negative as well as positive cash flows for some years, solving the equation gives more than one roots (i.e. more than one values of IRR).

These theoretical objections notwithstanding, IRR has become a very popular method for evaluating projects – almost as popular as NPV method. The reason lies in the fact that the IRR method does not require use of any 'arbitrary' discount rate for its use. So, it would be possible to calculate IRR merely from the project investment and cash flow data. Since the method gives a value of the time adjusted rate of return on the project, it is very easy for people to compare the IRR rate with the general interest rate for bank loans, inflation rate in the economy, the return on equity and the like for relating it to the external reality of day-to-day experience.

6.3 Summary

We discussed a number of techniques for selection of projects based on the financial criteria. Each technique has some special benefits and some likely pitfalls. The organizations usually have a preference for using one or the other method for project selection. Very often, the analysis using different techniques are carried out and the outcomes from them are weighed to come to a conclusion.

The different techniques for financial evaluation of a project provide very valuable guidance to the decision makers. However, the proverbial buck stops on the desk of the decision maker. In the final analysis, the knowledge, experience, risk tolerance, entrepreneurial capability and mature judgment of the decision makers is what plays the role of crucial importance in project selection and related investment decision.

CASE 2.1

Hector Gaming Company

Hector Gaming Company (HGC) is an educational gaming company specializing in young children's educational games. HGC has just completed their fourth year of operation. This year was a banner year for HGC. The company received a large influx of capital for growth by issuing stock privately through an investment banking firm. It appears the return on investment for this past year will be just over 25 percent with zero debt! The growth rate for the last two years has been approximately 80 percent each year. Parents and grandparents of young children have been buying HGC's products almost as fast as they are developed. Every member of the 56-person firm is enthusiastic and looking forward to helping the firm grow to be the largest and best educational gaming company in the world. The founder of the firm, Sally Peters, has been written up in *Young Entrepreneurs* as "the young entrepreneur to watch." She has been able to develop an organization culture in which all stakeholders are committed to innovation, continuous improvement, and organization learning.

Last year, 10 top managers of HGC worked with McKinley Consulting to develop the organization's strategic plan. This year the same 10 managers had a retreat in Aruba to formulate next year's strategic plan using the same process suggested by McKinley Consulting. Most executives seem to have a consensus of where the firm should go in the intermediate and long term. But there is little consensus on how this should be accomplished. Peters, now president of HGC, feels she may be losing control. The frequency of conflicts seems to be increasing. Some individuals are always requested for any new project created. When resource conflicts occur among projects, each project manager believes his or her project is most important. More projects are not meeting deadlines and are coming in over budget. Yesterday's management meeting revealed some top HGC talent have been working on an international business game for college students. This project does not fit the organization vision or market niche. At times it seems everyone is marching to his or her own drummer. Somehow more focus is needed to ensure everyone agrees on *how* strategy should be implemented, given the resources available to the organization.

Yesterday's meeting alarmed Peters. These emerging problems are coming at a bad time. Next week HGC is ramping up the size of the organization, number of new products per year, and marketing efforts. Fifteen new people will join HGC next month. Peters is concerned that policies be in place that will ensure the new people are used most productively. An additional potential problem looms on the horizon. Other gaming companies have noticed the success HGC is having in their niche market; one company tried to hire a key product development employee away from HGC. Peters wants HGC to be ready to meet any potential competition head on and to discourage any new entries into their market. Peters knows HGC is project driven; however, she is not as confident that she has a good handle on how such an organization should be managed—especially with such a fast growth rate and potential competition closer to becoming a reality. The magnitude of emerging problems demands quick attention and resolution.

Peters has hired you as a consultant. She has suggested the following format for your consulting contract. You are free to use another format if it will improve the effectiveness of the consulting engagement.

What is our major problem?
Identify some symptoms of the problem.
What is the major cause of the problem?

Provide a detailed action plan that attacks the problem. Be specific and provide examples that relate to HGC.

CASE 2.2

Film Prioritization

The purpose of this case is to give you experience in using a project priority system that ranks proposed projects by their contribution to the organization's objectives and strategic plan.

Company Profile

The company is the film division for a large entertainment conglomerate. The main office is located in Anaheim, California. In addition to the feature film division, the conglomerate includes theme parks, home videos, a television channel, interactive games, and theatrical productions. The company has been enjoying steady growth over the past 10 years. Last year total revenues increased by 12 percent to $21.2 billion. The company is engaged in negotiations to expand its theme park empire to mainland China and Poland. The film division generated $274 million in revenues, which was an increase of 7 percent over the past year. Profit margin was down 3 percent to 16 percent because of the poor response to three of the five major film releases for the year.

Company Mission

The mission for the firm:

Our overriding objective is to create shareholder value by continuing to be the world's premier entertainment company from a creative, strategic, and financial standpoint.

The film division supports this mission by producing four to six high-quality, family entertainment films for mass distribution each year. In recent years, the CEO of the company has advocated that the firm take a leadership position in championing environmental concerns.

Company "Must" Objectives

Every project must meet the must objectives as determined by executive management. It is important that selected film projects not violate such objectives of high strategic priority. There are three must objectives:

1. All projects meet current legal, safety, and environmental standards.
2. All film projects should receive a PG or lower advisory rating.
3. All projects should not have an adverse effect on current or planned operations within the larger company.

Company "Want" Objectives

Want objectives are assigned weights for their relative importance. Top management is responsible for formulating, ranking, and weighting objectives to ensure that projects support the company's strategy and mission. The following is a list of the company's want objectives:

1. Be nominated for and win an academy award for Best Picture of the Year.
2. Create at least one new animated character each year that can star in a cartoon or TV series.
3. Generate additional merchandise revenue (action figures, dolls, interactive games, music CDs).
4. Raise public consciousness about environmental issues and concerns.
5. Generate profit in excess of 18 percent.
6. Advance the state of the art in film animation, and preserve the firm's reputation.
7. Provide the basis for the development of a new ride at a company-owned theme park.

Assignment

You are a member of the priority team in charge of evaluating and selecting film proposals. Use the provided evaluation form to formally evaluate and rank each proposal. Be prepared to report your rankings and justify your decisions.

Assume that all of the projects have passed the estimated hurdle rate of 14 percent ROI. In addition to the brief film synopsis, the proposals include the following financial projections of theater and video sales: 80 percent chance of ROI, 50 percent chance of ROI, and 20 percent chance of ROI.

For example, for proposal #1 (Dalai Lama) there is an 80 percent chance that it will earn at least 8 percent return on investment (ROI), a 50-50 chance the ROI will be 18 percent, and a 20 percent chance that the ROI will be 24 percent.

Film Proposals

Project Proposal 1: My Life with Dalai Lama

An animated, biographical account of the Dalai Lama's childhood in Tibet based on the popular children's book *Tales from Nepal*. The Lama's life is told through the eyes of "Guoda," a field snake, and other local animals who befriend the Dalai and help him understand the principles of Buddhism.

Probability	80%	50%	20%
ROI	8%	18%	24%

Project Proposal 2: Heidi

A remake of the classic children's story with music written by award-winning composers Syskle and Obert. The big-budget film will feature top-name stars and breathtaking scenery of the Swiss Alps.

Probability	80%	50%	20%
ROI	2%	20%	30%

Project Proposal 3: The Year of the Echo

A low-budget documentary that celebrates the career of one of the most influential bands in rock-and-roll history. The film will be directed by new-wave director Elliot Cznerzy and will combine concert footage and behind-the-scenes interviews spanning the 25-year history of the rock band the Echos. In addition to great music, the film will focus on the death of one of the founding members from a heroin overdose and reveal the underworld of sex, lies, and drugs in the music industry.

Probability	80%	50%	20%
ROI	12%	14%	18%

Project Proposal 4: Escape from Rio Japuni

An animated feature set in the Amazon rainforest. The story centers around Pablo, a young jaguar who attempts to convince warring jungle animals that they must unite and escape the devastation of local clear cutting.

Probability	80%	50%	20%
ROI	15%	20%	24%

Project 5: Nadia!

The story of Nadia Comaneci, the famous Romanian gymnast who won three gold medals at the 1976 Summer Olympic Games. The low-budget film will document her life as a small child in Romania and how she was chosen by Romanian authorities to join their elite, state-run, athletic program. The film will highlight how Nadia maintained her independent spirit and love for gymnastics despite a harsh, regimented training program.

Probability	80%	50%	20%
ROI	8%	15%	20%

Project 6: Keiko-One Whale of a Story

The story of Keiko, the famous killer whale, will be told by an imaginary offspring Seiko, who in the distant future is telling her children about their famous grandfather. The big-budget film will integrate actual footage of the whale within a realistic animated environment using state-of-the-art computer imagery. The story will reveal how Keiko responded to his treatment by humans.

Probability	80%	50%	20%
ROI	6%	18%	25%

Project Priority Evaluation Form

Must objectives	Must meet if impacts	1	2	3	4	5	6	7
Meets all safety and environmental standards	Y = yes N = no N/A = not applicable							
PG or G rating	Y = yes N = no N/A = not applicable							
No adverse effect on other operations	Y = yes N = no N/A = not applicable							
Want objectives	Relative Importance 1–100	**Single project impact definitions**	Weighted Score	Weighted Score	Weighted Score	Weighted Score	Weighted Score	Weighted Score	Weighted Score
Be nominated for Best Picture of the Year	60	0 = No potential 1 = Low potential 2 = High potential							
Generate additional merchandise	10	0 = No potential 1 = Low potential 2 = High potential							
Create a new, major animated character	20	0 = No potential 1 = Low potential 2 = High potential							
Raise environmental concerns	55	0 = No potential 1 = Low potential 2 = High potential							
Generate profit greater than 18%	70	0 < 18% 1 = 18–22% 2 > 22%							
Advance state of film animation	40	0 = No impact 1 = Some impact 2 = Great impact							
Provide basis for new theme ride	10	0 = No potential 1 = Low potential 2 = High potential							
Total weighted score									
Priority									

Project 7: Grand Island

The true story of a group of junior-high biology students who discover that a fertilizer plant is dumping toxic wastes into a nearby river. The moderate-budget film depicts how students organize a grassroots campaign to fight local bureaucracy and ultimately force the fertilizer plant to restore the local ecosystem.

Probability	80%	50%	20%
ROI	9%	15%	20%

CHAPTER 3

Organization: Structure and Culture

Matrix management works, but it sure is difficult at times. All matrix managers must keep up their health and take Stress-Tabs.

—*A Project Manager*

Once management approves a project then the question becomes, how will the project be implemented? This chapter examines three different project management structures used by firms to implement projects: functional organization, dedicated project teams and matrix structure. Although not exhaustive, these structures and their variant forms represent the major approaches for organizing projects. The advantages and disadvantages of each of these structures are discussed as well as some of the critical factors that might lead a firm to choose one form over others.

Whether a firm chooses to complete projects within the traditional functional organization or through some form of matrix arrangement is only part of the story. Anyone who has worked for more than one organization realizes that there are often considerable differences in how projects are managed within certain firms with similar structures. Working in a matrix system at AT&T is different from working in a matrix environment at Hewlett-Packard. Many researchers attribute these differences to the organizational culture at AT&T and Hewlett-Packard. A simple explanation of *organizational culture* is that it reflects the "personality" of an organization. Just as each individual has a unique personality, so each organization has a unique culture. Toward the end of this chapter, we examine in more detail what organizational culture is and the impact that the culture of the parent organization has on organizing and managing projects.

Both the project management structure and the culture of the organization constitute major elements of the environment in which projects are implemented. It is important for project managers and participants to know the "lay of the land" so that they can avoid obstacles and take advantage of pathways to complete their projects.

Project Management Structures

A project management system provides a framework for launching and implementing project activities within a parent organization. A good system appropriately balances the needs of both the parent organization and the project by defining the interface between the project and parent organization in terms of authority, allocation of resources, and eventual integration of project outcomes into mainstream operations.

Many business organizations have struggled with creating a system for organizing projects while managing ongoing operations. One of the major reasons for this struggle is that projects contradict fundamental design principles associated with traditional organizations. Projects are unique, one-time efforts with a distinct beginning and end. Most organizations are designed to efficiently manage ongoing activities. Efficiency is achieved primarily by breaking down complex tasks into simplified, repetitive processes, as symbolized by assembly-line production methods. Projects are not routine and therefore can be like ducks out of water in these work environments. With this in mind, we will start the discussion of project management structures.

Organizing Projects within the Functional Organization

One approach to organizing projects is to simply manage them within the existing functional hierarchy of the organization. Once management decides to implement a project, the different segments of the project are delegated to the respective functional units with each unit responsible for completing its segment of the project (see Figure 3.1). Coordination is maintained through normal management channels. For example, a tool manufacturing firm decides to differentiate its product line by offering a series of tools specially designed for left-handed individuals. Top management decides to implement the project, and different segments of the project are distributed to appropriate areas. The industrial design department is responsible for modifying specifications to conform to the needs of left-handed users. The production department is responsible for devising the means for producing new tools according to these new design specifications. The marketing department is responsible for gauging demand and price as well as identifying distribution outlets. The overall project will be managed within the normal hierarchy, with the project being part of the working agenda of top management.

The functional organization is also commonly used when, given the nature of the project, one functional area plays a dominant role in completing the project or has a dominant interest in the success of the project. Under these circumstances, a high-ranking manager in that area is given the responsibility of coordinating the project. For example, the transfer of equipment and personnel to a new office would be managed by a top-ranking manager in the firm's facilities department. Likewise, a project involving the upgrading of the management information system would be managed by the information systems department. In both cases, most of the project work would be done within the specified department and coordination with other departments would occur through normal channels.

There are advantages and disadvantages for using the existing functional organization to administer and complete projects. The major advantages are the following:

1. **No Change.** Projects are completed within the basic functional structure of the parent organization. There is no radical alteration in the design and operation of the parent organization.
2. **Flexibility.** There is maximum flexibility in the use of staff. Appropriate specialists in different functional units can temporarily be assigned to work on the project and then return to their normal work. With a broad base of technical personnel available within each functional department, people can be switched among different projects with relative ease.
3. **In-Depth Expertise.** If the scope of the project is narrow and the proper functional unit is assigned primary responsibility, then in-depth expertise can be brought to bear on the most crucial aspects of the project.
4. **Easy Post-Project Transition.** Normal career paths within a functional division are maintained. While specialists can make significant contributions to projects, their functional field is their professional home and the focus of their professional growth and advancement.

Just as there are advantages for organizing projects within the existing functional organization, there are also disadvantages. These disadvantages are particularly pronounced when the scope of the project is broad and one functional department does not take the dominant technological and managerial lead on the project:

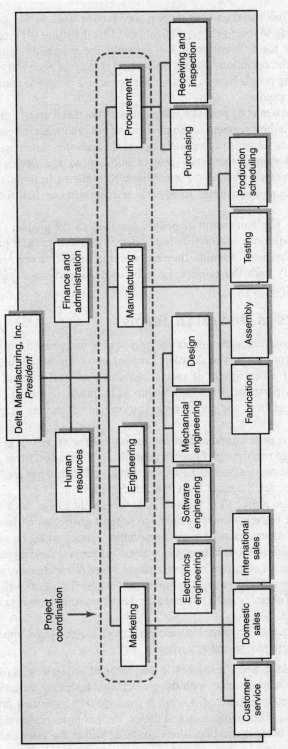

FIGURE 3.1   Functional Organizations

1. **Lack of Focus.** Each functional unit has its own core routine work to do; sometimes project responsibilities get pushed aside to meet primary obligations. This difficulty is compounded when the project has different priorities for different units. For example, the marketing department may consider the project urgent while the operations people considered it only of secondary importance. Imagine the tension if the marketing people have to wait for the operations people to complete their segment of the project before they proceed.

2. **Poor Integration.** There may be poor integration across functional units. Functional specialists tend to be concerned only with their segment of the project and not with what is best for the total project.

3. **Slow.** It generally takes longer to complete projects through this functional arrangement. This is in part attributable to slow response time—project information and decisions have to be circulated through normal management channels. Furthermore, the lack of horizontal, direct communication among functional groups contributes to rework as specialists realize the implications of others' actions after the fact.

4. **Lack of Ownership.** The motivation of people assigned to the project can be weak. The project may be seen as an additional burden that is not directly linked to their professional development or advancement. Furthermore, because they are working on only a segment of the project, professionals do not identify with the project. Lack of ownership discourages strong commitment to project-related activities.

Organizing Projects as Dedicated Teams

At the other end of the structural spectrum is the creation of independent project teams. These teams operate as separate units from the rest of the parent organization. Usually a full-time project manager is designated to pull together a core group of specialists who work full time on the project. The project manager recruits necessary personnel from both within and outside the parent company. The subsequent team is physically separated from the parent organization and given marching orders to complete the project (see Figure 3.2).

The interface between the parent organization and the project teams will vary. In some cases, the parent organization maintains a tight rein through financial controls. In other cases, firms grant the project manager maximum freedom to get the project done as he sees fit. Lockheed Martin has used this approach to develop next generation jet airplanes. See Snapshot from Practice: Skunk Works.

In the case of firms where projects are the dominant form of business, such as a construction firm or a consulting firm, the entire organization is designed to support project teams. Instead of one or two special projects, the organization consists of sets of quasi-independent teams working on specific projects. The main responsibility of traditional functional departments is to assist and support these project teams. For example, the marketing department is directed at generating new business that will lead to more projects, while the human resource department is responsible for managing a variety of personnel issues as well as recruiting and training new employees. This type of organization is referred to in the literature as a *Project Organization* and is graphically portrayed in Figure 3.3.

As in the case of functional organization, the dedicated project team approach has strengths and weaknesses. The following are recognized as strengths:

1. **Simple.** Other than taking away resources in the form of specialists assigned to the project, the functional organization remains intact with the project team operating independently.

2. **Fast.** Projects tend to get done more quickly when participants devote their full attention to the project and are not distracted by other obligations and duties. Furthermore, response time tends to be quicker under this arrangement because most decisions are made within the team and are not deferred up the hierarchy.

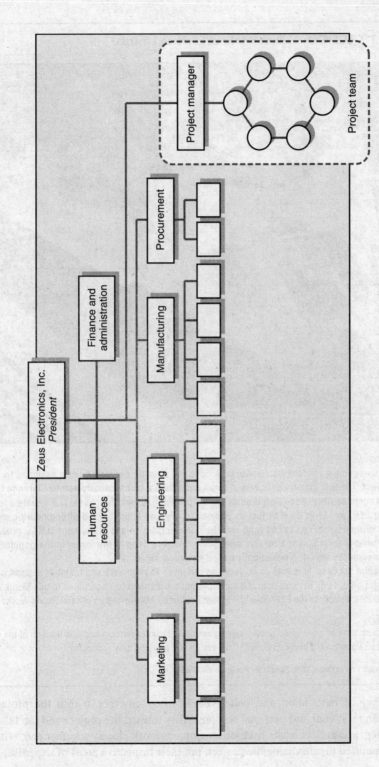

FIGURE 3.2   Dedicated Project Team

Snapshot from Practice   Skunk Works at Lockheed Martin*

Courtesy Lockheed Martin.

  In project management folklore, skunk works is code for a small, dedicated team assigned to a breakthrough project. The first skunk works was created more than a half a century ago by Clarence L. "Kelly" Johnson at Lockheed Aerospace Corporation. Kelly's project had two objectives: 1) to create a jet fighter, the Shooting Star, and 2) to do it as fast as possible. Kelly and a small band of engineering mavericks operated as a dedicated team unencumbered by red tape and the bureaucratic delays of the normal R&D process. The name was coined by team member Irvin Culver after the moonshine brewery deep in the forest in the popular cartoon strip Lil'Abner. The homemade whisky was euphemistically called kickapoo joy juice.

The project was a spectacular success. In just 43 days, Johnson's team of 23 engineers and teams of support personnel put together the first American fighter to fly at more than 500 miles per hour. Lockheed has continued to use Skunk Works to develop a string of high speed jets, including the F117 Stealth Fighter. Lockheed Martin has an official Skunk Works division. Their charter is:

The Skunk Works is a concentration of a few good people solving problems far in advance—and at a fraction of the cost—by applying the simplest, most straightforward methods possible to develop and produce new products.

* J., Miller, *Lockheed Martin's Skunk Works* (New York: Speciality Publications, 1996).

---

3. **Cohesive.** A high level of motivation and cohesiveness often emerges within the project team. Participants share a common goal and personal responsibility toward the project and the team.
4. **Cross-Functional Integration.** Specialists from different areas work closely together and, with proper guidance, become committed to optimizing the project, not their respective areas of expertise.

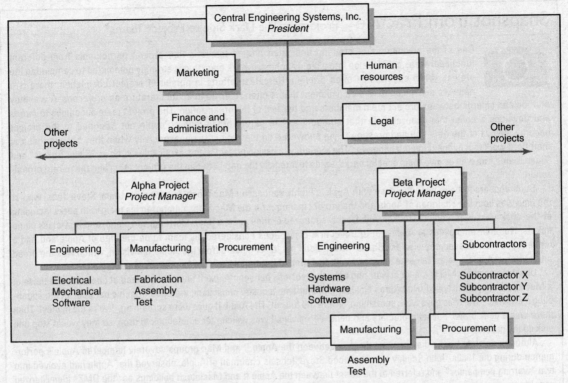

FIGURE 3.3   Project Organization Structure

In many cases, the project team approach is the optimum approach for completing a project when you view it solely from the standpoint of what is best for completing the project. Its weaknesses become more evident when the needs of the parent organization are taken into account:

1. **Expensive.** Not only have you created a new management position (project manager), but resources are also assigned on a full-time basis. This can result in duplication of efforts across projects and a loss of economies of scale.
2. **Internal Strife.** Sometimes dedicated project teams take on an entity of their own and a disease known as projectitis develops. See Snapshot from Practice: Projectitis—The Dark Side. A strong we–they divisiveness emerges between the project team and the parent organization. This divisiveness can undermine not only the integration of the eventual outcomes of the project into mainstream operations but also the assimilation of project team members back into their functional units once the project is completed.
3. **Limited Technological Expertise.** Creating self-contained teams inhibits maximum technological expertise being brought to bear on problems. Technical expertise is limited somewhat to the talents and experience of the specialists assigned to the project. While nothing prevents specialists from consulting with others in the functional division, the we–they syndrome and the fact that such help is not formally sanctioned by the organization discourage this from happening.
4. **Difficult Post-Project Transition.** Assigning full-time personnel to a project creates the dilemma of what to do with personnel after the project is completed. If other project work is not available, then the transition back to their original functional departments may be difficult because of their prolonged absence and the need to catch up with recent developments in their functional area.

Snapshot from Practice   Projectitis: The Dark Side to Project Teams*

One of the advantages of creating dedicated project teams is that project participants from different functional areas can develop into a highly cohesive work team that is strongly committed to completing the project. While such teams often produce Herculean efforts in pursuit of project completion, there is a negative dimension to this commitment that is often referred to in the literature as *projectitis*. A we–they attitude can emerge between project team members and the rest of the organization. The project team succumbs to *hubris* and develops a holier-than-thou attitude that antagonizes the parent organization. People not assigned to the project become jealous of the attention and prestige being showered on the project team, especially when they believe that it is their hard work that is financing the endeavor. The tendency to assign project teams exotic titles such as "Silver Bullets" and "Tiger Teams," as well as give them special perks, tends to intensify the gap between the project team and the parent organization.

Such appears to have been the case with Apple's highly successful Macintosh development team. Steve Jobs, who at the time was both the chairman of Apple and the project manager for the Mac team, pampered his team with perks including at-the-desk massages, coolers stocked with freshly squeezed orange juice, a Bosendorfer grand piano, and first-class plane tickets. No other employees at Apple got to travel first class. Jobs considered his team to be the elite of Apple and had a tendency to refer to everyone else as "Bozos" who "didn't get it." Engineers from the Apple II division, which was the bread and butter of Apple's sales, became incensed with the special treatment their colleagues were getting.

One evening at Ely McFly's, a local watering hole, the tensions between Apple II engineers seated at one table and those of a Mac team at another boiled over. Aaron Goldberg, a long-time industry consultant, watched from his barstool as the squabbling escalated. "The Mac guys were screaming, 'We're the future!' The Apple II guys were screaming, 'We're the money!' Then there was a geek brawl. Pocket protectors and pens were flying. I was waiting for a notebook to drop, so they would stop and pick up the papers."

Although comical from a distance, the discord between the Apple II and Mac groups severely hampered Apple's performance during the 1980s. John Sculley, who replaced Steve Jobs as chairman of Apple, observed that Apple had evolved into two "warring companies" and referred to the street between the Apple II and Macintosh buildings as "the DMZ" (demilitarized zone).

* J., Carlton, *Apple: The Inside Story of Intrigue, Egomania, and Business Blunders* (New York: Random House, 1997), pp. 13–14; J., Sculley, *Odyssey: Pepsi to Apple . . . A Journey of Adventure, Ideas, and the Future* (New York: Harper & Row, 1987), pp. 270–79.

Organizing Projects within a Matrix Arrangement

One of the biggest management innovations to emerge in the past 30 years has been the matrix organization. Matrix management is a hybrid organizational form in which a horizontal project management structure is "overlaid" on the normal functional hierarchy. In a matrix system, there are usually two chains of command, one along functional lines and the other along project lines. Instead of delegating segments of a project to different units or creating an autonomous team, project participants report simultaneously to both functional and project managers.

Companies apply this matrix arrangement in a variety of different ways. Some organizations set up temporary matrix systems to deal with specific projects, while "matrix" may be a permanent fixture in other organizations. Let us first look at its general application and then proceed to a more detailed discussion of finer points. Consider Figure 3.4. There are three projects currently under way: A, B, and C. All three project managers (PM A-C) report to a director of project management, who supervises all projects. Each project has an administrative assistant, although the one for project C is only part time.

Project A involves the design and expansion of an existing production line to accommodate new metal alloys. To accomplish this objective, project A has assigned to it 3.5 people from manufacturing and 6 people from engineering. These individuals are assigned to the project on a part-time or full-time basis, depending on the project's needs during various phases of the project. Project B involves the development of a new

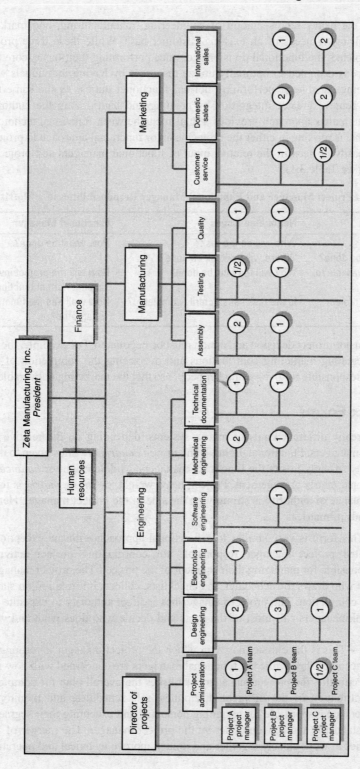

FIGURE 3.4 Matrix Organization Structure

product that requires the heavy representation of engineering, manufacturing, and marketing. Project C involves forecasting changing needs of an existing customer base. While these three projects, as well as others, are being completed, the functional divisions continue performing their basic, core activities.

The matrix structure is designed to optimally utilize resources by having individuals work on multiple projects as well as being capable of performing normal functional duties. At the same time, the matrix approach attempts to achieve greater integration by creating and legitimizing the authority of a project manager. In theory, the matrix approach provides a dual focus between functional/technical expertise and project requirements that is missing in either the project team or functional approach to project management. This focus can most easily be seen in the relative input of functional managers and project managers over key project decisions (see Table 3.1).

TABLE 3.1 **Division of Project Manager and Functional Manager Responsibilities in a Matrix Structure**

Project Manager	Negotiated Issues	Functional Manager
What has to be done?	Who will do the task?	How will it be done?
When should the task be done?	Where will the task be done?	
How much money is available to do the task?	Why will the task be done?	How will the project involvement impact normal functional activities?
How well has the total project been done?	Is the task satisfactorily completed?	How well has the functional input been integrated?

In principle every major project decision and action must be negotiated. For example, the project manager is responsible for integrating marketing contributions and overseeing the completion of the project. The marketing manager is responsible for overseeing her people so that the marketing deliverables are done right.

Different Matrix Forms

In practice there are really different kinds of matrix systems, depending on the relative authority of the project and functional managers. Functional, lightweight, or *weak matrix* are titles given to matrices in which the balance of authority strongly favors the functional managers. Middleweight or *balanced matrix* is used to describe the traditional matrix arrangement. Project, heavyweight, or *strong matrix* is used to describe a matrix in which the balance of authority is strongly on the side of the project manager. Here is a thumbnail sketch of the three kinds of matrices:

- **Weak matrix**—This form is very similar to a functional approach with the exception that there is a formally designated project manager responsible for coordinating project activities. Functional managers are responsible for managing their segment of the project. The project manager basically acts as a staff assistant who draws the schedules and checklists, collects information on status of work, and facilitates project completion. The project manager has indirect authority to expedite and monitor the project. Functional managers call most of the shots and decide who does what and when the work is completed.

- **Balanced matrix**—This is the classic matrix in which the project manager is responsible for defining what needs to be accomplished while the functional managers are concerned with how it will be accomplished. More specifically, the project manager establishes the overall plan for completing the project, integrates the contribution of the different disciplines, sets schedules, and monitors progress. The functional managers are responsible for assigning personnel and executing their segment of the project according to the standards and schedules set by the project manager. The merger of "what and how" requires both parties to work closely together and jointly approve technical and operational decisions.

- **Strong matrix**—This form attempts to create the "feel" of a project team within a matrix environment. The project manager controls most aspects of the project, including scope trade-offs and assignment of functional personnel. The project manager controls when and what specialists do and has final say on major project decisions. The functional manager has title over her people and is consulted on a need basis. In some situations a functional manager's department may serve as a "subcontractor" for the project, in which case they have more control over specialized work. For example, the development of a new series of laptop computers may require a team of experts from different disciplines working on the basic design and performance requirements within a project matrix arrangement. Once the specifications have been determined, final design and production of certain components (i.e., power source) may be assigned to respective functional groups to complete.

Matrix management both in general and in its specific forms has unique strengths and weaknesses. The advantages and disadvantages of matrix organizations in general are noted below, while only briefly highlighting specifics concerning different forms:

1. **Efficient.** Resources can be shared across multiple projects as well as within functional divisions. Individuals can divide their energy across multiple projects on an as-needed basis. This reduces duplication required in a projectized structure.
2. **Strong Project Focus.** A stronger project focus is provided by having a formally designated project manager who is responsible for coordinating and integrating contributions of different units. This helps sustain a holistic approach to problem solving that is often missing in the functional organization.
3. **Easier Post-Project Transition.** Because the project organization is overlaid on the functional divisions, specialists maintain ties with their functional group, so they have a homeport to return to once the project is completed.
4. **Flexible.** Matrix arrangements provide for flexible utilization of resources and expertise within the firm. In some cases functional units may provide individuals who are managed by the project manager. In other cases the contributions are monitored by the functional manager.

The strengths of the matrix structure are considerable. Unfortunately, so are the potential weaknesses. This is due in large part to the fact that a matrix structure is more complicated and the creation of multiple bosses represents a radical departure from the traditional hierarchical authority system.

Furthermore, one does not install a matrix structure overnight. Experts argue that it takes 3–5 years for a matrix system to fully mature. So many of the problems described below represent growing pains.

1. **Dysfunctional Conflict.** The matrix approach is predicated on tension between functional managers and project managers who bring critical expertise and perspectives to the project. Such tension is viewed as a necessary mechanism for achieving an appropriate balance between complex technical issues and unique project requirements. While the intent is noble, the effect is sometimes analogous to opening Pandora's box. Legitimate conflict can spill over to a more personal level, resulting from conflicting agendas and accountabilities. Worthy discussions can degenerate into heated arguments that engender animosity among the managers involved.
2. **Infighting.** Any situation in which equipment, resources, and people are being shared across projects and functional activities lends itself to conflict and competition for scarce resources. Infighting can occur among project managers, who are primarily interested in what is best for their project.
3. **Stressful.** Matrix management violates the management principle of unity of command. Project participants have at least two bosses—their functional head and one or more project managers. Working in a matrix environment can be extremely stressful. Imagine what it would be like to work in an environment in which you are being told to do three conflicting things by three different managers.

4. **Slow.** In theory, the presence of a project manager to coordinate the project should accelerate the completion of the project. In practice, decision making can get bogged down as agreements have to be forged across multiple functional groups. This is especially true for the balanced matrix.

When the three variant forms of the matrix approach are considered, we can see that advantages and disadvantages are not necessarily true for all three forms of matrix. The Strong matrix is likely to enhance project integration, diminish internal power struggles, and ultimately improve control of project activities and costs. On the downside, technical quality may suffer because functional areas have less control over their contributions. Finally, projectitis may emerge as the members develop a strong team identity.

The Weak matrix is likely to improve technical quality as well as provide a better system for managing conflict across projects because the functional manager assigns personnel to different projects. The problem is that functional control is often maintained at the expense of poor project integration. The Balanced matrix can achieve better balance between technical and project requirements, but it is a very delicate system to manage and is more likely to succumb to many of the problems associated with the matrix approach.

What Is the Right Project Management Structure?

There is growing empirical evidence that project success is directly linked to the amount of autonomy and authority project managers have over their projects. See Research Highlight: Relative Effectiveness of Different Project Management Structures. However, most of this research is based on what is best for managing specific projects. It is important to remember what was stated in the beginning of the chapter—that the best system balances the needs of the project with those of the parent organization. So what project structure should an organization use? This is a complicated question with no precise answers. A number of issues need to be considered at both the organization and project level.

Organization Considerations

At the organization level, the first question that needs to be asked is how important is project management to the success of the firm? What percentage of core work involves projects? If over 75 percent of work involves projects, then an organization should consider a fully projectized organization. If an organization has both standard products and projects, then a matrix arrangement would appear to be appropriate. If an organization has very few projects, then a less formal arrangement is probably all that is required. Dedicated teams could be created on an as-needed basis and the organization could outsource project work.

A second key question is resource availability. Remember, matrix evolved out of the necessity to share resources across multiple projects and functional domains while at the same time creating legitimate project leadership. For organizations that cannot afford to tie up critical personnel on individual projects, a matrix system would appear to be appropriate. An alternative would be to create a dedicated team but outsource project work when resources are not available internally.

Within the context of the first two questions, an organization needs to assess current practices and what changes are needed to more effectively manage projects. A strong project matrix is not installed overnight. The shift toward a greater emphasis on projects has a host of political implications that need to be worked through, requiring time and strong leadership. For example, we have observed many companies that make the transition from a functional organization to a matrix organization begin with a weak functional matrix. This is due in part to resistance by functional and department managers toward transferring authority to project managers. With time, these matrix structures eventually evolve into a project matrix. Many

Research Highlight

Relative Effectiveness of Different Project Management Structures*

Larson and Gobeli studied the relative efficacy of different project management structures. Their work is based on a sample of more than 1,600 project professionals and managers actively involved in project management within their organizations. Among the findings they report are the rated effectiveness of different structures for product development and construction projects. These results are summarized in Figure 3.5 and indicate a strong preference for either the project team or strong matrix. Both the functional approach and the weak matrix were rated ineffective, and the balanced matrix was considered only marginally effective.

Because these ratings may have been tempered by self-interest, with project managers advocating forms that give them more formal authority, the ratings of project managers were compared with those of top management and functional managers. No significant differences were found; the weak matrix and functional organization were considered the least effective even by functional managers.

This research was published at a time when matrix management was receiving a lot of negative press and when popular management media were advocating the dedicated project team approach. A key finding was that matrix management can be as effective as a project team—if the project manager is given significant control over project activities. The support is not without reservations; as one project manager reported, "Matrix management works, but it sure is difficult at times. All matrix managers must keep up their health and take Stress Tabs."

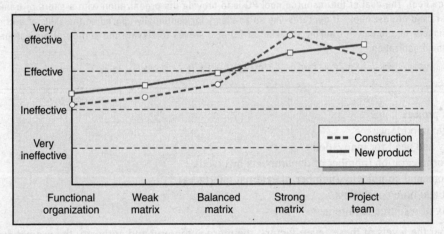

FIGURE 3.5   Rated Effectiveness of Different Project Structures by Type of Project

* E. W. Larson, and D. H. Gobeli, "Matrix Management: Contradictions and Insights," *California Management Review*, vol. 29, no. 4 (Summer 1987), p. 137.

organizations have created Project Management Offices to support project management efforts. See Snapshot from Practice: POs Project Offices.

Project Considerations

At the project level, the question is how much autonomy the project needs in order to be successfully completed. Hobbs and Ménard identify seven factors that should influence the choice of project management structure:

Snapshot from Practice   POs: Project Offices

Project offices (POs) were originally developed as a response to the poor track record many companies had in completing projects on time, within budget, and according to plan. They were often established to help matrix systems mature into more effective project delivery platforms.

Today, POs come in many different shapes and forms. One interesting way of classifying POs was set forth by Casey and Peck,* who describe certain POs in terms of being (1) a weather station, (2) a control tower, or (3) a resource pool. Each of these models performs a very different function for its organization.

- **Weather Station.** The primary function of the weather station PO is to track and monitor project performance. It is typically created to satisfy top management's need to stay on top of the portfolio of projects under way in the firm. Staff provides an independent forecast of project performance. The questions answered for specific projects include:
  - How are our projects progressing? Which ones are on track? Which ones are not?
  - How are we doing in terms of cost? Which projects are over or under budget?
  - What are the major problems confronting projects? Are contingency plans in place? What can the organization do to help the project?
- **Control Tower.** The primary function of the control tower PO is to improve project execution. It considers project management as a profession to be protected and advanced. Staff at the PO identify best practices and standards for project management excellence. They work as consultants and trainers to support project managers and their teams.
- **Resource Pool.** The goal of the resource pool PO is to provide the organization with a cadre of trained project managers and professionals. It operates like an academy for continually upgrading the skills of a firm's project professionals. In addition to training, this kind of PO also serves to elevate the stature of project management within the organization.

* W. Casey, and W. Peck, "Choosing the Right PMO Setup," *PM Network*, vol. 15, no. 2(2001), pp. 40–47.

- Size of project.
- Strategic importance.
- Novelty and need for innovation.
- Need for integration (number of departments involved).
- Environmental complexity (number of external interfaces).
- Budget and time constraints.
- Stability of resource requirements.

The higher the levels of these seven factors, the more autonomy and authority the project manager and project team need to be successful. This translates into using either a dedicated project team or a project matrix structure. For example, these structures should be used for large projects that are strategically critical and are new to the company, thus requiring much innovation. These structures would also be appropriate for complex, multidisciplinary projects that require input from many departments, as well as for projects that require constant contact with customers to assess their expectations. Dedicated project teams should also be used for urgent projects in which the nature of the work requires people working steadily from beginning to end.

Many firms that are heavily involved in project management have created a flexible management system that organizes projects according to project requirements. For example, Chaparral Steel, a mini-mill that produces steel bars and beams from scrap metal, classifies projects into three categories: advanced development, platform, and incremental. Advanced development projects are high-risk endeavors involving the creation of a breakthrough product or process. Platform projects are medium-risk projects involving system upgrades that yield new products and processes. Incremental projects are low-risk, short-term projects that involve minor adjustments in existing products and processes. At any point in time, Chaparral might have 40–50 projects underway, of which only one or two are advanced, three to five are platform projects, and the remainder are small, incremental projects. The incremental projects are almost all done within a weak matrix with the project manager coordinating the work of functional subgroups. A strong matrix is used to complete the platform projects, while dedicated project teams are typically created to complete the advanced development projects. More and more companies are using this "mix and match" approach to managing projects.

Organizational Culture

The decision for combining a discussion of project management structures and organizational cultures in this chapter can be traced to a conversation we, the authors, had with two project managers who work for a medium-sized information technology firm.

The managers were developing a new operating platform that would be critical to the future success of their company. When they tried to describe how this project was organized, one manager began to sketch out on a napkin a complicated structure involving 52 different teams, each with a project leader and a technical leader! In response to our further probing to understand how this system worked, the manager stopped short and proclaimed, "The key to making this structure work is the culture in our company. This approach would never work at company Y, where I worked before. But because of our culture here we are able to pull it off."

This comment, our observations of other firms, and research suggest there is a strong connection between project management structure, organizational culture, and project success. We have observed organizations successfully manage projects within the traditional functional organization because the culture encouraged cross-functional integration. Conversely we have seen matrix structures break down because the culture of the organization did not support the division of authority between project managers and functional managers. We have also observed companies relying on independent project teams because the dominant culture would not support the innovation and speed necessary for success.

What Is Organizational Culture?

Organizational culture refers to a system of shared norms, beliefs, values, and assumptions which binds people together, thereby creating shared meanings. This system is manifested by customs and habits that exemplify the values and beliefs of the organization. For example, egalitarianism may be expressed in the informal dress worn at a high-tech firm. Conversely, mandated uniforms at a department store reinforce respect for the hierarchy.

Culture reflects the personality of the organization and, similar to an individual's personality, can enable us to predict attitudes and behaviors of organizational members. Culture is also one of the defining aspects of an organization that sets it apart from other organizations even in the same industry.

Research suggests that there are 10 primary characteristics which, in aggregate, capture the essence of an organization's culture:

1. **Member identity**—the degree to which employees identify with the organization as a whole rather than with their type of job or field of professional expertise.
2. **Team emphasis**—the degree to which work activities are organized around groups rather than individuals.
3. **Management focus**—the degree to which management decisions take into account the effect of outcomes on people within the organization.

4. **Unit integration**—the degree to which units within the organization are encouraged to operate in a coordinated or interdependent manner.

5. **Control**—the degree to which rules, policies, and direct supervision are used to oversee and control employee behavior.

6. **Risk tolerance**—the degree to which employees are encouraged to be aggressive, innovative, and risk seeking.

7. **Reward criteria**—the degree to which rewards such as promotion and salary increases are allocated according to employee performance rather than seniority, favoritism, or other nonperformance factors.

8. **Conflict tolerance**—the degree to which employees are encouraged to air conflicts and criticisms openly.

9. **Means versus end orientation**—the degree to which management focuses on outcomes rather than on techniques and processes used to achieve those results.

10. **Open-systems focus**—the degree to which the organization monitors and responds to changes in the external environment.

As shown in Figure 3.6, each of these dimensions exists on a continuum. Assessing an organization according to these 10 dimensions provides a composite picture of the organization's culture. This picture becomes the basis for feelings of shared understanding that the members have about the organization, how things are done, and the way members are supposed to behave.

Culture performs several important functions in organizations. An organization's culture *provides a sense of identity* for its members. The more clearly an organization's shared perceptions and values are stated, the more strongly people can identify with their organization and feel a vital part of it. Identity generates commitment to the organization and reasons for members to devote energy and loyalty to the organization.

A second important function is that culture *helps legitimize the management system* of the organization. Culture helps clarify authority relationships. It provides reasons why people are in a position of authority and why their authority should be respected.

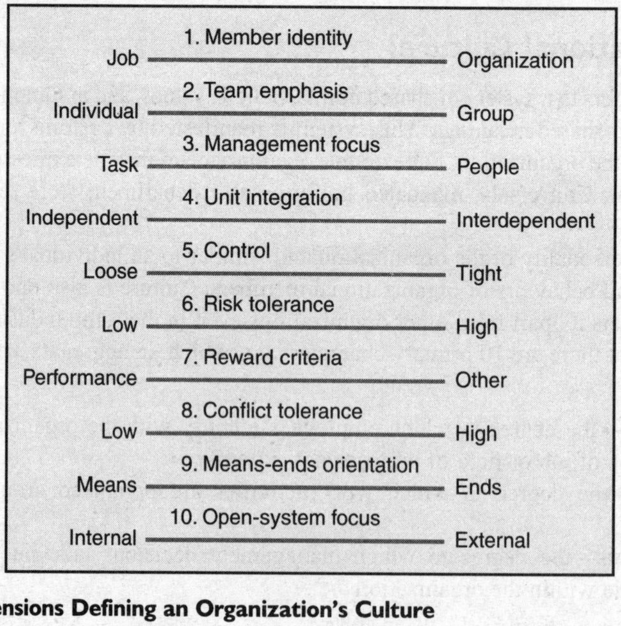

Job	1. Member identity	Organization
Individual	2. Team emphasis	Group
Task	3. Management focus	People
Independent	4. Unit integration	Interdependent
Loose	5. Control	Tight
Low	6. Risk tolerance	High
Performance	7. Reward criteria	Other
Low	8. Conflict tolerance	High
Means	9. Means-ends orientation	Ends
Internal	10. Open-system focus	External

FIGURE 3.6   Key Dimensions Defining an Organization's Culture

Most importantly, organizational culture *clarifies and reinforces standards of behavior.* Culture helps define what is permissible and inappropriate behavior. These standards span a wide range of behavior from dress code and working hours to challenging the judgment of superiors and collaborating with other departments. Ultimately, culture *helps create social order* within an organization. Imagine what it would be like if members didn't share similar beliefs, values, and assumptions—chaos! The customs, norms, and ideals conveyed by the culture of an organization provide the stability and predictability in behavior that is essential for an effective organization. See Snapshot from Practice: Software Development Teams at Microsoft for an example of this.

Although our discussion of organizational culture may appear to suggest one culture dominates the entire organization, in reality this is rarely the case. "Strong" or "thick" are adjectives used to denote a culture in which the organization's core values and customs are widely shared within the entire organization. Conversely, a "thin" or "weak" culture is one that is not widely shared or practiced within a firm.

Even within a strong organizational culture, there are likely to be subcultures often aligned within specific departments or specialty areas. As noted earlier in our discussion of project management structures, it is not uncommon for norms, values, and customs to develop within a specific field or profession such as marketing, finance, or operations. People working in the marketing department may have a different set of norms and values than those working in finance.

Countercultures sometimes emerge within organizations that embody a different set of values, beliefs, and customs—often in direct contradiction with the culture espoused by top management. How pervasive these subcultures and countercultures are affects the strength of the culture of the organization and the extent to which culture influences members' actions and responses.

Identifying Cultural Characteristics

Deciphering an organization's culture is a highly interpretative, subjective process that requires assessment of both current and past history. The student of culture cannot simply rely on what people report about their culture. The physical environment in which people work, as well as how people act and respond to different events that occur, must be examined. Figure 3.7 contains a worksheet for diagnosing the culture of an organization. Although by no means exhaustive, the checklist often yields clues about the norms, customs, and values of an organization:

1. **Study the physical characteristics of an organization.** What does the external architecture look like? What image does it convey? Is it unique? Are the buildings and offices the same quality for all employees? Or are modern buildings and fancier offices reserved for senior executives or managers from a specific department? What are the customs concerning dress? What symbols does the organization use to signal authority and status within the organization? These physical characteristics can shed light on who has real power within the organization, the extent to which the organization is internally differentiated, and how formal the organization is in its business dealings.

2. **Read about the organization.** Examine annual reports, mission statements, press releases, and internal newsletters. What do they describe? What principles are espoused in these documents? Do the reports emphasize the people who work for the organization and what they do or the financial performance of the firm? Each emphasis reflects a different culture. The first demonstrates concern for the people who make up the company. The second may suggest a concern for results and the bottom line.

3. **Observe how people interact within the organization.** What is their pace—is it slow and methodical or urgent and spontaneous? What rituals exist within the organization? What values do they express? Meetings can often yield insightful information. Who are the people at the meetings? Who does the talking? To whom do they talk? How candid is the conversation? Do people speak for the organization or for the individual

Snapshot from Practice   Software Development Teams at Microsoft*

Microsoft Corporation is the leading computer software company in the world. Microsoft's success stems in part from a corporate culture that supports teams of software developers to create and refine new products. No matter how big the project—even a complex one such as the development of the successful Windows 2000 operating system—the project is broken down into small parts that can be handled by teams of about 12 developers. The segment of the project each team is assigned is further subdivided so that each developer is assigned a specific part of the project to work on. Developers with greater experience are given more responsibilities than new members of the team, but the entire team knows that project success depends on the sum of their individual inputs.

Team members provide considerable support for each other. It is not uncommon to see two team members hunched over a computer screen trying to solve a problem. Team members can also be stern critics if a team member fails to perform at an acceptable level.

Developers are granted considerable autonomy in performing their work. At the same time behavior at Microsoft is governed by shared work culture that almost everyone follows. One set of informal rules governs the basic issue of working hours. Developers are free to adopt whatever work schedule suits them. If a developer has a sudden insight at

Michael Newman/PhotoEdit.

midnight, it is not unusual for people to work until dawn. Likewise, if a developer's child is sick, the developer can stay home to take care of the child, and do makeup work at some other time. Along with these "rules" on flexible working hours, almost all developers abide by another norm: They put in the hours necessary to get the job done, even if it requires staying up all night to work on a particularly difficult part of a program.

* K., Rebello, "Inside Microsoft," *Business Weekly*, July 15, 1996, pp. 56–67; B., Filipczak "Beyond the Gates of Microsoft," *Training*, September 1992, pp. 37–44.

department? What is the focus of the meetings? How much time is spent on various issues? Issues that are discussed repeatedly and at length are clues about the values of the organization's culture.

4. **Interpret stories and folklore surrounding the organization.** Look for similarities among stories told by different people. The subjects highlighted in recurring stories often reflect what is important to an organization's culture. For example, many of the stories that are repeated at Versatec, a Xerox subsidiary that makes graphic plotters for computers, involve their flamboyant cofounder, Renn Zaphiropoulos. According to company folklore, one of the very first things Renn did when the company was formed was to assemble the top management team at his home. They then devoted the weekend to handmaking a beautiful teak conference table around which all future decisions would be made. This table came to symbolize the importance of teamwork and maintaining high standards of performance, two essential qualities of the culture at Versatec.

Try to identify who the heroes and villains are in the folklore company. What do they suggest about the culture's ideals? Returning to the Versatec story, when the company was eventually purchased by Xerox many employees expressed concern that Versatec's informal, play hard/work hard culture would be overwhelmed by the bureaucracy at Xerox. Renn rallied the employees to superior levels of performance by arguing that if they exceeded Xerox's expectations they would be left alone. Autonomy has remained a fixture of Versatec's culture long after Renn's retirement.

It is also important to pay close attention to the basis for promotions and rewards. What do people see as the keys to getting ahead within the organization? What contributes to downfalls? These last two questions can yield important insights into the qualities and behaviors which the organization honors as well as the cultural taboos and behavioral land mines that can derail a career. For example, one project manager confided that a former colleague was sent to project management purgatory soon after publicly questioning the validity of a marketing report. From that point on, the project manager was extra careful to privately consult the marketing department whenever she had questions about their data.

```
┌─────────────────────────────────────────┐
│ I. Physical Characteristics             │
│ Architecture, office layout, decor, attire │
│ ──────────────────────                  │
│ ──────────────────────                  │
│                                         │
│ II. Public Documents                    │
│ Annual reports, internal newsletters, vision statements │
│ ──────────────────────                  │
│ ──────────────────────                  │
│                                         │
│ III. Behavior                           │
│ Pace, language, meetings, issues discussed, │
│ decision-making style, communication patterns, rituals │
│ ──────────────────────                  │
│ ──────────────────────                  │
│ ──────────────────────                  │
│                                         │
│ IV. Folklore                            │
│ Stories, anecdotes, heroines, heroes, villains │
│ ──────────────────────                  │
│ ──────────────────────                  │
└─────────────────────────────────────────┘
```

FIGURE 3.7   Organizational Culture Diagnosis Worksheet

With practice an observer can assess how strong the dominant culture of an organization is and the significance of subcultures and countercultures. Furthermore, learners can discern and identify where the culture of an organization stands on the 10 cultural dimensions presented earlier and, in essence, begin to build a cultural profile for a firm. Based on this profile, conclusions can be drawn about specific customs and norms that need to be adhered to as well as those behaviors and actions that violate the norms of a firm.

Implications of Organizational Culture for Organizing Projects

Project managers have to be able to operate in several, potentially diverse, organizational cultures. First, they have to interact with the culture of their parent organization as well as the subcultures of various departments (e.g., marketing, accounting). Second, they have to interact with the project's client or customer organizations. Finally, they have to interact in varying degrees with a host of other organizations connected to the project. These organizations include suppliers and vendors, subcontractors, consulting firms, government and regulatory agencies, and, in many cases, community groups. Many of these organizations are likely to have very different cultures. Project managers have to be able to read and speak the culture they are working in to develop strategies, plans, and responses that are likely to be understood and accepted. Still, the emphasis of this chapter is on the relationship between organizational culture and project management structure, and it is necessary to defer further discussion of these implications until Chapters 10–12, which focus on leadership, team building, and outsourcing.

Earlier we stated that we believe there are strong relationships among project management structure, organizational culture, and successful project management. To explore these relationships further, let us return to the dimensions that can be used to characterize the culture of an organization. When examining these dimensions we could hypothesize that certain aspects of the culture of an organization would support successful project management while other aspects would deter or interfere with effective management. Figure 3.8 attempts to identify which cultural characteristics create an environment conducive to completing most complex projects involving people from different disciplines.

Note that, in many cases, the ideal culture is not at either extreme. For example, a fertile project culture would likely be one in which management balances its focus on the needs of both the task and the people. An optimal culture would balance concern with output (ends) and processes to achieve those outcomes (means). In other cases, the ideal culture would be on one end of a dimension or the other. For example, because most projects require collaboration across disciplines, it would be desirable that the culture of the organization emphasize working in teams and identifying with the organization, not just the professional domain. Likewise it is important that the culture support a certain degree of risk taking and a tolerance for constructive conflict.

One organization that appears to fit this ideal profile is 3M. 3M has received acclaim for creating an entrepreneurial culture within a large corporate framework. The essence of its culture is captured in phrases that have been chanted often by 3Mers throughout its history: "Encourage experimental doodling." "Hire good people and leave them alone." "If you put fences around people, you get sheep. Give people the room they need." Freedom and autonomy to experiment are reflected in the "15 percent rule," which encourages technical people to spend up to 15 percent of their time on projects of their own choosing and initiative. This fertile culture has contributed to 3M's branching out into more than 60,000 products and 35 separate business units.

The metaphor we choose to describe the relationship between organizational culture and project management is that of a riverboat trip. Culture is the river and the project is the boat. Organizing and completing projects within an organization in which the culture is conducive to project management is like

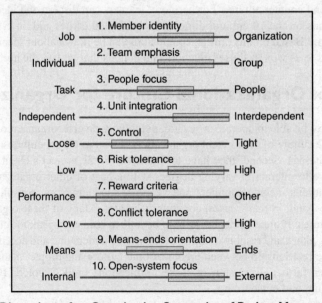

FIGURE 3.8   Cultural Dimensions of an Organization Supportive of Project Management

paddling downstream: much less effort is required. In many cases, the current can be so strong that steering is all that is required. Such is the case for projects that operate in a project-friendly environment where teamwork and cross-functional cooperation are the norms, where there is a deep commitment to excellence, and where healthy conflict is voiced and dealt with quickly and effectively.

Conversely, trying to complete a project in a toxic culture is like paddling upstream: much more time, effort, and attention are needed to reach the destination. This would be the situation in cultures that discourage teamwork and cooperation, that have a low tolerance for conflict, and where getting ahead is based less on performance and more on cultivating favorable relationships with superiors. In such cases, the project manager and her people not only have to overcome the natural obstacles of the project but also have to overcome the prevailing negative forces inherent in the culture of the organization.

The implications of this metaphor are important. Greater project authority and time are necessary to complete projects that encounter a strong, negative cultural current. Conversely, less formal authority and fewer dedicated resources are needed to complete projects in which the cultural currents generate behavior and cooperation essential to project success.

The key issue is the degree of interdependency between the parent organization and the project team. In cases where the prevalent organizational culture supports the behaviors essential to project completion, a weaker project management structure can be effective. For example, one of the major reasons Chaparral Steel is able to use a functional matrix to successfully complete incremental projects is that its culture contains strong norms for cooperation. Conversely, one of the reasons behind the failure of Kodak's "Factory of the Future" project in the mid-1980s was that the culture at that time did not support project management.

When the dominant organization culture inhibits collaboration and innovation, it is advisable to insulate the project team from the dominant culture. Here it becomes necessary to create a self-sufficient project team. If a dedicated project team is impossible because of resource constraints, then at least a project matrix should be used where the project manager has dominant control over the project. In both cases, the managerial strategy is to create a distinct team subculture in which a new set of norms, customs, and values evolve that will be conducive to project completion.

Under extreme circumstances this project culture could even represent a counterculture in that many of the norms and values are the antithesis of the dominant, parent culture. Such was the case when IBM decided to develop their personal computer quickly in 1980. They knew that the project could get bogged down by the overabundance of computer knowledge and bureaucracy in the company. They also realized that they would have to work closely with suppliers and make use of many non-IBM parts if they were to get to the market quickly. This was not the IBM way at the time, so IBM established the PC project team in a warehouse in Boca Raton, Florida, far from corporate headquarters and other corporate development facilities that existed within the organization.

Summary

This chapter examined two major characteristics of the parent organization that affect the implementation and completion of projects. The first is the formal structure of the organization and how it chooses to organize and manage projects. Although the individual project manager may have very little say as to how the firm chooses to manage projects, he or she must be able to recognize the options available as well as the inherent strengths and weaknesses of different approaches.

Three basic project management structures were described and assessed as to their weaknesses and strengths. Only under unique circumstances can a case be made for managing a project within the normal functional hierarchy. When thinking only in terms of what is best for the project, the creation of an independent project team is clearly favored. However, the most effective project management system appropriately balances the needs of the project with those of the parent organization. Matrix structures emerged out of the parent organization's need to share personnel and resources across multiple projects and operations while creating legitimate project focus. The matrix approach is a hybrid organizational form that combines elements of both the functional and project team forms in an attempt to realize the advantages of both.

The second major characteristic of the parent organization that was discussed in this chapter is the concept of organizational culture. Organizational culture is the pattern of beliefs and expectations shared by an organization's members. Culture includes the behavioral norms, customs, shared values, and the "rules of the game" for getting along and getting ahead within the organization. It is important for project managers to be "culture sensitive" so that they can develop appropriate strategies and responses and avoid violating key norms that would jeopardize their effectiveness within the organization.

The interaction between project management structure and organizational culture is a complicated one. We have suggested that in certain organizations, culture encourages the implementation of projects. In this environment the project management structure used plays a less decisive role in the success of the project. Conversely, for other organizations in which the culture stresses internal competition and differentiation, just the opposite may be true. The prevailing norms, customs, and attitudes inhibit effective project management, and the project management structure plays a more decisive role in the successful implementation of projects. At a minimum, under adverse cultural conditions, the project manager needs to have significant authority over the project team; under more extreme conditions firms should use dedicated project teams to complete critical projects. In both cases, the managerial strategy should be to insulate project work from the dominant culture so that a more positive "subculture" can emerge among project participants.

The project management structure of the organization and the culture of the organization are major elements of the environment in which a project is initiated. Subsequent chapters will examine how project managers and professionals work within this environment to successfully complete projects.

Key Terms

Balanced matrix	Organizational culture	Strong matrix
Dedicated project team	Projectitis	Weak matrix
Matrix	Project office (PO)	

Review Questions

1. What are the relative advantages and disadvantages of the functional, matrix, and dedicated team approaches to managing projects?
2. What distinguishes a weak matrix from a strong matrix?
3. Under what conditions would it be advisable to use a strong matrix instead of a dedicated project team?
4. Why is it important to assess the culture of an organization before deciding what project management structure should be used to complete a project?
5. What do you believe is more important for successfully completing a project—the formal project management structure or the culture of the parent organization?

Exercises

1. Going to college is analogous to working in a matrix environment in that most students take more than one class and must distribute their time across multiple classes. What problems does this situation create for you? How does it affect your performance? How could the system be better managed to make your life less difficult and more productive?

2. You work for LL Company, which manufacturers high-end optical scopes for hunting rifles. LL Company has been the market leader for the past 20 years and has decided to diversify by applying its technology to develop a top-quality binocular. What kind of project management structure would you recommend they use for this project? What information would you like to have to make this recommendation, and why?

3. You work for Barbata Electronics. Your R&D people believe they have come up with an affordable technology that will double the capacity of existing MP3 players and uses audio format that is superior to MP3. The project is code named KYSO (Knock Your Socks Off). What kind of project management structure would you recommend they use for the KYSO project? What information would you like to have to make this recommendation and why?

4. This chapter discussed the role of values and beliefs in forming an organization's culture. The topic of organization culture is big business on the Internet. Many companies use their Web pages to describe their mission, vision, and corporate values and beliefs. There also are many consulting firms that advertise how they help organizations to change their culture. The purpose of this exercise is for you to obtain information pertaining to the organizational culture for two different companies. You can go about this task by very simply searching on the key words "organizational culture" or "corporate vision and values." This search will identify numerous companies for you to use to answer the following questions. You may want to select companies that you would like to work for in the future.

    a. What are the espoused values and beliefs of the companies?
    b. Use the worksheet in Figure 3.7 to assess the Web page. What does the Web page reveal about the culture of this organization? Would this culture be conducive to effective project management?

5. Use the cultural dimensions listed in Figure 3.6 to assess the culture of your school. Instead of employees, consider students, and instead of management, use faculty. For example, member identity refers to the degree to which students identify with the school as a whole rather than their major or option. Either as individuals or in small groups rate the culture of your school on the 10 dimensions.

    a. What dimensions were easy to evaluate and which ones were not?
    b. How strong is the culture of your school?
    c. What functions does the culture serve for your school?
    d. Do you think the culture of your school is best suited to maximizing your learning? Why or why not?
    e. What kind of projects would be easy to implement in your school and what kind of projects would be difficult given the structure and culture of your school? Explain your answer.

6. You work as an analyst in the marketing department for Springfield International (SI). SI uses a weak matrix to develop new services. Management has created an extremely competitive organizational culture that places an emphasis upon achieving results above everything else. One of the project managers that you have been assigned to help has been pressuring you to make his project your number one priority. He also wants you to expand the scope of your work on his project beyond what your marketing manager believes is necessary or appropriate. The project manager is widely perceived as a rising star within SI.

Up to now you have been resisting the project manager's pressure and complying with your marketing manager's directives. However, your most recent interchange with the project manager ended by his saying, "I'm not happy with the level of help I am getting from you and I will remember this when I become VP of Marketing." How would you respond and why?

References

Block, T. R. and J. D., Frame, *The Project Office—A Key to Managing Projects Effectively* (Menlo Park, CA: Crisp Publications, 1998).

Block, T. R. and J. D. Frame, "Today's Project Office: Gauging Attitudes," *PM Network,* August, 2001.

Bowen, H. K., K. B. Clark, C. A. Holloway, and S. C. Wheelwright, *The Perpetual Enterprise Machine* (New York: Oxford University Press, 1994).

Brown, S. and K. R. Eisenhardt, "Product Development: Past Research, Present Findings, and Future Directions," *Academy of Management Review,* 20 (2) 1995, pp. 343–78.

Cameron, K. S. and R. E. Quinn, *Diagnosing and Changing Organizational Culture: Based on the Competing Values Framework* (Upper Saddle River, NJ: Prentice Hall, 1999).

Carlton, J., *Apple: The Inside Story of Intrigue, Egomania, and Business Blunders* (New York: Random House, 1997), pp. 13–14.

Casey, W. and W. Peck, "Choosing the Right PMO Setup," *PM Network,* 15 (2) 2001, pp. 40–47.

Collins, J. C. and J. I. Porras, *Built to Last: The Successful Habits of Visionary Companies* (New York: HarperCollins, 1994), pp. 150–58.

Deal, T. E. and A. A. Kennedy, *Corporate Cultures: The Rites and Rituals of Corporate Life* (Reading, MA: Addison-Wesley, 1982).

De Laat, P. B., "Matrix Management of Projects and Power Struggles: A Case Study of an R&D Laboratory," *IEEE Engineering Management Review* (Winter, 1995).

Filipczak, B., "Beyond the Gates of Microsoft," *Training,* September 1992, pp. 37–44.

Gallagher, R. S., *The Soul of an Organization: Understanding the Values That Drive Successful Corporate Cultures* (Chicago: Dearborn Trade Publishing, 2002).

Graham, R. J. and R. L. Englund, *Creating an Environment for Successful Projects: The Quest to Manage Project Management* (San Francisco: Jossey-Bass, 1997).

Gray, C., S. Dworatschek, D. H. Gobeli, H. Knoepfel, and E. W. Larson, "International Comparison of Project Organization Structures: Use and Effectiveness," *International Journal of Project Management,* vol. 8, no. 1 (February 1990), pp. 26–32.

Harrison, M. T. and J. M. Beyer, *The Culture of Organizations* (Englewood Cliffs, NJ: Prentice Hall, 1993).

Hobbs, B. and P. Ménard, "Organizational Choices for Project Management," in Paul Dinsmore (ed.), *The AMA Handbook of Project Management* (New York: AMACOM, 1993).

Hobday, M., "The Project-Based Organization: An Ideal Form for Managing Complex Products and Systems?" *Research Policy,* vol. 29, no.1 7, 2000.

Jassawalla, A. R. and H. C. Sashittal, "Cultures that Support Product-Innovation Processes," *Academy of Management Executive,* 15 (3) 2002, pp. 42–54.

Johnson, C. L., M. Smith, and L. K. Geary, *More Than My Share in All* (Washington, D.C.: Smithsonian Institute Publications, 1990).

Kerzner, H., *In Search of Excellence in Project Management* (New York: Von Nostrand Reinhold, 1997).

Kerzner, H., "Strategic Planning for the Project Office," *Project Management Journal,* 34 (2) 2003, pp. 13–25.

Larson, E. W. "Project Management Structures" in *The Wiley Handbook for Managing Projects,* P. Morris & J. Pinto (eds.) (New York: Wiley 2004), pp. 48–66.

Larson, E. W. and D. H. Gobeli, "Organizing for Product Development Projects," *Journal of Product Innovation Management,* vol. 5 (1988), pp. 180–90.

Larson, E. W., and D. H. Gobeli, "Matrix Management: Contradictions and Insights," *California Management Review,* vol. 29, no. 4 (Summer 1987), p. 137.

Larsson, U. (ed.), *Cultures of Creativity: The Centennial Exhibition of the Nobel Prize* (Canton, MA: Science History Publications, 2001).

Laslo, Z. and A. I. Goldberg, "Matrix Structures and Performance: The Search for Optimal Adjustments to Organizational Objectives?" *IEEE Transactions in Engineering Management,* vol. 48, no.1 2, 2001.

Lawrence, P. R. and J. W. Lorsch, *Organization and Environment* (Homewood, IL: Irwin, 1969).

Majchrzak, A. and Q. Wang, "Breaking the Functional Mind-Set in Process Organizations," *Harvard Business Review* (Sept.–Oct. 1996), pp. 93–99.

Miller, J., *Lockheed Martin's Skunk Works* (New York: Speciality Publications, 1996).

Olson, E. M., O. C. Walker, Jr., and R. W. Ruekert, "Organizing for Effective New Product Development: The Moderating Role of Product Innovativeness," *Journal of Marketing,* vol. 59 (January), 1995, pp. 48–62.

O'Reilly, C. A., J. Chatman, and D. F. Caldwell, "People and Organizational Culture: A Profile Comparison Approach to Assessing Person-Organization Fit," *Academy of Management Journal,* vol. 34, no. 3 (September 1991), pp. 487–516.

Pettegrew, A. M., "On Studying Organizational Culture," *Administrative Science Quarterly,* vol. 24, no. 4 (1979), pp. 570–81.

Powell, M. and J. Young, "The Project Management Support Office" in *The Wiley Handbook for Managing Projects,* P. Morris and J. Pinto, (eds.) (New York: Wiley, 2004) pp. 937–69.

Rebello, K., "Inside Microsoft," *Business Weekly,* July 15, 1996, pp. 56–67.

Schein, E., *Organizational Culture and Leadership: A Dynamic View* (San Francisco, CA: Jossey-Bass, 1985).

Sculley, J., *Odyssey: Pepsi to Apple . . . A Journey of Adventure, Ideas, and the Future* (New York: Harper & Row, 1987), pp. 270–79.

Shenhar, A. J., "From Theory to Practice: Toward a Typology of Project Management Styles," *IEEE Transactions in Engineering Management,* 41 (1) 1998, pp. 33–48.

Shenhar, A. J., D. Dvir T. Lechler and M. Poli, "One Size Does Not Fit All–True for Projects, True for Frameworks," *Frontiers of Project Management Research and Application,* Proceedings of PMI Research Conference, Seattle, 2002, pp. 99–106.

Smith, P. G. and D. G. Reinertsen, *Developing Products in Half the Time* (New York: Van Nostrand Reinhold, 1995).

Stuckenbruck, L. C., *Implementation of Project Management* (Upper Darby, PA: Project Management Institute, 1981).

Youker, R., "Organizational Alternatives for Project Management," *Project Management Quarterly,* vol. 8 (March 1977), pp. 24–33.

CASE 3.1

Moss and McAdams Accounting Firm

Bruce Palmer had worked for Moss and McAdams (M&M) for six years and was just promoted to account manager. His first assignment was to lead an audit of Johnsonville Trucks. He was quite pleased with the five accountants who had been assigned to his team, especially Zeke Olds. Olds was an Army vet who returned to school to get a double major in accounting and computer sciences. He was on top of the latest developments in financial information systems and had a reputation for coming up with innovative solutions to problems.

M&M was a well-established regional accounting firm with 160 employees located across six offices in Minnesota and Wisconsin. The main office, where Palmer worked, was in Green Bay, Wisconsin. In fact, one of the founding members, Seth Moss, played briefly for the hometown NFL Packers during the late 1950s. M&M's primary services were corporate audits and tax preparation. Over the last two years the partners decided to move more aggressively into the consulting business. M&M projected that consulting would represent 40 percent of their growth over the next five years.

M&M operated within a matrix structure. As new clients were recruited, a manager was assigned to the account. A manager might be assigned to several accounts, depending on the size and scope of the work. This was especially true in the case of tax preparation projects, where it was not uncommon for a manager to be assigned to 8 to 12 clients. Likewise, senior and staff accountants were assigned to multiple account teams. Ruby Sands was the office manager responsible for assigning personnel to different accounts at the Green Bay office. She did her best to assign staff to multiple projects under the same manager. This wasn't always possible, and sometimes accountants had to work on projects led by different managers.

M&M, like most accounting firms, had a tiered promotion system. New CPAs entered as junior or staff accountants. Within two years, their performance was reviewed and they were either asked to leave or promoted to senior accountant. Sometime during their fifth or sixth year, a decision was made to promote them to account manager. Finally, after 10 to 12 years with the firm, the manager was considered for promotion to partner. This was a very competitive position. During the last five years, only 20 percent of account managers at M&M had been promoted to partner. However, once a partner, they were virtually guaranteed the position for life and enjoyed significant increases in salary, benefits, and prestige. M&M had a reputation for being a results-driven organization; partner promotions were based on meeting deadlines, retaining clients, and generating revenue. The promotion team based its decision on the relative performance of the account manager in comparison to his or her cohorts.

One week into the Johnsonville audit, Palmer received a call from Sands to visit her office. There he was introduced to Ken Crosby, who recently joined M&M after working nine years for a Big 5 accounting firm. Crosby was recruited to manage special consulting projects. Sands reported that Crosby had just secured a major consulting project with Springfield Metals. This was a major coup for the firm: M&M had competed against two Big 5 accounting firms for the project. Sands went on to explain that she was working with Crosby to put together his team. Crosby insisted that Zeke Olds be assigned to his team. Sands told him that this would be impossible because Olds was already assigned to work on the Johnsonville audit. Crosby persisted, arguing that Olds's expertise was essential to the Springfield project. Sands decided to work out a compromise and have Olds split time across both projects.

At this time Crosby turned to Palmer and said, "I believe in keeping things simple. Why don't we agree that Olds works for me in the mornings and you in the afternoons. I'm sure we can work out any problems that come up. After all, we both work for the same firm."

Six Weeks Later

Palmer could scream whenever he remembered Crosby's words, "After all, we both work for the same firm." The first sign of trouble came during the first week of the new arrangement when Crosby called, begging to have Olds work all of Thursday on his project. They were conducting an extensive client visit, and Olds was critical to the assessment. After Palmer reluctantly agreed, Crosby said he owed him one. The next week when Palmer called Crosby to request that he return the favor, Crosby flatly refused and said any other time but not this week. Palmer tried again a week later and got the same response.

At first Olds showed up promptly at 1:00 P.M. at Palmer's office to work on the audit. Soon it became a habit to show up 30 to 60 minutes late. There was always a good reason. He was in a meeting in Springfield and couldn't just leave, or an urgent task took longer than planned. One time it was because Crosby took his entire team out to lunch at the new Thai restaurant—Olds was over an hour late because of slow service. In the beginning Olds would usually make up the time by working after hours, but Palmer could tell from conversations he overheard that this was creating tension at home.

What probably bothered Palmer the most were the e-mails and telephone calls Olds received from Crosby and his team members during the afternoons when he was supposed to be working for Palmer. A couple of times Palmer could have sworn that Olds was working on Crosby's project in his (Palmer's) office.

Palmer met with Crosby to talk about the problem and voice his complaints. Crosby acted surprised and even a little bit hurt. He promised things would change, but the pattern continued.

Palmer was becoming paranoid about Crosby. He knew that Crosby played golf with Olds on the weekends and could just imagine him badmouthing the Johnsonville project and pointing out how boring auditing work was. The sad fact was that there probably was some truth to what he was saying. The Johnsonville project was getting bogged down, and the team was slipping behind schedule. One of the contributing factors was Olds's performance. His work was not up to its usual standards. Palmer approached Olds about this, and Olds became defensive. Olds later apologized and confided that he found it difficult switching his thinking from consulting to auditing and then back to consulting. He promised to do better, and there was a slight improvement in his performance.

The last straw came when Olds asked to leave work early on Friday so that he could take his wife and kids to a Milwaukee Brewers baseball game. It turned out Springfield Metals had given Crosby their corporate tickets, and he decided to treat his team with box seats right behind the Brewers dugout. Palmer hated to do it, but he had to refuse the request. He felt guilty when he overheard Olds explaining to his son on the telephone why they couldn't go to the game.

Palmer finally decided to pick up the phone and request an urgent meeting with Sands to resolve the problem. He got up enough nerve and put in the call only to be told that Sands wouldn't be back in the office until next week. As he put the receiver down, he thought maybe things would get better.

Two Weeks Later

Sands showed up unexpectedly at Palmer's office and said they needed to talk about Olds. Palmer was delighted, thinking that now he could tell her what had been going on. But before he had a chance to speak, Sands told him that Olds had come to see her yesterday. She told him that Olds confessed that he was having a hard time working on both Crosby's and Palmer's projects. He was having difficulty concentrating on the auditing work in the afternoon because he was thinking about some of the consulting issues that had emerged during the morning. He was putting in extra hours to try to meet both of the projects' deadlines, and this was creating problems at home. The bottom line was that he was stressed out and couldn't deal with the situation. He asked that he be assigned full-time to Crosby's project. Sands went on to say that Olds didn't blame

Palmer, in fact he had a lot of nice things to say about him. He just enjoyed the consulting work more and found it more challenging. Sands concluded by saying, "We talked some more and ultimately I agreed with him. I hate to do this to you, Bruce, but Olds is a valuable employee, and I think this is the best decision for the firm."

1. If you were Palmer at the end of the case, how would you respond?
2. What, if anything, could Palmer have done to avoid losing Olds?
3. What advantages and disadvantages of a matrix type organization are apparent from this case?
4. What could the management at M&M do to more effectively manage situations like this?

CASE 3.2

ORION Systems (A)*

The office erupted into cheers when it was announced over the PA system that ORION had just been awarded the government contract to build the next generation of high-speed, light-rail trains. Everyone came over to shake Mike Rosas's hand and congratulate him. It was well known that Rosas would be the project manager for this important project, which would be code named Jaguar. Once the celebration subsided, Rosas gazed out the window and thought about what he had just gotten himself into.

The Jaguar project would be a high-profile project that would affect procurement of future contracts with the government. Increased competition had raised performance expectations regarding completion time, quality, reliability, and cost. He knew that major changes in how ORION organized and managed projects would be necessary to meet the expectations of the Jaguar project.

Project Management at Orion

ORION was a division of a large aerospace company with 7,000 employees. ORION evolved from a project organization into a matrix structure to conserve costs and better utilize limited resources. At any point in time, ORION could be working on three to five large projects such as the Jaguar project and 30 to 50 smaller projects. Project managers negotiated personnel assignments with the VP of operations, who ultimately decided project assignments. It was not uncommon for an engineer to be working on two to three projects during a week.

Figure C3.1 portrays how new-product development projects were organized at ORION. Project management was limited only to the design and development of the new product. Once the final design and prototype were completed, they were turned over to manufacturing for production and delivery to the customer. A four-person management team oversaw the completion of the project and their responsibilities are briefly described here:

- *Project manager*—responsible for all aspects of design and development of the product.
- *Planning and control manager*—responsible for building an overall project network, scheduling, managing the budget, controlling and evaluating the design and development program, and preparing status reports.
- *Electronics system engineer*—responsible for providing technical expertise on electronic systems issues.
- *Mechanics system engineer*—responsible for providing technical expertise on mechanical system issues.

---

* Prepared by Shlomo Cohen.

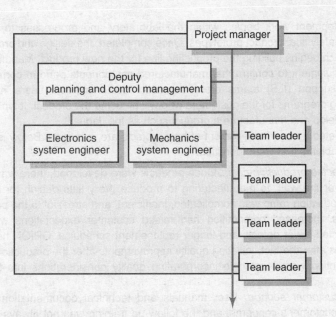

FIGURE C3.1 Organization of Product Development Projects at ORION

The core work was completed by 12 to 20 design teams. Each team had a leader, who was responsible for designing, developing, building, and testing a specific subsystem of the product. The size of individual teams varied from 5 to 15 engineers, depending on the scope of their work. These engineers split time across multiple projects.

Design engineers ran the show at ORION, and manufacturing, marketing, and other groups were expected to follow their lead. The special status of the design engineers was reinforced by the fact that they were actually paid on higher pay curves than the manufacturing engineers.

The overall product development and manufacturing process is captured in the master plan chart (Figure C3.2). New-product design and development evolves around five major reviews: system design review (SDR), preliminary design review (PDR), critical design review (CDR), test readiness review (TRR), and production readiness review (PRR).

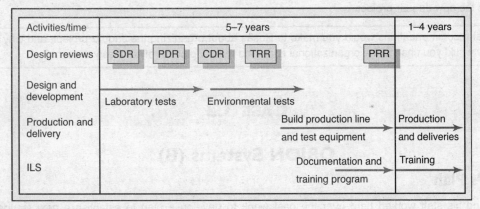

FIGURE C3.2 Traditional Master Plan at ORION

Design and development work begins within the laboratory and progresses to field tests of specific subsystems and ultimately final product prototypes. Once completed, the design and prototype are turned over to manufacturing, which begins building the production line for the new product. Manufacturing also develops the necessary test equipment to confirm that manufactured components perform correctly. During this time, integrated logistical support (ILS) teams prepare product documentation, users' manuals, maintenance programs, and training programs for the customers who will be using the product. It typically takes ORION six to seven years to develop and manufacture a product such as the Jaguar.

ORION just completed a major assessment of how projects are managed. Below is a brief description of some of the major problems that were identified:

- *Higher than expected production costs.* Once products were developed, there was a tendency for them to be "thrown over the wall" to manufacturing to produce. Very little design for manufacturability was done, and the production ramp was complicated, inefficient, and stressful to the people in the plant.
- *Quality concerns.* Increased competition had raised customer expectations with regard to quality. Customers expected fewer defects and longer replacement schedules. ORION had a tendency to deal with quality issues after the fact, initiating quality improvements after the production process was set up. Not enough attention was devoted to incorporating quality considerations into the original design of products.
- *Problems with customer support.* User manuals and technical documentation sometimes failed to address all of a customer's concerns, and the follow-up training was not always adequately prepared. These problems contributed to increased costs in customer service and a decline in customer satisfaction.
- *Lack of strong project ownership.* While everyone accepted that a matrix arrangement was the only way to accommodate all the projects at ORION, the shifting back and forth of personnel across multiple projects took its toll on the progress of individual projects. Members often failed to identify with individual projects and develop the sense of excitement that contributed to superior performance. The shuffling of personnel slowed down progress because additional time had to be devoted to bringing returning members up to speed on current developments.
- *Scope creep.* ORION was renowned for its engineering prowess. However, there was a tendency for design engineers to get so absorbed with the science of the project that they lost focus on the practical considerations. This led to costly delays and sometimes design modifications that were inconsistent with customer requirements.

Rosas was aware of these and other concerns as he sat down with his staff to figure out the best way to organize the new Jaguar project.

---

1. What recommendations would you make to Rosas about organizing the Jaguar project, and why?
2. How would you change the organizational chart and master plan to reflect these changes?

CASE 3.3

ORION Systems (B)

Rosas's Plan

Rosas and his staff worked hard over the past week to develop a plan to establish a new standard for completing projects at ORION. The Jaguar project management team will be expanded to seven managers,

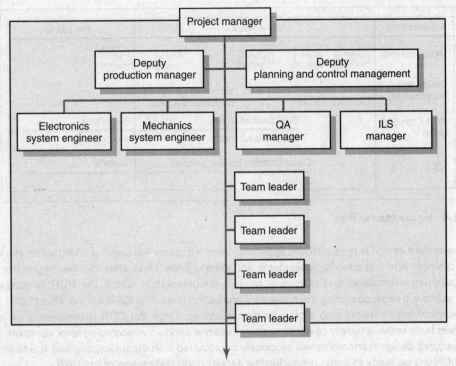

FIGURE C3.3 Proposed Project Organization for the Jaguar Project

who will be responsible for overseeing the completion of the project from design to delivery to the customer. A brief description of the responsibiiities for the three new positions follows (see Figure C3.3):

- *Production manager*—responsible for raising production issues during the design phase; responsible for building and managing the production line.
- *ILS (integrated logistical support) manager*—responsible for all activities that require project/customer support after delivery including customer training, documentation, and equipment testing.
- *QA (quality assurance) manager*—responsible for implementing a quality program that will enhance the reliability, availability and maintainability of the product.

These seven managers (the three just described plus the four discussed in Part A) will coordinate the completion of the project and see that their respective disciplines are factored into all major decisions. Rosas, as project manager, will work toward achieving consensus, but he will have the authority to intervene and make decisions if necessary.

The core work will be completed by 35 teams. Each team will have a "leader," who will be responsible for designing, developing, building, and testing a specific subsystem of the project. They will also be responsible for the quality and productivity of the subsystems and for doing the work on time and within budget.

Individual teams will consist of 5 to 12 members, and Rosas insists that at least half of each team be assigned to work full time on the project. This will help ensure continuity and enhance commitment to the project.

The second key feature to the plan is the development of the overall master plan for the project. This involves abandoning the traditional sequential approach to product development and adopting a concurrent engineering approach to the project (see Figure C3.4).

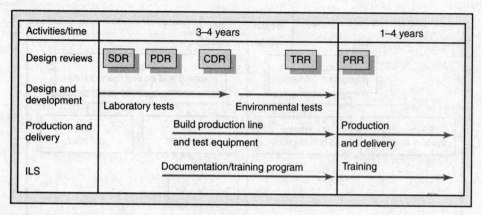

Activities/time	3–4 years			1–4 years
Design reviews	SDR PDR	CDR	TRR	PRR
Design and development	Laboratory tests	Environmental tests		
Production and delivery	Build production line and test equipment			Production and delivery
ILS	Documentation/training program			Training

FIGURE C3.4 Jaguar Master Plan

Once the system design is reviewed and approved, different teams will begin working within the laboratory to design, develop, and test specific subsystems and components. Soon after this has begun the ILS team will start gathering information and preparing product documentation. Once the PDR is completed, the production teams will begin designing the necessary production lines. The CDR will include not only resolution of major technical questions but also a plan for manufacturing. Once the CDR is completed, project teams will begin field tests under a variety of different environmental conditions according to government specifications. Subsequent design refinements will be closely coordinated with manufacturing and ILS teams so that, ideally, ORION will be ready to begin producing the Jaguar upon completion of the PRR.

Rosas believes that the phasing of the production and documentation work alongside the core development work will accelerate project completion, reduce production costs, and contribute to customer satisfaction.

1. What are the major changes between this plan and the way ORION has managed projects in the past?
2. How well do you believe these changes deal with the problems identified in Part A?
3. Who is likely to support this plan? Who is not likely to support this plan?

CHAPTER 4

Defining the Project

Select a dream

Use your dream to set a goal

Create a plan

Consider resources

Enhance skills and abilities

Spend time wisely

Start! Get organized and go

. . . it is one of those acro-whatevers,

said Pooh.[*]

Project managers in charge of a single small project can plan and schedule the project tasks without much formal planning and information. However, when the project manager must manage several small projects or a large complex project, a threshold is quickly reached in which the project manager can no longer cope with the detail.

This chapter describes a disciplined, structured method for selectively collecting information to use through all phases of the project life cycle, to meet the needs of all stakeholders (e.g., customer, project manager), and to measure performance against the strategic plan of the organization. The method suggested is a selective outline of the project called the *work breakdown structure*. The early stages of developing the outline serve to ensure that all tasks are identified and that participants of the project have an understanding of what is to be done. Once the outline and its detail are defined, an integrated information system can be developed to schedule work and allocate budgets. This baseline information is later used for control. In addition, the chapter will present a variant of the work breakdown structure called the *process breakdown structure* as well as responsibility matrices which are used for design and build projects. With the work of the project defined through the *work breakdown structure,* the chapter concludes with the process of creating a communication plan used to help coordinate project activities and follow progress.

The five generic steps described herein provide a structured approach for collecting the project information necessary for developing a work breakdown structure. These steps and the development of project networks found in the next chapters all take place concurrently, and several iterations are typically required to develop dates and budgets that can be used to manage the project. The old saying "We can control only what we have planned" is true; therefore, defining the project is the first step.

---

* Roger E. Allen and Stephen D. Allen, *Winnie-the-Pooh on Success* (New York: Penguin, 1997), p. 10.

Step 1: Defining the Project Scope

Defining the project scope sets the stage for developing a project plan. Project scope is a definition of the end result or mission of your project—a product or service for your client/customer. The primary purpose is to define as clearly as possible the deliverable(s) for the end user and to focus project plans. As fundamental and essential as scope definition appears, it is frequently overlooked by project leaders of well-managed, large corporations.

Research clearly shows that a poorly defined scope or mission is the most frequently mentioned barrier to project success. In a study involving more than 1,400 project managers in the United States and Canada, Gobeli and Larson found that approximately 50 percent of the planning problems relate to unclear definition of scope and goals. This and other studies suggest a strong correlation between project success and clear scope definition. The scope document directs focus on the project purpose throughout the life of the project for the customer and project participants.

The scope should be developed under the direction of the project manager and customer. The project manager is responsible for seeing that there is agreement with the owner on project objectives, deliverables at each stage of the project, technical requirements, and so forth. For example, a deliverable in the early stage might be specifications; for the second stage, three prototypes for production; for the third, a sufficient quantity to introduce to market; and finally, marketing promotion and training.

Your project scope definition is a document that will be published and used by the project owner and project participants for planning and measuring project success. *Scope* describes what you expect to deliver to your customer when the project is complete. Your project scope should define the results to be achieved in specific, tangible, and measurable terms.

Employing a Project Scope Checklist

Clearly, project scope is the keystone interlocking all elements of a project plan. To ensure that scope definition is complete, you may wish to use the following checklist:

Project Scope Checklist
1. Project objective
2. Deliverables
3. Milestones
4. Technical requirements
5. Limits and exclusions
6. Reviews with customer

1. **Project objective.** The first step of project scope definition is to define the overall objective to meet your customer's need(s). For example, as a result of extensive market research a computer software company decides to develop a program that automatically translates verbal sentences in English to Russian. The project should be completed within three years at a cost not to exceed $1.5 million. Another example is to design and produce a completely portable, hazardous waste, thermal treatment system in 13 months at a cost not to exceed $13 million. The project objective answers the questions of what, when, and how much.

2. **Deliverables.** The next step is to define major deliverables—the expected outputs over the life of the project. For example, deliverables in the early design phase of a project might be a list of specifications. In the second phase deliverables could be software coding and a technical manual. The next phase could be to test prototypes. The final phase could be final tests and approved software.

3. **Milestones.** A milestone is a significant event in a project that occurs at a point in time. The milestone schedule shows only major segments of work; it represents first, rough-cut estimates of time, cost, and resources for the project. The milestone schedule is built using the deliverables as a platform to identify major segments of work and an end date—for example, testing complete and finished by July 1 of the same year. Milestones should be natural, important control points in the project. Milestones should be easy for all project participants to recognize.

4. **Technical requirements.** More frequently than not, a product or service will have technical requirements to ensure proper performance. For example, a technical requirement for a personal computer might be the ability to accept 120-volt alternating current or 240-volt direct current without any adapters or user switches. Another well-known example is the ability of 911 emergency systems to identify the caller's phone number and location of the phone. Examples from information systems projects include speed and capacity of database systems and connectivity with alternative systems. For understanding the importance of key requirements, see Snapshot from Practice: Big Bertha.

5. **Limits and exclusions.** The limits of scope should be defined. Failure to do so can lead to false expectations and to expending resources and time on the wrong problem. Examples of limits are: local air transportation to and from base camps will be outsourced; system maintenance and repair will be done only up to one month after final inspection; client will be billed for additional training beyond that prescribed in the contract. Exclusions further define the boundary of the project by stating what is not included. Examples include: data will be collected by the client, not the contractor; a house will be built, but no landscaping or security devices added; software will be installed, but no training given.

6. **Reviews with customer.** Completion of the scope checklist ends with a review with your customer— internal or external. The main concern here is the understanding and agreement of expectations. Is the customer getting what he or she desires in deliverables? Does the project definition identify key accomplishments, budgets, timing, and performance requirements? Are questions of limits and exclusions covered? Clear communication in all these issues is imperative to avoid claims or misunderstanding.

Scope definition should be as brief as possible but complete; one or two pages are typical for small projects. See Snapshot from Practice: Scope Statement on page 95.

The above checklist is generic. Different industries and companies will develop unique checklists and templates to fit their needs and specific kinds of projects. Many companies engaged in contracted work refer to scope statements as *statements of work* (SOW). Other organizations use the term *project charter*. However, *project charter* has different meanings in the world of project management. One meaning is an expanded version of the scope statement, described above, that might include such items as risk limits, customer needs, spending limits, and even team composition. A second, and more useful meaning, which dates back to the original use of the word charter, is a document that authorizes the project manager to initiate and lead the project. This document is issued by upper management and provides the project manager with written authority to use organizational resources for project activities.

Many projects suffer from scope creep, which is the tendency for the project scope to expand over time— usually by changing requirements, specifications, and priorities. Scope creep can be reduced by carefully writing your scope statement. A scope statement that is too broad is an invitation for scope creep. Scope creep can have a positive or negative effect on the project, but in most cases scope creep means added costs and possible project delays. Changes in requirements, specifications, and priorities frequently result in cost overruns and delays. Examples are abundant—Denver airport baggage handling system; Boston's new freeway system ("The Big Dig"); China's fast train in Shanghai; and the list goes on. On software development projects, scope creep is manifested in bloated products in which added functionality undermines ease of use.

Snapshot from Practice   Big Bertha II versus the USGA's COR Requirements*

In 1991 Callaway Golf Equipment introduced their Big Bertha driver and revolutionized the golf equipment business. Big Bertha—named after the World War I German long-distance cannon—was much larger than conventional woods and lacked a hosel (the socket in the head of the club into which the shaft is inserted) so that the weight could be better distributed throughout the head. This innovative design gave the clubhead a larger sweet spot, which allowed a player to strike the golf ball off-center and not suffer much loss in distance or accuracy. Callaway has maintained its preeminent position in the golf industry by utilizing space-age technology to extend the accuracy and distance of golf equipment.

In 2000 Callaway introduced the Big Bertha ERC II forged titanium driver. The driver was technologically superior to any driver on the market. However, there was one big problem. The new version of Bertha did not conform to the coefficient of restitution (COR) requirement established by the United States Golf Association (USGA). As a result it was barred from use by golfers in North America who intended to play by USGA's Rules of Golf.

The USGA believed that the rapid technological advances in golf equipment made by Callaway Golf and other golf manufacturers were threatening the integrity of the game. Players were hitting balls so much farther and straighter that golf courses around the world were being redesigned to make them longer and more difficult.

So in 1998 the USGA established performance thresholds for all new golf equipment. In order to prevent manufacturers from developing more powerful clubs, the USGA limited the COR of new golf equipment to 0.83. The COR was calculated by firing a golf ball at a driver out of a cannon-like machine at 109 miles per hour. The speed that the ball returned to the cannon could not exceed 83 percent of its initial speed (90.47 mph). The USGA called the ratio of incoming to outgoing velocity the coefficient of restitution (COR). The intent of the USGA COR threshold was to limit the distance that golf balls could be hit since studies indicated that 0.01 increase in COR resulted in two extra yards of carry. The Big Bertha ERC II's COR was 0.86.

After numerous efforts to get USGA to change its technical requirements, Callaway's engineers went back to the drawing board and in 2002 introduced Great Big Bertha II, which conformed to USGA's 0.83 COR restriction.

* John E., Gamble. "Callaway Golf Company: Sustaining Advantage in a Changing Industry," in A. A. Thompson, J. E. Gamble, and A. J. Strickland, *Strategy: Winning in the Marketplace,* Boston: McGraw-Hill/Irwin, 2004, pp. C204–C228.

Snapshot from Practice   Scope Statement

Project Objective

To construct a high-quality, custom home within five months at cost not to exceed $350,000.

Deliverables

- A 2,200-square-foot, 2½-bath, 3-bedroom, finished home.
- A finished garage, insulated and sheetrocked.
- Kitchen appliances to include range, oven, microwave, and dishwasher.
- High-efficiency gas furnace with programmable thermostat.

Milestones

1. Permits approved—March 5
2. Foundation poured—March 14
3. Drywall in. Framing, sheathing, plumbing, electrical, and mechanical inspections passed—May 25
4. Final inspection—June 7

Technical Requirements

1. Home must meet local building codes.
2. All windows and doors must pass NFRC class 40 energy ratings.
3. Exterior wall insulation must meet an "R" factor of 21.
4. Ceiling insulation must meet an "R" factor of 38.
5. Floor insulation must meet an "R" factor of 25.
6. Garage will accommodate two large-size cars and one 20-foot Winnebago.
7. Structure must pass seismic stability codes.

Limits and Exclusions

1. The home will be built to the specifications and design of the original blueprints provided by the customer.
2. Owner responsible for landscaping.
3. Refrigerator is not included among kitchen appliances.
4. Air conditioning is not included but prewiring is included.
5. Contractor reserves the right to contract out services.
6. Contractor responsible for subcontracted work.
7. Site work limited to Monday through Friday, 8:00 A.M. to 6:00 P.M.

Customer Review

John and Joan Smith

If the project scope needs to change, it is critical to have a sound change control process in place that records the change and keeps a log of all project changes. The log identifies the change, impact, and those responsible for accepting or rejecting a proposed change.

Change control is one of the topics of Chapter 7. Project managers in the field constantly suggest that dealing with changing requirements is one of their most perplexing problems.

Step 2: Establishing Project Priorities

Quality and the ultimate success of a project are traditionally defined as meeting and/or exceeding the expectations of the customer and/or upper management in terms of cost (budget), time (schedule), and performance (scope) of the project (see Figure 4.1). The interrelationship among these criteria varies. For example, sometimes it is necessary to compromise the performance and scope of the project to get the project done quickly or less expensively. Often the longer a project takes, the more expensive it becomes. However, a positive correlation between cost and schedule may not always be true. Other times project costs can be reduced by using cheaper, less efficient labor or equipment that extends the duration of the project. Likewise, as will be seen in Chapter 9, project managers are

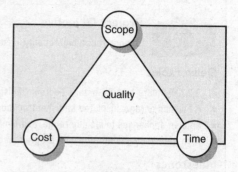

FIGURE 4.1   Project Management Trade-offs

often forced to expedite or "crash" certain key activities by adding additional labor, thereby raising the original cost of the project.

One of the primary jobs of a project manager is to manage the trade-offs among time, cost, and performance. To do so, project managers must define and understand the nature of the priorities of the project. They need to have a candid discussion with the project customer and upper management to establish the relative importance of each criterion. For example, what happens when the customer keeps adding requirements? Or if, midway through the project, a trade-off must be made between cost and expediting, which criterion has priority?

One technique found in practice that is useful for this purpose is completing a priority matrix for the project to identify which criterion is constrained, which should be enhanced, and which can be accepted:

Constrain. The original parameter is fixed. The project must meet the completion date, specifications and scope of the project, or budget.

Enhance. Given the scope of the project, which criterion should be optimized? In the case of time and cost, this usually means taking advantage of opportunities to either reduce costs or shorten the schedule. Conversely, with regard to performance, enhancing means adding value to the project.

Accept. For which criterion is it tolerable not to meet the original parameters? When trade-offs have to be made, is it permissible for the schedule to slip, to reduce the scope and performance of the project, or to go over budget?

Figure 4.2 displays the priority matrix for the development of a new cable modem. Because *time* to market is important to sales, the project manager is instructed to take advantage of every opportunity to reduce completion time. In doing so, going over *budget* is acceptable though not desirable. At the same time, the original *performance* specifications for the modem as well as reliability standards cannot be compromised.

Priorities vary from project to project. For example, for many software projects time to market is critical, and companies like Microsoft may defer original scope requirements to later versions in order to get to the market first. Alternatively, for special event projects (conferences, parades, tournaments) time is constrained once the date has been announced, and if the budget is tight, the project manager will compromise the scope of the project in order to complete the project on time.

Some would argue that all three criteria are always constrained and that good project managers should seek to optimize each criterion. If everything goes well on a project and no major problems or setbacks are encountered, their argument may be valid. However, this situation is rare, and project managers are often forced to make tough decisions that benefit one criterion while compromising the other two. The purpose of

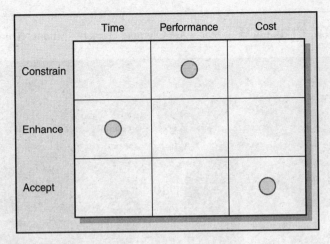

FIGURE 4.2 Project Priority Matrix

this exercise is to define and agree on what the priorities and constraints of the project are so that when "push comes to shove," the right decisions can be made.

There are likely to be natural limits to the extent managers can constrain, optimize, or accept any one criterion. It may be acceptable for the project to slip one month behind schedule but no further or to exceed the planned budget by as much as $20,000. Likewise, it may be desirable to finish a project a month early, but after that cost conservation should be the primary goal. Some project managers document these limits as part of creating the priority matrix.

In summary, developing a decision priority matrix for a project before the project begins is a useful exercise. It provides a forum for clearly establishing priorities with customers and top management so as to create shared expectations and avoid misunderstandings. The priority information is essential to the planning process, where adjustments can be made in the scope, schedule, and budget allocation. Finally, the matrix is useful midway in the project for approaching a problem that must be solved.

One caveat must be mentioned; during the course of a project, priorities may change. The customer may suddenly need the project completed one month sooner, or new directives from top management may emphasize cost saving initiatives. The project manager needs to be vigilant in order to anticipate and confirm changes in priorities and make appropriate adjustments.

Step 3: Creating the Work Breakdown Structure

Major Groupings Found in a WBS

Once the scope and deliverables have been identified, the work of the project can be successively subdivided into smaller and smaller work elements. The outcome of this hierarchical process is called the work breakdown structure (WBS). The WBS is a map of the project. Use of WBS helps to assure project managers that all products and work elements are identified, to integrate the project with the current organization, and to establish a basis for control. Basically, the WBS is an outline of the project with different levels of detail.

Figure 4.3 on page 100 shows the major groupings commonly used in the field to develop a hierarchical WBS. The WBS begins with the project as the final deliverable. Major project work deliverables/systems are identified first; then the subdeliverables necessary to accomplish the larger deliverables are defined. The

Snapshot from Practice   Year 2004 Olympic Games—Athens, Greece

AP/Wide World.

In the realm of event project management, the Olympic Games rank as one of the premier achievements.

Project Definition

Objective: To stage the Year 2004 Summer Olympic Games at specified locations in Greece beginning August 13 at a cost of $5.2 billion.

Client: Activities are underwritten by the Greek government. Many stakeholders and customers, e.g., citizens of Athens, local and national governments, the Greek people, the International Olympic Organization, the international community as a whole, the athletes, and Greek and international business communities.

Scope: Organizing all Games and ceremonies. Putting in place all technology and resources required to stage the Games. Handling public relations and fundraising.

Criteria for success: Trouble-free performance of Games. Level of public enthusiasm and enjoyment. Economic activity generated within Athens and Greece. Continued interest in future Olympic Games.

Project team: Athens Organizing Committee Olympic Games (AOCOG) was appointed as the project managers by legislation. Other organizations directly contributing to the success of the Games, such as the International Olympic Committee, Greek Olympic Committee, Athens City Council, and Olympic Coordination Authority (Greek government) have been made party to the Host City Contract. Olympic Coordination Authority is responsible for all the infrastructure projects, most of which are either already under way or are being reprogrammed to accommodate the Games. Completion of these projects on time is vital to the success of the Olympic Games.

WBS: The work breakdown structure for the project includes the following major areas: events; venues and facilities including accommodation; transport; media facilities and coordination; telecommunications; security arrangements; medical care; human resources including volunteers; cultural olympiad; pre-games training; information technology projects; opening and closing ceremonies; public relations; financing; test games and trial events; and sponsorship management and control of ambush marketing. Each of these items could be treated as a project in its own right. Precision coordination will be necessary to ensure that these, and therefore the entire Games project, are delivered on time.

Time, obviously, is the most critical dimension of the Athens 2004 Olympic Games project. Early on initial delays and confusion caused the International Olympic Committee (IOC) to consider moving the Olympics to a different city. This threat galvanized the Greek efforts. At the end of a three year, around the clock construction blitz, Olympic organizers finally silenced critics with all the venues ready for the August 13 opening ceremony. As in the past, Olympics cost was the dimension sacrificed with the projected cost doubling to the $8 to 12 billion range. The Greeks were also forced to scale back the scope of construction and compromise on quality. While the glass roof centerpiece for the Olympic Stadium was preserved, delays caused cancellation of a similar roof for the aquatic center. Secondary projects designed to spruce up the city had to be scaled back or cut. Unfinished work was hidden behind huge banners. Ribbons and flags were used to divert attention from sidewalks that were never smoothed out or the dreary concrete buildings that didn't get fresh paint.

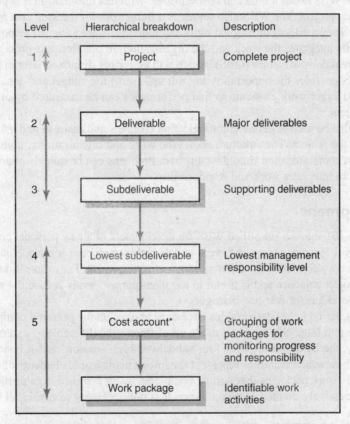

Level	Hierarchical breakdown	Description
1	Project	Complete project
2	Deliverable	Major deliverables
3	Subdeliverable	Supporting deliverables
4	Lowest subdeliverable	Lowest management responsibility level
5	Cost account*	Grouping of work packages for monitoring progress and responsibility
	Work package	Identifiable work activities

* This breakdown groups work packages by type of work within a deliverable and allows assignment of responsibility to an organizational unit. This extra step facilitates a system for monitoring project progress (discussed in Chapter 13).

FIGURE 4.3   Hierarchical Breakdown of the WBS

process is repeated until the subdeliverable detail is small enough to be manageable and where one person can be responsible. This subdeliverable is further divided into work packages. Because the lowest subdeliverable usually includes several work packages, the work packages are grouped by type of work—for example, hardware, programming, testing. These groupings within a subdeliverable are called cost accounts. This grouping facilitates a system for monitoring project progress by work, cost, and responsibility.

How WBS Helps the Project Manager

The WBS defines all the elements of the project in a hierarchical framework and establishes their relationships to the project end item(s). Think of the project as a large work package that is successively broken down into smaller work packages; the total project is the summation of all the smaller work packages. This hierarchical structure facilitates evaluation of cost, time, and technical performance at all levels in the organization over the life of the project. The WBS also provides management with information appropriate to each level. For example, top management deals primarily with major deliverables, while first-line supervisors deal with smaller subdeliverables and work packages.

Each item in the WBS needs a time and cost estimate. With this information it is possible to plan, schedule, and budget your project. The WBS also serves as a framework for tracking cost and work performance.

As the WBS is developed, organizational units and individuals are assigned responsibility for executing work packages. This integrates the work and the organization. In practice, this process is sometimes called the organization breakdown structure (OBS), which will be further discussed later in the chapter.

Use of the WBS provides the opportunity to "roll up" (sum) the budget and actual costs of the smaller work packages into larger work elements so that performance can be measured by organizational units and work accomplishment.

The WBS can also be used to define communication channels and assist in understanding and coordinating many parts of the project. The structure shows the work and organizational units responsible and suggests where written communication should be directed. Problems can be quickly addressed and coordinated because the structure integrates work and responsibility.

WBS Development

Figure 4.4 on page 101 shows a simplified WBS for development of a new personal computer project. At the top of the chart (level 1) is the project end item—a deliverable product or service. Note how the levels of the structure can represent information for different levels of management. For example, level 1 information represents the total project objective and is useful to top management; levels 2, 3, and 4 are suitable for middle management; and level 5 is for first-line managers.

Level 2 shows a partial list of deliverables necessary to develop the personal computer. One deliverable is the disk storage unit (shaded), which is made up of three subdeliverables—external USB, optical, and hard disks. Finally, the hard disk requires four subdeliverables—motor, circuit board, chassis frame, and read/write head. These subdeliverables represent the lowest manageable elements of the project. Each subdeliverable requires work packages that will be completed by an assigned organizational unit. Each deliverable will be successively divided in this manner. It is not necessary to divide all elements of the WBS to the same level.

The lowest level of the WBS is called a *work package*. Work packages are short-duration tasks that have a definite start and stop point, consume resources, and represent cost. Each work package is a control point. A work package manager is responsible for seeing that the package is completed on time, within budget, and according to technical specifications. Practice suggests a work package should not exceed 10 workdays or one

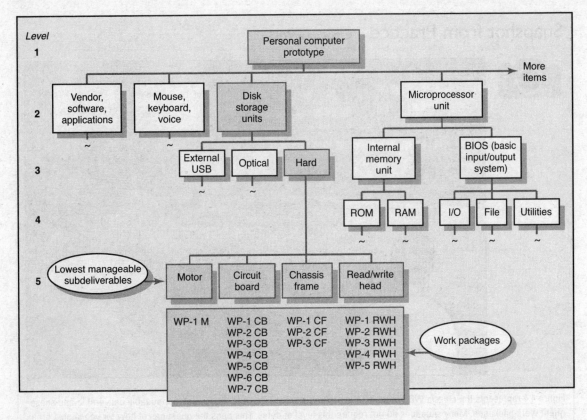

FIGURE 4.4   **Work Breakdown Structure**

reporting period. If a work package has a duration exceeding 10 days, check or monitoring points should be established within the duration, say, every three to five days, so progress and problems can be identified before too much time has passed. Each work package of the WBS should be as independent of other packages of the project as possible. No work package is described in more than one subdeliverable of the WBS.

There is an important difference from start to finish between the last work breakdown subdeliverable and a work package. Typically, a work breakdown subdeliverable includes the outcomes of more than one work package from perhaps two or three departments. Therefore, the subdeliverable does not have a duration of its own and does not consume resources or cost money directly. (In a sense, of course, a duration for a particular work breakdown element can be derived from identifying which work package must start first [earliest] and which package will be the latest to finish; the difference from start to finish becomes the duration for the subdeliverable.) The higher elements are used to identify deliverables at different phases in the project and to develop status reports during the execution stage of the project life cycle. Thus, the work package is the basic unit used for planning, scheduling, and controlling the project.

To review, each work package in the WBS

1. Defines work (what).
2. Identifies time to complete a work package (how long).
3. Identifies a time-phased budget to complete a work package (cost).
4. Identifies resources needed to complete a work package (how much).

Snapshot from Practice Creating a WBS

Figure 4.4 represents the classic WBS in which the project is broken down to the lowest manageable deliverable and subsequent work packages. Many situations do not require this level of detail. This begs the questions of how far you should break down the work.

There is no set answer to this question. However, here are some tips given by project managers:

Break down the work until you can do an estimate that is accurate enough for your purposes. If you are doing a ball-park estimate to see if the project is worthy of serious consideration, you probably do not need to break it down beyond major deliverables. On the other hand, if you are pricing a project to submit a competitive bid, then you are likely to go down to the work package level.

The WBS should conform to how you are going to schedule work. For example, if assignments are made in terms of days, then tasks should be limited as best as possible to one day or more to complete. Conversely, if hours are the smallest unit for scheduling, then work can be broken down to one-hour increments.

Final activities should have clearly defined start/end events. Avoid open-ended tasks like "research" or "market analysis." Take it down to the next level in which deliverables/outcomes are more clearly defined. Instead of ending with market analysis include items such as identify market share, list user requirements, or write a problem statement.

If accountability and control are important, then break the work down so that one individual is clearly responsible for the work. For example, instead of stopping at product design, take it to the next level and identify specific components of the design (i.e., electrical schematics, power source, etc.) that different individuals will be responsible for creating.

The bottom line is that the WBS should provide the level of detail needed to manage the specific project successfully.

5. Identifies a single person responsible for units of work (who).
6. Identifies monitoring points for measuring progress (how well).

Creating a WBS from scratch can be a daunting task. Project managers should take advantage of relevant examples from previous projects to begin the process.

WBSs are products of group efforts. If the project is small, the entire project team may be involved breaking down the project into its components. For large, complex projects, the people responsible for the major deliverables are likely to meet to establish the first two levels of deliverables. In turn, further detail would be delegated to the people responsible for the specific work. Collectively this information would be gathered and integrated into a formal WBS by a project support person. The final version would be reviewed by the inner echelon of the project team. Relevant stakeholders (most notably customers) would be consulted to confirm agreement and revise when appropriate.

Project teams developing their first WBS frequently forget that the structure should be end-item, output oriented. First attempts often result in a WBS that follows the organization structure—design, marketing, production, finance. If a WBS follows the organization structure, the focus will be on the organization function and processes rather than the project output or deliverables. In addition, a WBS with a process focus will become an accounting tool that records costs by function rather than a tool for "output" management. Every effort should be made to develop a WBS that is output oriented in order to concentrate on concrete deliverables. See Snapshot from Practice: Creating a WBS for more advice on creating a WBS. This process is discussed next.

Step 4: Integrating the WBS with the Organization

The WBS is used to link the organizational units responsible for performing the work. In practice, the outcome of this process is the organization breakdown structure (OBS). The OBS depicts how the firm has organized to discharge work responsibility. The purposes of the OBS are to provide a framework to summarize organization unit work performance, identify organization units responsible for work packages, and tie the organizational unit to cost control accounts. Recall, cost accounts group similar work packages (usually under the purview of a department). The OBS defines the organization subdeliverables in a hierarchical pattern in successively smaller and smaller units. Frequently, the traditional organization structure can be used. Even if the project is completely performed by a team, it is necessary to break down the team structure for assigning responsibility for budgets, time, and technical performance.

As in the WBS, the OBS assigns the lowest organizational unit the responsibility for work packages within a cost account. Herein lies one major strength of using WBS and OBS; they can be *integrated* as shown in Figure 4.5. The intersection of work packages and the organizational unit creates a project control point (cost account) that integrates work and responsibility. The intersection of the WBS and OBS represents the set of work packages necessary to complete the subdeliverable located immediately above and the organizational unit on the left responsible for accomplishing the packages at the intersection. Later we will use the intersection as a cost account for management control of projects. For example, the circuit board element requires completion of work packages whose primary responsibility will include the design, production, test, and software departments. Control can be checked from two directions— outcomes and responsibility. In the execution phase of the project, progress can be tracked vertically on deliverables (client's interest) and tracked horizontally by organization responsibility (management's interest).

Step 5: Coding the WBS for the Information System

Gaining the maximum usefulness of a breakdown structure depends on a coding system. The codes are used to define levels and elements in the WBS, organization elements, work packages, and budget and cost information. The codes allow reports to be consolidated at any level in the structure. The most commonly used scheme in practice is numeric indention. An example for the new computer project and the "Disk storage units" in Figure 4.5 is presented here:

1.0   Computer project
    1.1   Disk storage units
        1.1.1   External USB
        1.1.2   Optical
        1.1.3   Hard
            1.1.3.1   Motor
                1.1.3.1.1   Sourcing work package
                •
                •
            1.1.3.4   Read/write head
                1.1.3.4.1   Cost account
                1.1.3.4.2   Cost account
                    1.1.3.4.2.1   WP
                    1.1.3.4.2.2   WP
                    1.1.3.4.2.3   WP
                1.1.3.4.3   Cost account
                    •
                    •
                    •
                etc.

Note the project identification is 1.0. Each successive indention represents a lower element or work package. Ultimately the numeric scheme reaches down to the work package level, and all tasks and elements in the structure have an identification code. The "cost account" is the focal point because all budgets, work assignments, time, cost, and technical performance come together at this point.

This coding system can be extended to cover large projects. Additional schemes can be added for special reports. For example, adding a "–3" after the code could indicate a site location, an elevation, or a special account such as labor. Some letters can be used as special identifiers such as "M" for materials or "E" for engineers. You are not limited to only 10 subdivisions (0–9); you can extend each subdivision to large numbers—for example, .1–.99 or .1–.9999. If the project is small, you can use whole numbers. The following example is from a large, complex project:

$$3R–237A–P2–33.61$$

where 3R identifies the facility, 237A represents elevation and the area, P2 represents pipe two inches wide, and 33.6 represents the work package number. In practice most organizations are creative in combining letters and numbers to minimize the length of WBS codes.

Process Breakdown Structure

The WBS is best suited for design and build projects that have tangible outcomes such as an off-shore mining facility or a new car prototype. The project can be decomposed or broken down into major deliverables, subdeliverables, further subdeliverables, and ultimately to work packages. It is more difficult to apply WBS to less tangible, *process-oriented* projects in which the final outcome is a product of a series of steps or

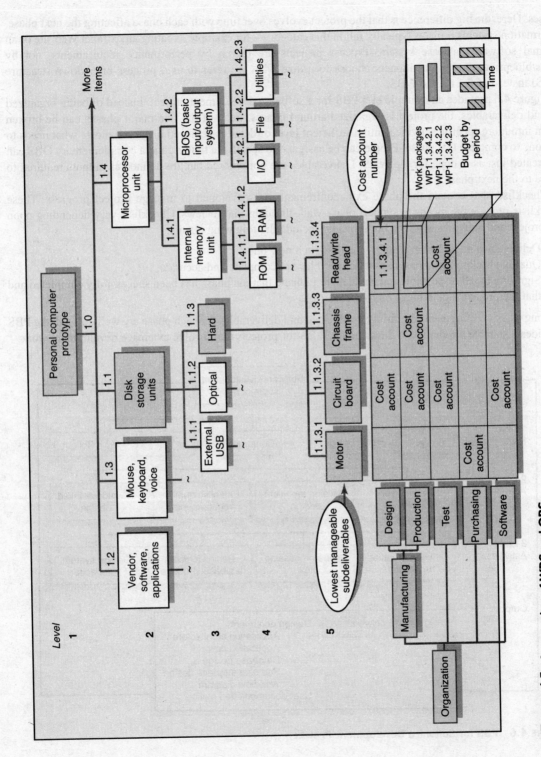

Figure 4.5 Integration of WBS and OBS

phases. Here, the big difference is that the project evolves over time with each phase affecting the next phase. Information systems projects typically fall in this category—for example, creating an extranet Web site or an internal software database system. Process projects are driven by performance requirements, not by plans/blueprints. Some practitioners choose to utilize what we refer to as a process breakdown structure (PBS) instead of the classic WBS.

Figure 4.6 provides an example of a PBS for a software development project. Instead of being organized around deliverables, the project is organized around phases. Each of the five major phases can be broken down into more specific activities until a sufficient level of detail is achieved to communicate what needs to be done to complete that phase. People can be assigned to specific activities, and a complementary OBS can be created just as is done for the WBS. Deliverables are not ignored but are defined as outputs required to move to the next phase.

Checklists that contain the phase exit requirements are developed to manage project progress. These checklists provide the means to support phase walk-throughs and reviews. Checklists vary depending upon the project and activities involved but typically include the following details:

- Deliverables needed to exit a phase and begin a new one.
- Quality checkpoints to ensure that deliverables are complete and accurate.
- Sign-offs by all responsible stakeholders to indicate that the phase has been successfully completed and that the project should move on to the next phase.

As long as exit requirements are firmly established and deliverables for each phase are well defined, the PBS provides a suitable alternative to the standard WBS for projects that involve extensive development work.

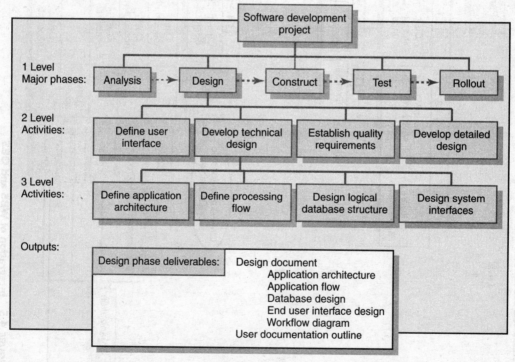

FIGURE 4.6   PBS for Software Development Project

Responsibility Matrices

In many cases, the size and scope of the project do not warrant an elaborate WBS or OBS. One tool that is widely used by project managers and task force leaders of small projects is the *responsibility matrix* (RM). The RM (sometimes called a linear responsibility chart) summarizes the tasks to be accomplished and who is responsible for what on a project. In its simplest form an RM consists of a chart listing all the project activities and the participants responsible for each activity. For example, Figure 4.7 illustrates an RM for a market research study. In this matrix the R is used to identify the committee member who is responsible for coordinating the efforts of other team members assigned to the task and making sure that the task is completed. The S is used to identify members of the five-person team who will support and/or assist the individual responsible. Simple RMs like this one are useful not only for organizing and assigning responsibilities for small projects but also for subprojects of large, more complex projects.

More complex RMs not only identify individual responsibilities but also clarify critical interfaces between units and individuals that require coordination. For example, Figure 4.8 is an RM for a larger, more complex project to develop a new piece of test equipment. Notice that within each cell a numeric coding scheme is used to define the nature of involvement on that specific task. Such an RM extends the WBS/OBS and provides a clear and concise method for depicting responsibility, authority, and communication channels.

Responsibility matrices provide a means for all participants in a project to view their responsibilities and agree on their assignments. They also help clarify the extent or type of authority exercised by each participant in performing an activity in which two or more parties have overlapping involvement. By using an RM and by defining authority, responsibility, and communications within its framework, the relationship between different organizational units and the work content of the project is made clear.

	Project Team				
Task	Richard	Dan	Dave	Linda	Elizabeth
Identify target customers	R	S		S	
Develop draft questionnaire	R	S	S		
Pilot-test questionnaire		R		S	
Finalize questionnaire	R	S	S	S	
Print questionnaire					R
Prepare mailing labels					R
Mail questionnaires					R
Receive and monitor returned questionnaires				R	S
Input response data			R		
Analyze results		R	S	S	
Prepare draft of report	S	R	S	S	
Prepare final report	R		S		

R = Responsible
S = Supports/assists

FIGURE 4.7   Responsibility Matrix for a Market Research Project

| | Organization | | | | | | | |
Deliverables	Design	Development	Documentation	Assembly	Testing	Purchasing	Quality Assur.	Manufacturing
Architectural designs	1	2			2		3	3
Hardware specifications	2	1				2	3	
Kernel specifications	1	3			3			3
Utilities specifications	2	1			3	3		
Hardware design	1			3				3
Disk drivers	3	1	2		3	3		
Memory management	1	3						
Operating system documentation	2	2	1	1	3	3	3	3
Prototypes	5		4				3	4
Integrated acceptance test	5	2	2		1		5	5

1 Responsible
2 Support
3 Consult
4 Notification
5 Approval

FIGURE 4.8   Responsibility Matrix for the Conveyor Belt Project

Project Communication Plan

Once the project deliverables and work are clearly identified, following up with an internal communication plan is vital. Stories abound of poor communication as a major contributor to project failure. Having a robust communications plan can go a long way toward mitigating project problems and can ensure that customers, team members, and other stakeholders have the information to do their jobs.

The communication plan is usually created by the project manager and/or the project team in the early stage of project planning.

Communication is a key component in coordinating and tracking project schedules, issues, and action items. The plan maps out the flow of information to different stakeholders and becomes an integral part of the overall project plan. The purpose of a project communication plan is to express what, who, how, and when information will be transmitted to project stakeholders so schedules, issues, and action items can be tracked.

Project communication plans address the following core questions:

- What information needs to be collected and when?
- Who will receive the information?
- What methods will be used to gather and store information?
- What are the limits, if any, on who has access to certain kinds of information?
- When will the information be communicated?
- How will it be communicated?

Developing a communication plan that answers these questions usually entails the following basic steps:

1. **Stakeholder analysis.** Identify the target groups. Typical groups could be the customer, sponsor, project team, project office, or anyone who needs project information to make decisions and/or contribute to project progress.
2. **Information needs.** What information is pertinent to stakeholders who contribute to the project's progress? For example, top management needs to know how the project is progressing, whether it is encountering critical problems, and the extent to which project goals are being realized. This information is required so that they can make strategic decisions and manage the portfolio of projects. Project team members need to see schedules, task lists, specifications, and the like, so they know what needs to be done next. External groups need to know any changes in the schedule and performance requirements of the components they are providing. Frequent information needs found in communication plans are:

Project status reports	Deliverable issues
Changes in scope	Team status meetings
Gating decisions	Accepted request changes
Action items	Milestone reports

3. **Sources of information.** When the information needs are identified, the next step is to determine the sources of information. That is, where does the information reside? How will it be collected? For example, information relating to the milestone report, team meetings, and project status meetings would be found in the minutes and reports of various groups.
4. **Dissemination modes.** In today's world, traditional status report meetings are being supplemented by e-mail, teleconferencing, Lotus Notes, SharePoint, and a variety of database sharing programs to circulate information. In particular, many companies are using the Web to create a "virtual project office" to store project information. Project management software feeds information directly to the Web site so

that different people have immediate access to relevant project information. In some cases, appropriate information is routed automatically to key stakeholders. Backup paper hardcopy to specific stakeholders is still critical for many project changes and action items.

5. **Responsibility and timing.** Determine who will send out the information. For example, a common practice is to have secretaries of meetings forward the minutes or specific information to the appropriate stakeholders. In some cases the responsibility lies with the project manager or project office. Timing and frequency of distribution appropriate to the information need to be established.

The advantage of establishing a communication plan is that instead of responding to information requests, you are controlling the flow of information. This reduces confusion and unnecessary interruptions, and it can provide project managers greater autonomy. Why? By reporting on a regular basis how things are going and what is happening, you allow senior management to feel more comfortable about letting the team complete the project without interference. See Figure 4.9 for a sample Shale Oil Research Project Communication Plan.

The importance of establishing up-front a plan for communicating important project information cannot be overstated. Many of the problems that plague a project can be traced back to insufficient time devoted to establishing a well-grounded internal communication plan.

What Information	Target Audience	When?	Method of Communication	Provider
Milestone report	Senior management and project manager	Bimonthly	E-mail and hardcopy	Project office
Project status reports & agendas	Staff and customer	Weekly	E-mail and hardcopy	Project manager
Team status reports	Project manager and project office	Weekly	E-mail	Team recorder
Issues report	Staff and customer	Weekly	E-mail	Team recorder
Escalation reports	Staff and customer	When needed	Meeting and hardcopy	Project manager
Outsourcing performance	Staff and customer	Bimonthly	Meeting	Project manager
Accepted change requests	Project office, senior mgmt., customer, staff, and project mgr.	Anytime	E-mail and hardcopy	Design department
Oversight gate decisions	Senior management and project manager	As required	E-mail meeting report	Oversight group or project office

FIGURE 4.9   Shale Oil Research Project Communication Plan

Summary

The project scope definition, priorities, and breakdown structure are the keys to nearly every aspect of managing the project. The scope definition provides focus and emphasis on the end item(s) of the project. Establishing project priorities allows managers to make appropriate trade-off decisions. The structure helps ensure all tasks of the project are identified and provides two views of the project—one on deliverables and one on organization responsibility. The WBS avoids having the project driven by organization function or by a finance system. The structure forces attention to realistic requirements of personnel, hardware, and budgets. Use of the structure provides a powerful framework for project control that identifies deviations from plan, identifies responsibility, and spots areas for improved performance. No well-developed project plan or control system is possible without a disciplined, structured approach. The WBS, OBS, and cost account codes provide this discipline. The WBS will serve as the database for developing the project network which establishes the timing of work, people, equipment, and costs.

PBS is often used for process-based projects with ill-defined deliverables. In small projects responsibility matrices may be used to clarify individual responsibility.

Clearly defining your project is the first and most important step in planning. The absence of a clearly defined project plan consistently shows up as the major reason for project failures. Whether you use a WBS, PBS, or responsibility matrix will depend primarily on the size and nature of your project. Whatever method you use, definition of your project should be adequate to allow for good control as the project is being implemented. Follow-up with a clear communication plan for coordinating and tracking project progress will help keep important stakeholders informed and avoid some potential problems.

Key Terms

Cost account	Process breakdown	Work breakdown structure
Milestone	structure (PBS)	(WBS)
Organization breakdown	Responsibility matrix	Work package
structure (OBS)	Scope creep	
Priority matrix	Scope statement	

Review Questions

1. What are the six elements of a typical scope statement?
2. What questions does a project objective answer? What would be an example of a good project objective?
3. What does it mean if the priorities of a project include: Time-constrain, Scope-accept, and Cost-enhance?
4. What kinds of information are included in a work package?
5. When would it be appropriate to create a responsibility matrix rather than a full-blown WBS?
6. How does a communication plan benefit management of projects?

Exercises

1. You are in charge of organizing a dinner-dance concert for a local charity. You have reserved a hall that will seat 30 couples and have hired a jazz combo.

   a. Develop a scope statement for this project that contains examples of all the elements. Assume that the event will occur in 4 weeks and provide your best guess estimate of the dates for milestones.

   b. What would the priorities likely be for this project?

2. In small groups, identify real life examples of a project that would fit each of the following priority scenarios:

   a. Time-constrain, Scope-enhance, Cost-accept

   b. Time-accept, Scope-constrain, Cost-accept

   c. Time-constrain, Scope-accept, Cost-enhance

3. Develop a WBS for a project in which you are going to build a bicycle. Try to identify all of the major components and provide three levels of detail.

4. You are the father or mother of a family of four (kids ages 13 and 15) planning a weekend camping trip. Develop a responsibility matrix for the work that needs to be done prior to starting your trip.

5. Develop a WBS for a local stage play. Be sure to identify the deliverables and organizational units (people) responsible. How would you code your system? Give an example of the work packages in one of your cost accounts. Develop a corresponding OBS which identifies who is responsible for what.

6. Use an example of a project you are familiar with or are interested in. Identify the deliverables and organizational units (people) responsible. How would you code your system? Give an example of the work packages in one of your cost accounts.

7. Develop a communication plan for an airport security project. The project entails installing the hardware and software system that (1) scans a passenger's eyes, (2) fingerprints the passenger, and (3) transmits the information to a central location for evaluation.

8. Go to an Internet search engine (e.g., Google) and type in "project communication plan." Check three or four that have ".gov" as their source. How are they similar or dissimilar? What would be your conclusion concerning the importance of an internal communication plan?

References

Ashley, D. B., et al., "Determinants of Construction Project Success," *Project Management Journal,* 18 (2) June 1987, p. 72.

Chilmeran, A. H., "Keeping Costs on Track," *PM Network,* 19 (2) 2004, pp. 45–51.

Gobeli, D. H. and E. W. Larson, "Project Management Problems" *Engineering Management Journal, 2,* 1990, pp. 31–36.

Ingebretsen, M., "Taming the Beast," *PM Network,* July 2003, pp. 30–35.

Katz, D. M., "Case Study: Beware 'Scope Creep' on ERP Projects," *CFO.com,* March 27, 2001.

Kerzner, H., *Project Management: A Systems Approach to Planning,* 8th edition (New York: Van Nostrand Reinhold, 2003).

Lewis, J. P., *Project Planning, Scheduling and Controlling,* 3rd edition (Burr Ridge, IL: McGraw-Hill, 2000).

Luby, R. E., D. Peel, and W. Swahl, "Component-Based Work Breakdown Structure," *Project Management Journal,* 26 (2) December 1995, pp. 38–44.

Murch, R., *Project Management: Best Practices for IT Professionals* (Upper Darby, NJ: Prentice Hall, 2001).

Pinto, J. K. and D. P. Slevin, "Critical Success Factors Across the Project Life Cycle," *Project Management Journal,* 19 (3) June 1988, p. 72.

Pitagorsky, G., "Realistic Project Planning Promotes Success," *Engineer's Digest,* 29 (1) 2001.

PMI Standards Committee, *Guide to the Project Management Body of Knowledge* (Newton Square, PA: Project Management Institute, 2000).

Posner, B. Z., "What It Takes to Be a Good Project Manager," *Project Management Journal,* 18 (1) March 1987, p. 52.

Raz, T. and S. Globerson, "Effective Sizing and Content Definition of Work Packages," *Project Management Journal,* 29 (4) 1998, pp. 17–23.

Tate, K. and K. Hendrix, "Chartering IT Projects," *Proceedings, 30th Annual, Project Management Institute* (Philadelphia, PA. 1999), CD.

Zimmerman, E., "Preventing Scope Creep," *Manage,* February 2000.

APPENDIX 4.1

Project Scope Management

Definitions of Project and Project Scope

PMBOK® Guide defines project as *"A temporary endeavor undertaken to create a unique product, service or result"* and project scope as *"The work that must be performed to deliver a product, service or result with specified features and functions"*. These very definitions of project and project scope underscore the importance accorded to scope management processes. Organizations undertake projects, which act as vehicles of change and instruments for implementing the organization's strategic initiatives, and project scope includes the work to be accomplished for this purpose. Therefore, project scope management is indeed the heart of planning and execution of the project.

Key Issues in Project Scope Management

PMBOK® Guide defines scope management processes as *"The processes required to ensure that the project scope includes all the work required and only the work required, to complete the project successfully."*

From the nature of project scope and project scope management as defined above, we see that managing the project scope is essentially focusing on defining and controlling what is, and what is not included in the project. With this sharp focus on inclusion and exclusion of the work in the project scope viewpoint, three important or key issues in project scope management are identified and listed below:

- *Prevent indiscriminate scope creep* to ensure that the project thrust remains focused and resources are not frittered away
- *Include all deliverables in project work and complete them satisfactorily* to ensure that all work planned to be included for meeting he project objectives is completed to the satisfaction of the stakeholders.

- *Use discretion in permitting some scope changes* which are crucial for meeting the project objectives though they may not have been properly spelt out at the stage of defining scope.

Project Scope Management Processes

Five scope management processes are identified which collectively address the above mentioned key issues of scope management. Of the five scope management processes, three are in the planning group and two are in the monitoring and controlling group.

Planning Group includes three processes:

1. Collect Requirements
2. Define Scope, and
3. Create WBS

Monitoring and Controlling Group includes two processes:

1. Verify Scope, and
2. Control Scope

Before we understand how these processes collectively manage to carry out the task of project scope management as defined above, let us first learn more about each process.

1. Collect Requirements

Collect Requirements is the process of defining and documenting the needs to meet the project objectives.

The satisfaction of the needs of key stakeholders (project sponsor within the organization, client for whom the project is performed, or other key stakeholders) provides the measure for judging the success of a project. The starting point for crystallizing the project objectives, therefore, would be collecting and analyzing the needs of the stakeholders, which a particular project is authorized to meet. No doubt, the primary vision of the project objectives would be included in the project charter (or similar project authorizing document) issued at the start of the project. However, often all necessary details are not visualized at the very start of the project. As the project planning is taken up and the details for project work are mapped out, some important changes in the work necessary to meet the project objective become apparent. The collect requirement process addresses this issue by going back once more to the stakeholders and ensuring that the project scope includes such refinements and the project scope fully reflects the key stakeholders' needs for which the project is authorized.

We will now take a closer look at the major Inputs, outputs and tools & techniques for this process.

Major Inputs

The major inputs to the process are:

- *Formal interviews (including recorded minutes)*
- *Group discussions of key stakeholders*
- *Questionnaires and surveys*
- *Inviting reactions on a preliminary scheme or prototype* (For a software project, the proto-typical web-pages for key documents and the demonstration of general operating scheme could be very valuable.)

Tools & Techniques

The technique for collecting requirements is essentially close interaction with the key stakeholders to unearth their real needs. It might include:

- Interviews with the stakeholders
- Group Discussions
- Focused questionnaire and surveys

Major Outputs

Major output of the process is the requirements documentation. It formally documents the business need for the project. The Contents of formal documentation of the requirements also include unambiguous, omplete and consistent statement of the requirements and the criteria for acceptance set down by the key stakeholders.

2. Define Scope

Define scope is the process of developing a detailed description of the project and the product of the project.

Preparation of detailed scope statement is critical for project success. In this process, detailed description of the project and the product of the project is developed. The project objectives are analyzed to arrive at the major deliverables, which must be created to meet the objectives. The criteria for acceptance of the product and the major deliverables (the performance requirements, technical specifications and criteria for satisfaction of theses work components) are defined and specified. The work excluded from the project scope is explicitly spelled out. The assumptions and constraints taken into account in project planning are listed and analyzed. Finally, preliminary estimates for project cost and schedule are also developed for general guidelines. In this manner, this process provides the blueprint of detailed project planning leading to the next scope management process (Create Work Breakdown Structure – WBS) which involves more detailed project planning.

The major inputs, tools & techniques and outputs for this process are discussed below.

Major Inputs

Major inputs for defining the scope are the project objectives, major deliverables and criteria for acceptance for the product of the project. This basic information is elaborated and further refined by the process of direct reference with the key stakeholders in the Collect Requirements process. In addition to these two inputs for the process scope contents, the organization's process assets (policies and procedures for planning and executing projects, earlier used templates for drafting project scope statement, lessons learnt from earlier similar projects, etc.) are other helpful inputs for defining project scope.

Tools & Techniques

Preparing the project scope statement requires essentially drafting a comprehensive project scope document. Therefore, the techniques and tools employed would depend on:

- *Product analysis*—the form and nature of the project's product
- *Identification of project execution approach*—based on evaluation of the available alternatives and selecting the most appropriate for the situation.
- *Expert Judgment*—the expertise developed by the project manager from his experience in handling similar projects earlier and

Output

Output of the process is *Project Scope Statement.* Along with Project Charter, Project Scope Statement forms the basis for all subsequent project decisions, conflict resolution and tradeoffs during the execution phase. Contents of a typical *Project Scope Statement* would be:

- *Project Objectives*—a comprehensive statement of the project objectives based on the directives in the project charter document and analyzed and confirmed by collect requirement process
- *Product scope description*—characteristics of the product, service or result described in the project charter, including the performance requirements, detailed technical specifications, applicable quality standards and project satisfaction criteria
- *Project deliverables and project acceptance criteria*—Deliverable is a unique and verifiable product, result or capability that must be produced to complete the project phase or process. It is necessary that deliverables are defined and described in concrete terms and are subject to objectively measurable results or characteristics.
- *Project boundaries*—specific mention of exclusions to avoid misunderstanding and unwarranted expectations from the project
- *Project Constraints & assumptions*—which have been taken into account for project planning
- *Project Management Guidelines*
  - Project Cost
  - Major milestones & project schedule
  - Quality aspects and acceptance requirements
  - Project management Team & project organization

Compare the above list with the 'Snapshot from Practice Scope Statement' given in this chapter (page 119) and observe the similarities.

3. Create WBS

Create WBS is the process of subdividing the project deliverables and project work into smaller and more manageable components. WBS is defined as *"A deliverable oriented hierarchical decomposition of the work to be executed by the project team to accomplish the project objectives and create the required deliverables. It organizes and defines the total scope of the project".*

Each descending level represents an increasingly detailed definition of the project work. The WBS is decomposed until meaningful work packages are defined. In this manner, this process ensures that all work necessary for the project is included in the project plan, accurate estimates for resource requirements and time are developed and responsibility is assigned for executing each work package. On completion of all work packages planned in the WBS, the total scope of project work is covered.

The WBS structure includes unique identifiers from the code of accounts and accordingly provides a hierarchical structure for summation of costs, schedules, and resource information. As one of the special tools used in project management, its purpose is:

To define
Solution strategy or general approach, and Implementation tactics.
To support more accurate estimates of project duration and cost than can be made at the project level.
To assign the responsibility of each work package or major component/sub-component to an individual, group, department or outside agency (Responsibility Assignment Matrix).
To provide a basis for estimating project resources: Departmental or subcontractor support.

The Inputs, Outputs and Tools and Techniques for the process are briefly mentioned below.

Major Inputs

The main inputs for creating the WBS structure are

- *The project scope statement*—the document produced from Define Scope process
- *The requirements documentation*—the document prepared from the Collect Requirements process, and
- *The organizational process assets*—viz. the organization's past experience of planning and executing similar projects, policies & procedures, templates for creating a WBS and the lessons learnt from earlier projects

Tools & Techniques

The technique is to gradually decompose the main deliverables into smaller and better defined elements till work packages level is reached. The mode of decomposition would depend on the project's product and the industry practice. It may be based on the phases of the project life cycle or the external agencies or departments employed for project work or the major deliverables consisting of work spread across different life cycle phases and performing agencies.

Major Outputs

WBS, WBS Dictionary, and the scope baseline are the main outputs for the process.

WBS, the hierarchical breakdown of project deliverables into work packages, is described before.

WBS Dictionary is an important accompanying document of WBS and contains detailed description of the work and technical documentation of each work package. It is a document that supports WBS and includes all detailed information, which a brief tabular structure of the WBS cannot hold. WBS Dictionary holds code of account identifier, description of work, performance specifications, technical specification (drawings and standards), quality requirements, schedule milestones and contract information.

Scope Baseline is the scope component of the project management plan and describes the collection of the project scope statement, WBS and WBS Dictionary.

The Contents of a Typical Work Package

A work package should include the following:

- Unique identification from a code of accounts
- Detailed technical or performance specification set down in WBS dictionary
- Estimated / Budgeted Cost
- Estimated time duration or expected milestone
- Preceding and succeeding project activity or work package
- Assigned Responsibility (RAM)
- Applicable standard of acceptance or quality level

Heuristics for Preparing WBS

It is very important to know how far the decomposition of the major deliverable should be carried out. General principle is that such decomposition should be carried out until resulting work package would unambiguously define the total scope of work in the work package. This would cover the technical and performance specifications, the resource requirements and cost, the sequencing of activities with expected start and end times of the activities. Each work package should have its unique identification number for control and it should be possible to assign independent responsibility for the entire work package.

The following guidelines could be helpful in deciding the degree of decomposition of project scope into work packages during 'Create WBS' process.

- Tendency to decompose to a very high degree or leave unduly large work package should be curbed. Work packages should ordinarily not be smaller than 1% to 2 % of the total project scope and not greater than 8-10 % of the scope. Generally decomposing the project into 5-10 major deliverables is found satisfactory.
- It should be possible to assign unambiguously responsibility for individual work packages.
- It should be possible to provide complete technical and performance specifications for work included in each work package.
- It should be possible to estimate the time required to carry out the activity for the work package.
- It should be possible to estimate the resources required and cost to be incurred for the work package.
- The interface between the sequential work packages should be clearly demarcated and no portion of work should remain outside the WBS.

4. Verify Scope

Verify scope is the process of formalizing the acceptance of the completed project deliverables.

This process belongs to monitoring and controlling process group and it is meant to ensure that all deliverables and work packages planned in the WBS are completed to the satisfaction of the sponsor or key stakeholders and are formally accepted by the stakeholders. The process requires carrying out Inspection and testing to ensure that the deliverables meet the necessary performance and technical specifications

Major Inputs

For this process, the major inputs are:

1. Project management Plan
   - Project Scope Statement
   - WBS and WBS Dictionary
2. Requirements Documentation
3. Validated Deliverables

Tools and Techniques

Tools and techniques for verification are inspection and testing (activities involving physical inspection), measurement of technical specifications and performance testing to verify that the completed deliverable meets the product satisfaction criteria set down in the project scope.

Major Outputs

After the testing and inspection, the deliverable is formally accepted to meet the criteria for its acceptance set down in the project scope statement and elaborated in the WBS and WBS Dictionary. If this testing reveals the necessity of adding any more project work, the change requests are originated. Summing up, the outputs from the process are:

- Accepted Deliverables
- Change Requests

5. Control Scope

Control Scope is the process of monitoring the status of the project and product scope and managing changes to the scope baseline.

This process would ensure that all requested changes and recommended corrective actions found during scope verification are suitably processed through policies and procedures set down in *Integrated Change Control Process* – like forms for change requests, authority levels, impact evaluation of suggested change on cost and schedule, etc. Approved changes should be incorporated in the project plan updates (i.e. project planning documents like WBS, Project Schedule, Project Cost and Budget, Quality Plans, etc.).

The Inputs, Outputs and Tools and Techniques for the process are briefly described below.

Inputs

Like the standard feed-back control loop, the inputs for the Control Scope process are planned versus actual performance. So, the requirements set down in the components of the Project Management Plan (*WBS* and *WBS Dictionary, Project Schedule, Quality Standards*) and *Product Requirements* documentation included in project plan are one set of inputs and the actual work performance results found from inspection and testing during Verify Scope process are another set of inputs.

Techniques

The technique for cost control involves analyzing the variance between the standards set down in the project plan documents and actual work performance results from Verify Scope process.

Outputs

The main outputs from this process are:

- Change Requests (for including approved corrective or preventive actions to ensure that the deliverable meets the project satisfaction criteria)
- Project Plan Updates (for incorporating the approved changes into the Project Plan and revising the cost and time schedule taking into account impacts of the accepted changes on the project budget and project schedule), and
- Work Performance Measurements (actual versus planned for communicating to the stakeholders)

How Five Scope Management Processes Collectively Address Key Issues of Scope Management

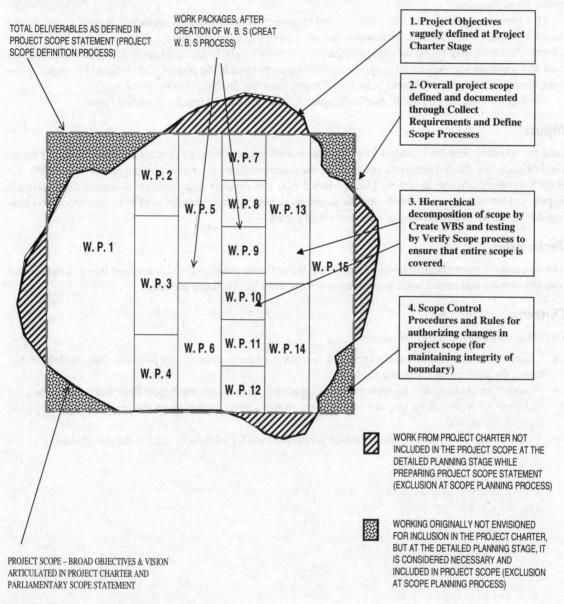

TOTAL DELIVERABLES AS DEFINED IN PROJECT SCOPE STATEMENT (PROJECT SCOPE DEFINITION PROCESS)

WORK PACKAGES, AFTER CREATION OF W. B. S (CREAT W. B. S PROCESS)

1. Project Objectives vaguely defined at Project Charter Stage

2. Overall project scope defined and documented through Collect Requirements and Define Scope Processes

3. Hierarchical decomposition of scope by Create WBS and testing by Verify Scope process to ensure that entire scope is covered.

4. Scope Control Procedures and Rules for authorizing changes in project scope (for maintaining integrity of boundary)

W. P. 1
W. P. 2
W. P. 3
W. P. 4
W. P. 5
W. P. 6
W. P. 7
W. P. 8
W. P. 9
W. P. 10
W. P. 11
W. P. 12
W. P. 13
W. P. 14
W. P. 15

WORK FROM PROJECT CHARTER NOT INCLUDED IN THE PROJECT SCOPE AT THE DETAILED PLANNING STAGE WHILE PREPARING PROJECT SCOPE STATEMENT (EXCLUSION AT SCOPE PLANNING PROCESS)

WORKING ORIGINALLY NOT ENVISIONED FOR INCLUSION IN THE PROJECT CHARTER, BUT AT THE DETAILED PLANNING STAGE, IT IS CONSIDERED NECESSARY AND INCLUDED IN PROJECT SCOPE (EXCLUSION AT SCOPE PLANNING PROCESS)

PROJECT SCOPE – BROAD OBJECTIVES & VISION ARTICULATED IN PROJECT CHARTER AND PARLIAMENTARY SCOPE STATEMENT

FIGURE 4.8 Scope Management Processes

APPENDIX 4.2

Project Communications Management

Great natural leaders as well as successful corporate managers are usually blessed with distinctly superior skills for all forms for communication – verbal as well as written, formal as well as informal. This natural skill in communication of an experienced general management professional, no doubt, would be an important asset for project communication also. However, it would be possible for most project managers to bear in mind the special characteristics of project communication and learn to manage project communication to the satisfaction of all key stakeholders.

The logical organization of the project communication involves:

- Identifying the key stakeholders, determining their information needs and formulating the communication plan for desired flow of project information
- Setting up efficient systems for collection, storage and retrieval of the information for future use
- Collecting and distributing project information & reporting performance in a timely manner

Project Communication Management includes the processes required to ensure timely and appropriate generation, collection, distribution, storage, retrieval and ultimate disposition of project information. **(PMBOK Guide, 4th Edition)**

PMBOK lists 5 processes in project communication management.

1. Identify Stakeholders	(Initiating Process Group)
2. Plan Communications	(Planning Process Group)
3. Distribute Information	(Executing Process Group)
4. Manage Stakeholders, and	(Monitoring & Controlling Group)
5. Report Performance	(Executing Process Group)

Let us study these processes, their inputs, tools & techniques and outputs.

1. Identify Stakeholders (Initiating Process Group)
(and their needs for communication)

The process involves identifying all people or organizations impacted by the project, and documenting relevant information regarding their interests, involvement, and impact on the project success.

A project stakeholder is defined as any person or organization actively involved in the project, whose interests might be positively or negatively affected by the project and who in turn might exert significant influence on the project deliverables and outcome. This definition would identify for every project the following key stakeholders—the direct customer for the project's product (especially the senior corporate officers of the customer dealing with the project) and the ultimate users or general public. Some are listed as follows:

- The project performing organization (and its senior project officers)
- Project sponsor, the person or organization that provides financial resources and non-financial support for the project and immediate superiors in the organization
- Project management team and PMO (if it exists for the organization)

- Project team members
- Project manager
- Contractors for supplying materials or services for the project

The key inputs, tools and techniques and outputs are as follows:

Key Inputs

The key inputs for the process are:

- Project Charter (By providing information about who are the project sponsor, customers, key project team members and which groups or department participate in the project; their interest and likely impact on the project)
- Procurement Documents (By providing information on the client, other contracting parties, and the terms of contract)
- Enterprise Environmental Factors (By providing information about the organizational practices and culture and the government or industry standards and practices)
- Organizational Process Assets (By providing information on stakeholders of previous projects)

Tools and Techniques

The main tools for the process are:

- Stakeholder Analysis—Identification of stakeholders and collecting information on their roles, interests, and expectations, and
- Expert Judgment—Judgment of senior managers and subject matter experts would be useful in identifying the stakeholders and their interests and influence.

Outputs

Stakeholder Register and Stakeholder Management Strategy are main outputs.

Stakeholder Register should include details identifying the stakeholder (name, organization, address, contact details, etc.), assessment of the stakeholders' requirements and expectations (what information, in what degree of details and at what frequency) and potential influence. All stakeholders are not interested in all project related information; in fact the information overload itself (resulting from an attempt to tell all project details to everybody) may turn out to be one of the barriers in communication. Generally, the closer the stakeholder is to the project, the more detailed information he would demand. The project sponsor and higher levels of corporate management would simply require at certain time intervals or project life cycle phase gate an overview of the general direction the project has taken and to what extent the actual performance appears to be conforming to or deviating from the original plans. The user departments and project team members, on the other hand, might want more frequent updating and more detailed briefing.

Stakeholder Management Strategy should include the approach for managing the involvement and influence of the stakeholders during the entire project life cycle. Once the stakeholders are identified and their specific need for information and the timing or frequency for receiving the information is determined the next step of developing the communication plan can be taken up. In this manner, the formal system for project communication should be designed after taking into account:

- Who needs information
- What type and in what degree of details the information is needed
- Preferred mode of communication (verbal/meetings, informal written reports, formal written reports, etc.), and
- The timing and frequency of reporting

2. Plan Communication (Planning Process Group)

It is the process of determining the project stakeholders' information needs and defining a communication approach.

Once the stakeholders' needs for communication are determined, the communication plan is formulated. Essentially, it is to define and plan who needs what specific information, when they need it, in what detail they need it, the frequency of update and the preferred form of receiving the information. In most medium and large size projects, communication planning is formally done during the early stages of the project and the reports, the report formats, frequency of reporting, the persons receiving the specific reports, medium of delivery and other details are settled and followed.

Inputs

The stakeholder register and *strategy for managing the stakeholders* (the outputs of the previously discussed process "Define Stakeholders") are the main inputs for planning communication. Other inputs are *organizational process assets* (essentially for lessons learned from earlier projects on communication planning) and *enterprise environmental factors* (the project environment and communication technology most suitable for a specific communication).

Tools and Techniques

The following tools and technologies associated with communication planning should be taken into account:

- *Analysis of communication requirement*—The data from the main inputs for the earlier process (Define Stakeholders), the stakeholders' needs for information need to be analyzed in light of the number of communication channels, hierarchical or free form communication channels, organizational structure and whether the stakeholders are internal or external to plan project communications.
- *Communication technology*—This tool concerns the nature of technology to be used for project communication – verbal or written communication, urgency of communication and availability of suitable technology, project duration and environment.
- *Communication models*—This part is concerned with understanding the basic communication model and exploiting it for effective and efficient communication and preventing the lapses likely to occur. A somewhat more detailed discussion on general model for communication is offered in general principles for effective communication.
- *Communication methods*—The broad classification of whether the communication would be
  - (a) *Interactive communication* (meetings or phone calls) – most effective but most time and effort consuming; desirable or necessary for critical communication to key stakeholders.
  - (b) *"Push" Communication* (reports, e-mails, minutes of meetings, etc. sent periodically) which does not check whether the recipient actually received and understood the message; suitable for routine periodic updates to a larger audience of stakeholders, and
  - (c) *"Pull" Communication* (making available access to information)- least expensive and quite suitable for wider circulation of a relatively large volume of information.

Outputs

The output of the Plan Communication process is the **Communication Management Plan**. It essentially includes detailed account of who needs what specific information (developed from stakeholders register and strategy to mange stakeholders), when they need it, in what detail they need it, the frequency of update and the preferred form of receiving the information. Somewhat more detailed discussion on the nature and contents of the project communication plan is given below.

Nature and Contents of a Project Communication Plan

This is a very important planning document for all projects especially for the organizations performing projects on a contract basis. Most project managers and senior managers stress the need for effective communications in the project and the communication management plan should address to it by encompassing the entire spectrum of the key stakeholders' needs. It should, therefore, include:

- The list of major reports that would be prepared for communication during the project life cycle—Ordinarily, this list should include major project planning documents (project charter, scope statement, cost estimate and budget, Gantt chart for major project milestones, quality plan, risk register, major technical documentations like facilities design report for an infrastructures project, and communication plan) as well as periodic status reports and phase-gate review reports.
- The format, content and the level of details to be included in these reports—Often, the organizations have some tradition about what these reports should contain, and in that case, it should be followed generally with any specific modification required to suit the needs of the project in hand.
- The list of details regarding which stakeholders should receive which reports and the frequency of reporting—To avoid the information overload and distributing an avalanche of project information to all stakeholders, a judicious selection of the recipients of each report should be prepared on the need-to-know basis and the organization hierarchy.
- Methods or technologies used to convey the information- This aspect should cover how the communication would be handled, by issue of formal hard copy reports, formal presentations in meetings, informal memoranda and e-mails, project meetings and minutes of meetings, prints of drawings and technical specifications for review or execution, and
- The person(s) or group responsible for preparing and issue of specific communication.

3. Distribute Information (Executing Process Group)

Distribute Information is the process of making relevant information available to project stakeholders according to the project communication plan.

The communication management plan includes the framework for all formal and informal communications during the project: the details of who will get what information in what form and what frequency and the responsibility for generating and distributing the information. As the project is executed, the results of work performance become available in the concrete deliverables form. The physical inspection and performance testing during the scope verification process give the actual status of the work. The mode for information distribution (whether formal or informal and whether written or verbal) is also actually determined during the planning stage and all that is required to be done is actual compilation and distribution of the project status information to the stakeholders according to the communication plan reporting scheme.

The inputs, tools and techniques and outputs of the Distribute Information process are as follows:

Inputs

The main inputs for the process 'Distribute Information' are:

- *Project Communications Management Plan:* the output of the Plan Communications process (and a subsidiary of the Project Management Plan),
- *Performance Reports:* The information on the project status on the reporting date, including inspection & testing results, and updated forecast for based on the progress so far.

Tools and Techniques

The main techniques for distributing information are based on

- *Communication Methods:* The communication methods planned may include interactive mode (face-to-face meetings or telephone calls, etc.), "push" communication mode(written reports, e-mails, minutes of meetings etc. distributed periodically without any interaction with the recipient) or "pull" communication methods(making access to necessary information available through intra-net or similar 'publicly available' project documents)
- *Information Distribution Tools:* Information can be distributed by written or verbal communication. The written documents may be in the form of hard copy reports, electronic communication (e-mails, voice mails, fax, etc.) or use of project management software and other intra-net data sharing.

Outputs

The main outputs of the process are:

- *Project Reports:* Formal written reports issued at specific occasion or according to pre- decided frequency
- *Project Meetings and Presentations*
- *Organizational Process Assets- Lessons Learned Documents:* This is an important and special category of information to be distributed. For every project, during the execution phase, some previously unexpected situation occurs. The reasons behind development of such a situation and the remedial measures or the handling technique used for successfully overcoming the problem are very useful part of the organization's learning. The project team should always be vigilant to record such lessons learned details and circulate them throughout the organization for the benefit of other current or future projects.

4. Manage Stakeholders' Expectations (Executing Process Group)

Manage Stakeholders' Expectations is the process of communicating and working with stakeholders to meet their needs and addressing issues as they occur.

This process in the executing process group involves:

- Actively managing the expectations of the stakeholders to increase their stake in the project
- Addressing their concerns before they turn into sticky issues, and
- Clarifying and resolving the issues already identified

Inputs

Of course, the Project Communication Plan, a part of the Project Management Plan, is the first logical input. The major inputs for this process are *Stakeholder Register* and *Stakeholder Management Strategy* identified earlier. In case of major projects, it may also be desirable to use as inputs *Issue Logs* (used to document, monitor and resolve issues raised by key stakeholders) and *Change Logs* (used for documenting the changes accepted during the project planning and execution phases and their impact on project cost, time and risk to be communicated to the stakeholders).

Tools and Techniques

Essentially the techniques for managing the key stakeholders require application of good interpersonal and management skills and effective communication methods. Interpersonal skills like building trust, resolving conflict, overcoming resistance and active listening hold key to successful management of stakeholders' expectations. Amongst managerial skills specially called for are negotiation skills, good written communication, good presentation skills and some times, public speaking.

Outputs

The outputs of this process are updates of project documents (updates of stakeholders register, issue logs and change logs) and Change Requests originated to accommodate the stakeholders' need not included in the original project scope.

5. Report Performance (Monitoring and Controlling Process Group)

Report Performance is the process of collecting and distributing performance information including status reports, progress measurement and forecasts.

This process addresses the key issues of project communication.

- Communicating the exact up-to-date status of the project,
- Its analysis and critical review, and
- Forecasts for project completion (including time and cost)

Inputs

By its very nature, this process gives a comparative evaluation of the planned or expected outcomes for the project and the actual results achieved for major deliverables. Therefore the inputs would require on one hand the inputs from the planned or expected outcomes (scope baseline, project schedule and milestones for major deliverables) and budget forecasts (project cost management). On the other hand, it would require the exact current status of the project deliverables (viz. work performance information on the actual work progress in creating deliverables, cost and schedule) and work performance measurements (comparative evaluation of the planned versus actual work completed, cost and time).

Tools and Techniques

The techniques applicable for this process are summarized below.

- *Variance Analysis:*
  Essentially variance analysis is determining the difference between the actual performance and the planned value (in the project scope baseline, budget and schedule).
- *Forecasting Methods:*
  Performance report should include a forecast of the project outcomes at completion based on the progress so far. Forecasting may be based simply on a judgment by the project manager (or his team member responsible for a particular deliverable) for small, simple or familiar project. Elaborate forecasting techniques like Time Series, Causal/Econometric Analysis, Probabilistic forecasts based on simulation or Earned Value Management techniques may be desirable for complex or mega projects.
- *Communication Methods:*
  Status review meetings, e-mails on project progress or formal written reports submitted for project deliverables could be used for reporting performance.
- *Reporting Systems:*
  Different organizations use various systems for collecting information from different reports and consolidating them for report performance. Several specialized software also serve as excellent tools.

Outputs

The main outputs of the process are:

- *Performance Reports:* This is the main output of the process. The contents of a typical performance report are discussed in more detail below.
- *Change Requests* (Based on analysis of performance reports to bring back the orientation of the project to align with the basic project objectives)
- *Organizational Process Assets Updates* (Essentially lessons learnt in the form of Report Formats and performance analysis technique updates)

Contents of a Typical Performance Report

Performance report summarizes the information on the status of the project and its normative evaluation by comparing the actual performance with the planned values. At the same time, it should summarize the unresolved risks and issues as well as the forecasts for expected time and cost at completion. Accordingly, a typical performance report might include:

- Summary of current status of the project in terms of core areas of scope, time, cost and quality
- Analysis of the performance by comparison with the planned values
- Status of unresolved risks ad issues
- Forecast for project completion (time, budget, any major scope change from original)

  Some additional important concepts in project communication deserve special attention.

  1. Communication Channels In Free And Hierarchical Information Flows and Their Suitability For Project Communication
  2. Written and Verbal Communication

1. Communication Channels in Free and Hierarchical Information Flows and Their Suitability for Project Communication

Project communication is essentially the flow of information between the people engaged in the project activities. In that context, the communication process can be visualized as a network, where the people involved in the communication are the nodes and the active or permissible channels of communication between any two persons would be the lines joining these nodes.

From a network analysis point of view, there are two basic forms of communication networks:

Hierarchical Information Flow Network: This is the formal communication network in many organizations. The instructions or orders pass down from the higher levels or upper management to the next lower level and feedbacks or site information flow upward from the lower levels to the next higher managerial level and so forth.

The network basically looks like a set of straight lines connecting the nodes representing successively lower managerial levels. The merits of this communication network are that there is a strict accountability for communication and all instructions or orders pass down the command chain and all feedbacks pass up the command chain properly filtered for content and relevance. The drawback in the network is that there is a considerable time delay between the origination of the instruction or command at top management level and its receipt and execution at the lower operating level. Similar time delay occurs also in case of any important feedback passing from the operating level to the top management.

Free And Open Flow Information Network: In this form of communication network, everyone is free to communicate to every one else without any restriction. The network represents the exchanges for information likely in any unstructured assembly or meeting.

The network looks like a star with the straight lines connecting all nodes to each other. For a network with "n" persons in the communicating network (i.e. "n" nodes in the diagram), the number of communication channels (i.e. the number of straight lines joining the nodes in the diagram) would be "n (n – 1)/2". For a number of people as small as 10, this network would have 45 channels of communication; it would be really a cacophony in an open meeting, if all people choose to exercise their right to communicate! This type of communication network is ideal for brainstorming and visualizing a vast number of ideas or options for actions, when the situation is fluid and no single source has predominantly superior feedback to give. When a specific time-bound action based on instructions from some superior source of knowledge or skill is required, this form of network is wasteful and delaying the action in a crisis situation.

A combination of both basic forms is generally used for project communications. In a large project organization, the project manager may communicate through assistant project managers or department heads essentially using a hierarchical network, while the assistant project managers or section heads may have among themselves set up a free flow network. The project life cycle stage would also influence the form of communication network to be chosen. During the early planning phase of the project life cycle, it would be preferable to have the free flow and open communication channels for a large number of ideas and options to emerge for consideration. During the execution and monitoring stage, on the other hand, it would be generally preferable to limit the free communication and adopt some restricted form of communication channels.

2. Written and Verbal Communication

Sometimes, a project manager wonders whether he should use verbal communication or written. The general rule is to use the written mode for all formal documents. They may be in the following forms:

- The technical feasibility and economic viability reports
- The project charter and project scope statement
- The Project Plan (along with its subsidiary plans for cost, time, quality and risk management etc.)
- Project design basis and design reports for infrastructure projects
- Lessons learned reports and quality or cost audits, and
- Monthly status reports

This tradition is probably the reason for the humorous apocryphal saying that, "The weight of the paper work for a construction project equals the weight of the concrete cast!" Written communication is slower, impersonal, and takes effort. However, its merits are that accurate, detailed and well thought out presentation of complex ideas and information can be made and a permanent record of the project events is available for later analysis.

The anecdotal and news-of-the-moment communication should be informal and so preferably, verbal. Where a person-to-person explanation is necessary, verbal communication is, of course, a must. But even when the formal documented communication is used, an informal discussion with the team members or key stakeholders, along with the issue of formal document, lends it a personal touch and helps set up good rapport. Verbal communications are a two-way affair, so the listener has a chance to seek clarifications and receive the full impact of the message conveyed, while the sender can get assurance of message having been properly received and understood. The other obvious advantages of verbal communication (person-to-person talk or telephone calls)are that it takes much less effort and time.

The written communication can be in the form of hard copies of printed/typed reports, e-mails or intra-net transmittals. E-mail has the facility of being a written record and yet to the extent that it is usually some-what informal, sent in a relatively shorter time and with less effort. Intra-net transmittals, especially of project schedule files of large projects are very convenient to use; again they could be updated with small effort and short time.

Ability for effective verbal and written communication is an important part of the skill set desired from a project management professional. So, conscious efforts should be made to hone this skill.

CASE 4.1

Manchester United Soccer Club

Nicolette Larson was loading the dishwasher with her husband, Kevin, and telling him about the first meeting of the Manchester United Tournament Organizing Committee. Nicolette, a self-confessed "soccer mom," had been elected tournament director and was responsible for organizing the club's first summer tournament.

Manchester United Soccer Club (MUSC) located in Manchester, New Hampshire, was formed in 1992 as a way of bringing recreational players to a higher level of competition and preparing them for the State Olympic Development Program and/or high school teams. The club currently has 24 boys and girls (ranging in age from under 9 to 16) on teams affiliated with the Hampshire Soccer Association and the Granite State Girls Soccer League. The club's board of directors decided in the fall to sponsor a summer invitational soc-cer tournament to generate revenue. Given the boom in youth soccer, hosting summer tournaments has become a popular method for raising funds. MUSC teams regularly compete in three to four tournaments each summer at different locales in New England. These tournaments have been reported to generate between $50,000 and $70,000 for the host club.

MUSC needs additional revenue to refurbish and expand the number of soccer fields at the Rock Rimmon soccer complex. Funds would also be used to augment the club's scholarship program, which provides finan-cial aid to players who cannot afford the $450 annual club dues.

Nicolette gave her husband a blow-by-blow account of what transpired during the first tournament com-mittee meeting that night. She started the meeting by having everyone introduce themselves and by pro-claiming how excited she was that the club was going to sponsor its own tournament. She then suggested that the committee brainstorm what needed to be done to pull off the event; she would record their ideas on a flipchart.

What emerged was a free-for-all of ideas and suggestions. One member immediately stressed the impor-tance of having qualified referees and spent several minutes describing in detail how his son's team was robbed in a poorly officiated championship game. This was followed by other stories of injustice on the soccer field. Another member suggested that they needed to quickly contact the local colleges to see if they could use their fields. The committee spent more than 30 minutes talking about how they should screen teams and how much they should charge as an entry fee. An argument broke out over whether they should reward the win-ning teams in each age bracket with medals or trophies. Many members felt that medals were too cheap, while others thought the trophies would be too expensive. Someone suggested that they seek local corporate spon-sors to help fund the tournament. The proposed sale of tournament T-shirts and sweatshirts was followed by a general critique of the different shirts parents had acquired at different tournaments. One member advocated that they recruit an artist he knew to develop a unique silk-screen design for the tournament. The meeting adjourned 30 minutes late with only half of the members remaining until the end. Nicolette drove home with seven sheets of ideas and a headache.

As Kevin poured a glass of water for the two aspirin Nicolette was about to take, he tried to comfort her by saying that organizing this tournament would be a big project not unlike the projects he works on at his engineering and design firm. He offered to sit down with her the next night and help her plan the project. He suggested that the first thing they needed to do was to develop a WBS for the project.

1. Make a list of the major deliverables for the project and use them to develop a draft of the work breakdown structure for the tournament that contains at least three levels of detail. What are the major deliverables associated with hosting an event such as a soccer tournament?
2. How would developing a WBS alleviate some of the problems that occurred during the first meeting and help Nicolette organize and plan the project?
3. Where can Nicolette find additional information to help her develop a WBS for the tournament?
4. How could Nicolette and her task force use the WBS to generate cost estimates for the tournament? Why would this be useful information?

CASE 4.2

Hotel Pulkeshi International
(A Case Focusing on Project Scope Management)

Introduction

Work Breakdown Structure (WBS) is the basic tool for planning the project work. This case focuses on illustrating the technique for preparing WBS by preparation of a WBS for a construction project. The case includes description of the project initiation processes and presents a specimen of the Project Scope Statement modeled on the PMBOK® Guide recommendations. A WBS specimen based on the case details and conforming to the guidelines given in the Practice Standard for Work Breakdown Structure published by PMI is also presented at the end.

How would you describe a luxuriously furnished well-appointed conference room in sylvan surroundings, where you can look out of the French window and see a small man-made lake with some lotus in full bloom and a black swan majestically floating? Most people would be tempted to use the cliché "a Five-Star Facility". But in this case it would be an understatement; it was the Head Office Conference Room of the famous *Coronation Hotels* chain—"Seven Star Facility" would be a more appropriate description.

The centre mahogany table spotlessly polished and with a beautiful 51 candles chandelier overhanging above, was surrounded by plush chairs adequate in number to seat at least 20 people. But there were only five people at the table now. At the head of the table sat Soli Jamashedji, the aging patriarch and founder of the Coronation Hotels chain. In a side chair, slightly drawn away from the table was a young man in his early thirties with rimless glasses, Padmanabhan Iyer or Paddy, as addressed by most people in the organization. He was one of the top graduates of IIM– Ahmedabad, where he had studied after his basic degree in computer science at IIT- Delhi. Soli used to lean a lot on him for business analysis using modern management analytical techniques, particularly in connection with mergers and acquisitions or setting up hotels at new locations. Other three senior officers at the table were Saurav Chakraborti (Director—Marketing), Satpal Singh (Executive Director- Operations) and Manish Shah (Director—Finance).

The principal agenda for the meeting was of taking the decision on the future expansion plans of the Coronation Hotels. After the early pleasantries exchange, Saurav started presenting his findings. He pointed out that, "In view of the increasing emphasis on the development of the tourism industry, the flow of the foreigners and NRIs visiting India in the next five years was expected to increase by 12-15 % per annum between 2005-06 to 2010-11 by the Government of India as well as several independent economic survey institutions. Earlier, most foreign tourists used to limit their itinerary to Delhi, Agra and Taj Mahal, some metropolitan cities (Mumbai, Banglore, Mysore), cave sculptures of Khajuraho or Ajanta-Ellora, tiger sanctuaries of Bandhavgarh or Kanha forest and similar well-trodden tourist circuits. However, recently a trend was noticed that an increasing part of these tourists wanted to go for out of the way or unusual destinations. One such cluster of locations could be in the northern Karanatak region—Badami (the capital of the Chalukya dynasty), Bijapur (famous for Chand Bibi who fought emperor Akabar), Vijayanagar Dynasty's Hampi and even Banglore-Mysore nearby."

Saurav spread out a small map of India and pointed out, " Here; here is Badami—now a small sleeping urban town in North Karnataka, but once the capital of the mighty Chalukya Dynasty king Pulkeshi-II, who stopped the emperor Harsh Vardhan's mighty and victorious army on the banks of river Narmada ... and .." Before he could complete, Manish stopped him with a friendly banter, "Yes, yes Saurav; we got your point. You suggest that we sat up a new hotel nearby? What capacity? What investment? Any preliminary market survey of likely occupancy figures? Apparently, this location would be of interest to the history buffs; so, are there any other well-known or interesting historical sites nearby? How far and convenient to visit Badami from the nearest airport?"

Saurav looked back disapprovingly but quietly continued, "Patience, Manish! We have done the preliminary market survey, investment and feasibility analysis in our group and the site looks very promising. Mr. Jamashedji is aware of all this. Now is the time to do some hard nose assessment and even some detailed planning if we generally agree on the proposal". Satpal Singh chipped in, "Yes, we have also been receivi inquiries from our patrons at Banglore and Mysore hotels, if they could go to and stay at one of our hotels iii Bijapur or Badami; so it may be worth a detailed study".

"O.K. fellows; looks like a good starting point", Jamshedji concluded and then he looked at Paddy and said, " Paddy, start working and get all the details and have all the dope on the proposal for us to take the decision in the next operating committee meeting six weeks from now". The discussion in the meeting shifted to other subjects.

Paddy had under his command Strategic Planning Group, a crack core team of 10 brilliant executives—accountants, engineers, and market research personnel. The team collected the necessary data and prepared the base case feasibility report. They also carried out risk analysis and ran some computer simulation based on it (Jamashedji always chided Paddy by remarking whether the computer simulation analytical tool, *Monte Carlo Analysis*, was named so as an implied admission of the gambling nature of the analysis). *Sensitivity Analysis* was carried out for determining the effect on the profitability of the new venture if the real life scenario in future turned out different from the base case assumptions. They also studied the hotel capacity expansion in phases and carried out the *Decision Tree Analysis* to arrive at the optimum hotel room capacity for the first phase – 100 rooms. Paddy's team found that the new hotel location in vicinity of Badami would be an attractive investment proposition. Paddy christened the project *Hotel Pulkeshi International* after the famous Chalukya dynasty emperor.

At the next operating committee meeting, Paddy presented the brief technical details of the project (likely optional locations, an architect's impressions of the hotel, general floor lay outs, land and site development cost, construction and furnishing costs, etc.) and the financial projections worked out by his team in cooperation with the finance group (projections of the next five years likely operating results in terms of occupancy, operating cost and profitability and the net cash flows).

Jamashedji felt pleased with the way Paddy and his group worked out the data for decision making. After some discussions on the project assumptions and the working paper details underlying the summery, the committee gave a green signal for going ahead. "Then gentlemen, we agree to go ahead with Hotel Pulkeshi International project at Badami, right? Satpal, you pick out a good project manager for this project, and get him started working on the project". Then after a pause of half a minute, he added, with a wink in his eye, "But before that, Paddy, you prepare the Project Charter and Project Scope Statement like that bald professor of project management used to harp on in the 1-day project management seminar you insisted on me to attend last month". Everybody thought it was a joke and started to smile, when Jamashedji added, "No, I am serious; what he said makes sense".

Attachment 1 shows the Project Scope Statement prepared by Paddy's strategic planning group.

Satpal Singh zeroed in on Ram Prasad as the project manager to be appointed for Hotel Pulkeshi International. Ram Prasad was also an IIT-Kanpur trained civil engineer, who had joined the Coronation Hotels group seven years back. He had an impressive track record of efficient management of civil construction projects before he joined the Coronation Group. In Coronation, he got gradually involved with the entire gamut of the hotel projects and the last project, *Hotel Sabaramati*, which was managed under his independent command, earned him good reputation. There was some unspoken rivalry between Ram Prasad and Paddy. Ram Prasad looked upon numbers churning office engineers as something amiss of their basic profession. Paddy thought that the real business of business was after all the bottom line of the entire operations. Paddy had some latent contempt for these hard core engineering people. Satpal Singh was somewhat aware of this and decided to exploit the situation for effective management of project Hotel Pulkeshi Iternational.

"Ram, we are happy to select you to be the project manager for our newest hotel project, *Hotel Pulkeshi Iternational*", Satpal told him, "Here are the market research and project feasibility study data for the project to give you a grounding in the overall strategy." Then he pulled out another set of file papers from his folder and said, "These papers contain the Project Charter and Project Scope Statement prepared by the Strategic Planning Group—your good friend Paddy. Paddy appears to nurse the grouse that we engineers are not focused on the overall project objectives and get lost among the trees and miss the forest. I want you to show him what we actually accomplish in bricks and mortars and not just paper projects. But I also want to show that you could be as systematic in your project planning as he himself could ever hope to be. Get the point? Start with preparing a systematic Work Breakdown Structure (WBS) for the project. I understand that is the cornerstone in the modern project management planning. Let us discuss it on Monday two weeks from now", then he looked at the calendar and added, "December 19, 3 PM; fine? Anything you want in terms of resources just let me know and you would have them".

Ram Prasad came back to his room and worked day and night with his core project team of seven people (one architect and landscape designer, two civil engineers, one mechanical/utility engineer, one electrical engineer, one accounts manager, one interior designer). He prepared the overall project management plan and an impressive WBS using the guidelines given in the *Practice Standard for **Work Breakdown Structure*** published by the Project Management Institute (PMI), USA as shown in **Attactment 2**.

ATTACHMENT 1

Project Scope Statement
(Hotel Pulkeshi International)

The Coronation Hotels Group proposes to set up a new hotel in the vicinity of Badami, Karnataka State. The broad parameters of the scope of this project are given below:

The facilities shall conform to the construction, layout, furnishing, and operating standards currently followed at all other Coronation Group locations and would permit the new facility to be classified as a Five Star Facility according to the International Hotel Management Association guidelines.

1. Project Objectives

The project objectives are to set up a new 100-rooms capacity 5-star hotel in the vicinity of Badami, Karnataka

- To take advantage of the niche group of foreign tourists to southern India
- To maintain Coronation's market share among the premier hotel accommodations, and
- To earn a net return of 20 % per annum on equity investment

2. General Description of Facilities

The facilities should conform to the following general requirements:

- The overall layout, the architecture and landscaping of the entire facility should be spacious and give an impression of a luxury five star hotel. The master plan should include a provision for the expansion of the facility to a total 500 rooms hotel in future.
- The initial capacity of the hotel would be 100 air conditioned fully carpeted guest rooms, each with facility for 2 guests accommodation. The rooms shall be furnished according to current Coronation Group hotels standard and should include suitable number of single or double beds, a writing table, two sofa chairs with a small service table, a small fridge, a TV set, outlets for intercom and outside phones, an outlet for internet connection for lap-top computers, and other usual amenities.
- Hotel should include three restaurants serving Indian, western and Chinese cuisine; a coffee shop, a bar and a central kitchen for giving room service to guests.
- A swimming pool and gym facilities for guests.
- Two large halls suitable for assembly of 150-200 persons for use in case of some prestigious occasions or receptions.
- Four small conference rooms with capacities to accommodate 20 to 35 guests for company meetings or conferences.
- Other facilities like a medicines shop, souvenirs and personal needs shop and several shops to be given on a franchise basis to outsiders to set up arts, sculptures, novelties, fancy textiles shops and the like.

This description of facilities is not exhaustive and will need to be reviewed and planned during the detailed planning stage.

3. Project Assumptions

The basic assumptions for success in meeting project objectives are as follows:

1. The company board formally approves the project latest by January 31, 2007.
2. The statutory approvals necessary for setting up the hotel are received by March 31, 2007.
3. Preliminary funding arrangements are in place for the project cash outflows to begi3n latest by June 1, 2007.
4. The foreign tourist flow and its niche clientele composition materializes as per current projections
5. The occupancy rates of minimum 70 % during the off seasons and full occupancy during the peak periods are maintained.
6. The key persons for the project team are assigned to the project by March 31, 2007.

4. Project Deliverables

The first level project deliverables are:

- Acquisition of land, site development and landscaping
- Necessary statutory approvals for starting the project and on an ongoing basis as needed
- Construction of buildings and structures
- Setting up utilities facilities (water, electricity, firefighting, etc.)
- Furnishing; Main furniture hardware and soft furnishing
- Recruitment and training of staff
- Preliminary marketing
- Project management for on-time and within-budget completion of the project deliverables to meet the project satisfaction criteria

5. Preliminary Project Schedule

Assuming that the basic statutory approvals and financing arrangements are in place for the project construction to start by June 2007, the following milestones are envisaged:

Site selection and acquisition	August 31, 2007
Detailed planning of the facility	September 30, 2007
Award of civil construction contract	October 15, 2007
Start of civil construction at the site	November 1, 2007
Completion of basic buildings and structures	September 30, 2008
Final finishing and furnishing	November 30, 2008
Recruitment of new key staff and training completion	December 15, 2008
Functionally complete in operation to serve guests	January 1, 2009

6. Preliminary Cost Estimate

The preliminary cost estimate for the project is Rs 145 crores as follows:

		(Rs in crores)
Land & site development		12.00
Buildings, Structures & Furnishings		
Civil construction	45.00	
Utilities & facilities	15.00	
Furnishings	38.00	
Landscape & gardens	2.00	100.00
Preliminary & pre-operative expenses		18.00
Provision for contingency (@ 10 %, rounded up)		15.00
Total Project Cost		**Rs 145.00 crores**

ATTACHMENT 2

Work Breakdown Structure (WBS)
(Hotel Pulkeshi Iternational)

1. Confirm needs analysis and refine project planning

1.1 Confirm the needs for service
1.2 Confirm the market size, quality of service and hotel capacity
1.3 Verify the project assumptions
1.4 Prepare refined cost estimate for the project and check with the preliminary cost estimate
1.5 Prepare preliminary schedule and check its compatibility with the expected completion
1.6 Verify the cash flow and project feasibility assumptions
1.7 Prepare detailed project management plan

2. Acquire land, carry out site development and landscaping

2.1 Evaluate available sites and select the site
2.2 Negotiate land acquisition with the suppliers and purchase land
2.3 Carry out land survey and load bearing tests for soil
2.4 Carry our site development activities
    2.4.1 Construct approach roads
    2.4.2 Construct boundary wall or fence
    2.4.3 Start overall leveling and fine leveling of the main hotel building area
    2.4.4 Arrange for water supply and electricity
    2.4.5 Plant trees near the outskirts or clear areas

3. Obtain necessary statutory approvals (for project start and on-going basis)

3.1 Receive approval for building construction plan
3.2 Receive electricity supply related approvals
    3.2.1 Load sanction and initial connection
    3.2.2 Electricity Inspectorate – approval after construction inspection
3.3 Receive approvals from water supply authority
    3.3. 1 Load sanction and initial connection
    3.4 Receive drainage and effluents connection approvals
    3.5 Receive building completion certificate and occupancy certificate

4. Prepare Master Plan for the premises

4.1 Select and appoint architect
4.2 Prepare the master plan for property development (incl. future expansion)

5. Prepare building construction plans

5.1 Prepare overall floor-wise hotel layout plans

    5.2 Prepare detailed civil engineering designs

        5.2.1 Columns and plinth beams layout and sizing

        5.2.2 Slab designs

        5.2.3 Construction details for lintels, staircase, walls, windows and doors

        5.2.4. Colour scheme and finishes

        5.2.5 Specifications for flooring, fittings and fixtures

    5.3 Prepare water piping and drainage piping plans

    5.4 Prepare electrical cables layouts

    5.5 Prepare fire escapes and sprinkler layout plans

    5.6 Prepare air conditioning scheme and ducting layouts

    5.6 Prepare telephone and intercom network layouts

6. Carry out construction activities at the site

    6.1 Select road construction contractor and construct internal roads

    6.2 Construct the main building

        6.2.1 Select the prime contractor for all construction work (civil engineering, electrical, water & drainage, air conditioning, telephones, fire fighting systems, etc.)

        6.2.2 Construct RCC structure (columns, beams, slabs, walls, windows)

        6.2.3 Install electric cabling

        6.2.4 Install water & drainage piping

        6.2.5 Install central ac equipment and distribution ducting

        6.2.6 Install telephone network lines

        6.2.7 Install sprinklers and fire safety equipment

        6.2.8 Finish flooring, ceiling and painting

    6.3 Construct ancillary buildings

    6.4 Complete landscaping, plant shrubs, bushes and lawns

7. Furnish the hotel facilities

    7.1 Prepare the Master Plan for interior decoration

    7.2 Install entrance lobby and floor lobbies furniture

    7.3 Install room furniture – beds, sofas, tables, fridges, etc.

    7.4 Install soft furniture – curtains, mattresses, art works frames, etc.

8. Recruit and train staff

    8.1 Get key and supervisory staff assigned from other operating locations

    8.2 Recruit other supervisory staff and train

    8.3 Recruit daily operating workers and train

9 Manage project effectively and efficiently

    9.1 Acquire project team, communicate the overall scheme and start project work

    9.2 Prepare detailed cost estimate and month-wise budget for cash out-flows

    9.3 Prepare detailed project activities network and project schedule using MS Projects

    9.4 Prepare detailed communication plan.

9.5 Execute, monitor & control the project activities according to project management plan

9.6 Close the contracts

10. Preliminary commercial activities

10.1 Keep the central marketing group informed of the project progress

10.2 Invite the Chairman Soli Jamashedji, Executive Director Satpal Singh, other directors and Karnataka Tourism Development Minister for hotel inauguration

CASE 4.3

Process Development at Union Chemicals
(A Case Study Focusing on Project Communication Management)

Introduction

The project success, no doubt, requires effectively managing the core project management issues of scope, time, cost and quality. In the midst of hectic project activities, a hard working, conscientious project manager might some time neglect paying attention to the soft skills of project management viz. interpersonal skills in leading and managing the team, conflict management, negotiation, and managing project communication for key stakeholders. This case study focuses on a project communication management and especially on the importance of managing the communication needs of the key stakeholders for project success. Failing to manage the communication needs of the key stakeholders, the project manager in the case, though successful in addressing all key project objectives, is forced to quit disgraced.

It was Monday, February 1. The siren blew at 5-30 pm and within only a few minutes the staff bus of Union Chemicals started getting filled up with the middle level staff entitled to travel by the company bus. Girish Pandya also stepped in and without exchanging any pleasantry with the colleagues already sitting in the bus, he headed straight to the back corner seat and buried his head in the current copy of the Time magazine.

Hey Girish, after a long many months, I found you quitting the work on time and coming with us plebeians in this bus. Why, you have already solved all problems of the high pressure alpha-naphthol process or what?" Patankar chided Girish while sliding into the next seat in the bus. "Leave me alone, Sidh! I am really dead tired to-day." said Girish. Though he continued to bury his head into the open pages of the magazine, Girish's mind was not there. He was pondering over how the project to develop new process for manufacture of alpha-naphthol ran the course in the last five months.

History

Girish Pandya was a mechanical engineer with a reasonably bright academic career and had proved a competent shift-in-charge for one of the production departments at Union Chemical's plant. His real strength, however, was his ability think out of the box and the sound grasp of fundamental engineering principles—"engineering fundas" as the students' jargon referred to them. This enabled him to come out now and then with an altogether unconventional solution to production problems, which came up from time to time in the production department and baffled the group.

Union Chemicals was a subsidiary of a U.K. based large multinational company of the same name, with the parent organization having a noteworthy presence in the U.K. The UK Company had been manufacturing and marketing a number of specialty chemicals in the UK. Some of the chemicals, which fell out of favour with the UK parent company due to the concerns raised by the environmentalists and the Green Brigade, were licensed to the Indian subsidiary for manufacture in India and distribution world-wide—especially to south-east Asian countries.

Indian subsidiary of Union Chemicals remained a routine manufacturing operation for a number of chemicals. With the globalization trend, the parent company decided on the strategy of trying to exploit the opportunity of availability of competent low cost technical personnel in India to shift a part of its research effort to India. A well-equipped laboratory for such research effort and development department to build and operate pilot plants was set up for development of a new process or trying out important modifications in a process step in an already commercially established process. These two departments, staffed with academically high-flying PhDs in chemistry or chemical engineering, soon occupied the position of the blue-eyed boys of the top management. Dr. Arnav Patel headed this departmental group. Raman Shah headed four production departments at the plant, each department concerned with one specific chemical. There was an understandable rivalry between Dr. Patel and Mr. Shah, and Dr. Patel had started to edge out Raman Shah.

Selection of the Project Manager

In later part of 2003, there was a buzz that the UK company had landed a big process research contract and that Union Chemical's Indian operations may be given a piece of the cake. Every one had thought that the assignment will be passed on to Dr. Arnav Patel's group and he would sprint ahead in the race to be the next CEO of Union Chemical's India operations.

On September 18, 2003, Raman Shah called Girish into his office just around 5:20 PM. Girish's first reaction was to get upset at the prospect of missing his regular staff bus travel to home and his impatience showed through his body language. The seasoned manager, that Raman Shah was, did not miss the signal. "Girish, I have called you for something very important. You can afford to miss your staff bus travel today, but you dare not miss the bus of opportunity I want to talk to you about. Our parent company has passed on a part of the high-pressure alpha-naphthol process research project to us in India—**under my charge**. We need to set up a small pilot plant based on the preliminary chemical process information developed by the head office R & D group. I want you to head that pilot plant effort!"

"But why not Dr. Arnav Patel's group? They have some good Ph.Ds strutting around. And, then of all the people, why me? I haven't got even a Master's degree – I am just a graduate mechanical engineer, not even a chemist!" blurted Girish unbelieving of the great opportunity, which appeared to knock at his door – the opportunity, which he had not even dared to dream.

"Good questions, Girish. I like your practical no-nonsense approach. In fact, that is precisely why I want to choose you for heading the effort. You are highly creative and you have sound knowledge of engineering fundamentals; I have personally seen it in working. The new process for alpha-naphthol will require very high-pressure reaction and separation process steps and so your creativity and sound engineering will be a real asset. And why our department? Because, we do make another naphthalene based intermediate and so our production department has a group of persons quite familiar with the basic raw material. Since you mentioned, let me share with you, off the records of course, my personal opinion of those chemistry PhDs of Arnav, they are just good at mixing colored solutions in the test tubes—nothing more. Our head office has also found out that they usually have no clue about the engineering aspects of a commercial production process for a chemical plant. That's why they want me to take the lead on this. It will be my baby! The project will be a feather in my cap!", Raman would not miss an opportunity to express his low opinion of the work Dr.

Arnav Patel and his group did. Then he continued, "And now let me tell you, what's in it for you. Well, if you can swing this process development work, you will be department head jumping four of your seniors in the queue. I have great confidence in your ability to deliver the results. For the time being, you will work at your current level only till the process development succeeds and work very hard, say 14 hours a day, but the opportunity is really big if you make it. " Girish did not have to think very long to accept the offer, though he asked for a week's time for thinking over in that evening meeting.

The Project Start

Like proverbial true love, the path of a project is also not strewn with roses.

The first obstacle that Girish faced was getting the sanction for the resources for setting up the pilot plant. For setting up a small pilot plant would require first understanding the basic chemistry of the laboratory scale process developed by the head office. The next step would be to prepare designs of the pilot plant equipment and prepare detailed engineering specifications for procurement. Procuring the equipment, installing them, carrying out trial runs and making suitable modifications in the equipment and processing steps based on trial results were the next project phases. After staying back at the plant and working very late evenings for a whole week, Girish came up with the basic pilot plant scheme and the cost of setting up the project.

"The project will cost Rs 6.5 millions and take 6 months", Girish announced the next week Monday morning to Raman.

"What? Rs 5 million are the budget sanctioned by the head office. We have to keep project cost within it. And we have to also complete it within 4 months." Raman almost shouted, though in fact the head office had given the outer limit for this work to be 6 months.

Girish leafed back and forth his sheaf of papers with detailed list of items and cost and started to explain his cost estimate basis. Raman just waved him aside and said, "Forget those numbers. Rework them and bring the project cost to total Rs 4.9 millions. We must meet HO project cost expectations to start with. If the project succeeds, we will run the overrun request after the project completion - nobody will grudge it then."

"But, sir, ... " Girish stuttered.

"Do as I say. If you want to be all that truthful and accurate, forget the assignment. I can pull out some other, even more senior engineer, for this assignment."

Girish did not have much choice except to follow Raman's instructions.

Project Execution

Selecting the project team was the next hurdle. The project would require as team members an engineer from the design and drafting department, an engineer for procurement and a chemist for testing the raw materials, in-process streams and final product. " I will get you Shashi Rana from the Materials Department and Sudhakar Joshi from Engineering & Design Department to work with you. At the end of six weeks, we have to submit the first interim report of the project status to HO; Mr. Williams, the Process Development-Head at HO will himself be in the video conference meeting to discuss the report; so just get on the work as fast as you can."

Shashi Rana was a young but very promising engineer and Girish and Shashi started to work on the equipment procurement in real earnest. The process required a high temperature hydrolysis reaction (at over 220 degrees C) in an aqueous medium. The corrosive nature of the reactants and high pressure requirements called for a special metering pump built with stainless steel 316 L. The reactor and some pipe fittings also required to be special – and not off the shelf items. Shashi and Girish started a close follow up with the vendors for the special items – discussing and clearing the technical difficulties that vendors brought up from time to time and visiting the shops for inspection and first-hand information.

All this kept Girish so busy that his interim report at the end of the six weeks was merely 2 pages long. HO had expected a much more elaborate submission from the Indian subsidiary and may be referrals to them for some help or clarifications all along in the 6-week period! Since Girish did not contact HO, Mr. Williams himself started calling India to talk with the project manager and most of the times, he was told that Girish was visiting the vendor's shop or in the Engineering & Design Department reviewing the drawings. Mr. Williams expressed his displeasure to Raman Shah.

Raman Shah called Girish to his office. Girish was full of enthusiasm for the headway he could make in engineering design and procurement in spite of the heavy odds. Raman Shah threw cold water on his enthusiasm. "What a 2-page rag sheets-like report you submitted for 6-weeks status report! Mr. Williams was furious. He also said you were never available, whenever he called you."

"I and Shashi were at the vendor's shops to test out the components of the metering pump, so that it would surely work... "

"Your job as a project manager is to manage the project—not to test the components. Weren't you telling me that at the project management program, you recently took at that institution, they stressed on the importance of project communication—especially managing the communication needs of the key stakeholders and all that? HO and Mr. Williams are our key stakeholders for the project-understand? Write out a detailed report now ... preferably before the end of the next week. Submit with an explanation that for some unforeseen problems, you could not submit your formal 6-week report on time, so you chose to send a short interim report to meet dead line. The video conference meeting will follow it in 2-day."

For all the hard work he had done for the past six weeks and the promise for success, which it showed, this was a bitter pill to swallow for Girish. His 2-page report, if anybody had read closely, would have earned him kudos for the extraordinary work he and his team had put. The HO and Raman merely wanted reams of papers rather than concrete results, he felt. For the whole next week, Girish sat at his desk and drafted and redrafted report parts with elaborate tables and graphs, paying attention to the report language, report format and fonts and colour scheme of the graphs! The final 70-page report looked beautiful and for that very reason, Girish hated it and himself for being forced to spend time in so unproductive activities.

But Girish's troubles were not over. HO went over the report with a fine comb and had several queries based on the reading. The e-mails between HO and Girish started crossing the continents faster and more furious than ever, when finally Mr. Williams again called Raman Shah and explained that he was quite unhappy with the way the project was managed and he would have to consider sending his engineer, Dr. Rudolph, to India to oversee Girish's work, if the situation does not improve soon.

In the mean time, Girish's problems with his other senior colleagues at the plant also multiplied. The Materials Department Head complained to Raman Shah that Girish had started overloading Shashi Rana so much with this project work that she was unable to manage her other assignments in the department. "Besides, I have no clue about what Girish and Shashi are doing. If it is that entire important and prestigious project, why am I not in the list of project report recipients? Girish has never even dropped in my office and let me know what is happening in the project or how our department can contribute". So, this was what really hurt the Materials Department Head. "I would have to ask Shashi to pay attention to other projects." He warned.

The Head of Design & Engineering Department was also equally upset about his being in the dark. He told Raman Shah, "Raman, Girish is doing some design & engineering work on that high pressure hydrolysis process. I had worked on similar two process designs earlier. I could have given him some really useful tips on the design and engineering specifications for the components. Girish never even talked with me. He just sits with Sudhakar Joshi, calculates design parameters, prepares some sketches and specifications and runs around. If the things don't work, Girish will blame Sudhakar and CEO will blame me why I did not intervene and help."

Raman gave some lame excuses, but he himself really had not detailed up-to-date information on the project. So, what could he share with the Head of Engineering & Design?

In the mean time, six more weeks passed and all the equipment and components arrived at the site. Begging the maintenance mechanical and electrical supervisors, Girish got them installed even though some work overflowed into the week-ends requiring overtime – just as a personal favour to himself. The time came for submission of the second status report. Girish now had to take papers home and work late till early morning three days in a row. His wife remarked, "In the last three months, you have not been at home for more than a few hours to eat and sleep. You haven't got a decent raise in the last three years, so what is all this hard work for? " Girish could not explain her the reality he faced; he just stood silent and looked down to avoid her accusing gaze.

Finally the report was ready and it included good news if some one could really read and understand it rather than flip over it. Girish, however, was not lucky in this respect. Raman Shah remarked, "You appear to go out even beyond your own project cost estimate. I won't be able to explain such huge overruns on project cost". CEO passed on to Dr.Arnav Patel a copy of the report for review. He remarked, "Looks like not meticulously designed set of experiments. You see, if Girish had contacted me earlier, I would have helped him with a much better and more economical experiments set using the principles of Design of Experiments (DOE)." But Dr. Ramanathan, in charge of testing laboratory, was some what more kind," Get done with whatever tests you want during regular working hours; no overtime or week-ends, please." Girish again had to use his personal relationships with Dr. Ramanathan's staff and actually got testing done, even during week-ends when necessary, to expedite the project.

The first results, though promising, were not adequate for finalizing the design parameters for a commercial process. The main reaction was good, but some side- reactions also occurred, which reduced the overall yield to 84 %. At the same time, the product purity was 97.2 %. A minimum yield of 90 % and product purity of 98.5% were necessary for process commercialization. Girish went through with redesign of some components to permit the operating conditions for a 10 degrees higher temperature and 150 psi higher pressure. By the end of 16 weeks, the redesigned set up was ready for the next set of trial runs. This was when the four months project schedule conveyed by Girish to HO at the start of the project was to come to a close. Mr. Williams was furiously looking for some final results and report as promise by the Indian subsidiary. He decided that the time had come for his more active intervention.

He summoned Raman Shah, "Look Raman, you have let us down badly. You don't realize but the process development part the India Company is working on, is only a small miniscule part. Not even the tip of the iceberg. We cannot allow India Company to jeopardize our multi-million pounds research project contract. I am sending Dr. Rudolph to India; he will be there on February 1. Mind well, it is not too soon; it would be fifteen days beyond the deadline you yourself had scheduled!"

Girish did not see the Republic Day parade on TV on the national holiday. He was doing the final test run on the modified pilot plant. Shashi Rana and Sudhakar Joshi were also there. The test appeared to run quite well and the laboratory results and analysis would be over by January 29. Mahatma Gandhi Assassination Day, January 30, was observed as a holiday at the plant. Girish was at home—the very first time at home in the last five months. He was dead tired—every bone in his body ached; every nerve in his mind had gone numb. The first phone call he received that day was from Raman Shah. " Dr. Rudolph will reach here day after tomorrow. Are you ready with all the briefings for him? We have already missed the 4-month project schedule dead line. We also would not be able to hide that the project will have large cost overruns. You better prepare some good briefing to win him over. " The next call he received was from Shashi Rana, " Hey, you are at home? I thought you would also be with us at the laboratory. You should be right here at the plant for celebration! Our last trial run is successful beyond our imagination. We got 98.7 % product purity at 91.3 % yield. Did you hear? **98.7 % product purity at 91.3 % yield**! " The third call was again from Raman Shah,

"By the way, Girish, who have you arranged to go and receive Dr. Rudolph at the airport? And what about booking his accommodation at Taj Intercontinental Hotel? I hope, you would personally go there. You are quite negligent in dealing with some of these crucial issues".

Girish sat stunned after Shah's call. The entire five months period passed in front of his eyes like a review. He had worked night and day and offered blood and sweat for making the project a success. Now, how will HO hierarchy see it? Dr. Rudolph visited India and straightened out the pilot plant project! Yes! very timely intervention by Dr. Williams of HO, who kept a hawk-eye on the entire project. Excellent cooperation and coordination by India plant, particularly Raman Shah! Forget the Head Office, even his own superior here in the India plant, Raman Shah, did not realize the pains we took to succeed. And while doing the project work, he had surely not made friends with other senior department heads in the plant, nor the seniors in own department. It was a desperate situation. He had to move out. He decided, "there is no future for me to continue working here now."

He sat deeply immersed in himself for good one hour. Then he moved over to the phone, dialed Raman Shah and started speaking in as calm a voice as he could keep, "Sir, please arrange for some one else to receive Dr. Rudolph. In fact, please ask some one else to take charge of whatever is left in the project from now onwards. After all, as you explained me on the first day, the project is 'your baby' and 'the feather in your cap'. By the way, the second set of trial runs have succeeded and we could get yield and purity required—Shashi told me on the phone- so my conscience is clear about meeting my commitments. I would hand over my resignation the first thing on the February, 1, morning". Then, without waiting to listen to the response, he put the phone down.

Epilogue

Union Chemicals, UK, made a grand success of the research project contract and the contribution from the Indian subsidiary in working on a critical research component was not lost sight of. Raman Shah was promoted as the next CEO of Union Chemicals, India.

Questions for Case Discussion

1. In your opinion,
   - Did the project succeed?
   - Did Girish Pandya succeed as a Project Manager?
2. Using the background of this case, discuss the project communication management and its importance in successful project management.
3. PMBOK lists 5 processes in project communication management:
   - Identify Stakeholders
   - Plan Communications
   - Distribute Information
   - Report Performance and
   - Manage Stakeholders
4. Discuss Girish Pandya's project communication management in context of the above processes.

CHAPTER 5

Estimating Project Times and Costs

Project estimation is indeed a yardstick for project cost control. And if the yardstick is faulty, you start on the "wrong foot." . . . we exhort you not to underestimate the estimate.*

Given the urgency to start work on the project, managers sometimes minimize or avoid the effort to follow through on estimating project time and cost. This attitude is a huge mistake and costly. There are important reasons to make the effort and incur the cost of estimating for your project. Exhibit 5.1 summarizes some key reasons.

EXHIBIT 5.1 Why Estimating Time and Cost Are Important

- Estimates are needed to support good decisions.
- Estimates are needed to schedule work.
- Estimates are needed to determine how long the project should take and its cost.
- Estimates are needed to determine whether the project is worth doing.
- Estimates are needed to develop cash flow needs.
- Estimates are needed to determine how well the project is progressing.
- Estimates are needed to develop time-phased budgets and establish the project baseline.

Estimating is the process of forecasting or approximating the time and cost of completing project deliverables. Estimating processes are frequently classified as top-down and bottom-up. Top-down estimates are usually done by senior management. Management will often derive estimates from analogy, group consensus, or mathematical relationships. Bottom-up estimates are typically performed by the people who are doing the work. Their estimates are based on estimates of elements found in the work breakdown structure.

All project stakeholders prefer accurate cost and time estimates, but they also understand the inherent uncertainty in all projects. Inaccurate estimates lead to false expectations and consumer dissatisfaction. Accuracy is improved with greater effort, but is it worth the time and cost—estimating costs money! Project estimating becomes a trade-off, balancing the benefits of better accuracy against the costs for securing increased accuracy.

Cost, time, and budget estimates are the lifeline for control; they serve as the standard for comparison of actual and plan throughout the life of the project. Project status reports depend on reliable estimates as the

---

* O. P. Kharbanda and J. K. Pinto, *What Made Gertie Gallop: Learning from Project Failures* (New York: Von Nostrand Reinhold, 1996), p. 73.

major input for measuring variances and taking corrective action. Ideally, the project manager, and in most cases the customer, would prefer to have a database of detailed schedule and cost estimates for every work package in the project. Regrettably, such detailed data gathering is not always possible or practical and other methods are used to develop project estimates.

Factors Influencing the Quality of Estimates

A typical statement in the field is the desire to "have a 95 percent probability of meeting time and cost estimates." *Past experience* is a good starting point for developing time and cost estimates. But past experience estimates must almost always be refined by other considerations to reach the 95 percent probability level. Factors related to the uniqueness of the project will have a strong influence on the accuracy of estimates. Project, people, and external factors all need to be considered to improve quality of estimates for project times and costs.

Planning Horizon

The quality of the estimate depends on the *planning horizon;* estimates of current events are close to 100 percent accurate but are reduced for more distant events. The accuracy of time and cost estimates should improve as you move from the conceptual phase to the point where individual work packages are defined.

Project Duration

Time to implement new *technology* has a habit of expanding in an increasing, nonlinear fashion. Sometimes poorly written scope specifications for new technology result in errors in estimating times and costs. Long-duration projects increase the uncertainty in estimates.

People

The *people* factor can also introduce errors in estimating times and cost. For example, accuracy of estimates depends on the skills of the people making the estimates. A close match of people skills to the task will influence productivity and learning time. Similarly, whether members of the project team have worked together before on similar projects will influence the time it takes to coalesce into an effective team. Sometimes factors such as staff turnover can influence estimates. It should be noted that adding new people to a project increases time spent communicating. Typically, people have only five to six productive hours available for each working day; the other hours are taken up with indirect work, such as meetings, paperwork, answering e-mail.

Project Structure and Organization

Which *project structure* is chosen to manage the project will influence time and cost estimates. One of the major advantages of a dedicated project team discussed earlier is the speed gained from concentrated focus and localized project decisions. This speed comes at an additional cost of tying up personnel full time. Conversely, projects operating in a matrix environment may reduce costs by more efficiently sharing personnel across projects but may take longer to complete since attention is divided and coordination demands are higher.

Padding Estimates

In some cases people are inclined to *pad estimates.* For example, if you are asked how long it takes you to drive to the airport, you might give an average time of 30 minutes, assuming a 50/50 chance of getting there in 30 minutes. If you are asked the fastest you could possibly get there, you might reduce the driving time to 20 minutes. Finally, if you are asked how long the drive would take if you absolutely had to be there to meet with the president, it is likely you would increase the estimate to say 50 minutes to ensure not being late. In work situations where you are asked for time and cost estimates, most of us are inclined to add a little padding to increase the probability and reduce the risk of being late. If everyone at all levels of the project adds a little padding to reduce risk, the project duration and cost are seriously overstated. This phenomenon causes some managers or owners to call for a 10–15 percent cut in time and/or cost for the project. Of course the next time the game is played, the person estimating cost and/or time will pad the estimate to 20 percent or more. Clearly such games defeat chances for realistic estimates, which is what is needed to be competitive.

Organization Culture

Organization culture can significantly influence project estimates. In some organizations padding estimates is tolerated and even privately encouraged. Other organizations place a premium on accuracy and strongly discourage estimating gamesmanship. Organizations vary in the importance they attach to estimates. The prevailing belief in some organizations is that detailed estimating takes too much time and is not worth the effort or that it's impossible to predict the future. Other organizations subscribe to the belief that accurate estimates are the bedrock of effective project management. Organization culture shapes every dimension of project management; estimating is not immune to this influence.

Other Factors

Finally, *nonproject factors* can impact time and cost estimates. For example, equipment downtime can alter time estimates. National holidays, vacations, and legal limits can influence project estimates. Project priority can influence resource assignment and impact time and cost.

Project estimating is a complex process. The quality of time and cost estimates can be improved when these variables are considered in making the estimates. Estimates of time and cost together allow the manager to develop a time-phased budget, which is imperative for project control. Before discussing macro and micro estimating methods for times and costs, a review of estimating guidelines will remind us of some of the important "rules of the game" that can improve estimating.

Estimating Guidelines for Times, Costs, and Resources

Managers recognize time, cost, and resource estimates must be accurate if project planning, scheduling, and controlling are to be effective. However, there is substantial evidence suggesting poor estimates are a major contributor to projects that have failed. Therefore, every effort should be made to see that initial estimates are as accurate as possible since the choice of no estimates leaves a great deal to luck and is not palatable to serious project managers. Even though a project has never been done before, a manager can follow seven guidelines to develop useful work package estimates.

1. **Responsibility.** At the work package level, estimates should be made by the person(s) most familiar with the task. Draw on their expertise! Except for supertechnical tasks, those responsible for getting the job done on schedule and within budget are usually first-line supervisors or technicians who are experienced and familiar with the type of work involved. These people will not have some preconceived, imposed duration for a deliverable in mind. They will give an estimate based on experience and best judgment. A secondary benefit of using those responsible is the hope they will "buy in" to seeing that the estimate materializes when they implement the work package. If those involved are not consulted, it

will be difficult to hold them responsible for failure to achieve the estimated time. Finally, drawing on the expertise of team members who will be responsible helps to build communication channels early.

2. **Use several people to estimate.** It is well known that a cost or time estimate usually has a better chance of being reasonable and realistic when several people with relevant experience and/or knowledge of the task are used. True, people bring different biases based on their experience. But discussion of the individual differences in their estimate leads to consensus and tends to eliminate extreme estimate errors. This approach is similar to the Delphi estimating method, which can also be used.

3. **Normal conditions.** When task time, cost, and resource estimates are determined, they are based on certain assumptions. *Estimates should be based on normal conditions, efficient methods, and a normal level of resources.* Normal conditions are sometimes difficult to discern, but it is necessary to have a consensus in the organization as to what normal conditions mean in this project. If the normal workday is eight hours, the time estimate should be based on an eight-hour day. Similarly, if the normal workday is two shifts, the time estimate should be based on a two-shift workday. Any time estimate should reflect efficient methods for the resources normally available. The time estimate should represent the normal level of resources—people or equipment. For example, if three programmers are available for coding or two road graders are available for road construction, time and cost estimates should be based on these normal levels of resources unless it is anticipated the project will change what is currently viewed as "normal." In addition, possible conflicts in demand for resources on parallel or concurrent activities should not be considered at this stage. The need for adding resources will be examined when resource scheduling is discussed in a later chapter.

4. **Time units.** Specific time units to use should be selected early in the development phase of the project network. *All task time estimates need consistent time units.* Estimates of time must consider whether normal time is represented by calendar days, workdays, workweeks, person days, single shift, hours, minutes, etc. In practice the use of workdays is the dominant choice for expressing task duration. However, in projects such as a heart transplant operation, minutes probably would be more appropriate as a time unit. One such project that used minutes as the time unit was the movement of patients from an old hospital to an elegant new one across town. Since there were several life-endangering moves, minutes were used to ensure patient safety so proper emergency life-support systems would be available if needed. The point is, network analysis requires a standard unit of time. When computer programs allow more than one option, some notation should be made of any variance from the standard unit of time. If the standard unit of time is a five-day workweek and the estimated activity duration is in calendar days, it must be converted to the normal workweek.

5. **Independence.** Estimators should treat each task as independent of other tasks that might be integrated by the WBS. Use of first-line managers usually results in considering tasks independently; this is good. Top managers are prone to aggregate many tasks into one time estimate and then deductively make the individual task time estimates add to the total. If tasks are in a chain and performed by the same group or department, it is best not to ask for all the time estimates in the sequence at once to avoid the tendency for a planner or a supervisor to look at the whole path and try to adjust individual task times in the sequence to meet an arbitrary imposed schedule or some rough "guesstimate" of the total time for the whole path or segment of the project. This tendency does not reflect the uncertainties of individual activities and generally results in optimistic task time estimates. In summary, each task time estimate should be considered independently of other activities.

6. **Contingencies.** *Work package estimates should not include allowances for contingencies.* The estimate should assume normal or average conditions even though every work package will not materialize as

planned. For this reason top management needs to create an extra fund for contingencies that can be used to cover unforeseen events.

7. **Adding risk assessment to the estimate helps to avoid surprises to stakeholders.** It is obvious some tasks carry more time and cost risks than others. For example, a new technology usually carries more time and cost risks than a proven process. Simply identifying the degree of risk lets stakeholders consider alternative methods and alter process decisions. A simple breakdown by optimistic, most likely, and pessimistic for task time could provide valuable information regarding time and cost. See Chapter 7 for further discussion of project risk.

Where applicable, these guidelines will greatly help to avoid many of the pitfalls found so often in practice.

Top-Down versus Bottom-Up Estimating

Since estimating efforts cost money, the time and detail devoted to estimating is an important decision. Yet, when estimating is considered, you as a project manager may hear statements such as these:

> *Rough order of magnitude is good enough. Spending time on detailed estimating wastes money.*
> *Time is everything; our survival depends on getting there first! Time and cost*
> *accuracy is not an issue.*
> *The project is internal. We don't need to worry about cost.*
> *The project is so small, we don't need to bother with estimates. Just do it.*
>
> *We were burned once. I want a detailed estimate of every task by the people responsible.*

However, there are sound reasons for using top-down or bottom-up estimates. Table 5.1 depicts conditions that suggest when one approach is preferred over another.

TABLE 5.1   Conditions for Preferring Top-Down or Bottom-Up Time and Cost Estimates

Condition	Top-Down Estimates	Bottom-Up Estimates
Strategic decision making	X	
Cost and time important		X
High uncertainty	X	
Internal, small project	X	
Fixed-price contract		X
Customer wants details		X
Unstable scope	X	

Top-down estimates usually are derived from someone who uses experience and/or information to determine the project duration and total cost. These estimates are sometimes made by top managers who have very little knowledge of the processes used to complete the project. For example, a mayor of a major city making a speech noted that a new law building would be constructed at a cost of $23 million and would be ready for occupancy in two and one-half years. Although the mayor probably asked for an estimate from someone, the estimate could have come from a luncheon meeting with a local contractor who wrote an estimate (guesstimate) on a napkin. This is an extreme example, but in a relative sense this scenario is frequently played out in practice. See Snapshot from Practice: Council Fumes, for another example of this. But the question is, *do these estimates represent low-cost, efficient methods?* Do the top-down estimates of project time and cost become a self-fulfilling prophecy in terms of setting time and cost parameters?

Snapshot from Practice   Council Fumes as Tram Tale Unfolds*

Portland, Oregon's, Willamette riverfront development has exploded with seven condominium towers and a new health sciences center under construction. The health science complex is to be linked with Oregon Health Sciences University (OHSU), which is high on a nearby hill, with an aerial cable tram.

The aerial tram linking the waterfront district to OHSU is to support the university expansion, to increase biotechnology research, and to become Portland's icon equivalent to Seattle's Space Needle. All of the hype turned south when news from a hearing suggested that the real budget for the tram construction, originally estimated at $15 million, is going to be about $55–$60 million, nearly triple the original estimate. The estimate could even go higher. Commissioners want to find out why city staff knowingly relied on flawed estimates. Mike Lindberg, president of the nonprofit Aerial Transportation Inc., acknowledged "the $15 million number was not a good number. It was simply a guesstimate." Commissioner Erik Sten said, "Those numbers were presented as much more firm than they appear to have been. . . . It appears the actual design wasn't costed out. That's pretty shoddy."

* *The Oregonian*, January 13, 2006, by Frank Ryan, pages A1 and A14, and April 2, 2006, page A1.

If possible and practical, you want to push the estimating process down to the work package level for bottom-up estimates that establish low-cost, efficient methods. This process can take place after the project has been defined in detail. Good sense suggests project estimates should come from the people most knowledgeable about the estimate needed. The use of several people with relevant experience with the task can improve the time and cost estimate. The bottom-up approach at the work package level can serve as a check on cost elements in the WBS by rolling up the work packages and associated cost accounts to major deliverables. Similarly, resource requirements can be checked. Later, the time, resource, and cost estimates from the work packages can be consolidated into time-phased networks, resource schedules, and budgets that are used for control.

The bottom-up approach also provides the customer with an opportunity to compare the low-cost, efficient method approach with any imposed restrictions. For example, if the project completion duration is imposed at two years and your bottom-up analysis tells you the project will take two and one-half years, the client can now consider the trade-off of the low-cost method versus compressing the project to two years—or in rare cases canceling the project. Similar trade-offs can be compared for different levels of resources or increases in technical performance. The assumption is any movement away from the low-cost, efficient method will increase costs—e.g., overtime. The preferred approach in defining the project is to make rough top-down estimates, develop the WBS/OBS, make bottom-up estimates, develop schedules and budgets, and reconcile differences between top-down and bottom-up estimates. Hopefully, these steps will be done *before* final negotiation with either an internal or external customer. In conclusion, the ideal approach is for the project manager to allow enough time for both the top-down and bottom-up estimates to be worked out so a complete plan based on reliable estimates can be offered to the customer. In this way false expectations are minimized for all stakeholders and negotiation is reduced.

Methods for Estimating Project Times and Costs

Top-Down Approaches for Estimating Project Times and Costs

At the strategic level top-down estimating methods are used to evaluate the project proposal. Sometimes much of the information needed to derive accurate time and cost estimates is not available in the initial phase of the project—for example, design is not finalized. In these situations top-down estimates are used until the tasks in the WBS are clearly defined.

Consensus Methods

This method simply uses the pooled experience of senior and/or middle managers to estimate the total project duration and cost. This typically involves a meeting where experts discuss, argue, and ultimately reach a decision as to their best guess estimate. Firms seeking greater rigor will use the Delphi method to make these macro estimates. See Snapshot from Practice: The Delphi Method.

It is important to recognize that these first top-down estimates are only a rough cut and typically occur in the "conceptual" stage of the project. The top-down estimates are helpful in initial development of a complete plan. However, such estimates are sometimes significantly off the mark because little detailed information is gathered. At this level individual work items are not identified. Or, in a few cases, the top-down estimates are not realistic because top management "wants the project." Nevertheless, the initial top-down estimates are helpful in determining whether the project warrants more formal planning, which would include more detailed estimates. Be careful that macro estimates made by senior managers are not dictated to lower level managers who might feel compelled to accept the estimates even if they believe resources are inadequate.

Snapshot from Practice   The Delphi Method

Originally developed by the RAND Corporation in 1969 for technological forecasting, the *Delphi Method* is a group decision process about the likelihood that certain events will occur. The Delphi Method makes use of a panel of experts familiar with the kind of project in question. The notion is that well-informed individuals, calling on their insights and experience, are better equipped to estimate project costs/times than theoretical approaches or statistical methods. Their responses to estimate questionnaires are anonymous, and they are provided with a summary of opinions.

Experts are then encouraged to reconsider, and if appropriate to change their previous estimate in light of the replies of other experts. After two or three rounds it is believed that the group will converge toward the "best" response through this consensus process. The midpoint of responses is statistically categorized by the median score. In each succeeding round of questionnaires, the range of responses by the panelists will presumably decrease and the median will move toward what is deemed to be the "correct" estimate.

One distinct advantage of the Delphi Method is that the experts never need to be brought together physically. The process also does not require complete agreement by all panelists, since the majority opinion is represented by the median. Since the responses are anonymous, the pitfalls of ego, domineering personalities and the "bandwagon or halo effect" in responses are all avoided. On the other hand, future developments are not always predicted correctly by iterative consensus nor by experts, but at times by creative, "off the wall" thinking.

Although your authors prefer to avoid the top-down approach if possible, we have witnessed surprising accuracy in estimating project duration and cost in isolated cases. Some examples are building a manufacturing plant, building a distribution warehouse, developing air control for skyscraper buildings, and road construction. However, we have also witnessed some horrendous miscalculations, usually in areas where the technology is new and unproven. Top-down methods can be useful if experience and judgment have been accurate in the past.

Ratio Methods

Top-down methods (sometimes called parametric) usually use ratios, or surrogates, to estimate project times or costs. Top-down approaches are often used in the concept or "need" phase of a project to get an initial duration and cost estimate for the project. For example, contractors frequently use number of square feet to estimate the cost and time to build a house; that is, a house of 2,700 square feet might cost $160 per square foot (2,700 feet $\times$ $160 per foot equals $432,000). Likewise, knowing the square feet and dollars per square foot, experience suggests it should take approximately 100 days to complete. Two other common examples of top-down cost estimates are the cost for a new plant estimated by capacity size, or a software product estimated by features and complexity.

Apportion Methods

This method is an extension to the ratio method. Apportionment is used when projects closely follow past projects in features and costs. Given good historical data, estimates can be made quickly with little effort and reasonable accuracy. This method is very common in projects that are relatively standard but have some small variation or customization.

Anyone who has borrowed money from a bank to build a house has been exposed to this process. Given an estimated total cost for the house, banks and the FHA (Federal Housing Authority) authorize pay to the contractor by completion of specific segments of the house. For example, foundation might represent 3 percent of the total loan, framing 25 percent, electric, plumbing and heating 15 percent, etc. Payments are

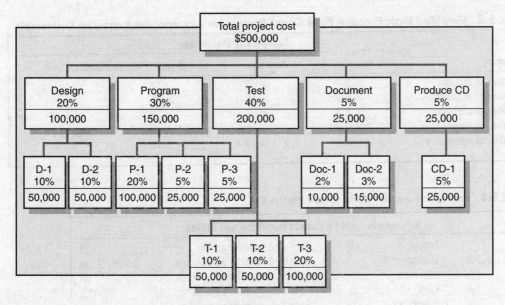

FIGURE 5.1   Apportion Method of Allocating Project Costs Using the Work Breakdown Structure

made as these items are completed. An analogous process is used by some companies that apportion costs to deliverables in the WBS—given average cost percentages from past projects. Figure 5.1 presents an example similar to one found in practice. Assuming the total project cost is estimated, using a top-down estimate, to be $500,000, the costs are apportioned as a percentage of the total cost. For example, the costs apportioned to the "Document" deliverable are 5 percent of the total, or $25,000. The subdeliverables "Doc-1 and Doc-2" are allocated 2 and 3 percent of the total—$10,000 and $15,000, respectively.

Function Point Methods for Software and System Projects

In the software industry, software development projects are frequently estimated using weighted macro variables called "function points" or major parameters such as number of inputs, number of outputs, number of inquiries, number of data files, and number of interfaces. These weighted variables are adjusted for a complexity factor and added. The total adjusted count provides the basis for estimating the labor effort and cost for a project (usually using a regression formula derived from data of past projects). This latter method assumes adequate historical data by type of software project for the industry—for example, MIS systems. In the U.S. software industry, one-person month represents on average five function points. A person working one month can generate on average (across all types of software projects) about five function points. Of course each organization needs to develop its own average for its specific type of work. Such historical data provide a basis for estimating the project duration. Variations of this top-down approach are used by companies such as IBM, Bank of America, Sears Roebuck, HP, AT & T, Ford Motors, GE, Du Pont and many others. See Table 5.2 and Table 5.3 for a simplified example of function point count methodology.

From historical data the organization developed the weighting scheme for complexity found in Table 5.2. Function points are derived from multiplying the number of kinds of elements by weighted complexity.

Table 5.3 shows the data collected for a specific task or deliverable: Patient Admitting and Billing—the number of inputs, outputs, inquiries, files and interfaces along with the expected complexity rating. Finally, the application of the element count is applied and the function point count total is 660. Given this count and

TABLE 5.2   Simplified Basic Function Point Count Process for a Prospective Project or Deliverable

Element	Complexity Weighting			Total
	Low	Average	High	
Number of *inputs*	_____ × 2 +	_____ × 3 +	_____ × 4	= _____
Number of *outputs*	_____ × 3 +	_____ × 6 +	_____ × 9	= _____
Number of *inquiries*	_____ × 2 +	_____ × 4 +	_____ × 6	= _____
Number of *files*	_____ × 5 +	_____ × 8 +	_____ × 12	= _____
Number of *interfaces*	_____ × 5 +	_____ × 10 +	_____ × 15	= _____

TABLE 5.3   Example: Function Point Count Method

Software Project 13: Patient Admitting and Billing			
15	Inputs	Rated complexity as low	(2)
5	Outputs	Rated complexity as average	(6)
10	Inquiries	Rated complexity as average	(4)
30	Files	Rated complexity as high	(12)
20	Interfaces	Rated complexity as average	(10)

Application of Complexity Factor					
Element	Count	Low	Average	High	Total
Inputs	15	× 2			= 30
Outputs	5		× 6		= 30
Inquiries	10		× 4		= 40
Files	30			× 12	= 360
Interfaces	20		× 10		= 200
				Total	660

the fact that one person month has historically been equal to 5 function points, the job will require 132 person months (660/5 = 132). Assuming you have 10 programmers who can work on this task, the duration would be approximately 13 months. The cost is easily derived by multiplying the labor rate per month times 132 person months. For example, if the monthly programmer rate is $4,000, then the estimated cost would be $528,000 (132 × 4,000). Although function point metrics are useful, their accuracy depends on adequate historical data, currency of data, and relevancy of the project/deliverable to past averages.

Learning Curves

Some projects require that the same task, group of tasks, or product be repeated several times. Managers know intuitively that the time to perform a task improves with repetition. This phenomenon is especially true of tasks that are labor intensive. In these circumstances the pattern of improvement phenomenon can be used to predict the reduction in time to perform the task. From empirical evidence across *all* industries, the pattern of this improvement has been quantified in the *learning curve* (also known as improvement curve, experience curve, and industrial progress curve), which is described by the following relationship:

Each time the output quantity doubles, the unit labor hours are reduced at a constant rate.

In practice the improvement ratio may vary from 60 percent, representing very large improvement, to 100 percent, representing no improvement at all. Generally, as the difficulty of the work decreases the expected improvement also decreases and the improvement ratio that is used becomes greater. One significant factor to consider is the proportion of labor in the task in relation to machine-paced work. Obviously, a lower percentage of improvement can occur only in operations with high labor content. Appendix 5.1 at the end of the chapter provides a detailed example of how the improvement phenomenon can be used to estimate time and cost for repetitive tasks.

The main disadvantage of top-down approaches to estimating is simply that the time and cost for a specific task are not considered. Grouping many tasks into a common basket encourages errors of omission and the use of imposed times and costs.

Micro estimating methods are usually more accurate than macro methods. The bottom-up approach at the work package level can serve as a check on cost elements in the WBS by rolling up the work packages and associated cost accounts to major deliverables. Similarly, resource requirements can be checked. Later, the time, resource, and cost estimates from the work packages can be consolidated into time-phased networks, resource schedules, and budgets that are used for control.

Bottom-Up Approaches for Estimating Project Times and Costs

Template Methods

If the project is similar to past projects, the costs from past projects can be used as a starting point for the new project. Differences in the new project can be noted and past times and costs adjusted to reflect these differences. For example, a ship repair drydock firm has a set of standard repair projects (i.e., templates for overhaul, electrical, mechanical) that are used as starting points for estimating the cost and duration of any new project. Differences from the appropriate standardized project are noted (for times, costs, and resources) and changes are made. This approach enables the firm to develop a potential schedule, estimate costs, and develop a budget in a very short time span. Development of such templates in a database can quickly reduce estimate errors.

Parametric Procedures Applied to Specific Tasks

Just as parametric techniques such as cost per square foot can be the source of top-down estimates, the same technique can be applied to specific tasks. For example, as part of an MS Office conversion project, 36 different computer workstations needed to be converted. Based on past conversion projects, the project manager determined that on average one person could convert three workstations per day. Therefore the task of converting the 36 workstations would take three technicians four days [(36/3)/3]. Similarly, to estimate the wallpapering allowance on a house remodel, the contractor figured a cost of $5 per square yard of wallpaper and $2 per yard to install it, for a total cost of $7. By measuring the length and height of all the walls she was able to calculate the total area in square yards and multiply it by $7.

Detailed Estimates for the WBS Work Packages

Probably the most reliable method for estimating time and cost is to use the WBS and to ask the people responsible for the work package to make the estimates. They know from experience or know where to find the information to estimate work package durations—especially those that depend on labor hours and costs. When work packages have significant uncertainty associated with the time to complete, it is a prudent policy to require three time estimates—low, average, and high. Figure 5.2 presents a template training form using three time estimates for work packages by three different estimators. The form illustrates how this information

WBS ID	Description	Estimator 1			Estimator 2			Estimator 3			Estimator Averages			Ratio*
		Low Est. Days	Aver. Est. Days	High Est. Days	Low Est. Days	Aver. Est. Days	High Est. Days	Low Est. Days	Aver. Est. Days	High Est. Days	Aver. Low Days	Aver. Days	Aver. High Days	Range/ Aver.
102	Engineering	95	100	105	97	100	103	93	96	100	95.0	98.7	102.7	0.08
103	Project Management	14	15	17	14	16	18	13	14	15	13.7	15.0	16.7	0.20
104	R/W Property Acceptances	44	48	52	45	50	52	43	46	49	44.0	48.0	51.0	0.15
105	Base Maps	36	38	40	36	37	39	35	36	37	35.7	37.0	38.7	0.08
106	Coordinate Utilities	7	8	9	7	8	9	8	9	10	7.3	8.3	9.3	0.24
107	EPA Acceptance	13	14	15	14	15	16	13	15	17	13.3	14.7	16.0	0.18
108	Alignment Surveys	32	35	38	32	35	37	32	34	35	32.0	34.7	36.7	0.14

Project Number: *17*
Project Description: *Road Diversion Project*

Project Manager: *Kathleen Walling*
Date: *5 - 07*

* Note: = ABS (Average Low - Average High)/Average
This ratio indicates the degree of variability in the estimates.

FIGURE 5.2   SB45 Support Cost Estimate Worksheet

can identify large differences among estimators and how the use of averages can give a more balanced time estimate. This time estimating approach gives the project manager and owner an opportunity to assess the risks associated with project times (and thus, costs). The approach helps to reduce surprises as the project progresses. The three-time estimate approach also provides a basis for assessing risk and determining the contingency fund. (See Chapter 7 for a discussion of contingency funds.)

A Hybrid: Phase Estimating

This approach begins with a top-down estimate for the project and then refines estimates for phases of the project as it is implemented. Some projects by their nature cannot be rigorously defined because of the uncertainty of design or the final product. Although rare, such projects do exist. These projects are often found in aerospace projects, IT projects, new technology projects, and construction projects where design is incomplete. In these projects, phase or life-cycle estimating is frequently used.

Phase estimating is used when an unusual amount of uncertainty surrounds a project and it is impractical to estimate times and costs for the entire project. Phase estimating uses a two-estimate system over the life of the project. A detailed estimate is developed for the immediate phase and a macro estimate is made for the remaining phases of the project. Figure 5.3 depicts the phases of a project and the progression of estimates over its life.

For example, when the project need is determined, a macro estimate of the project cost and duration is made so analysis and decisions can be made. Simultaneously a detailed estimate is made for deriving project specifications and a macro estimate for the remainder of the project. As the project progresses and specifications are solidified, a detailed estimate for design is made and a macro estimate for the remainder of the

Snapshot from Practice   Estimate Accuracy

The smaller the element of a work package, the more accurate the overall estimate is likely to be. The extent of this improvement varies by type of project. The table below is developed to reflect this observation. For example, information technology projects that determine their time and cost estimates in the conceptual stage can expect their "actuals" to err up to 200 percent over cost and duration and, perhaps, as much as 30 percent under estimates. Conversely, estimates for buildings, roads, etc., made after the work packages are clearly defined, have a smaller error in actual costs and times of 15 percent over estimate and 5 percent less than estimate. Although these estimates vary by project, they can serve as ballpark numbers for project stakeholders selecting how project time and cost estimates will be derived.

Time and Cost Estimate Accuracy by Type of Project

	Bricks and Mortar	Information Technology
Conceptual stage	+60% to −30%	+200% to −30%
Deliverables defined	+30% to −15%	+100% to −15%
Work packages defined	+15% to −5%	+50% to −5%

Phase	Need 1	Specifications 2	Design 3	Produce 4	Deliver 5
1		Macro estimate			
2		Detailed estimate	Macro estimate		
3			Detailed estimate	Macro estimate	
4				Detailed estimate	Macro estimate
5					Detailed estimate

FIGURE 5.3   Phase Estimating over Project Life Cycle

project is computed. Clearly, as the project progresses through its life cycle and more information is available, the reliability of the estimates should be improving.

Phase estimating is preferred by those working on projects where the final product is not known and the uncertainty is very large—for example, the integration of wireless phones and computers. The commitment to cost and schedule is only necessary over the next phase of the project and commitment to unrealistic future schedules and costs based on poor information is avoided. This progressive macro/micro method provides a stronger basis for using schedule and cost estimates to manage progress during the next phase.

Unfortunately your customer—internal or external—will want an accurate estimate of schedule and cost the moment the decision is made to implement the project. Additionally, the customer who is paying for the project often perceives phase estimating as a blank check because costs and schedules are not firm over most of the project life cycle. Even though the reasons for phase estimating are sound and legitimate, most customers have to be sold on its legitimacy. A major advantage for the customer is the opportunity to change features, re-evaluate, or even cancel the project in each new phase. In conclusion, phase estimating is very useful in projects that possess huge uncertainties concerning the final nature (shape, size, features) of the project.

See Figure 5.4 for a summary of the differences between top-down and bottom-up estimates.

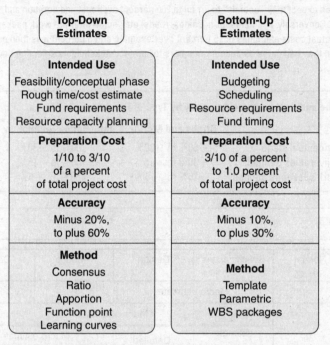

FIGURE 5.4   Top-Down and Bottom-Up Estimates

Obtaining accurate estimates is a challenge. Committed organizations accept the challenge of coming up with meaningful estimates and invest heavily in developing their capacity to do so. Accurate estimates reduce uncertainty and support a discipline for effectively managing projects.

Level of Detail

Level of detail is different for different levels of management. At any level the detail should be no more than is necessary and sufficient. Top management interests usually center on the total project and major milestone events that mark major accomplishments—e.g., "Build Oil Platform in the North Sea" or "Complete Prototype." Middle management might center on one segment of the project or one milestone. First-line managers' interests may be limited to one task or work package. One of the beauties of WBS is the ability to aggregate network information so each level of management can have the kind of information necessary to make decisions.

Getting the level of detail in the WBS to match management needs for effective implementation is crucial, but the delicate balance is difficult to find. See Snapshot from Practice: Level of Detail. The level of detail in the WBS varies with the complexity of the project; the need for control; the project size, cost, duration;

Snapshot from Practice   Level of Detail—Rule of Thumb

Practicing project managers advocate keeping the level of detail to a minimum. But there are limits to this suggestion. One of the most frequent errors of new project managers is to forget that the task time estimate will be used to control schedule and cost performance. A frequent rule of thumb used by practicing project managers says that a task duration should not exceed 5 workdays or at the most 10 workdays, if workdays are the time units used for the project. Such a rule probably will result in a more detailed network, but the additional detail pays off in controlling schedule and cost as the project progresses.

Suppose the task is "build prototype computer-controlled conveyor belt," the time estimate is 40 workdays, and the budget $300,000. It may be better to divide the task into seven or eight smaller tasks for control purposes. If one of the smaller tasks gets behind because of problems or a poor time estimate, it will be possible to take corrective action quickly and avoid delaying successive tasks and the project. If the single task of 40 workdays is used, it is possible that no corrective action would be taken until day 40, since many people have a tendency to "wait and see" or avoid admitting they are behind or passing on bad news; the result may mean far more than 5 days behind schedule.

The 5- to 10-day rule of thumb applies to cost and performance goals. If using the rule of thumb suggested above results in too many network tasks, an alternative is available, but it has conditions. The activity time can be extended beyond the 5- to 10-day rule only *IF* control monitoring checkpoints for segments of the task can be established so clear measures of progress can be identified by a specific percent complete.

This information is invaluable to the control process of measuring schedule and cost performance—for example, payments for contract work are paid on "percent complete" basis. Defining a task with clear definable start and end points and intermediate points enhances the chances of early detection of problems, corrective action, and on-time project completion.

---

and other factors. If the structure reflects excessive detail, there is a tendency to break the work effort into department assignments. This tendency can become a barrier to success, since the emphasis will be on departmental outcomes rather than on deliverable outcomes. Excessive detail also means more unproductive paperwork. Note that if the level of the WBS is increased by one, the number of cost accounts may increase geometrically. On the other hand, if the level of detail is not adequate, an organization unit may find the structure falls short of meeting its needs. Fortunately, the WBS has built-in flexibility. Participating organization units may expand their portion of the structure to meet their special needs. For example, the engineering department may wish to further break their work on a deliverable into smaller packages by electrical, civil, and mechanical. Similarly, the marketing department may wish to break their new product promotion into TV, radio, periodicals, and newspapers.

Types of Costs

Assuming work packages are defined, detailed cost estimates can be made. Here are typical kinds of costs found in a project:

1. Direct costs
   a. Labor
   b. Materials
   c. Equipment
   d. Other

2. Project overhead costs

3. General and administrative (G&A) overhead costs

The total project cost estimate is broken down in this fashion to sharpen the control process and improve decision making.

Direct Costs

These costs are clearly chargeable to a specific work package. Direct costs can be influenced by the project manager, project team, and individuals implementing the work package. These costs represent real cash outflows and must be paid as the project progresses; therefore, direct costs are usually separated from overhead costs. Lower-level project rollups frequently include only direct costs.

Direct Overhead Costs

Direct overhead rates more closely pinpoint which resources of the organization are being used in the project. Direct overhead costs can be tied to project deliverables or work packages. Examples include the salary of the project manager and temporary rental space for the project team. Although overhead is not an immediate out-of-pocket expense, it is *real* and must be covered in the long run if the firm is to remain viable. These rates are usually a ratio of the dollar value of the resources used—e.g., direct labor, materials, equipment. For example, a direct labor burden rate of 20 percent would add a direct overhead charge of 20 percent to the direct labor cost estimate. A direct charge rate of 50 percent for materials would carry an additional 50 percent charge to the material cost estimate. Selective direct overhead charges provide a more accurate project (job or work package) cost, rather than using a blanket overhead rate for the whole project.

General and Administrative (G&A) Overhead Costs

These represent organization costs that are not directly linked to a specific project. These costs are carried for the duration of the project. Examples include organization costs across all products and projects such as advertising, accounting, and senior management above the project level. Allocation of G&A costs varies from organization to organization. However, G&A costs are usually allocated as a percent of total direct cost, or a percent of the total of a specific direct cost such as labor, materials, or equipment.

Given the totals of direct and overhead costs for individual work packages, it is possible to cumulate the costs for any deliverable or for the entire project. A percentage can be added for profit if you are a contractor. A breakdown of costs for a proposed contract bid is presented in Figure 5.5.

Direct costs	$80,000
Direct overhead	$20,000
Total direct costs	$100,000
G&A overhead (20%)	$20,000
Total costs	$120,000
Profit (20%)	$24,000
Total bid	$144,000

FIGURE 5.5   Contract Bid Summary Costs

Perceptions of costs and budgets vary depending on their users. The project manager must be very aware of these differences when setting up the project budget and when communicating these differences to others. Figure 5.6 depicts these different perceptions. The project manager can commit costs months before the resource is used. This information is useful to the financial officer of the organization in forecasting future cash outflows. The project manager is interested in when the budgeted cost is expected to occur, and when the budgeted cost actually is charged (earned); the respective timings of these two cost figures are used to measure project schedule and cost variances.

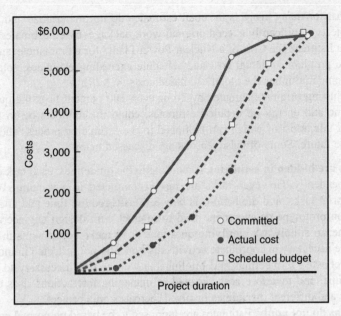

FIGURE 5.6   Three Views of Cost

Snapshot from Practice   How Do You Estimate the Cost of a Nuclear Power Plant?

O. P. Kharbanda in his book (co-authored with Jeffrey Pinto) *What Made Gertie Gallop: Learning from Project Failures* makes the important point that estimating is as much an art as a skill. For example, early in his career (1960s), he was involved with the fabrication of a nuclear reactor in India at a time when the local facilities were not geared for such sophisticated jobs. Having had no experience in building complex equipment with (almost) unheard of tolerances and precision, it was virtually impossible to create a reasonable advance estimate of the cost. The estimators did the best they could, then added a little more than normal margin before quoting a price to the client.

Soon after, O. P. happened to attend a week-long international nuclear power conference that included stalwarts in this field from all over the world. About midweek, he was fortunate to come face-to-face with the chief engineer of the company that had supplied the first reactor to India, identical in design to the one his company had recently bid on. This was the chance of a lifetime to finally get the inside information on accurate cost estimating. In fact, the expert confessed that his company lost "their shirt" on the Indian reactor. Then in reply to the innocent question, "How do you estimate a nuclear reactor?" the expert answered with cool confidence, "Do your normal cautious estimating, add more than normal margin and then after a short pause, double it!" O. P. confessed that in their ignorance, they had skipped the last vital step, but this short, casual conversation proved most valuable. "We were forewarned, we took it seriously, and got forearmed. It saved us several millions of dollars."

Refining Estimates

As described earlier in Chapter 4, detailed work package estimates are aggregated and "rolled up" by deliverable to estimate the total direct cost of the project. Similarly, estimated durations are entered into the project network to establish the project schedule and determine the overall duration of the project.

Experience tells us that for many projects the total estimates do not materialize and the actual costs and schedule of some projects significantly exceed original work package–based estimates. See Snapshot from Practice: How Do You Estimate the Cost of a Nuclear Power Plant? for a dramatic example of this. In order to compensate for the problem of actual cost and schedule exceeding estimates, some project managers adjust total costs by some multiplier (i.e., total estimated costs × 1.20).

The practice of adjusting original estimates by 20 or even 100 percent begs the question of why, after investing so much time and energy on detailed estimates, could the numbers be so far off? There are a number of reasons for this, most of which can be traced to the estimating process and the inherent uncertainty of predicting the future. Some of these reasons are discussed below.

- **Interaction costs are hidden in estimates.** According to the guidelines, each task estimate is supposed to be done independently. However, tasks are rarely completed in a vacuum. Work on one task is dependent upon prior tasks, and the hand-offs between tasks require time and attention. For example, people working on prototype development need to interact with design engineers after the design is completed, whether to simply ask clarifying questions or to make adjustments in the original design. Similarly, the time necessary to coordinate activities is typically not reflected in independent estimates. Coordination is reflected in meetings and briefings as well as time necessary to resolve disconnects between tasks. Time, and therefore cost, devoted to managing interactions rises exponentially as the number of people and different disciplines involved increases on a project.

- **Normal conditions do not apply.** Estimates are supposed to be based on normal conditions. While this is a good starting point, it rarely holds true in real life. This is especially true when it comes to the availability of resources. Resource shortages, whether in the form of people, equipment, or materials, can extend original estimates. For example, under normal conditions four bulldozers are typically used to clear a certain site size in five days, but the availability of only three bulldozers would extend the task duration to eight days. Similarly, the decision to outsource certain tasks can increase costs as well as extend task durations since time is added to acclimating outsiders to the particulars of the project and the culture of the organization.

- **Things go wrong on projects.** Design flaws are revealed after the fact, extreme weather conditions occur, accidents happen, and so forth. Although you shouldn't plan for these risks to happen when estimating a particular task, the likelihood and impact of such events need to be considered.

- **Changes in project scope and plans.** As one gets further and further into the project, a manager obtains a better understanding of what needs to be done to accomplish the project. This may lead to major changes in project plans and costs. Likewise, if the project is a commercial project, changes often have to be made midstream to respond to new demands by the customer and/or competition. Unstable project scopes are a major source of cost overruns. While every effort should be made up front to nail down the project scope, it is becoming increasingly difficult to do so in our rapidly changing world.

The reality is that for many projects not all of the information needed to make accurate estimates is available, and it is impossible to predict the future. The dilemma is that without solid estimates, the credibility of the project plan is eroded. Deadlines become meaningless, budgets become rubbery, and accountability becomes problematic.

Challenges similar to those described above will influence the final time and cost estimates. Even with the best estimating efforts, it may be necessary to revise estimates based on relevant information *prior* to establishing a baseline schedule and budget.

Effective organizations adjust estimates of specific tasks once risks, resources, and particulars of the situation have been more clearly defined. They recognize that the rolled up estimates generated from a detailed estimate based on the WBS are just the starting point. As they delve further into the project-planning process, they make appropriate revisions both in the time and cost of specific activities. They factor the final assignment of resources into the project budget and schedule. For example, when they realize that only three instead of four bulldozers are available to clear a site, they adjust both the time and cost of that activity. They adjust estimates to account for specific actions to mitigate potential risks on the project. For example, to reduce the chances of design code errors, they would add the cost of independent testers to the schedule and budget. Finally, organizations adjust estimates to take into account abnormal conditions. For example, if soil samples reveal excessive ground water, then they adjust foundation costs and times.

There will always be some mistakes, omissions, and adjustments that will require additional changes in estimates. Fortunately every project should have a change management system in place to accommodate these situations and any impact on the project baseline. Change management and contingency funds will be discussed later in Chapter 7.

Creating a Database for Estimating

The best way to improve estimates is to collect and archive data on past project estimates and actuals. Saving historical data—estimates and actuals—provides a knowledge base for improving project time and cost estimating. Creating an estimating database is a "best practice" among leading project management organizations.

Some organizations have large estimating departments of professional estimators—e.g., Boeing, Kodak, IBM—that have developed large time and cost databases. Others collect these data through the project office. This database approach allows the project estimator to select a specific work package item from the database for inclusion. The estimator then makes any necessary adjustments concerning the materials, labor, and equipment. Of course any items not found in the database can be added to the project—and ultimately to the

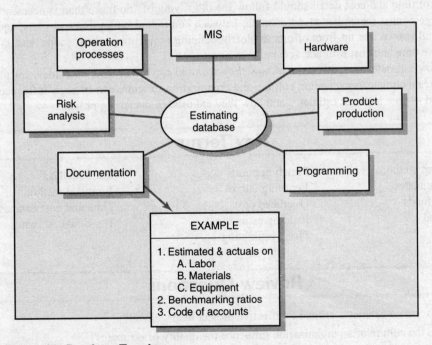

FIGURE 5.7   Estimating Database Templates

database if desired. Again, the quality of the database estimates depends on the experience of the estimators, but over time the data quality should improve. Such structured databases serve as feedback for estimators and as benchmarks for cost and time for each project. In addition, comparison of estimate and actual for different projects can suggest the degree of risk inherent in estimates. See Figure 5.7 for the structure of a database similar to those found in practice.

Summary

Quality time and cost estimates are the bedrock of project control. Past experience is the best starting point for these estimates. The quality of estimates is influenced by other factors such as people, technology, and downtimes. The key for getting estimates that represent realistic average times and costs is to have an organization culture that allows errors in estimates without incriminations. If times represent average time, we should expect that 50 percent will be less than the estimate and 50 percent will exceed the estimate. The use of teams that are highly motivated can help in keeping task times and costs near the average. For this reason, it is crucial to get the team to buy into time and cost estimates.

Using top-down estimates is good for initial and strategic decision making or in situations where the costs associated with developing better estimates have little benefit. However, in most cases the bottom-up approach to estimating is preferred and more reliable because it assesses each work package, rather than the whole project, section, or deliverable of a project. Estimating time and costs for each work package facilitates development of the project schedule and a time-phased budget, which are needed to control the project as it is implemented. Using the estimating guidelines will help eliminate many common mistakes made by those unacquainted with estimating times and costs for project control. Establishing a time and cost estimating database fits well with the learning organization philosophy.

The level of time and cost detail should follow the old saying of "no more than is necessary and sufficient." Managers must remember to differentiate between committed outlays, actual costs, and scheduled costs. It is well known that up-front efforts in clearly defining project objectives, scope, and specifications vastly improve time and cost estimate accuracy.

Finally, how estimates are gathered and how they are used can affect their usefulness for planning and control. The team climate, organization culture, and organization structure can strongly influence the importance attached to time and cost estimates and how they are used in managing projects.

Key Terms

Apportionment methods	Function points	Ratio methods
Bottom-up estimates	Learning curves	Template method
Contingency funds	Overhead costs	Time and cost databases
Delphi method	Padding estimates	Top-down estimates
Direct costs	Phase estimating	

Review Questions

1. Why are accurate estimates critical to effective project management?
2. How does the culture of an organization influence the quality of estimates?

3. What are the differences between bottom-up and top-down estimating approaches? Under what conditions would you prefer one over the other?

4. What are the major types of costs? Which costs are controllable by the project manager?

Exercises

1. Mrs. Tolstoy and her husband, Serge, are planning their dream house. The lot for the house sits high on a hill with a beautiful view of the Appalachian Mountains. The plans for the house show the size of the house to be 2,900 square feet. The average price for a lot and house similar to this one has been $120 per square foot. Fortunately, Serge is a retired plumber and feels he can save money by installing the plumbing himself. Mrs. Tolstoy feels she can take care of the interior decorating.

    The following average cost information is available from a local bank that makes loans to local contractors and disperses progress payments to contractors when specific tasks are verified as complete.

24%	Excavation and framing complete
8%	Roof and fireplace complete
3%	Wiring roughed in
6%	Plumbing roughed in
5%	Siding on
17%	Windows, insulation, walks, plaster, and garage complete
9%	Furnace installed
4%	Plumbing fixtures installed
10%	Exterior paint, light fixtures installed, finish hardware installed
6%	Carpet and trim installed
4%	Interior decorating
4%	Floors laid and finished

    a. What is the estimated cost for the Tolstoy's house if they use contractors to complete all of the house?

    b. Estimate what the cost of the house would be if the Tolstoys use their talents to do some of the work themselves.

2. Below is a project WBS with cost apportioned by percents. If the total project cost is estimated to be $600,000, what are the estimated costs for the following deliverables?

    a. Design?

    b. Programming?

    c. In-house testing?

    What weaknesses are inherent in this estimating approach?

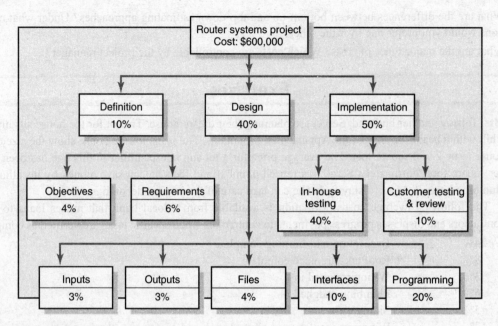

EXERCISE 5.2   WBS Figure

3. Firewall Project XT. Using the "complexity weighting" scheme shown in Table 5.2 and the function point complexity weighted table shown below, estimate the total function point count. Assume historical data suggest five function points equal one person a month and six people can work on the project.

Complexity Weight Table		
Number of inputs	10	Rated complexity low
Number of outputs	20	Rated complexity average
Number of inquires	10	Rated complexity average
Number of files	30	Rated complexity high
Number of interfaces	50	Rated complexity high

a. What is the estimated project duration?

b. If 20 people are available for the project, what is the estimated project duration?

c. If the project must be completed in six months, how many people will be needed for the project?

References

Dalkey, N. C., D. L. Rourke, R. Lewis, and D. Snyder, *Studies in the Quality of Life: Delphi and Decision Making* (Lexington, MA: Lexington Books, 1972).

Gray, N. S., "Secrets to Creating the Elusive 'Accurate Estimate,'" *PM Network,* 15 (8) August 2001, p. 56.

Jeffery, R., G. C. Low, and M. Barnes, "A Comparison of Function Point Counting Techniques," *IEEE Transactions on Software Engineering,* 19 (5) 1993, pp. 529–32.

Jones, C., *Applied Software Measurement* (New York: McGraw-Hill, 1991).

Jones, C., *Estimating Software Costs* (New York: McGraw-Hill, 1998).

Kharbanda, O. P., and J. K. Pinto, *What Made Gertie Gallop: Learning from Project Failures* (New York: Von Nostrand Reinhold, 1996).

Magne, E., K. Emhjellenm, and P. Osmundsen, "Cost Estimation Overruns in the North Sea," *Project Management Journal* 34 (1) 2003, pp. 23–29.

McLeod, G., and D. Smith, *Managing Information Technology Projects* (Cambridge, MA: Course Technology, 1996).

Milosevic, D. Z., *Project Management ToolBox* (Upper Saddle River, NJ: John Wiley, 2003), p. 229.

Pressman, R. S., *Software Engineering: A Practitioner's Approach, 4th edition* (New York: McGraw-Hill, 1997).

Symons, C. R., "Function Point Analysis: Difficulties and Improvements," *IEEE Transactions on Software Engineering,* 14 (1) 1988, pp. 2–11.

APPENDIX 5.1

Learning Curves for Estimating

A forecast estimate of the time required to perform a work package or task is a basic necessity for scheduling the project. In some cases, the manager simply uses judgment and past experience to estimate work package time, or may use historical records of similar tasks.

Most managers and workers intuitively know that improvement in the amount of time required to perform a task or group of tasks occurs with repetition. A worker can perform a task better/quicker the second time and each succeeding time she/he performs it (without any technological change). It is this pattern of improvement that is important to the project manager and project scheduler.

This improvement from repetition generally results in a reduction of labor hours for the accomplishment of tasks and results in lowers project costs. From empirical evidence across *all* industries, the pattern of this improvement has been quantified in the *learning curve* (also known as improvement curve, experience curve, and industrial progress curve), which is described by the following relationship:

Each time the output quantity doubles, the unit labor hours are reduced at a constant rate.

For example, assume that a manufacturer has a new contract for 16 prototype units and a total of 800 labor hours were required for the first unit. Past experience has indicated that on similar types of units the improvement rate was 80 percent. This relationship of improvement in labor hours is shown below:

Unit		Labor Hours
1		800
2	800 × .80 =	640
4	640 × .80 =	512
8	512 × .80 =	410
16	410 × .80 =	328

By using Table A5.1 unit values, similar labor hours per unit can be determined. Looking across the 16 unit level and down the 80 percent column, we find a ratio of .4096. By multiplying this ratio times the labor hours for the first unit, we obtained the per unit value:

$$.4096 \times 800 = 328 \text{ hours or } 327.68$$

That is, the 16th unit should require close to 328 labor hours, assuming an 80 percent improvement ratio.

Obviously, a project manager may need more than a single unit value for estimating the time for some work packages. The cumulative values in Table A5.2 provide factors for computing the cumulative total labor hours of all units. In the previous example, for the first 16 units, the total labor hours required would be

$$800 \times 8.920 = 7,136 \text{ hours}$$

By dividing the total cumulative hours (7,136) by the units, the average unit labor hours can be obtained:

$$7,136 \text{ labor hours}/16 \text{ units} = 446 \text{ average labor hours per unit}$$

Note how the labor hours for the 16th unit (328) differs from average for all 16 units (446). The project manager, knowing the average labor costs and processing costs, could estimate the total prototype costs. (The mathematical derivation of factors found in Tables A5.1 and A5.2 can be found in Jelen, F. C. and J. H. Black, *Cost and Optimization Engineering,* 2nd ed. (New York: McGraw-Hill, 1983.)

Follow-On Contract Example

Assume the project manager gets a follow-on order of 74 units, how should she estimate labor hours and cost? Going to the cumulative Table A5.2 we find at the 80 percent ratio and 90 total units intersection—a 30.35 ratio.

$800 \times 30.35 =$	24,280 labor hours for 90 units
Less previous 16 units =	7,136
Total follow-on order =	17,144 labor hours
17,144/74 equals 232 average labor hours per unit	

Labor hours for the 90th unit can be obtained from Table A5.1: $.2349 \times 800 = 187.9$ labor hours. (For ratios between given values, simply estimate.)

Exercise A5.1

Norwegian Satellite Development Company
Cost estimates
for
World Satellite Telephone Exchange Project

NSDC has a contract to produce eight satellites to support a worldwide telephone system (for Alaska Telecom, Inc.) that allows individuals to use a single, portable telephone in any location on earth to call in and out. NSDC will develop and produce the eight units. NSDC has estimated that the R&D costs will be NOK (Norwegian Krone) 12,000,000. Material costs are expected to be NOK 6,000,000. They have estimated the design and production of the first satellite will require 100,000 labor hours and an 80 percent improvement curve is expected. Skilled labor cost is NOK 300 per hour. Desired profit for all projects is 25 percent of total costs.

TABLE A5.1 Learning Curves Unit Values

Unit	60%	65%	70%	75%	80%	85%	90%	95%
1	1.0000	1.0000	1.0000	1.0000	1.0000	1.0000	1.0000	1.0000
2	.6000	.6500	.7000	.7500	.8000	.8500	.9000	.9500
3	.4450	.5052	.5682	.6338	.7021	.7729	.8462	.9219
4	.3600	.4225	.4900	.5625	.6400	.7225	.8100	.9025
5	.3054	.3678	.4368	.5127	.5956	.6857	.7830	.8877
6	.2670	.3284	.3977	.4754	.5617	.6570	.7616	.8758
7	.2383	.2984	.3674	.4459	.5345	.6337	.7439	.8659
8	.2160	.2746	.3430	.4219	.5120	.6141	.7290	.8574
9	.1980	.2552	.3228	.4017	.4930	.5974	.7161	.8499
10	.1832	.2391	.3058	.3846	.4765	.5828	.7047	.8433
12	.1602	.2135	.2784	.3565	.4493	.5584	.6854	.8320
14	.1430	.1940	.2572	.3344	.4276	.5386	.6696	.8226
16	.1296	.1785	.2401	.3164	.4096	.5220	.6561	.8145
18	.1188	.1659	.2260	.3013	.3944	.5078	.6445	.8074
20	.1099	.1554	.2141	.2884	.3812	.4954	.6342	.8012
22	.1025	.1465	.2038	.2772	.3697	.4844	.6251	.7955
24	.0961	.1387	.1949	.2674	.3595	.4747	.6169	.7904
25	.0933	.1353	.1908	.2629	.3548	.4701	.6131	.7880
30	.0815	.1208	.1737	.2437	.3346	.4505	.5963	.7775
35	.0728	.1097	.1605	.2286	.3184	.4345	.5825	.7687
40	.0660	.1010	.1498	.2163	.3050	.4211	.5708	.7611
45	.0605	.0939	.1410	.2060	.2936	.4096	.5607	.7545
50	.0560	.0879	.1336	.1972	.2838	.3996	.5518	.7486
60	.0489	.0785	.1216	.1828	.2676	.3829	.5367	.7386
70	.0437	.0713	.1123	.1715	.2547	.3693	.5243	.7302
80	.0396	.0657	.1049	.1622	.2440	.3579	.5137	.7231
90	.0363	.0610	.0987	.1545	.2349	.3482	.5046	.7168
100	.0336	.0572	.0935	.1479	.2271	.3397	.4966	.7112
120	.0294	.0510	.0851	.1371	.2141	.3255	.4830	.7017
140	.0262	.0464	.0786	.1287	.2038	.3139	.4718	.6937
160	.0237	.0427	.0734	.1217	.1952	.3042	.4623	.6869
180	.0218	.0397	.0691	.1159	.1879	.2959	.4541	.6809
200	.0201	.0371	.0655	.1109	.1816	.2887	.4469	.6757
250	.0171	.0323	.0584	.1011	.1691	.2740	.4320	.6646
300	.0149	.0289	.0531	.0937	.1594	.2625	.4202	.5557
350	.0133	.0262	.0491	.0879	.1517	.2532	.4105	.6482
400	.0121	.0241	.0458	.0832	.1453	.2454	.4022	.6419
450	.0111	.0224	.0431	.0792	.1399	.2387	.3951	.6363
500	.0103	.0210	.0408	.0758	.1352	.2329	.3888	.6314
600	.0090	.0188	.0372	.0703	.1275	.2232	.3782	.6229
700	.0080	.0171	.0344	.0659	.1214	.2152	.3694	.6158
800	.0073	.0157	.0321	.0624	.1163	.2086	.3620	.6098
900	.0067	.0146	.0302	.0594	.1119	.2029	.3556	.6045
1,000	.0062	.0137	.0286	.0569	.1082	.1980	.3499	.5998
1,200	.0054	.0122	.0260	.0527	.1020	.1897	.3404	.5918
1,400	.0048	.0111	.0240	.0495	.0971	.1830	.3325	.5850
1,600	.0044	.0102	.0225	.0468	.0930	.1773	.3258	.5793
1,800	.0040	.0095	.0211	.0446	.0895	.1725	.3200	.5743
2,000	.0037	.0089	.0200	.0427	.0866	.1683	.3149	.5698
2,500	.0031	.0077	.0178	.0389	.0606	.1597	.3044	.5605
3,000	.0027	.0069	.0162	.0360	.0760	.1530	.2961	.5530

TABLE A5.2   Learning Curves Cumulative Values

Units	60%	65%	70%	75%	80%	85%	90%	95%
1	1.000	1.000	1.000	1.000	1.000	1.000	1.000	1.000
2	1.600	1.650	1.700	1.750	1.800	1.850	1.900	1.950
3	2.045	2.155	2.268	2.384	2.502	2.623	2.746	2.872
4	2.405	2.578	2.758	2.946	3.142	3.345	3.556	3.774
5	2.710	2.946	3.195	3.459	3.738	4.031	4.339	4.662
6	2.977	3.274	3.593	3.934	4.299	4.688	5.101	5.538
7	3.216	3.572	3.960	4.380	4.834	5.322	5.845	6.404
8	3.432	3.847	4.303	4.802	5.346	5.936	6.574	7.261
9	3.630	4.102	4.626	5.204	5.839	6.533	7.290	8.111
10	3.813	4.341	4.931	5.589	6.315	7.116	7.994	8.955
12	4.144	4.780	5.501	6.315	7.227	8.244	9.374	10.62
14	4.438	5.177	6.026	6.994	8.092	9.331	10.72	12.27
16	4.704	5.541	6.514	7.635	8.920	10.38	12.04	13.91
18	4.946	5.879	6.972	8.245	9.716	11.41	13.33	15.52
20	5.171	6.195	7.407	8.828	10.48	12.40	14.64	17.13
22	5.379	6.492	7.819	9.388	11.23	13.38	15.86	18.72
24	5.574	6.773	8.213	9.928	11.95	14.33	17.10	20.31
25	5.668	6.909	8.404	10.19	12.31	14.80	17.71	21.10
30	6.097	7.540	9.305	11.45	14.02	17.09	20.73	25.00
35	6.478	8.109	10.13	12.72	15.64	19.29	23.67	28.86
40	6.821	8.631	10.90	13.72	17.19	21.43	26.54	32.68
45	7.134	9.114	11.62	14.77	18.68	23.50	29.37	36.47
50	7.422	9.565	12.31	15.78	20.12	25.51	32.14	40.22
60	7.941	10.39	13.57	17.67	22.87	29.41	37.57	47.65
70	8.401	11.13	14.74	19.43	25.47	33.17	42.87	54.99
80	8.814	11.82	15.82	21.09	27.96	36.80	48.05	62.25
90	9.191	12.45	16.83	22.67	30.35	40.32	53.14	69.45
100	9.539	13.03	17.79	24.18	32.65	43.75	58.14	76.59
120	10.16	14.16	19.57	27.02	37.05	50.39	67.93	90.71
140	10.72	15.08	21.20	29.67	41.22	56.78	77.46	104.7
160	11.21	15.97	22.72	32.17	45.20	62.95	86.80	118.5
180	11.67	16.79	24.14	34.54	49.03	68.95	95.96	132.1
200	12.09	17.55	25.48	36.80	52.72	74.79	105.0	145.7
250	13.01	19.28	28.56	42.08	61.47	88.83	126.9	179.2
300	13.81	20.81	31.34	46.94	69.66	102.2	148.2	212.2
350	14.51	22.18	33.89	51.48	77.43	115.1	169.0	244.8
400	15.14	23.44	36.26	55.75	84.85	127.6	189.3	277.0
450	15.72	24.60	38.48	59.80	91.97	139.7	209.2	309.0
500	16.26	25.68	40.58	63.68	98.85	151.5	228.8	340.6
600	17.21	27.67	44.47	70.97	112.0	174.2	267.1	403.3
700	18.06	29.45	48.04	77.77	124.4	196.1	304.5	465.3
800	18.82	31.09	51.36	84.18	136.3	217.3	341.0	526.5
900	19.51	32.60	54.46	90.26	147.7	237.9	376.9	587.2
1,000	20.15	34.01	57.40	96.07	158.7	257.9	412.2	647.4
1,200	21.30	36.59	62.85	107.0	179.7	296.6	481.2	766.6
1,400	22.32	38.92	67.85	117.2	199.6	333.9	548.4	884.2
1,600	23.23	41.04	72.49	126.8	218.6	369.9	614.2	1001.
1,800	24.06	43.00	76.85	135.9	236.8	404.9	678.8	1116.
2,000	24.83	44.84	80.96	144.7	254.4	438.9	742.3	1230.
2,500	26.53	48.97	90.39	165.0	296.1	520.8	897.0	1513.
3,000	27.99	52.62	98.90	183.7	335.2	598.9	1047.	1791.

A. How many labor hours should the eighth satellite require?

B. How many labor hours for the whole project of eight satellites?

C. What price would you ask for the project? Why?

D. Midway through the project your design and production people realize that a 75 percent improvement curve is more appropriate. What impact does this have on the project?

E. Near the end of the project Deutsch Telefon AG has requested a cost estimate for four satellites identical to those you have already produced. What price will you quote them? Justify your price.

APPENDIX 5.2

Project Cost Management

1. Nature of Project Cost Management

Project Cost Management involves managing the processes for planning, estimating, budgeting and controlling project costs in order to complete all project activities included in the project within the approved budget.

The cornerstones of project management are managing the project scope, time and cost. For successful project management, these triple constraints need to be managed effectively and simultaneously. However, often, the project cost management performance turns out to be more crucial than performance in other areas.

- First, most organizations always find themselves short of the resources they need for their operation and strategic growth. Hence, any cost overrun on a major project would put severe strains on the company's resources available for other projects and operations.

- Secondly, the project cost is likely to leave a life-long impact on the viability of the project and may be the entire organization. The higher interest and depreciation charges associated with the project cost overruns would plague the project's product for its entire life.

Hence, project managers need to pay close attention to all aspects of cost management.

2. Cost Management Plan

Cost Management Plan is the overarching document in the project cost management which sets the framework, basic policies and procedures for all three cost management processes. It is a component of the integrated *project management plan*. The document would address the issues like:

- Specifying the precision level and the policies and procedures for preparing project cost estimates and control documents

- In some cases, the project team does not have access to actual costs in monetary terms; cost management plan could provide basis for substituting the monetary values by some other suitable measure for resource costs (man-hours or man-days for labour and some valuable material quantity units like reinforcing steels in tones or cement bags for civil construction)

- Providing linkage to the organization's accounting practices and codes for recording and reporting project costs

- Specifying formats for reports for cost estimates, budgets, variance reports, earned value management and other project cost related reporting

3. Cost Management Processes

PMBOK® Guide, 4th Edition, includes two processes of planning nature and one process of monitoring and controlling nature in project cost management.

1. *Estimate Costs* (Planning Process Group): Estimating or predicting the likely cost of the resources required to complete all activities for the project work
2. *Determine Budget* (Planning Process Group): Allocating the costs to individual project work activities according to the project network and developing an authorized cost baseline – the time-phased outflow of funds for project work
3. *Control Cost* (Monitoring and Controlling Process Group): Monitoring and controlling the project cost during execution phase by influencing the factors having impact on the project cost

3.1 Cost Estimating

The cost estimating process involves developing an approximate estimate of the resources required to complete all activities for completing the project in monetary terms.

The key words to note here are "resources required to complete all activities in monetary terms" and "approximate". Firstly, the cost estimates are usually expressed in monetary units; however, sometimes the project manager or project team does not have access to certain cost elements. In such cases, a suitable comparable unit for a measure of resource could be substituted e.g. the number of man-hours for software or engineering consultancy industry or number of cement bags for construction industry. Secondly, depending on the details worked out in project planning the availability of resource cost, the rigor employed in developing the cost estimates and the accuracy of cost estimate would vary, but it would always remain *approximate* till the last cost element is accounted for.

For cost estimates desired during the different phases of the project life cycle, the degree of reliability of the cost estimate, the management levels participating in the estimating process, and the time and cost involved in preparing the estimates would be different. Similarly, the tools and techniques employed for developing the cost estimates would also be different. The subsequent sections take up discussion of these issues.

3.1.1 Need for Different Types of Cost Estimates During the Project Life Cycle

Cost estimating is not a one-time activity during the project life cycle. Cost estimates may need to be developed

- before formal initiation of the project during the project selection phase
- during the project initiation stage for setting the preliminary project cost boundary
- during the planning stage with gradual and successive refinements as the project planning matures to develop detailed project budget for use in project monitoring and control, and
- during the monitoring and controlling phase for devising alternative cost influencing plans for cost control

The rigour and degree of the reliability or accuracy of the cost estimate required at the above project phases are distinctly different and, therefore, different types of cost estimates are developed to suit project needs. **The accompanying figure (on page 202) shows a process flow diagram,** *which presents the type of cost estimate desired at different stages in the selection phase of the project life cycle and the cost estimating technique associated with preparing such estimates.*

Keeping in view its business strategy, an organization would think of a project idea. It would need to decide whether the project as conceived is within the reach of the resources the organization can raise. It would need at this first decision- making gate an order of magnitude cost estimate, which does not necessarily have high accuracy (say, + 40%). The estimates would be prepared with minimal efforts and time expenditure, under almost direct supervision and direction of the top management. The estimates are based on expert judgment and historical project cost data of some similar projects from the company's archives or published data—using *an analogous cost estimating technique*, one of the top-down cost estimating techniques.

If the investment estimate is within reach of the organization or alternatively if the project's characteristics (capacity, technology, sophistication, etc.) can be modified to bring the investment within the resources which the organization can raise, the company would like to refine its cost estimate to work out the technical feasibility and economic viability of the project. The accuracy and rigor demanded from the project cost estimate at this decision making gate is somewhat higher (say, ± 30%).Though the estimate is worked out using a top-down estimating technique, *parametric cost estimating technique*, project details are worked out to specify the major deliverables or major systems and the quantity of the parameter influencing the system cost is determined. For example, for an infrastructure project, the parameter for site development cost would be area of plot, parameter for building cost would be floor area of buildings, parameter for material handling system would be the tonnage capacity (tons/hr or cubic meter per day, etc.), parameter for electrical system would be the KVA rating of distributed power, etc. The *Function Points Analysis* would provide similar parameter for software project cost estimation. Along with the project cost estimate, the operating costs are also worked out. With these details, the technical feasibility of the project and economic viability of the project can be worked out. If the project is technically feasible and return on capital employed meets the norms set by the organization for project acceptance, the second decision- making gate for project selection is cleared.

Since the organization may be considering at a point of time several alternative proposals for investment, it might commit more resources for working out the project details, including the total project cost to the next higher level of accuracy, say ± 15 to 20%, which would be adequate for final selection and formal authorization of the project. The cost estimating technique employed at this stage would be one of the bottom-up cost estimating techniques, based on working out adequate project details to enable a far more reliable cost boundary for formal initiation of the project. At this stage, the middle and operating managerial levels would also be involved. The project would be analyzed into specific deliverables and sub-deliverables up to work package stage and well–defined technical parameters and associated cost would be worked out. Rolling these cost elements up, the total project cost, investment and schedule of capital expenditure would be ready for the formal initiation of the project.

Once the project is formally launched, the project team would set down the major and minor deliverables and prepare a work breakdown structure up to work packages and major project activities for which reliable cost estimates would be available. The cost estimating technique would be essentially one of the bottom-up cost estimating techniques and the accuracy of the cost estimate would depend on the details worked out in project planning, say ± 10% to ± 5%.

It is not necessary that all organizations need to go through each of the above decision-making gates as described above. However, the above description illustrates the need for developing different types of cost estimates during the life cycle of the project and the different techniques employed for developing these estimates. In the next two sections, different types of cost estimates and different types of cost estimating techniques are discussed.

As described in the preceding section, the type of project cost estimates desired to meet the project needs would determine:

- The accuracy or overall dependability of the estimate
- Type of detailed information worked out to develop the estimate

- Tools and techniques used for developing the estimate
- Effort, time and cost associated with development of the estimates, and
- The managerial level at which the major estimating work is carried out or directed

3.1.2 Classification Based on Cost Estimating Approach

One classification of the project cost estimates is based on the cost estimating technique used and associated nature of information flow during the estimate preparation and the degree of details worked out during the cost estimating process. When the cost estimates are developed at the top management level without working out project details and passed down to the operating level, the estimates are called top-down type of an estimate and the technique is called top-down cost estimating technique. On the other hand, when the cost estimates are developed at lower or operating levels after working out adequate project details and sent up to top management for approval or decision-making, the estimates are called bottom-up type of an estimate and the technique is called bottom-up cost estimating technique.

Top-Down Cost Estimates

The top management plays a predominant role in developing the Top-Down Cost Estimate. Such estimates are prepared by the top management for taking a broad overview and are meant to serve as the first decision-making gate for the project. The estimates are prepared without detailed project information, in a relatively short time span and without involvement of middle or operating managerial levels. The merits of such estimates is that they require less effort and time and they reflect the top management's experience and judgment in taking a comprehensive overview without getting bogged down into the details. Their main disadvantage is less accuracy (as they are developed without working out adequate project details) and some possible resistance in their willing acceptance at the operating level later.

Bottom-Up Cost Estimates

On the other hand, Bottom-Up Cost Estimates are developed at operating or middle management levels after working out sufficient project details. They are prepared at the detailed project planning stage and are intended for budgetary control during the project execution phase. Work break down structure for the project is prepared up to individual work packages and costs for the work packages or major activities are estimated. These individual cost elements are rolled up to come up with the total project cost. Understandably, Bottom-Up estimates require much greater effort, cost and time to prepare. The plus point is the increased accuracy and its full acceptance by the operating group during execution.

A Composite of Top-Down and Bottom-Up Estimates

Frequently, a combination of the Top-Down and Bottom-Up techniques is practiced by most organizations using an iterative mode. After the preliminary approval by the top management accompanied by a Top-Down budget for the project, the middle and operating levels develop detailed planning and work break-down structure, work out the costs and roll them up to develop the Bottom- Up Cost Estimate for its review and approval by the top management. After the review, discussions and necessary revisions by the top management, the approved project cost estimate is passed down for project budgeting.

3.1.3 Classification Based on the Degree of Accuracy of the Cost Estimate (ASCE Classification)

The American Society of Cost Engineers (ASCE) has developed a classification of the types of project cost estimates essentially based on the degree of accuracy of the cost estimates. The descriptive name of the cost estimate gives a general idea of the accuracy, rigor, availability of supporting details and techniques used for developing the estimate and similar information. For example order of magnitude or ball park estimate by its very name suggests the estimate to be rough and ready estimate, developed at a short notice with little effort and availability and scant details. On the other hand, definitive or detailed estimate names imply much greater accuracy of the estimate, developed after working out considerable details and with large effort.

Different organizations use different nomenclatures for indicating the type of estimate, its accuracy and project phase for which it is meant. Table A5.1 gives the nomenclature used by ASCE for classifying cost estimates into five categories. The table also gives associated accuracy, effort levels ordinarily spent, nature and degree of supporting details, managerial level at which the estimating work is done and the tools and techniques ordinarily employed to develop the estimate.

TABLE A5.1   Classification of Estimates American Association of Cost Engineers (AACE)

	Order of Magnitude	"Ball Park" Study Estimates	Preliminary Cost Estimate	Definitive Cost Estimate	Detailed Cost Estimate
Purpose	As the first decision making gate for project initiation	As the second decision making gate for project initiation	Authorization of Preliminary budget	Authorization of Project Budget	Cost data to be used for detailed project planning and accountable budgetary controls
Basis	Scale-up ratios or cost escalation factors from known cost of similar plants No process flow sheets No system designs No equipment details No technology details	Basic technology or Process flow identified But incomplete information on details	Well defined engineering or technology information with Flow sheets List of equipments Preliminary specifications	A detailed scope of all project deliverables, including: The flow sheets, Equipment lists with specifications, Preliminary lay-outs, and Budgetary quotes for critical equipment	A thorough list of work packages With detailed technical work contents and cost elements details
Accuracy	± 40 %	± 30 %	± 20 %	± 10 %	± 5 %
Efforts/ Costs	Minimal level efforts	Low effort level	Medium level efforts	Somewhat extensive efforts and costs depending on the nature of the project	Extensive efforts and associated costs
Duration Required	Very brief	Brief	A time-bound short duration program	Somewhat extensive duration	As necessary for detailed project planning
Organization Level	Top management	Top & Middle management	Upper middle level management	Upper middle level & lower middle management	Operating level for project activity – and supervised by middle upper management

3.1.4 Techniques for Developing Cost Estimates

Technique employed for developing the project cost estimate would be geared to the type of cost estimate desired to meet the organization's need at a particular phase of the project life cycle. Ordinarily, at the project selection stage, one of the top-down cost estimating techniques (Analogous or Parametric cost estimating) is used. For detailed project planning and setting the project budget for monitoring and control, the technique used is some variation of the Bottom-up cost estimating techniques (Definitive or Detailed Cost Estimating techniques based on work packages and corresponding cost elements, or resource rates and corresponding requirements of resources worked out in detail). Table A5.2 presents at a glance the purpose, necessary inputs, typical process steps in the technique, characteristics of the output, and expected accuracy from these techniques. Somewhat detailed illustration of the analogous, parametric and definitive cost estimating techniques is presented in the **Case 5.1, National Acetylene Company** at the end of this section.

3.1.4.1 Analogous Cost Estimating Technique

This is one of the Top-Down types of cost estimating techniques and it is essentially used at the project selection stage by the top management. As the name suggests, the technique is based on using the actual historical costs of similar previous projects (analogues) as the basis for estimating the cost of the project in hand. The degree of similarity between the analogues selected for basis and the expert judgment of the estimator play a critical role in the accuracy of the estimate developed. In general, the analogous estimates are not supposed to be very accurate and could be off by as much as +/– 40 %, if the analogous projects used for reference are not closely similar to the proposed project.

The technique starts with collection of actual historical data of costs of similar projects and any readily available project details like the year of analogue project construction, location, capacity, technology employed, etc. either from the organization's own earlier projects files or from published technical or commercial data. From this data, the cost of the proposed plant is deduced, which may require expert judgment to make allowances as far as available information would permit for differences between the selected analogous project and the proposed project for the following aspects:

- The differences in the general price levels between projects construction years
- The project capacities
- Other project details in terms of product quality requirements, feedstock, and degree of automation or sophistication desired, etc.

The merits of the technique are that it would require relatively less effort, cost and time to develop the estimate; the chief disadvantage is low level of accuracy or reliability.

3.1.4.2 Parametric Cost Estimating Technique

This is also a Top-Down type of cost estimating techniques and often used at the project selection stage by the top management; however, the technique is based on quantitative analysis of the important factors or parameters, which influence cost and hence it accuracy or reliability is higher (say, ± 30 % or better) than analogous cost estimating.

The principle underlying the technique is that the cost of a project is predominantly influenced by the value of a few important parameters, like the tonnage in structural steel construction, code lines or functional point value for a software project, storage capacity for a system of tankages, square foot area in case of building, man-hours in case of certain labour contracts, kilowatt rating for electric power distribution system, etc. Generally the correlation between these parameters and costs is readily available (say Rs 4,000 per square feet, or Rs 300 per man-hour) from the organization's project archives or published in industry and

TABLE A5.2   Cost Estimating Tools and Techniques

	Analogous Estimating	Parametric Estimating	Bottom-Up Estimating	Resource Cost Rate Estimating
Purpose	Preparing an Order of Magnitude estimate at the project selection stage for estimating project investment —first decision making gate for project selection	Preparing Ballpark or Study Estimate for determining the technical feasibility and economic viability of the project—second decision making gate for project selection	Preparing Detailed Cost Estimate to serve as: ■ The final decision making gate at project selection for ranking the alternative projects, or ■ Detailed project planning tool; for working out cost baseline and budget for monitoring and controlling the project.	Useful to an organization for developing cost of projects requiring use of a different mix of certain common resources (materials, equipment, labour). Specially useful for a contracting organization working on job-work projects (construction work, software projects, consultancy etc.)
Inputs	Actual historical cost data of a previous similar project (Analogue) and any available additional useful details (capacity, technology, process, etc.)	■ Preliminary boundaries for the project size, schedule, degree of sophistication ■ Analysis of proposed project into top level systems or deliverables and system parameters influencing costs ■ Cost data of projects with similar cost influencing parameters.	■ Project charter and Project scope statement ■ Work Breakdown structure ■ Enterprise environmental factors ■ Organizational process assets ■ Risk Analysis, reserve Analysis, Quality requirements	■ Work breakdown structure up to work packages level and further analysis of the resources requirements (material, labour, infrastructure equipment use, etc.) ■ Resources rates worked out from the company's historical costs and projections based on them
Technique	Estimate the cost of the proposed project by allowing for the differences in the analogue and proposed projects using expert judgment for: ■ Different times and locations ■ Different capacities ■ Different quality requirements	Analyze the proposed project into major systems and deliverables Work out system's parameters influencing the cost From comparison of the system parameters and costs of other projects, deduce the costs of major deliverables or systems and roll up these	■ Analyze the project charter, project scope statement and work breakdown structure up to work packages level ■ Estimate the cost of individual work packages from the cost elements involved in the work package to serve as budget	■ Apply the projected resource cost rates worked out from historical data (accounts) to individual work package ■ Estimate the cost of work packages to serve as budget for detailed planning and monitoring and controlling

TABLE A5.2 Cost Estimating Tools and Techniques (Contd.)

	Analogous Estimating	Parametric Estimating	Bottom-Up Estimating	Resource Cost Rate Estimating
	■ Degree of sophistication	elements to work out total project cost	■ Roll up the cost estimates of the work packages to develop the total project cost	■ Roll up the cost of work packages to develop the total project cost
Output & Characteristics	■ Top-Down Estimating Technique ■ Generally used at top managerial level ■ Requires less effort, cost and time for preparation ■ Accuracy very low (± 40 %)	■ Top-Down Estimating Technique ■ Generally used at top or high middle managerial levels ■ Effort, cost and time for preparation more than analogous but less than detailed ■ Accuracy low (± 30 %)	■ Bottom-up cost estimating ■ Generally used at middle and operating levels ■ Considerable, effort, cost and time required for such estimate ■ Accuracy depends on the rigor and details – from ± 10 to ± 5 %	■ Bottom-up cost estimating ■ Generally used at middle and operating levels ■ Considerable, effort, cost and time required for such estimate ■ Accuracy depends on the rigor and details – from ± 10 to ± 5 %

trade literature. Statistical methods (Regression Analysis) can be used for analyzing the cost data and influencing parameter from project archives if relationship is not available readily.

The first step in the technique is the analysis of the project into the main deliverables and sub- deliverables (in some cases, systems and sub-systems), identifying the cost influencing parameters associated with those deliverables or systems and estimating their values. Then using the generally known cost- parameter relationships, the costs of different deliverables can be estimated and rolling them up and the total cost of the project can be estimated. Depending upon the degree of details and sophistication used in the project analysis and the reliability of the relationship correlating project parameter and cost, reasonably accurate estimates can be developed.

Like analogous cost estimating, the fact that this technique would require relatively less effort, cost and time than most bottom-up estimating techniques is the main merit of the technique. The low level of accuracy or reliability is the disadvantage. Compared to analogous estimating, the technique is more reliable; on the other hand, it would require more inputs in terms of effort, cost and time.

3.1.4.3 Bottom-up Estimating Techniques

A variety of bottom-up techniques is used for detailed project planning or project control. Definitive or Detailed cost estimates are prepared at the detailed planning stage or setting up project cost budgets for cost control use. These techniques based on bottom-up cost estimating require the project team to work out the details commensurate with the desired overall accuracy of the estimate (say ± 5 to ± 10 % in detailed planning or project cost control phases).

The general procedure for the technique involves developing a work breakdown structure detailed enough to arrive at the level of work packages for which the cost data can be estimated. If work breakdown structure has enough details, the accuracy of the overall estimate would be high, even if the accuracy of cost estimate of individual packages is not very high. The underlying reason is that the overestimates of some work packages would cancel out the underestimates of other work packages and the overall total project cost estimate would be reasonably accurate. Understandably, the effort, cost and time required to develop a bottom-up cost estimate are high and would depend on the degree of details of the project analysis. The project management team has to use discretion to work out details to such a degree as would be adequate for practical project management and control.

3.1.4.4 Determining Resource Cost Rates

This technique is one of the bottom-up techniques of cost estimating and it relies on the analysis of organization's historical cost data (accounting data). Generally, this technique is more commonly used by the organizations working on contracting for outsiders' projects—providing products or services (civil construction projects, piping or electrical work contracts, consulting contracts, software development projects, general business process outsourcing type of project, etc). This technique can enable development of sufficiently accurate cost estimates (say, from ± 5 % to ± 15 %) depending upon the degree of details and sophistication used in the project analysis.

From the analysis of its books of accounts, the contracting organization works out and keeps ready for use the resource costs rates (for example, Rs 10,000 per ton fabrication labour, Rs 1000 per man-day for software coding work, Rs 200,000/- deployment charge and Rs 30,000 per day hiring charges for a crane, etc.). For working out the resource rates, the costs are sorted into costs directly related to the use of the resource and indirect or overhead costs. The indirect costs are then apportioned or allocated to different resource rates using some rationale for allocation. The composite resource rates for use in the estimates for bidding on contracts are worked out by adding the direct costs and the corresponding allocated cost per unit of resource rate.

PLACE OF COST ESTIMATING TECHNIQUES IN PROJECT LIFE CYCLE

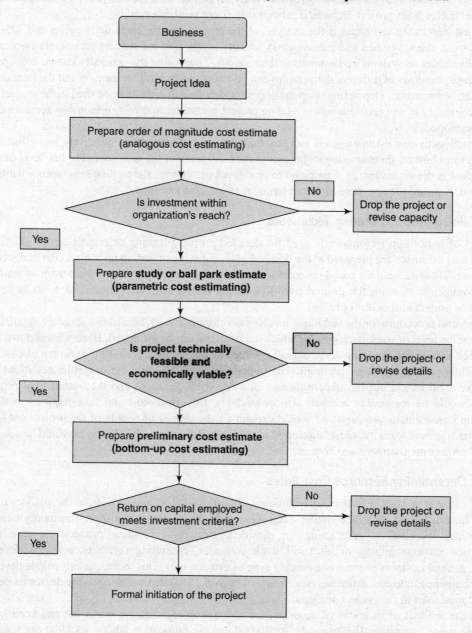

The project on hand is analyzed into the major deliverables and sub-deliverables and the corresponding use of resources for the deliverables is worked out. Using the composite resource rates and the quantity of resources required for deliverables, the cost for each major deliverable, and in turn the total cost of the project is estimated. This cost is suitably modified by providing the margin or reserve necessary to manage the project risks and operating profits to arrive at the contract bid price. Quotations from vendors or published information in trade or industry literature may also be useful for working out resource rates for works which the organization may need to outsource.

3.1.5 Inputs, Tools and Techniques and Outputs of Cost Estimating Process

The inputs, tools and techniques and outputs for the cost estimating process according to PMBOK® Guide, 4th Edition, are as follows:

Inputs

Basically, for estimating the cost of work package or activity, we would need to know
  1. What precisely is required to be done
  2. The direct cost for materials, labour and services, and
  3. The charges for use of the infrastructure and technology required to carry out the work

As discussed in detail in earlier section, the type of the cost estimate and the technique used for preparing the estimate would determine the exact nature of inputs. Keeping these basic requirements in focus, the following general process inputs listed in the PMBOK® Guide, Fourth Edition become self-explanatory:

- *Project Scope Statement* describes the business need and justification for the project and hence it provides the broad perspective of what detailed planning project work should include.
- *Work Breakdown Structure (WBS)* and accompanying document *WBS Dictionary* provide the breakdown of the major deliverables into individual components, for which suitable technical or functional details can be specified and the corresponding costs determined.
- *Enterprise Environmental Factors* cover at what prices and under what commercial terms the materials, products and services are available in the market; these may be available from the published data base or specific inquiries.
- *Organizational Process Assets* include
    - The organization's knowledge data base (historical information of costs on earlier projects and data archived in project files), and
    - The organization's own cost estimating procedures (cost estimating templates, cost estimating policies, quality or safety standards used for products and services, etc.)

Tools & Techniques

The tools and techniques are essentially concerned with how the input data is processed to turn out the desired outputs. As discussed in earlier section, depending on the project life cycle phase and project needs, different techniques are employed. They require different levels of rigor and development of details are employed for project cost estimating.

Analogous and parametric cost estimating techniques are generally used at the project selection stage or early life cycle of the project. Bottom-up estimating is used for detailed project planning and developing the project budgets. When an organization is engaged in executing a number of projects on contractual basis for other companies using a common pool of resources, the project costs are worked out from the quantum of resource requirements and the resource cost rates based on historical (accounting) information.

Accordingly, the comprehensive list of tools and techniques for estimating costs includes:

- *Analogous Estimating* technique uses historical data of past project costs with suitable broad adjustments made for the differences between the project on hand and the earlier project, for which cost data is available.

- *Parametric Estimating Technique* involves a preliminary analysis of the project deliverables and the key parameters determining the deliverables cost.
- *Determining Resource Cost Rates* is the technique for estimating the cost of projects, which use the common resource pool for the project work. This technique is often used for organizations providing contractual services for projects for initial bid preparation as well as cost control during execution.
- *Bottom-up Estimating* is based on working out the costs of individual work packages constituting the major deliverables and then aggregating the costs by trolling up the cost elements to arrive at the total project cost. For detailed project planning, budgeting and cost control during execution phase, the numbers worked out by this technique are generally used. This technique usually yield very reliable cost estimates because the technique is based on focusing on detailed analysis, and secondly, if sufficient number of activities are included in the total project cost, the pluses and minuses in the errors would tend to cancel out each other to enable increased overall accuracy.
- *Vendor Bid Analysis* is necessary when historical data or commercial data base is not available for the combination of products and services constituting the work package, specific products or services. In this situation, the offers received from vendors against requests for proposals for specific work packages are used for estimating the costs.
- *Reserve Analysis* is necessary for making a provision for contingency to allow for uncertainty in cost estimates due to either some minor changes in scope of work packages or escalation in the cost of material or service rates. The usual practice is to provide a reserve of a certain per cent (say, 5 to 10 %) of the subtotal of estimated cost of all other cost elements.
- *Cost of Quality* should be factored in while preparing the cost estimate. It includes the costs associated with attaining the desired level of quality in the project work. It would be the sum total of the cost of conformance (cost for building into the product quality and testing) and the cost of non-conformance (cost of rework, scrap and cost related to warranties and product liability).

Outputs

- *Activity Cost Estimate* is the obvious output of the cost estimating process. However, two necessary important outputs from the cost estimating technique are some times not obvious and they are discussed in some details below.
- *Requested Changes and Update of Cost Management Plan* The very process of estimating cost of activities and the accompanying activity analysis may throw up other alternative and more economical approaches for planning and executing the project. If some of the alternatives are distinctly favorable to the project, the change request would originate from the cost management processes (say, change in the intermediate product or service specifications, grouping of activities, etc.). There would be corresponding update of the cost management plan.
- *Supporting Details for Activity Cost Estimates* It is not enough that the cost estimator provides some number representing the estimated cost of the project activity or the entire project. Other project stake holders, who have not been involved in the estimating process themselves, would find it difficult to fully grasp the impact of the cost estimate in absence of supporting details: Therefore, it is highly desirable for a cost estimate to be accompanied by the following supporting details:
  - The basis and *modus operandi* used for developing the cost estimate
  - The degree of in-depth analysis carried out to develop the cost and which should reflect in terms of the accuracy or reliability of the cost estimate (± 10 % or ± 30 %?) according to estimator
  - Documentation of major assumptions and constraints forming the estimate basis
  - Cost of important parameter (say, the cost of steel and cement for a construction project, expected price escalation on a yearly basis for long duration projects, etc.)

3.2 Cost Budgeting

Project budgeting is the process of adding up the cost estimates of the individual project activities or work packages to develop a time-phased cost baseline for measuring project cost performance and which would serve as a standard for monitoring and controlling the project during the execution phase of the project. The project budget, after its formal approval, represents the organization's commitment of the resources allocated to the project during the budget period. At the same time, the budget also serves as a standard for measuring the project cost performance and thus it also functions as a valuable instrument for project cost control.

3.2.1 Process for Developing Project Budgets

Since the project budget is a time-phased aggregation of the cost estimates for the individual activities or work packages, for developing the project budget, we must know not only the cost estimate for individual activities or work packages, but also when they will be needed. Accordingly, the process of developing project budget would involve the following steps:

1. Develop cost estimates of individual activities or work packages (the outputs of earlier cost estimating process)
2. Set down the precedence or succession order of the activities to develop the project network and in turn the project schedule (the output of project schedule process)
3. Allocate to different budgetary time periods the cost of work packages according to the project schedule
4. For each budgetary period, aggregate the costs to be incurred during the period for all work packages scheduled during that period
5. The individual budgetary period costs give the cash outflows for each period and the cumulative cost would give the project cost baseline

The following simple illustration will clarify the steps described above. For the sake of simplicity, the illustration is focused on developing project budget for 3 project work packages with the cost estimates and precedence-succession given in the following table:

Work Package	Estimated Total Cost	Estimated Time Required	Preceding Work Package	Succeeding Work Package
A	Rs 10,000`	1 month	Start	B and C
B	Rs 40,000	2 months	A	D
C	Rs 90,000	3 months	A	E (not included here)
D	Rs 7000	1 month	B	F (not included here)

Based on this simple network portion and estimated costs, the project budget for the first four months would be as follows:

Work Package	Estimated Total Cost	Estimated Time Required	1st Month	2nd Month	3rd Month	4th Month
A	Rs 10,000`	1 month	Rs10,000	—	—	—
B	Rs 40,000	2 months	—	Rs 20,000	Rs 20,000	—
C	Rs 90,000	3 months	—	Rs 30,000	Rs 30,000	Rs 30,000
D	Rs 7000	1 month	—	—	—	Rs 7,000
Month- wise Project Budget			Rs 10,000	Rs 50,000	Rs 50,000	Rs 37,000

3.2.2 Inputs, Tools and Techniques and Outputs of Cost Budgeting Process

The inputs, tools and techniques and outputs for the cost budgeting process according to PMBOK® Guide, 4th Edition, are as follows:

Inputs

Cost budgeting would require, as inputs, data on the activity or project costs and the time during which these costs are to be incurred. With this basic process mapping and taking into account the overall project constraints, the following inputs, as enumerated by PMI® in its PMBOK® Guide, Fourth Edition, can be identified:

- *Project Charter* and *Project Scope Statement* giving the funding constraints for the project.
- *Contractual Obligations* give the constraints on account of payment terms for products or services to be procured.
- *Activity Cost Estimates* and *Activity Cost Estimate Support Details* (outputs of the cost estimating process) give the actual costs to be incurred.
- *Project Schedule and Resource Calendars* give the time periods in which the costs on the activities are to be incurred.
- Work Breakdown Structure (WBS) and WBS Dictionary give independent checks on whether the activity costs and their spending periods are suitable to meet the overall project objectives.

Tools and Techniques

The basic technique for preparing project budgets and cost base line is *Aggregating Costs* of different activities or work packages keeping in view the project schedule for carrying out these expenses. However, when such detailed analysis of cost of activities and project schedule is not done in case of some projects (either because they are too small or simple or they are quite similar to the other projects routinely executed by the organization), *Parametric Estimating* of costs and working out cost base line directly could be a practical and viable option for budgeting technique.Finally, the expenditure on project has to be within the funding limits of the organization and hence *Funding Limit Reconciliation* is another tool used during the cost budgeting process.

Outputs

The budgeting process develops time-phased estimates for individual project activity and the overall project cost baseline from cumulative rolling up of these costs. With that background, the following outputs are listed in PMBOK by PMI:

- *Cost Baseline:* It is the cumulative time phased budget for project activities and the entire project, against which the project performance would be measured during the execution phase for monitoring and control
- *Project Funding Requirements:* From period-wise expenditure worked out in the budget, the project funding requirements are developed.
- *Update of Cost Management Plan and Origin of Change Request:* The funding constraints may impose changes in the project plan to execute work in a manner that can be satisfactorily funded by the organization from the resources available at its command. The change request originated from the budgeting process and the corresponding up-date in project cost management plan are other outputs from the budgeting process.

3.3 Project Cost Control

Project cost control is the process for influencing the factors that impact the cost baseline, getting approved such project changes for better control of the project cost and managing such desirable changes effectively.

The cost of carrying out any activity would depend on the precise specifications for the work to be done and the time frame in which it is to be carried out. Usually there is some leeway in the precise specifications or the time frame for its execution—for example, whether a premium price should be paid for a particular product or service for the project and similarly whether premium for earlier delivery should be paid (which might justify, in turn, overtime payments, permit overuse of other resources, etc.). The project manager has to continuously watch the cost baseline or budget on one hand and the performance reports in terms of actual work during specific time periods on the other hand. From the cost variance data generated from this analysis, project manager should proactively manage the factors, which will favorably influence the cost of the project. For a vast majority of the projects, controlling the project cost and project schedule are the prime goals of project management and hence, cost control assumes great importance in project management.

The classic feedback control loop is the model for this process. The standard for cost performance expected from the project is given by the project cost baseline (output of the cost budgeting process). The actual cost performance of the project is available from the actual work carried out at a specific stage and the cost incurred for completing the work at that stage. The difference between the two *cost variance*, provides the project manager directional map for what factors impacting the cost should be influenced for improved cost control.

3.3.1 Inputs, Tools & Techniques and Outputs of Cost Control Process

The inputs, tools and techniques and outputs for the cost controlling process according to PMBOK® Guide, 4th Edition, are as follows:

Inputs

A comprehensive list of inputs is given below. The first two inputs listed in PMBOK Guide provide the standards against which the actual cost performance on the project is to be measured. The next two inputs listed provide the details of the actual project cost performance

- *Cost Baseline*—Cost baseline provides the time-phased budget for individual work package or activity and also for the entire project; hence, it provides the standard for measuring the cost performance of the project for the purpose of monitoring and controlling.
- *Project Funding Requirements*—Based on the mandatory dependencies, the project network and the corresponding project funding requirements may be initially worked out. Depending on the constraints and convenience of organizing these fund flows, some modification in the final budget document might have been incorporated. Cost Control needs to take into account project funding requirement as an input.
- *Performance Reports*—These provide information on actual progress of work and the corresponding cost during specific time periods, and
- *Work Performance Information*—These may be somewhat more comprehensive than periodic performance reports mentioned above. They may also include status and cost of the work, packages or activities during the execution, a review of the completed and balance work and the forecast for completion in terms of time and cost.

The project integration management would necessitate the consideration of *Project Management Plan* and *Approved Change Requests* as additional inputs for cost control process.

Tools & Techniques

Techniques for cost control aim at

- Analysis of the cost performance on the project by comparing the actual performance against the budgetary standards and cost baseline (cost variance), and
- Forecasting the project performance (estimated time and cost to complete the total project)

Accordingly the main tools and techniques for cost control are:

- *Project Performance Reviews* have been traditionally employed for analysis of actual cost performance of the project.
- *Cost Variance Analysis,* based on the calculation of variance from the budget or cost baseline, is the common tool employed. Use of the company's proprietary *Project Management Software* may be helpful in such an analysis.
- *Earned Value Management (EVM),* a cost control technique, which has recently become popular, aims at an integrated control of the scope, cost and schedule performance of the project. In view of the importance gained by this technique, a somewhat detailed discussion on it is separately presented in Chapter 13, in 'Development of an Earned Value Cost or Schedule system'.

The organization may use a *Forecasting* technique developed to meet its own needs. *Earned Value Management* includes a technique for developing a forecast for estimated time and cost for project at completion.

Outputs

Three most important outputs of the cost control process are:

- *Cost Performance Measurements*—the variances from the budget in traditional cost control and *Cost Performance Index (CPI) and Schedule Performance Index(SPI)* metrics for EVM technique
- *Forecasted Completion*—the estimated time and cost for project completion, again either calculated in the traditional way or calculated using the EVM technique, and most importantly
- *Corrective Actions*—the steps to be taken to influence the factors, which would impact the cost performance in the desired direction

The secondary outputs from the process would be *Updates in Cost Estimate* (as a part of forecasting performance), *Requested Changes* (as a part of the corrective actions to influence the factors impacting the cost), *Updates in Project management Plan* (as a part of the integration management of the project reflecting the cost management aspects).

CASE 5.1

Sharp Printing, AG

Three years ago the Sharp Printing (SP) strategic management group set a goal of having a color laser printer available for the consumer and small business market for less than $200. A few months later the senior management met off-site to discuss the new product. The results of this meeting were a set of general technical specifications along with major deliverables, a product launch date, and a cost estimate based on prior experience.

Shortly afterward, a meeting was arranged for middle management explaining the project goals, major responsibilities, the project start date, and importance of meeting the product launch date within the cost estimate. Members of all departments involved attended the meeting. Excitement was high. Although everyone saw the risks as high, the promised rewards for the company and the personnel were emblazoned in their minds. A few participants questioned the legitimacy of the project duration and cost estimates. A couple of R&D people were worried about the technology required to produce the high-quality product for less than $200. But given the excitement of the moment, everyone agreed the project was worth doing and doable. The color laser printer project was to have the highest project priority in the company.

Lauren was selected to be the project manager. She had 15 years of experience in printer design and manufacture, which included successful management of several projects related to printers for commercial markets. Since she was one of those uncomfortable with the project cost and time estimates, she felt getting good bottom-up time and cost estimates for the deliverables was her first concern. She quickly had a meeting with the significant stakeholders to create a WBS identifying the work packages and organizational unit responsible for implementing the work packages. Lauren stressed she wanted time and cost estimates from those who would do the work or were the most knowledgeable, if possible. Getting estimates from more than one source was encouraged. Estimates were due in two weeks.

The compiled estimates were placed in the WBS/OBS. The corresponding cost estimate seemed to be in error. The cost estimate was $1,250,000 over the senior management estimate; this represents about a 20 percent overrun! The time estimate from the developed project network was only four months over the top management time estimate. Another meeting was scheduled with the significant stakeholders to check the estimates and to brainstorm for alternative solutions; the cost and time estimates appeared to be reasonable. Some of the suggestions for the brainstorming session are listed below.

- Change scope.
- Outsource technology design.
- Use the priority matrix (found in Chapter 4) to get top management to clarify their priorities.
- Partner with another organization or build a research consortium to share costs and to share the newly developed technology and production methods.
- Cancel the project.
- Commission a break-even study for the laser printer.

Very little in the way of concrete savings was identified, although there was consensus that time could be compressed to the market launch date, but at additional costs.

Lauren met with the marketing (Connor), production (Kim), and design (Gage) managers who yielded some ideas for cutting costs, but nothing significant enough to have a large impact. Gage remarked, "I wouldn't want to be the one to deliver the message to top management that their cost estimate is $1,250,000 off! Good luck, Lauren."

---

1. At this point, what would you do if you were the project manager?
2. Was top management acting correctly in developing an estimate?
3. What estimating techniques should be used for a mission critical project such as this?

CASE 5.2

National Acetylene Company

(Project Cost Estimation for Manufacturing Facility)

Introduction

It may be necessary to develop cost estimates for project selection, for the initiation phase of the project for project authorization, and finally for development of detailed budgeted costs used for monitoring and controlling project cost. The case presents scenarios for application of three common cost estimating techniques (analogous, parametric and detailed cost estimating techniques), and associated rigour and accuracy of the estimate.

In January 1992, Vishnu Mhatre, General Manager-Strategic Business Planning at National Acetylene Company, sat at his table poring over the several investment proposals for setting up manufacturing facilities for the company's diversification plan. Suddenly, it flashed in his mind to his surprise at why he had overlooked the obvious option for his company's diversification plan: setting up a calcium carbide unit with backward integration of the company's current operation! Of course, it was true that setting up a reasonable sized calcium carbide plant needed a substantial investment and National Acetylene did not have that kind of funds available for investment earlier. But the company had done rather well in the two years. Only the other day, while he was chatting with Mr. Padhye, Director-Finance, Padhye had mentioned that the company may be in a position to consider investment proposals for around Rs 25 crores. Mhatre wondered whether that kind of investment would be adequate for setting up an economically viable calcium carbide manufacturing plant. He decided to act fast and wanted to keep on hand at least a preliminary investment proposal for discussion at the quarterly directors' meeting scheduled next week, if the opportunity was within reach available resources.

National Acetylene Company (NAC) was one of the reputed suppliers of bottled acetylene gas for oxy-acetylene type welding processes in Pune. It purchased calcium carbide from a supplier located in a different state and generated acetylene by hydrolyzing it in its plant. Acetylene generated from hydrolysis of calcium carbide is absorbed in the acetone and filled in the gas cylinders supplied to the customers. Acetylene being a highly explosive gas, the plant for generating and filling acetylene in the cylinders required expertise in the design of the plant, which required minute attention to a number of details. In view of these technological barriers and somewhat higher capital investment, the entry by new entrants would not be easy. Considering the rapidly growing market for bottled acetylene in the area with the increased steel fabrication activity, NAC decided to expand its scale of operation. The top management also wanted to look at the opportunity for backward integration to set up a captive facility for production of 10,000 tonnes calcium carbide.

The plant for production of calcium carbide required a large capital investment and consequently arranging for institutional finance from a development bank (for setting up the production facility) was inevitable. The viability of the project depended to a great extent on the accuracy of the estimate for the capital cost of the project. Mhatre would have to head the efforts for the detailed feasibility report. He knew that he would have to be very careful not only in estimating the cost for setting up the plant, but also in preparing its presentation, which would be acceptable to the financial institution without much hassle.

Mhatre realized that before the final commitment to go ahead, he would need to develop a fairly reliable estimate for the calcium carbide plant cost. However, for the preliminary consideration, it would be sufficient for him to check out if the opportunity would be within reach. There was not much time for detailed cost estimate, which could be used for a firm investment decision; but surely he would have to come up with a "ball park" figure for the investment.

He called his assistant, Avinash Rane and explained to him that he wanted to develop a rough estimate for the cost of setting up calcium carbide plant with an annual production capacity of 10,000 tonnes per annum "The technical literature from U.S mentions the economically viable plant's size to be at least 50,000 tonnes; but that may be too big for us in India. Besides, I suspect that investment for that size plant may also be out of our reach. "Mhatre explained the idea underlying his choice of capacity.

"I entirely agree with you, Sir. I will start work right away. By the way, when do you need this?" Avinash asked.

"Yesterday, my friend! Drop everything else on your hand; just concentrate on this one. The board meeting is next Thursday and I want to have a preliminary discussion on the proposal in that meeting if the cost looks right. So you have 3 days to come up with this number."

"But, you know the kind of information we process and the details we work into our investment proposals; how can we ... " Avinash left the sentence unfinished.

"I understand, Avinash, that you do not like to prepare proposals without reliable investment, operating costs and market size figures. I admire your professional approach and I would prefer to take that myself if the situation permitted. In fact, we will do precisely that, if we get a go-ahead signal in the next week's meeting. But right now, we just don't have enough time. If we miss this quarterly meeting, we will simply lose 3 months; that is plain and simple. What I want is some idea of cost ..."

"How much accuracy would be good enough for this exercise?" Avinash interrupted "If I say +40 %?"

"Well, then let me tell you how I plan to proceed. I will look up the investment figures of calcium carbide plants in the last few years, so that we can have a look at them and prepare our guestimate for preliminary discussions. I would also carry out rough and ready preliminary plant design and work out the important parameters on which the plant cost would depend and their current costs. Based on this data, I will prepare my cost estimates for your review in the next three days. If you find them acceptable and the investment outlay within our reach and interest, we can use some consultant's service for developing a definitive cost estimate for taking the final investment decision."

Avinash moved towards the cabin door. Before stepping out, however, he just held the door half open and added, "And you will have to relax your deadline for my vinyl acetate operating cost report for a week".

What Avinash presented for discussion after two days is shown in Exhibit 1. The investment estimates thrown up from the data looked encouraging and Metallurgical Consultants, a reputed company for metallurgical projects, was commissioned to prepare a Definitive Cost Estimate. The executive summary of the consultant's report included the project cost details briefly extracted in Exhibit 2.

EXHIBIT 1   Data Collected for Developing Cost Estimate for A 10, 000 Tonnes Capacity Calcium Carbide Plant

1. Data for developing a cost estimate from the historical information:
In 1982, Raymond Carbide set up a plant for production of calcium carbide. It was similar in scope—a stand alone calcium carbide manufacturing plant and not connected with any other manufacturing facility.

The source of data: Raymond Carbide's Annual Shareholders' Report, 1983.
- The Production capacity of the plant: 20,000 tonnes per annum on 3-shift continuous basis
- Project location: Jadughoda, Bihar
- Cost of project: Rs 24 crores
- Reserve Bank Wholesale Price Index for Materials for 1982: 282
- Reserve Bank Wholesale Price Index for Materials for 1992: 340
- Relative costs of construction labour in Bihar/ Maharashtra :75 :100
- Breakdown of project cost into materials and labour: 90 % cost for purchased equipment and construction materials; 10 % cost for construction labour at the site

2. Basic design parameters for 10,000 TPA capacity calcium carbide plant and available current cost data for the parameters
Based on the preliminary plant design calculations, the following parameters having an important bearing on the plant cost have been identified and worked out.. The current estimated cost for these parameters have been also collected and presented in the table on next page.

	Available Cost Data	Parameter Unit Value	Requirements for 10,000 TPA Project
			(Costs in Rs crores)
Plant site land area, sq.m	Rs 200,000	1000 sq.m	40,000 sq.m
Site development	Rs 20,000	1000 sq.m	40,000 sq.m
Plant buildings	Rs 8,000	1.0	sq. m 3,000 sq.m
Warehouses for Storage	Rs 5,000	1.0	sq. m 3,000 sq.m
Raw Material Handling System	Rs 40 lakhs	2.0 T/hr	10.0 T/hr
Electric Furnace	Rs 5 crores	40 T batch	80 T/batch
Product Handling System	Rs 50 lakhs	2.0 T/hr	10.0 T/hr
Electric Sub-station	Rs 1.6 crores	1.0 Mw	2.5 MW

EXHIBIT 2   Definitive Cost Estimate

Mr. Mhatre commissioned Metallurgical Consultants for preparing a detailed feasibility report for the project. The report submitted by Metallurgical Consultants had about 300 pages and contained a 20 pages chapter on the project cost estimate supported by budgetary quotations for critical or major equipment or sub-systems.

A section on the project cost estimate from the **executive summary of the report** *is extracted and presented below.*

Extract from Metallurgical Consultants Project Report

The cost of **New Fixed Investment** *for the project to set up a plant for an annual production of 10,000 tonnes calcium carbide from purchased calcium carbonate and petroleum coke at Pune is estimated at Rs 24.20 crores + 10 % . The estimate is valid for the plant construction to start latest by September 1992 and the construction to be completed in the next 18 months period. The breakdown of the cost* **(at WBS Level 1)** *follows:*

		(Cost in Rs lakhs)
Land and site development		78.50
Buildings		
▪ *Warehouses for raw materials storage*	98.00	
▪ *Main production plant building*	320.00	
▪ *Warehouse for finished product*	45.00	
▪ *Ancillary buildings (workshop, etc.)*	28.00	
▪ *Plant office and Quality Test Laboratory*	16.00	
Sub-total buildings		507.00
Plant & Machinery		
▪ *Purchased equipment at the site*	956.50	
▪ *Installation expenses*	137.00	
▪ *Auxiliary equipment*	282.00	
Sub-total plant & machinery		1375.50
Lump sum Technical Know-how fees		75.00
Detailed Engineering & Site Construction Supervision		92.00
Miscellaneous Fixed Assets		72.00
Sub-total		2200.00
Provision for Contingency		220.00
Total cost for New Fixed Investment		2420.00

Basis for the Cost Estimate:

- *The cost for land is taken from the offers for land prices available in the Pune industrial belt. The site development costs for earthwork is based on the database available with the company from earlier project.*
- *The preliminary layout and sizing of the plant is carried out to determine the size and the type of construction for the proposed production unit. The requirements for storage of raw materials and finished products (providing for 6 weeks storage capacity) have also been worked out for preliminary sizing of these buildings. Again, the building costs have been estimated using parametric costing for similar constructions from our database. For this estimate, the price of structural steel is taken at Rs 15,800 per tonne, reinforcing steel at Rs 14,300 per tonne and cement at Rs 2200 per tonne.*
- *Preliminary flow sheet for the production process was prepared and the list of all major production equipment was finalized. Preliminary brief specifications for inviting budgetary quotations from equipment suppliers were worked out, the quotations were invited (some on telephones) and used for this estimate. The installation expenses include the civil foundations, mechanical erection at the site and electric power cabling and earthing. The provision for auxiliary equipment (laboratory and fire fighting equipment) and miscellaneous fixed assets (office equipment, telecom equipment, cars and trucks) is based on our experience for similar recent projects. Provision for technical know-how fees is according to the draft technical collaboration agreement made available by National Acetylene.*
- *The total provision for contingency is made at 10 % – 5 % to take care of for scope changes necessary during detailed project planning and execution and 5 % for price escalations.*

Questions for Discussion

1. Develop
   - The 'Order of Magnitude' cost estimate using the data in the first part of Exhibit 1 using analogous cost estimating technique.
   - Develop the 'Ball Park' cost estimate using the data in the second part of Exhibit 1 using parametric cost estimating technique.
2. The Definitive Cost Estimate is the most reliable or accurate; why did Mhatre go through the exercise of developing the cost estimate using other techniques successively? Explain why the Definitive Cost Estimate report include a substantial amount of supporting details.

CASE 5.3

Infotech Corporation

(Project Cost Estimation for a Software Project)

Introduction

The case presents scenario and data necessary for application of resource rate technique generally used for estimating costs for software projects, for engineering project consulting, and construction contracting sectors.

Infotech Corporation (Infotech) specialized in providing special business solutions to the customers. For this purpose, Infotech adopted the commercially available software to the client's special business needs by designing the proper interface between the available ready software packages and the customer's requirements, design of special forms and short commands for simple user-friendly operations. This process required system design, code writing, testing and technical write up for training and operating manuals. The company employed 10 system designers, 30 software coding persons, 5 testers and 2 technical writers. It also included another 15 people in the supervisory, management and support function categories.

Infotech had a good reputation in the industry and could retain skilled professionals with its payscales and liberal leave plans. The average salary of Infotech's employee was Rs 45,000 per month for system designers, Rs 20,000 per month for coding department, Rs 20,000 per month for testers and Rs 25,000 per month for technical writers. The company also offered all its employees two weeks paid vacation, 11 days paid public holidays, 7 days sick leave and 7 days casual leave The company required each employee to work 40 hours per week on a regular basis with Saturdays and Sundays off. The company's policy was to understaff its operation to some extent, which required some overtime working routine for most employees, but with liberal overtime payment scales (overtime payment at 50 % over regular rates), the employees generally accepted the work culture.

Before 2001, Infotech could get away with its bids based on 'Dollar Economy' pricing and providing arbitrary 450 % overheads on its direct costs. But gradually the competition increased and Infotech found it necessary to develop a reliable costing system for the job bids based on realistic overhead costs and profit margins. **Exhibit 1** lists a brief summary of the company's expenses on different heads.

EXHIBIT I   Summary of Annual Operating Costs Budget for 2002

		(All expenses in Rs lakhs)
Salaries and Wages		
■ System Designers	54.0	
■ Coders	72.0	
■ Testers	12.0	
■ Technical writers	6.0	
■ Supervisory and managerial staff	166.0	
■ Supporting subordinate staff	40.0	
Sub-total salaries and wages		**350.0**
Other staff related expenses		
■ Professional Meetings	12.0	
■ Travel	48.0	
■ Training	10.0	
Sub-total other staff related expenses		**70.0**
Other Office Overheads		
■ Rent	20.0	
■ Insurance	12.0	
■ Electricity charges	24.0	
■ Telephones	36.0	
■ Stationery	8.0	
Sub-total other office overheads		**100.0**
Equipment Depreciation		**12.0**
Interest payments on loans		**48.0**
Total Annual Expenses		**580.0**

In August 2002, Mr. Vasudevan, Sales Manger, visited the office of one of its regular clients, Sundaram Computers and met their outsourcing manager Ms Vidyalaksmi. Infotech had established a relationship of trust with Sundaram Computers and whenever Sundaram found itself shorthanded to complete some critical assignments on time, it outsourced some modules from Infotech. Vidyalakshmi told Vasudevan that they wanted to outsource some database development work to Infotech, if it could adhere to a rather tight delivery schedule and she passed on to him the Database Schema, Entity Relations Diagrams and the summary of functionalities expected by the client from the preliminary work carried out by Sundaram. Vidyalaksmi emphasized that Sundaram wanted a firm fixed price contract offer for the assignment and delivery time would be the essence of the contract. Vasudevan returned to his office and immediately assigned the project cell to complete on an urgent basis a study of the work involved and the estimate of man hours. He also asked the project department to check out if the December 15 delivery can be met in light of the on-going jobs on hand in the regular course and if not what would be the extent of overtime work required. The project cell completed the study in the next two days and sent to Vasudevan the summary of the man hours estimate for Sundaram Project as shown in **Exhibit 2**.

EXHIBIT 2 Man-hours Estimate for Sundaram Computers

Estimate Summary

Total 1600 man-hours are estimated to be required for Sundaram Computers project with the break-down given in Table C5.1 below:

Basis for Estimate

1. A preliminary Function Point Analysis was carried out to estimate the man-hours. The numbers for man-hours from Function Point Analysis were compared with the actual man- hours spent by us for a somewhat similar database assignment for ICICI in October 2001 and they matched well.

2. The estimates are based on normal working man-hours. Since this is a high pressure job with the project to be completed by December 15 and we have some prior commitments, .we should provide for doing at least 20 % of the work on this project overtime.

3. The estimate provided is for only the direct man-hours. All supporting service man-hours and organizational overheads would have to be accounted separately.

TABLE C5.1 Category-wise Estimate of Man-hours for Sundaram Computers

Task	Skill-set Required	Man-hours
Preliminary Study & Overall Scheme	System Designer	40
Plan System Architecture	System Designer	360
Design (Detailed Code-writing)		
Module (a)	Programmers (C ++ platform)	330
Module (b)	Programmers (Oracle platform)	470
Writing Test Specification and Testing	Program Testers	200
Preparing Instruction Manual	Technical Writers	50
Project Management (@ 10 % of above sub-total)	Project Leads	150
Total Estimated Man-hours		1600

Based on this data, Vasudevan proposed to quote Rs 18.5 lakhs for a firm fixed price contract and sent the following note to Infotech's Executive Vice President for getting his approval.

August 14, 2002

From : G. Vasudevan
To: M. Vishvamohan

Subject: Making a FFP Contract Offer to Sundaram Computers

Sundaram Computers have approached us for making a FFP contract offer for two data-base related modules, a part of their contracted offer to their client. Their technical specifications were studied by the project cell and their estimate is total 1600 man-hours for the job.

I have worked out our offer based on the following:

- Estimate of category-wise man-hours prepared by the project cell and the man-hour rate worked for each category from our current salary scale
- Provision of 20% overtime work taking into account the required delivery and our current work-load
- The allocation of overhead expenses based on our annual budget for 2002
- Provision of 15 % contingency on the project cost worked out as above
- A mark-up of about 30 % on our project cost

Accordingly, I propose to quote Rs 18.5 lakh for FFP contract. The relevant work papers are enclosed. Request your approval.

Vasudevan

On receiving Vishvamohan's approval, Vasudevan promptly approached Sundaram Computers with their offer. Two days later, Vidyalakshmi called Vasudevan "You appear to have padded up your offer a lot. We can't pay you that price. We appreciate the quality of your work and your reliability in meeting deadlines. So, we would be quite happy to outsource this work to you but not at that price; we just don't have that kind of margin on this job. Let me make you a fair counter offer. If you would be ready to accept Rs 13.50 lakh total for a firm fixed price contract, the job is yours. In that case, collect the purchase order and the balance technical details and start the work right away."

Vasudevan was reasonably confident of Vishvamohan accepting whatever recommendation he would make concerning Sundaram's counteroffer. He knew that Infotech order backlog was not heavy. He sat down studying the papers and thinking out what course of action Infotech should take.

Questions for Discussion

This case requires application of 'Resource Rate' technique, which is generally employed by organizations executing projects for clients as contract work (like engineering contractors, software companies, etc.).
1. Develop the cost of project for Sundarm Computers based on the available data.
2. Should Infotech accept the Sundaram's counter offer?

CHAPTER 6

Developing a Project Plan

I keep six honest serving-men (they taught me all I knew); their names are What and Why and When and How and Where and Who.

Rudyard Kipling

Developing the Project Network

The project network is the tool used for planning, scheduling, and monitoring project progress. The network is developed from the information collected for the WBS and is a graphic flow chart of the project job plan. The network depicts the project activities that must be completed, the logical sequences, the interdependencies of the activities to be completed, and in most cases the times for the activities to start and finish along with the longest path(s) through the network—the *critical path*. The network is the framework for the project information system that will be used by the project managers to make decisions concerning project time, cost, and performance.

Developing the project networks takes time for someone or some group to develop; therefore, they cost money! Are networks really worth the struggle? The answer is definitely yes, except in cases where the project is considered trivial or very short in duration. The network is easily understood by others because the network presents a graphic display of the flow and sequence of work through the project. Once the network is developed, it is very easy to modify or change when unexpected events occur as the project progresses. For example, if materials for an activity are delayed, the impact can be quickly assessed and the whole project revised in only a few minutes with the computer. These revisions can be communicated to all project participants quickly (for example, via e-mail or project Web site).

The project network provides other invaluable information and insights. It provides the basis for scheduling labor and equipment. It enhances communication that melds all managers and groups together in meeting the time, cost, and performance objectives of the project. It provides an estimate of project duration rather than picking a project completion date from a hat or someone's preferred date. The network gives the times when activities can start and finish and when they can be delayed. It provides the basis for budgeting the cash flow of the project. It identifies which activities are "critical" and, therefore, should not be delayed if the project is to be completed as planned. It highlights which activities to consider if the project needs to be compressed to meet a deadline.

There are other reasons project networks are worth their weight in gold. Basically, project networks minimize surprises by getting the plan out early and allowing corrective feedback. A commonly heard statement from practitioners is that the project network represents three-quarters of the planning process. Perhaps this is an exaggeration, but it signals the perceived importance of the network to project managers in the field.

From Work Package to Network

Project networks are developed from the WBS. The project network is a visual flow diagram of the sequence, interrelationships, and dependencies of all the activities that must be accomplished to complete the project. *An activity is an element in the project that consumes time—for example, work or waiting.* Work packages from the WBS are used to build the activities found in the project network. An activity can include one or more work packages. The activities are placed in a sequence that provides for orderly completion of the project. Networks are built using nodes (boxes) and arrows (lines). The node depicts an activity, and the arrow shows dependency and project flow.

Integrating the work packages and the network represents a point where the management process often fails in practice. The primary explanations for this failure are that (1) different groups (people) are used to define work packages and activities and (2) the WBS is poorly constructed and not deliverable/output oriented. Integration of the WBS and project network is crucial to effective project management. The project manager must be careful to guarantee continuity by having some of the same people who defined the WBS and work packages develop the network activities.

Networks provide the project schedule by identifying dependencies, sequencing, and timing of activities, which the WBS is not designed to do. The primary inputs for developing a project network plan are work packages. Remember, a work package is defined independently of other work packages, has definite start and finish points, requires specific resources, includes technical specifications, and has cost estimates for the package. However, dependency, sequencing, and timing of each of these factors are not included in the work package. A network activity can include one or more work packages.

Figure 6.1 shows a segment of the WBS example from Chapter 4 and how the information is used to develop a project network. The lowest level deliverable in Figure 6.1 is "circuit board." The cost accounts (design, production, test, software) denote project work, organization unit responsible, and time-phased budgets for the work packages. Each cost account represents one or more work packages. For example, the design cost account has two work packages (D-1-1 and D-1-2)—specifications and documentation. The software and production accounts also have two work packages. Developing a network requires sequencing tasks from all work packages that have measurable work.

Figure 6.1 traces how work packages are used to develop a project network. You can trace the use of work packages by the coding scheme. For example, activity A uses work packages D-1-1 and D-1-2 (specifications and documentation), while activity C uses work package S-22-1. This methodology of selecting work packages to describe activities is used to develop the project network, which sequences and times project activities. Care must be taken to include all work packages. *The manager derives activity time estimates from the task times in the work package.* For example, activity B (proto 1) requires five weeks to complete; activity K (test) requires three weeks to complete. After computing the activity early and late times, the manager can schedule resources and time-phase budgets (with dates).

Constructing a Project Network

Terminology

Every field has its jargon that allows colleagues to communicate comfortably with each other about the techniques they use. Project managers are no exception. Here are some terms used in building project networks.

Activity. For project managers, an *activity* is an element of the project that requires time. It may or may not require resources. Typically an activity consumes time—either while people work or while

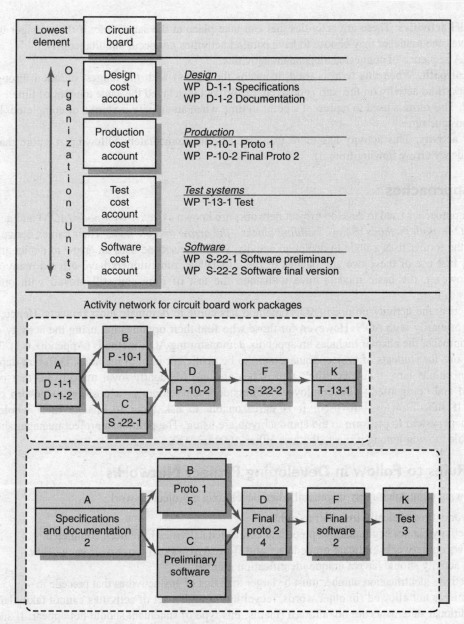

FIGURE 6.1   WBS/Work Packages to Network

people wait. Examples of the latter are time waiting for contracts to be signed, materials to arrive, drug approval by the government, budget clearance, etc. Activities usually represent one or more tasks from a work package. Descriptions of activities should use a verb/noun format: for example, develop product specifications.

Merge activity. This is an activity that has more than one activity immediately preceding it (more than one dependency arrow flowing to it).

Parallel activities. These are activities that can take place at the same time, if the manager wishes. However, the manager may choose to have parallel activities *not* occur simultaneously.

Path. A sequence of connected, dependent activities.

Critical path. When this term is used, it means the path(s) with the longest duration through the network; if an activity on the path is delayed, the project is delayed the same amount of time.

Event. This term is used to represent a point in time when an activity is started or completed. It does not consume time.

Burst activity. This activity has more than one activity immediately following it (more than one dependency arrow flowing from it).

Two Approaches

The two approaches used to develop project networks are known as *activity-on-node (AON)* and *activity-on-arrow (AOA). Both methods use two building blocks—the arrow and the node.* Their names derive from the fact that the former uses a node to depict an activity, while the second uses an arrow to depict an activity. From the first use of these two approaches in the late 1950s, practitioners have offered many enhancements; however, the basic models have withstood the test of time and still prevail with only minor variations in form.

In practice, the activity-on-node (AON) method has come to dominate most projects. Hence, this text will deal primarily with AON. However, for those who find their organization using the activity-on-arrow (AOA) approach, the chapter includes an appendix demonstrating AOA methods (Appendix 6.1). There are good reasons for students of project management to be proficient in both methods. Different departments and organizations have their "favorite" approaches and are frequently loyal to software that is already purchased and being used. New employees or outsiders are seldom in a position to govern choice of method. If subcontractors are used, it is unreasonable to ask them to change their whole project management system to conform to the approach you are using. The point is, a project manager should feel comfortable moving among projects that use either AON or AOA.

Basic Rules to Follow in Developing Project Networks

The following eight rules apply in general when developing a project network:

1. Networks flow typically from left to right.
2. An activity cannot begin until all preceding connected activities have been completed.
3. Arrows on networks indicate precedence and flow. Arrows can cross over each other.
4. Each activity should have a unique identification number.
5. An activity identification number must be larger than that of any activities that precede it.
6. Looping is not allowed (in other words, recycling through a set of activities cannot take place).
7. Conditional statements are not allowed (that is, this type of statement should not appear: If successful, do something; if not, do nothing).
8. Experience suggests that when there are multiple starts, a common start node can be used to indicate a clear project beginning on the network. Similarly, a single project end node can be used to indicate a clear ending.

Read the Snapshot from Practice: The Yellow Sticky Approach (page 153) to see how these rules are used to create project networks.

Activity-on-Node (AON) Fundamentals

The wide availability of personal computers and graphics programs has served as an impetus for use of the activity-on-node (AON) method (sometimes called the *precedence diagram method*). Figure 6.2 shows a few typical uses of building blocks for the AON network construction. An **activity** is represented by a *node* (box). The node can take many forms, but in recent years the node represented as a rectangle (box) has dominated. The dependencies among activities are depicted by *arrows* between the rectangles (boxes) on the AON network. The arrows indicate how the activities are related and the sequence in which things must be accomplished. The length and slope of the arrow are arbitrary and set for convenience of drawing the network. The letters in the boxes serve here to identify the activities while you learn the fundamentals of network construction and analysis. In practice, activities have identification numbers and descriptions.

There are three basic relationships that must be established for activities included in a project network. The relationships can be found by answering the following three questions for each activity:

1. Which activities must be completed immediately *before* this activity? These activities are called *predecessor* activities.

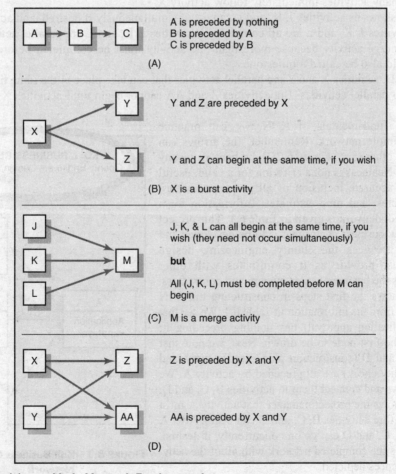

FIGURE 6.2   Activity-on-Node Network Fundamentals

2. Which activities must immediately *follow* this activity? These activities are called *successor* activities.
3. Which activities can occur *while* this activity is taking place? This is known as a *concurrent* or *parallel* relationship.

Sometimes a manager can use only questions 1 and 3 to establish relationships. This information allows the network analyst to construct a graphic flow chart of the sequence and logical interdependencies of project activities.

Figure 6.2A is analogous to a list of things to do where you complete the task at the top of the list first and then move to the second task, etc. This figure tells the project manager that activity A must be completed before activity B can begin, and activity B must be completed before activity C can begin.

Figure 6.2B tells us that activities Y and Z cannot begin until activity X is completed. This figure also indicates that activities Y and Z can occur concurrently or simultaneously if the project manager wishes; however, it is not a necessary condition. For example, pouring concrete driveway (activity Y) can take place while landscape planting (activity Z) is being accomplished, but land clearing (activity X) must be completed before activities Y and Z can start. Activities Y and Z are considered *parallel* activities. Parallel paths allow concurrent effort, which may shorten time to do a series of activities. Activity X is sometimes referred to as a *burst* activity because more than one arrow bursts from the node. The number of arrows indicates how many activities immediately follow activity X.

Figure 6.2C shows us activities J, K, and L can occur simultaneously if desired, and activity M cannot begin until activities J, K, and L are all completed. Activities J, K, and L are parallel activities. Activity M is called a *merge* activity because more than one activity must be completed before M can begin. Activity M could also be called a milestone.

In Figure 6.2D, activities X and Y are parallel activities that can take place at the same time; activities Z and AA are also parallel activities. But activities Z and AA cannot begin until activities X and Y are both completed.

Given these fundamentals of AON, we can practice developing a simple network. Remember, the arrows can cross over each other (e.g., Figure 6.2D), be bent, or be any length or slope. Neatness is not a criterion for a valid, useful network—only accurate inclusion of all project activities, their dependencies, and time estimates. Information for a simplified project network is given in Table 6.1. This project represents a new business center that is to be developed and the work and services the county engineering design department must provide as it coordinates with other groups—such as the business center owners and contractors.

Figure 6.3 shows the first steps in constructing the AON project network from the information in Table 6.1. We see that activity A (application approval) has nothing preceding it; therefore, it is the first node to be drawn. Next, we note that activities B, C, and D (construction plans, traffic study, and service availability check) are all preceded by activity A. We draw three arrows and connect them to activities B, C, and D. This segment shows the project manager that activity A must be completed before activities B, C, and D can begin. After A is completed, B, C, and D can go on concurrently, if desired. Figure 6.4 shows the completed network with all of the activities and precedences depicted.

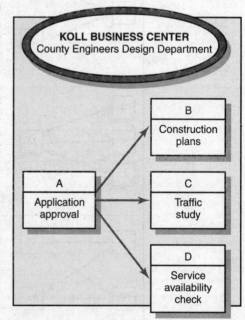

FIGURE 6.3 Koll Business Center—Partial Network

TABLE 6.1   Network Information

	KOLL BUSINESS CENTER County Engineers Design Department	
Activity	**Description**	**Preceding Activity**
A	Application approval	None
B	Construction plans	A
C	Traffic study	A
D	Service availability check	A
E	Staff report	B, C
F	Commission approval	B, C, D
G	Wait for construction	F
H	Occupancy	E, G

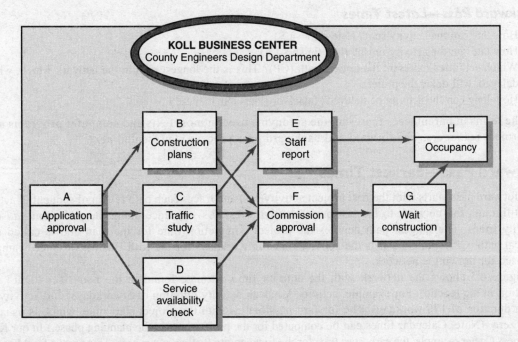

FIGURE 6.4   Koll Business Center—Complete Network

At this point our project network presents us with a graphic map of the project activities with sequences and dependencies. This information is tremendously valuable to those managing the project. However, estimating the duration for each activity will further increase the value of the network. A realistic project plan and schedule require reliable time estimates for project activities. The addition of time to the network allows us to estimate how long the project will take. When activities can or must start, when resources must be available, which activities can be delayed, and when the project is estimated to be complete are all determined from the times assigned. Deriving an activity time estimate necessitates early assessment of resource needs in terms of material, equipment, and people. In essence the project network with activity time estimates links planning, scheduling, and controlling of projects.

Network Computation Process

Drawing the project network places the activities in the right sequence for computing start and finish times of activities. Activity time estimates are taken from the task times in the work package and added to the network (review Figure 6.2). Performing a few simple computations allows the project manager to complete a process known as the forward and backward pass. Completion of the *forward and backward pass* will answer the following questions:

Forward Pass—Earliest Times

1. How soon can the activity start? (early start—ES)
2. How soon can the activity finish? (early finish—EF)
3. How soon can the project be finished? (expected time—TE)

Backward Pass—Latest Times

1. How late can the activity start? (late start—LS)
2. How late can the activity finish? (late finish—LF)
3. Which activities represent the critical path (CP)? This is the longest path in the network which, when delayed, will delay the project.
4. How long can the activity be delayed? (slack or float—SL)

The terms in parentheses represent the acronyms used in most texts and computer programs and by project managers. The forward and backward pass process is presented next.

Forward Pass—Earliest Times

The forward pass starts with the first project activity(ies) and traces each path (chain of sequential activities) through the network to the last project activity(ies). As you trace along the path, you *add* the activity times. The longest path denotes the project completion time for the plan and is called the critical path (CP). Table 6.2 lists the activity times in workdays for the Koll Business Center example we used for drawing a network.

Figure 6.5 shows the network with the activity time estimate found in the node (see "Dur" for duration in the legend). For example, activity A has an activity duration of 5 workdays, and activity G has a duration of 170 workdays. The forward pass begins with the project start time, which is usually time zero. (Note: Calendar times can be computed for the project later in the planning phase.) In our Koll Business Center example, the early start time for the first activity (activity A) is zero. This time is found in the upper left corner of the activity A node in Figure 6.6. The early finish for activity A is 5 (ES + Dur = EF or 0 + 5 = 5). Next, we see that activity A is the predecessor for activities B, C, and D. Therefore, the earliest these activities can begin is the instant in time when activity A is completed; this time is 5 workdays. You can now see in Figure 6.6 that activities B, C, and D can all start the moment activity A is complete and, therefore, have an early start (ES) of 5. Using the formula ES + Dur = EF, the early finish (EF) times for activities B, C, and D are 20, 15, and 10. What is the ES for activity E, then, which is a merge activity? Is it 15 or 20? The answer is 20 because all activities immediately preceding activity E (B and C) must be completed before activity E can begin. Because activity B will take the longest to complete, it controls the ES of activity E. The same process is used for determining the ES for activity F. It is preceded by activities B, C, and D. The controlling early finish (EF) time is activity B, which has the

Snapshot from Practice   The Yellow Sticky Approach
(for Constructing a Project Network)

In practice small project networks (25 to 100 activities) are frequently developed using yellow Post-it® stickers. The meeting requirements and process for the project team are described herein.

The following are the requirements for such a project:

1. Project team members and a facilitator.
2. One yellow sticker (3 × 4 inches or larger) for each activity with the description of the activity printed on the sticker.
3. Erasable whiteboard with marker pen (a long, 4-foot-wide piece of butcher paper can be used in place of the whiteboard).

All of the yellow stickers are placed in easy view of all team members. The team begins by identifying those activity stickers that have no predecessors. Each of these activity stickers is then attached to the whiteboard. A start node is drawn, and a dependency arrow is connected to each activity.

Given the initial network start activities, each activity is examined for immediate successor activities. These activities are attached to the whiteboard and dependency arrows drawn. This process is continued until all of the yellow stickers are attached to the whiteboard with dependency arrows. (Note: The process can be reversed, beginning with those activities that have no successor activities and connecting them to a project end node. The predecessor activities are selected for each activity and attached to the whiteboard with dependency arrows marked.)

When the process is complete, the dependencies are recorded in the project software, which develops a computer-designed network along with the critical path(s) and early, late, and slack times. This methodology sensitizes team members early to the interdependencies among activities of the project. But more importantly, the methodology empowers team members by giving them input to the important decisions that they must implement later.

TABLE 6.2   Network Information

KOLL BUSINESS CENTER County Engineers Design Department			
Activity	**Description**	**Preceding Activity**	**Activity Time**
A	Application approval	None	5
B	Construction plans	A	15
C	Traffic study	A	10
D	Service availability check	A	5
E	Staff report	B, C	15
F	Commission approval	B, C, D	10
G	Wait for construction	F	170
H	Occupancy	E, G	35

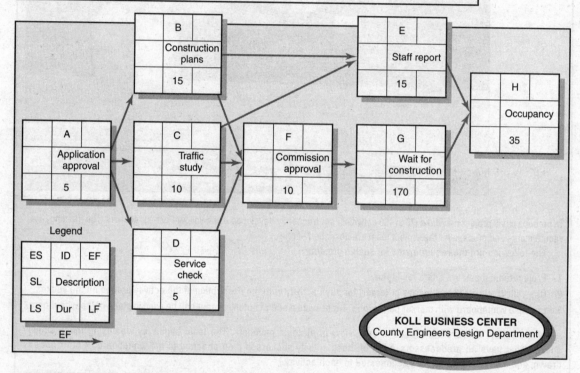

FIGURE 6.5   Activity-on-Node Network

longer early finish (20 versus 15 and 10) of the immediate predecessors (activities B, C, and D) of activity F. Stated differently, the forward pass assumes every activity will start the instant in time when the last of its predecessors is finished.

The forward pass requires that you remember just three things when computing early activity times:

1. You *add* activity times along each path in the network (ES + Dur = EF).
2. You carry the early finish (EF) to the next activity where it becomes its early start (ES), *unless*
3. The next succeeding activity is a *merge* activity. In this case you select the *largest* early finish number (EF) of *all* its immediate predecessor activities.

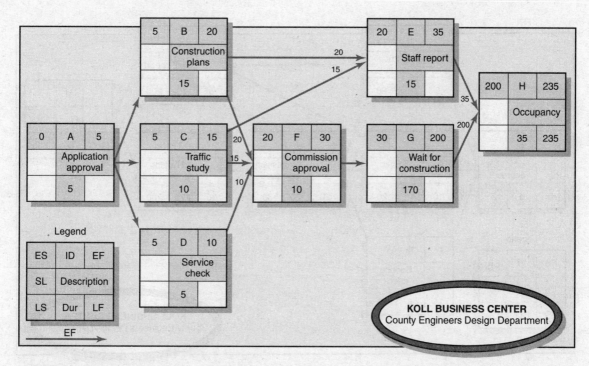

FIGURE 6.6   Activity-on-Node Network Forward Pass

In our example in Figure 6.6, the EF for activity F (30) is carried to activity G, where it becomes its ES (30). We see activity H is a merge activity and therefore find the largest EF of its immediate predecessors (activities E and G). In this case, the choice is between the EF times of 35 and 200; the choice for the ES of activity H is 200. The EF for activity H (235) becomes the earliest the project can be expected to be completed (TE) under normal conditions. The three questions derived from the forward pass have been answered; that is, early start (ES), early finish (EF), and the project duration (TE) times have been computed. The backward pass is the next process to learn.

Backward Pass—Latest Times

The backward pass starts with the last project activity(ies) on the network. You trace backward on each path *subtracting* activity times to find the late start (LS) and finish times (LF) for each activity. Before the backward pass can be computed, the late finish for the last project activity(ies) must be selected. In early planning stages, this time is usually set equal to the early finish (EF) of the last project activity (or in the case of multiple finish activities, the activity with the largest EF). In some cases an imposed project duration deadline exists, and this date will be used. Let us assume for planning purposes we can accept the EF project duration (TE) equal to 235 workdays. The LF for activity H becomes 235 workdays (EF = LF) (see Figure 6.7).

The backward pass is similar to the forward pass; you need to remember three things:

1. You *subtract* activity times along each path starting with the project end activity (LF − Dur = LS).
2. You carry the LS to the next preceding activity to establish its LF, *unless*
3. The next preceding activity is a *burst* activity; in this case you select the *smallest* LS of all its immediate successor activities to establish its LF.

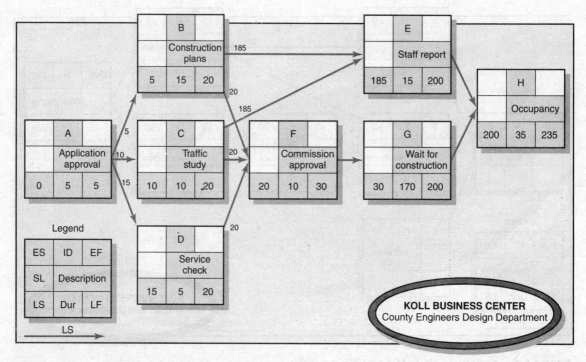

FIGURE 6.7   Activity-on-Node Network Backward Pass

Let's apply these rules to our Koll Business Center example. Beginning with activity H (occupancy) and an LF of 235 workdays, the LS for activity H is 200 workdays (LF − Dur = LS or 235 − 35 = 200). The LS for activity H becomes the LF for activities E and G. The LS for activities E and G becomes 185 (200 − 15 = 185) and 30 workdays (200 − 170 = 30), respectively. Next, the LS for activity G becomes the LF for activity F, and its LS becomes 20. At this point we see that activities B and C are *burst* activities that tie to activities E and F. The late finish for activity B is controlled by the LS of activities E and F. The LS for activity E is 185 days and for activity F, 20 days. Follow the arrows backward from activities E and F to activity B. Note that LS times for activities E and F have been placed to the right of the node so you can select the *smallest* time—20 days. The latest activity B can finish is 20 days, or activity F will be delayed and hence the project. The LF for activity C is identical to activity B because it is also controlled by the LS of activities E and F. Activity D simply picks up its LF from activity F. By computing the LS (LF − Dur = LS) for activities B, C, and D, we can determine the LF for activity A, which is a *burst* activity. You see that the finish of activity A is controlled by activity B, which has the smallest LS of activities B, C, and D. Because the LS for activity B is time period 5, the LF for activity A is 5, and its LS is time period zero. The backward pass is complete, and the latest activity times are known.

Determining Slack (or Float)

When the forward and backward passes have been computed, it is possible to determine which activities can be delayed by computing "slack" or "float." Total slack or float for an activity is simply the difference between the LS and ES (LS − ES = SL) or between LF and EF (LF − EF = SL). For example, the slack for activity C is 5 days, for activity D is 10 days, and for activity G is zero (see Figure 6.8). *Total slack* tells

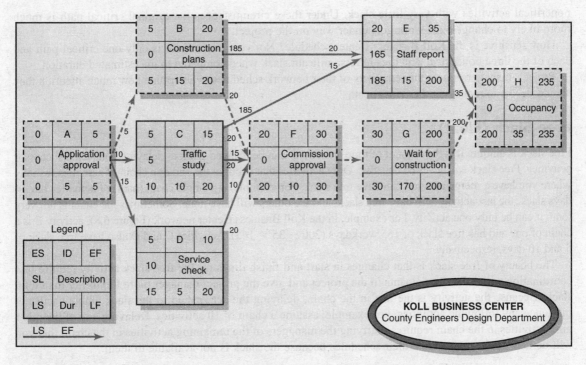

FIGURE 6.8 Activity-on-Node Network with Slack

us the amount of time an activity can be delayed and yet not delay the project. If slack of one activity in a path is used, the ES for all activities that follow in the chain will be delayed and their slack reduced. Use of total slack must be coordinated with all participants in the activities that follow in the chain.

After slack for each activity is computed, the critical path(s) is (are) easily identified. When the LF = EF for the end project activity, the critical path can be identified as those activities that also have LF = EF or a slack of zero (LF − EF = 0 or LS − ES = 0). *The critical path is the network path(s) that has (have) the least slack in common.* This awkward arrangement of words is necessary because a problem arises when the project finish activity has an LF that differs from the EF found in the forward pass—for example, an imposed duration date. If this is the case, the slack on the critical path will *not* be zero; it will be the difference between the project EF and the imposed LF of the last project activity. For example, if the EF for the project is 235 days, but the imposed LF or target date is set at 220 days, all activities on the critical path would have a slack of minus 15 days. Of course, this would result in a late start of − 15 days for the first project activity—a good trick if the project is to start now. Negative slack occurs in practice when the critical path is delayed.

In Figure 6.8 the critical path is marked with dashed arrows and nodes—activities A, B, F, G, and H. Delay of any of these activities will delay the total project by the same number of days. Critical activities typically represent about 10 percent of the activities of the project. Therefore, project managers pay close attention to the critical path activities to be sure they are not delayed. See Snapshot from Practice: The Critical Path.

We use the term sensitivity to reflect the likelihood the original critical path(s) will change once the project is initiated. Sensitivity is a function of the number of critical or near-critical paths. A network schedule that has only one critical path and noncritical activities that enjoy significant slack would be labeled insensitive. Conversely, a sensitive network would be one or more than critical paths and/or noncritical activities with very little slack. Under these circumstances the original critical path is much more likely to change once work gets under way on the project.

How sensitive is the Koll Business Center schedule? Not very, since there is only one critical path and each of the three noncritical activities have significant slack when compared to the estimated duration.

Projects managers assess the sensitivity of their network schedules to determine how much attention they should devote to managing the critical path.

Free Slack (Float)

Free slack is unique. It is the amount of time an activity can be delayed without delaying connected successor activities. Free slack can never be negative. Only activities that occur at the end of a chain of activities (usually where you have a merge activity) can have free slack. For example, if a single chain (path) of activities has 14 days slack, the last activity will have free slack, and the others will have none. Sometimes the chain is not very long; it can be only one activity. For example, in the Koll Business Center network (Figure 6.8), activity E is a chain of one and has free slack of 165 workdays ($200 - 35 = 165$). Activities C and D also have free slack of 5 and 10 days, respectively.

The beauty of free slack is that changes in start and finish times for the free slack activity require less coordination with other participants in the project and give the project manager more flexibility than total slack. Because the activity is the last in the chain, delaying the activity up to the slack amount will not influence any following activities. For example, assume a chain of 10 activities. Delaying any of the other nine activities in the chain requires notifying the managers of the remaining activities in the chain that you will be late, so they can adjust their schedules because the slack is not available to them.

Snapshot from Practice　The Critical Path

The critical path method (CPM) has long been considered the "Holy Grail" of project management. Here are comments made by veteran project managers when asked about the significance of the critical path in managing projects:

- I try to make it a point whenever possible to put my best people on critical activities or on those activities that stand the greatest chance of becoming critical.
- I pay extra attention when doing risk assessment to identifying those risks that can impact the critical path, either directly or indirectly, by making a noncritical activity so late that it becomes critical. When I've got money to spend to reduce risks, it usually gets spent on critical tasks.
- I don't have time to monitor all the activities on a big project, but I make it a point to keep in touch with the people who are working on critical activities. When I have the time, they are the ones I visit to find out firsthand how things are going. It's amazing how much more I can find out from talking to the rank and file who are doing the work and by reading the facial expressions of people—much more than I can gain from a number-driven status report.
- When I get calls from other managers asking to "borrow" people or equipment, I'm much more generous when it involves resources from working on noncritical activities. For example, if another project manager needs an electrical engineer who is assigned to a task with five days of slack, I'm willing to share that engineer with another project manager for two to three days.
- The most obvious reason the critical path is important is because these are the activities that impact completion time. If I suddenly get a call from above saying they need my project done two weeks earlier than planned, the critical path is where I schedule the overtime and add extra resources to get the project done more quickly. In the same way, if the project schedule begins to slip, it's the critical activities I focus on to get back on schedule.

Using the Forward and Backward Pass Information

What does a slack of 10 workdays for activity D (Service check) mean for the project manager? In this specific case it means activity D can be delayed 10 days. In a larger sense the project manager soon learns that slack is important because it allows flexibility in scheduling scarce project resources—personnel and equipment—that are used on more than one parallel activity or another project.

Knowing the four activity times of ES, LS, EF, and LF is invaluable for the planning, scheduling, and controlling phases of the project. The ES and LF tell the project manager the time interval in which the activity should be completed. For example, activity E (Staff report) must be completed within the time interval 20 and 200 workdays; the activity can start as early as day 20 or finish as late as day 200. Conversely, activity F (Commission approval), must start on day 20, or the project will be delayed.

When the critical path is known, it is possible to tightly manage the resources of the activities on the critical path so no mistakes are made that will result in delays. In addition, if for some reason the project must be expedited to meet an earlier date, it is possible to select those activities, or combination of activities, that will cost the least to shorten the project. Similarly, if the critical path is delayed and the time must be made up by shortening some activity or activities on the critical path to make up any negative slack, it is possible to identify the activities on the critical path that cost the least to shorten. If there are other paths with very little slack, it may be necessary to shorten activities on those paths also.

Level of Detail for Activities

Time-phasing work and budgets of the project mandate careful definition of the activities that make up the project network. Typically an activity represents one or more tasks from a work package. How many tasks you include in each activity sets the level of detail. In some cases it is possible to end up with too much information to manage, and this can result in increased overhead costs. Managers of small projects have been able to minimize the level of detail by eliminating some of the preliminary steps to drawing networks. Larger firms also recognize the cost of information overload and are working to cut down the level of detail in networks and in most other dimensions of the project.

Practical Considerations

Network Logic Errors

Project network techniques have certain logic rules that must be followed. One rule is that conditional statements such as "if test successful build proto, if failure redesign" are not permitted. The network is not a decision tree; it is a project plan that we assume will materialize. If conditional statements were allowed, the forward and backward pass would make little sense. Although in reality a plan seldom materializes as we expect in every detail, it is a reasonable initial assumption. You shall see that once a network plan is developed, it is an easy step to make revisions to accommodate changes.

Another rule that defeats the project network and computation process is *looping*. Looping is an attempt by the planner to return to an earlier activity. Recall that the activity identification numbers should always be higher for the activities following an activity in question; this rule helps to avoid the illogical precedence relationships among the activities. An activity should only occur once; if it is to occur again, the activity should have a new name and identification number and should be placed in the right sequence on the network. Figure 6.9 shows an illogical loop. If this loop were allowed to exist, this path would perpetually repeat itself. Many computer programs catch this type of logic error.

Activity Numbering

Each activity needs a unique identification code—usually a number. In practice very elegant schemes exist. Most schemes number activities in ascending order, that is, each succeeding activity has a larger number so that the flow of the project activities is toward project completion. It is customary to leave gaps between numbers (1, 5, 10, 15 . . .). Gaps are desirable so you can add missing or new activities later. Because it is nearly impossible to draw a project network perfectly, numbering networks is frequently not done until after the network is complete.

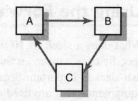

FIGURE 6.9   Illogical Loop

In practice you will find computer programs that accept numeric, alphabetic, or a combination of activity designations. Combination designations are often used to identify cost, work skill, departments, and locations. As a general rule, activity numbering systems should be ascending and as simple as possible. The intent is to make it as easy as you can for project participants to follow work through the network and locate specific activities.

Use of Computers to Develop Networks

All of the tools and techniques discussed in this chapter can be used with computer software currently available. Two examples are shown in Figures 6.10 and 6.11. Figure 6.10 presents a generic AON computer output for the Air Control project. The critical path is identified by the unshaded nodes (activities 1, 4, 6, 7, and 8). The activity description is shown on the top line of the activity node. The activity identification and duration are found on the right side of the node. The early start and early finish are on the left side of the node. The project starts on January 1 and is planned to finish February 14.

Figure 6.11 presents an early start Gantt bar chart. Bar charts are popular because they present an easy-to-understand, clear picture on a time-scaled horizon. They are used during planning, resource scheduling, and status reporting. The format is a two-dimensional representation of the project schedule, with activities down the rows and time across the horizontal axis. In this computer output the gray bars represent the activity durations. The extended lines from the bars represent slack. For example, "software development" has a duration of 18 time units (shaded area of the bar) and 20 days slack (represented by the extended line). The bar also indicates the activity has an early start of January 3, would end January 20, but can finish as late as February 9 because it has 20 days of slack. When calendar dates are used on the time axis, Gantt charts provide a clear overview of the project schedule and can be often found posted on the walls of project offices. Unfortunately, when projects have many dependency relationships, the dependency lines soon become overwhelming and defeat the simplicity of the Gantt chart.

Project management software can be a tremendous help in the hands of those who understand and are familiar with the tools and techniques discussed in this text. However, there is nothing more dangerous than someone using the software with little or no knowledge of how the software derives its output. Mistakes in input are very common and require someone skilled in the concepts, tools, and information system to recognize that errors exist so false actions are avoided.

Calendar Dates

Ultimately you will want to assign calendar dates to your project activities. If a computer program is not used, dates are assigned manually. Lay out a calendar of workdays (exclude nonworkdays), and number them. Then relate the calendar workdays to the workdays on your project network. Most computer programs will assign calendar dates automatically after you identify start dates, time units, nonworkdays, and other information.

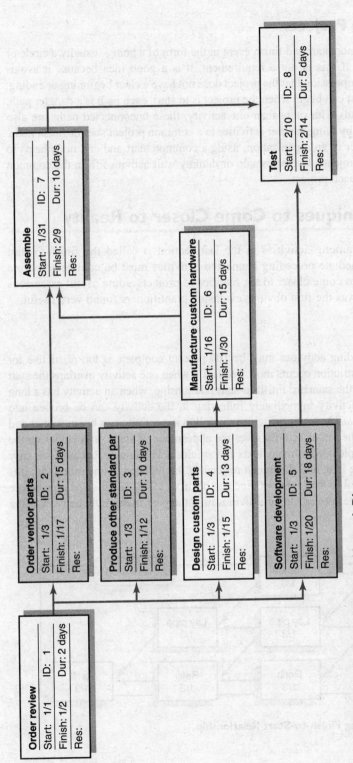

FIGURE 6.10   Air Control Project—Network Diagram

ID	Duration	Task Name	Start	Finish	Late Start	Late Finish	Free Slack	Total Slack
1	2 days	Order review	Tue 1/1	Wed 1/2	Tue 1/1	Wed 1/2	0 days	0 days
2	15 days	Order vendor parts	Thu 1/3	Thu 1/17	Wed 1/16	Wed 1/30	13 days	13 days
3	10 days	Produce other standard parts	Thu 1/3	Sat 1/12	Mon 1/21	Wed 1/30	18 days	18 days
4	13 days	Design custom parts	Thu 1/3	Tue 1/15	Tue 1/15	Sat 2/9	0 days	20 days
5	18 days	Software development	Thu 1/3	Sun 1/20	Wed 1/23	Sat 2/9	20 days	20 days
6	15 days	Manufacture custom hardware	Wed 1/16	Wed 1/30	Wed 1/16	Wed 1/30	0 days	0 days
7	10 days	Assemble	Thu 1/31	Sat 2/9	Thu 1/31	Sat 2/9	0 days	0 days
8	5 days	Test	Sun 2/10	Thu 2/14	Sun 2/10	Thu 2/14	0 days	0 days

FIGURE 6.11   Air Control Project—Gantt Chart

Multiple Starts and Multiple Projects

Some computer programs require a common start and finish event in the form of a node—usually a circle or rectangle—for a project network. Even if this is not a requirement, it is a good idea because it avoids "dangler" paths. Dangler paths give the impression that the project does not have a clear beginning or ending. If a project has more than one activity that can begin when the project is to start, each path is a dangler path. The same is true if a project network ends with more than one activity; these unconnected paths are also called danglers. Danglers can be avoided by tying dangler activities to a common project start or finish node.

When several projects are tied together in an organization, using a common start and end node helps to identify the total planning period of all projects. Use of pseudo or dummy wait activities from the common start node allows different start dates for each project.

Extended Network Techniques to Come Closer to Reality

The method for showing relationships among activities in the last section is called the finish-to-start relationship because it assumes all immediate preceding connected activities must be completed before the next activity can begin. In an effort to come closer to the realities of projects, some useful extensions have been added. The use of *laddering* was the first obvious extension practitioners found very useful.

Laddering

The assumption that all immediate preceding activities must be 100 percent complete is too restrictive for some situations found in practice. This restriction occurs most frequently when one activity overlaps the start of another and has a long duration. Under the standard finish-to-start relationship, when an activity has a long duration and will delay the start of an activity immediately following it, the activity can be broken into segments and the network drawn using a *laddering* approach so the following activity can begin sooner and not delay the work. This segmenting of the larger activity gives the appearance of steps on a ladder on the network, thus the name. The classic example used in many texts and articles is laying pipe, because it is easy to visualize. The trench must be dug, pipe laid, and the trench refilled. If the pipeline is one mile long, it is not necessary to dig one mile of trench before the laying of pipe can begin or to lay one mile of pipe before refill can begin. Figure 6.12 shows how these overlapping activities might appear in an AON network using the standard finish-to-start approach.

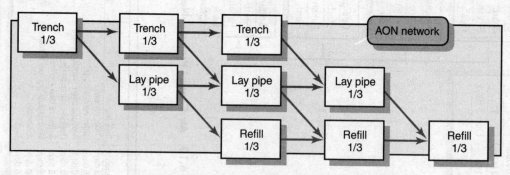

FIGURE 6.12   Example of Laddering Using Finish-to-Start Relationship

Use of Lags

The use of *lags* has been developed to offer greater flexibility in network construction. *A lag is the minimum amount of time a dependent activity must be delayed to begin or end.* The use of lags in project networks occurs for two primary reasons:

1. When activities of long duration delay the start or finish of successor activities, the network designer normally breaks the activity into smaller activities to avoid the long delay of the successor activity. Use of lags can avoid such delays and reduce network detail.
2. Lags can be used to constrain the start and finish of an activity.

The most commonly used relationship extensions are start-to-start, finish-to-finish, and combinations of these two. These relationship patterns are discussed in this section.

Finish-to-Start Relationship

The finish-to-start relationship represents the typical, generic network style used in the early part of the chapter. However, there are situations in which the next activity in a sequence must be delayed even when the preceding activity is complete. For example, removing concrete forms cannot begin until the poured cement has cured for two time units. Figure 6.13 shows this lag relationship for AON networks. Finish-to-start lags are frequently used when ordering materials. For example, it may take 1 day to place orders but take 19 days to receive the goods. The use of finish-to-start allows the activity duration to be only 1 day and the lag 19 days. This approach ensures the activity cost is tied to placing the order only rather than charging the activity for 20 days of work. This same finish-to-start lag relationship is useful to depict transportation, legal, and mail lags.

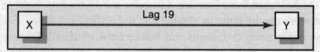

FIGURE 6.13   Finish-to-Start Relationship

The use of finish-to-start lags should be carefully checked to ensure their validity. Conservative project managers or those responsible for completion of activities have been known to use lags as a means of building in a "slush" factor to reduce the risk of being late. A simple rule to follow is that the use of finish-to-start lags must be justified and approved by someone responsible for a large section of the project. The legitimacy of lags is not usually difficult to discern. The legitimate use of the additional relationship shown can greatly enhance the network by more closely representing the realities of the project.

Start-to-Start Relationship

An alternative to segmenting the activities as we did earlier is to use a start-to-start relationship. Typical start-to-start relationships are shown in Figure 6.14. Figure 6.14A shows the start-to-start relationship with zero lag, while Figure 6.14B shows the same relationship with a lag of five time units. It is important to note that the relationship may be used with or without a lag. If time is assigned, it is usually shown on the dependency arrow of an AON network.

In Figure 6.14B, activity Q cannot begin until five time units after activity P begins. This type of relationship typically depicts a situation in which you can perform a portion of one activity and begin a following activity before completing the first. This relationship can be used on the pipe-laying project. Figure 6.15 shows the project using an AON network. The start-to-start relationship reduces network detail and project delays by using lag relationships.

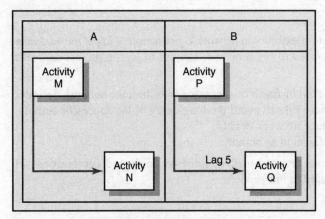

FIGURE 6.14　Start-to-Start Relationship

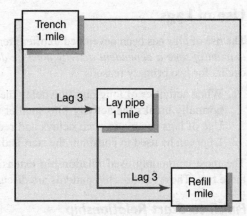

FIGURE 6.15　Use of Lags to Reduce Detail

It is possible to find compression opportunities by changing finish-to-start relations to start-to-start relationships. A review of finish-to-start critical activities may point out opportunities that can be revised to be parallel by using start-to-start relationships. For example, in place of a finish-to-start activity "design house, then build foundation," a start-to-start relationship could be used in which the foundation can be started, say, five days (lag) after design has started—assuming the design of the foundation is the first part of the total design activity. This start-to-start relationship with a small lag allows a sequential activity to be worked on in parallel and to compress the duration of the critical path. This same concept is frequently found in projects in which concurrent engineering is used to speed completion of a project. Concurrent engineering, which is highlighted in the Snapshot from Practice: Concurrent Engineering, basically breaks activities into smaller segments so that work can be done in parallel and the project expedited. Start-to-start relationships can depict the concurrent engineering conditions and reduce network detail. Of course, the same result can be accomplished by breaking an activity into small packages that can be implemented in parallel, but this latter approach increases the network and tracking detail significantly.

Finish-to-Finish Relationship

This relationship is found in Figure 6.17. The finish of one activity depends on the finish of another activity. For example, testing cannot be completed any earlier than four days after the prototype is complete. Note that this is not a finish-to-start relationship because the testing of subcomponents can begin before the prototype is completed, but four days of "system" testing is required after the prototype is finished.

Start-to-Finish Relationship

This relationship represents situations in which the finish of an activity depends on the start of another activity. For example, system documentation cannot end until three days after testing has started (see Figure 6.18). Here all the relevant information to complete the system documentation is produced after the first three days of testing.

Combinations of Lag Relationships

More than one lag relationship can be attached to an activity. These relationships are usually start-to-start and finish-to-finish combinations tied to two activities. For example, debug cannot begin until two time units after coding has started. Coding must be finished four days before debug can be finished (see Figure 6.19).

Snapshot from Practice   Concurrent Engineering*

The In the old days, when a new product development project was initiated by a firm, it would start its sequential journey in the research and development department. Concepts and ideas would be worked out and the results passed to the engineering department, which sometimes reworked the whole product. This result would be passed to manufacturing, where it might be reworked once more in order to ensure the product could be manufactured using existing machinery and operations. Quality improvements were initiated after the fact once defects and improvement opportunities were discovered during production. This sequential approach to product development required a great deal of time, and it was not uncommon for the final product to be totally unrecognizable when compared to original specifications.

Given the emphasis on speed to the market, companies have abandoned the sequential approach to product development and have adopted a more holistic approach titled concurrent engineering. In a nutshell, *concurrent engineering* entails the active involvement of all the relevant specialty areas throughout the design and development process. The traditional chainlike sequence of finish-to-start relationships is replaced by a series of start-to-start lag relationships as soon as meaningful work can be initiated for the next phase. Figure 6.16 summarizes the dramatic gains in time to market achieved by this approach.

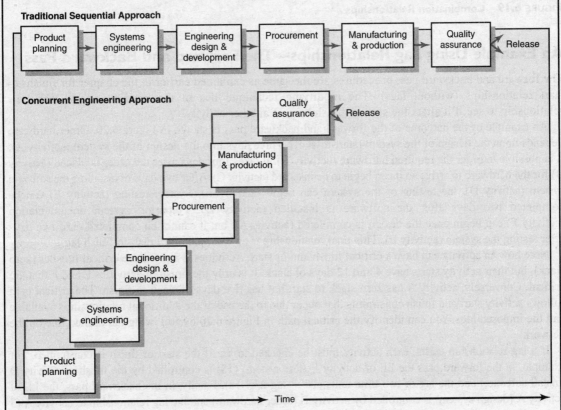

FIGURE 6.16   New Product Development Process

For example, this approach was used by Chrysler Corporation to design its new line of SC cars including the popular *Neon* sedan. From the very beginning specialists from marketing, engineering, design, manufacturing, quality assurance, and other relevant departments were involved in every stage of the project. Not only did the project meet all of its objectives, it was completed six months ahead of schedule.

* O. Suris, "Competitors Blinded by Chrysler's Neon," *The Wall Street Journal*, January 10, 1994.

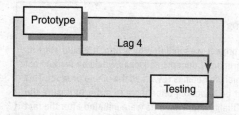

FIGURE 6.17   Finish-to-Finish Relationship

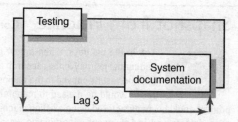

FIGURE 6.18   Start-to-Finish Relationship

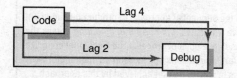

FIGURE 6.19   Combination Relationships

An Example Using Lag Relationships—The Forward and Backward Pass

The forward and backward pass procedures are the same as explained earlier in the chapter for finish-to-start relationships (without lags). The modifying technique lies in the need to check each new relationship to see if it alters the start or finish time of another activity.

An example of the outcome of the forward and backward pass is shown in Figure 6.20. Order hardware depends upon the design of the system (start-to-start). Three days into the design of the system (activity A), it is possible to order the required hardware (activity B). It takes four days after the order is placed (activity B) for the hardware to arrive so it can begin to be installed (activity C). After two days of installing the software system (activity D), the testing of the system can begin (activity E). System testing (activity E) can be completed two days after the software is installed (activity D). Preparing system documentation (activity F) can begin once the design is completed (activity A), but it cannot be completed until two days after testing the system (activity E). This final relationship is an example of a finish-to-finish lag.

Note how an activity can have a critical finish and/or start. Activities E and F have critical finishes (zero slack), but their activity starts have 4 and 12 days of slack. It is only the finish of activities E and F that are critical. Conversely, activity A has zero slack to start but has five days of slack to finish. The critical path follows activity start and finish constraints that occur due to the use of the additional relationships available and the imposed lags. You can identify the critical path in Figure 6.20 by following the dashed line on the network.

If a lag relationship exists, each activity must be checked to see if the start or finish is constrained. For example, in the forward pass the EF of activity E (test system) (18) is controlled by the finish of activity D (install software) and the lag of two time units (16 + lag 2 = 18). Finally, in the backward pass, the LS of activity A (design system) is controlled by activity B (order hardware) and the lag relationship to activity A (3 − 3 = 0).

Hammock Activities

Another of the extended techniques uses a *hammock activity*. This type of activity derives its name because it spans over a segment of a project. The hammock activity duration is determined *after* the network plan is drawn. The Snapshot from Practice: Hammock Activities describes how the hammock activity is used.

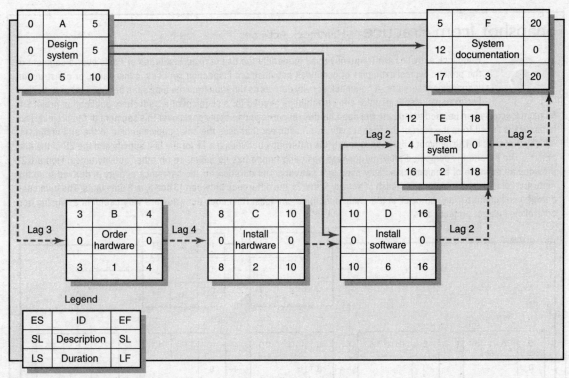

FIGURE 6.20   Network Using Lags

Summary

Many project managers feel the project network is their most valuable exercise and planning document. Project networks sequence and time-phase the project work, resources, and budgets. Work package tasks are used to develop activities for networks. Every project manager should feel comfortable working in an AON environment. The AON method uses nodes (boxes) for activities and arrows for dependencies. The forward and backward passes establish early and late times for activities. Although most project managers use computers to generate networks and activity times, they find a keen understanding of network development and the ability to compute activity times is invaluable in the field. Computers break down; input errors give false information; some decisions must be made without computer "what if" analysis. Project managers who are well acquainted with network development and AON methods and who are able to compute activity times will encounter fewer problems than project managers less well acquainted. Project networks help to ensure there are no surprises.

Several extensions and modifications have been appended to the original AON method. Lags allow the project planner to more closely replicate the actual conditions found in practice. The use of lags can result in the start or finish of an activity becoming critical. Some computer software simply calls the whole activity critical rather than identifying the start or finish as being critical. Caution should be taken to ensure that lags are not used as a buffer for possible errors in estimating time. Finally, hammock activities are useful in tracking costs of resources used for a particular segment of a project. Hammock activities can also be used to reduce the size of a project network by grouping activities for simplification and clarity. All of the discussed refinements to the original AON methodology contribute toward better planning and control of projects.

Snapshot from Practice   Hammock Activities

Hammock activities are frequently used to identify the use of fixed resources or costs over a segment of the project. Typical examples of hammock activities are inspection services, consultants, or construction management services. A hammock activity derives its duration from the time span between other activities. For example, a special color copy machine is needed for a segment of a tradeshow publication project. A hammock activity can be used to indicate the need for this resource and to apply costs over this segment of the project. This hammock is linked from the start of the first activity in the segment that uses the color copy machine to the end of the last activity that uses it. The hammock duration is simply the difference between the EF for the last activity and the ES of the first activity. The duration is computed after the forward pass and hence has no influence on other activity times. Figure 6.21 provides an example of a hammock activity used in a network. The duration for the hammock activity is derived from the early start of activity B and the early finish of activity F; that is, the difference between 13 and 5, or 8 time units. The hammock duration will change if any ES or EF in the chain-sequence changes. Hammock activities are very useful in assigning and controlling indirect project costs.

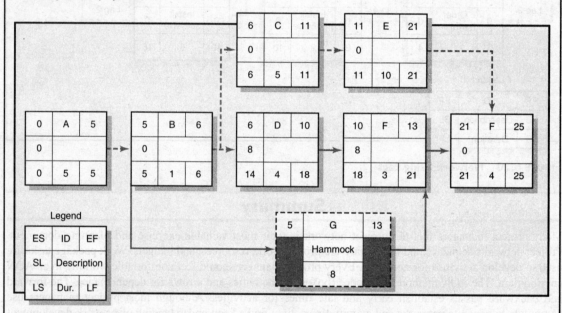

FIGURE 6.21   Hammock Activity Example

Another major use of hammock activities is to aggregate sections of a project. This is similar to developing a subnetwork, but the precedence is still preserved. This approach is sometimes used to present a "macro network" for upper management levels. Using a hammock activity to group activities can facilitate getting the right level of detail for specific sections of a project.

Key Terms

Activity

Activity-on-arrow (AOA)

Activity-on-node (AON)

Burst activity

Concurrent engineering

Critical path

Early and late times

Gantt chart

Hammock activity

Lag relationship

Merge activity

Network sensitivity

Parallel activity

Slack/float—total and free

Review Questions

1. How does the WBS differ from the project network?
2. How are WBS and project networks linked?
3. Why bother creating a WBS? Why not go straight to a project network and forget the WBS?
4. Why is slack important to the project manager?
5. What is the difference between free slack and total slack?
6. Why are lags used in developing project networks?
7. What is a hammock activity, and when is it used?

Exercises

Creating a Project Network

1. Here is a work breakdown structure for a wedding. Use the method described in the Snapshot from Practice: The Yellow Sticky Approach to create a network for this project.

Note: Do not include summary tasks in the network (i.e., 1.3, Ceremony, is a summary task; 1.2, Marriage license, is not a summary task). Do not consider who would be doing the task in building the network. For example, do not arrange "hiring a band" to occur after "florist" because the same person is responsible for doing both tasks. Focus only on technical dependencies between tasks.

Hint: Start with the last activity (wedding reception), and work your way back to the start of the project. Build the logical sequence of tasks by asking the following question: In order to have or do this, what must be accomplished immediately before this? Once completed, check forward in time by asking this question: Is this task(s) the only thing that is needed immediately before the start of the next task?

Work Breakdown Structure

1. Wedding project
   - 1.1 Decide on date
   - 1.2 Marriage license
   - 1.3 Ceremony
      - *1.3.1 Rent church*
      - *1.3.2 Florist*
      - *1.3.3 Create/print programs*
      - *1.3.4 Hire photographer*
      - *1.3.5 Wedding ceremony*
   - 1.4 Guests
      - *1.4.1 Develop guest list*
      - *1.4.2 Order invitations*
      - *1.4.3 Address and mail invitations*
      - *1.4.4 Track RSVPs*

1.5 Reception

    1.5.1 Reserve reception hall

    1.5.2 Food and beverage

        1.5.2.1 Choose caterer

        1.5.2.2 Decide on menu

        1.5.2.3 Make final order

    1.5.3 Hire band

    1.5.4 Decorate reception hall

    1.5.5 Wedding reception

Drawing AON Networks

2. Draw a project network from the following information.

Activity	Predecessor
A	None
B	A
C	A
D	A, B, C
E	D
F	D, E

3. Given the following information, draw a project network.

Activity	Predecessor
A	None
B	A
C	A
D	A
E	B
F	C, D
G	E
H	G, F

4. Use the following information to draw a project network.

Activity	Predecessor
A	None
B	A
C	A
D	B
E	B
F	C
G	D, E
H	F
I	F
J	G, H
K	J, I

5. Draw an AON project network from the following information.

Activity	Predecessor
A	None
B	None
C	None
D	A, B
E	C
F	D, E
G	E
H	F, G
I	H

6. Use the following information to draw a project network.

Activity	Predecessor
A	None
B	None
C	A
D	B
E	C, D
F	E
G	E
H	E
I	F
J	G, H
K	H, I, J

AON Network Times

7. From the following information, develop an AON project network. Complete the forward and backward pass, compute the activity slack, and identify the critical path.

Activity	Predecessor	Time (weeks)
A	None	4
B	A	5
C	A	4
D	B	3
E	C, D	6
F	D	2
G	E, F	5

What is the critical path?
How many weeks to complete?
What is the slack for activity C? For activity F?

8. The marketing department of a bank is developing a new mortgage plan for housing contractors. Draw a project network given the information below. Complete the forward and backward pass, compute the activity slack, and identify the critical path.

Activity	Predecessor	Time (weeks)
A	None	3
B	None	4
C	A	2
D	C	5
E	B	7
F	D, E	1
G	D	4
H	F, G	5

What is the critical path?

How many weeks to complete?

What is the slack for activity F? For activity G?

9. The project information for the custom order project of the Air Control Company is presented here. Draw a project network for this project. Compute the early and late activity times and the slack times. Identify the critical path.

ID	Activity	Predecessor	Time
A	Order review	None	2
B	Order standard parts	A	15
C	Produce standard parts	A	10
D	Design custom parts	A	13
E	Software development	A	18
F	Manufacture custom hardware	C, D	15
G	Assemble	B, F	10
H	Test	E, G	5

10. J. Wold, project manager of Print Software, Inc., wants you to prepare a project network; compute the early, late, and slack activity times; determine the planned project duration; and identify the critical path. His assistant has collected the following information for the Color Printer Drivers Software Project:

ID	Description	Predecessor	Time
A	External specifications	None	8
B	Review design features	A	2
C	Document new features	A	3
D	Write software	A	60
E	Program and test	B	60
F	Edit and publish notes	C	2
G	Review manual	D	2
H	Alpha site	E, F	20
I	Print manual	G	10
J	Beta site	H, I	10
K	Manufacture	J	12
L	Release and ship	K	3

11. A large eastern city is requesting federal funding for a park-and-ride project. One of the requirements in the request application is a network plan for the design phase of the project. Catherine Walker, the chief engineer, wants you to develop a project network plan to meet this requirement. She has gathered the activity time estimates and their dependencies shown here. Show your project network with the activity early, late, and slack times. Mark the critical path.

ID	Description	Predecessor	Time
A	Survey	None	5
B	Soils report	A	20
C	Traffic design	A	30
D	Lot layout	A	5
E	Approve design	B, C, D	80
F	Illumination	E	15
G	Drainage	E	30
H	Landscape	E	25
I	Signing	E	20
J	Bid proposal	F, G, H, I	10

12. Given the project network that follows, complete a bar chart for the project. Use the timeline to align your bars. Be sure to show slack for noncritical activities.

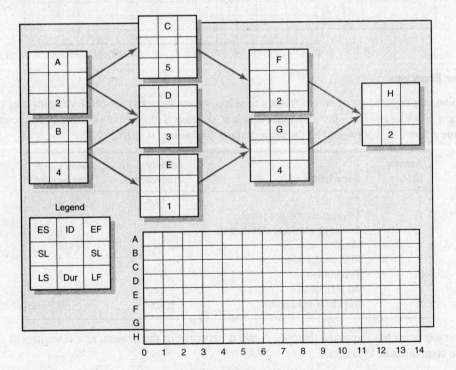

13. Given the project network that follows, complete a bar chart for the project. Use the timeline to align your bars. Be sure to show slack for noncritical activities.

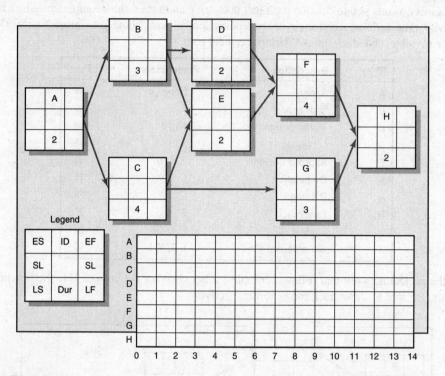

Computer Exercises

14. The planning department of an electronics firm has set up the activities for developing and production of a new CD Player. Given the information below, develop a project network using Microsoft Project. Assume a five-day workweek and the project starts on January 4, 2010.

Activity ID	Description	Activity Predecessor	Activity Time (weeks)
1	Staff	None	2
2	Develop market program	1	3
3	Select channels of distribution	1	8
4	Patent	1	12
5	Pilot production	1	4
6	Test market	5	4
7	Ad promotion	2	4
8	Set up for production	4, 6	16

The project team has requested that you create a network for the project, and determine if the project can be completed in 45 weeks.

15. Using Microsoft Project, set up the network and determine the critical path for Phase 1 of the project. The project workweek will be 5 days (M—F).

Whistler Ski Resort Project

Given the coming 2010 Winter Olympics in Vancouver and Whistler, BC, Canada, and the fact that the number of skiing visitors to Whistler has been increasing at an exciting rate, the Whistler Ski Association has been considering construction of another ski lodge and ski complex. The results of an economic feasibility study just completed by members of the staff show that a winter resort complex near the base of Whistler Mountain could be a very profitable venture. The area is accessible by car, bus, train, and air. The board of directors has voted to build the ten-million dollar complex recommended in the study. Unfortunately, due to the short summer season, the complex will have to be built in stages. The first stage (year 1) will contain a day lodge, chair lift, rope tow, generator house (for electricity), and a parking lot designed to accommodate 400 cars and 30 buses. The second and third stages will include a hotel, ice rink, pool, shops, two additional chair lifts, and other attractions. The board has decided that stage one should begin no later than April 1 and be completed by October 1, in time for the next skiing season. You have been assigned the task of project manager, and it is your job to coordinate the ordering of materials and construction activities to ensure the project's completion by the required date.

After looking into the possible sources of materials, you are confronted with the following time estimates. Materials for the chair lift and rope tow will take 30 days and 12 days, respectively, to arrive once the order is submitted. Lumber for the day lodge, generator hut, and foundations will take 9 days to arrive. The electrical and plumbing materials for the day lodge will take 12 days to arrive. The generator will take 12 days to arrive. Before actual construction can begin on the various facilities, a road to the site must be built; this will take 6 days. As soon as the road is in, clearing can begin concurrently on the sites of the day lodge, generator house, chair lift, and rope tow. It is estimated that the clearing task at each site will take 6 days, 3 days, 36 days, and 6 days, respectively. The clearing of the main ski slopes can begin after the area for the chair lift has been cleared; this will take 84 days.

The foundation for the day lodge will take 12 days to complete. Construction of the main framework will take an additional 18 days. After the framework is completed, electrical wiring and plumbing can be installed concurrently. These should take 24 and 30 days, respectively. Finally, the finishing construction on the day lodge can begin; this will take 36 days.

Installation of the chair lift towers (67 days) can begin once the site is cleared, lumber delivered, and the foundation completed (6 days). Also, when the chair lift site has been cleared, construction of a permanent road to the upper towers can be started; this will take 24 days. While the towers are being installed, the electric motor to drive the chair lift can be installed; the motor can be installed in 24 days. Once the towers are completed and the motor installed, it will take 3 days to install the cable and an additional 12 days to install the chairs.

Installation of the towers for the rope tow can begin once the site is cleared and the foundation is built and poured; it takes 4 days to build the foundation, pour the concrete and let it cure, and 20 days to install the towers for the rope tow. While the towers are being erected, installation of the electric motor to drive the rope tow can begin; this activity will take 24 days. After the towers and motor are installed, the rope tow can be strung in 1 day. The parking lot can be cleared once the rope tow is finished; this task will take 18 days.

The foundation for the generator house can begin at the same time as the foundation for the lodge; this will take 6 days. The main framework for the generator house can begin once the foundation is completed; framing will take 12 days. After the house is framed, the diesel generator can be installed in 18 days. Finishing construction on the generator house can now begin and will take 12 more days.

Assignment:

1. Identify the critical path on your network.
2. Can the project be completed by October 1?

Optical Disk Preinstallation Project

16. The optical disk project team has started gathering the information necessary to develop the project network—predecessor activities and activity times in weeks. The results of their meeting are found in the following table.

Activity	Description	Duration	Predecessor
1	Define scope	6	None
2	Define customer problems	3	1
3	Define data records and relationships	5	1
4	Mass storage requirements	5	2, 3
5	Consultant needs analysis	10	2, 3
6	Prepare installation network	3	4, 5
7	Estimate costs and budget	2	4, 5
8	Design section "point" system	1	4, 5
9	Write request proposal	5	4, 5
10	Compile vendor list	3	4, 5
11	Prepare mgmt. control system	5	6, 7
12	Prepare comparison report	5	9, 10
13	Compare system "philosophies"	3	8, 12
14	Compare total installation	2	8, 12
15	Compare cost of support	3	8, 12
16	Compare customer satisfaction level	10	8, 12
17	Assign philosophies points	1	13
18	Assign installation cost	1	14
19	Assign support cost	1	15
20	Assign customer satisfaction points	1	16
21	Select best system	1	11, 17, 18, 19, 20
22	Order system	1	21

The project team has requested that you create a network for the project, and determine if the project can be completed in 45 weeks.

Lag Exercises

17. From the following information, draw the project network. Compute the early, late, and slack times for each activity. Identify the critical path. (Hint: Draw the finish-to-start relationships first.)

ID	Duration	Finish-to-Start Predecessor	Finish-to-Start Lag	Additional Lag Relationships	Lag
A	5	None	0	None	0
B	10	A	0	None	0
C	15	A	0	Start-finish C to D	20
D	5	B	5	Start-start D to E	5
				Finish-finish D to E	25
E	20	B	0	Finish-finish E to F	0
F	15	D	0	None	
G	10	C	10	Finish-finish G to F	10
H	20	F	0	None	

18. Given the following information, draw the project network. Compute the early, late, and slack times for the project network. Which activities on the critical path have only the start or finish of the activity on the critical path?

ID	Duration	Finish-to-Start Predecessor	Finish-to-Start Lag	Additional Lag Relationships	Lag
A	2	None	0	None	0
B	4	A	0	None	0
C	6	A	0	Finish-finish C to F	7
D	8	A	0	None	0
E	18	B	0	Finish-finish E to G	9
		C	10		
F	2	D	0	None	
G	5	F	0	Start-start G to H	10
H	5	None	0	None	0
I	14	E	0	Finish-finish I to J	5
J	15	G, H	0	None	

19. Given the information in the following lag exercises, compute the early, late, and slack times for the project network. Which activities on the critical path have only the start or finish of the activity on the critical path?

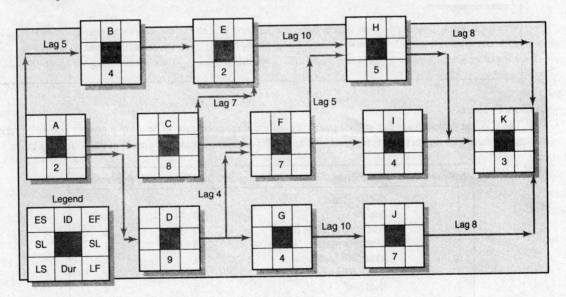

20. Given the network below, compute the early, late, and slack time for each activity.

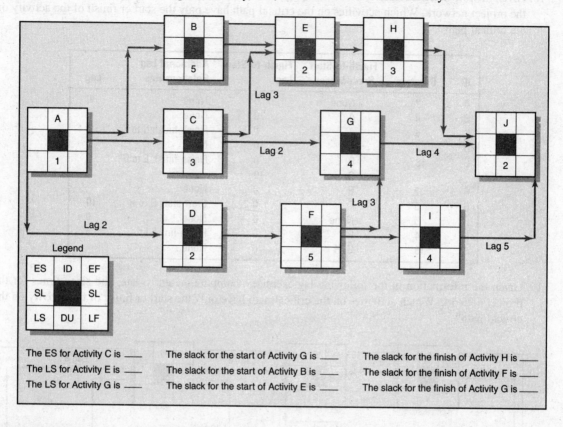

The ES for Activity C is ____   The slack for the start of Activity G is ____   The slack for the finish of Activity H is ____

The LS for Activity E is ____   The slack for the start of Activity B is ____   The slack for the finish of Activity F is ____

The LS for Activity G is ____   The slack for the start of Activity E is ____   The slack for the finish of Activity G is ____

CyClon Project

21. The CyClon project team has started gathering information necessary to develop a project network-predecessor activities and activity time in days. The results of their meeting are found in the following table:

Activity	Description	Duration	Predecessor
1	**Cyclon Project**		
2	Design	10	
3	Procure prototype parts	10	2
4	Fabricate parts	8	2
5	Assemble prototype	4	3, 4
6	Laboratory test	7	5
7	Field test	10	6
8	Adjust design	6	7
9	Order stock components	10	8
10	Order custom components	15	8
11	Assemble test production unit	10	9, 10
12	Test unit	5	11
13	Document results	3	12

Part A. Create a network based on the above information. How long will the project take? What is the critical path?

Part B. Upon further review the team recognizes that they missed three finish-to-start lags. Procure prototype parts will involve only 2 days of work but it will take 8 days for the parts to be delivered. Likewise, Order stock components will take 2 days of work and 8 days for delivery and Order custom components 2 days of work and 13 days for delivery.

Reconfigure the CyClon schedule by entering the three finish-to-start lags. What impact did these lags have on the original schedule? On the amount of work required to complete the project?

Part C. Management is still not happy with the schedule and wants the project completed as soon as possible. Unfortunately, they are not willing to approve additional resources. One team member pointed out that the network contained only finish-to-start relationships and that it might be possible to reduce project duration by creating start-to-start lags. After much deliberation the team concluded that the following relationships could be converted into start-to-start lags:

- Procure prototype parts could start 6 days after the start of Design.
- Fabricate parts could start 9 days after the start of Design.
- Laboratory test could begin 1 day after the start of Assemble prototype.
- Field test could start 5 days after the start of Laboratory test.
- Adjust design could begin 7 days after the start of Field test.
- Order stock and Order custom components could begin 5 days after Adjust design.
- Test unit could begin 9 days after the start of Assemble test production unit.
- Document results could start 3 days after the start of Test unit.

Reconfigure the CyClon schedule by entering all nine start-to-start lags. What impact did these lags have on the original schedule (Part A)? How long will the project take? Is there a change in the critical path? Is there a change in the sensitivity of the network? Why would management like this solution?

APPENDIX 6.1

Activity-on-Arrow Method

Description

The activity-on-arrow (AOA) approach also uses the arrow and node as network building blocks. However, in this approach *the arrow represents an individual project activity that requires time*. The length and slope of the arrow have no significance. *The node represents an event; it is usually presented as a small circle.* Events represent points in time but do not consume time. Each activity on the network has a start and end event node. For example, if the activity were "install software," the start event could be "start installing software" and the end event could be "finish software installation." Event nodes are numbered with the start node having a smaller number than the end event node (see Figure A6.1). These two numbers are used to identify the activity start node to finish node (79–80). As we shall see shortly, an event node can serve as a start or end node for one or more activities, and an end event node can serve as a start node for one or more activities that immediately follow.

Figure A6.2 illustrates several methods for showing AOA activity relationships in a project network. Figure A6.2A simply tells the project manager that activity X must be completed before activity Y can begin. Activity X can also be identified as activity 10–11. Note that event 11 is the finish event for activity X and the start event for activity Y. All AOA networks use this method to link activities and establish dependencies among activities.

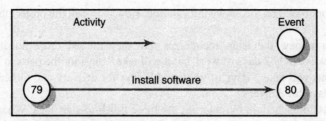

FIGURE A6.1 AOA Network Building Blocks

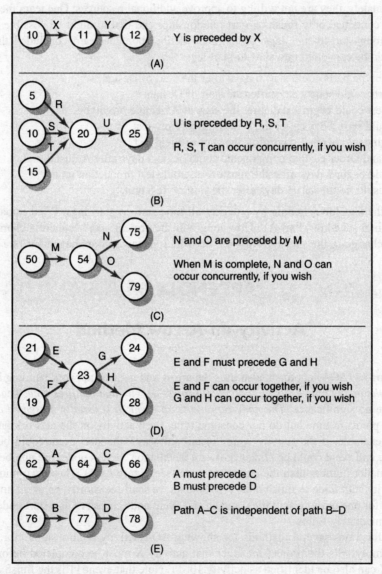

FIGURE A6.2 Activity-on-Arrow Network Fundamentals

Figure A6.2B tells us that activities R, S, and T are parallel, that is, independent, and can occur concurrently if the project manager wishes; however, activities R, S, and T must all be completed before activity U can begin. Observe how event 20 is a common ending event for activities R, S, and T and the start event for activity U. Figure 6.2C shows that activity M must be completed before activities N and O can begin. When activity M is complete, activities N and O are considered independent and can occur simultaneously if you wish. Event 54 is called a burst event because more than one activity arrow leaves (bursts from) it. Figure A6.2D tells us activity E and F can go on together, but both must be completed before activities G and H can begin. Event 23 is both a merge event and a burst event. Theoretically, an event is unlimited in the number of activities (arrows) that can lead into (merge) or out of (burst from) it. Figure A6.2E illustrates parallel paths A–C and B–D. Activity A must precede activity C and B precede D. Paths A–C and B–D are independent of each other. Let us apply these fundamentals to the simple Koll Business Center project.

Design of an AOA Project Network

You are now ready to use the information in Table A6.1 to draw an AOA network of the Koll Business Center. From the information given, the first four activities can be drawn as shown in Figure A6.3. Activity A (1–2) (Application approval) must be completed before activities B (2–4), C (2–3), and D (2–5) can begin.

TABLE A6.1   Network Information

KOLL BUSINESS CENTER County Engineers Design Department			
Activity	Description	Preceding Activity	Activity Time
A	Application approval	None	5
B	Construction plans	A	15
C	Traffic study	A	10
D	Service availability check	A	5
E	Staff report	B, C	15
F	Commission approval	B, C, D	10
G	Wait for construction	F	170
H	Occupancy	E, G	35

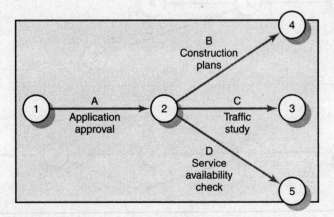

FIGURE A6.3   Partial Koll Business Center AOA Network

At this point we run into a problem common in AOA networks. Activity E is preceded by activities B and C. The natural inclination is to draw your activity arrows for B and C from event 2 straight to event 4, which is the beginning event for activity E. However, the result would be that activities B and C would both have the same identification numbers (2–4). In cases like this where two or more activities are parallel and have the same start and finish nodes, a dummy activity is inserted to ensure each activity has its unique identification number. A dummy activity is depicted by a dashed arrow and its duration is zero. The dummy activity could be inserted before or after either activity B or C as shown in Figure A6.4 (see parts A through D). In Figure A6.4E we placed it after activity C with its own identification of X or 3–4.

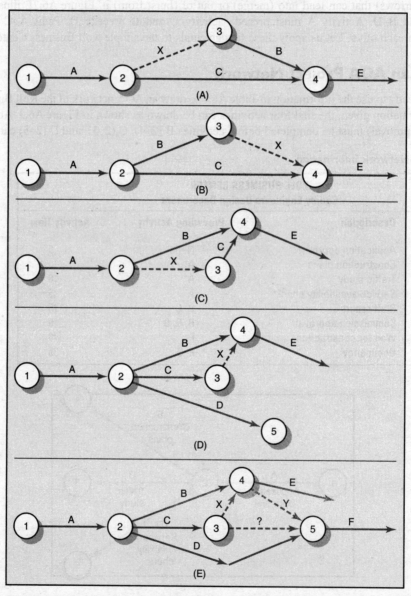

FIGURE A6.4   Partial AOA Koll Business Center Network

Activity F in Figure A6.4E denotes another network problem in which activity dependencies exist but it is not convenient to connect the activities. In this case, the dummy activity can be used to maintain the logic of the network dependencies. Activity F is preceded by activities B, C, and D. Dummy activity Y (4–5) is necessary because activity B precedes both E and F. The dummy activity maintains the intended logic and sequence. Dummy activity 3–5 can be removed because it is redundant; that is, its removal does not change the intended relationships—the end event 4 precedes activity F. Typically, the first pass in drawing your network will include many dummy activities. After several passes forward and backward through the network, you will find ways to remove some of the dummy activities that are there solely to maintain logic. However, when two or more parallel activities have the same beginning and ending event nodes, dummy activities cannot be avoided. Figure A6.5 has a completed network for the Koll design project.

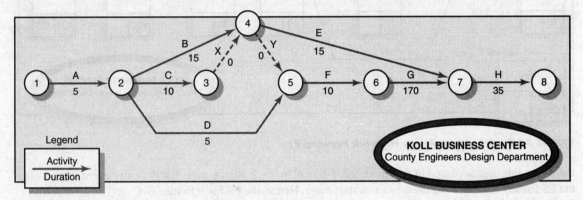

FIGURE A6.5   Activity-on-Arrow Network

In this simple project network no activity networks cross over each other, a situation which is very rare. Remember the length and slope of the arrows is arbitrary. The activity durations are included and found below the arrows, near the middle. You should work through the AOA network exercises before moving to the next section. Your familiarity with the activity/event approach will help your initial understanding of the forward and backward pass on an AOA network.

Forward Pass—Earliest Times

The forward pass in AOA uses the same concepts found in the AON procedure. The major difference lies in recognition and use of events to set early and late start and finish times for activities. Figure A6.6 shows the Koll design project with all the activity durations and early start and finish times. Also near each event is a box that will allow us to record event times and slack. In the field this box is sometimes called a "T-box" because the shape within the box forms the letter T. There are many variations of the T-box found in the field, but they all use the basic T format.

The forward pass starts with the first activity(ies) and traces each path through the network. As in AON, you *add* (cumulate) the activity times along the path. When you come to a merge event, you select the largest early finish (EF) of all the activities merging to that event. Let's work through Figure A6.6. Event 1 is the project start event; therefore, the earliest that event can occur is time zero. This early event time for event 1 is placed in the lower left side of the event box. The early event time is also the ES for any activity bursting from an event. Therefore, the zero in the box for event 1 is also the early start for activity A. The early finish for activity A is 5 workdays (ES + Dur = EF or 0 + 5 = 5). The EF for the activity is placed at the head of the arrow. The earliest event 2 can occur is the instant activity A is complete, which is 5 workdays;

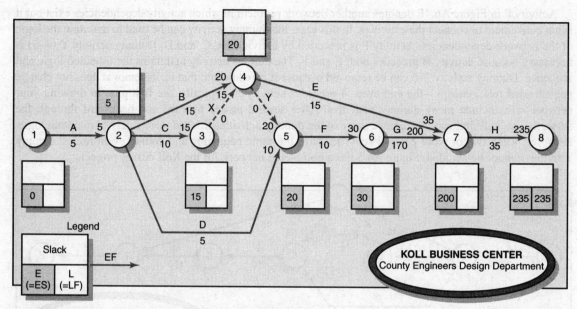

FIGURE A6.6   Activity-on-Arrow Network Forward Pass

therefore, this time is placed in the lower left T-box of event 2. Again, note that the early event time is also the ES for any activity using the event as a start event. Hence, the ES for activities B, C, and D is 5 workdays. The EF for activity B is 20 (ES + Dur = EF), for activity C is 15, and for activity D is 10. (See the head of the arrow for each activity.) The ES for the dummy activity (3–4) is 15, and its EF is 15 (15 + 0 = 15). Although the dummy activity has zero duration, it must be included in the forward and backward pass computations.

At this point you must determine the early event times for events 4 and 5. Both are merge events that require selection among activities merging into these events. Event 4 has B and X, the dummy activity (3–4). The largest EF for these two activities (20 and 15) is 20, which controls the early event time for event 4. Similarly, event 5 is controlled by activities D and Y. Because activity Y has the largest early finish (20 versus 10 workdays for activity D), it establishes the early event time for event 5 and activity F. Times are cumulated until merge event 7. The EFs for activities E and G are 35 and 200 workdays, respectively. Thus, event 7 and activity H have early times of 200 workdays. The early finish for the project is 235 workdays. Assuming we accept this planned duration of 235 days for the project, the LF for event 8 becomes 235 days, and you are ready to compute the backward pass.

Backward Pass—Latest Times

The backward pass procedure is similar to that used in the AON procedure. You start with the last project event node(s) and *subtract* activity times along each path (LF − Dur = LS) until you reach a burst event. When this happens, you pick the *smallest* LS of all the activities bursting from the event; this number denotes the latest that event can occur and not delay the project. Let's trace the backward pass for part of the Koll design project.

Figure A6.7 displays the late times for the events and activities. The late start for activity H is 200 days (LF − Dur = LS or 235 − 35 = 200). This time is found at the tail of the arrow. Because event 7 is not a burst event, the late start for activity H becomes the late time for event 7. This procedure continues until you reach event 4, which is a burst event. The LS for activity E is 185 and for activity Y is 20. The smallest time is 20

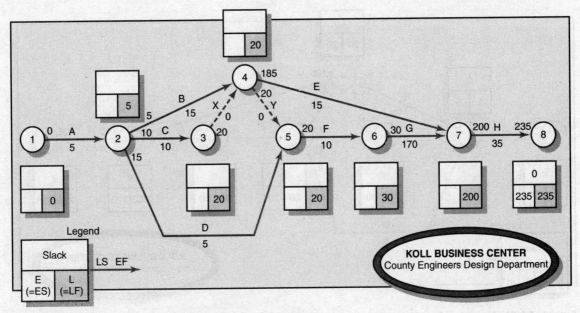

FIGURE A6.7   Activity-on-Arrow Network Backward Pass

days and is the late time for event 4. The next burst event is event 2. Here the LS for activities B, C, and D are 5, 10, and 15 days, respectively. Activity B controls the late event time for event 2, which is 5 workdays. The late event time is also the LF for any activity using the event as an end event. For example, the late time for event 7 is 200 workdays; thus, activities E and G can finish no later than day 200, or the project will be delayed.

With the backward pass complete, the slack and critical path can be identified. Figure A6.8 presents the completed network. The event slack is entered above the T in the event box. Activity slack is the difference between LS and ES or LF and EF. For example, the slack for activity E is 165 days—LS − ES (185 − 20 = 165) or LF − EF (200 − 35 = 165). What are the slack values for activities B, C, and D? The answers are zero workdays (5 − 5 = 0 or 20 − 20 = 0), 5 workdays (10 − 5 = 5 or 20 − 15 = 5), and 10 workdays (15 − 5 = 10 or 20 − 10 = 10), respectively. The critical path is A, B, Y, F, G, H.

Compare the networks found in Figure A6.8 and in chapter text Figure 6.8 to see the differences between the AOA and AON methods. As in the AON method, if the early and late time for the end project event are the same (L = E or LF = EF), the slack on the critical path will be zero. If the times are not the same, the slack on the critical path will equal the difference (L − E or LF − EF).

Computer-Generated Networks

Figure A6.9 presents a generic AOA computer output for the custom order project. AOA networks identify activities by the beginning and ending nodes—for example, the software development activity is identified as activity 2–6. Its duration is 18 time units; ES = 2; EF = 20; LS = 22; and LF = 40 time units. The critical path is 1-2-3-4-5-6-7. Compare the AOA computer output in Figure A6.9 with the AON computer output in chapter Figure 6.10. Bar charts are identical to those developed for AON networks; see chapter Figure 6.11.

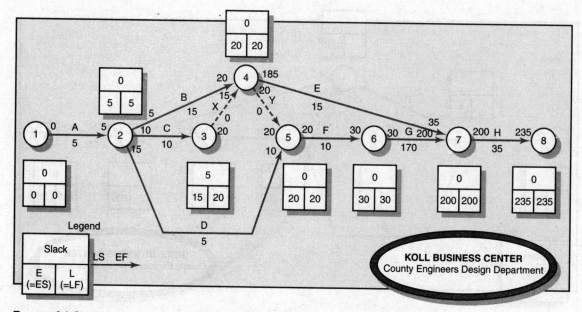

FIGURE A6.8 Activity-on-Arrow Network Backward Pass, Forward Pass, and Slack

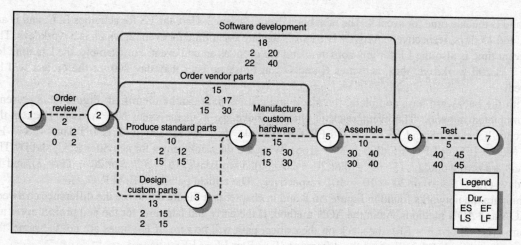

FIGURE A6.9 Air Control, Inc. Custom Order Project—AOA Network Diagram

Choice of Method—AON or AOA

Your choice of method depends on the importance of various advantages and disadvantages of each method. Table A6.2 will assist you in making your choice.

TABLE A6.2 Comparison of AON and AOA Methods

AON Method
Advantages
1. No dummy activities are used.
2. Events are not used.
3. AON is easy to draw if dependencies are not intense.
4. Activity emphasis is easily understood by first-level managers.
5. The CPM approach uses deterministic times to construct networks.
Disadvantages
1. Path tracing by activity number is difficult. If the network is not available, computer outputs must list the predecessor and successor activities for each activity.
2. Network drawing and understanding are more difficult when dependencies are numerous.

AOA Method
Advantages
1. Path tracing is simplified by activity/event numbering scheme.
2. AOA is easier to draw if dependencies are intense.
3. Key events or milestones can easily be flagged.
Disadvantages
1. Use of dummy activities increases data requirements.
2. Emphasis on events can detract from activities. Activity delays cause events and projects to be late.

Summary

In AOA networks, dummy activities meet two needs. First, when two parallel activities have the same start and end nodes, a dummy must be inserted to give each activity a unique identification number (see activity X in Figure A6.8). Next, dummy activities can be used to clarify dependency relationships (see activity Y in Figure A6.8). Dummy activities are very useful when activity dependencies are far apart on the network. In AOA networks the early event time is the ES for any activity emanating from the event. Conversely, the late event time is the LF for any activity merging to the event. The major advantage of the AOA method is the avoidance of having to list all the predecessor and successor activities for each activity in the network so activity sequence and dependency can be traced when a network is not available or shows incomplete information. Computer output is reduced manyfold.

Review Questions

1. How do the building blocks of AON and AOA differ?
2. What are the purposes of dummy or pseudo activities?
3. How do activities differ from events?

Appendix Exercises

1. Use the information found in the text exercises 3 and 4 (page 173) to draw AOA networks.
2. Use the information found in the text exercise 11 to draw an AOA network. Include the activity times and event nodes on the network as shown in Figure A6.5.

3. Given the project network that follows, compute the early, late, and slack times for the project. Be sure to show the early finish and late start times on your network.

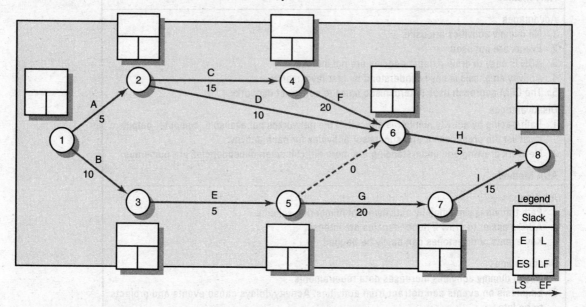

4. Given the project network that follows, compute the early, late, and slack times for the project. Be sure to show the early finish and late start times on your network.

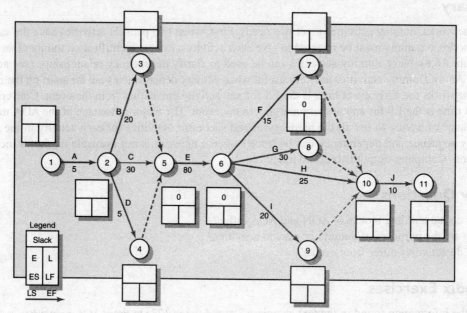

5. Given the project network that follows, complete the bar chart for this project. Use the timeline to align your bars. Be sure to use the legend to show slack for noncritical activities.

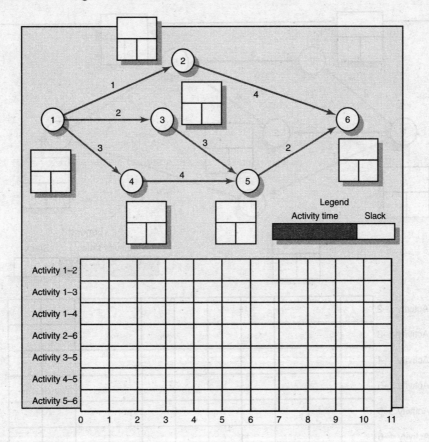

6. Given the project network that follows, draw a bar chart for this project. Use the timeline to align your bars. Be sure to show slack for noncritical activities.

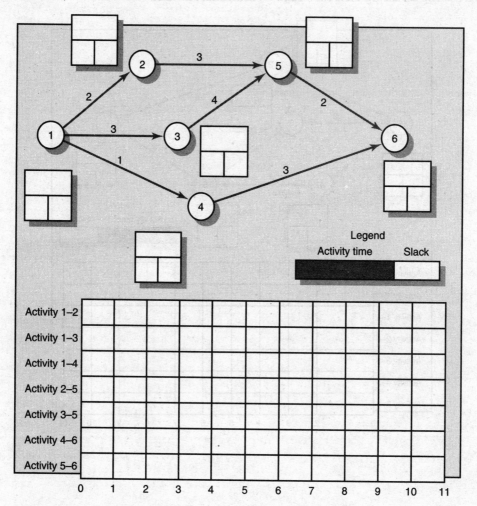

APPENDIX 6.2

Project Time Management

1. Introduction

1.1 Importance of Time Management

Project time management, along with project scope and project cost management, is one of the three core areas of project management. The reason for importance of time management is rooted in three factors:

- *Essential Nature of Projects:* By definition, the projects are temporary endeavors to create a unique product, service or result. They are authorized with definite starting dates and definite completion dates to accomplish the objectives and these essential constraints for project must be observed during all project work. Often, the windows of opportunity for exploiting the value of the product of the project are open for only a small specific time slot—like timing for introduction of a new product for developing a new technology or a product complying with a new technology, for release of large volume of production to the customers or consumers at opportune times, etc. If the projects do not deliver the project objectives in the schedule earmarked for them, their value to the organization is greatly diminished and sometimes the time, effort and resources spent on a project delayed may turn out to be just entirely wasteful. The cliché," Time is money", is literally very true for projects and project management.

- *Incremental Costs Associated with Schedule Delay:* Again, often, the project delay results in the loss of focus by the project team and sometimes even by the entire organization. With loss of momentum and enthusiasm, which invariably accompany project delays, the focus on quality gets diffused, the effort level slackens and the period costs associated with the time mount up. The analysis of a vast number of projects confirms the conclusion that projects with delayed schedule are invariably associated with large cost overruns.

- *Irreversible Recovery of Time Delays:* The project manager and his team must attend to effective time management right from the start, for lost time cannot be recovered at any cost. If the work done for project deliverable does not meet quality standards or criteria for project success, may be with extra efforts and costs, some recovery might be possible. It may be possible to compensate the overruns of some project activities by cost economy in some others. But, in case of unacceptable project delays and missing the opportunities, there is no such safety net.

Therefore, all project methodology lay strong emphasis on managing project time.

1.2 Key Issues in Time Management

The superstructure for effective management of time rests on three pillars. We shall briefly discuss these principles below before taking up discussion on the time management processes described in PMBOK® Guide and the inputs, tools and techniques and outputs for them.

1.2.1 Well Prepared Project Plans

The effective management of project time begins with a well prepared project plan which essentially involves following the logical process steps mentioned below.

(i) *Identification and definition of activities:* A thorough review of the work packages developed in work breakdown structure is carried out and all activities necessary for accomplishing the work packages are identified and listed. In order to compile this list, the project team must have access to the knowledge or expertise in the industry practice and knowledge of the project's product or service characteristics for understanding the project scope and the nature of work involved in project activities. This exercise has to be carried out very patiently and thoroughly (particularly for projects new to the organization) so that no activity necessary for project work slips between the tables.

The next step is focusing on each activity and determining the nature, quality standard & performance requirements and the quantum of work for completing each activity. With these two steps, a comprehensive list of well defined activities would be available with the project team.

(ii) *Sequencing the activities:* Sequencing the activities from the list is the next logical step in planning. Often, the sequencing of activities is natural and follows a logical approach and conformance to physical requirements for carrying out the work (like casting the foundation and columns before building the superstructure). However, there is a pitfall to watch out for. Sometimes the dependency of an activity on completion of another activity is not mandatory but a specific activity sequence is adopted only due to traditional practice in the industry. It is desirable to question the dependency of each activity on the prior activity and spot opportunities for good planning (by fast tracking and parallel paths for network).

(iii) *Estimating resources and time required for each activity:* In most project work, the availability of resources to the organization or resources released for a particular project is a constraint and the time required for an activity often depends on the quality and availability of resources. Therefore, it is often necessary to decide on the resources available for carrying out an activity and the estimated time for an activity simultaneously. While doing this, it is important to keep in mind this relationship, so that if there is a need to rework the project schedule at a later stage to crash activity duration, the project team would be able to take an informed decision.

(iv) *Develop Project Network and Project Schedule:* Using the list of defined activities arranged in a sequence showing the precedence and succession connections between them, the project network is mapped out. Note that except the project start and project end, every activity should have one or more activities preceding it and one or more activities succeeding it. The forward path and backward path analysis of project network would reveal a critical path, which would determine the minimum time for project duration from the start and all activities on the critical path which must be completed for completing the project.

(v) *Tailoring the schedule to project constraints or sponsor's requirements:* If the project schedule resulting from this network plan meets the project sponsor's requirements, there would be no further work necessary for planning project schedule. More often, the sponsor's needs would necessitate a shorter project schedule than the first pass on the critical path for the network would come out with. This would start another round of review of the project network activities with a view to cut down the project schedule. This could be done by carrying out fast tracking of activities (some activities originally planned to be carried out sequentially are taken up simultaneously or in parallel) or activities crashing (making additional resources available at additional cost to reduce the activity duration). This network tweaking process is continued till the overall schedule meets the project sponsor's requirements.

The modern project planning software are a great help in project planning. The project planning software (like Microsoft Project ® , Prima Vera® or other proprietary software) are very helpful in the steps of activities listing and orderly arranging the list, developing the project network and project schedule, and going through the iterative modification rounds necessary to develop a satisfactory project schedule.

1.2.2 Vigilant monitoring of progress and prompt corrective actions

Once an effective planning is accomplished, it needs to be vigilantly followed to ensure that project is completed in the planned schedule. A planning approach which could be helpful would be to carry out a risk analysis for schedule delays and prepare plans to go into action if the risk occurs. A more proactive approach would be to watch out for risk triggers and take the steps envisaged in the risk management plan promptly as soon as the trigger is pressed.

The first necessity for schedule control is close monitoring of the performance. Once the variance between the planned schedule and actual performance is noted, the schedule compression techniques should be deployed.

Frequently, the villain of the piece turns out to be inadequately controlled scope changes. Scope creep has a tendency to cause cost overruns as well as schedule delays. An effective integrated change control procedures and scope control measures would contribute significantly to schedule control also.

Another useful technique is to take a calculated risk for rework or repair and apply suitable leads or lags between the preceding and succeeding activities. In this approach, as soon as the preceding activity is completed to a degree sufficient to permit availability of information or set up physical condition suitable to start the succeeding activity, it should be taken up for execution without waiting for the preceding activity to reach its proper completion.

1.2.3 Proactive integrated schedule management

Understanding and applying the principles based on relationships between project scope, quality, cost and time can be useful for project schedule management. The classical representation of this relationship visualizes the scope, time and cost as the sides of a triangle; change in any one side length is likely to change the lengths of other sides. As every project manager knows, the activity durations and project schedule are not absolute unchangeable quantities. It would be possible to reduce some part of the scope or relax a quality standard in order to save time. It might also be possible to use more expensive resources or larger quantum of resources to crash an activity time at the risk of cost overrun. It might be possible to take a chance and take a short cut to compress the activity duration with activities executed in parallel network paths. All these decisions require a project manager to understand thoroughly the effect the variation in parameters would have on the set of activities and project under management. The project manager should also have clear conception of the project sponsor's requirements and priorities so that the right trade-off among the available options could be chosen (for example, whether scope should be reduced or quality standard should be relaxed for cutting down activity duration or whether preventing a minor delay in schedule is worth the risk of significant cost overrun, or adding a feature considered valuable by the sponsor, etc.).

2. Project Time Management Processes

(PMBOK® GUIDE, 4TH EDITION, APPROACH)

The detailed description of the process for development of the project plan and step-wise illustration of the technique for developing and analyzing the project network to find the critical path is the subject matter of this chapter. The readers interested in step-wise instructions for learning the technique should devote time and effort to the relevant sections of this chapter. This section of the appendix is devoted merely to present the approach for time management given in the PMBOK® Guide for the sake of reference and comparison.

PMBOK® Guide, 4th Edition, 2008 recommends total six processes to cover the above discussed methodology for time management. Five processes are in the planning group and one process is in the monitoring and controlling group.

Planning Process Group

1. Define Activities
2. Sequence Activities
3. Estimate Activity Resources

4. Estimate Activity Durations
5. Develop Schedule

Monitoring and Controlling Process Group

1. Control Schedule

The inputs, techniques and tools and outputs for these processes are briefly described below.

2.1 Define Activities

This process is involved with identifying the activities to complete a specific work package or deliverable, define the activity attributes and develop a comprehensive list of all activities necessary for meeting the project objectives. The decomposition carried out at the WBS stage is taken one step further and the work package is decomposed into one or more better defined and more manageable activities in order to come up with a list of activities with activity identification code. The difference in decomposition degree is for bringing out the actual attributes of the activity like the actual work to be carried out, predecessor and successor activities, resource requirements, assumptions & constraints, and leads & lags possibilities. Imposed or planned milestones for completion of critical activities are worked out and flagged.

PMBOK® Guide includes the following inputs, tools and techniques and outputs for this process.

Inputs

Scope Baseline is the first input. Work packages included in the WBS part of the baseline and their technical and performance specifications included in the WBS Dictionary provide the starting point. The work packages are further decomposed as explained above to prepare the activities list. *Organizational Process Assets* (activity lists and templates for activity lists in the earlier similar projects) and *Enterprise environmental Factors* (Project Management Information System and other specific activity listing and definition practices of the organization) are other likely inputs.

Tools and Techniques

The use of *Decomposition* (decomposition of work packages into one or more actual activity to be carried out), *Templates* (activity lists from similar projects) and *Expert Judgment* (based on knowledge and experience of similar earlier projects) as possible techniques should be self evident.

Rolling Wave Planning This technique requires special mention and explanation. When the project is likely to extend for a long period (over one or two years) or when the nature of the project activities cannot be chalked out accurately in advance (such conditions are likely in project requiring application of new technology, development of a new product or a research project), the rolling wave planning technique is very relevant. The technique is based on carrying out detailed planning for only the near future phase of the project about which sufficient details can be worked out. The planning without detailed activity lists and attributes for the more distant or less clearly visualized future phase of the project is done only at high level of planning. When the project work to be carried out in the next phase becomes clear enough, the detailed planning of that phase for activity lists and attributes is taken up.

Outputs

Activity Lists (A comprehensive list of all activities, with identification code, obtained by sufficient decomposition of work packages), *Activity Attributes* (the actual work to be carried out, predecessor and successor activities, nature of resource requirements, assumptions & constraints, leads and lags possibilities) and *Milestones List* (mandatory or planned completion dates worked out for critical activities) are outputs from the process.

2.2 Sequence Activities

As the name suggests, the process involves determining and recording the precedence or succession relationship between the project activities and their attributes (identified in the earlier process). The logical relationship between the activities is the basis for sequencing. Every activity, except the start and end of the project, would have some precedent or succeeding activity.

While developing the network diagram, the nature of dependency between the activities (whether mandatory, discretionary or external) and the precise relationships between the start and finish of preceding and succeeding activities (Finish-to-Start, Finish-to-Finish, Start-to-Start and Start-to-Finish) should be is examined.

PMBOK® Guide includes the following inputs, tools and techniques and outputs for the process.

Inputs

Activity list, *Activity Attributes*, and *Milestones List*, the outputs of the earlier Define Activities process, are natural logical inputs for this process. Other inputs are the *Organizational Process Assets* (data from networks of project files for similar projects) and *Project Scope Statement* (as a double check to ensure that no material deliverable or performance requirement from the original scope is missed out while preparing the WBS and WBS Dictionary).

Tools and Techniques

The techniques required to develop the network diagram from the activities list involves:

- Determining the nature of dependencies
- Employing a suitable diagrammatic method, and
- Applying suitable leads and lags between closely related activities

These are described in detail and illustrated in the main chapter text. Here only brief listing is done for the sake of comprehensive coverage.

Determining the nature of dependencies

The dependencies could be:

- Mandatory Dependencies (dependencies in the inherent nature of the work or contractual requirements)
- Discretionary Dependencies (dependencies adopted from the industry or organization practices by tradition; these dependencies could be challenged and altered for network development, if the project team desires).
- External Dependencies (when activities are dependent on some external agency outside the close control of the project team—e.g. statutory approvals for project work, delivery of critical components by a monopoly supplier, etc.)

Diagrammatic Method (Precedence Diagrammatic Method or PDM Method)

By systematic application of the network diagrammatic methods, the project network is developed. PMBOK® Guide, 4th Edition lists only one technique and that is Precedence Diagramming Method or 'Activities-onNodes' (AON) method. This method is more commonly employed by proprietary project network software. The earlier edition also listed another technique, 'Activities-on-Arrows' (AOA) method.

The diagrammatic technique requires the dependencies to be classified according to whether the relationship between the activities is:

- Finish-to-Start (The preceding activity must be completed before the succeeding activity can start. This is the most common relationship for mandatory dependencies)
- Finish-to-Finish (The succeeding activity cannot be completed unless the preceding activity is completed)

- Start-to-Start (The succeeding activity can be started only after the start of the preceding activity)
- Start-to-Finish (The preceding activity can be finished only after the start of the succeeding activity)

Applying suitable leads and lags between closely related activities

Often, the succeeding activity need not wait for the completion of the preceding activity fully. The preceding activity would need to be completed only partly before the necessary information or physical working condition suitable for start of the succeeding activity may be set up. For example, for installing a 3-kilometer-long underground piping, the pipe fabrication and installation need not wait till the entire 3 kilometers stretch is excavated. The pipe laying activity can be started with providing a lag of a few days after the start of excavation. Spotting the possibility of such suitable leads and lags can lead to an improved project schedule. *Organizational Process Assets* (use of templates for project networks of similar projects from archives) is also an effort and time saving technique.

Outputs

Project Schedule Network Diagram is the out put of the process. This diagram shows only all activities and the interrelationship between the activities. It does not include estimates for activity duration and so the time estimate for completion of the project or even the groups of activities for the project cannot be determined from the network at this stage.

2.3 Estimate Activity Resources

Estimating the resources for activities necessary to actually carry out the work for completing the project deliverable is a very important process from the point of actual project execution. The planning necessary for execution of the project activities has to be based on the knowledge and experience with the industry and the 'product oriented processes', so that requirements of technology, equipment, materials & supplies, and man-power for actually carrying out the project work can be estimated realistically. The project manager and project team's success very much depends on how knowledgeable or experienced the team is about the industry and project nature.

Inputs

Activity List and *Activity Attributes* are the logical starting points. *Enterprise Environmental factors* (the quality and availability of resources in the market place and the organization) and *Organizational Process Assets* (organization's policies and procedures for recruiting, compensation and working conditions for employees and for contractual work, etc.) are other inputs.

Tools and Techniques

Industry Practice Data from Published Sources, Bottom-Up Estimating (if ready-made estimates for exactly the same work are not available but the estimates can be built from component for which the estimates might be available) and *Expert Judgment* readily suggest themselves as tools. Looking for and evaluating *Alternative Methods* for more efficient use of resources could also be a very useful tool.

Outputs

The output from the process would be essentially the *Resource Requirements* [the equipment, materials & supplies and personnel (with skill levels) required] for carrying out an activity.

2.4 Estimate Activity Durations

The process involves estimating the time periods required for completing the individual activity with the availability of identified resources. From the scope of work for the activity and the quality and available quantity of resources, the duration can be estimated for individual activity.

Inputs

Activity List and *Activity Attributes* are again the logical starting points.

Enterprise Environmental factors (the quality and availability of resources in the market place and the organization and industry practices for work) is another input.

Resource Availability Calendar is another important input for converting the network from the number of days to working project calendar.

Tools and Techniques

The estimating techniques for activity duration follow the general pattern of estimations.

Analogous Estimation: The estimator compares the activity to be planned with a similar activity carried out for a similar project in the past and the time taken for the activity. The duration estimate is worked out by applying adjustment factors to reflect the differences in quality standards and sizes of the present and comparable past activity.

Parametric Estimation: In this technique, a parameter critical for estimating the duration is defined and from the earlier duration data for a unit value of the identified parameter (the weld length per day or excavation cubic meters per day, etc.) an estimate for activity duration is developed.

Three-point Estimate This method is based on Beta type statistical distribution theory as applied to PERT (Program Evaluation & Review Technique) for network evaluations. Three estimates are developed for the activity duration by way of the most likely (T_{lik}), Optimistic (T_{opt}) and Pessimistic (T_{pess}). From these three estimates, the expected value of the activity duration (T_{exp}) is calculated by the following formula:

$$T_{exp} = (T_{opt} + 4T_{lik} + T_{pess})/6$$

Reserve Analysis (contingency provision or time buffer added to activity duration for managing risk) and *Expert Judgment* are other tools for the process.

Outputs

Activity Duration Estimates is the main output of the process.

2.5 Develop Schedule

This process helps the project manager to take an overview of all project activities and develop the project schedule by unifying and analyzing the outputs from all earlier mentioned time management planning processes.

The steps involved in developing the project schedule are as follows:

 (i) Start with the project network, the output of the Sequence Activities process.

 (ii) Fill in the activity duration estimate for individual activity in the network—an output of Estimate Activity Duration process

 (iii) Make the forward and backward pass exercises for the network and develop the schedule for the entire project and the *Critical Path for the Project* (the path through all activities having no slack between the latest permissible and earliest possible start for each activity)

 (iv) If the project schedule developed this way is acceptable to the project sponsor or client, the schedule is firmed up

 (v) Often, the schedule worked out this way does not meet the desired project schedule. In that case, the activities on the critical path would be reviewed and techniques for schedule compression (activity time crashing and fast tracking) would be applied

 (vi) The iteration is continued till a satisfactory project plan and corresponding project schedule are developed

It is important to note that project management software play a very important part in this process. For any but the simplest project, the manual exercise is almost impossible,—very tedious, time consuming and error prone. For a medium to large size project, use of project management software is almost mandatory. When a number of iterations are necessary for developing a satisfactory project plan, the project management software proves its value. Secondly, the schedule developed on the software is also very convenient for periodic review during the monitoring and controlling phase.

PMBOK® Guide, 4th Edition, 2008 describes the following inputs, tools and techniques and outputs of the process.

Inputs

The following inputs in the PMBOK® Guide list are in essence the planning data developed from the earlier time management processes:

- *Activity List* and *Activity Attributes* (outputs of Define Activity process)
- *Project Schedule Network Diagrams* (output of Sequence Activity process)
- *Activity Resource Requirements* (output of Estimate Activity Resources)
- *Activity Duration Estimates* (output of Estimate Activity Duration process)

The other inputs essentially map project schedule to the project constraints and project success criteria:

- *Project Scope Statement* (Assumptions, constraints and criteria for project success)
- *Enterprise Environmental Factors* (External environmental constraints)
- *Organizational Process Assets* (The lessons learned and all the help which the organization's knowledge base and project archives can offer)

Tools and Techniques

The technique involved is essentially unifying and analyzing the time-related data for activities and their network relationship to develop the project schedule. Once the first-cut project schedule is ready, it would be necessary to go through the necessary iterations applying schedule compression techniques till satisfactory project schedule is developed.

The list given in PMBOK® Guide includes two types of techniques.

1. Unifying and analyzing the time data and network

- Schedule Network Analysis (Developing the first cut schedule from analysis and unification of various time data and network from earlier processes)
- Use of project management software for developing schedule

2. Optimizing the project schedule to Meet Project Objectives

- Critical Path and Critical Chain Methods (The analytical techniques for developing optimum schedule from the first schedule developed from unified network)
- Applying Leads and Lags (Optimizing the schedule)
- Schedule Compression (Modifying the schedule to meet objectives set for project success)
- Resource Leveling(Optimizing the overall project plan taking into account resource availability and resource calendar)

Outputs

Of the four outputs of the process, the main output of the process is project schedule. A brief description of the nature of project schedule and its contents would be in place here.

Project Schedule: It is the complete or comprehensive document for project time management. It shows the planned start date, planned completion date and duration of each activity. Summary milestones for start and completion of a group of activities for a project phase and the entire project are also readily available. When some proprietary software for project managements are used, their special features would enable the project team to include into the project schedule document additional useful project planning details like resource calendar, resource requirements, resource costs, assumptions and constraints for individual activity. The project schedule can be presented in tabular form or any of the following graphical formats:

- *Gantt Charts:* A bar chart with horizontal bars representing important activities labeled and placed in a series of rows and the corresponding horizontal bar lengths on the date line showing the milestones for start and finish of the activities. Strictly speaking, a Gantt Chart is not supposed to show the dependency relationships or leads and lags between the activities, but Gantt Charts for Project Schedule generally include these details.
- *Project Schedule Network Diagrams:* These diagrams show the project network, the activities, the precedence or succeeding dependency relationship of the activities and the critical path for the network. Each activity is represented by a rectangular block and the block labeled to show the activity code, activity duration, scheduled start and completion dates, the slack between the earliest and latest start dates and whether it lies on the critical path for the project.

Proprietary project management software would have several additional features, which would include provisions for activity attributes notes, resource calendars and resource assignments to activities, resource costs and even earned value management calculations. In addition, tracking the project status for monitoring and controlling the project schedule in graphical forms could also be facilitated by the software.

Other outputs of the process are:

Schedule Baseline: It is a project schedule accepted and approved by the management and forms the component part of the project management plan.

Schedule Data: This would include besides the basic milestones for project activities, activity list, activity attributes, activity duration estimates, resource requirements, assumptions and constraints in developing the schedule, and provision of contingency reserve or time buffer to manage schedule.

2.6 Control Schedule

Control Schedule is the sixth process of the time management processes and the only one in the monitoring and controlling group. It is concerned with tracking the actual status of the project activities and ensuring that the project activities adhere to the planned project schedule.

The typical activities carried out for this process include:

- Tracking the progress of all project activities
- Determining the schedule variance and taking corrective steps when the actual work performance lags behind the planned schedule (using fast tracking or activity crashing techniques)
- Anticipate schedule delays and proactively manage the project changes and risks to keep the project schedule on the track
- Forecasting the milestones for completion of the critical activities and the whole project

Inputs

Like all monitoring and controlling processes, the inputs for the process are the planned standard for comparison (*Project Management Plan* and *Project Schedule* in this case) and the actual status on the control date (*Work Performance Report* in this case).

Tools and Techniques

The three types of tools necessary for Control Schedule process are that of tracking the project status and finding the variances, taking proactive measures to keep and bring the project schedule on track and the project management software to facilitate the data record and its graphical presentation. These three types of tools are briefly described below.

- *Schedule Variance Analysis* and *Performance Reviews* are tools related to data handling and helping to know the exact schedule status and assess the need for corrective action.
- *Resource Leveling, Adjusting Leads and Lags*, and *Schedule Compression Techniques* form the project manager's arsenal for pro-active correction measures for controlling schedule.
- *Project Management Software* (proprietary software) help to facilitate recording schedule data and its graphical representation.

Outputs

Work Performance Reports showing the schedule variance and schedule variance index (using the Earned Value Management technique) is the important output.

Updates of Project Documents (particularly the schedule and cost baselines) and *Forecast for Project Completion* are other important outputs.

CASE 6.1

Advantage Energy Technology Data Center Migration*

Brian Smith, network administrator at Advanced Energy Technology (AET), has been given the responsibility of implementing the migration of a large data center to a new office location. Careful planning is needed because AET operates in the highly competitive petroleum industry. AET is one of five national software companies which provide an accounting and business management package for oil jobbers and gasoline distributors. A few years ago, AET jumped into the "application service provider" world. Their large data center provides clients with remote access to AET's complete suite of application software systems. Traditionally, one of AET's primary competitive advantages has been the company's trademark IT reliability. Due to the complexity of this project, Brian will have to use a parallel method of implementation. Although this will increase project costs, a parallel approach is essential if reliability is not to be compromised.

Currently, AET's data center is located on the second floor of a renovated old bank building in downtown, Corvallis, Oregon. The company is moving to a new, one-level building located in the recently developed industrial complex at the Corvallis International Airport. On February 1, Brian is formally assigned the task by the Vice-President of Operations, Dan Whitmore, with the following guidelines:

- From start to finish, it is anticipated the entire project will take three to four months to complete.
- It is essential that AET's 235 clients suffer no downtime.

Whitmore advises Brian to come back to the Executive Committee on February 15, with a presentation on the scope of the project that includes costs, "first-cut" timeline, and proposed project team members.

Brian had some preliminary discussions with some of AET's managers and directors from each of the functional departments and then arranged for a full-day scope meeting on February 4 with a few of the managers and technical representatives from operations, systems, facilities, and applications. The scope team determined the following:

- Three to four months is a feasible project timeline and first-cut cost estimate is $80,000–$90,000 (this includes the infrastructure upgrade of the new site).
- Critical to the "no-downtime" requirement is the need to completely rely on AET's remote disaster recovery "hot" site for full functionality.
- Brian will serve as project manager of a team consisting of one team member each from facilities, operations/systems, operations/telecommunications, systems & applications, and customer service.

Brian's Executive Committee report was positively received and, after a few modifications and recommendations, he was formally charged with responsibility for the project. Brian recruited his team and scheduled their first team meeting (March 1) as the initial task of his project planning process.

Once the initial meeting is conducted Brian can hire the contractors to renovate the new data center. During this time Brian will figure out how to design the network. Brian estimates that screening and hiring a contractor will take about one week and that the network design will take about two weeks. The new center requires a new ventilation system. The manufacturer's requirements include an ambient temperature of 67 degrees to keep all of the data servers running at optimal speeds. The ventilation system has a lead time of three weeks. Brian will also need to order new racks to hold the servers, switches, and other network devices. The racks have a two-week delivery time.

The data center supervisor requested that Brian replace all of the old power supplies and data cables. Brian will need to order these as well. Because Brian has a great relationship with the vendor, they guarantee that it will take only one week lead time for the power supplies and the data cables. Once the new ventilation system and racks arrive, Brian can begin installing them. It will take one week to install the ventilation system and three weeks to install the racks. The renovation of the new data center can begin as soon as the contractors have been hired. The contractors tell Brian that construction will take 20 days. Once the construction begins and before Brian installs the ventilation system and racks, the city inspector must approve the construction of the raised floor.

The city inspector will take two days to approve the infrastructure. After the city inspection and after the new power supplies and cables have arrived, Brian can install the power supplies and run the cables. Brian estimates that it will take five days to install the power supplies and one week to run all of the data cables. Before Brian can assign an actual date for taking the network off line and switching to the hot remote site, he must get approval from the each of the functional units ("Switchover Approval"). Meetings with each of the functional units will require one week. During this time he can initiate a power check to ensure that each of the racks has sufficient voltage. This will require only one day.

Upon completion of the power check, he can take one week to install his test servers. The test servers will test all of the primary network functions and act as a safeguard before the network is taken off line. The batteries must be charged, ventilation installed, and test servers up and running before management can be assured that the new infrastructure is safe, which will take two days. Then they will sign off the Primary Systems check, taking one day of intense meetings. They will also set an official date for the network move.

Brian is happy that everything has gone well thus far and is convinced that the move will go just as smoothly. Now that an official date is set, the network will be shut down for a day. Brian must move all of the network components to the new data center. Brian will do the move over the weekend—two days—when user traffic is at low point.

Assignment

1. Generate a priority matrix for AET's system move.
2. Develop a WBS for Brian's project. Include duration (days) and predecessors.
3. Using a project planning tool, generate a network diagram for this project.
   (Note: Base your plan on the following guidelines: eight-hour days, seven-day weeks, no holiday breaks, March 1, 2010 is the project start date.)

CASE 6.2

Greendale Stadium Case

The G&E Company is preparing a bid to build the new 47,000 seat Greendale baseball stadium. The construction must start July 1, 2006, and be completed in time for the start of the 2009 season. A penalty clause of $100,000 per day of delay beyond May 20, 2009, is written into the contract.

Ben Keith, the president of the company, expressed optimism at obtaining the contract and revealed that the company could net as much as $2 million on the project. He also said if they are successful, the prospects for future projects are quite good since there is a projected renaissance in building classic ball parks with modern luxury boxes.

Assignment

Given the information provided in Table 6.3, construct a network schedule for the stadium project and answer the following questions:

1. Will the project be able to be completed by the May 20 deadline? How long will it take?
2. What is the critical path for the project?
3. Based on the schedule would you recommend that G&E pursue this contact? Why? Include a one-page Gantt chart for the stadium schedule.

TABLE 6.3   Greendale Stadium Case

ID	Activity	Duration	Predecessor(s)
1	*Baseball Stadium*		
2	Clear stadium site	70 days	—
3	Demolish building	30 days	2
4	Set up construction site	70 days	3
5	Drive support piling	120 days	2
6	Pour lower concrete bowl	120 days	5
7	Pour main concourse	120 days	3,6
8	Install playing field	90 days	3,6
9	Construct upper steel bowl	120 days	3,6
10	Install seats	140 days	7,9
11	Build luxury boxes	90 days	7,9
12	Install Jumbotron	30 days	7,9
13	Stadium infrastructure	120 days	7,9
14	Construct steel canopy	75 days	10
15	Light installation	30 days	14
16	Build roof supports	90 days	6
17	Construct roof	180 days	16
18	Install roof tracks	90 days	16
19	Install roof	90 days	17,18
20	Inspection	20 days	8,11,13,15,19

Case Appendix: Technical Details of the Baseball Stadium

The baseball stadium is an outdoor structure with a retractable roof. The project begins with clearing the site, an activity that lasts 70 days. Once the site is clear, work can start simultaneously on the structure itself and demolishing an adjacent building site. This demolition is necessary to create a construction stage for storing materials and equipment. It will take 30 days to demolish the buildings and another 70 days to set up the construction site.

The work on the stadium begins by driving 160 support pilings, which will take 120 days. Next comes the pouring of the lower concrete bowl (120 days). Once this is done and the construction site has been set up, then the pouring of the main concourse (120 days), the installation of the playing field (90 days), and the construction of the upper steel bowl can occur (120 days).

Once the concourse and upper bowl are completed, work can start simultaneously on building the luxury boxes (90 days), installing the seats (140 days), installing the Jumbotron (30 days), and installing stadium infrastructure (120 days) which includes: bathrooms, lockers, restaurants, etc. Once the seats are installed then the steel canopy can be constructed (75 days) followed by the installation of the lights (30 days).

The retractable roof represents the most significant technical challenge to the project. Building the roof track supports (90 days) can begin after the lower concrete bowl is constructed. At this time the dimensions of the roof can be finalized and the construction of the roof at a separate site can begin (180 days). After the roof supports are completed then the roof tracks can be installed (90 days). Once the tracks and the roof are completed then the roof can be installed and made operational (90 days). Once all activities are completed it will take 20 days to inspect the stadium.

For purposes of this case assume the following:

1. The following holidays are observed: January 1, Memorial Day (last Monday in May), July 4th, Labor Day (first Monday in September), Thanksgiving Day (4th Thursday in November), December 25 and 26.
2. If a holiday falls on a Saturday then Friday will be given as an extra day off, and if it falls on a Sunday then Monday will be given as a day off.
3. The construction crew work Monday through Friday.

CHAPTER 7

Managing Risk

No great deed is done by falterers who ask for certainty.

George Eliot

Every project manager understands risks are inherent in projects. No amount of planning can overcome *risk,* or the inability to control chance events. In the context of projects, risk is an uncertain event or condition that, if it occurs, has a positive or negative effect on project objectives. A risk has a cause and, if it occurs, a consequence. For example, a cause may be a flu virus or change in scope requirements. The event is that team members get striken with the flu or the product has to be redesigned. If either of these uncertain events occurs, it will impact the cost, schedule, and quality of the project.

Some potential risk events can be identified before the project starts—such as equipment malfunction or change in technical requirements. Risks can be anticipated consequences, like schedule slippages or cost overruns. Risks can be beyond imagination like the September 11, 2001, attack on the Twin Towers in New York City.

While risks can have positive consequences such as unexpected price reduction in materials, the focus of this chapter is on what can go wrong and the risk management process.

Risk management attempts to recognize and manage potential and unforeseen trouble spots that may occur when the project is implemented. Risk management identifies as many risk events as possible (what can go wrong), minimizes their impact (what can be done about the event before the project begins), manages responses to those events that do materialize (contingency plans), and provides contingency funds to cover risk events that actually materialize.

For a humorous, but ultimately embarrassing example of poor risk management see Snapshot from Practice: Giant Popsicle Gone Wrong.

Risk Management Process

Figure 7.1 presents a graphic model of the risk management challenge. The chances of a risk event occurring (e.g., an error in time estimates, cost estimates, or design technology) are greatest in the concept, planning, and start-up phases of the project. The cost impact of a risk event in the project is less if the event occurs earlier rather than later. The early stages of the project represent the period when the opportunity for minimizing the impact or working around a potential risk exists. Conversely, as the project passes the halfway implementation mark, the cost of a risk event occurring increases rapidly. For example, the risk event of a design flaw occurring after a prototype has been made has a greater cost or time impact than if the event occurred in the start-up phase of the project. Clearly, identifying project risk events and deciding a response before the project begins is a more prudent approach than not attempting to manage risk.

The cost of mismanaged risk control early on in the project is magnified by the ill-fated 1999 NASA Mars Climate Orbiter. Investigations revealed that Lockheed Martin botched the design of critical navigation

Snapshot from Practice   Giant Popsicle Gone Wrong*

An attempt to erect the world's largest Popsicle in New York City ended with a scene straight out of a disaster film, but much stickier.

The 25-foot-tall, 17½-ton treat of frozen juice melted faster than expected, flooding Union Square in downtown Manhattan with kiwi-strawberry–flavored fluid.

Bicyclists wiped out in the stream of goo. Pedestrians slipped. Traffic was, well, frozen. Firefighters closed off several streets and used hoses to wash away the thick, sweet slime.

The Snapple Company, a leading maker of soft beverages, had been trying to promote a new line of frozen treats by setting a record for the world's largest Popsicle, but called off the stunt before the frozen giant was pulled fully upright by a construction crane.

Authorities said they were worried the 2½-story popsicle would collapse.

Organizers were not sure why it melted so quickly. "We planned for it. We just didn't expect for it to happen so fast," said Snapple spokeswoman Lauren Radcliffe. She said the company would offer to pay the city for the clean-up costs.

* Associated Press, June 23, 2005.

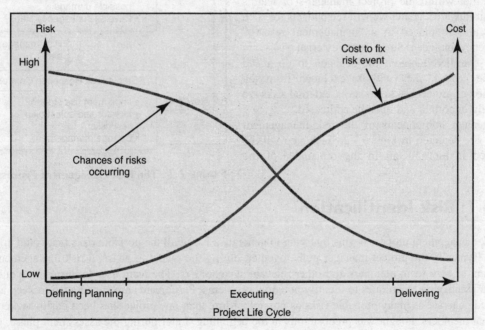

FIGURE 7.1   Risk Event Graph

software. While flight computers on the ground did calculations based on pounds of thrust per second, the spacecraft's computer software used metric units called newtons. A check to see if the values were compatible was never done.

"Our check and balances processes did not catch an error like this that should have been caught," said Ed Weiler, NASA's associate administrator for space science. "That is the bottom line. Processes that were in place were not followed." (*Orlando Sentinel,* 1999.) After the nine-month journey to the Red Planet the $125 million probe approached Mars at too low an altitude and burned up in the planet's atmosphere.

Risk management is a proactive approach rather than reactive. It is a preventive process designed to ensure that surprises are reduced and that negative consequences associated with undesirable events are minimized. It also prepares the project manager to take risk when a time, cost, and/or technical advantage is possible. Successful management of project risk gives the project manager better control over the future and can significantly improve chances of reaching project objectives on time, within budget, and meeting required technical (functional) performance.

The sources of project risks are unlimited. There are sources external to the organization, such as inflation, market acceptance, exchange rates, and government regulations. In practice, these risk events are often referred to as "threats" to differentiate them from those that are not within the project manager's or team's responsibility area. (Later we will see budgets for such risk events are placed in a "management reserve" contingency budget.) Since such external risks are usually considered before the decision to go ahead with the project, they will be excluded from the discussion of project risks. However, external risks are extremely important and must be addressed.

The major components of the risk management process are depicted in Figure 7.2. Each step will be examined in more detail in the remainder of the chapter.

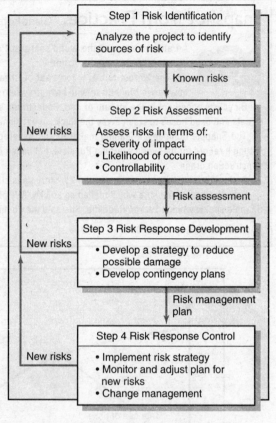

FIGURE 7.2   The Risk Management Process

Step 1: Risk Identification

The risk management process begins by trying to generate a list of all the possible risks that could affect the project. Typically the project manager pulls together, during the planning phase, a risk management team consisting of core team members and other relevant stakeholders. The team uses brainstorming and other problem identifying techniques to identify potential problems. Participants are encouraged to keep an open mind and generate as many probable risks as possible. More than one project has been bushwhacked by an event that members thought was preposterous in the beginning. Later during the assessment phase, participants will have a chance to analyze and filter out unreasonable risks.

One common mistake that is made early in the risk identification process is to focus on objectives and not on the events that could produce consequences. For example, team members may identify failing to meet schedule as a major risk. What they need to focus on are the events that could cause this to happen (i.e., poor estimates, adverse weather, shipping delays, etc.). Only by focusing on actual events can potential solutions be found.

Organizations use risk breakdown structures (RBSs) in conjunction with work breakdown structures (WBSs) to help management teams identify and eventually analyze risks. Figure 7.3 provides a generic example of an RBS. The focus at the beginning should be on risks that can affect the whole project as opposed to a specific section of the project or network.

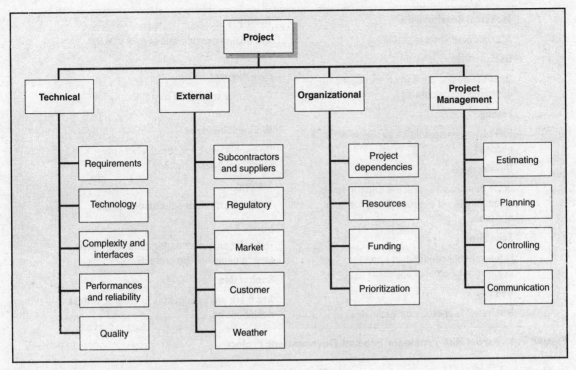

FIGURE 7.3   The Risk Breakdown Structure (RBS)

After the macro risks have been identified, specific areas can be checked. An effective tool for identifying specific risks is the work breakdown structure. Use of the WBS reduces the chance a risk event will be missed. On large projects multiple risk teams are organized around specific deliverables and submit their risk management reports to the project manager.

A risk profile is another useful tool. A risk profile is a list of questions that address traditional areas of uncertainty on a project. These questions have been developed and refined from previous, similar projects. Figure 7.4 provides a partial example of a risk profile.

Good risk profiles, like RBSs, are tailored to the type of project in question. For example, building an information system is different from building a new car. They are organization specific. Risk profiles recognize the unique strengths and weaknesses of the firm. Finally, risk profiles address both technical and management risks. For example, the profile shown in Figure 7.4 asks questions about design *(Does the design depend upon unrealistic assumptions?)* and work environment *(Do people cooperate across functional boundaries?)*.

Risk profiles are generated and maintained usually by personnel from the project office. They are updated and refined during the postproject audit (see Chapter 14). These profiles, when kept up to date, can be a powerful resource in the risk management process. The collective experience of the firm's past projects resides in their questions.

Historical records can complement or be used when formal risk profiles are not available. Project teams can investigate what happened on similar projects in the past to identify potential risks. For example, a project manager can check the on-time performance of selected vendors to gauge the threat of shipping delays. IT project managers can access "best practices" papers detailing other companies' experiences converting software systems. Inquiries should not be limited to recorded data. Savvy project managers tap the wisdom of others by seeking the advice of veteran project managers.

Technical Requirements	Quality
Are the requirements stable?	Are quality considerations built into the design?
Design	**Management**
Does the design depend on unrealistic or optimistic assumptions?	Do people know who has authority for what?
Testing	**Work Environment**
Will testing equipment be available when needed?	Do people work cooperatively across functional boundaries?
Development	**Staffing**
Is the development process supported by a compatible set of procedures, methods, and tools?	Is staff inexperienced or understaffed?
	Customer
Schedule	Does the customer understand what it will take to complete the project?
Is the schedule dependent upon the completion of other projects?	**Contractors**
Budget	Are there any ambiguities in contractor task definitions?
How reliable are the cost estimates?	

FIGURE 7.4   Partial Risk Profile for Product Development Project

The risk identification process should not be limited to just the core team. Input from customers, sponsors, subcontractors, vendors, and other stakeholders should be solicited. Relevant stakeholders can be formally interviewed or included on the risk management team. Not only do these players have a valuable perspective, but by involving them in the risk management process they also become more committed to project success.

One of the keys to success in risk identification is attitude. While a "can do" attitude is essential during implementation, project managers have to encourage critical thinking when it comes to risk identification. The goal is to find potential problems before they happen.

The RBS and risk profiles are useful tools for making sure no stones are left unturned. At the same time, when done well the number of risks identified can be overwhelming and a bit discouraging. Initial optimism can be replaced with griping and cries of "what have we gotten ourselves into?" It is important that project managers set the right tone and complete the risk management process so members regain confidence in themselves and the project.

Step 2: Risk Assessment

Step 1 produces a list of potential risks. Not all of these risks deserve attention. Some are trivial and can be ignored, while others pose serious threats to the welfare of the project. Managers have to develop methods for sifting through the list of risks, eliminating inconsequential or redundant ones and stratifying worthy ones in terms of importance and need for attention.

Scenario analysis is the easiest and most commonly used technique for analyzing risks. Team members assess the significance of each risk event in terms of:

- Probability of the event.
- Impact of the event.

Simply stated, risks need to be evaluated in terms of the likelihood the event is going to occur and the impact or consequences of its occurrence. The risk of a project manager being struck by lightning at a work site would have major negative impact on the project, but the likelihood is so low it is not worthy of consideration. Conversely, people do change jobs, so an event like the loss of key project personnel would have not only an adverse impact but also a high likelihood of occurring in some organizations. If so, then it would be wise for that organization to be proactive and mitigate this risk by developing incentive schemes for retaining specialists and/or engaging in cross-training to reduce the impact of turnover.

The quality and credibility of the risk analysis process requires that different levels of risk probabilities and impacts be defined. These definitions vary and should be tailored to the specific nature and needs of the project. For example, a relatively simple scale ranging from "very unlikely" to "almost certainly" may suffice for one project, whereas another project may use more precise numerical probabilities (e.g., 0.1, 0.3, 0.5, …).

Impact scales can be a bit more problematic since adverse risks affect project objectives differently. For example, a component failure may cause only a slight delay in project schedule but a major increase in project cost. If controlling cost is a high priority, then the impact would be severe. If, on the other hand, time is more critical than cost, then the impact would be minor.

Because impact ultimately needs to be assessed in terms of project priorities, different kinds of impact scales are used. Some scales may simply use rank-order descriptors, such as "low," "moderate," "high," and "very high," whereas others use numeric weights (e.g., 1–10). Some may focus on the project in general while others focus on specific project objectives. The risk management team needs to establish up front what distinguishes a 1 from a 3 or "moderate" impact from "severe" impact. Figure 7.5 provides an example of how impact scales could be defined given the project objectives of cost, time, scope, and quality.

Documentation of scenario analyses can be seen in various risk assessment forms used by companies. Figure 7.6 is a partial example of a risk assessment form used on an IS project involving the upgrade from Windows Office XP to Windows Vista.

Project Objective	Relative or Numerical Scale				
	1 Very Low	2 Low	3 Moderate	4 High	5 Very High
Cost	Insignificant cost increase	< 10% cost increase	10–20% cost increase	20–40% cost increase	> 40% cost increase
Time	Insignificant time increase	< 5% time increase	5–10% time increase	10–20% time increase	> 20% time increase
Scope	Scope decrease barely noticeable	Minor areas of scope affected	Major areas of scope affected	Scope reduction unacceptable to sponsor	Project end item is effectively useless
Quality	Quality degradation barely noticeable	Only very demanding applications are affected	Quality reduction requires sponsor approval	Quality reduction unacceptable to sponsor	Project end item is effectively useless

FIGURE 7.5   Defined Conditions for Impact Scales of a Risk on Major Project Objectives (Examples for negative impacts only)

Risk Event	Likelihood	Impact	Detection Difficulty	When
Interface problems	4	4	4	Conversion
System freezing	2	5	5	Start-up
User backlash	4	3	3	Postinstallation
Hardware malfunctioning	1	5	5	Installation

FIGURE 7.6 Risk Assessment Form

Notice that in addition to evaluating the severity and probablity of risk events the team also assesses when the event might occur and its detection difficulty. Detection difficulty is a measure of how easy it would be to detect that the event was going to occur in time to take mitigating action, that is, how much warning would we have?

Often organizations find it useful to categorize the severity of different risks into some form of risk assessment matrix. The matrix is typically structured around the impact and likelihood of the risk event. For example, the risk matrix presented in Figure 7.7 consists of a 5 × 5 array of elements with each element representing a different set of impact and likelihood values.

The matrix is divided into red, yellow, and green zones representing major, moderate, and minor risks, respectively. The red zone is centered on the top right corner of the matrix (high impact/high likelihood),

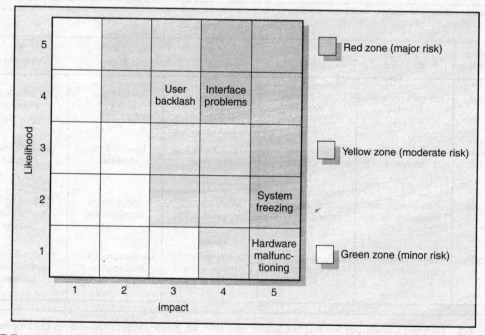

FIGURE 7.7 Risk Severity Matrix

while the green zone is centered on the bottom left corner (low impact/low likelihood). The moderate risk, yellow zone extends down the middle of the matrix. Since impact is generally considered more important than likelihood (a 10 percent chance of losing $1,000,000 is usually considered a more severe risk than a 90 percent chance of losing $1,000), the red zone (major risk) extends farther down the high impact column.

Using the Windows Vista project again as an example, interface problems and system freezing would be placed in the red zone (major risk), while user backlash and hardware malfunctioning would be placed in the yellow zone (moderate risk).

The risk severity matrix provides a basis for prioritizing which risks to address. Red zone risks receive first priority followed by yellow zone risks. Green zone risks are typically considered inconsequential and ignored unless their status changes.

Failure Mode and Effects Analysis (FMEA) extends the risk severity matrix by including ease of detection in the equation:

$$\text{Impact} \times \text{Probability} \times \text{Detection} = \text{Risk Value}$$

Each of the three dimensions is rated according to a five-point scale. For example, detection is defined as the ability of the project team to discern that the risk event is imminent. A score of 1 would be given if even a chimpanzee could spot the risk coming. The highest detection score of 5 would be given to events that could only be discovered after it is too late (i.e., system freezing). Similar anchored scales would be applied for severity of impact and the probability of the event occurring. The weighting of the risks is then based on their overall score. For example, a risk with an impact in the "1" zone with a very low probability and an easy detection score might score a 1 ($1 \times 1 \times 1 = 1$). Conversely, a high-impact risk with a high probability and impossible to detect would score 125 ($5 \times 5 \times 5 = 125$). This broad range of numerical scores allows for easy stratification of risk according to overall significance.

No assessment scheme is absolutely foolproof. For example, the weakness of the FMEA approach is that a risk event rated Impact = 1, Probability = 5, and Detection = 5 would receive the same weighted score as an event rated Impact = 5, Probability = 5, and Detection = 1! This underscores the importance of *not* treating risk assessment as simply an exercise in mathematics. There is no substitute for thoughtful discussion of key risk events.

Probability Analysis

There are many statistical techniques available to the project manager that can assist in assessing project risk. Decision trees have been used to assess alternative courses of action using expected values. Statistical variations of net present value (NPV) have been used to assess cash flow risks in projects. Correlations between past projects' cash flow and S-curves (cumulative project cost curve—baseline—over the life of the project) have been used to assess cash flow risks.

PERT (program evaluation and review technique) and PERT simulation can be used to review activity and project risk. PERT and related techniques take a more macro perspective by looking at overall cost and schedule risks. Here the focus is not on individual events but on the likelihood the project will be completed on time and within budget. These methods are useful in assessing the overall risk of the project and the need for such things as contingency funds, resources, and time. The use of PERT simulation is increasing because it uses the same data required for PERT, and software to perform the simulation is readily available.

Basically PERT simulation assumes a statistical distribution (range between optimistic and pessimistic) for each activity duration; it then simulates the network (perhaps over 1,000 simulations) using a random number generator. The outcome is the relative probability, called a criticality index, of an activity becoming critical under the many different, possible activity durations for each activity. PERT simulation also provides a list of potential critical paths and their respective probabilities of occurring. Having this information available can greatly facilitate identifying and assessing schedule risk. (See Appendix 7.1 at the end of this chapter for a more detailed description and discussion.)

Step 3: Risk Response Development

When a risk event is identified and assessed, a decision must be made concerning which response is appropriate for the specific event. Responses to risk can be classified as mitigating, avoiding, transferring, sharing, or retaining.

Mitigating Risk

Reducing risk is usually the first alternative considered. There are basically two strategies for mitigating risk: (1) reduce the likelihood that the event will occur and/or (2) reduce the impact that the adverse event would have on the project. Most risk teams focus first on reducing the likelihood of risk events since, if successful, this may eliminate the need to consider the potentially costly second strategy.

Testing and prototyping are frequently used to prevent problems from surfacing later in a project. An example of testing can be found in an information systems project. The project team was responsible for installing a new operating system in their parent company. Before implementing the project, the team tested the new system on a smaller isolated network. By doing so they discovered a variety of problems and were able to come up with solutions prior to implementation. The team still encountered problems with the installation but the number and severity were greatly reduced.

Often identifying the root causes of an event is useful. For example, the fear that a vendor will be unable to supply customized components on time may be attributable to (1) poor vendor relationships, (2) design miscommunication, and (3) lack of motivation. As a result of this analysis the project manager may decide to take his counterpart to lunch to clear the air, invite the vendor to attend design meetings, and restructure the contract to include incentives for on-time delivery.

Other examples of reducing the probability of risks occurring are scheduling outdoor work during the summer months, investing in up-front safety training, and choosing high-quality materials and equipment.

When the concerns are that duration and costs have been underestimated, managers will augment estimates to compensate for the uncertainties. It is common to use a ratio between old and new project to adjust time or cost. The ratio typically serves as a constant. For example, if past projects have taken 10 minutes per line of computer code, a constant of 1.10 (which represents a 10 percent increase) would be used for the proposed project time estimates because the new project is more difficult than prior projects.

An alternative mitigation strategy is to reduce the impact of the risk if it occurs. For example, a bridge-building project illustrates risk reduction. A new bridge project for a coastal port was to use an innovative, continuous cement-pouring process developed by an Australian firm to save large sums of money and time. The major risk was that the continuous pouring process for each major section of the bridge could not be interrupted. Any interruption would require that the whole cement section (hundreds of cubic yards) be torn down and started over. An assessment of possible risks centered on delivery of the cement from the cement factory. Trucks could be delayed, or the factory could break down. Such risks would result in tremendous rework costs and delays. Risk was reduced by having two additional portable cement plants built nearby on different highways within 20 miles of the bridge project in case the main factory supply was interrupted. These two portable plants carried raw materials for a whole bridge section, and extra trucks were on immediate standby each time continuous pouring was required. Similar risk reduction scenarios are apparent in system and software development projects where parallel innovation processes are used in case one fails.

Snapshot from Practice   From Dome to Dust*

On March 26, 2000, the largest concrete domed structure in the world was reduced to a pile of rubble in a dramatic implosion lasting less than 20 seconds. According to Mark Loizeaux, whose Maryland-based Controlled Demolition Inc. was hired to bring the 24-year-old Seattle Kingdome down, "We don't blow things up. We use explosives as an engine, but gravity is the catalyst that will bring it down."

Destroying the Kingdome was the most complicated of the 7,000 demolitions Loizeaux's company has undertaken. Nearly three months of preparations were needed to implode the dome at a total cost of $9 million. The Kingdome was considered to be one of the strongest structures in the world containing over 25,000 tons of concrete with each of its 40 vaulted ribs incorporating seven lengths of two-and-one-quarter-inch reinforcing steel bar.

Strands of orange detonating cord—basically dynamite in a string that explodes at the lightning pace of 24,000 feet per second—connected six pielike divisions of the Kingdome to a nearby control center.

Throughout each section, Controlled Demolition workers drilled nearly 1,000 holes and packed them with high-velocity gelatin explosives the size of hot dogs. Large charges were placed about one-third of the way up each dome rib, smaller charges were put farther up the ribs. When the detonation button was pushed, blasting caps set off a chain reaction of explosions in each section reducing the stadium to rubble.

While the actual implosion was a technical tour-de-force, risk management was a critical part of the project's success. To minimize damage to surrounding buildings, the explosive charges were wrapped in a layer of chain-link fencing covered with thick sheets of geotextile polypropylene fabric to contain flying concrete. Nearby buildings were protected in various manners depending on the structure and proximity to the Dome. Measures included sealing air-handling units, taping seams on doors and windows, covering floors and windows with plywood and draping reinforced polyethylene sheeting around the outside.

To help absorb the impact, air-conditioning units removed from the interior were stacked with other material to create a barrier around the perimeter of the work area.

Hundreds of police officers and security personnel were used to cordon off an area extending roughly 1,000 feet from the Dome from overzealous spectators. Traffic was closed for a larger area. Accommodations were provided for people and pets who lived within the restricted zone.

Eight water trucks, eight sweeper units, and more than 100 workers were deployed immediately after the blast to control dust and begin the cleanup.

As a side note, one-third of the concrete will be crushed and used in the foundation of a new $430 million outdoor football stadium which is being built in its place. The rest of the concrete will be carted away and used in roadbeds and foundations throughout the Seattle area.

*New York Times—Sunday Magazine (March 19, 2000); Seattle Times (March 27, 2000) Web site.

The Dome to Dust Snapshot from Practice details the steps Controlled Demolition took to minimize damage when they imploded the Seattle Kingdome.

Avoiding Risk

Risk avoidance is changing the project plan to eliminate the risk or condition. Although it is impossible to eliminate all risk events, some specific risks may be avoided before you launch the project. For example, adopting proven technology instead of experimental technology can eliminate technical failure. Choosing an Australian supplier as opposed to an Indonesian supplier would virtually eliminate the chance that political unrest would disrupt the supply of critical materials. See the WAP versus JAVA Snapshot from Practice to see how Ellipsus Systems avoided a potentially critical technical risk.

Snapshot from Practice   WAP or JAVA?*

Ellipsus Systems, AB, located in Vaxjo, Sweden, is a software design company whose products link corporate computer systems to mobile phones. Critical to the company's success is making the right technology decisions, especially around the standards and protocols its software uses. As wireless and mobile devices continue to take hold, there are two major emerging technical standards. One standard is WAP (Wireless Application Protocol). The second standard, Java, is based on Internet programming standards created by Sun Microsystems.

Rikard Kjellberg, one of Ellipsus's founders, was facing a conundrum: which standard to use? In one, Java was dominant; in the other, WAP was dominant. WAP was first to market. It generated huge excitement, and as Nokia prepared to launch the first wireless phone in late 1999, engineers across Europe left secure jobs to form WAP start-ups. At the same time some negative perceptions were developing about systems based on the WAP standard. Due to the slow response time, a Swedish newspaper ran a story titled "WAP is Crap." Java, on the other hand, had yet to establish itself with no commercial handsets available at the time.

Kjellberg's solution was to have projects in his company's portfolio based on both standards. Ellipsus built early proto-types of both systems and took them to a trade show, with both systems sitting side by side. "We knew within an hour which way to go," says Douglas Davies, the COO. Ellipsus began securing million dollar contracts to supply its Java-based system to leading U.S. operators.

* David Pringle, "How the U.S. took the wireless lead away from Europe," *The Wall Street Journal Europe,* 20 February 2002 http://www.network365.com/news.jsp?id=145 (accessed 10, November 2003).

Transferring Risk

Passing risk to another party is common; this transfer does not change risk. Passing risk to another party almost always results in paying a premium for this exemption. Fixed-price contracts are the classic example of transferring risk from an owner to a contractor. The contractor understands his or her firm will pay for any risk event that materializes; therefore, a monetary risk factor is added to the contract bid price. Before deciding to transfer risk, the owner should decide which party can best control activities that would lead to the risk occurring. Also, is the contractor capable of absorbing the risk? Clearly identifying and documenting responsibility for absorbing risk is imperative.

Another more obvious way to transfer risk is insurance. However, in most cases this is impractical because defining the project risk event and conditions to an insurance broker who is unfamiliar with the project is difficult and usually expensive. Of course, low-probability and high-consequence risk events such as acts of God are more easily defined and insured. Performance bonds, warranties, and guarantees are other financial instruments used to transfer risk.

Sharing Risk

Risk sharing allocates proportions of risk to different parties. An example of risk sharing was the Airbus A340. Research and development risks were allocated among European countries including Britain and France. Alternatively, the entertainment industry formed a consortium to define a common operating format for Digital Video Disc (DVD) to ensure compatibility across products. Other forms of risk sharing are emerging.

On large, international construction projects like petrochemical plants and oil refineries, host countries are insisting on contracts that enforce Build-Own-Operate-Transfer (BOOT) provisions. Here the prime project organization is expected not only to build the facility, but also to take over ownership until its operation capacity has been proven and all the debugging has occurred before final transfer of ownership to the client. In such cases, the host country and project firm agree to share the financial risk of ownership until the project has been completed and capabilities proven.

Sharing risk has also been used to cut project costs and encourage innovation. Partnering (see Chapter 12) between an owner and contractors has prompted the development of continuous improvement procedures to encourage contractors to suggest innovative ways for project implementation. The new method will probably include additional start-up costs and the risk that the new process may not work. Usually the risk costs and benefits of the improved process are shared on a 50/50 basis between the owner and contracting firms.

Retaining Risk

In some cases a conscious decision is made to accept the risk of an event occurring. Some risks are so large it is not feasible to consider transferring or reducing the event (e.g., an earthquake or flood). The project owner assumes the risk because the chance of such an event occurring is slim. In other cases risks identified in the budget reserve can simply be absorbed if they materialize. The risk is retained by developing a contingency plan to implement if the risk materializes. In a few cases a risk event can be ignored and a cost overrun accepted should the risk event occur.

The more effort given to risk response before the project begins, the better the chances are for minimizing project surprises. Knowing that the response to a risk event will be retained, transferred, or shared greatly reduces stress and uncertainty when the risk event occurs. Again, control is possible with this structured approach.

Contingency Planning

A contingency plan is an alternative plan that will be used if a possible foreseen risk event becomes a reality. The contingency plan represents actions that will reduce or mitigate the negative impact of the risk event. Like all plans, the contingency plan answers the questions of what, where, when, and how much action will take place. The absence of a contingency plan, when a risk event occurs, can cause a manager to delay or postpone the decision to implement a remedy. This postponement can lead to panic, and acceptance of the first remedy suggested. Such after-the-event decision making under pressure can be potentially dangerous and costly. Contingency planning evaluates alternative remedies for possible foreseen events before the risk event occurs and selects the best plan among alternatives. This early contingency planning facilitates a smooth transition to the remedy or work-around plan. The availability of a contingency plan can significantly increase the chances for project success.

Conditions for activating the implementation of the contingency plan should be decided and clearly documented. The plan should include a cost estimate and identify the source of funding. All parties affected should agree to the contingency plan and have authority to make commitments. Because implementation of a contingency plan embodies disruption in the sequence of work, all contingency plans should be communicated to team members so that surprise and resistance are minimized.

Here is an example: A high-tech niche computer company intends to introduce a new "platform" product at a very specific target date. The project's 47 teams all agree delays will not be acceptable. Their contingency plans for two large component suppliers demonstrate how seriously risk management is viewed. One supplier's plant sits on the San Andreas Fault. The contingency plan has an alternative supplier, who is constantly updated, producing a replica of the component in another plant. Another supplier in Toronto, Canada, presents a delivery risk on their due date because of potential bad weather. This contingency plan calls for a chartered plane (already contracted to be on standby) if overland transportation presents a delay problem. To outsiders these plans must seem a bit extreme, but in high-tech industries where time to market is king, risks of identified events are taken seriously.

Risk response matrices such as the one shown in Figure 7.8 are useful for summarizing how the project team plans to manage risks that have been identified. Again, the Windows Vista project is used to illustrate this kind of matrix. The first step is to identify whether to reduce, share, transfer, or accept the risk. The team decided to reduce the chances of the system freezing by experimenting with a prototype of the system. Prototype experimentation not only allows them to identify and fix conversion "bugs" before the actual installation, but it also yields information that could be useful in enhancing acceptance by end-users. The project team is then able to identify and document changes between the old and new system that will be incorporated in the training the users receive. The risk of equipment malfunctioning is transferred by choosing a reliable supplier with a strong warranty program.

Risk Event	Response	Contingency Plan	Trigger	Who Is Responsible
Interface problems	Reduce	Work around until help comes	Not solved within 24 hours	Nils
System freezing	Reduce	Reinstall OS	Still frozen after one hour	Emmylou
User backlash	Reduce	Increase staff support	Call from top management	Eddie
Equipment malfunctions	Transfer	Order different brand	Replacement doesn't work	Jim

FIGURE 7.8　Risk Response Matrix

The next step is to identify contingency plans in case the risk still occurs. For example, if interface problems prove insurmountable, then the team would attempt a work-around until vendor experts arrived to help solve the problem. If the system freezes after installation, the team will first try to reinstall the software. If user dissatisfaction is high, then the IS department will provide more staff support. If the team is unable to get reliable equipment from the original supplier, then it will order a different brand from a second dealer. The team also needs to discuss and agree what would "trigger" implementation of the contingency plan. In the case of the system freezing, the trigger is not being able to unfreeze the system within one hour or, in the case of user backlash, an angry call from top management. Finally, the individual responsible for monitoring the potential risk and initiating the contingency plan needs to be assigned. Smart project managers establish protocols for contingency responses before they are needed. For an example of the importance of establishing protocols see the Risk Management at the Top of the World Snapshot from Practice on next page.

Some of the most common methods for handling risk are discussed here.

Technical Risks

Technical risks are problematic; they can often be the kind that cause the project to be shut down. What if the system or process does not work? Contingency or backup plans are made for those possibilities that are foreseen. For example, Carrier Transicold was involved in developing a new Phoenix refrigeration unit for truck-trailer applications. This new unit was to use rounded panels made of bonded metals, which at the time was new technology for Transicold. Furthermore, one of its competitors had tried unsuccessfully to

Snapshot from Practice   Risk Management at the Top of the World*

Into Thin Air, Jon Krakauer's gripping account of an ill-fated attempt to climb Mount Everest in which six climbers died, provides testimony to the risks of extreme mountain climbing. Thirteen days after the tragedy, David Breashears successfully led a film crew to the summit. Their footage can be seen in the spectacular IMAX film, *Everest.*

Accounts of Mount Everest expeditions provide insights into project risk management. First, most climbers spend more than three weeks acclimating their bodies to high-altitude conditions. Native Sherpas are used extensively to carry supplies and set up each of the four base camps that will be used during the final stages of the climb. To reduce the impact of hypoxia, lightheadness, and disorientation caused by shortage of oxygen, most climbers use oxygen masks and bottles during the final ascent. If lucky enough not to be one of the first expeditions of the season, the path to the summit should be staked out and roped by previous climbers. Climbing guides receive last-minute weather reports by radio to confirm whether the weather conditions warrant the risk. Finally, for added insurance, most climbers join their Sherpas in an elaborate *puja* ritual intended to summon the divine support of the gods before beginning their ascent.

All of these efforts pale next to the sheer physical and mental rigors of making the final climb from base camp IV to

Bobby Model/National Geographic Image Collection.

the summit. This is what climbers refer to as the "death zone" because beyond 26,000 feet the mind and body begin to quickly deteriorate despite supplemental oxygen. Under fair conditions it takes around 18 hours to make the round-trip to the top and back to the base camp. Climbers leave as early as 1:00 A.M. in order to make it back before night falls and total exhaustion sets in.

The greatest danger in climbing Mount Everest is not reaching the summit but making it back to the base camp. One out of every five climbers who make it to the summit dies during their descent. The key is establishing a contingency plan in case the climbers encounter hard going or the weather changes. Guides establish a predetermined turnaround time (i.e., 2:00 P.M.) to ensure a safe return no matter how close the climbers are to the summit. Accepting the time takes tremendous discipline. One who was caught up by time was solo climber Goran Krupp. He turned back 1,000 feet from the top after bicycling 8,000 miles from Stockholm to Katmandu!

Many lives have been lost by failing to adhere to the turnback time and pushing forward to the summit. As one climber put it, "With enough determination, any bloody idiot can get up the hill. The trick is to get back down alive."

* Jon Krakauer, *Into Thin Air* (New York: Doubleday, 1997), p. 190; Broughton Coburn, *Everest: Mountain without Mercy* (New York: National Geographic Society, 1997).

incorporate similar bonded metals in their products. The project team was eager to make the new technology work, but it wasn't until the very end of the project that they were able to get the new adhesives to bond adequately to complete the project. Throughout the project, the team maintained a welded-panel fabrication approach just in case they were unsuccessful. If this contingency approach had been needed, it would have increased production costs, but the project still would have been completed on time.

In addition to backup strategies, project managers need to develop methods to quickly assess whether technical uncertainties can be resolved. The use of sophisticated CAD programs has greatly helped resolve design problems. At the same time, Smith and Reinertsen, in their book *Developing Products in Half the Time,* argue that there is no substitute for making something and seeing how it works, feels, or looks. They suggest that one should first identify the high-risk technical areas, then build models or design experiments to resolve the risk as quickly as possible. By isolating and testing the key technical questions early on in a project, project feasibility can be quickly determined and necessary adjustments made such as reworking the process or in some cases closing down the project. Usually the owner and project manager make decisions concerning technical risks.

Schedule Risks

Often organizations will defer the threat of a project coming in late until it surfaces. Here contingency funds are set aside to expedite or "crash" the project to get it back on track. Crashing, or reducing project duration, is accomplished by shortening (compressing) one or more activities on the critical path. This comes with additional costs and risk. Techniques for managing this situation are discussed in Chapter 9. Some contingency plans can avoid costly procedures. For example, schedules can be altered by working activities in parallel or using start-to-start lag relationships. Also, using the best people for high-risk tasks can relieve or lessen the chance of some risk events occurring.

Cost Risks

Projects of long duration need some contingency for price changes—which are usually upward. The important point to remember when reviewing price is to avoid the trap of using one lump sum to cover price risks. For example, if inflation has been running about 3 percent, some managers add 3 percent for all resources used in the project. This lump-sum approach does not address exactly where price protection is needed and fails to provide for tracking and control. Price risks should be evaluated item by item. Some purchases and contracts will not change over the life of the project. Those that may change should be identified and estimates made of the magnitude of change. This approach ensures control of the contingency funds as the project is implemented.

Funding Risks

What if the funding for the project is cut by 25 percent or completion projections indicate that costs will greatly exceed available funds? What are the chances of the project being canceled before completion? Seasoned project managers recognize that a complete risk assessment must include an evaluation of funding supply. This is especially true for publicly funded projects. Case in point was the ill-fated RAH-66 Comanche helicopter which was being developed for the U.S. Army by Sikorsky Aircraft Corp. and Boeing Co. Eight billion dollars had been invested to develop a new age combat and reconnaissance helicopter, when in February 2004, the Defense Department recommended that the project be canceled. The cancellation reflected a need to cut costs and a switch toward using unmanned aircraft for surveillance as well as attack missions.

Just as government projects are subject to changes in strategy and political agenda, business firms frequently undergo changes in priorities and top management. The pet projects of the new CEO replace the pet projects of the former CEO. Resources become tight and one way to fund new projects is to cancel other projects.

Severe budget cuts or lack of adequate funding can have a devastating effect on a project. Typically, when such a fate occurs, there is a need to scale back the scope of the project to what is possible. "All-or-nothing projects" are ripe targets to budget cutters. This was the case of the Comanche helicopter once the decision was made to move away from manned reconnaissance aircraft. Here the "chunkability" of the project can be an advantage. For example, freeway projects can fall short of the original intentions but still add value for each mile completed.

On a much smaller scale, similar funding risks may exist for more mundane projects. For example, a building contractor may find that due to a sudden downturn in the stock market the owners can no longer afford to build their dream house. Or an IS consulting firm may be left empty handed when a client files for bankruptcy. In the former case the contractor may have as a contingency selling the house on the open market, while unfortunately the consulting firm will have to join the long line of creditors.

Contingency Funding and Time Buffers

Contingency funds are established to cover project risks—identified and unknown. When, where, and how much money will be spent is not known until the risk event occurs. Project "owners" are often reluctant to set up project contingency funds that seem to imply the project plan might be a poor one. Some perceive the contingency fund as an add-on slush fund. Others say they will face the risk when it materializes. Usually such reluctance to establish contingency reserves can be overcome with documented risk identification, assessment, contingency plans, and plans for when and how funds will be disbursed.

The size and amount of contingency reserves depend on uncertainty inherent in the project. Uncertainty is reflected in the "newness" of the project, inaccurate time and cost estimates, technical unknowns, unstable scope, and problems not anticipated. In practice, contingencies run from 1 to 10 percent in projects similar to past projects. However, in unique and high-technology projects it is not uncommon to find contingencies running in the 20 to 60 percent range. Use and rate of consumption of reserves must be closely monitored and controlled. Simply picking a percentage of the baseline, say, 5 percent, and calling it the contingency reserve is not a sound approach. Also, adding up all the identified contingency allotments and throwing them into one pot is not conducive to sound control of the reserve fund.

In practice, the contingency reserve fund is typically divided into budget and management reserve funds for control purposes. Budget reserves are set up to cover identified risks; these reserves are those allocated to specific segments or deliverables of the project. Management reserves are set up to cover unidentified risks and are allocated to risks associated with the total project. The risks are separated because their use requires approval from different levels of project authority. Because all risks are probabilistic, the reserves are not included in the baseline for each work package or activity; they are only activated when a risk occurs. If an identified risk does not occur and its chance of occurring is past, the fund allocated to the risk should be deducted from the budget reserve. (This removes the temptation to use budget reserves for other issues or problems.) Of course if the risk does occur, funds are removed from the reserve and added to the cost baseline.

It is important that contingency allowances be independent of the original time and cost estimates. These allowances need to be clearly distinguished to avoid time and budget game playing.

Budget Reserves

These reserves are identified for specific work packages or segments of a project found in the baseline budget or work breakdown structure. For example, a reserve amount might be added to "computer coding" to cover the risk of "testing" showing a coding problem. The reserve amount is determined by costing out the accepted contingency or recovery plan. The budget reserve should be communicated to the project team. This openness suggests trust and encourages good cost performance. However, distributing budget reserves should be the responsibility of both the project manager and the team members responsible for implementing the specific segment of the project. If the risk does not materialize, the funds are removed from the budget reserve. Thus, budget reserves decrease as the project progresses.

Management Reserves

These reserve funds are needed to cover major unforeseen risks and, hence, are applied to the total project. For example, a major scope change may appear necessary midway in the project. Because this change was not anticipated or identified, it is covered from the management reserve. Management reserves are established *after* budget reserves are identified and funds established. These reserves are independent of budget reserves and are controlled by the project manager and the "owner" of the project. The "owner" can be internal (top management) or external to the project organization. Most management reserves are set using historical data and judgments concerning the uniqueness and complexity of the project.

Placing technical contingencies in the management reserve is a special case. Identifying possible technical (functional) risks is often associated with a new, untried, innovative process or product. Because there is a chance the innovation may not work out, a fallback plan is necessary. This type of risk is beyond the control of the project manager. Hence, technical reserves are held in the management reserve and controlled by the owner or top management. The owner and project manager decide when the contingency plan will be implemented and the reserve funds used. It is assumed there is a high probability these funds will never be used.

Table 7.1 shows the development of a contingency fund estimate for a hypothetical project. Note how budget and management reserves are kept separate; control is easily tracked using this format.

TABLE 7.1   Contingency Fund Estimate (Thousands of Dollars)

Activity	Budget Baseline	Budget Reserve	Project Budget
Design	$500	$15	$515
Code	900	80	980
Test	20	2	22
Subtotal	$1,420	$97	$1,517
Management reserve	—	—	50
Total	$1,420	$97	$1,567

Time Buffers

Just as contingency funds are established to absorb unplanned costs, managers use time buffers to cushion against potential delays in the project. And like contingency funds, the amount of time is dependent upon the inherent uncertainty of project. The more uncertain the project the more time should be reserved for the schedule. The strategy is to assign extra time at critical moments in the project. For example, buffers are added to

A. activities with severe risks.
B. merge activities that are prone to delays due to one or more preceding activities being late.
C. noncritical activities to reduce the likelihood that they will create another critical path.
D. activities that require scarce resources to ensure that the resources are available when needed.

In the face of overall schedule uncertainty, buffers are sometimes added to the end of the project. For example, a 300-working-day project may have a 30-day project buffer. While the extra 30 days would not appear on the schedule, it is available if needed. Like management reserves, this buffer typically requires the authorization of top management. A more systematic approach to buffer management is discussed in the Chapter 8 Appendix on critical chain project management.

Step 4: Risk Response Control

The last step in the risk management process is risk control—executing the risk response strategy, monitoring triggering events, initiating contingency plans, and watching for new risks. Establishing a change management system to deal with events that require formal changes in the scope, budget, and/or schedule of the project is an essential element of risk control.

Project managers need to monitor risks just like they track project progress. Risk assessment and updating needs to be part of every status meeting and progress report system. The project team needs to be on constant alert for new, unforeseen risks. Management needs to be sensitive that others may not be forthright in acknowledging new risks and problems. Admitting that there might be a bug in the design code or that different components are not compatible reflects poorly on individual performance. If the prevailing organizational culture is one where mistakes are punished severely, then it is only human nature to protect oneself. Similarly, if bad news is greeted harshly and there is a propensity to "kill the messenger," then participants will be reluctant to speak freely. The tendency to suppress bad news is compounded when individual responsibility is vague and the project team is under extreme pressure from top management to get the project done quickly.

Project managers need to establish an environment in which participants feel comfortable raising concerns and admitting mistakes. The norm should be that mistakes are acceptable, hiding mistakes is intolerable. Problems should be embraced not denied. Participants should be encouraged to identify problems and new risks. Here a positive attitude by the project manager toward risks is a key.

On large, complex projects it may be prudent to repeat the risk identification/assessment exercise with fresh information. Risk profiles should be reviewed to test to see if the original responses held true. Relevant stakeholders should be brought into the discussion. While this may not be practical on an ongoing basis, project managers should touch base with them on a regular basis or hold special stakeholder meetings to review the status of risks on the project.

A second key for controlling the cost of risks is documenting responsibility. This can be problematic in projects involving multiple organizations and contractors. Responsibility for risk is frequently passed on to others with the statement, "That is not my worry." This mentality is dangerous. Each identified risk should be assigned (or shared) by mutual agreement of the owner, project manager, and the contractor or person having line responsibility for the work package or segment of the project. It is best to have the line person responsible approve the use of budget reserve funds and monitor their rate of usage. If management reserve funds are required, the line person should play an active role in estimating additional costs and funds needed to complete the project. Having line personnel participate in the process focuses attention on the management reserve, control of its rate of usage, and early warning of potential risk events. If risk management is not formalized, responsibility and responses to risk will be ignored—*it is not my area.*

The bottom line is that project managers and team members need to be vigilant in monitoring potential risks and identify new land mines that could derail a project. Risk assessment has to be part of the working agenda of status meetings and when new risks emerge they need to be analyzed and incorporated into the risk management process.

Change Control Management

A major element of the risk control process is change management. Every detail of a project plan will not materialize as expected. Coping with and controlling project changes present a formidable challenge for most project managers. Changes come from many sources such as the project customer, owner, project manager, team members, and occurrence of risk events. Most changes easily fall into three categories:

1. Scope changes in the form of design or additions represent big changes; for example, customer requests for a new feature or a redesign that will improve the product.
2. Implementation of contingency plans, when risk events occur, represent changes in baseline costs and schedules.
3. Improvement changes suggested by project team members represent another category.

Because change is inevitable, a well-defined change review and control process should be set up early in the project planning cycle.

Change control systems involve reporting, controlling, and recording changes to the project baseline. (Note: Some organizations consider change control systems part of configuration management.) In practice most change control systems are designed to accomplish the following:

1. Identify proposed changes.
2. List expected effects of proposed change(s) on schedule and budget.
3. Review, evaluate, and approve or disapprove changes formally.
4. Negotiate and resolve conflicts of change, conditions, and cost.
5. Communicate changes to parties affected.
6. Assign responsibility for implementing change.
7. Adjust master schedule and budget.
8. Track all changes that are to be implemented.

As part of the project communication plan, stakeholders define up front the communication and decision-making process that will be used to evaluate and accept changes. The process can be captured in a flow diagram like the one presented in Figure 7.9. On small projects this process may simply entail approval of a small group of stakeholders. On larger projects more elaborate decision-making processes are established, with different processes being used for different kinds of change. For example, changes in performance requirements may require multiple sign-offs, including the project sponsor and client, while switching suppliers may be authorized by the project manager. Regardless of the nature of the project, the goal is to establish the process for introducing necessary changes in the project in a timely and effective manner.

Of particular importance is assessing the impact of the change on the project. Often solutions to immediate problems have adverse consequence on other aspects of a project. For example, in overcoming a problem with the exhaust system for a hybrid automobile, the design engineers contributed to the prototype exceeding weight parameters. It is important that the implications of changes are assessed by people with appropriate expertise and perspective. On construction projects this is often the responsibility of the architecture firm, while "software architects" perform a similar function on software development efforts.

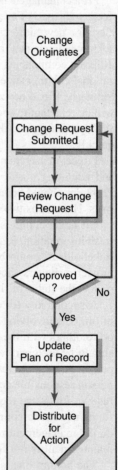

FIGURE 7.9
Change Control Process

Organizations use change request forms and logs to track proposed changes. An example of a simplified change request form is depicted in Figure 7.10. Typically change request forms include a description of the change, the impact of not approving the change, the impact of the change on project scope/schedule/cost, and defined signature paths for review as well as a tracking log number.

An abridged version of a change request log for a construction project is presented in Figure 7.11. These logs are used to monitor change requests. They typically summarize the status of all outstanding change requests and include such useful information as source and date of the change, document codes for related information, cost estimates, and the current status of the request.

Project name _Irish/Chinese culture exchange_   **Project sponsor** _Irish embassy_

Request number _12_   **Date** _June 6, 2xxx_

Originator _Jennifer McDonald_   **Change requested by** _Chinese culture office_

Description of requested change

1. _Request river dancers to replace small Irish dance group._
2. _Request one combination dance with river dancers and China ballet group._

Reason for change

River dancers will enhance stature of event. The group is well known and loved by Chinese people.

Areas of impact of proposed change–describe each on separate sheet

[X] Scope   [X] Cost   [ ] Other _____

[ ] Schedule   [ ] Risk

Disposition	Priority	Funding Source
[ ] Approve	[ ] Emergency	[ ] Mgmt. reserve
[X] Approve as amended	[X] Urgent	[ ] Budget reserve
[ ] Disapprove	[ ] Low	[X] Customer
[ ] Deferred		[ ] Other

Sign-off Approvals

Project manager _William O'Mally_   Date _June 12, 2xxx_

Project sponsor _Kenneth Thompson_   Date _June 13, 2xxx_

Project customer _Hong Lee_   Date _June 18, 2xxx_

Other _____   Date _____

FIGURE 7.10   Sample Change Request

OWNER REQUESTED CHANGE STATUS REPORT—OPEN ITEMS							OSU—WEATHERFORD
			DATES				
RC#	DESCRIPTION	REFERENCE DOCUMENT	DATE REC'D	DATE SUBMIT	AMOUNT	STATUS	COMMENTS
51	Sewer work offset				−188,129	OPEN	FUNDING FROM OTHER SOURCE
52	Stainless Plates at restroom Shower Valves	ASI 56	1/5/2008	3/30/2008	9,308	APPROVED	
53	Waterproofing Options	ASI 77	1/13/2008		169,386	OPEN	
54	Change Electrical floor box spec change	RFI 113	12/5/2008	3/29/2008	2,544	SUBMIT	
55	VE Option for Style and rail doors	Door samples	1/14/2008		−20,000	ROM	
56	Pressure Wash C tower	Owner request	3/15/2008	3/30/2008	14,861	SUBMIT	
57	Fire Lite glass in stairs	Owner request			8,000	QUOTE	ROM BASED ON FIRELITE NT
58	Cyber Café added tele/OFOI equipment	ASI 65	1/30/2008	3/29/2008	4,628	APPROVED	
59	Additional Dampers in C wing	ASI 68	2/4/2008	3/29/2008	1,085	SUBMIT	
60	Revise Corridor ceilings	ASI 72	2/13/2008	3/31/2008	−3,755	SUBMIT	

OPEN—Requires estimate   SUBMIT—RC letter submitted   ASI—Architect's supplemental instructions
ROM—Rough Order magnitde   APPROVED—RC letter approved   RFI—Request for information
QUOTE—Subcontractor quotes   REVISE—RC letter to be reviewed

FIGURE 7.11   Change Request Log

Every approved change must be identified and integrated into the plan of record through changes in the project WBS and baseline schedule. The plan of record is the current official plan for the project in terms of scope, budget, and schedule. The plan of record serves as a change management benchmark for future change requests as well as the baseline for evaluating project progress.

If the change control system is not integrated with the WBS and baseline, project plans and control will soon self-destruct. Thus, one of the keys to a successful change control process is document, document, document! The benefits derived from change control systems are the following:

1. Inconsequential changes are discouraged by the formal process.
2. Costs of changes are maintained in a log.
3. Integrity of the WBS and performance measures is maintained.
4. Allocation and use of budget and management reserve funds are tracked.
5. Responsibility for implementation is clarified.
6. Effect of changes is visible to all parties involved.
7. Implementation of change is monitored.
8 Scope changes will be quickly reflected in baseline and performance measures.

Clearly, change control is important and requires that someone or some group be responsible for approving changes, keeping the process updated, and communicating changes to the project team and relevant stakeholders. Project control depends heavily on keeping the change control process current. This historical record can be used for satisfying customer inquiries, identifying problems in post-project audits, and estimating future project costs.

Summary

To put the processes discussed in this chapter in proper perspective one should recognize that the essence of project management is risk management. Every technique in this book is really a risk management technique. Each in its own way tries to prevent something bad from happening. Project selection systems try to reduce the likelihood that projects will not contribute to the mission of the firm. Project scope statements, among other things, are designed to avoid costly misunderstandings and reduce scope creep. Work breakdown structures reduce the likelihood that some vital part of the project will be omitted or that the budget estimates are unrealistic. Teambuilding reduces the likelihood of dysfunctional conflict and break-downs in coordination. All of the techniques try to increase stakeholder satisfaction and increase the chances of project success.

From this perspective managers engage in risk management activities to compensate for the uncertainty inherent in project management and that things never go according to plan. Risk management is proactive not reactive. It reduces the number of surprises and leads to a better understanding of the most likely outcomes of negative events.

Although many managers believe that in the final analysis, risk assessment and contingency depend on subjective judgment, some standard method for identifying, assessing, and responding to risks should be included in all projects. The very process of identifying project risks forces some discipline at all levels of project management and improves project performance.

Contingency plans increase the chance that the project can be completed on time and within budget. Contingency plans can be simple "work-arounds" or elaborate detailed plans. Responsibility for risks should be clearly identified and documented. It is desirable and prudent to keep a reserve as a hedge against project risks. Budget reserves are linked to the WBS and should be communicated to the project team. Control of management reserves should remain with the owner, project manager, and line person responsible. Use of contingency reserves should be closely monitored, controlled, and reviewed throughout the project life cycle.

Experience clearly indicates that using a formal, structured process to handle possible foreseen and unforeseen project risk events minimizes surprises, costs, delays, stress, and misunderstandings. Risk management is an iterative process that occurs throughout the lifespan of the project. When risk events occur or changes are necessary, using an effective change control process to quickly approve and record changes will facilitate measuring performance against schedule and cost. Ultimately successful risk management requires a culture in which threats are embraced not denied and problems are identified not hidden.

Key Terms

Avoiding risk	Mitigating risk	Scenario analysis
Budget reserve	Risk	Sharing risk
Change management system	Risk breakdown structure (RBS)	Time buffer
Contingency plan	Risk profile	Transferring risk
Management reserve	Risk severity matrix	

Review Questions

1. Project risks can/cannot be eliminated if the project is carefully planned. Explain.
2. The chances of risk events occurring and their respective costs increasing change over the project life cycle. What is the significance of this phenomenon to a project manager?
3. What is the difference between avoiding a risk and accepting a risk?
4. What is the difference between mitigating a risk and contingency planning?
5. Explain the difference between budget reserves and management reserves.
6. How are the work breakdown structure and change control connected?
7. What are the likely outcomes if a change control process is not used? Why?

Exercises

1. Gather a small team of students. Think of a project most students would understand; the kinds of tasks involved should also be familiar. Identify and assess major and minor risks inherent to the project. Decide on a response type. Develop a contingency plan for two to four identified risks. Estimate costs. Assign contingency reserves. How much reserve would your team estimate for the whole project? Justify your choices and estimates.
2. You have been assigned to a project risk team of five members. Because this is the first time your organization has formally set up a risk team for a project, it is hoped that your team will develop a process that can be used on all future projects. Your first team meeting is next Monday morning. Each team member has been asked to prepare for the meeting by developing, in as much detail as possible, an outline that describes how you believe the team should proceed in handling project risks. Each team member will hand out their proposed outline at the beginning of the meeting. Your outline should include but not be limited to the following information:
   a. Team objectives.
   b. Process for handling risk events.
   c. Team activities.
   d. Team outputs.
3. The Manchester United Soccer Tournament project team (Review Manchester United case at the end of Chapter 4) has identified the following potential risks to their project:
   a. Referees failing to show up at designated games.
   b. Fighting between teams.
   c. Pivotal error committed by a referee that determines the outcome of a game.
   d. Abusive behavior along the sidelines by parents.
   e. Inadequate parking.
   f. Not enough teams sign up for different age brackets.
   g. Serious injury.
   How would you recommend that they respond (i.e., avoid, accept, . . .) to these risks and why?
4. Search the World Wide Web (WWW) using the key words: "best practices, project management." What did you find? How might this information be useful to a project manager?

References

Atkinson, W., "Beyond the Basics," *PM Network,* May 2003, pp. 38–43.

Baker, B., and R. Menon, "Politics and Project Performance: The Fourth Dimension of Project Management," *PM Network,* 9 (11) November 1995, pp. 16–21.

Carr, M. J., S. L. Konda, I. Monarch, F. C. Ulrich, and C. F. Walker, "Taxonomy-Based Risk Identification," *Technical Report CMU/SEI-93-TR 6, Software Engineering Institute,* Carnegie Mellon University, Pittsburgh, 1993.

Ford, E. C., J. Duncan, A. G. Bedeian, P. M. Ginter, M. D. Rousculp, and A. M. Adams, "Mitigating Risks, Visible Hands, Inevitable Disasters, and Soft Variables: Management Research that Matters to Managers," *Academy of Management Executive,* 19 (4) November 2005, pp. 24–38.

Graves, R., "Qualitative Risk Assessment," *PM Network,* 14 (10) October 2000, pp. 61–66.

Gray, C. F., and R. Reinman, "PERT Simulation: A Dynamic Approach to the PERT Technique," *Journal of Systems Management,* March 1969, pp. 18–23.

Hamburger, D. H., "The Project Manager: Risk Taker and Contingency Planner," *Project Management Journal,* 21 (4) 1990, pp. 11–16.

Hulett, D. T., "Project Schedule Risk Assessment," *Project Management Journal,* 26 (1) 1995, pp. 21–31.

Ingebretson, M., "In No Uncertain Terms," *PM Network,* 2002, pp. 28–32.

Levine, H. A., "Risk Management for Dummies: Managing Schedule, Cost and Technical Risk, and Contingency," *PM Network,* 9 (10) October 1995, pp. 31–33.

"Math Mistake Proved Fatal to Mars Orbiter," *The Orlando Sentinel,* November 23, 1999.

Pavlik, A., "Project Troubleshooting: Tiger Teams for Reactive Risk Management," *Project Management Journal,* 35 (4) December 2004, pp. 5–14.

Pinto, J. K., *Project Management: Achieving Competitive Advantage* (Upper Saddle River, NJ: Pearson, 2007).

Pritchard, C. L., "Advanced Risk-How Big Is Your Crystal Ball?" Proceedings of the 31st Annual Project Management Institute 2000 Seminars and Symposium, (Houston, TX, 2000) CD, pp. 933–36.

Project Management Body of Knowledge (Newton Square, PA: Project Management Institute, 2000), pp. 127–46.

Schuler, J. R., "Decision Analysis in Projects: Monte Carlo Simulation," *PM Network,* 7 (1) January 1994, pp. 30–36.

Smith, P. G., and G. M. Merritt, *Proactive Risk Management: Controlling Uncertainty in Product Development* (New York: Productivity Press, 2002).

Smith, P. G., and D. G. Reinertsen, *Developing Products in Half the Time* (New York: Van Nostrand Reinhold, 1995).

APPENDIX 7.1

PERT and PERT Simulation

PERT—Program Evaluation Review Technique

In 1958 the Special Office of the Navy and the Booze, Allen, and Hamilton consulting firm developed PERT (program evaluation and review technique) to schedule the more than 3,300 contractors of the Polaris submarine project and to cover uncertainty of activity time estimates.

PERT is almost identical to the critical path method (CPM) technique except it assumes each activity duration has a range that follows a statistical distribution. PERT uses three time estimates for each activity. Basically, this means each activity duration can range from an optimistic time to a pessimistic time, and a weighted average can be computed for each activity. Because project activities usually represent work, and because work tends to stay behind once it gets behind, the PERT developers chose an approximation of the *beta distribution* to represent activity durations. This distribution is known to be flexible and can accommodate empirical data that do not follow a normal distribution. The activity durations can be skewed more toward the high or low end of the data range. Figure A7.1A depicts a *beta distribution* for activity durations that is skewed toward the right and is representative of work that tends to stay late once it is behind. The distribution for the project duration is represented by a normal (symmetrical) distribution shown in Figure A7.1B. The project distribution represents the sum of the weighted averages of the activities on the critical path(s).

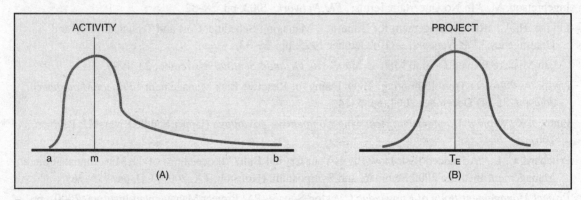

FIGURE A7.1   Activity and Project Frequency Distributions

Knowing the weighted average and variances for each activity allows the project planner to compute the probability of meeting different project durations. Follow the steps described in the hypothetical example given next. (The jargon is difficult for those not familiar with statistics, but the process is relatively simple after working through a couple of examples.)

The weighted average activity time is computed by the following formula:

$$t_e = \frac{a + 4m + b}{6} \qquad (7.1)$$

where t_e = weighted average activity time

   a = optimistic activity time (1 chance in 100 of completing the activity earlier under *normal* conditions)

     b = pessimistic activity time (1 chance in 100 of completing the activity later under *normal* conditions)

    m = most likely activity time

When the three time estimates have been specified, this equation is used to compute the weighted average duration for each activity. The average (deterministic) value is placed on the project network as in the CPM method and the early, late, slack, and project completion times are computed as they are in the CPM method.

    The variability in the activity time estimates is approximated by the following equations: Equation 7.2 represents the standard deviation for the *activity*. Equation 7.3 represents the standard deviation for the *project*. Note the standard deviation of the activity is squared in this equation; this is also called variance. This sum includes only activities on the critical path(s) or path being reviewed.

$$\sigma_{t_e} = \left(\frac{b - a}{6}\right) \tag{7.2}$$

$$\sigma_{T_E} = \sqrt{\Sigma \sigma t_e^2} \tag{7.3}$$

Finally, the average project duration (T_E) is the sum of all the average activity times along the critical path (sum of t_e), and it follows a normal distribution.

    Knowing the average project duration and the variances of activities allows the probability of completing the project (or segment of the project) by a specific time to be computed using standard statistical tables. The equation below (Equation 7.4) is used to compute the "Z" value found in statistical tables (Z = number of standard deviations from the mean), which, in turn, tells the probability of completing the project in the time specified.

$$Z = \frac{T_S - T_E}{\sqrt{\Sigma \sigma t_e^2}} \tag{7.4}$$

where T_E = critical path duration

          T_S = scheduled project duration

          Z = probability (of meeting scheduled duration) found in statistical Table A7.2

A Hypothetical Example Using the PERT Technique

The activity times and variances are given in Table A7.1. The project network is presented in Figure A7.2. This figure shows the project network as AOA and AON. The AON network is presented as a reminder that PERT can use AON networks as well as AOA.

TABLE A7.1   **Activity Times and Variances**

Activity	a	m	b	t_e	$[(b - a)/6]^2$
1–2	17	29	47	30	25
2–3	6	12	24	13	9
2–4	16	19	28	20	4
3–5	13	16	19	16	1
4–5	2	5	14	6	4
5–6	2	5	8	5	1

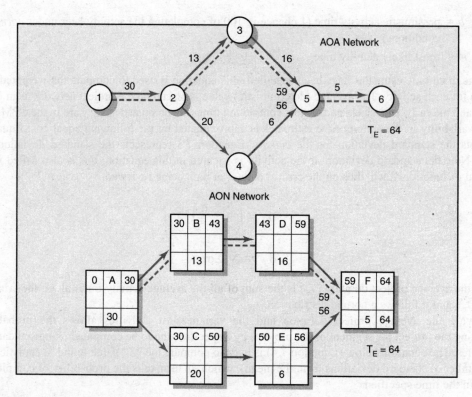

FIGURE A7.2   Hypothetical Network

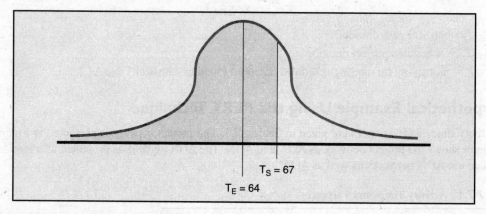

FIGURE A7.3   Possible Project Durations

The expected project duration (T_E) is 64 time units; the critical path is 1, 2, 3, 5, 6. With this information, the probability of completing the project by a specific date can easily be computed using standard statistical methods. For example, what is the probability the project will be completed before a scheduled time (T_S) of 67? The normal curve for the project would appear as shown in Figure A7.3.

Using the formula for the Z value, the probability can be computed as follows:

$$Z = \frac{T_S - T_E}{\sqrt{\Sigma \sigma_{t_e}^2}}$$

$$= \frac{67 - 64}{\sqrt{25 + 9 + 1 + 1}}$$

$$= \frac{+3}{\sqrt{36}}$$

$$= +0.50$$

$$P = 0.69$$

Reading from Table A7.2, a Z value of $+0.5$ gives a probability of 0.69, which is interpreted to mean there is a 69 percent chance of completing the project on or before 67 time units.

Conversely, the probability of completing the project by time period 60 is computed as follows:

$$Z = \frac{60 - 64}{\sqrt{25 + 9 + 1 + 1}}$$

$$= \frac{-4}{\sqrt{36}}$$

$$= -0.67$$

$$P \approx 0.26$$

From Table A7.2, a Z value of -0.67 gives an approximate probability of 0.26, which is interpreted to mean there is about a 26 percent chance of completing the project on or before 60 time units. Note that this same type of calculation can be made for any path or segment of a path in the network.

When such probabilities are available to management, trade-off decisions can be made to accept or reduce the risk associated with a particular project duration. For example, if the project manager wishes to improve the chances of completing the project by 64 time units, at least two choices are available. First, management can spend money up front to change conditions that will reduce the duration of one or more activities on the critical path. A more prudent, second alternative would be to allocate money to a contingency fund and wait to see how the project is progressing as it is implemented.

TABLE A7.2

Z Value	Probability	Z Value	Probability
22.0	0.02	+2.0	0.98
21.5	0.07	+1.5	0.93
21.0	0.16	+1.0	0.84
20.7	0.24	+0.7	0.76
20.5	0.31	+0.5	0.69
20.3	0.38	+0.3	0.62
20.1	0.36	+0.1	0.54

APPENDIX 7.2

Project Risk Management

1. General Perception of Risks and Project Risks

According to general perception, risk is an uncertain event (i.e. the event having unknown probability of its occurrence) having an unexpected and undesirable impact on some desired objectives or plans. In this sense, the risk is inherently present in all future plans, actions and all business related decisions, whether they are in the course of routine day-to-day work or operation on one hand or unique and specific task as in the case of a project.

(PMI®'s definition of risk and approach to risk management are somewhat different; they are described from Section 3 onwards in this appendix.)

Distinction between risk management for operations and projects
However, there are some important distinctions between the risks occurring during routine operations and the risks associated with the projects.

- Firstly, the projects require carrying out activities, which are not routinely carried out within the organization or which involve interactions with external agencies which are not necessary for routine operations. Therefore, unless conscious effort to think through the project risks is made, these risks do not become apparent and if a plan to manage the risks is not prepared in advance and ready for going into action, prompt effective and efficient measures for management of the risk would not be available for implementation.
- Secondly, the project decisions taken during implementing major capital projects are irreversible and some of them would leave a very significant effect on the organization over a long period of time. Some crucial decisions taken during the project life cycle significantly affect the operating mode, efficiency and economic viability of the organization. The successful projects set the organizations on path of growth and prosperity and all inadequately handled risks or lapses in project management haunt the organization's operations for years. Managing the risks for a major project is, therefore, important for long term health of the organization over and beyond managing the health of the project itself.

Risk categories
Risks are generally classified into three categories.

- *Known Risks:* These risks have occurred in the past and they are known to the project team. They are readily identified and suitable strategy for handling them is usually planned. Though, it is not necessary that they should occur on the project in hand or when they are very likely to occur cannot be determined. Therefore, planning in advance to handle such risks is strongly recommended. Building a high plinth level building in flood prone area is a risk of this nature.
- *Known–Unknown risks:* These types of risks are an instance of risks which have some time occurred in the past but their probability is low as well as quite unknown and the project team may not have handled similar risks before. Therefore, sort of tried and proven track record of risk handling strategy may not be available. Building in an earthquake prone zone is an instance of this. The project team's skill in analyzing and planning to handle risks is put to test for handling such risks.
- *Unknown-Unknown Risks:* These are the types of risks which no one in the project team is able to foresee and no risk planning is possible. Striking of Tsunami on Tamil Nadu coast line a few years back was risk of this nature.

Project Risks during Different Phases of the Project Life Cycle

Risk management processes need to be actively used by the project team for the entire project life cycle, since future events are unpredictable and risks could occur during any project phase. However, the severity and frequency of common risks to projects keep on getting smaller as the project moves from initiating and planning to closing phase of the project life cycle. Therefore, ordinarily, major effort for risk identification, analysis and response plans takes at the initiation and planning phases.

2. Proactive Management of Project Risks

2.1 Importance of Pro-active Risk Management

In earlier eras, an approach towards formal planning for risk management was reflected in the stance taken by some hard boiled off-the-cuff managing project managers: "No necessity of all that plan, we will cross the bridge when we reach it." Or that "I don't want my team to think of all those negative thoughts associated with risk planning." The answer to this approach can be summed up in a witty repartee made in defense of preventive maintenance program: "You can pay for the maintenance now or later—later it would be much much more".

This off-the-cuff risk management approach has been now mostly replaced by proactive approach, which analyses the project risks and maps out in advance the strategy for mitigating the risk in case it arose. So much so, that risk management is considered now one of the prime responsibilities of a project manager. The risk analysis does not ensure that the project would be free from all risks, but the preparation in advance for managing the risk if it occurred would definitely reduce the negative impact and bring the exposure from project risk to the organization's risk tolerance level. Also, don't forget, as mentioned earlier, that risk is not just a crisis or an accident waiting to happen. It could as well be some opportunity and the risk planning process would keep project team geared up to profit from some windfall opportunity, if good fortune smiles.

2.2 The Steps in Pro-active Risk Management

The steps involved in proactive risk management may be summed up as follows:

Phase I: Risk Identification

This phase of risk management is concerned with collecting data, such as:

- Identifying the likely risk events and their probability
- Identification of the risk drivers (conditions which might increase or decrease the probability of the risk event)
- Impacts of risk events on scope, time, cost, and quality
- Identification of impact drivers (factors which might increase or decrease the degree of impact of the risk event if it occurred, on scope, time, cost and quality)

All this is much easier said than done. For making this process more amenable to application, the use of techniques like Delphi Technique, Brainstorming and Checklists developed on the basis of earlier project experiences, etc has been suggested. All the same, the experience and expertise of the project team is of prime importance in this phase of project risk management.

Phase II: Risk Analysis—Qualitative and Quantitative Approaches

This phase is concerned with analyzing the risk data collected in the earlier phase, which would include:

- Calculating the expected value of negative impact on outcome for each risk event from the probability of risk event and impact if occurred
- Ranking the risk events for prioritization according to the expected value and preparing a Risk Table or Risk Map

- Carrying out further detailed analysis of some selected and prioritized risks using sophisticated quantitative techniques like Sensitivity Analysis, Decision Trees and Monte Carlo Simulation

Once the data for risk analysis is collected, its analysis for prioritization or sophisticated quantitative analysis for more informed direction for managing the risk are straight forward as far as their techniques of application go.

Phase III: Formulating Risk Management Strategies

This phase is concerned with formulating plans to pro-actively manage the prioritized risks. It should be remembered that there could be several causes for a single risk and that a risk event, if it occurred, could impact negatively several project objectives. The risk management strategy should take this into consideration. The roles and responsibilities of the persons or organizations assigned to manage specific risks and the risk triggers are also documented. The strategies commonly used for handling negative risks are:

- Avoidance — Modifying the project plan to bye-pass the risk associated activity or replace it with another, which would not be subject to the identified risk
- Transfer — Transferring the risk management to a third party at a known cost for risk management
- Mitigating the negative impact — Reducing the negative impact of the risk, in case the risk did occur, and
- Acceptance — Accepting the risk, if either there is no practical way to avoid, transfer or mitigate the risk or that it would not be economically viable to undertake managing that risk proactively.

Phase IV: Control and Documentation—Developing and Maintaining Risk Register

The final step in risk management is developing a comprehensive document with the detailed risk management plans, activities for monitoring and controlling the risk, and recording the outcomes and residual risks after main risk event is over. The record might include.

- List of identified risk events with risk event drivers, likely impacts of consequences and impact drivers
- Planned response for each major risk event
- Responsibility for managing each risk
- Identification of the trigger to activate risk response action
- Recording in the Risk Register the risk management activities and their outcomes with impacts on project objectives of scope, time, cost and quality
- Residual risk after the main event and any new risks on the horizon

3. Approach for Risk Management Recommended in PMBOK® Guide, 4TH Edition

Risk Definition: Risk is defined as an uncertain event or condition that, if it occurred, it would have a positive or negative effect on the project's objectives.

There is an important distinction between this definition of risk and the general conception of risk. PMI's definition includes "positive as well as negative effects" and therefore connotes both good as well as bad effects, while the common perception of risk is associated with only bad effects or harmful events. Risk management according to PMI®, therefore, encompasses measures to minimize the negative impacts and to leverage the positive impacts on project objectives (scope, time, cost and quality).

Risk Management Processes

Total six processes have been identified for project risk management; five processes are in the planning process group and one process in the monitoring and controlling group. The general approach for project risk management follows the proactive risk management described in the earlier section.

- *Plan Risk Management (Planning Process Group):* This process sets down the guideline and procedures for how the project risk management activities would be carried out. This would include policies and procedures for identification and analysis of risks, developing plan for managing the prioritized risks and implementing the plan for the tracking the risk management process through out the project life cycle.
- *Identify Risks (Planning Process Group):* This process involves determining which risks may affect the project outcomes and recording their characteristics and impacts on project outcomes.
- *Perform Qualitative Risk Analysis (Planning Process Group):* This process aims at prioritizing the identified risks by assessing the probability of risk occurrence, the value of impact if the risk event occurred and calculating the expected value of impact from theses assessments.
- *Perform Quantitative Risk Analysis (Planning Process Group):* The process of numerical analysis of the major or prioritized risks to arrive at the probabilistic estimate for different likely outcomes.
- *Plan Risk Responses (Planning Process Group):* This process examines each of the prioritized risks and plans the strategy for managing them (avoiding, transferring, mitigating the impact or accepting the risk), the identification of triggers for risks and the primary responsibility for managing the risk if it occurs.
- *Monitor and Control Risks (Monitoring and controlling process group):* This is the process of implementing the risk response plans, tracking identified risks, monitoring residual risks and identifying new risks throughout the project life cycle.

In the rest of this section, we will briefly describe these risk management processes and their inputs, tools and techniques and outputs.

3.1 Plan Risk Management

This process defines how to conduct the risk management activities for a project. The guidelines and procedures developed during this process are set down in The Risk Management Plan, a document which describes methodology for:

- Identifying and listing the risk events
- Carrying out qualitative and quantitative risk analysis to prioritize the risks and develop numerical probabilistic estimate for different risk exposures if risks occurred
- Planning the strategy for managing the prioritized risks including the approach, identification of risk trigger and assigning the primary responsibility of managing the risk
- Implementing the risk response plans

By its very nature, since this process would provide the basic guidelines for the entire risk management efforts, it needs to start at the very early stage of the project planning and should be completed as early as practicable during the planning phase.

Inputs

Components of project management plan: The first set of important inputs for risk planning come from the project management plan components. By closely analyzing the tasks involved for the work packages and WBS, the perception of risks associated with the tasks can be obtained. The degree of variation or range in the cost estimates and time duration estimates, similarly point out the degree of uncertainty in the activity cost and activity time duration and hence the corresponding nature of risks. Analysis of quality management plan would reveal the likely pitfalls and risks in attaining the desired quality in product of the project. Analysis and challenging of the assumptions and constraints in the project scope statement would give a sense of the risk arising out of the assumptions not working out.

Enterprise environmental factors: Risk planning also requires to look at what is happening outside the project environment and how the uncertainties in the external environment (in the other divisions of the organization, the industry trends and overall macroeconomic factors) would pose risks to the project. The risk tolerance of the project sponsors and other key stakeholders is also important in the approach to be taken for risk planning.

Organizational process assets: The lessons learned on earlier similar projects, particularly the nature of risks faced and the risk management techniques successfully used can provide good insight into risk planning process.

Tools and Techniques

Analysis: The extensive data input from various sources for risk planning mentioned above requires thorough analysis to provide the basis for preparing the risk management plan.

Meetings with project team members and stakeholders: Being an uncharted territory, the collective wisdom of knowledgeable team members and stakeholders is very useful resource for perceiving and planning for risk events.

Outputs

Output of the process is the *Risk Management Plan*. This is the basic document which will guide planning for all subsequent risk management activities. The contents of Risk management Plan might include:

- *How to identify risk, and analyze and prioritize it (Methodology)*—the sources for risk identification, probability estimating procedures, risk categories, methods assessing the impacts and methods for performing qualitative and quantitative analysis
- *Who will do risk management?* The assignment of risk management tasks to different project team members with well-defined roles and responsibilities.
- *At what cost* This would cover the provision of contingency funds in the project budget in the cost management plan and provision in the project plan for some specific expenses for measures for avoiding or mitigating risks
- *What Category of risk: (Risk Breakdown Structure):* A risk categorization structure, developed from the experience on earlier projects, could be also useful in risk planning. Such formal structure for risk categorization, called Risk Breakdown Structure, is shown in Figure 7.3 in this chapter.
- *How much, risk exposure would be tolerated by stakeholders:* From the analysis of stakeholders risk tolerance, guidelines for risk management can be formulated.
- *How to define risk probability and impacts based on risk tolerance:* Clarity in applying uniform and rational methods for estimating the risk probabilities and their classification into relative seriousness or importance is the backbone of sound qualitative and quantitative analysis of risks. Risk management plan gives the desired definitions.
- *How to report:* Finally, the risk management plan provides the formats and templates for risk management report in the form of the risk register.

3.2 Identify Risk

This process involves determining which risks may affect the project outcomes and recording their characteristics and impacts on project outcomes. The general description of the process is described in the "Step 1: Risk Identification" of this chapter.

However, for the sake of making comprehensive coverage of the treatment of this subject and this process in PMBOK® Guide, 4th Edition, the inputs, tools and techniques, and outputs are briefly enumerated below.

Inputs

Risk Management Plan This is the most important and distinctive input for the process. Provision for risk management activities in the budget and schedule, the responsibility and roles assigned for risk management, risk breakdown structure and definitions of risk probability and impact described in the Risk Management Plan are important inputs.

In addition, a number of inputs for Risk Identify process and Plan Risk Management are common. *Activity Cost Estimate* and *Activity Duration Estimate, Scope Baseline, Stakeholders' Register, Risk tolerance profiles of the stakeholders*, and templates and risk management techniques, *the Lessons Learned from the project files* could also provide useful inputs.

Tools and Techniques

Review and Analysis of project planning documents—Project Charter, Project Scope Statement, Assumptions and Constraints, Major Contracts, Quality Plan and other earlier projects files would be an important tool.

Checklist Analysis—Risk Checklist from earlier projects and Risk breakdown structure is another important input. In article 6 in this section, a specimen of the checklist for risk identification is given.

Two techniques depend on benefiting from the collective wisdom of project team members (*Brainstorming*) and for reaching a consensus among experts about the perceived risks (*Delphi Technique*). They are more useful for projects with unusual technical processes or project activities.

Analysis of assumptions and challenging them systematically could also be a helpful tool for identifying techniques.

Analytical techniques like *SWOT Analysis* and *Cause-and-Effect Diagrams* can also be used as tools.

Output

Risk Register: The primary output from the process is Risk Register. It is also a primary out put from other risk management processes described later in this section. Risk Register is defined in PMBOK® Guide as a document containing the results of the qualitative risk analysis, quantitative risk analysis and risk response planning. The Risk Register details all identified risks including description, category, cause, probability of occurring, impact(s) on objectives, proposed responses, owners and current status.

Risk Register is a comprehensive reference document concerned with almost all risk management processes. It evolves into its finished final form as the successive risk management processes are carried out. In view of its great importance as a risk management document, a detailed note on Risk Register is provided in Section 4.

3.3 Perform Qualitative Risk Analysis

This process aims at prioritizing the identified risks by assessing the probability of risk occurrence, the value of impact if the risk event occurred and calculating the risk value or risk exposure. This risk exposure or risk value is calculated from the assessment of the probability and impact of each risk identified in the Risk Register developed in the earlier process.

Inputs

The list of risks identified and recorded into the *Risk Register* and the definitions for assessing the probability and impact of the risk in the *Risk Management Plan* are the two main inputs. The *Project Scope Statement* and information base from earlier projects (Organizational Process Assets) are other two inputs.

Tools and Techniques

The expected value of the risk (also called 'risk value' or 'risk exposure') is calculated by the product of risk probability and impact if the risk occurred.

Expected Value of Risk = (Risk Probability) × (Impact of risk on scope, cost or time)

The risks are prioritized based on the expected value off the risk—the higher the expected value, the greater the priority for risk planning and management. **In Step 2: Risk Assessment" in this chapter, an illustration of the definitions of risk probability and impact, risk value, and risk severity matrix developed from the risk value are described in detail.**

Outputs

Risk Register Updates: The output from qualitative analysis of risks is a further refinement of the risk register document already created during the Identify Risk process. The updates would include the assessment of the risk values and the prioritization of risks based on the risk values, classification of risks into categories and any general trends spotted during the qualitative analysis process. A detailed note on Risk Register is provided in Section 4.

3.4 Perform Quantitative Risk Analysis

The process of numerical analysis of the major or prioritized risks listed in the risk register document after its updating to reflect qualitative risk analysis conclusions. The quantitative risk analysis aims at working out a probabilistic estimate for different likely outcomes using some specialized analytical techniques.

Monte Carlo Simulation, This technique for quantitative risk analysis is based on building a model and carrying out simulation for the project outcomes based on the individual data point generated to correspond to its probability. The final output would be a plot of the cumulative probability of occurrence plotted against project cost or project schedule. From this graph, it would be possible to read out the probability of any desired project cost or project schedule.

To illustrate the nature of output from Monte Carlo simulation, it would be possible read out from the plot the probability of occurrence of a specific cost chosen from the entire range of possible project costs (e.g. 'The probability would be 75 % for the project to be completed in some specific project cost, say Rs 30 crores,' or say 'For the project to be completed at the cost of Rs 38 crores, the probability is 95 %', etc.). Similarly, from the Monte Carlo simulation for project network, the probability for some specific project schedule from the entire range of likely project completion times could be read out. (e.g. The probability for completing the project in 45 weeks is 75 % or that the probability would be 90% for the project to be completed in say, 54 weeks, etc.)

The Sensitivity Analysis focuses on estimating the relative variation in the project outcomes of interest (cost or time) when a unit variation occurs in one of the variables while keeping all other variables constant. It is useful in examining the impact of individual risk factors on the overall project risk and thus it can help select the critical factors for focusing.

Decision Tree Analysis technique helps to analyze the risks and benefits associated with investment decision strategy when the investments could be made in phases.

Inputs

Risk Management Plan and *Risk Register* (its updated version after qualitative analysis) provide one set of inputs. *The cost management plan and schedule management plan* provide another set of data. With this dataset, the quantitative analysis is carried out using some of the above described techniques.

Outputs

The output from the process is further update of Risk Register. A detailed note in Section 4.

3.5 Plan Risk Response

This process is concerned with developing the options for reducing the threats to project outcomes from negative risks and enhancing the opportunities from the positive risks and selecting the strategy for optimum results from the options developed. The process involves:

- Analyzing the data in the risk register (the list of prioritized risks from qualitative analysis and the results and trends spotted from quantitative risk analysis) and the methodology and responsibility assignments in the Risk management Plan
- Developing options for individual risks and selecting the strategy from the available options of risk handling (avoiding, transferring, mitigating and accepting)
- Developing risk response plan for incorporation as an update into the risk register (selected strategy for each prioritized risk, assigning the risk management responsibility, and identifying the triggers), and
- Calculating contingency reserves position

Inputs

Risk Register (including its updates from qualitative and quantitative analysis) and *Risk Management Plan* (for methodology, responsibility assignments and risk tolerance thresholds of key stakeholders) provide the main inputs.

Tools and Techniques

PMBOK® Guide makes distinction between the strategies for handling positive and negative risks. The strategies for negative risk include avoiding, transferring, mitigating and accepting the risk. The strategies for handling opportunities (or positive risks) include exploiting, sharing, enhancing and accepting. These techniques for responding to the risks are described in detail in "Step: 3 Risk response Development" of this chapter.

Outputs

Risk Register Updates: The output of the process is a detailed plan of actions for prioritized risks, which is incorporated as an update in the risk register. The updates would include:

- The list of prioritized risks and recommended strategy for handling it
- The provision of budget for risk management activities
- Provision of time required for risk management activity in the project schedule
- The assignment of roles and responsibilities for handling risks
- The residual and secondary risks

Updates of project plan components and *Project Documents* in light of risk response plan are the other outputs.

3.6 Monitor and Control Risk

This is the process of implementing all the planning for risk management carried out in the earlier five risk planning processes. It includes:

- Tracking identified and prioritized risks
- Watching out for risk triggers and putting into action the measures planned for handling the risks
- Monitoring the residual risks and identifying the new risks after handling the main risk is over
- Evaluating the effectiveness of risk management throughout the project life cycle
- Adjusting the contingency reserves in project budget and time buffers in light of the current position

Inputs

Like all monitoring and controlling processes, the inputs for this process are:

- *Risk Register* and *Project Management Plan* as the desired outcome or standard to be achieved, and
- *Work Performance Information* and *Performance Reports* as the actual results obtained.

Tools and Techniques

Variance Analysis: By comparing the variance between what is actually achieved with what was planned to be achieved, the degree and effectiveness of risk management is assessed and the direction for corrective measures for further risk management is set.

Risk Audits: This is another technique, like quality audits, of getting an independent assessment of how the risk management for the project is handled.

Reassessment of risk scenario: The process requires continuously reassessing the risk scenario and its reassessment.

Outputs

The outputs of the process are *Risk Register Updates* (outcomes of actual risk handling activities and risk audit conclusions), and *updates in the Project Plan* and *Updates in the project documents* (technical documentation and assumptions).

4. Risk Register

(Its gradual development during carrying out risk management planning processes)

While discussing Project Risk Management, PMBOK® Guide, 4th Edition, introduces the concept of Risk Register, a document comprehensively dealing with all project risk issues.

4.1 Risk Register Definition

Risk Register is defined as **"The document containing the results of the qualitative risk analysis, quantitative risk analysis and risk response planning. The Risk Register details all identified risks, including description, category, cause, probability of occurring, impact(s) on objectives, proposed responses, owners and current status"** (PMBOK® Guide, 4th Edition, 2008).

4.2 Development of Risk Register

Risk Register is a comprehensive reference document concerned with almost all risk management processes described in PMBOK® Guide. It evolves into its finished final form as the successive risk management processes are carried out. To start with, it would be important to note that PMBOK's definition of risk has slightly different connotations from the generally accepted idea. PMBOK defines risk as "An uncertain event or condition that, if it occurs, has a positive or negative effect on project's objectives (viz. scope, schedule, cost and quality)". The term risk is used in general parlance to refer to only negative or unfavourable aspect of the uncertain event or condition, while PMBOK includes in the term also favourable aspect and possibility of exploiting the opportunity.

The initiation of Risk Register and its progressive elaboration proceeds during the risk management processes as follows:

4.2.1 Identify Risk

Risk Register comes into existence with the process "Identify Risk". Risk Register is the output of this process and includes entries of all risks identified at that stage; as additional risks are identifies at the later planning or executing stage, the entries for them are made. At this stage the Risk Register includes just two data sets:

- *List of Identified Risk:* This would include the risk identification, its brief description, the causes for the risk and the likely impact on project objectives (scope, schedule, cost or quality)
- *List of potential responses:* The preliminary analysis of the risk and the likely response to manage the risk

4.2.2 Perform Qualitative Risk Analysis

During this process, each of the identified risk from the risk register list is analyzed to assess the probability of the risk event to occur and the impact it would have if the risk occurred on project scope, cost, schedule or quality. Using this data, the expected value of the risk impact is evaluated (Expected value of impact = probability of risk x the impact in event of risk occurrence). Once these assessments are worked out, a relative ranking of the risk can be carried out to prioritize further analysis and response planning. So, at this stage of risk management process, the Risk Register includes three additional data for each identified list entry in the form of Probability, Impact on Occurrence, and Expected Value of Impact. The ranking based expected value of impact would be the basis for qualitative analysis.

4.2.3 Perform Quantitative Risk Analysis

A detailed quantitative risk analysis may be carried out for selected risks based on the prioritization derived from qualitative analysis of risk. Quantitative analysis would require collection of data for more reliable estimate of probability and impacts on outcome and the use of quantitative techniques like Monte Carlo Simulation, Decision Tree Analysis and Sensitivity Analysis. Quantitative analysis of risk is therefore far more refined and reliable and comes out with the probabilistic analysis of achieving the time and cost objectives even in the event of risk occurrence. At this stage, therefore, the results from quantitative risk in the Risk Register, analysis are added against the specific entries.

4.2.4 Plan Risk Response

From the prioritized list of risks from the qualitative or quantitative risk analysis, the suitable responses are devised from the four available strategies for risk management. These strategies are:

- *Avoid Risk:* Change project plan suitably to prevent risk arising by eliminating the work likely to involve risk.
- *Transfer Risk:* Transfer the risk to an agent more experienced or capable of handling the work associated with the risk (Outsourcing) or transfer the consequence of risk to a third party (insurance).
- *Mitigate Risk:* Adopt such measures in project plan and execution which would decrease the probability of occurrence of risk or reduce the impact of risk in case it occurred.
- *Acceptance:* It is sometimes physically impossible or economically unviable to manage a risk and accepting it in case it occurs is the only way left.

After this risk management process, the Risk Register would be further updated to include the planned response to the identified risk entries. At this stage, the main agency or person responsible for managing the risk, if it occurred, and the risk trigger, giving advance warning of the increased likelihood of risk occurrence.

4.2.5 Monitor and Control Risk

During this process, the Risk Register is periodically reviewed and updated to current status of the project. The retired risks are removed from the active list of Risk Register and some new risks arising out of mitigation measures taken for managing some risks outcome are added. At the end of the project, Risk Register would provide a very valuable record of lessons learned for how a similar project in future can be planned and executed more effectively.

4.3 The Contents of Risk Register

The contents of Risk Register, after undergoing all updating from sequential risk management processes would be as listed below. An Excel® format worksheet may be prepared and used with suitable columns to include these contents. These attributes, as evident from the above description of risk management processes are sequentially added in developing the Risk Register and not at a one go.

List of Identified Risks (Identify Risk)

Attributes Against Each Risk Entry:

- Description risk event—including causes, impact on which specific objectives (Identify Risk)
- Probability of risk occurrence (Perform Qualitative Risk Analysis)
- Impact in event the risk event occurred (Perform Qualitative Risk Analysis)
- Expected value of risk event (Perform Qualitative Risk Analysis)
- Prioritized ranking or ordering of the list entries (Perform Qualitative Risk Analysis)
- Probabilistic assessment of risk event (Perform Quantitative Risk Analysis)
- Description of strategies for risk management (Plan Risk Response)
- Responsibility assigned for managing risk (Plan Risk Response)
- Description of risk trigger (Plan Risk Response)

The Risk Register would be periodicaly reviewed and updated during monitoring and controlling phase.

4.4. Specimen for Risk Register (Template)

A tabular template for the Risk Register is presented in the accompanying figure. The columns ordinarily included in the Risk Register template and some guidance on how to complete the risk analysis and update the risk register document are briefly described below.

(i) *Risk Event*

Care should be exercised to clearly articulate the event and not confuse with the impact on project outcome if the risk occurs. So "Cost Overrun" is not a correct articulation of risk; it is the negative impact of some risk. The risk itself may be inflation and price rise of materials, inadequately understood and agree requirements, overtime, etc.

(ii) *Risk event drivers*

Financial Risks, Technical Risks, Commercial risks, Project Planning and Execution Risks, Contractual or Legal Risks

(iii) Probability of each risk event driver

(iv) Likely negative impact on project objectives outcomes

- Scope
- Cost
- Schedule
- Quality

(v) Impact Drivers in case the risk does occur (e.g. High tides timings, heavy rains, the cleanliness of drains, evacuation plans vulnerable population in low lying areas, readiness of emergency assistance services, communications in case of risk analysis for flooding of Mumbai roads during monsoon)

(vi) Planned response for each major risk event / event driver Avoidance / Transfer /Sharing Risk/Impact mitigation /Acceptance or retaining risk

(vii) Risk Response Plan for each major risk
  - Responsibility for risk management (risk owners)
  - Agreed risk response planned
  - Trigger
  - Residual risks
  - Budget for risk response

(viii) Contingency provision for risk management in
  - Project cost
  - Project schedule

5. Check-List for Risk Identification

Financial Risks (Financial Viability)—exposure to loss due to

  - Huge project cost overruns
  - Unexpectedly large delay in project implementation
  - Total failure in development or use of new technology or material
  - Acts of God
  - Delayed returns from project
  - Returns not up to expectation
  - Project failing in meeting all objectives

Technical Risks (Technical Feasibility)—due to

  - Requirement for use of unproven technology
  - Unavailability of skilled personnel for use of the technology
  - Use of an operation previously not used
  - Use of new materials

Commercial Risks (Business Plan Failure)—due to

  - Total market development not up to expectation
  - Failure in capturing planned market share (quality/price constraints)
  - Project delay and corresponding delayed cash inflows
  - Product pricing and cost unfavourable compared to projections

Project Planning and Execution Risks—due to

  - Failure in meeting criteria for project success (scope management)
  - Project cost overruns (cost management)
  - Schedule delay (time management)

Contractual or Legal Risk

  - Discrepancy between estimated and contracted cost
  - Project late delivery penalty
  - Third party litigations
  - Failure in meeting environmental or other legal requirements for communities around the project sites.

"Contingency Planning" section in this chapter describes in details the categories of risks listed in the check list. Interested readers should revisit it for more extensive discussion.

CASE 7.1

Alaska Fly-Fishing Expedition*

You are sitting around the fire at a lodge in Dillingham, Alaska, discussing a fishing expedition you are planning with your colleagues at Great Alaska Adventures (GAA). Earlier in the day you received a fax from the president of BlueNote, Inc. The president wants to reward her top management team by taking them on an all-expense-paid fly-fishing adventure in Alaska. She would like GAA to organize and lead the expedition.

You have just finished a preliminary scope statement for the project (see below). You are now brainstorming potential risks associated with the project.

1. Brainstorm potential risks associated with this project. Try to come up with at least five different risks.
2. Use a risk assessment form similar to Figure 7.6 to analyze identified risks.
3. Develop a risk response matrix similar to Figure 7.8 to outline how you would deal with each of the risks.

Project Scope Statement

Project Objective

To organize and lead a five-day fly-fishing expedition down the Tikchik River system in Alaska from June 21 to 25 at a cost not to exceed $27,000.

Deliverables

- Provide air transportation from Dillingham, Alaska, to Camp I and from Camp II back to Dillingham.
- Provide river transportation consisting of two eight-man drift boats with outboard motors.
- Provide three meals a day for the five days spent on the river.
- Provide four hours fly-fishing instruction.
- Provide overnight accommodations at the Dillingham lodge plus three four-man tents with cots, bedding, and lanterns.
- Provide four experienced river guides who are also fly fishermen.
- Provide fishing licenses for all guests.

Milestones

1. Contract signed January 22.
2. Guests arrive in Dillingham June 20.
3. Depart by plane to Base Camp I June 21.
4. Depart by plane from Base Camp II to Dillingham June 25.

Technical Requirements

1. Fly in air transportation to and from base camps.
2. Boat transportation within the Tikchik River system.
3. Digital cellular communication devices.
4. Camps and fishing conform to state of Alaska requirements.

---

* This case was prepared with the assistance of Stuart Morigeau.

Limits and Exclusions

1. Guests are responsible for travel arrangements to and from Dillingham, Alaska.
2. Guests are responsible for their own fly-fishing equipment and clothing.
3. Local air transportation to and from base camps will be outsourced.
4. Tour guides are not responsible for the number of King Salmon caught by guests.

Customer Review

The president of BlueNote, Inc.

CASE 7.2

Silver Fiddle Construction

You are the president of Silver Fiddle Construction (SFC), which specializes in building high-quality, customized homes in the Grand Junction, Colorado, area. You have just been hired by the Czopeks to build their dream home. You operate as a general contractor and employ only a part-time bookkeeper. You subcontract work to local trade professionals. Housing construction in Grand Junction is booming. You are tentatively scheduled to complete 11 houses this year. You have promised the Czopeks that the final costs will range from $450,000 to $500,000 and that it will take five months to complete the house once groundbreaking has begun. The Czopeks are willing to have the project delayed in order to save costs.

You have just finished a preliminary scope statement for the project (see below). You are now brainstorming potential risks associated with the project.

1. Identify potential risks associated with this project. Try to come up with at least five different risks.
2. Use a risk assessment form similar to Figure 7.6 to analyze identified risks.
3. Develop a risk response matrix similar to Figure 7.8 to outline how you would deal with each of the risks.

Project Scope Statement

Project Objective

To construct a high-quality, custom home within five months at a cost not to exceed $500,000.

Deliverables

- A 2,500-square-foot, 2½-bath, 3-bedroom, finished home.
- A finished garage, insulated and sheetrocked.
- Kitchen appliances to include range, oven, microwave, and dishwasher.
- High-efficiency gas furnace with programmable thermostat.

Milestones

1. Permits approved July 5.
2. Foundation poured July 12.
3. "Dry in"—framing, sheathing, plumbing, electrical, and mechanical inspections—passed September 25.
4. Final inspection November 7.

Technical Requirements

1. Home must meet local building codes.
2. All windows and doors must pass NFRC class 40 energy ratings.
3. Exterior wall insulation must meet an "R" factor of 21.
4. Ceiling insulation must meet an "R" factor of 38.
5. Floor insulation must meet an "R" factor of 25.
6. Garage will accommodate two cars and one 28-foot-long Winnebago.
7. Structure must pass seismic stability codes.

Limits and Exclusions

1. The home will be built to the specifications and design of the original blueprints provided by the customer.
2. Owner is responsible for landscaping.
3. Refrigerator is not included among kitchen appliances.
4. Air conditioning is not included, but house is prewired for it.
5. SFC reserves the right to contract out services.

Customer Review

"Bolo" and Izabella Czopek.

CASE 7.3

Peak LAN Project

Peak Systems is a small, information systems consulting firm located in Meridian, Louisiana. Peak has just been hired to design and install a local area network (LAN) for the city of Meridian's social welfare agency. You are the manager for the project, which includes one Peak professional and two interns from a local university. You have just finished a preliminary scope statement for the project (see below). You are now brainstorming potential risks associated with the project.

1. Identify potential risks associated with this project. Try to come up with at least five different risks.
2. Use a risk assessment form similar to Figure 7.6 to analyze identified risks.
3. Develop a risk response matrix similar to Figure 7.8 to outline how you would deal with each of the risks.

Project Scope Statement

Project Objective

To design and install a local area network (LAN) within one month with a budget not to exceed $90,000 for the Meridian Social Service Agency.

Deliverables

- Twenty workstations and twenty laptop computers.
- Server with dual-core processors.

- Two color laser printers.
- Windows Vista server and workstation operating system.
- Four hours of introduction training for client's personnel.
- Sixteen hours of training for client network administrator.
- Fully operational LAN system.

Milestones

1. Hardware January 22.
2. Setting users' priority and authorization January 26.
3. In-house whole network test completed February 1.
4. Client site test completed February 2.
5. Training completed February 16.

Technical Requirements

1. Workstations with 17-inch flat panel monitors, dual-core processo   1 GB RAM, 8X DVD+RW, wireless card, Ethernet card, 80 GB hard drive.
2. Laptops with 12-inch display monitor, dual-core processors, 512 MB RAM, 8X DVD+RW, wireless card, Ethernet card, 60 GB hard drive and weigh less than 4½ lbs.
3. Wireless network interface cards and Ethernet connections.
4. System must support Windows Vista platform.
5. System must provide secure external access for field workers.

Limits and Exclusions

1. System maintenance and repair only up to one month after final inspection.
2. Warranties transferred to client.
3. Only responsible for installing software designated by the client two weeks before the start of the project.
4. Client will be billed for additional training beyond that prescribed in the contract.

Customer Review

Director of the city of Meridian's Social Service Agency.

CASE 7.4

XSU Spring Concert

You are a member of the X State University (XSU) student body entertainment committee. Your committee has agreed to sponsor a Spring concert. The motive behind this concert is to offer a safe alternative to Hasta Weekend. Hasta Weekend is a spring event in which students from XSU rent houseboats and engage in heavy partying. Traditionally this occurs during the last weekend in May. Unfortunately, the partying has a long history of getting out of hand, sometimes leading to fatal accidents. After one such tragedy last Spring, your committee wants to offer an alternative experience for those who are eager to celebrate the change in weather and the pending end of the school year.

You have just finished a preliminary scope statement for the project (see below). You are now brain-storming potential risks associated with the project.

1. Identify potential risks associated with this project. Try to come up with at least five different risks.
2. Use a risk assessment form similar to Figure 7.6 to analyze identified risks.
3. Develop a risk response matrix similar to Figure 7.8 to outline how you would deal with each of the risks.

Project Scope Statement

Project Objective

To organize and deliver an eight-hour concert at Wahoo Stadium at a cost not to exceed $50,000 on the last Saturday in May.

Deliverables

- Local advertising.
- Concert security.
- Separate Beer Garden.
- Eight hours of music and entertainment.
- Food venues.
- Souvenir concert t-shirts.
- Secure all licenses and approvals.
- Secure sponsors.

Milestones

1. Secure all permissions and approvals by January 15.
2. Sign big-name artist by February 15.
3. Complete artist roster by April 1.
4. Secure vendor contracts by April 15.
5. Setup completed on May 27.
6. Concert on May 28.
7. Clean-up completed by May 31.

Technical Requirements

1. Professional sound stage and system.
2. At least one big-name artist.
3. At least seven performing acts.
4. Restroom facilities for 10,000 people.
5. Parking available for 1,000 cars.
6. Compliance with XSU and city requirements/ordinances.

Limits and Exclusions

1. Performers responsible for travel arrangements to and from XSU.
2. Vendors contribute a set percentage of sales.
3. Concert must be over by 11:30 P.M.

CASE 7.5

International Capital, Inc.—Part A

International Capital, Inc. (IC), is a small investment banking firm that specializes in securing funds for small- to medium-sized firms. IC is able to use a standardized project format for each engagement. Only activity times and unusual circumstances change the standard network. Beth Brown has been assigned to this client as project manager partner and has compiled the network information and activity times for the latest client as follows:

Activity	Description	Immediate Predecessor
A	Start story draft using template	—
B	Research client firm	—
C	Create "due diligence" rough draft	A, B
D	Coordinate needs proposal with client	C
E	Estimate future demand and cash flows	C
F	Draft future plans for client company	E
G	Create and approve legal documents	C
H	Integrate all drafts into first-draft proposal	D, F, G
I	Line up potential sources of capital	G, F
J	Check, approve, and print final legal proposal	H
K	Sign contracts and transfer funds	I, J

	Time in Workdays		
Activity	Optimistic	Most Likely	Pessimistic
A	4	7	10
B	2	4	8
C	2	5	8
D	16	19	28
E	6	9	24
F	1	7	13
G	4	10	28
H	2	5	14
I	5	8	17
J	2	5	8
K	17	29	45

Managerial Report

Brown and other broker partners have a policy of passing their plan through a project review committee of colleagues. This committee traditionally checks that all details are covered, times are realistic, and resources are available. Brown wishes you to develop a report that presents a planned schedule and expected project completion time in workdays. Include a project network in your report. The average duration for a sourcing capital project is 70 workdays. IC partners have agreed it is good business to set up projects with a 95 percent chance of attaining the plan. How does this project stack up with the average project? What would the average have to be to ensure a 95 percent chance of completing the project in 70 workdays?

CASE 7.6

Venugopal's Dilemma
(Illustration of Monte Carlo Simulation:
A Technique for Quantitative Risk Analysis)

Introduction

Quantitative risk analysis techniques find application for projects of large scope, cost and associated risks. The case describes a project situation, where a popular quantitative risk analysis technique, Monte Carlo Simulation, is effectively applied. The idea underlying this case presentation is to bring awareness about (i) what a simulation based quantitative risk analysis can accomplish, (ii) the general framework and nature of input data require for carrying out the analysis, and (iii) the type of inferences which this technique would develop—the graphical output of the cumulative probability for different likely project outcomes suitable for taking calculated risks. The details of actual simulation technique (available from the textbooks on quantitative analytical methods) are not presented here. The quantitative techniques themselves are sound in concept and relatively straight forward in application. However, for their meaningful application, the input data would need to be collected with great care and judgment.

When Ram Kumar Sharma returned from his U.S. visit, he was just thrilled and eager to display the goldmine opportunity he discovered during the trip. On a routine call to one of his company's customers, where their team of twelve programmers was working on a review of the Y2K impact on the software already used by the customer for over a decade, he happened to meet the outsourcing director of the client. From discussion over a dinner in the evening, Sharma learnt about the client's plan to invite a tender for a good size business solution IT project. The project appeared to have a potential for attractive margins and so he extended his stay there for two days more and collected the details of the tender and the competitors likely to participate in the tendering process.

Sharma was bubbling with enthusiasm and pride while talking about the opportunity that he had discovered. Vice President, Venugopal was, however, not that enthused. He could see some of the project risks and their likely impacts. All the same, the opportunity was too attractive to be bypassed without a second look.

Venugopal could see that if they landed the contract, it would be indeed a very attractive opportunity of earning over Rs 700 to 950 million. But the competition was also strong and his company would have to spend up front a good sum even to prepare the bid. With over Rs 300,000 per day cost of a team of hundred workers likely to be involved for bid preparation and assuming that the team might require eight weeks for the work involved in preparing the details for making the bid, the minimum up-front cost of developing the bid was Rs 12 million—not small for his company. The cost could even swell up to Rs 24 millions. What was more, there were certain risk elements in the cost for bid preparation, which were subject to variation in a range. *Obtaining the estimate for the cost of bid preparation with a known degree of certainty or confidence was crucial in deciding whether his company should undertake the exercise and spend the money in bid preparation.*

The bid was to be prepared for a medium sized IT system consisting of two mainframe computer installations supporting 80 work stations. The software would consist of the off-the-shelf applications as well as some customization and integration. The system was to be installed (hardware part also) and the users were to be trained. Part of the bid was also for full hardware and software support for 10 years after the system was installed. All this information was obtained by Sharma from the discussion with the client, but the specific requirements, especially the identity of the software application would not be known till the tender was formally issued.

With his vast experience, Venugopal could easily take an overview of the bid preparation activities and break them down into main six or seven work packages. The next step he took was to mull over the likely contents of the work packages and make a very rough estimate of the work effort and corresponding costs for each work package. This six-hours exercise helped to clarify some issues, but Venugopal still did not feel comfortable about the element of risk involved in preparing the bid. Sharma kept on reassuring Venugopal that the client was very happy with the quality of outsourcing work carried out by them for the client so far and that they would have a high chance of winning the tender if they came out with a technically sound and cost effective proposal. This encouraged Venugopal to take a chance for preparing the bid, but before he could decide on that course, he needed some degree of confidence on the exact outlay he would have to be ready to commit for bidding. Venugopal decided to discuss this with Dr. Sesha Iyanger, one of his brilliant new associate, who had a good grounding in quantitative techniques for estimation.

Over a cup of coffee, Venugopal gave Dr. Sesha the essential details of the situation and summarized with a remark, " I would be ready to commit a specific sum for preparing bid, but I would like to know how much chance I have in being able to prepare the bid in that budget. In other words, I would want to *take a calculated risk*; I would like to know the answers to the questions like:

- What are the chances of my preparing the bid within a budget of, say Rs 12 million?, or
- What budget I must be prepared to sanction if I want to have the confidence of over 90% in completing preparation of bid within that budget ?or, for that matter, or
- What would be the most likely (50 % confidence level) cost for preparing the bid?"

Dr. Sesha said, "Well, you have rightly described it as a gambling situation, but there are certain simulation modeling techniques for quantitative risk analysis, which could give you the answers you are looking for. The analysis could tell you the degree of confidence you can have on preparing the bid within a certain budget. For example, the analysis could give you an inference that the probability of your preparing the bid within a certain budget, say Rs 12 million, is 60 % or 70 %. Or that if you want to have a degree of confidence to be around 95 %, you must be prepared to sanction a higher budget, say Rs 16 million. Interestingly, the technique is called *Monte Carlo* Simulation—probably an implicit admission of the nature of gambling uncertainty in the tool and reminding me of an old James Bond movie, Casino Royal, where he was shown sitting at a gaming table at Monte Carlo.

The technique consists of *creating a scenario by picking at random one of the likely outcomes* (say, cost or time duration) *of each of the elements constituting the total work and working out from these individual estimates the total outcome (say, cost or time for the entire project).* The computer would carry out this exercise for the desired number of scenarios (say 100 or 500) and give you the total cost or time for the project for each scenario. The cumulative frequency distribution of the resulting total cost or time period is plotted against the total project cost or time. From this graph, you could read the degree of confidence, which you can associate with any particular value of total project cost or project schedule. *The technique is statistically sound in concept, but, as you realize, the quality of the output would depend on the quality and reliability of the input data.*

Also, let me assure you, this would not take too much work or time. Our new age computers and the standard soft wares available on them, say Excel, could be used to work out such quantitative risk analysis in a day at the most. Just give me an idea of the nature of distribution, which the cost of individual packages would take, their minimum and maximum likely values and I will work out a Monte Carlo simulation model, from which you can gauge the degree of confidence that can be associated with any specific budget you may be prepared to sanction."

Venugopal found the technique interesting and worth exploring. He sat down and worked out the details necessary for the data required to give to Dr. Sesha (Exhibit 1).

Two days later, Dr. Sesha came back to Venugopal and showed him the graph of the cumulative probability of completing the bid versus the bid budget (Exhibit 2).

Venugopal was quite impressed by what he saw. He kept on mulling over studying the graph, drawing the inferences, which could be drawn from it and to what extent the data he gave for the analysis was trustworthy and if the data could be refined for greater reliability.

Well, the quantitative risk analysis could take it just so far. It was now left to Venugopal to keep simmering within and looking at various of issues for decision making: the overall company strategy, financial position of the company, the likely market scenario in the next 12 months, the risk tolerance of the other board members at this stage, and the risks and pay-offs from the successful or unsuccessful outcomes of the bid.

Exhibit I

Identification of Activities for Bid Preparation

Venugopal identified seven activities to be the parts of preparing a bid. The corresponding work packages are described below.

Project Management	This work package covers compiling the final documentation for the bid and the cost of project management for preparing the bid.
System Design	This work package covers preparing the overall specifications of the system, design of system architecture and technical specifications of component products required to build the system estimating the cost of man-hours for system design, and
Purchased Software	This work package covers identifying the suppliers for proprietary software included in the system design, obtain technical specifications and quotes for provision within the bid. It also covers preparing proposal text describing the software features and how they meet the client's tender specifications.
Software Development	This work package covers: (a) Defining the requirements for software to be developed and integrating tasks departmentally and developing the estimate of time and cost, and (b) Estimating the time and cost for integration of the departmentally developed software with the overall system.
Installation	This work package covers estimating the time and cost of installing the hardware, proprietary software and departmentally developed software for building the system to meet the functional requirements and the desired features.
Training and Initial Support	This work package covers estimating the training requirements, the cost of preparing and compiling the training manual, the time and cost of personal training of key operating staff of the client, and describing the scope of training offered in the proposal.
Post-installation Support	This work package covers estimating the cost of post-installation support and including its description in the proposal.

Exhibit 1 (Continued)

Summary of Work Packages Cost Estimates For Quantitative Risk Analysis

Work Package	Estimated Cost in Rs lakhs (Effort in Man days)		
	Minimum	*Likely*	*Maximum*
Project Management	30.0	34.5	36.0
	(100)	(115)	(120)
System Design	42.0	54.0	60.0
	(140)	(180)	(200)
Purchased Software	4.5	7.5	9.0
Software Development	21.0	24.0	30.0
and Integration tasks	(70)	(80)	(100)
Installation	4.5	6.0	9.0
	(15)	(20)	(30)
Training and Initial Support	4.5	6.0	9.0
	(15)	(20)	(30)
Post-installation Support	2.5	4.0	5.0
	(8)	(10)	(13)
Total Cost in Rs. Lakhs	109	136	158
(Rs million)	(10.9)	(13.6)	(15.8)
Total Effort in Man-days	(348)	(425)	(493)

Basis for Estimates: 1. Man-days estimated from references to the project archives for similar projects and confirmed by preliminary function points analysis

2. Average cost of man-days taken at Rs 3,000/- per man-day, (salary and allocated overheads) based on the current year budgeted costs.

Exhibit 2

THE CUMULATIVE PROBABILITY VERSUS BID COST (RS LAKHS)
Tabular Data and Graph Worked out By Dr. Shesha Iyanger

From the graph given below, Venugopal can get the inferences he desired from the quantitative risk analysis.

1. The probability of completing the bid within the budgeted cost of Rs 12 millions is less than 5 %. In other words the degree of confidence for completing the bid within Rs 12 million budget is less than 5 %.
2. For the degree of confidence to be 90 %, the budget to be sanctioned for bid preparation must be Rs 14.2 million.
3. The most likely cost (50 % confidence level) for the bid preparation would be Rs 13.4 million.

VENUGOPAL'S DILEMMA (Cumulative Probability vs Bid Cost (Rs Lakhs)

Data Table

Cumulative probability	Bid Cost (Rs Lakhs)
0	118
2	120
2	122
8	124
12	126
20	128
30	130
40	132
52	134
70	136
80	138
88	140
94	142
98	144
100	146

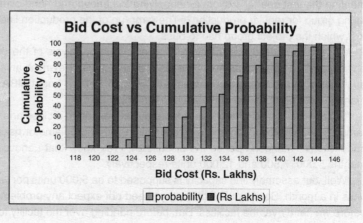

CASE 7.7

Supercomp Systems Manufacturing

Introduction

Qualitative risk analysis is an important risk management process used for prioritizing risks. The technique requires developing a cause-effect diagram linking the risk event drivers and risk impact drivers with the impact on the cost or schedule if the risk event occurred. From the probability of the risk event and the corresponding impact on the project cost or schedule, the expected value of the risk is estimated. This expected value is used for prioritizing risks and developing the risk management plan. The case below describes a scenario of qualitative risk management for a project for a manufacturing organization.

Four executives sat at the conference room table of Supercomp Systems Manufacturing Ltd with intense facial expressions. The group had been closely working together on a project to develop and market a new slim lap-top computer, lighter by a kilo than the models available in the market. Their project brief included developing the prototype, setting up the production line and overseeing for the first three months the production operation for the smooth transfer of the project to the manufacturing group.

The project group had burnt mid-night oil and devised ingenious ways to develop the proto-type. Lenovo, the Chinese computer giant considered introducing in the U.S.A. the lap-top computer under development by Supercomp as one of its low-cost models in the product line. Lenovo contracted with Supecomp to bankroll the cost of development for the proto-type and purchase at the contracted price about 25,000 units to be supplied in the first three months for seed marketing. Lenovo indicated to Supercomp that if the product was well accepted in the U.S.A., they expected the market to grow up to 15,000 units per week within a year and, accordingly, suggested Supercomp to set up the manufacturing line with a capacity for at least 5000 units per week to start with.

One look at the proto-type model and Nimish Mehta, the Executive Vice-President, realized that Supercomp had a real winner with this product. To reap the full benefits from the new product, he mused, it was crucial to ramp up the production and establish the brand and the position as a pioneer before the competitors came up with their 'me-too' imitations. "You have done very well so far", Nimish addressed Mahesh, who was the leader of the cross-functional product development team," How set you guys are in meeting the first quarter's quota for supplying to Lenovo and hand over the project facilities to our manufacturing group for regular production?" The ramp-up of the production line was indeed the final and crucial acid test which the project group had to pass.

Mahesh had called this meeting for a review and analysis of the risks in meeting the project's ramp-up objectives. The other members of the team were Asutosh Kejarival, an accountant, B. Subramaniam, a senior engineer from production department and Raman Seth, a bright MBA leading a newly set-up supply chain management group in the materials department.

"Sixteen months" efforts of our group are now coming to a close and we must pass the test of successfully ramping up the production and win recognition. What problems or risks do we foresee and what can we do about them?" Mahesh opened the discussion," You know that Lenovo has to be supplied for the first three months 5,000, 7,500 and 12,000 units respectively."

"Well, our assembly line capacity is supposed to be 5,000 units per week on a 3-shifts basis or over 20,000 units in a month. So, it would look that we need not expect any problems in meeting the first 3- months quota before we hand over the facilities. But, before handing over the facility to manufacturing, we need to establish that the production capacity of the assembly line is 5,000 units per week. We may have a problem there. My experience from all these years is that we do face problems in ramping up production. I expect the production rate in the first three months to be about 10,000 units, say 40-45% of the required monthly output. Use only 45% of the sales forecast to be met in the first three months; that is the bitter truth. So we will have a problem in demonstrating the production capacity of the assembly line before handing it over for manufacturing", Subramaniam explained.

"Do you mean every time the manufacturing ramp up is launched, the output is a meager, less than half the capacity in the first quarter? We would lose a gross margin of several million dollars. Wait a minute! I will calculate the exact number and come back." Kejarival was surprised.

"Not every time. But most times say, seven times out of ten !" Subbu shot back.

The euphoria of the project team, which developed a new winning product in a record time, sank. There was a silence for a minute, while Kejarival flipped his papers back and forth, noted down some numbers and punched in his calculator. " Over U.S Dollars six and a half millions", he announced looking up from the calculator, " Dollars 6,505,191 to be precise. That is the loss in gross revenue if we fail to meet the first quarter's production targets."

" How do you get all these funny accuracy in your numbers, right down to a Dollar?", Subbu asked teasingly.

"It is elementary Dr. Watson!" Kejarival mimicked the famous Sherlock Holmes quote, "Our sale price to Lenovo is U.S.$ 995/- per piece and the cost of goods sold (COGS) is projected to be U.S.$ 512.24 cents per unit. Now, using these sales price and COGS numbers, if we fail to supply 55 % of the projected requirement, we stand to lose US $ six and a half million five thousand one hundred and ninety one." Kejarival paused for the impact. "Work it out yourself!"

"That is a big risk. A very big risk. This would top all the ten risks in our list in terms of exposure." Mahesh took charge of the situation, "This is the risk we should take up first for our analysis and try all that we can do to minimize the exposure. Here, look at this table and chart. This is where this risk and exposure would fall on this graph." He pointed out on the graph sheet.

"Mahesh, you are talking of our assembly line capacity. But have you considered the capacity of Tandon Printed Circuit Boards? He won't be able to supply new PCBs to our design at the rate we need." Subbu came out with the first possible hitch in ramping up.

"Don't worry about Tandon." Raman Seth interjected, " While I considered the possible suppliers for the PCBs, I did have preliminary evaluation of Tandon's production capacity. Managing that supply chain is my responsibility and I will work with Tandon to make sure that he supplies as many PCBs as we need for the first quarter. We are still six months ahead of the launch. I will visit his shop and we will re-assess the capacity and then help him augment his capacity with assurances for guaranteed off take of the production or something like that. But, you have a point here, Subbu. For a long term strategy, I should develop an alternative supplier of PCBs also."

"That would go a long way, Raman"! Mahesh observed, " Do work with Tandon to make sure that we get the PCBs we want." Then turning towards Subbu, he asked," Tell me, if our assembly line capacity is 5,000 per week, why can't we get that output at that rate in the first three months? "

"These are new machines. New control panels! New assembly jigs! No one in our plant has operated or maintained these types of machines. There is something like 'Learning Curve Principle'—for a new operation, each time the output is doubled, the worker hours per unit decrease by a fixed percentage of the previous value. People take some time to get used to new machines and new methods. They need to be trained." Subbu explained

"Well, then, since this is the first priority risk in our project, let us manage this risk actively" Mahesh suggested, " We still have a few months to go before the launch. Let us have an intensive training program for the selected work force."

"We must do that if we want to meet the targets. While we do that, let us give special attention to the third shift crew. They are the ones who are usually the greatest defaulters on the production targets." Subbu suggested.

"Well, it is not my field of expertise, but I would like to venture here a thought", Raman spoke out slowly. He was the youngest of the group and was understandably circumspect in putting forth such ideas before his senior and more experienced colleagues. "The sale price is fixed and the sales department has booked orders at these prices. So probably there is not much we can do. But Asutosh, how did you work out the cost of goods sold per unit with accuracy down to cents?"

"Raman, the cost of goods sold (COGS) includes all direct costs of raw materials and labour, all indirect materials and indirect labour, other factory overheads and provision for depreciation for the new assembly line machinery. Most of the data input is from our group members here; all I have done is simple arithmetic, using the proper accounting procedures," Kejarival replied.

"But then, it looks to me like there could be a leeway in saving something from the direct material & labour costs." Raman ventured again.

Mahesh saw the merit in Raman's idea and immediately supported it, "Yes, I think we should form a production cost review team that would look with a magnifying glass into all operating costs. We can definitely form a small section of our project team to do that." After a short pause, he added, " Well, let us do it right away. I would christen the team as the Super Lenovo Team. Let us make the list of people to work in it."

"Before we make some big ramp up plans and commit expenses, Mahesh, please get a confirmation from the sales that indeed they will sell those units to Lenovo. I have noticed that many times the sales projections promise you the moon before the product is in hand. Once the product is available, all kinds of rationalizations are offered for not being able to sell such as the high price, the competitor's product features, sales personnel training... Long list they come up with." Kejarival butted in.

"I will surely get a firm commitment from them", Mahesh assured, before the meeting dispersed.

Questions and Homework

1. Identify event drivers and impact drivers for the risk event and construct a cause—effect diagram for the risk event.

2. Estimate expected values of impact for different risk events and prioritize the risks for developing a risk register.

CHAPTER 8

Scheduling Resources and Costs

Project network times are not a schedule until resources have been assigned. Cost estimates are not a budget until they have been time-phased.

We have consistently stressed that up-front planning results in big payoffs. For those who have diligently worked through the earlier planning processes chapters, you are nearly ready to launch your project. This chapter completes the final two planning tasks that become the master plan for your project—resource and cost scheduling. (See Figure 8.1.) This process uses the resource schedule to assign *time-phased* costs that provide the project budget *baseline*. Given this time-phased baseline, comparisons can be made with actual and planned schedule and costs. This chapter first discusses the process for developing the project resource schedule. This resource schedule will be used to assign the time-phased budgeted values to create a project budget baseline.

There are always more project proposals than there are available resources. The priority system needs to select projects that best contribute to the organization's objectives, within the constraints of the resources available. If all projects and their respective resources are computer scheduled, the feasibility and impact of adding a new project to those in process can be quickly assessed. With this information the project priority team will add a new project only if resources are available to be formally committed to that specific project. This chapter examines methods of scheduling resources so the team can make realistic judgments of resource availability and project durations. The project manager uses the same schedule for implementing the project. If changes occur during project implementation, the computer schedule is easily updated and the effects easily assessed.

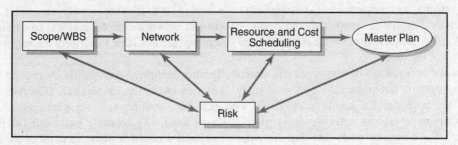

FIGURE 8.1   Project Planning Process

Overview of the Resource Scheduling Problem

After staff and other resources were assigned to her project, a project manager listed the following questions that still needed to be addressed:

- Will the assigned labor and/or equipment be adequate and available to deal with my project?
- Will outside contractors have to be used?
- Do unforeseen resource dependencies exist? Is there a new critical path?
- How much flexibility do we have in using resources?
- Is the original deadline realistic?

Clearly, this project director has a good understanding of the problems she is facing. Any project scheduling system should facilitate finding quick, easy answers to these questions.

The planned network and activity project duration times found in previous chapters fail to deal with resource usage and availability. The time estimates for the work packages and network times were made independently with the implicit assumption that resources would be available. This may or may not be the case.

If resources are adequate but the demand varies widely over the life of the project, it may be desirable to even out resource demand by delaying noncritical activities (using slack) to lower peak demand and, thus, increase resource utilization. This process is called *resource leveling* or *smoothing*.

On the other hand, if resources are not adequate to meet peak demands, the late start of some activities must be delayed, and the duration of the project may be increased. This process is called *resource-constrained scheduling*. One research study by your author of more than 50 projects found that planned project network durations were increased 38 percent when resources were scheduled.

The consequences of failing to schedule limited resources are a costly activity and project delays usually manifest themselves midway in the project when quick corrective action is difficult. An additional consequence of failing to schedule resources is ignoring the peaks and valleys of resource usage over the duration of the project. Because project resources are usually overcommitted and because resources seldom line up by availability and need, procedures are needed to deal with these problems. This chapter addresses methods available to project managers for dealing with resource utilization and availability through resource leveling and resource-constrained scheduling.

Up to now the start and sequence of activities has been based solely on technical or logical considerations. For example, a project network for framing a house might show three activities in a sequence: (1) pour foundation, (2) build frame, and (3) cover roof. A network for a new software project could place the activities in the network, as a sequence of (1) design, (2) code, and (3) test. In other words, you cannot logically perform activity 2 until 1 is completed, and so on. The project network depicts technical constraints. (See Figure 8.2A). The network assumes the personnel and equipment are available to perform the required work. This is often not the case!

The absence or shortage of resources can drastically alter technical constraints. A project network planner may assume adequate resources and show activities occurring in parallel. However, parallel activities hold potential for resource conflicts. For example, assume you are planning a wedding reception that includes four activities—(1) plan, (2) hire band, (3) decorate hall, and (4) purchase refreshments. Each activity takes one day. Activities 2, 3, and 4 could be done in parallel by different people. There is no technical reason or dependency of one on another (see Figure 8.2B). However, if one person must perform all activities, the resource constraint requires the activities be performed in sequence or series. Clearly the consequence is a delay of these activities and a very different set of

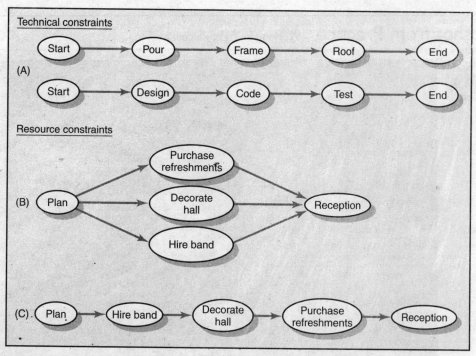

FIGURE 8.2 Constraint Examples

network relationships (see Figure 8.2C). Note that the resource dependency takes priority over the technological dependency but *does not violate the technological dependency;* that is, hire, decorate, and purchase may now have to take place in sequence rather than concurrently, but they must all be completed before the reception can take place.

The interrelationships and interactions among time and resource constraints are complex for even small project networks. Some effort to examine these interactions before the project begins frequently uncovers surprising problems. Project managers who do not consider resource availability in moderately complex projects usually learn of the problem when it is too late to correct. A deficit of resources can significantly alter project dependency relationships, completion dates, and project costs. Project managers must be careful to schedule resources to ensure availability in the right quantities and at the right time. Fortunately, there are computer software programs that can identify resource problems during the early project planning phase when corrective changes can be considered. These programs only require activity resource needs and availability information to schedule resources.

See the Snapshot from Practice: Working in Tight Places for a third constraint that impinges on project schedules.

Types of Resource Constraints

Resources are people, equipment, and material that can be drawn on to accomplish something. In projects the availability or unavailability of resources will often influence the way projects are managed.

Snapshot from Practice   Working in Tight Places

Digital Vision/Punchstock.

In rare situations, physical factors cause activities that would normally occur in parallel to be constrained by contractual or environmental conditions. For example, in theory the renovation of a sailboat compartment might involve four to five tasks that can be done independently. However, since space allows only one person to work at one time, all tasks have to be performed sequentially. Likewise, on a mining project it may be physically possible for only two miners to work in a shaft at a time. Another example would be the erection of a communication tower and nearby groundwork. For safety considerations, the contract prohibits groundwork within 2,000 feet of the tower construction.

The procedures for handling physical factors are similar to those used for resource constraints.

1. People   This is the most obvious and important project resource. Human resources are usually classified by the skills they bring to the project—for example, programmer, mechanical engineer, welder, inspector, marketing director, supervisor. In rare cases some skills are interchangeable, but usually with a loss of productivity. The many differing skills of human resources add to the complexity of scheduling projects.

2. Materials   Project materials cover a large spectrum: for example, chemicals for a scientific project, concrete for a road project, survey data for a marketing project.

Material availability and shortages have been blamed for the delay of many projects. When it is known that a lack of availability of materials is important and probable, materials should be included in the project network plan and schedule. For example, delivery and placement of an oil rig tower in a Siberian oil field has a very small time window during one summer month. Any delivery delay means a one-year, costly delay. Another example in which material was the major resource scheduled was the resurfacing and replacement of some structures on the Golden Gate Bridge in San Francisco. Work on the project was limited to the hours between midnight and 5:00 A.M. with a penalty of $1,000 per minute for any work taking place after 5:00 A.M. Scheduling the arrival of replacement structures was an extremely important part of managing the five-hour work-time window of the project. Scheduling materials has also become important in developing products where time-to-market can result in loss of market share.

3. Equipment   Equipment is usually presented by type, size, and quantity. In some cases equipment can be interchanged to improve schedules, but this is not typical. Equipment is often overlooked as a constraint. The most common oversight is to assume the resource pool is more than adequate for the project. For example, if a project needs one earth-moving tractor six months from now and the organization owns four, it is common to assume the resource will not delay the pending project. However, when the earth-moving tractor is due on-site in six months, all four machines in the pool might be occupied on other projects. In multiproject environments it is prudent to use a common resource pool for all projects. This approach forces a check of resource availability across all projects and reserves the equipment for specific project needs in the future. Recognition of equipment constraints before the project begins can avoid high crashing or delay costs.

Classification of a Scheduling Problem

Most of the scheduling methods available today require the project manager to classify the project as either *time constrained* or *resource constrained*. Project managers need to consult their priority matrix (see Figure 4.2) to determine which case fits their project. One simple test to determine if the project is time or resource constrained is to ask, "If the critical path is delayed, will resources be added to get back on schedule?" If the answer is yes, assume the project is time constrained; if no, assume the project is resource constrained.

A _time-constrained project_ is one that must be completed by an imposed date. If required, resources can be added to ensure the project is completed by a specific date. Although time is the critical factor, resource usage should be no more than is necessary and sufficient.

A _resource-constrained project_ is one that assumes the level of resources available cannot be exceeded. If the resources are inadequate, it will be acceptable to delay the project, but as little as possible.

In scheduling terms, time constrained means time (project duration) is fixed and resources are flexible, while resource constrained means resources are fixed and time is flexible. Methods for scheduling these projects are presented in the next section.

Resource Allocation Methods

Assumptions

Ease of demonstrating the allocation methods available requires some limiting assumptions to keep attention on the heart of the problem. The rest of the chapter depends entirely on the assumptions noted here. First, splitting activities will not be allowed. This means once an activity is placed in the schedule, assume it will be worked on continuously until it is finished; hence, an activity cannot be started, stopped for a period of time, and then finished. Second, the level of resources used for an activity cannot be changed. These limiting assumptions do not exist in practice, but simplify learning. It is easy for new project managers to deal with the reality of splitting activities and changing the level of resources when they meet them on the job.

Time-Constrained Projects: Smoothing Resource Demand

Scheduling time-constrained projects focuses on resource *utilization.* When demand for a specific resource type is erratic, it is difficult to manage, and utilization may be very poor. Practitioners have attacked the utilization problem using resource leveling techniques that balance or smooth demand for a resource. Basically, all leveling techniques delay noncritical activities by using positive slack to reduce peak demand and fill in the valleys for the resources. An example will demonstrate the basic procedure for a time-constrained project. See Figure 8.3.

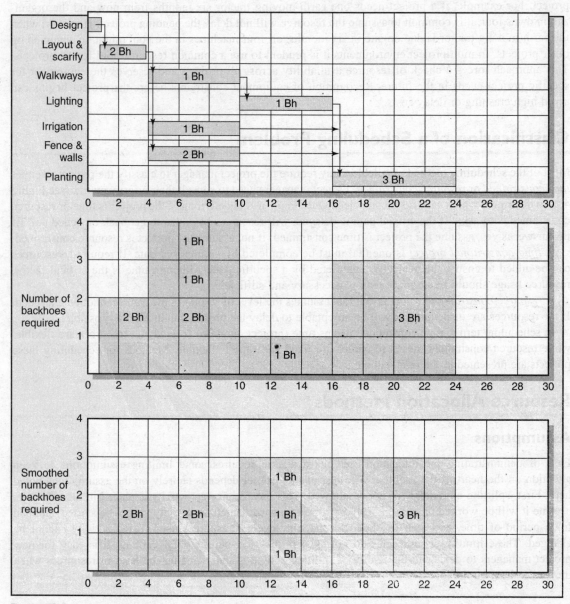

FIGURE 8.3   Botanical Garden

For the purpose of demonstration, the Botanical Garden project uses only one resource (backhoes); all backhoes are interchangeable. The top bar chart shows the activities on a time scale. The dependencies are shown with the vertical connecting arrows. The horizontal arrows following activities represent activity slack (for example, irrigation requires six days to complete and has six days slack). The number of backhoes needed for each task is shown in the shaded activity duration block (rectangle). After the land has been scarified and the plan laid out, work can begin on the walkways, irrigation, and fencing and retaining walls simultaneously. The middle chart shows the resource profile for the backhoes. For periods 4 through 10, four backhoes are needed.

Because this project is declared time constrained, the goal will be to reduce the peak requirement for the resource and thereby increase the utilization of the resource. A quick examination of the ES (early start) resource load chart suggests only two activities have slack that can be used to reduce the peak—fence and walls provide the best choice for smoothing the resource needs. Another choice could be irrigation, but it would result in an up and down resource profile. The choice will probably center on the activity that is perceived as having the least risk of being late. The smoothed resource loading chart shows the results of delaying the fence and walls activity. Note the differences in the resource profiles. The important point is the resources needed over the life of the project have been reduced from four to three (25 percent). In addition the profile has been smoothed, which should be easier to manage.

The Botanical Garden project schedule reached the three goals of smoothing:

- The peak of demand for the resource was reduced.
- Resources over the life of the project have been reduced.
- The fluctuations in resource demand were minimized.

The latter improves the utilization of resources. Backhoes are not easily moved from location to location. There are costs associated with changing the level of resources needed. The same analogy applies to the movement of people back and forth among projects. It is well known that people are more efficient if they can focus their effort on one project rather than multitasking their time among, say, three projects.

The downside of leveling is a loss of flexibility that occurs from reducing slack. The risk of activities delaying the project also increases because slack reduction can create more critical activities and/or near-critical activities. Pushing leveling too far for a perfectly level resource profile is risky. Every activity then becomes critical.

The Botanical Garden example gives a sense of the time-constrained problem and the smoothing approach. However, in practice the magnitude of the problem is very complex for even small projects. Manual solutions are not practical. Fortunately, the software packages available today have very good routines for leveling project resources. Typically, they use activities that have the most slack to level project resources. The rationale is those activities with the most slack pose the least risk. Although this is generally true, other risk factors such as reduction of flexibility to use reassigned resources on other activities or the nature of the activity (easy, complex) are not addressed using such a simple rationale. It is easy to experiment with many alternatives to find the one that best fits your project and minimizes risk of delaying the project.

Resource-Constrained Projects

When the number of people and/or equipment is not adequate to meet peak demand requirements and it is impossible to obtain more, the project manager faces a resource-constrained problem. Something has to give. The trick is to prioritize and allocate resources to minimize project delay without exceeding the resource limit or altering the technical network relationships.

The resource scheduling problem is a large combinatorial one. This means even a modest-size project network with only a few resource types might have several thousand feasible solutions. A few researchers have demonstrated *optimum* mathematical solutions to the resource allocation problem but only for small networks and very few resource types. The massive data requirements for larger problems make pure mathematical solutions (e.g., linear programming) impractical. An alternative approach to the problem has been the use of heuristics (rules of thumb) to solve large combinatorial problems. These practical decision or priority rules have been in place for many years.

Heuristics do not always yield an optimal schedule, but they are very capable of yielding a "good" schedule for very complex networks with many types of resources. The efficiency of different rules and combinations of rules has been well documented. However, because each project is unique, it is wise to test several sets of heuristics on a network to determine the priority allocation rules that minimize project delay. The computer software available today makes it very easy for the project manager to create a good resource schedule for the project. A simple example of the heuristic approach is illustrated here.

Heuristics allocate resources to activities to minimize project delay; that is, heuristics prioritize which activities are allocated resources and which activities are delayed when resources are not adequate. The following scheduling heuristics have been found to consistently minimize project delay over a large variety of projects. Schedule activities using the following heuristic priority rules in the order presented:

1. Minimum slack.
2. Smallest duration.
3. Lowest activity identification number.

The parallel method is the most widely used approach to apply heuristics. The parallel method is an iterative process that starts at the first time period of the project and schedules period-by-period any activities eligible to start. In any period when two or more activities require the same resource, the priority rules are applied. For example, if in period 5 three activities are eligible to start (i.e., have the same ES) and require the same resource, the first activity placed in the schedule would be the activity with the least slack (rule 1). However, if all activities have the same slack, the next rule would be invoked (rule 2), and the activity with the smallest duration would be placed in the schedule first. In very rare cases, when all eligible activities have the same slack and the same duration, the tie is broken by the lowest activity identification number (rule 3), since each activity has a unique ID number.

When a resource limit has been reached, the early start (ES) for succeeding activities not yet in the schedule will be delayed (and all successor activities not having free slack) and their slack reduced. In subsequent periods the procedure is repeated until the project is scheduled. The procedure is demonstrated next, see Figure 8.4. The shaded areas in the resource loading chart represent the "scheduling interval" of the *time constrained* schedule (ES through LF). You can schedule the resource any place *within* the interval and not delay the project. Scheduling the activity beyond the LF will delay the project.

The programmers are limited to three. Follow the actions described in Figures 8.4 and 8.5. Note how the limit of three programmers starts to delay the project.

Observe how it is necessary to update each period to reflect changes in activity early start and slack times so the heuristics can reflect changing priorities. When using the parallel scheduling method, the network in Figure 8.5 on page 243 reflects the new schedule date of 14 time units, rather than the time-constrained project duration of 12 time units. The network has also been revised to reflect new start, finish, and slack times for each activity. Note that activity 6 is still critical and has a slack of 0 time units because no resources are available (they are being used on activities 2 and 5). Compare the slack for each activity found in Figures 8.4 and 8.5; slack has been reduced significantly. Note that activity 4 has only 2 units of slack

The Parallel Method:

Period	Action
0–1	Only activity 1 is eligible. It requires 2 programmers. Load activity 1 into schedule. <div align="center">See Figure 8.4</div>
1–2	No activities are eligible to be scheduled.
2–3	Activities 2, 3, and 4 are eligible to be scheduled. Activity 3 has the least slack (0)— apply rule 1. Load Activity 3 into schedule. Activity 2 is next with slack of 2; however, activity 2 requires 2 programmers and only 1 is available. Delay activity 2. Update: ES = 3, slack = 1. The next eligible activity is activity 4, since it only requires 1 programmer. Load activity 4 into schedule. <div align="center">See Figure 8.5</div>
3–4	Activity 2 is eligible but exceeds limit of 3 programmers in pool. Delay activity 2. Update: ES = 4, slack = 0.
4–5	Activity 2 is eligible but exceeds limit of 3 programmers in pool. Delay activity 2. Update: ES = 5, LF = 11, slack = –1. Delay activity 7. Update: ES = 11, LF = 13, slack = –1.
5–6	Activity 2 is eligible but exceeds limit of 3 programmers in pool. Delay activity 2. Update: ES = 6, LF = 12, slack = –2. Delay activity 7. Update: ES = 12, LF = 14, slack = –2.
6–7	Activities 2, 5, and 6 are eligible with slack of –2, 2, and 0, respectively. Load activity 2 into schedule (rule 1). Because activity 6 has 0 slack, it is the next eligible activity. Load activity 6 into schedule (rule 1). The programmer limit of 3 is reached. Delay activity 5. Update: ES = 7, slack = 1.
7–8	Limit is reached. No programmers available. Delay activity 5. Update: ES = 8, slack = 0.
8–9	Limit is reached. No programmers available. Delay activity 5. Update: ES = 9, LF = 11, slack = –1.
9–10	Limit is reached. No programmers available. Delay activity 5. Update: ES = 10, LF = 12, slack = –2.
10–11	Activity 5 is eligible. Load activity 5 into schedule. (Note: Activity 6 does not have slack because there are no programmers available— 3 maximum.)
11–12	No eligible activities.
12–13	Activity 7 is eligible. Load activity 7 into schedule.

rather than what appears to be 6 slack units. This occurs because only three programmers are available, and they are needed to satisfy the resource requirements of activities 2 and 5. Note that the number of critical activities (1, 2, 3, 5, 6, 7) has increased from four to six.

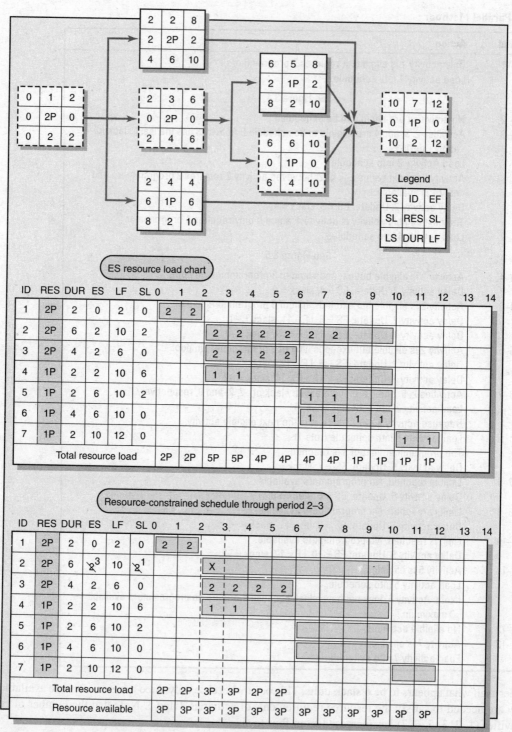

FIGURE 8.4   Resource-Constrained Schedule through Period 2–3

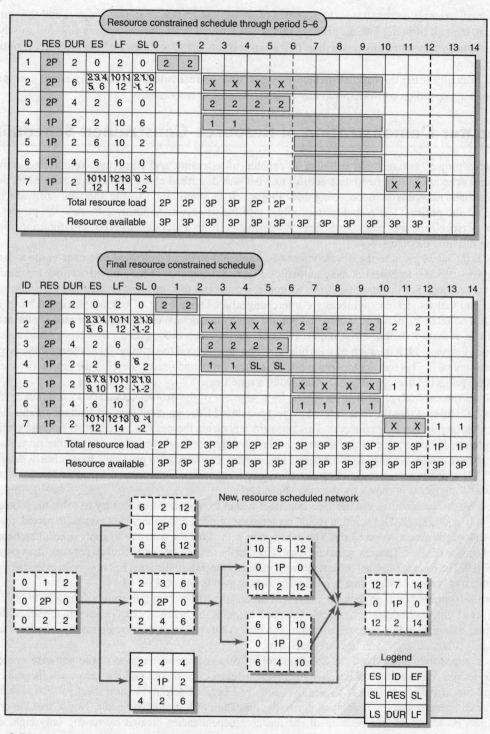

FIGURE 8.5   Resource Constrained Schedule through Period 5–6

This small example demonstrates the scenario of scheduling resources in real projects and the resulting increase in the risk of being late. In practice this is not a trivial problem! Managers who fail to schedule resources usually encounter this scheduling risk when it is too late to work around the problem, resulting in a project delay.

Since manually using the parallel method is impractical on real-world projects because of size, project managers will depend on software programs to schedule project resources.

Computer Demonstration of Resource-Constrained Scheduling

Fortunately, project management software is capable of assessing and resolving complicated resource-constrained schedules using heuristics similar to what was described above. We will use the EMR project to demonstrate how this is done using MS Project. It is important to note that the software is not "managing" the project. The software is simply a tool the project manager uses to view the project from different perspectives and conditions. See the Snapshot from Practice on page 250 for more tips on assessing resource problems.

EMR is the name given to the development of a handheld electronic medical reference guide to be used by emergency medical technicians and paramedics. Figure 8.6 contains a time-limited network for the design phase of the project. For the purpose of this example, we assume that only design engineers are required for the tasks and that the design engineers are interchangeable. The number of engineers required to perform each task is noted in the network, where 500 percent means five design engineers are needed for the activity. For example, activity 5, feature specs, requires four design engineers (400 percent). The project begins January 1, and ends February 14, a duration of 45 workdays. The time-limited (constrained) bar chart for the project is shown in Figure 8.7. This bar chart incorporates the same information used to develop the project network, but presents the project in the form of a bar chart along a time line.

Finally, a resource usage chart is presented for a segment of the project—January 15 to January 23; see Figure 8.8A. Observe that the time-limited project requires 21 design engineers on January 18 and 19 (168 hrs/8 hrs per engineer = 21 engineers). This segment represents the peak requirement for design engineers for the project. However, due to the shortage of design engineers and commitments to other projects, only eight engineers can be assigned to the project. This creates overallocation problems more clearly detailed in Figure 8.8B, which is a resource loading chart for design engineers. Notice that the peak is 21 engineers and the limit of 8 engineers is shown by the gray shaded area.

To resolve this problem we use the "leveling" tool within the software and first try to solve the problem by leveling only within slack. This solution would preserve the original finish date. However, as expected, this does not solve all of the allocation problems. The next option is to allow the software to apply scheduling heuristics and level outside of slack. The new schedule is contained in the revised, resource-limited network chart presented in Figure 8.9. The resource-limited project network indicates the project duration has now been extended to 2/26, or 57 workdays (versus 45 days time limited). The critical path is now 2, 3, 9, 13.

Figure 8.10 presents the project bar chart and the results of leveling the project schedule to reflect the availability of only eight design engineers. The application of the heuristics can be seen in the scheduling of the internal, external, and feature specification activities. All three activities were originally scheduled to start immediately after activity 1, architectural decisions.

This is impossible, since the three activities collectively require 14 engineers. The software chooses to schedule activity 5 first because this activity is on the original critical path and has zero slack (heuristic # 1). Next, and concurrently, activity 4 is chosen over activity 3 because activity 4 has a shorter duration (heuristic # 2); internal specs, activity 3, is delayed due to the limitation of 8 design engineers. Notice that the original critical path no longer applies because of the resource dependencies created by having only eight design engineers.

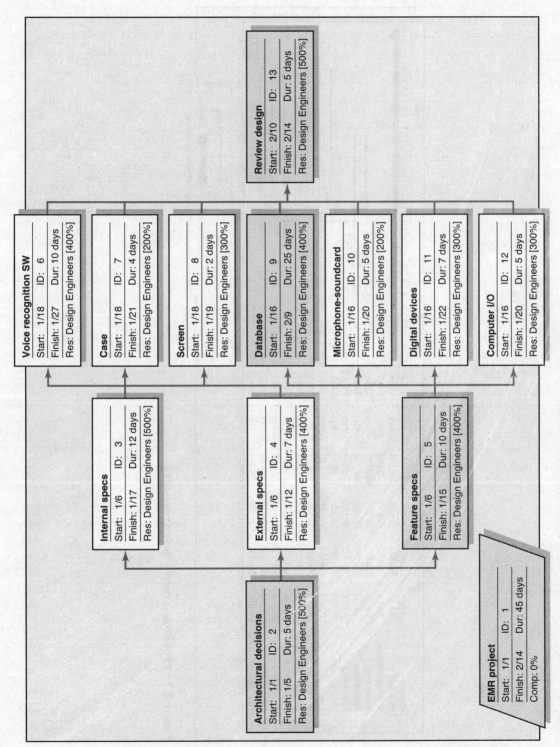

Review design
Start: 2/10   ID: 13
Finish: 2/14   Dur: 5 days
Res: Design Engineers [500%]

Voice recognition SW
Start: 1/18   ID: 6
Finish: 1/27   Dur: 10 days
Res: Design Engineers [400%]

Case
Start: 1/18   ID: 7
Finish: 1/21   Dur: 4 days
Res: Design Engineers [200%]

Screen
Start: 1/18   ID: 8
Finish: 1/19   Dur: 2 days
Res: Design Engineers [300%]

Database
Start: 1/16   ID: 9
Finish: 2/9   Dur: 25 days
Res: Design Engineers [400%]

Microphone-soundcard
Start: 1/16   ID: 10
Finish: 1/20   Dur: 5 days
Res: Design Engineers [200%]

Digital devices
Start: 1/16   ID: 11
Finish: 1/22   Dur: 7 days
Res: Design Engineers [300%]

Computer I/O
Start: 1/16   ID: 12
Finish: 1/20   Dur: 5 days
Res: Design Engineers [300%]

Internal specs
Start: 1/6   ID: 3
Finish: 1/17   Dur: 12 days
Res: Design Engineers [500%]

External specs
Start: 1/6   ID: 4
Finish: 1/12   Dur: 7 days
Res: Design Engineers [400%]

Feature specs
Start: 1/6   ID: 5
Finish: 1/15   Dur: 10 days
Res: Design Engineers [400%]

Architectural decisions
Start: 1/1   ID: 2   Dur: 5 days
Finish: 1/5
Res: Design Engineers [500%]

EMR project
Start: 1/1   ID: 1   Dur: 45 days
Finish: 2/14
Comp: 0%

FIGURE 8.6   **EMR Project Network View Schedule before Resources Leveled**

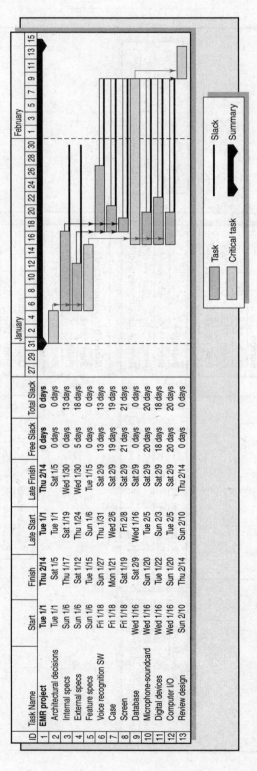

ID	Task Name	Start	Finish	Late Start	Late Finish	Free Slack	Total Slack
1	**EMR project**	**Tue 1/1**	**Thu 2/14**	**Tue 1/1**	**Thu 2/14**	**0 days**	**0 days**
2	Architectural decisions	Tue 1/1	Sat 1/5	Tue 1/1	Sat 1/5	0 days	0 days
3	Internal specs	Sun 1/6	Thu 1/17	Sat 1/19	Wed 1/30	0 days	13 days
4	External specs	Sun 1/6	Sat 1/12	Thu 1/24	Wed 1/30	5 days	18 days
5	Feature specs	Sun 1/6	Tue 1/15	Sun 1/6	Tue 1/15	0 days	0 days
6	Voice recognition SW	Fri 1/18	Sun 1/27	Thu 1/31	Sat 2/9	13 days	13 days
7	Case	Fri 1/18	Mon 1/21	Wed 2/6	Sat 2/9	19 days	19 days
8	Screen	Fri 1/18	Sat 1/19	Fri 2/8	Sat 2/9	21 days	21 days
9	Database	Wed 1/16	Sat 2/9	Wed 1/16	Sat 2/9	0 days	0 days
10	Microphone-soundcard	Wed 1/16	Sun 1/20	Tue 2/5	Sat 2/9	20 days	20 days
11	Digital devices	Wed 1/16	Tue 1/22	Sun 2/3	Sat 2/9	18 days	18 days
12	Computer I/O	Wed 1/16	Sun 1/20	Tue 2/5	Sat 2/9	20 days	20 days
13	Review design	Sun 2/10	Thu 2/14	Sun 2/10	Thu 2/14	0 days	0 days

FIGURE 8.7   EMR Project before Resources Added

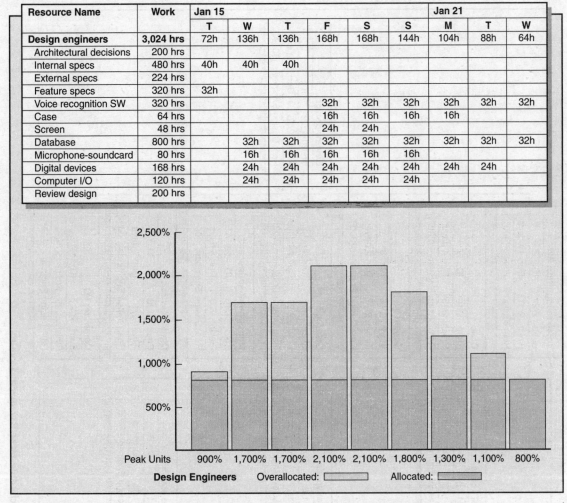

Resource Name	Work	Jan 15						Jan 21		
		T	W	T	F	S	S	M	T	W
Design engineers	**3,024 hrs**	72h	136h	136h	168h	168h	144h	104h	88h	64h
Architectural decisions	200 hrs									
Internal specs	480 hrs	40h	40h	40h						
External specs	224 hrs									
Feature specs	320 hrs	32h								
Voice recognition SW	320 hrs				32h	32h	32h	32h	32h	32h
Case	64 hrs				16h	16h	16h	16h		
Screen	48 hrs				24h	24h				
Database	800 hrs		32h	32h	32h	32h	32h	32h	32h	32h
Microphone-soundcard	80 hrs		16h	16h	16h	16h	16h			
Digital devices	168 hrs		24h	24h	24h	24h	24h	24h	24h	
Computer I/O	120 hrs		24h	24h	24h	24h	24h			
Review design	200 hrs									

Peak Units: 900% 1,700% 1,700% 2,100% 2,100% 1,800% 1,300% 1,100% 800%

Design Engineers   Overallocated: ☐   Allocated: ▨

FIGURE 8.8A   EMR Project—Time-Constrained Resource Usage View, January 15–23

Compare the bar chart in Figure 8.10 with the time-limited bar chart in Figure 8.7. For example, note the different start dates for activity 8 (screen). In the time-limited plan (Figure 8.7), the start date for activity 8 is 1/18, while the start date in the resource limited schedule (Figure 8.10) is 2/16, almost a month later!

While resource bar graphs are commonly used to illustrate overallocation problems, we prefer to view resource usage tables like the one presented in Figure 8.8A. This table tells you when you have an overallocation problem and identifies activities that are causing the overallocation.

The Impacts of Resource-Constrained Scheduling

Like leveling schedules, the limited resource schedule usually reduces slack, reduces flexibility by using slack to ensure delay is minimized, and increases the number of critical and near-critical activities. Scheduling complexity is increased because resource constraints are added to technical constraints; start times may now have two constraints. The traditional critical path concept of sequential activities from the

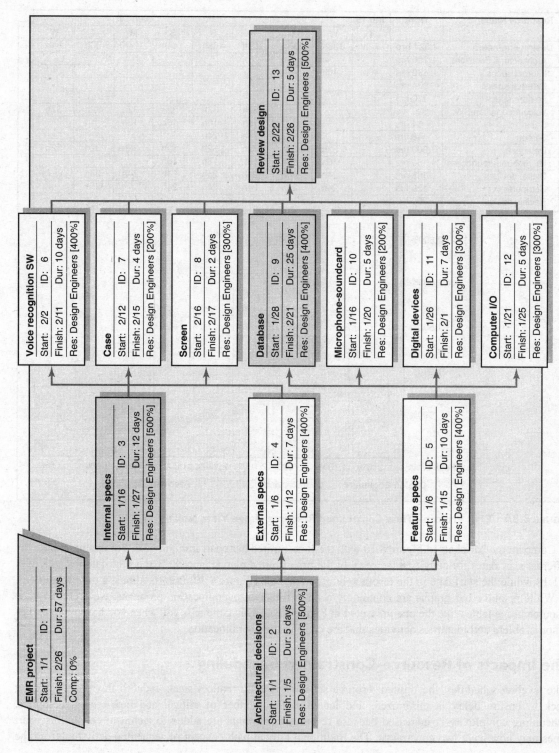

FIGURE 8.9 EMR Project Network View Schedule after Resources Leveled

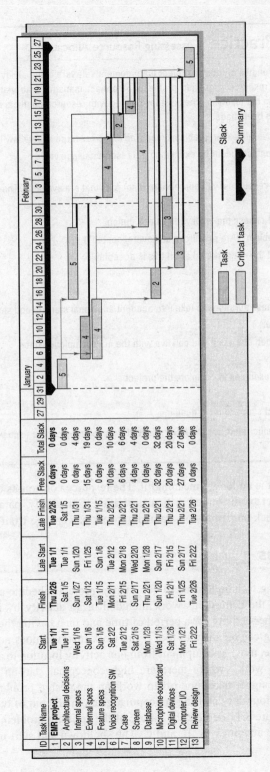

FIGURE 8.10 EMR Project Resources Leveled

Snapshot from Practice   Assessing Resource Allocation

One of the strengths of today's project management software is the ability to identify and provide options for resolving resource allocation problems. A project manager who uses MS Project to plan projects shared with us the following checklist for dealing with resource conflicts after preliminary assignment of resources has been made.

1. Assess whether you have overallocation problems (see *Red* in the resource sheet view.)
2. Identify where and when conflicts occur by examining the resource usage view.
3. Resolve the problem by
   a. Replacing overallocated resources with appropriate resources that are available. Then ask if this solves the problem.
   If not:
   b. Use the leveling tool and choose the level within slack option.
      i Does this solve the problem? (Are resources still overallocated?)
      ii Check the sensitivity of the network and ask if this is acceptable.
   If not:
   c. Consider splitting tasks.
      i Make sure to readjust task durations to take into account additional start-up and shutdown time.
4. If 3 does not work then either:
   a. Use level tool default option and ask if you can live with the new completion date.
   If not:
   b. Negotiate for additional resources to complete the project.
   If not possible
   c. Consider reducing project scope to meet deadline.

While this checklist makes specific references to MS Project, the same steps can be used with most project management software.

---

start to the end of the project is no longer meaningful. The resource constraints can break the sequence and leave the network with a set of disjointed critical activities. Conversely, parallel activities can become sequential. Activities with slack on a time-constrained network can change from critical to noncritical.

Splitting Activities

Splitting tasks is a scheduling technique used to get a better project schedule and/or to increase resource utilization. A planner splits the continuous work included in an activity by interrupting the work and sending the resource to another activity for a period of time and then having the resource resume work on the original activity. Splitting can be a useful tool if the work involved does not include large start-up or shutdown costs—for example, moving equipment from one activity location to another. The most common error is to interrupt "people work," where there are high conceptual start-up and shutdown costs. For example, having a bridge designer take time off to work on the design problem of another project may cause this individual to lose four days shifting conceptual gears in and out of two activities. The cost may be hidden, but it is real. Figure 8.11 depicts the nature of the splitting problem. The original activity has been split into three separate activities: A, B, and C. The shutdown and start-up times lengthen the time for the original activity.

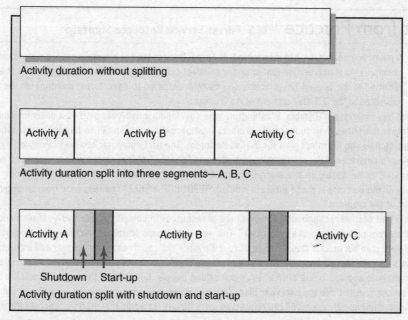

FIGURE 8.11   Splitting Activities

Some have argued that the propensity to deal with resource shortages by splitting is a major reason why projects fail to meet schedule. We agree. Planners should avoid the use of splitting as much as possible, except in situations where splitting costs are known to be small or when there is no alternative for resolving the resource problem. Computer software offers the splitting option for each activity; use it sparingly. See Snapshot from Practice: Assessing Resource Allocation.

Benefits of Scheduling Resources

It is important to remember that, if resources are truly limited and activity time estimates are accurate, the resource-constrained schedule *will* materialize as the project is implemented—*not* the time-constrained schedule! Therefore, failure to schedule limited resources can lead to serious problems for a project manager. The benefit of creating this schedule *before* the project begins leaves time for considering reasonable alternatives. If the scheduled delay is unacceptable or the risk of being delayed too high, the assumption of being resource constrained can be reassessed. Cost-time trade-offs can be considered. In some cases priorities may be changed. See Snapshot from Practice: U.S. Forest Service Resource Shortage.

Resource schedules provide the information needed to prepare time-phased work package budgets with dates. Once established, they provide a quick means for a project manager to gauge the impact of unforeseen events such as turnover, equipment breakdowns, or transfer of project personnel. Resource schedules also allow project managers to assess how much flexibility they have over certain resources. This is useful when they receive requests from other managers to borrow or share resources. Honoring such requests creates goodwill and an "IOU" that can be cashed in during a time of need.

Snapshot from Practice   U.S. Forest Service Resource Shortage

A major segment of work in managing U.S. Forest Service (USFS) forests is selling mature timber to logging companies that harvest the timber under contract conditions monitored by the Service. The proceeds are returned to the federal government. The budget allocated to each forest depends on the two-year plan submitted to the U.S. Department of Agriculture.

Olympic Forest headquarters in Olympia, Washington, was developing a two-year plan as a basis for funding. All of the districts in the forest submitted their timber sale projects (numbering more than 50) to headquarters, where they were compiled and aggregated into a project plan for the whole forest. The first computer run was reviewed by a small group of senior managers to determine if the plan was reasonable and "doable." Management was pleased and relieved to note all projects appeared to be doable in the two-year time frame until a question was raised concerning the computer printout. "Why are all the columns in these projects labeled 'RESOURCE' blank?" The response from an engineer was, "We don't use that part of the program."

The discussion that ensued recognized the importance of resources in completing the two-year plan and ended with a request to "try the program with resources included." The new output was startling. The two-year program turned into a three-and-a-half-year plan because of the shortage of specific labor skills such as road engineer and environmental impact specialist. Analysis showed that adding only three skilled people would allow the two-year plan to be completed on time. In addition, further analysis showed hiring only a few more skilled people, beyond the three, would allow an extra year of projects to also be compressed into the two-year plan. This would result in additional revenue of more than $3 million. The Department of Agriculture quickly approved the requested extra dollars for additional staff to generate the extra revenue.

Assigning Project Work

When making individual assignments, project managers should match, as best they can, the demands and requirements of specific work with the qualifications and experience of available participants. In doing so, there is a natural tendency to assign the best people the most difficult tasks. Project managers need to be careful not to overdo this. Over time these people may grow to resent the fact that they are always given the toughest assignments. At the same time, less experienced participants may resent the fact that they are never given the opportunity to expand their skill/knowledge base. Project managers need to balance task performance with the need to develop the talents of people assigned to the project.

Project managers not only need to decide who does what but who works with whom. A number of factors need to be considered in deciding who should work together. First, to minimize unnecessary tension, managers should pick people with compatible work habits and personalities but who complement each other (i.e., one person's weakness is the other person's strength). For example, one person may be brilliant at solving complex problems but sloppy at documenting his or her progress. It would be wise to pair this person with an individual who is good at paying attention to details. Experience is another factor. Veterans should be teamed up with new hires—not only so they can share their experience but also to help socialize the newcomers to the customs and norms of the organization. Finally, future needs should be considered. If managers have some people who have never worked together before but who have to later on in the project, they may be wise to take advantage of opportunities to have these people work together early on so that they can become familiar with each other. Finally, see the Snapshot in Practice: Managing Geeks for some interesting thoughts about how Novell, Inc., puts together teams.

Snapshot from Practice   Managing Geeks*

Eric Schmidt, after a successful career at Sun Microsystems, took over struggling Novell, Inc., and helped turn it around within two years. One of the keys to his success is his ability to manage the technical wizards who develop the sophisticated systems, hardware, and software that are the backbone of electronically driven companies. He uses the term "geek" (and he can, since he is one, with a Ph.D. in computer science) to describe this group of technologists who rule the cyberworld.

Schmidt has some interesting ideas about assigning geeks to projects. He believes that putting geeks together in project teams with other geeks creates productive peer pressure. Geeks care a great deal about how other geeks perceive them. They are good at judging the quality of technical work and are quick to praise as well as criticize each other's work. Some geeks can be unbearably arrogant, but Schmidt claims that having them work together on projects is the best way to control them—by letting them control each other.

At the same time, Schmidt argues that too many geeks spoil the soup. By this he means that, when there are too many geeks on a development team, there is a tendency for intense technical navel gazing. Members lose sight of deadlines, and delays are inevitable. To combat this tendency, he recommends using geeks only in small groups. He urges breaking up large projects into smaller, more manageable projects so that small teams of geeks can be assigned to them. This keeps the project on time and makes the teams responsible to each other.

* Mitchel Russ, "How to Manage Geeks," *Fast Company* (June 1999), pp. 175–80.

Multiproject Resource Schedules

For clarity we have discussed key resource allocation issues within the context of a single project. In reality resource allocation generally occurs in a multiproject environment where the demands of one project have to be reconciled with the needs of other projects. Organizations must develop and manage systems for efficiently allocating and scheduling resources across several projects with different priorities, resource requirements, sets of activities, and risks. The system must be dynamic and capable of accommodating new projects as well as reallocating resources once project work is completed. While the same resource issues and principles that apply to a single project also apply to this multiproject environment, application and solutions are more complex, given the interdependency among projects.

The following lists three of the more common problems encountered in managing multiproject resource schedules. Note that these are macro manifestations of single-project problems that are now magnified in a multiproject environment:

1. **Overall schedule slippage.** Because projects often share resources, delays in one project can have a ripple effect and delay other projects. For example, work on one software development project can grind to a halt because the coders scheduled for the next critical task are late in completing their work on another development project.
2. **Inefficient resource utilization.** Because projects have different schedules and requirements, there are peaks and valleys in overall resource demands. For example, a firm may have a staff of 10 electricians to meet peak demands when, under normal conditions, only 5 electricians are required.
3. **Resource bottlenecks.** Delays and schedules are extended as a result of shortages of critical resources that are required by multiple projects. For example, at one Lattice Semiconductor facility, project schedules were delayed because of competition over access to test equipment necessary to debug programs. Likewise, several projects at a U.S. forest area were extended because there was only one silviculturist on the staff.

Snapshot from Practice   Multiple Project Resource Scheduling

The case for a central source to oversee project resource scheduling is well known by practitioners. Here is a synopsis of a conversation with one middle manager.

Interviewer: Congratulations on acceptance of your multiproject scheduling proposal. Everyone tells me you were very convincing.

Middle Manager: Thanks. Gaining acceptance was easy this time. The board quickly recognized we have no choice if we are to keep ahead of competition by placing our resources on the right projects.

Interviewer: Have you presented this to the board before?

Middle Manager: Yes, but not this company. I presented the same spiel to the firm I worked for two years ago. For their annual review meeting I was charged to present a proposal suggesting the need and benefits of central capacity resource planning for managing the projects of the firm.

I tried to build a case for bringing projects under one umbrella to standardize practices and to forecast and assign key people to mission critical projects. I explained how benefits such as resource demands will be aligned with mission critical projects, proactive resource planning, and a tool for catching resource bottlenecks and resolving conflicts.

Almost everyone agreed the idea was a good one. I felt good about the presentation and felt confident something was going to happen. But the idea never really got off the ground; it just faded into the sunset.

With hindsight, managers really did not trust colleagues in other departments, so they only gave half-hearted support to central resource planning. Managers wanted to protect their turf and ensure that they would not have to give up power. The culture there was simply too inflexible for the world we live in today. They are still struggling with constant conflicts among projects.

I'm glad I made the switch to this firm. The culture here is much more team-oriented. Management is committed to improving performance.

To deal with these problems, more and more companies create project offices or departments to oversee the scheduling of resources across multiple projects. One approach to multiple project resource scheduling is to use a first come–first served rule. A project queue system is created in which projects currently underway take precedence over new projects. New project schedules are based on the projected availability of resources. This queuing tends to lead to more reliable completion estimates and is preferred on contracted projects that have stiff penalties for being late. The disadvantages of this deceptively simple approach are that it does not optimally utilize resources or take into account the priority of the project. See the Snapshot from Practice: Multiple Project Resource Scheduling.

Many companies utilize more elaborate processes for scheduling resources to increase the capacity of the organization to initiate projects. Most of these methods approach the problem by treating individual projects as part of one big project and adapting the scheduling heuristics previously introduced to this "megaproject." Project schedulers monitor resource usage and provide updated schedules based on progress and resource availability across all projects. One major improvement in project management software in recent years is the ability to prioritize resource allocation to specific projects. Projects can be prioritized in ascending order (e.g., 1, 2, 3, 4, . . .), and these priorities will override scheduling heuristics so that resources go to the project highest on the priority list. (Note: This improvement fits perfectly with organizations that use project priority models similar to those described in Chapter 2.) Centralized project scheduling also makes it easier to identify resource bottlenecks that stifle progress on projects. Once identified, the impact of the bottlenecks can be documented and used to justify acquiring additional equipment, recruiting critical personnel, or delaying the project.

Finally, many companies are using outsourcing as a means for dealing with their resource allocation problems. In some cases, a company will reduce the number of projects they have to manage internally to only core projects and outsource noncritical projects to contractors and consulting firms. In other cases, specific segments of projects are outsourced to overcome resource deficiencies and scheduling problems. Companies may hire temporary workers to expedite certain activities that are falling behind schedule or contract project work during peak periods when there are insufficient internal resources to meet the demands of all projects. The ability to more efficiently manage the ebbs and flows of project work is one of the major driving forces behind outsourcing today.

Using the Resource Schedule to Develop a Project Cost Baseline

Once resource assignments have been finalized we are able to develop a baseline budget schedule for the project. Using your project schedule, you can *time-phase* work packages and assign them to their respective scheduled activities to develop a budget schedule over the life of your project. Understanding the reason for time-phasing your budget is very important. Without a time-phased budget good project schedule and cost control are impossible.

Why a Time-Phased Budget Baseline Is Needed

The need for a time-phased budget baseline is demonstrated in the following scenario. The development of a new product is to be completed in 10 weeks at an estimated cost of $400,000 per week for a total cost of $4 million. Management wants a status report at the end of five weeks. The following information has been collected:

- Planned costs for the first five weeks are $2,000,000.
- Actual costs for the first five months are $2,400,000.

How are we doing? It would be easy to draw the conclusion there is a $400,000 cost overrun. But we really have no way of knowing. The $400,000 may represent money spent to move the project ahead of schedule. Assume another set of data at the end of five weeks:

- Planned costs for the first five weeks are $2,000,000.
- Actual costs for the first five weeks are $1,700,000.

Is the project costing $300,000 less than we expected? Perhaps. But the $300,000 may represent the fact that the project is behind schedule and work has not started. Could it be the project is behind schedule and over cost? We cannot tell from these data. The many systems found in the real world that use only planned funds (a constant burn rate) and actual costs can provide false and misleading information. There is no way to be certain how much of the physical work has been accomplished. *These systems do not measure how much work was accomplished for the money spent! Hence, without time-phasing cost to match your project schedule, it is impossible to have reliable information for control purposes.*

Creating a Time-Phased Budget

By using information from your WBS and resource schedule, you can create a time-phased cost baseline. Remember from the WBS for the PC Project in Chapters 4 and 5 we integrated the WBS and OBS organization breakdown structure so the work packages could be tracked by deliverable and organization responsible. See Figure 8.12 for an example of the PC Prototype Project arranged by deliverable and organization unit responsible. For each intersection point of the WBS/OBS matrix, you see work package

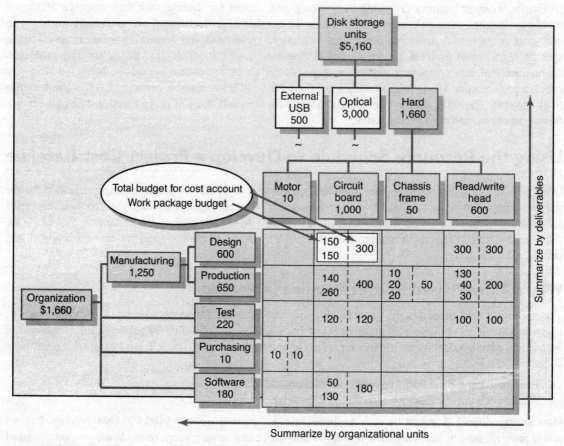

FIGURE 8.12   Direct Labor Budget Rollup ($000)

budgets and the total cost. The total cost at each intersection is called a cost or control account. For example, at the intersection of the Read/write head deliverable and the Production department we see there are three work packages with a total budget of $200,000. The sum of all cost accounts in a column should represent the total costs for the deliverable. Conversely, the sum of the cost accounts in a row should represent the costs or budget for the organizational unit responsible to accomplish the work. You can continue to "roll up" costs on the WBS/OBS to total project costs. This WBS provides the information you can use to time phase work packages and assign them to their respective scheduled activities over the life of the project.

Recall, from the development of your work breakdown structure for each work package, the following information needed to be developed:

1. Define work (what).
2. Identify time to complete a work package (how long).
3. Identify a time-phased budget to complete a work package (cost).
4. Identify resources needed to complete a work package (how much).
5. Identify a single person responsible for units of work (who).
6. Identify monitoring points for measuring progress (how well).

Number three, time-phasing the work package, is critical for the final step of creating your budget baseline. The process of time-phasing work packages, which is illustrated next, is demonstated in Figure 8.13. The work package has a duration of three weeks. Assuming labor, materials, and equipment are tracked separately, the work package costs for labor are distributed over the three weeks as they are expect to occur— $40,000, $30,000, and $50,000 for each week, respectively. When the three-week work package is placed in the network schedule, the costs are distributed to the time-phased budget for the same three scheduled weeks. Fortunately, most single WPs become an activity and the process of distributing costs is relatively simple. That is, the relationship is one-for-one. Such budget timing is directly from the work package to the activity.

Work Package Time-Phased Budget
Labor cost only

Work Package Description ___Test___   Page ___1___ of ___1___

Work Package ID ___1.1.3.2.3___   Project ___PC Protoype___

Deliverable ___Circuit board___   Date ___3/24/xx___

Responsible organization unit ___Test___   Estimator ___CEG___

Work Package Duration ___3___ weeks   Total labor cost ___$120___

Time-Phased Labor Budget ($000)

Work Package	Resource	Labor rate	Work Periods--Weeks					
			1	2	3	4	5	Total
Code 1.1.3.2.3	Quality testers	$xxxx/ week	$40	$30	$50			$120

FIGURE 8.13   Time-Phased Work Package Budget (labor cost only)

In a few instances an activity will include more than one work package, where the packages are assigned to *one responsible person or department and deliverable*. In this case the work packages are consolidated into one activity. As seen in Figure 8.14, this activity includes two WPs. The first, WP-1.1.3.2.4.1 (Code), is distributed over the first three weeks. The second, WP-1.1.3.2.4.2 (Integration), is sequenced over weeks 3 and 4. The actvity duration is four weeks. When the activity is placed in the schedule, the costs are distributed starting with the schedule start—$20,000, $15,000, $75,000, and $70,000, respectively.

These time-phased budgets for work packages are lifted from your WBS and are placed in your project schedule as they are expected to occur over the life of the project. The outcome of these budget allocations is the project *cost* baseline (also called planned value—PV), which is used to determine cost and schedule variances as the project is implemented.

Figure 8.15 shows the Patient Entry Project network schedule, which is used to place the time-phased work packages' budgets in the baseline. Figure 8.16 presents the project time-phased budget for the Patient Entry Project and the cumulative graph of the project budget baseline. In this figure you can see how the time-phased work package costs were placed into the network and how the cumulative project budget graph for a project is developed. Notice that costs do not have to be distributed linearly, but the costs should be placed as you expect them to occur.

Work Package Time-Phased Budget
Labor cost only

Work Package Description ___Software___

Work Package ID _**1.1.3.2.4.1 and 1.1.3.2.4.2**_

Deliverable ___Circuit board___

Responsible organization unit _Software_

Work Package Duration ___4___ weeks

Page ___1___ of ___1___

Project ___PC Protoype___

Date ___3/24/xx___

Estimator ___LGG___

Total labor cost ___$180___

Time-Phased Labor Budget ($000)

Work Package	Resource	Labor rate	Work Periods--Weeks					
			1	2	3	4	5	Total
Code **1.1.3.2.4.1**	Program'rs	$2,000/ week	$20	$15	$15			$50
Integration **1.1.3.2.4.2**	System/ program'rs	$2,500/ week			$60	$70		$130
Total			$20	$15	$75	$70		$180

FIGURE 8.14   Two Time-Phased Work Packages (labor cost only)

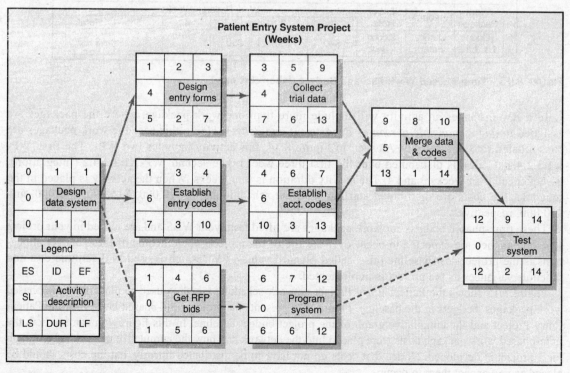

FIGURE 8.15   Patient Entry Project Network

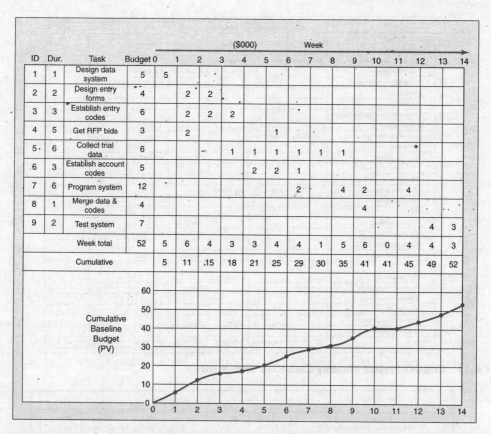

FIGURE 8.16   Patient Entry Time-Phased Work Packages Assigned

You have now developed complete time and cost plans for your project. These project baselines will be used to compare planned schedule and costs using an integrative system called *earned value*. The application and use of project baselines to measure performance are discussed in detail in Chapter 13. With your project budget baseline established, you are also able to generate cash flow statements for your project like the one presented in Figure 8.17. Such statements prepare the firm to cover costs over the lifespan of the project. Finally, with resource assignments finalized you are able to generate resource usage schedules for your project (see Figure 8.18). These schedules map out the full deployment of personnel and equipment and can be used to generate individual work schedules.

	January	February	March	April	May	June	July
CEBOO Project							
Hardware							
Hardware specifications	$11,480.00	$24,840.00	$3,360.00				
Hardware design			$23,120.00	$29,920.00	$14,960.00		
Hardware documentation					$14,080.00	$24,320.00	
Prototypes							
Order GXs							
Assemble preproduction models							
Operating system							
Kernel specifications	$5,320.00	$9,880.00					
Drivers							
OC drivers				$3,360.00	$12,320.00	$11,760.00	$12,880.00
Serial VO drivers							
Memory management							
Operating system documentation		$10,240.00	$21,760.00				
Network interface							
Utilities							
Utilities specifications				$8,400.00			
Routine utilities				$5,760.00	$21,120.00	$20,160.00	$10,560.00
Complex utilities							
Utilities documentation				$7,680.00	$17,920.00		
Shell							
System integration							
Architectural decisions	$20,400.00						
Integration first phase							
System H/S test							
Project documentation							
Integration acceptance test							
Total	$37,200.00	$44,960.00	$48,240.00	$55,120.00	$80,400.00	$56,240.00	$23,440.00

FIGURE 8.17   CEBOO Project Monthly Cash Flow Statement

	12/30/07	1/6/08	1/13/08	1/20/08	1/27/08	2/03/08
I. Suzuki	24 hrs	40 hrs	40 hrs	40 hrs	40 hrs	40 hrs
Hardware specifications				24 hrs	40 hrs	40 hrs
Hardware design						
Hardware documentation						
Operating system documentation						
Utilities documentation						
Architectural decisions	24 hrs	40 hrs	40 hrs	16 hrs		
J. Lopez	24 hrs	40 hrs	40 hrs	40 hrs	40 hrs	40 hrs
Hardware specifications				12 hrs	20 hrs	20 hrs
Hardware design						
Prototypes						
Kernel specifications				12 hrs	20 hrs	20 hrs
Utilities specifications						
Architectural decisions	24 hrs	40 hrs	40 hrs	16 hrs		
Integration first phase						
J.J. Putz				24 hrs	40 hrs	40 hrs
Hardware documentation						
Kernel specifications				24 hrs	40 hrs	40 hrs
Operating system documentation						
Utilities documentetion						
Project documentation						
R. Sexon				24 hrs	40 hrs	40 hrs
Hardware specifications				24 hrs	40 hrs	40 hrs
Prototypes						
Assemble preproduction models						
OC drivers						
Complex utilities						
Integration first phase						
System H/S test						
Integration acceptance test						

FIGURE 8.18   CEBOO Project Weekly Resource Usage Schedule

Summary

Usage and availability of resources are major problem areas for project managers. Attention to these areas in developing a project schedule can point out resource bottlenecks before the project begins. Project managers should understand the ramifications of failing to schedule resources. The results of resource scheduling are frequently significantly different from the results of the standard CPM method.

With the rapid changes in technology and emphasis on time-to-market, catching resource usage and availability problems before the project starts can save the costs of crashing project activities later. Any resource deviations from plan and schedule that occur when the project is being implemented can be quickly recorded and the effect noted. Without this immediate update capability, the real negative effect of a change may not be known until it happens. Tying resource availability to a multiproject, multiresource system supports a project priority process that selects projects by their contribution to the organization's objectives and strategic plan.

Assignment of individuals to projects may not fit well with those assigned by computer software routines. In these cases overriding the computer solution to accommodate individual differences and skills is almost always the best choice.

The project resource schedule is important because it serves as your time baseline, which is used for measuring time differences between plan and actual. The resource schedule serves as the basis for developing your time-phased project cost budget baseline. The baseline (planned value, PV) is the sum of the cost accounts, and each cost account is the sum of the work packages in the cost account. Remember, if your budgeted costs are not time-phased, you really have no reliable way to measure performance. Although there are several types of project costs, the cost baseline is usually limited to direct costs (such as labor, materials, equipment) that are under the control of the project manager; other indirect costs can be added to project costs separately.

Key Terms

Heuristic	Resource-constrained projects	Time-constrained projects
Leveling/smoothing	Resource profile	Time-phased baseline
Planned value (PV)	Splitting	

Review Questions

1. How does resource scheduling tie to project priority?
2. How does resource scheduling reduce flexibility in managing projects?
3. Present six reasons scheduling resources is an important task.
4. How can outsourcing project work alleviate the three most common problems associated with multiproject resource scheduling?
5. Explain the risks associated with leveling resources, compressing or crashing projects, and imposed durations or "catch-up" as the project is being implemented.
6. Why is it critical to develop a time-phased baseline?

Exercises

1. Given the network plan that follows, compute the early, late, and slack times. What is the project duration? Using any approach you wish (e.g., trial and error), develop a loading chart for resources, Electrical Engineers (EE), and resource, Mechanical Engineers (ME). Assume only one of each resource exists. Given your resource schedule, compute the early, late, and slack times for your project. Which activities are now critical? What is the project duration now? Could something like this happen in real projects?

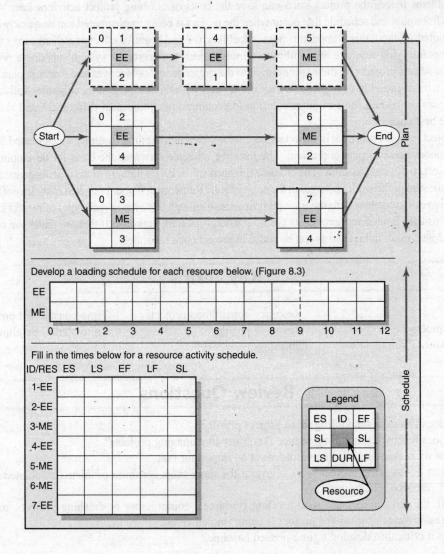

Develop a loading schedule for each resource below. (Figure 8.3)

Fill in the times below for a resource activity schedule.

ID/RES	ES	LS	EF	LF	SL
1-EE					
2-EE					
3-ME					
4-EE					
5-ME					
6-ME					
7-EE					

Legend

ES	ID	EF
SL		SL
LS	DUR	LF

Resource

2. Given the network plan that follows, compute the early, late, and slack times. What is the project duration? Using any approach you wish (e.g., trial and error), develop a loading chart for resources Carpenters (C) and Electricians (E). Assume only one Carpenter is available and two Electricians are available. Given your resource schedule, compute the early, late, and slack times for your project. Which activities are now critical? What is the project duration now?

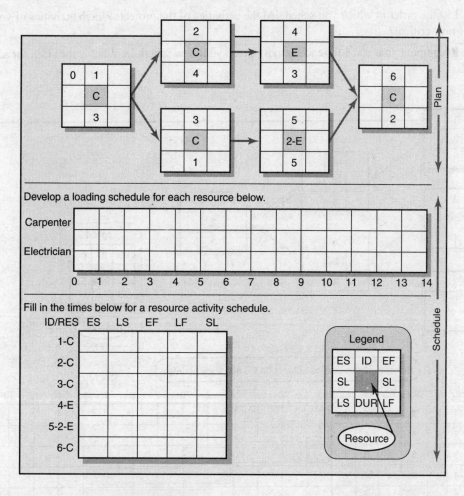

3. Compute the early, late, and slack times for the activities in the network that follows, assuming a time-constrained network. Which activities are critical? What is the timeconstrained project duration?

   Note: Recall, in the schedule resource load chart the *time-constrained* "scheduling interval (ES through LF) has been shaded. Any resource scheduled beyond the shaded area will delay the project.

   Assume you have only three resources and you are using a computer that uses software that schedules projects by the parallel method and following heuristics. Schedule only one period at a time!

   Minimum slack
   Smallest duration
   Lowest identification number

Keep a log of each activity change and update you make each period—e.g., period 0–1, 1–2, 2–3, etc. (Use a format similar to the one on page 241.) The log should include any changes or updates in ES and slack times each period, activities scheduled, and activities delayed. (Hint: Remember to maintain the technical dependencies of the network.) Use the resource load chart to assist you in scheduling (see pages 242–243).

List the order in which you scheduled the activities of the project. Which activities of your schedule are now critical?

Recompute your slack for each activity given your new schedule. What is the slack for activity 1? 4? 5?

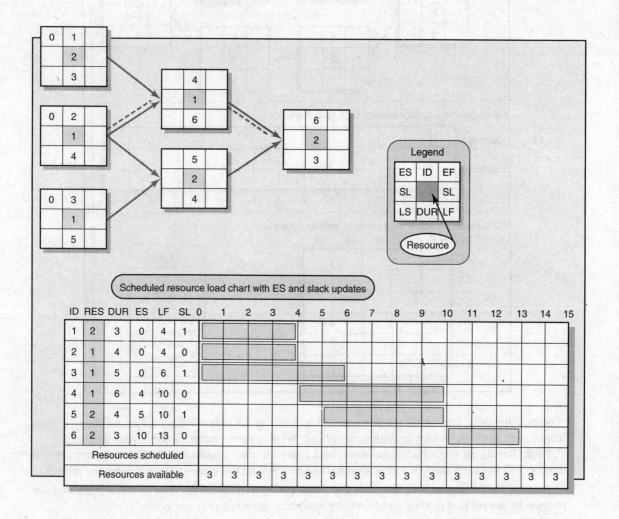

4. Develop a resource schedule in the loading chart that follows. Use the parallel method and heuristics given. Be sure to update each period as the computer would do. Note: Activities 2, 3, 5, and 6 use two of the resource skills. Three of the resource skills are available.

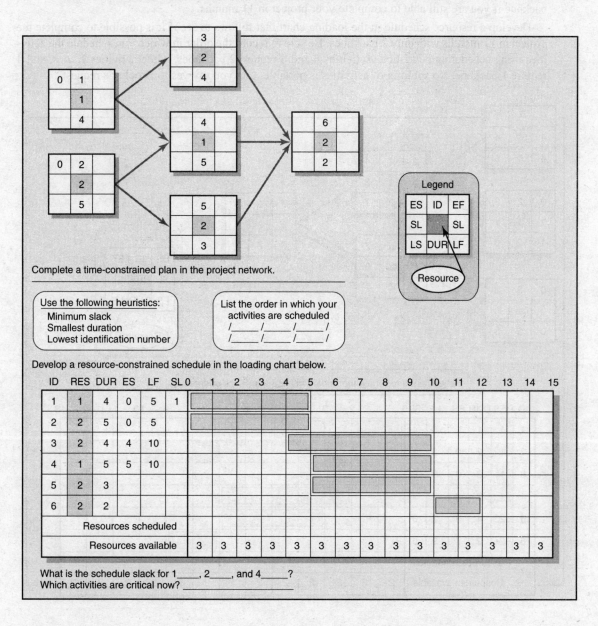

Complete a time-constrained plan in the project network.

Use the following heuristics:
  Minimum slack
  Smallest duration
  Lowest identification number

List the order in which your activities are scheduled
/_____/_____/_____/
/_____/_____/_____/

Develop a resource-constrained schedule in the loading chart below.

ID	RES	DUR	ES	LF	SL	0	1	2	3	4	5	6	7	8	9	10	11	12	13	14	15
1	1	4	0	5	1																
2	2	5	0	5																	
3	2	4	4	10																	
4	1	5	5	10																	
5	2	3																			
6	2	2																			
Resources scheduled																					
Resources available						3	3	3	3	3	3	3	3	3	3	3	3	3	3	3	

What is the schedule slack for 1_____, 2_____, and 4_____?
Which activities are critical now? _____

5. You have prepared the following schedule for a project in which the key resource is a backhoe. This schedule is contingent on having 3 backhoes. You receive a call from your partner, Brooker, who desperately needs 1 of your backhoes. You tell Brooker you would be willing to let him have the backhoe if you are still able to complete your project in 11 months.

Develop a resource schedule in the loading chart that follows to see if it is possible to complete the project in 11 months with only 2 backhoes. Be sure to record the order in which you schedule the activities using scheduling heuristics. Activities 5 and 6 require 2 backhoes, while activities 1, 2, 3, and 4 require 1 backhoe. No splitting of activities is possible. Can you say yes to Brooker's request?

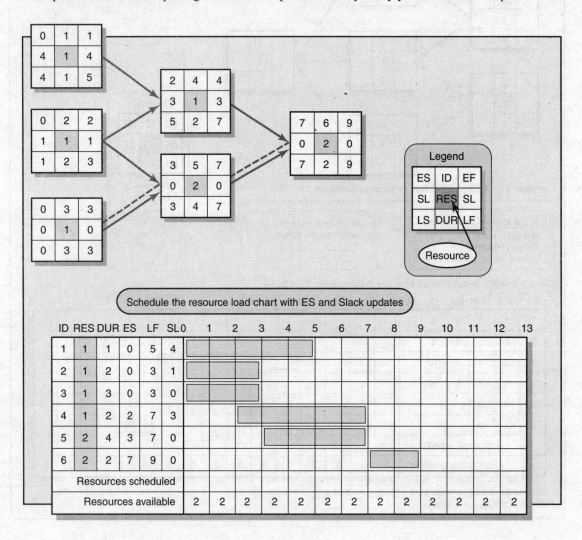

6. Given the time-phased work packages, complete the baseline budget form for the project.

Time-phased budget ($ 000)

Task	Budget	0	1	2	3	4	5	6	7	8	9	10
Activity 1	4	4										
Activity 2	6		1	3	2							
Activity 3	10		2	4	2	2						
Activity 4	8						2	3	3			
Activity 5	3									2	1	
Total	31											
Cumulative												

7. Given the time-phased work packages and network, complete the baseline budget form for the project.

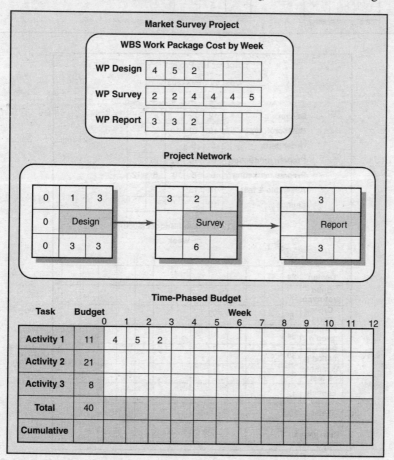

8. Given the time-phased work packages and network, complete the baseline budget form for the project.

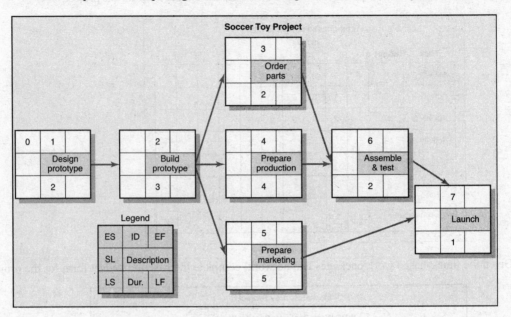

Soccer Toy Project

Cost by Week ($00)

	◄1	◄2	◄3	◄4	◄5
Design	12	12			
Build prototype	10	10	10		
Order parts	5	5			
Prepare production	16	10	22	16	
Prepare marketing	6	6	0	6	12
Assemble & test	18	18			
Launch	12				

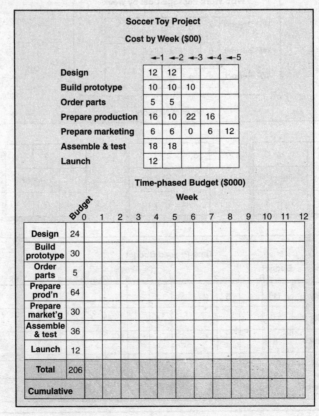

Time-phased Budget ($000)

Week

	Budget	0	1	2	3	4	5	6	7	8	9	10	11	12
Design	24													
Build prototype	30													
Order parts	5													
Prepare prod'n	64													
Prepare market'g	30													
Assemble & test	36													
Launch	12													
Total	206													
Cumulative														

References

Arrow, K. J., and L. Hurowicz, *Studies in Resource Allocation Process* (New York: Cambridge University Press, 1997).

Brucker, P., A. Drexl, R. Mohring, L. Newmann, and E. Pesch, "Resource-constrained Project Scheduling: Notation, Classification, Models and Methods," *European Journal of Operational Research,* Vol. 112, 1999, pp. 3–42.

Burgess, A. R., and J. B. Kellebrew, "Variations in Activity Level on Cyclical Arrow Diagrams," *Journal of Industrial Engineering,* Vol. 13, March–April 1962, pp. 76–83.

Charnes, A., and W. W. Cooper, "A Network Interpretation and Direct Sub Dual Algorithm for Critical Path Scheduling," *Journal of Industrial Engineering,* July–August 1962.

Demeulemeester, E. L., and W. S. Herroelen, *Project Scheduling: A Research Handbook* (Norwell, Mass: Kluwer Academic Publishers, 2002).

Fendly, L. G., "Towards the Development of a Complete Multi Project Scheduling System," *Journal of Industrial Engineering,* Vol. 19, 1968, pp. 505–15.

Reinersten, D., "Is It Always a Bad Idea to Add Resources to a Late Project?" *Electric Design,* October 30, 2000, pp. 17–18.

Talbot, B. F., and J. H. Patterson, "Optimal Methods for Scheduling Under Resource Constraints," *Project Management Journal,* December 1979.

Wiest, J. D., "A Heuristic Model for Scheduling Large Projects with Unlimited Resources," *Management Science,* Vol. 18, February 1967, pp. 359–77.

Woodworth, B. M., and C. J. Willie, "A Heuristic Algorithm for Resource Leveling in Multiproject, Multiresource Scheduling," *Decision Sciences,* Vol. 6, July 1975, pp. 525–40.

Woodworth, B. M., and S. Shanahan, "Identifying the Critical Sequence in a Resource Constrained Project," *International Journal of Project Management,* Vol. 6, 1988, pp. 89–96.

APPENDIX 8.1

The Critical-Chain Approach

In practice, project managers carefully manage slack on sensitive resource-limited projects. If possible, they will add slack at the end of the project by committing to a completion date that goes beyond the scheduled date. For example, the plans say the project should be completed on April 1, although the official completion date is May 1. Other managers take a more aggressive approach to managing slack within the schedule. They use an early start schedule and prohibit use of slack on any activity or work package to be used unless authorized by the project manager. Progress by percent complete and by remaining time are carefully monitored. Activities that are beating estimated completion times are reported so that succeeding activities can start ahead of schedule. This ensures that the time gained is used to start a succeeding activity earlier and time is not wasted. The overall intent is to create and save slack as a time buffer to complete the project early or to cover delay problems that may creep up on critical activities or paths.

Eliyahu Goldratt, who championed the "theory of constraints" in his popular book *The Goal,* advocates an alternative approach to managing slack. He has coined the term "critical-chain" to recognize that the project network may be constrained by both resource and technical dependencies. Each type of constraint can create task dependencies, and in the case of resource constraints, new task dependencies can be created! Remember how resource constrains shifted the critical path? If not, visit Figure 8.5 again. The critical chain refers to the longest string of dependencies that exist on the project. Chain is used instead of path, since the latter tends to be associated with just technical dependencies not resource dependencies. Goldratt uses the critical chain concept to develop strategies for accelerating the completion of projects. These strategies are based on his observations about time estimates of individual activities.

Time Estimates

Goldratt argues that there is a natural tendency for people to add safety (just-in-case) time to their estimations. It is believed that those who estimate activity times provide an estimate that has about an 80 to 90 percent chance of being completed on or before the estimated time. Hence, the median time (50/50 chance) is overestimated by approximately 30 to 40 percent. For example, a programmer may estimate that there is a 50/50 chance that he can complete an activity in six days. However, to ensure success and to protect against potential problems, he adds three days of safety time and reports that it will take nine days to complete the task. In this case the median (50/50) time is overestimated by approximately 50 percent. He now has a 50/50 chance of completing the project three days ahead of the schedule. If this hidden contingency is pervasive across a project, then most activities in theory should be completed ahead of schedule.

Not only do workers add safety, but project managers like to add safety to ensure that they will be able to bring the project in ahead of schedule. They will add a month to a nine-month project to cover any delays or risks that might spring up. This situation raises an interesting paradox:

> *Why, if there is a tendency to overestimate activity durations, and add safety to the end of a project, do so many projects come in behind schedule?*

Critical Chain Project Management (CCPM) offers several explanations:

- *Parkinson's law:* Work fills the time available. Why hustle to complete a task today when it isn't due until tomorrow? Not only will the pace of work be dictated by deadline, but workers will take advantage of perceived free time to catch up on others things. This is especially true in matrix environments where workers will use this time to clear work backlog on other projects and duties.
- *Self-protection:* Participants fail to report early finishes out of fear that management will adjust their future standards and demand more next time. For example, if a team member estimates that a task will take seven days and delivers it in five, the next time he is asked for an estimate, the project manager may want to trim the estimate based on past performance. Peer pressure may also be a factor here: to avoid being labeled a "rate buster," members may not report early finishes.
- *Dropped baton:* Goldratt uses the metaphor of project as relay race to illustrate the impact of poor coordination. Just as a runner's time is lost if the next runner is not ready to receive the baton, so is the time gained from completing a task early lost if the next group of people are not ready to receive the project work. Poor communication and inflexible resource schedules prevent progress from occurring.
- *Excessive multitasking:* The norm in most organizations is to have project personnel work on several projects, activities, or assignments at the same time. This leads to costly interruptions and excessive task splitting. As pointed out on p. 250, this adds time to each activity. When looked at in isolation the time loss may seem minimal, but when taken as a whole the transition costs can be staggering.
- *Resource bottlenecks:* In multiproject organizations projects are frequently delayed because test equipment or other necessary resources are tied up on other project work.

- *Student syndrome (procrastination):* Goldratt asserts that just as students delay writing a term paper until the last minute, workers delay starting tasks when they perceive that they have more than enough time to complete the task. The problem with delaying the start of a task is that obstacles are often not detected until the task is under way. By postponing the start of the task, the opportunity to cope with these obstacles and complete the task on time is compromised.

Critical-Chain in Action

CCPM's solution to reducing project time overruns is to insist on people using the "true 50/50" activity time estimates (rather than estimates which have an 80 to 90 percent chance of being completed before the estimated time); the 50/50 estimates result in a project duration about one-half the low risk of 80 to 90 percent estimates. This requires a corporate culture which values accurate estimates and refrains from blaming people for not meeting deadlines. According to CCPM, using 50/50 estimates will discourage Parkinson's law, the student syndrome, and self protection from coming into play because there is less "free time" available. Productivity will be increased as individuals try to meet tighter deadlines. Similarly, the compressed time schedule reduces the likelihood of the dropped baton effect.

CCPM recommends inserting time buffers into the schedule to act as "shock absorbers" to protect the project completion date against task durations taking longer than the 50/50 estimate. The rationale is that by using 50/50 estimates you are in essence taking out all of the "safety" in individual tasks. CCPM also recommends using portions of this collective safety strategically by inserting time buffers where potential problems are likely to occur. There are three kinds of buffers in CCPM:

- *Project buffer:* First, since all activities along the critical chain have inherent *uncertainty* that is difficult to predict, project duration is uncertain. Therefore, a project time buffer is added to the expected *project duration*. CCPM recommends using roughly 50 percent of the aggregate safety. For example, if the modified schedule reduces the project duration by 20 days from 50 to 30, then a 10-day project buffer would be used.
- *Feeder buffers:* Buffers are added to the network where noncritical paths merge with the critical chain. These buffers protect the critical chain from being delayed.
- *Resource buffers:* Time buffers are inserted where scarce resources are needed for an activity. Resource time buffers come in at least two forms. One form is a time buffer attached to a critical resource to ensure that the resource is on call and available when needed. This preserves the relay race. The second form of time buffer is added to activities preceding the work of a scarce resource. This kind of buffer protects against resource bottlenecks by increasing the likelihood that the preceding activity will be completed when the resource is available.

All buffers reduce the risk of the project duration being late and increase the chance of early project completion.

Critical-Chain Versus Traditional Scheduling Approach

To illustrate how CCPM affects scheduling let's compare it with the traditional approach to project scheduling. We will first resolve resource problems the way described in Chapter 8 and then the CCPM method. Figure A8.1A shows the *planned* Air Control project network without any concern for resources. That is, activities are assumed to be independent and resources will be made available and/or are interchangeable. Figure A8.1B depicts the bar chart for the project. The blue bars represent the durations of critical activities; the clear bars represent the durations of noncritical activities; the light gray bars represent slack. Note that the duration is 45 days and the critical path is represented by activities 1, 4, 6, 7, and 8.

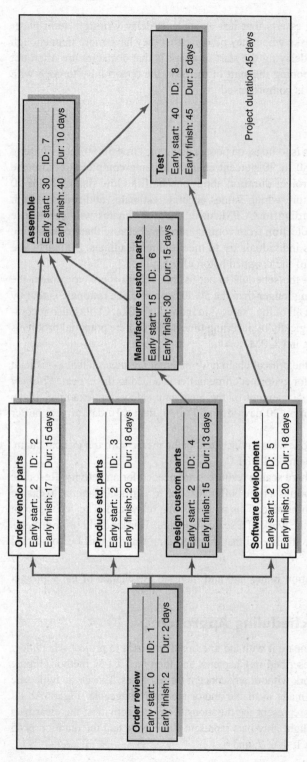

FIGURE A8.1A   Air Control Project: Time Plan without Resources

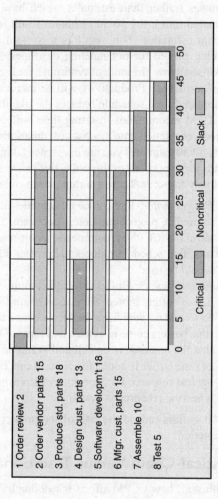

FIGURE A8.1B   Air Control Project: Time Plan without Resources

Parallel activities hold potential for resource conflicts. This is the case in this project. Ryan is the resource for activities 3 and 6. If you insert Ryan in the bar chart in Figure A8.1B for activities 3 and 6, you can see activity 3 overlaps activity 6 by five days—an impossible situation. Because Ryan cannot work two activities simultaneously and no other person can take his place, a resource dependency exists. The result is that two activities (3 and 6) that were assumed to be independent now become dependent. Something has to give! Figure A8.2A shows the Air Control project network with the resources included. A pseudo-dashed arrow has been added to the network to indicate the resource dependency. The bar chart in Figure A8.2B reflects the revised schedule resolving the overallocation of Ryan. Given the new schedule, slack for some activities has changed. More importantly, the critical path has changed. It is now 1, 3, 6, 7, 8. The resource schedule shows the new project duration to be 50 days rather than 45 days.

Now let's apply the CCPM approach to the Air Control project. Figure A8.3 details many of the changes. First, notice that task estimates now represent approximations of the 50/50 rule. Second, observe that not all of the activities on the critical-chain are technically linked. Manufacture custom parts is included because of previously defined resource dependency. Third, a project time buffer is added at the end of schedule. Finally, feeder buffers are inserted at each point where a noncritical activity merges with the critical chain.

The impact the CCPM approach has on the project schedule can best be seen in the Gantt chart presented in Figure A8.4. Notice first the late start times for each of the three noncritical activities. For example, under the critical path method, order vendor parts and software development would be scheduled to begin immediately after the order review. Instead they are scheduled later in the project. Three-day feeder buffers have been added to each of these activities to absorb any delays that might occur in these activities. Finally, instead of taking 50 days the project is now estimated to take only 27 days with a 10-day project buffer!

This example provides an opportunity for explaining the differences between buffers and slack. Slack is spare time inherent in the schedule of noncritical activities and can be determined by differences between the early start and late start of a specific activity. Buffers, on the other hand, are dedicated time blocks reserved to cover most likely contingencies and are monitored closely so, if they are not needed, subsequent activities can proceed on schedule. Buffers are needed in part because the estimates are based on 50/50 approximations, and therefore roughly half of the activities will take longer than planned. To protect against these extended activity durations, buffers are inserted to minimize the impact on the schedule. Buffers are not part of the project schedule and are used only when sound management dictates it.

While not depicted in the figures, an example of a resource buffer would be to add six days to Ryan's schedule (remember he is the critical resource that caused the schedule to be extended). This would ensure that he could continue to work on the project beyond the 18th day in case either produce standard parts and/or manufacture custom parts takes longer than planned. Progress on these two tasks would be monitored closely, and his schedule would be adjusted accordingly.

CCPM and Splitting Tasks

Buffers do not address the insidious effects of pervasive task splitting, especially in a multiproject environment where workers are juggling different project assignments. CCPM has three recommendations that will help to reduce the impact of splitting activities:

1. Reduce the number of projects so people are not assigned to as many projects concurrently.
2. Control start dates of projects to accommodate resource shortages. Don't start projects until sufficient resources are available to work full time on the project.
3. Contract (lock in) for resources *before* the project begins.

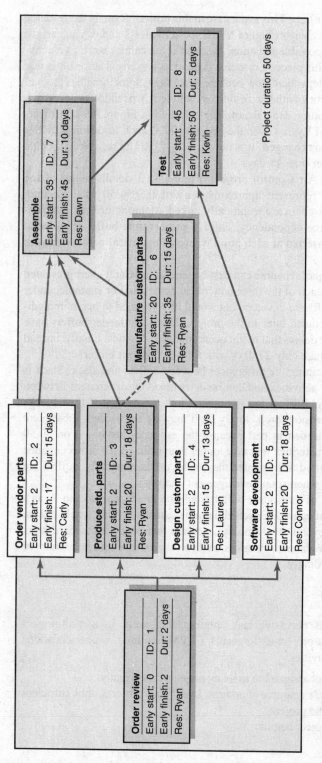

FIGURE A8.2A   Air Control Project: Schedule with Resources Limited

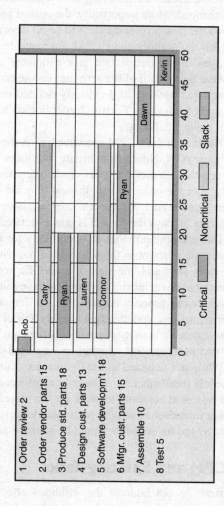

FIGURE A8.2B   Air Control Project: Schedule with Resources Limited

Monitoring Project Performance

The CCPM method uses buffers to monitor project time performance. Remember that as shown in Figure A8.3 a project buffer is used to insulate the project against delays along the critical-chain. For monitoring purposes, this buffer is typically divided into three zones—OK, Watch and Plan, and Act, respectively (see Figure A8.5). As the buffer begins to decrease and moves into the second zone, alarms are set off to seek corrective action. To be truly effective, buffer management requires comparing buffer usage with actual progress on the project. For example, if the project is 75 percent complete and you have only used 50 percent of the project buffer, then the project is in pretty good shape. Conversely, if the project is only 25 percent complete and 50 percent of the buffer has already been used, you are in trouble and corrective action is needed. A method for estimating percentage complete is described in Chapter 13.

The CCPM Method Today

CCPM has generated considerable debate within the project management community. While sound in theory, support at this time is limited but growing. For example, Harris Semiconductor was able to build a new automated wafer fabrication facility within 13 months using CCPM methods when the industry standard for such a facility is 26–36 months. The Israeli aircraft industry has used CCPM techniques to reduce average maintenance work on aircraft from two months to two weeks. The U.S. Air Force and Navy as well as Boeing, Lucent Technologies, Intel, GM, and 3M are applying critical-chain principles to their multi-project environments.

CCPM is not without critics. First, CCPM does not address the biggest cause of project delays, which is an ill-defined and unstable project scope. Second, some critics challenge Goldratt's assumptions about human behavior. They question the tendency of experts to pad estimates and that employees act deliberately against the organization for their own interest and benefit. They also object to the insinuation that trained professionals would exhibit the student syndrome habits. Third, evidence of success is almost exclusively anecdotal and based on single case studies. The lack of systematic evidence raises questions about generalizability of application. CCPM may prove to work best for only certain kinds of projects.

One of the keys to implementing CCPM is the culture of the organization. If the organization honors noble efforts that fail to meet estimates as it does efforts that do meet estimates, then greater acceptance will occur. Conversely, if management treats honest failure differently from success, then resistance will be high. Organizations adopting the CCPM approach have to invest significant energy to obtaining "buy-in" on the part of all participants to its core principles and allaying the fears that this system may generate.

Appendix Summary

Regardless of where one stands in the debate, the CCPM approach deserves credit for bringing resource dependency to the forefront, highlighting the modern ills of multitasking, and forcing us to rethink conventional methods of project scheduling.

Appendix Exercises

1. Check out the Goldratt Institute's homepage at *http://www.goldratt.com* for current information on the application of critical-chain techniques to project management.
2. Apply critical-chain scheduling principles to the Print Software, Inc., project presented in Chapter 6 on page 175. Revise the estimated time durations by 50 percent except round up the odd time durations (i.e., 3 becomes 4). Draw a CCPM network diagram similar to the one contained in Figure A8.3 for the Print Software project as well as a Gantt chart similar to Figure A8.4. How would these diagrams differ from the ones generated using the traditional scheduling technique?

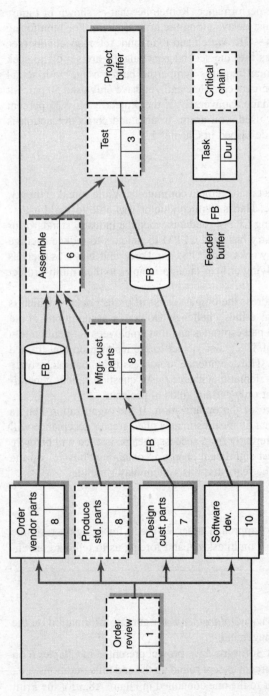

FIGURE A8.3 Air Control Project: CCPM Network

Activity	DUR	LS	LF	Buffer
1. Order review	1	0	1	0
2. Order vendor parts	8	7	15	3
3. Produce std. parts	8	1	9	0
4. Design cust. parts	7	1	8	3
5. Software dev.	10	11	21	3
6. Mfgr. cust. parts	8	11	19	0
7. Assemble	6	18	24	0
8. Test	3	24	27	12

FIGURE A8.4 Air Control Project Gantt Chart: CCPM Network

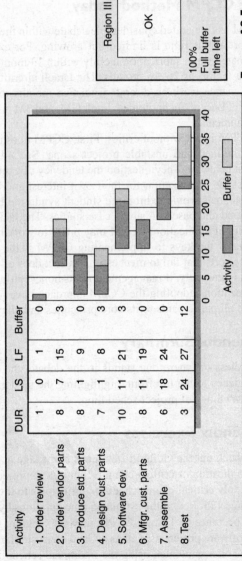

FIGURE A8.5 Project Control— Buffer Management

APPENDIX REFERENCES

Goldratt, *Critical Chain* (Great Barrington, MA: North River Press, 1997).

Herroelen, W., R. Leus, and E. Demeulemeester, "Critical Chain Project Scheduling: Do Not Oversimplify," *Project Management Journal,* Vol. 33 (4), 2002, pp. 48–60.

Leach, L. P., "Critical Chain Project Management," *Proceedings of 29th Annual Project Management Institute, 1998, Seminars and Symposium* (Newtown, PA: Project Management Institute, 1998), pp. 1239–44.

Levine, H. A., "Shared Contingency: Exploring the Critical Chain," *PM Network,* October 1999, pp. 35–38.

Newbold, R. C., *Project Management in the Fast Lane: Applying the Theory of Constraints* (Boca Raton, FL: St. Lucie Press, 1998).

Noreen, E., D. Smith, and J. Mackey, *The Theory of Constraints and Its Implication for Management Accounting* (Great Barrington, MA: North River Press, 1995).

Raz, T., R. Barnes, and D. Dvir, "A Critical Look at Critical Chain Project Management," *Project Management Journal,* December 2003, pp. 24–32.

Sood, S., "Taming Uncertainty: Critical-Chain Buffer Management Helps Minimize Risk in the Project Equation," *PM Network,* March 2003, pp. 57–59.

Zalmanson, E., "Readers Feedback," *PM Network,* Vol. 15 (1), 2001, p. 4.

CASE 8.1

Power Train, Ltd.

We have smashing systems for reporting, tracking, and controlling costs on design projects. Our planning of projects is better than any I have seen at other companies. Our scheduling seemed to serve us well when we were small and we had only a few projects. Now that we have many more projects and schedule using multiproject software, there are too many occasions when the right people are not assigned to the projects deemed important to our success. This situation is costing us big money, headaches, and stress!

Claude Jones, VP, Design and Operations

History

Power Train, Ltd. (PT), was founded in 1960 by Daniel Gage, a skilled mechanical engineer and machinist. Prior to founding PT he worked for three years as design engineer for a company that designed and built transmissions for military tanks and trucks. It was a natural transition for Dan to start a company designing and building power trains for farm tractor companies. Today, Dan is no longer active in the management of PT but is still revered as its founder. He and his family still own 25 percent of the company, which went public in 1988. PT has been growing at a 6 percent clip for the last five years but expects industry growth to level off as supply exceeds demand.

Today, PT continues its proud tradition of designing and building the best-quality power trains for manufacturers of farm tractors and equipment. The company employs 178 design engineers and has about 1,800 production and support staff. Contract design projects for tractor manufacturers represent a major portion of PT's revenue. At any given time, about 45 to 60 design projects are going on concurrently. A small portion of their design work is for military vehicles. PT only accepts military contracts that involve very advanced, new technology and are cost plus.

A new phenomenon has attracted management of PT to look into a larger market. Last year a large Swedish truck manufacturer approached PT to consider designing power trains for its trucks. As the industry consolidates, the opportunities for PT should increase because these large firms are moving to more outsourcing to cut infrastructure costs and stay very flexible. Only last week a PT design engineer spoke to a German truck manufacturing manager at a conference. The German manager was already exploring outsourcing of drive trains to Porsche and was very pleased to be reminded of PT's expertise in the area. A meeting is set up for next month.

Claude Jones

Claude Jones joined PT in 1989 as a new MBA from the University of Edinburgh. He worked as a mechanical engineer for U.K. Hydraulics for five years prior to returning to school for the MBA. "I just wanted to be part of the management team and where the action is." Jones moved quickly through the ranks. Today he is the vice president of design and operations. Sitting at his desk, Jones is pondering the conflicts and confusion that seem to be increasing in scheduling people to projects. He gets a real rush at the thought of designing power trains for large trucks; however, given their current project scheduling problems, a large increase in business would only compound their problems. Somehow these conflicts in scheduling have to be resolved before any serious thought can be given to expanding into design of power transmissions for truck manufacturers.

Jones is thinking of the problems PT had in the last year. The MF project is the first to come to mind. The project was not terribly complex and did not require their best design engineers. Unfortunately, the scheduling software assigned one of the most creative and expensive engineers to the MF project. A similar situation, but reversed, happened on the Deer project. This project involved a big customer and new hydrostatic technology for small tractors. In this project the scheduling software assigned engineers who were not familiar with small tractor transmissions. Somehow, thinks Jones, the right people need to be scheduled to the right projects. Upon reflection, this problem with scheduling has been increasing since PT went to multiproject scheduling. Maybe a project office is needed to keep on top of these problems.

A meeting with the information technology team and software vendors was positive but not very helpful because these people are not really into detailed scheduling problems. The vendors provided all sorts of evidence suggesting the heuristics used—least slack, shortest duration, and identification number—are absolutely efficient in scheduling people and minimizing project delays. One project software vendor, Lauren, kept saying their software would allow PT to customize the scheduling of projects and people to almost any variation selected. Lauren repeated over and over, "If the standard heuristics do not meet your requirements, create your own heuristics that do." Lauren even volunteered to assist in setting up the system. But she is not willing to spend time on the problem until PT can describe to her exactly what criteria will be used (and their sequence) to select and schedule people to projects.

What Next?

Potential expansion into the truck power train business is not feasible until the confusion in project scheduling is solved or reduced significantly. Jones is ready to tackle this problem, but he is not sure where to start.

CHAPTER 9

Reducing Project Duration

In skating over thin ice our safety is in our speed

—*Ralph Waldo Emerson*

Imagine the following scenarios:

—After finalizing your project schedule, you realize the estimated completion date is two months beyond what your boss publicly promised an important customer.

—Five months into the project, you realize that you are already three weeks behind the drop dead date for the project.

—Four months into a project top management changes its priorities and now tells you that money is not an issue. Complete the project ASAP!

What do you do?

This chapter addresses strategies for reducing project duration either prior to setting the baseline for the project or in the midst of project execution. Choice of options is based on the constraints surrounding the project. Here the project priority matrix introduced in Chapter 4 comes into play. For example, there are many more options available for reducing project time if you are not resource constrained than if you cannot spend more than your original budget. We will begin first by examining the reasons for reducing project duration followed by a discussion of different options for accelerating project completion. The chapter will conclude with the classic time-cost framework for selecting which activities to "crash." Crash is a term that has emerged in the Project Management lexicon for shortening the duration of an activity or project beyond when it can be normally done.

Rationale for Reducing Project Duration

There are few circumstances in which a project manager or owner would not wish to reduce the time to complete a project. Reducing the time of a critical activity in a project can be done but almost always results in a higher direct cost; thus, the manager faces a cost-time trade-off problem—is the reduction in time worth the additional cost? Cost-time situations focus on reducing the critical path that determines the project completion date.

There are many good reasons for attempting to reduce the duration of a project. One of the more important reasons today is time to market. Intense global competition and rapid technological advances have made speed a competitive advantage. To succeed, companies have to spot new opportunities, launch project teams, and bring new products or services to the marketplace in a flash. Perhaps in no industry does speed matter as much as in

Snapshot from Practice   Cell-Phone Wars*

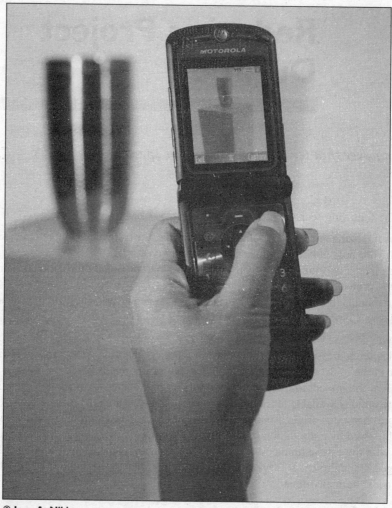

© Lars A. Niki.

Speed has been critical in business ever since the California Gold Rush. The cell-phone industry is a good example of an intensely competitive business that places a premium on speed. In 2005 Motorola came out with the RAZR, its ultrathin cell phone with camera and music player. Samsung Group answered seven months later with the Blade . Then on February 1, 2006, Motorola released SLVR, a phone that is even more svelte than its predecessor. Nokia entered the fray with N80, which added Wi-Fi Web browsing to the product mix. "It's like having a popular night-club. You have to keep opening new ones. To stay cool, you have to speed up," says Michael Greeson, president of market researcher Diffusion Group, Inc.

In order to survive, Motorola, Nokia, and other cell-phone manufacturers have become masters at project management. They have been able to cut the market release time of new phones from 12–18 months to 6–9 months. What is at stake is over 500 million in forecasted sales of new cell phones each year.

* Steve Hamm, "Is Your Company Fast Enough?" *BusinessWeek*, March 27, 2006, pp. 68–76.

Snapshot from Practice Responding to the Northridge Earthquake*

David Butow/Corbis.

On January 17, 1994, a 6.8-magnitude earthquake struck the Los Angeles basin, near suburban Northridge, causing 60 deaths, thousands of injuries, and billions of dollars in property damage. Nowhere was the destructive power of nature more evident than in the collapsed sections of the freeway system that disrupted the daily commute of an estimated 1 million Los Angelenos. The Northridge earthquake posed one of the greatest challenges to the California Department of Transportation (CalTrans) in its nearly 100-year history. To expedite the recovery process, Governor Pete Wilson signed an emergency declaration allowing CalTrans to streamline contracting procedures and offer attractive incentives for completing work ahead of schedule. For each day that the schedule was beaten, a sizable bonus was to be awarded. Conversely, for each day over the deadline, the contractor would be penalized the same amount. The amount ($50,000 to $200,000) varied depending on the importance of the work.

The incentive scheme proved to be a powerful motivator for the freeway reconstruction contractors. C. C. Myers, Inc., of Rancho Cordova, California, won the contract for the reconstruction of the Interstate 10 bridges. Myers pulled out all stops to finish the project in a blistering 66 days—a whopping 74 days ahead of schedule—and earning a $14.8 million bonus! Myers took every opportunity to save time and streamline operations. They greatly expanded the workforce. For example, 134 ironworkers were employed instead of the normal 15. Special lighting equipment was set up so that work could be performed around the clock. Likewise, the sites were prepared and special materials were used so that work could continue despite inclement weather that would normally shut down construction. The work was scheduled much like an assembly line so that critical activities were followed by the next critical activity. A generous incentive scheme was devised to reward teamwork and reach milestones early. Carpenters and ironworkers competed as teams against each other to see who could finish first.

Although C. C. Myers received a substantial bonus for finishing early, they spent a lot of money on overtime, bonuses, special equipment, and other premiums to keep the job rolling along. CalTrans supported Myers's efforts. With reconstruction work going on 24 hours a day, including jackhammering and pile-driving, CalTrans temporarily housed many families in local motels. CalTrans even erected a temporary plastic soundwall to help reduce the construction noise traveling to a nearby apartment complex. The double-layer curtain, 450 feet long and 20 feet high, was designed to reduce construction noise by 10 decibels.

Despite the difficulties and expense incurred by around-the-clock freeway building, most of Los Angeles cheered CalTrans's quake recovery efforts. The Governor's Office of Planning and Research issued a report concluding that for every day the Santa Monica Freeway was closed, it cost the local economy more than $1 million.

* Jerry B. Baxter, "Responding to the Northridge Earthquake," *PM Network* (November 1994), pp. 13–22.

the electronics industry. For example, a rule of thumb for moderate- to high-technology firms is that a six-month delay in bringing a product to market can result in a gross profit loss of market share of about 35 percent. In these cases, high-technology firms typically assume that the time savings and avoidance of lost profits are worth any additional costs to reduce time without any formal analysis. See the Snapshot from Practice: Cell-Phone Wars for more on this.

Another common reason for reducing project time occurs when unforeseen delays—for example, adverse weather, design flaws, and equipment breakdown—cause substantial delays midway in the project. Getting back on schedule usually requires compressing the time on some of the remaining critical activities. The additional costs of getting back on schedule need to be compared with the consequences of being late. This is especially true when time is a top priority.

Incentive contracts can make reduction of project time rewarding—usually for both the project contractor and owner. For example, a contractor finished a bridge across a lake 18 months early and received more than $6 million for the early completion. The availability of the bridge to the surrounding community 18 months early to reduce traffic gridlock made the incentive cost to the community seem small to users. In another example, in a continuous improvement arrangement, the joint effort of the owner and contractor resulted in early completion of a river lock and a 50/50 split of the savings to the owner and contractor. See Snapshot from Practice: Northridge Earthquake for a situation in which a contractor went to great lengths to complete a project as quickly as possible.

"Imposed deadlines" is another reason for accelerating project completion. For example, a politician makes a public statement that a new law building will be available in two years. Or the president of a software company remarks in a speech that new advanced software will be available in one year. Such statements too often become imposed project duration dates—without any consideration of the problems or cost of meeting such a date. The project duration time is set while the project is in its "concept" phase before or without any detailed scheduling of all the activities in the project. This phenomenon occurs very frequently in practice! Unfortunately, this practice almost always leads to a higher cost project than one that is planned using low-cost and detailed planning. In addition, quality is sometimes compromised to meet deadlines. More important, these increased costs of imposed duration dates are seldom recognized or noted by project participants.

Sometimes very high overhead costs are recognized before the project begins. In these cases it is prudent to examine the direct costs of shortening the critical path versus the overhead cost savings. Usually there are opportunities to shorten a few critical activities at less than the daily overhead rate. Under specific conditions (which are not rare), huge savings are possible with little risk.

Finally there are times when it is important to reassign key equipment and/or people to new projects. Under these circumstances, the cost of compressing the project can be compared with the costs of not releasing key equipment or people.

Options for Accelerating Project Completion

Managers have several effective methods for crashing specific project activities when resources are not constrained. Several of these are summarized below.

Options When Resources Are Not Constrained

Adding Resources

The most common method for shortening project time is to assign additional staff and equipment to activities. There are limits, however, as to how much speed can be gained by adding staff. Doubling the size of the workforce will not necessarily reduce completion time by half. The relationship would be correct only when tasks can be partitioned so minimal communication is needed between workers, as in harvesting

Snapshot from Practice   Outsourcing in Bio-Tech Picks Up Speed*

In the face of increasing time-to-market pressures, many bio-tech firms are turning to outsourcing to expedite the drug development process. Panos Kalaritis, vice president of operations for Irix Pharmaceuticals, says that outsourcing process development can accelerate a drug's evolution by allowing a pharmaceutical company to continue research while a contractor works on process optimization. Susan Dexter of Lonza Biologics identified different types of outsourcing contracts including agreements for product development, clinical trial supplies, in-market or commercial supplies, and technology transfer. Often, she said, a given project can encompass more than one of the above stages over a period of several years.

Using a contractor, said Paul Henricks, business manager for Patheon Inc., gives the client company access to specialized knowledge and infrastructure as well as flexible resources and capacity. The sponsoring company can also manage risks by sharing responsibilities through outsourcing.

"Communication is key to a successful outsourcing relationship," said Dan Gold, vice president of process development for Covance, which was formerly Corning Bio. "Contractors and sponsors should both assign project managers, and the two must work together to maintain, track, and document project completion. There must be a concerted effort on the part of both parties to work as partners to complete the project."

* Mathew Lerner, "Outsourcing in Bio-Technology Picks Up Speed," *Chemical Market Reporter*, Vol. 251, No. 14 (2002), p. 17.

a crop by hand or repaving a highway. Most projects are not set up that way; additional workers increase the communication requirements to coordinate their efforts. For example, doubling a team by adding two workers requires six times as much pairwise intercommunication than is required in the original two-person team. Not only is more time needed to coordinate and manage a larger team; there is the additional delay of training the new people and getting them up to speed on the project. The end result is captured in Brooks' law: Adding manpower to a late software project makes it later.

Frederick Brooks formulated this principle based on his experience as a project manager for IBM's System/360 software project during the early 1960s. Subsequent research concluded that adding more people to a late project does not necessarily cause the project to be later. The key is whether the new staff is added early so there is sufficient time to make up for lost ground once the new members have been fully assimilated.

Outsourcing Project Work

A common method for shortening the project time is to subcontract an activity. The subcontractor may have access to superior technology or expertise that will accelerate the completion of the activity. For example, contracting for a backhoe can accomplish in two hours what it can take a team of laborers two days to do. Likewise, by hiring a consulting firm that specializes in ADSI programming, a firm may be able to cut in half the time it would take for less experienced, internal programmers to do the work. Subcontracting also frees up resources that can be assigned to a critical activity and will ideally result in a shorter project duration. See Snapshot from Practice: Outsourcing Bio-Tech. Outsourcing will be addressed more fully in Chapter 12.

Scheduling Overtime

The easiest way to add more labor to a project is not to add more people, but to schedule overtime. If a team works 50 hours a week instead of 40, it might accomplish 25 percent more. By scheduling overtime you avoid the additional costs of coordination and communication encountered when new people are added. If people involved are salaried workers, there may be no real additional cost for the extra work. Another advantage is that there are fewer distractions when people work outside normal hours.

Overtime has disadvantages. First, hourly workers are typically paid time and a half for overtime and double time for weekends and holidays. Sustained overtime work by salaried employees may incur intangible costs such as divorce, burnout, and turnover. The latter is a key organizational concern when there is a shortage of workers. Furthermore, it is an oversimplification to assume that, over an extended period of time, a person is as productive during his or her eleventh hour at work as during his or her third hour of work. There are natural limits to what is humanly possible, and extended overtime may actually lead to an overall decline in productivity when fatigue sets in.

Overtime and working longer hours is the preferred choice for accelerating project completion, especially when the project team is salaried. The key is to use overtime judiciously. Remember a project is a marathon not a sprint! You do not want to run out of energy before the finish line.

Establish a Core Project Team

As discussed in Chapter 3, one of the advantages of creating a dedicated core team to complete a project is speed. Assigning professionals full time to a project avoids the hidden cost of multitasking in which people are forced to juggle the demands of multiple projects. Professionals are allowed to devote their undivided attention to a specific project. This singular focus creates a shared goal that can bind a diverse set of professionals into a highly cohesive team capable of accelerating project completion. Factors that contribute to the emergence of high-performing project teams will be discussed in detail in Chapter 11.

Do It Twice—Fast and Correctly

If you are in a hurry, try building a "quick and dirty" short-term solution, then go back and do it the right way. For example, the Rose Garden stadium in Portland, Oregon, was supposed to be completely finished in time for the start of the 1995–1996 National Basketball Association (NBA) season. Delays made this impossible, so the construction crew set up temporary bleachers to accommodate the opening-night crowd. The additional costs of doing it twice are often more than compensated for by the benefits of satisfying the deadline.

Options When Resources Are Constrained

A project manager has fewer options for accelerating project completion when additional resources are either not available or the budget is severely constrained. This is especially true once the schedule has been established. Below are some of these options.

Fast-Tracking

Sometimes it is possible to rearrange the logic of the project network so that critical activities are done in parallel (concurrently) rather than sequentially. This alternative is a good one if the project situation is right. When this alternative is given serious attention, it is amazing to observe how creative project team members can be in finding ways to restructure sequential activities in parallel. As noted in Chapter 6, one of the most common methods for restructuring activities is to change a finish-to-start relationship to a start-to-start relationship. For example, instead of waiting for the final design to be approved, manufacturing engineers can begin building the production line as soon as key specifications have been established. Changing activities from sequential to parallel usually requires closer coordination among those responsible for the activities affected but can produce tremendous time savings.

Critical-Chain

Critical-chain project management (CCPM) is designed to accelerate project completion. As discussed in Chapter 8, the jury is still out in terms of its applicability. Still CCPM principles appear sound and worthy

Snapshot from Practice   The Fastest House in the World*

AP/Wide World.

On March 13, 1999, Habitat for Humanity New Zealand built a fully operational, four-bedroom house in Auckland in 3 hours, 44 minutes, and 59 seconds from floor to roof complete with curtains, running showers, lawn, and fence. In doing so they became the fastest house builders in the world.

"We made a significant decimation of the record," said Habitat New Zealand's Chief Executive Graeme Lee. "The previous record of 4 hours, 39 minutes, 8 seconds, held by a Habitat chapter in Nashville, USA, was made with a three-bedroom home, and we built one with four bedrooms and used only 140 volunteers on the site." The rules provide for construction to commence from an established floor platform. The house is complete when it meets the local building code, and the family can move in.

The project took 14 months to plan. CCPM principles were applied using ProChain Software to finalize project schedule. The critical-chain was recalculated 150–200 times and then analyzed to optimize the resulting new sequence of operations. This reiterative process was used to progressively develop the fastest plan.

One of the keys to efficiency was the use of "Laserbilt" prefabricated walls made from 36mm particleboard using technology that had been invented by a company in New Zealand. Another time saver was the use of a crane which lowered the wooden roof frame (built on adjacent land) onto the four walls.

Once the roof was on the walls, roofing iron was put on. Meanwhile, the wall sheathing was attached to outside walls and windows fitted, with painters almost painting the face of the hammers as sheath nailing was completed. Inside, vinyl was laid first in the utility areas while painters started in the bedrooms. After the vinyl, the bathrooms were fitted and curtains hung. On the outside, while the roofing was being installed, decks and steps were constructed, a front path laid, mail box and clothesline installed, wooden fence constructed around the perimeter, three trees planted, and lawns leveled and seeded.

Post-project assessment revealed that even further time could have been gained. The management rule was to be "One tradesperson in one room at one time," but enthusiasm took over and people were doing whatever they could wherever they could, especially toward the end. The project manager estimated that if greater discipline had been exercised and if people moved out of the house as soon as they had completed their task, another 15 minutes would have been shaved from the record.

Habitat for Humanity is an international charitable organization that builds simple, affordable houses and sells them on a no-interest, no-profit basis to needy families.

*"A Four Bedroom House in Three Hours, 44 Minutes & 59 Seconds," Avraham Y. Goldratt Institute, *www.goldratt.com*. "Fastest House in the World," Habitat for Humanity International, *www.habitat.org*.

of experimentation if speed is essential. At the same time, it would be difficult to apply CCPM midstream in a project. CCPM requires considerable training and a shift in habits and perspectives that take time to adopt. Although there have been reports of immediate gains, especially in terms of completion times, a long-term management commitment is probably necessary to reap full benefits. See the Snapshot from Practice: The Fastest House in the World for an extreme example of CCPM application.

Reducing Project Scope

Probably the most common response for meeting unattainable deadlines is to reduce or scale back the scope of the project. This invariably leads to a reduction in the functionality of the project. For example, the new car will average only 25 mpg instead of 30, or the software product will have fewer features than originally planned. While scaling back the scope of the project can lead to big savings in both time and money, it may come at a cost of reducing the value of the project. If the car gets lower gas mileage, will it stand up to competitive models? Will customers still want the software minus the features?

The key to reducing a project scope without reducing value is to reassess the true specifications of the project. Often requirements are added under best-case, blue-sky scenarios and represent desirables, but not essentials. Here it is important to talk to the customer and/or project sponsors and explain the situation—you can get it your way but not until February. This may force them to accept an extension or to add money to expedite the project. If not, then a healthy discussion of what the essential requirements are and what items can be compromised in order to meet the deadline needs to take place. More intense re-examination of requirements may actually improve the value of the project by getting it done more quickly and for a lower cost.

Calculating the savings of reduced project scope begins with the work breakdown structure. Reducing functionality means certain tasks, deliverables, or requirements can be reduced or even eliminated. These tasks need to be found and the schedule adjusted. Focus should be on changes in activities on the critical path.

Compromise Quality

Reducing quality is always an option, but it is rarely acceptable or used. If quality is sacrificed, it may be possible to reduce the time of an activity on the critical path.

In practice the methods most commonly used to crash projects are scheduling overtime, outsourcing, and adding resources. Each of these maintains the essence of the original plan. Options that depart from the original project plan include do it twice and fast-tracking. Rethinking of project scope, customer needs, and timing become major considerations for these techniques.

Project Cost–Duration Graph

Nothing on the horizon suggests that the need to shorten project time will change. The challenge for the project manager is to use a quick, logical method to compare the benefits of reducing project time with the cost. When sound, logical methods are absent, it is difficult to isolate those activities that will have the greatest impact on reducing project time at least cost. This section describes a procedure for identifying the costs of reducing project time so that comparisons can be made with the benefits of getting the project completed sooner. The method requires gathering direct and indirect costs for specific project durations. Critical activities are searched to find the lowest direct-cost activities that will shorten the project duration. Total cost for specific project durations are computed and then compared with the benefits of reducing project time—before the project begins or while it is in progress.

Explanation of Project Costs

The general nature of project costs is illustrated in Figure 9.1. The total cost for each duration is the sum of the indirect and direct costs. Indirect costs continue for the life of the project. Hence, any reduction in project duration means a reduction in indirect costs. Direct costs on the graph grow at an increasing rate as the project duration is reduced from its original planned duration. With the information from a graph such as this for a project, managers can quickly judge any alternative such as meeting a time-to-market deadline. Further discussion of indirect and direct costs is necessary before demonstrating a procedure for developing the information for a graph similar to the one depicted in Figure 9.1.

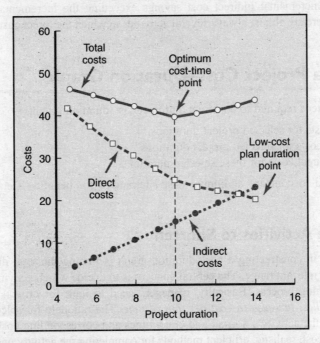

FIGURE 9.1   Project Cost–Duration Graph

Project Indirect Costs

Indirect costs generally represent overhead costs such as supervision, administration, consultants, and interest. Indirect costs cannot be associated with any particular work package or activity, hence the term. Indirect costs vary directly with time. That is, any reduction in time should result in a reduction of indirect costs. For example, if the daily costs of supervision, administration, and consultants are $2,000, any reduction in project duration would represent a savings of $2,000 per day. If indirect costs are a significant percentage of total project costs, reductions in project time can represent very real savings (assuming the indirect resources can be utilized elsewhere).

Project Direct Costs

Direct costs commonly represent labor, materials, equipment, and sometimes subcontractors. Direct costs are assigned directly to a work package and activity, hence the term. The ideal assumption is that direct costs for an activity time represent normal costs, which typically mean low-cost, efficient methods for a normal time.

When project durations are imposed, direct costs may no longer represent low-cost, efficient methods. Costs for the imposed duration date will be higher than for a project duration developed from ideal normal times for activities. Because direct costs are assumed to be developed from normal methods and time, any reduction in activity time should add to the costs of the activity. The sum of the costs of all the work packages or activities represents the total direct costs for the project.

The major plight faced in creating the information for a graph similar to Figure 9.1 is computing the direct cost of shortening individual critical activities and then finding the total direct cost for each project duration as project time is compressed; the process requires selecting those critical activities that cost the least to shorten. (Note: The graph implies that there is always an optimum cost-time point. This is only true if shortening a schedule has incremental indirect cost savings exceeding the incremental direct cost incurred. However, in practice there are almost always several activities in which the direct costs of shortening are less than the indirect costs.)

Constructing a Project Cost–Duration Graph

There are three major steps required to construct a project cost–duration graph:

1. Find total direct costs for selected project durations.
2. Find total indirect costs for selected project durations.
3. Sum direct and indirect costs for these selected durations.

The graph is then used to compare additional cost alternatives for benefits. Details of these steps are presented here.

Determining the Activities to Shorten

The most difficult task in constructing a cost–duration graph is finding the total direct costs for specific project durations over a relevant range. The central concern is to decide which activities to shorten and how far to carry the shortening process. Basically, managers need to look for critical activities that can be shortened with the *smallest increase in cost per unit of time.* The rationale for selecting critical activities depends on identifying the activity's normal and crash times and corresponding costs. *Normal time* for an activity represents low-cost, realistic, efficient methods for completing the activity under normal conditions. Shortening an activity is called *crashing.* The shortest possible time an activity can realistically be completed in is called its *crash time.* The direct cost for completing an activity in its crash time is called *crash cost.* Both normal and crash times and costs are collected from personnel most familiar with completing the activity. Figure 9.2 depicts a hypothetical cost–duration graph for an activity.

The normal time for the activity is 10 time units, and the corresponding cost is $400. The crash time for the activity is five time units and $800. The intersection of the normal time and cost represents the original low-cost, early-start schedule. The crash point represents the maximum time an activity can be compressed. The heavy line connecting the normal and crash points represents the slope, which assumes the cost of reducing the time of the activity is constant *per unit of time.* The assumptions underlying the use of this graph are as follows:

1. The cost-time relationship is linear.
2. Normal time assumes low-cost, efficient methods to complete the activity.
3. Crash time represents a limit—the greatest time reduction possible under realistic conditions.
4. Slope represents cost per unit of time.
5. All accelerations must occur within the normal and crash times.

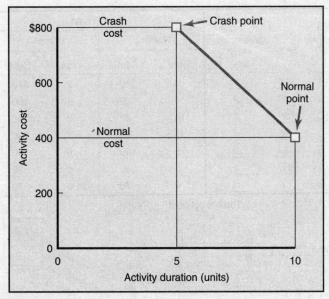

FIGURE 9.2 Activity Graph

Knowing the slope of activities allows managers to compare which critical activities to shorten. The less steep the cost slope of an activity, the less it costs to shorten one time period; a steeper slope means it will cost more to shorten one time unit. The cost per unit of time or slope for any activity is computed by the following equation:

$$\text{Cost slope} = \frac{\text{Rise}}{\text{Run}} = \frac{\text{Crash cost} - \text{Normal cost}}{\text{Normal time} - \text{Crash time}}$$

$$= \frac{CC - NC}{NT - CT} = \frac{\$800 - \$400}{10 - 5}$$

$$= \frac{\$400}{5} = \$80 \text{ per unit of time}$$

In Figure 9.2 the rise is the y axis (cost) and the run is the x axis (duration). The slope of the cost line is $80 for each time unit the activity is reduced; the limit reduction of the activity time is five time units. Comparison of the slopes of all critical activities allows us to determine which activity(ies) to shorten to minimize total direct cost. Given the preliminary project schedule (or one in progress) with all activities set to their early-start times, the process of searching critical activities as candidates for reduction can begin. The total direct cost for each specific compressed project duration must be found.

A Simplified Example

Figure 9.3A presents normal and crash times and costs for each activity, the computed slope and time reduction limit, the total direct cost, and the project network with a duration of 25 time units. Note the total direct cost for the 25-period duration is $450. This is an anchor point to begin the procedure of shortening the critical path(s) and finding the total direct costs for each specific duration less than 25 time units. The

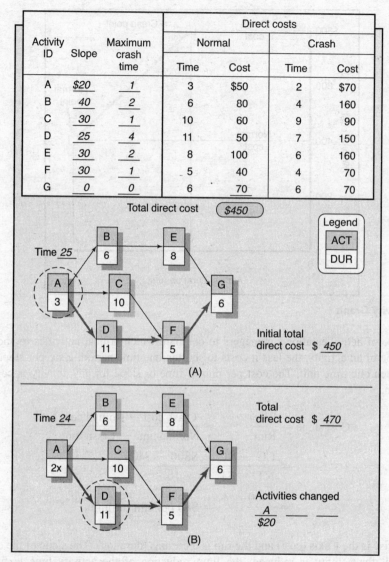

| | | | Direct costs | | | |
| | | | Normal | | Crash | |
Activity ID	Slope	Maximum crash time	Time	Cost	Time	Cost
A	$20	1	3	$50	2	$70
B	40	2	6	80	4	160
C	30	1	10	60	9	90
D	25	4	11	50	7	150
E	30	2	8	100	6	160
F	30	1	5	40	4	70
G	0	0	6	70	6	70

Total direct cost $450

Legend
ACT
DUR

Time 25

B 6
E 8
A 3
C 10
D 11
F 5
G 6

Initial total direct cost $ 450

(A)

Time 24

B 6
E 8
A 2x
C 10
D 11
F 5
G 6

Total direct cost $ 470

Activities changed
A
$20

(B)

FIGURE 9.3   Cost–Duration Trade-off Example

maximum time reduction of an activity is simply the difference between the normal and crash times for an activity. For example, activity D can be reduced from a normal time of 11 time units to a crash time of 7 time units, or a maximum of 4 time units. The positive slope for activity D is computed as follows:

$$\text{Slope} = \frac{\text{Crash cost} - \text{Normal cost}}{\text{Normal time} - \text{Crash time}} = \frac{\$150 - \$50}{11 - 7}$$

$$= \frac{\$100}{4} = \$25 \text{ per period reduced}$$

The network shows the critical path to be activities A, D, F, G. Because it is impossible to shorten activity G, activity A is circled because it is the least-cost candidate; that is, its slope ($20) is less than the slopes for activities D and F ($25 and $30). Reducing activity A one time unit cuts the project duration to 24 time units but increases the total direct costs to $470 ($450 + $20 = $470). Figure 9.3B reflects these changes. The duration of activity A has been reduced to two time units; the "x" indicates the activity cannot be reduced any further. Activity D is circled because it costs the least ($25) to shorten the project to 23 time units. Compare the cost of activity F. The total direct cost for a project duration of 23 time units is $495 (see Figure 9.4A).

Observe that the project network in Figure 9.4A now has two critical paths—A, C, F, G and A, D, F, G. Reducing the project to 22 time units will require that activity F be reduced; thus, it is circled. This change is reflected in Figure 9.4B. The total direct cost for 22 time units is $525. This reduction has created a third critical path—A, B, E, G; all activities are critical. The least-cost method for reducing the project duration to

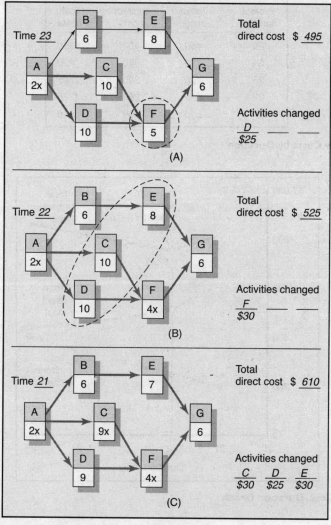

FIGURE 9.4   Cost–Duration Trade-off Example (continued)

21 time units is the combination of the circled activities C, D, E which cost $30, $25, $30, respectively, and increase total direct costs to $610. The results of these changes are depicted in Figure 9.4C. Although some activities can still be reduced (those without the "x" next to the activity time), no activity or combination of activities will result in a reduction in the project duration.

With the total direct costs for the array of specific project durations found, the next step is to collect the indirect costs for these same durations. These costs are typically a rate per day and are easily obtained from the accounting department. Figure 9.5 presents the total direct costs, total indirect costs, and total project costs. These same costs are plotted in Figure 9.6. This graph shows that the optimum cost-time duration is 22 time units and $775. Assuming the project will actually materialize as planned, any movement away from this time duration will increase project costs. The movement from 25 to 22 time units occurs because, in this range, the absolute slopes of the indirect costs are greater than the direct cost slopes.

Project duration	Direct costs	+	Indirect costs	=	Total costs
25	450		400		$850
24	470		350		820
23	495		300		795
22	525		250		775
21	610		200		810

FIGURE 9.5   Summary Costs by Duration

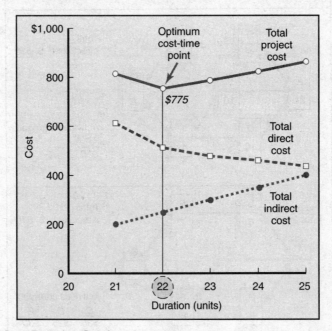

FIGURE 9.6   Project Cost–Duration Graph

Practical Considerations

Using the Project Cost–Duration Graph

This graph, as presented in Figures 9.1 and 9.6, is valuable to compare any proposed alternative or change with the optimum cost and time. More importantly, the creation of such a graph keeps the importance of indirect costs in the forefront of decision making. Indirect costs are frequently forgotten in the field when the pressure for action is intense. Finally, such a graph can be used before the project begins or while the project is in progress. Creating the graph in the preproject planning phase without an imposed duration is the first choice because normal time is more meaningful. Creating the graph in the project planning phase with an imposed duration is less desirable because normal time is made to fit the imposed date and is probably not low cost. Creating the graph after the project has started is the least desirable because some alternatives may be ruled out of the decision process. Managers may choose not to use the formal procedure demonstrated. However, regardless of the method used, the principles and concepts inherent in the formal procedure are highly applicable in practice and should be considered in any cost–duration trade-off decision.

Crash Times

Collecting crash times for even a moderate-size project can be difficult. The meaning of crash time is difficult to communicate. What is meant when you define crash time as "the shortest time you can realistically complete an activity"? Crash time is open to different interpretations and judgments. Some estimators feel very uncomfortable providing crash times. Regardless of the comfort level, the accuracy of crash times and costs is frequently rough at best, when compared with normal time and cost.

Linearity Assumption

Because the accuracy of compressed activity times and costs is questionable, the concern of some theorists—that the relationship between cost and time is not linear but curvilinear—is seldom a concern for practicing managers. Reasonable, quick comparisons can be made using the linear assumption. The simple approach is adequate for most projects. There are rare situations in which activities cannot be crashed by single time units. Instead, crashing is "all or nothing." For example, activity A will take 10 days (for say $1,000) or it will take 7 days (for say $1,500), but no options exist in which activity A will take 8 or 9 days to complete. In a few rare cases of very large, complex, long-duration projects, the use of present value techniques may be useful; such techniques are beyond the scope of this text.

Choice of Activities to Crash Revisited

The cost–time crashing method relies on choosing the cheapest method for reducing the duration of the project. There are other factors that should be assessed beyond simply cost. First, the inherent risks involved in crashing particular activities need to be considered. Some activities are riskier to crash than others. For example, accelerating the completion of a software design code may not be wise if it increases the likelihood of errors surfacing downstream. Conversely, crashing a more expensive activity may be wise if fewer inherent risks are involved.

Second, the timing of activities needs to be considered. Crashing a critical activity early in the project may result in wasted money if some other critical activity is finished early or some noncritical path becomes the new critical path. In such cases, the money spent early is gone and no benefit comes from early completion by crashing the activity. Conversely, it may be wise to crash an early critical activity when later activities are likely to be delayed and absorb the time gained. Then the manager would still have the option of crashing final activities to get back on schedule.

Finally, the impact crashing would have on the morale and motivation of the project team needs to be assessed. If the least-cost method repeatedly signals a subgroup to accelerate progress, fatigue and resentment may set in. Conversely, if overtime pay is involved, other team members may resent not having access to this benefit. This situation can lead to tension within the entire project team. Good project managers gauge the response that crashing activities will have on the entire project team. See Snapshot from Practice: I'll Bet You . . . for a novel approach to motivating employees to work faster.

Time Reduction Decisions and Sensitivity

Should the project owner or project manager go for the optimum cost-time? The answer is, "It depends." Risk must be considered. Recall from our example that the optimum project time point represented a reduced project cost and was less than the original normal project time (review Figure 9.6). The project direct-cost line near the normal point is usually relatively flat. Because indirect costs for the project are usually greater in the same range, the optimum cost-time point is less than the normal time point. Logic of the cost-time procedure suggests managers should reduce the project duration to the lowest total cost point and duration.

How far to reduce the project time from the normal time toward the optimum depends on the *sensitivity* of the project network. A network is sensitive if it has several critical or near-critical paths. In our example project movement toward the optimum time requires spending money to reduce critical activities, resulting in slack reduction and/or more critical paths and activities. Slack reduction in a project with several near-critical paths increases the risk of being late. The practical outcome can be a higher total project cost if some near-critical activities are delayed and become critical; the money spent reducing activities on the original critical path would be wasted. Sensitive networks require careful analysis. The bottom line is that compression of projects with several near-critical paths reduces scheduling flexibility and increases the risk of delaying the project. The outcome of such analysis will probably suggest only a partial movement from the normal time toward the optimum time.

There is a positive situation where moving toward the optimum time can result in very real, large savings—this occurs when the network is *insensitive*. A project network is insensitive if it has a dominant critical path, that is, no near-critical paths. In this project circumstance, movement from the normal time point toward the optimum time will *not* create new or near-critical activities. The bottom line here is that the reduction of the slack of noncritical activities increases the risk of their becoming critical only slightly when compared with the effect in a sensitive network. Insensitive networks hold the greatest potential for real, sometimes large, savings in total project costs with a minimum risk of noncritical activities becoming critical.

Insensitive networks are not a rarity in practice; they occur in perhaps 25 percent of all projects. For example, a light rail project team observed from their network a dominant critical path and relatively high indirect costs. It soon became clear that by spending some dollars on a few critical activities, very large savings of indirect costs could be realized. Savings of several million dollars were spent extending the rail line and adding another station. The logic found in this example is just as applicable to small projects as large ones. Insensitive networks with high indirect costs can produce large savings.

Ultimately, deciding if and which activities to crash is a judgment call requiring careful consideration of the options available, the costs and risks involved, and the importance of meeting a deadline.

Snapshot from Practice   I'll Bet You . . .

Michael Newman/Photoedit.

The focus of this chapter has been on how project managers crash activities by typically assigning additional manpower and equipment to cut significant time off of scheduled tasks. Project managers often encounter situations in which they need to motivate individuals to accelerate the completion of a specific, critical task. Imagine the following scenario.

Brue Young just received a priority assignment from corporate headquarters. The preliminary engineering sketches that were due tomorrow need to be e-mailed to the West Coast by 4:00 P.M. today so that the model shop can begin construction of a prototype to present to top management. He approaches Danny Whitten, the draftsman responsible for the task, whose initial response is, "That's impossible!" While he agrees that it would be very difficult he does not believe that it is as impossible as Danny suggests or that Danny truly believes that. What should he do?

He tells Danny that he knows this is going to be a rush job, but he is confident that he can do it. When Danny balks, he responds, "I tell you what, I'll make a bet with you. If you are able to finish the design by 4:00, I'll make sure you get two of the company's tickets to tomorrow night's Celtics–Knicks basketball game." Danny accepts the challenge, works feverishly to complete the assignment, and is able to take his daughter to her first professional basketball game.

Conversations with project managers reveal that many use bets like this one to motivate extraordinary performance. These bets range from tickets to sporting and entertainment events to gift certificates at high-class restaurants to a well-deserved afternoon off. For bets to work they need to adhere to the principles of expectancy theory of motivation. Boiled down to simple terms, expectancy theory rests on three key questions:

1. Can I do it (Is it possible to meet the challenge)?
2. Will I get it (Can I demonstrate that I met the challenge and can I trust the project manager will deliver his/her end of the bargain)?
3. Is it worth it (Is the payoff of sufficient personal value to warrant the risk and extra effort)?

If in the mind of the participant the answer to any of these three questions is no, then the person is unlikely to accept the challenge. However, when the answers are affirmative, then the individual is likely to accept the bet and be motivated to meet the challenge.

Bets can be effective motivational tools and add an element of excitement and fun to project work. But, the following practical advice should be heeded:

1. The bet has greater significance if it also benefits family members or significant others. Being able to take a son or daughter to a professional basketball game allows that individual to "score points" at home through work. These bets also recognize and reward the support project members receive from their families and reinforces the importance of their work to loved ones.
2. Bets should be used sparingly; otherwise everything can become negotiable. They should be used only under special circumstances that require extraordinary effort.
3. Individual bets should involve clearly recognizable individual effort, otherwise others may become jealous and discord may occur within a group. As long as others see it as requiring truly remarkable, "beyond the call of duty" effort, they will consider it fair and warranted.

What if Cost, Not Time, Is the Issue?

In today's fast-paced world, there appears to be a greater emphasis on getting things done quickly. Still, organizations are always looking for ways to get things done cheaply. This is especially true for fixed-bid projects, where profit margin is derived from the difference between the bid and actual cost of the project. Every dollar saved is a dollar in your pocket. Sometimes, in order to secure a contract, bids are tight, which puts added pressure on cost containment. In other cases, there are financial incentives tied to cost containment.

Even in situations where cost is transferred to customers there is pressure to reduce cost. Cost overruns make for unhappy customers and can damage future business opportunities. Budgets can be fixed or cut, and when contingency funds are exhausted, then cost overruns have to be made up with remaining activities.

As discussed earlier, shortening project duration may come at the expense of overtime, adding additional personnel, and using more expensive equipment and/or materials. Conversely, sometimes cost savings can be generated by extending the duration of a project. This may allow for a smaller workforce, less-skilled (expensive) labor, and even cheaper equipment and materials to be used. Below are some of the more commonly used options for cutting costs.

Reduce Project Scope

Just as scaling back the scope of the project can gain time, delivering less than what was originally planned also produces significant savings. Again, calculating the savings of a reduced project scope begins with the work breakdown structure. However, since time is not the issue, you do not need to focus on critical activities.

Have Owner Take on More Responsibility

One way of reducing project costs is identifying tasks that customers can do themselves. Homeowners frequently use this method to reduce costs on home improvement projects. For example, to reduce the cost of a bathroom remodel, a homeowner may agree to paint the room instead of paying the contractor to do it. On IS projects, a customer may agree to take on some of the responsibility for testing equipment or providing in-house training. Naturally, this arrangement is best negotiated before the project begins. Customers are less receptive to this idea if you suddenly spring it on them. An advantage of this method is that, while costs are lowered, the original scope is retained. Clearly this option is limited to areas in which the customer has expertise and the capability to pick up the tasks.

Outsourcing Project Activities or Even the Entire Project

When estimates exceed budget, it not only makes sense to re-examine the scope but also search for cheaper ways to complete the project. Perhaps instead of relying on internal resources, it would be more cost effective to outsource segments or even the entire project, opening up work to external price competition. Specialized subcontractors often enjoy unique advantages, such as material discounts for large quantities, as well as equipment that not only gets the work done more quickly but also less expensively. They may have lower overhead and labor costs. For example, to reduce costs of software projects, many American firms outsource work to firms operating in India where the salary of a software engineer is one-third that of an American software engineer. However, outsourcing means you have less control over the project and will need to have clearly definable deliverables.

Brainstorming Cost Savings Options

Just as project team members can be a rich source of ideas for accelerating project activities, they can offer tangible ways for reducing project costs. For example, one project manager reported that his team was able to come up with over $75,000 worth of cost saving suggestions without jeopardizing the scope of the project. Project managers should not underestimate the value of simply asking if there is a cheaper, better way.

Summary

The need for reducing the project duration occurs for many reasons such as imposed duration dates, time-to-market considerations, incentive contracts, key resource needs, high overhead costs, or simply unforeseen delays. These situations are very common in practice and are known as cost-time trade-off decisions. This chapter presented a logical, formal process for assessing the implications of situations that involve shortening the project duration. Crashing the project duration increases the *risk* of being late. How far to reduce the project duration from the normal time toward the optimum depends on the *sensitivity* of the project network. A sensitive network is one that has several critical or near-critical paths. Great care should be taken when shortening sensitive networks to avoid increasing project risks. Conversely, insensitive networks represent opportunities for potentially large project cost savings by eliminating some overhead costs with little downside risk.

Alternative strategies for reducing project time were discussed within the context of whether or not the project is resource limited. Project acceleration typically comes at a cost of either spending money for more resources or compromising the scope of the project. If the latter is the case, then it is essential that all relevant stakeholders be consulted so that everyone accepts the changes that have to be made. One other key point is the difference in implementing time-reducing activities in the midst of project execution versus incorporating them into the project plan. You typically have far fewer options once the project is underway than before it begins. This is especially true if you want to take advantage of the new scheduling methodologies such as fast-tracking and critical-chain. Time spent up front considering alternatives and developing contingency plans will lead to time savings in the end.

Key Terms

Crash point	Fast-tracking	Project cost–duration
Crash time	Indirect costs	graph
Direct costs	Outsourcing	

Review Questions

1. What are five common reasons for crashing a project?
2. What are the advantages and disadvantages of reducing project scope to accelerate a project? What can be done to reduce the disadvantages?
3. Why is scheduling overtime a popular choice for getting projects back on schedule? What are the potential problems for relying on this option?
4. Identify four indirect costs you might find on a moderately complex project. Why are these costs classified as indirect?

5. How can a cost–duration graph be used by the project manager? Explain.
6. Reducing the project duration increases the risk of being late. Explain.
7. It is possible to shorten the critical path and save money. Explain how.

Exercises

1. Draw a project network from the following information.

Activity	Predecessor	Duration
A	None	2
B	A	4
C	A	3
D	A	2
E	B	3
F	C	6
G	C, D	5
H	E, F	6
I	G	5
J	H, I	5

Activities B and H can be shortened to a minimum of 2 weeks. Which activity would you shorten to reduce the project duration by 2 weeks? Why?

2. Assume the network and data that follow. Compute the total direct cost for each project duration. If the indirect costs for each project duration are $400 (19 time units), $350 (18), $300 (17), and $250 (16), compute the total project cost for each duration. Plot the total direct, indirect, and project costs for each of these durations on a cost-time graph. What is the optimum cost-time schedule for the project? What is this cost?

Act.	Crash Cost (Slope)	Maximum Crash Time	Normal Time	Normal Cost
A	20	1	3	50
B	60	2	5	60
C	40	1	3	70
D	0	0	10	50
E	50	3	6	100
F	100	3	7	90
G	70	1	5	50
				$470

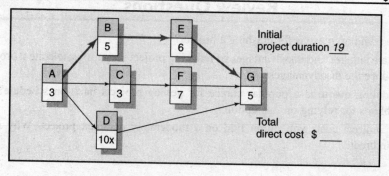

3. Given the data and information that follow, compute the total direct cost for each project duration. If the indirect costs for each project duration are $90 (15 time units), $70 (14), $50 (13), $40 (12), and $30 (11), compute the total project cost for each duration. What is the optimum cost-time schedule for the project? What is this cost?

Act.	Crash Cost (Slope)	Maximum Crash Time	Normal Time	Normal Cost
A	20	1	5	50
B	60	2	3	60
C	0	0	4	70
D	10	1	2	50
E	60	3	5	100
F	100	1	2	90
G	30	1	5	50
H	40	0	2	60
I	200	1	3	200
				$730

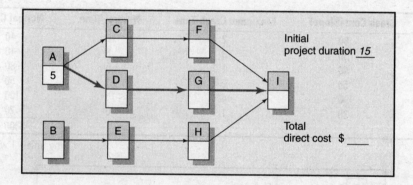

Initial project duration 15

Total direct cost $ ____

4. If the indirect costs for each duration are $1,200 for 16 weeks, $1,130 for 15 weeks, $1,000 for 14 weeks, $900 for 13 weeks, $860 for 12 weeks, $820 for 11 weeks and $790 for 10 weeks, compute the total costs for each duration. Plot these costs on a graph. What is the optimum cost-time schedule?

Act.	Crash Cost (Slope)	Maximum Crash Time	Normal Time	Normal Cost
A	10	1	4	30
B	70	2	7	60
C	0	0	1	80
D	20	2	4	40
E	50	3	5	110
F	200	3	5	90
G	30	1	2	60
H	40	1	2	70
I	0	0	2	140
				$680

Time unit = 1 week

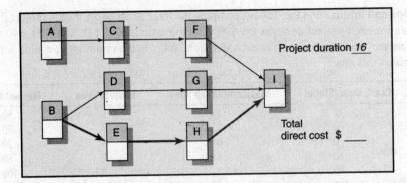

5. If the indirect costs for each duration are $300 for 27 weeks, $240 for 26 weeks, $180 for 25 weeks, $120 for 24 weeks, $60 for 23 weeks, and $50 for 22 weeks, compute the direct, indirect and total costs for each duration. What is the optimum cost-time schedule? The customer offers you $10 dollars for every week you shorten the project from your original network. Would you take it? If so for how many weeks?

Act.	Crash Cost (Slope)	Maximum Crash Time	Normal Time	Normal Cost
A	80	2	10	40
B	30	3	8	10
C	40	1	5	80
D	50	2	11	50
E	100	4	15	100
F	30	1	6	20
				$300

Time unit = 1 week

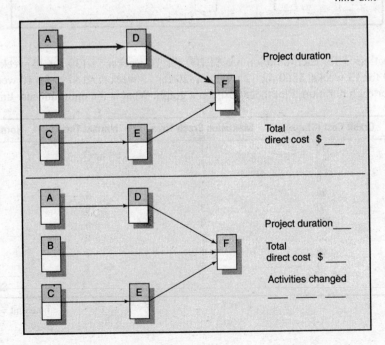

6. Use the information contained below to compress one time unit per move using the least cost method. Reduce the schedule until you reach the crash point of the network. For each move identify what activity(s) was crashed, the adjusted total cost, and explain your choice if you have to choose between activities that cost the same.

   Note: Crash point of the network is the point in which the duration cannot be reduced any further.

Activity ID	Slope	Maximum Crash Time	Normal Time	Normal Cost	Crash Time	Crash Cost
A	—	0	4	$50	0	—
B`	$40	3	5	70	2	$190
C	40	1	5	80	4	40
D	40	2	4	40	2	120
E	40	2	5	60	3	140
F	40	1	5	50	4	90
G	30	1	4	70	3	160
H	30	1	4	80	3	110
I	—	0	3	50	0	—

Total direct normal costs—$550

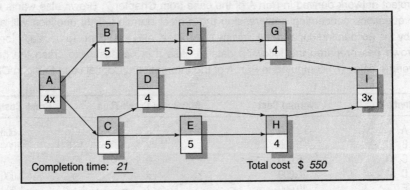

Completion time: _21_   Total cost $ _550_

References

Abdel-Hamid, T., and S. Madnick, *Software Project Dynamics: An Integrated Approach* (Englewood Cliffs, NJ: Prentice Hall, 1991).

Baker, B. M., "Cost/Time Trade-off Analysis for the Critical Path Method," *Journal of the Operational Research Society,* 48 (12), 1997, pp. 1241–44.

Brooks, F. P., Jr., *The Mythical Man-Month: Essays on Software Engineering Anniversary Edition* (Reading, MA: Addison-Wesley Longman, Inc., 1994), pp. 15–26.

DeMarco, T., *Slack: Getting Past Burnout, Busywork, and the Myth of Total Efficiency* (New York: Broadway, 2002).

Ibbs, C. W., S. A. Lee, and M. I. Li, "Fast-Tracking's Impact on Project Change," *Project Management Journal,* 29 (4), 1998, pp. 35–42.

Khang, D. B., and M.Yin, "Time, Cost, and Quality Tradeoff in Project Management," *International Journal of Project Management,* 17 (4), 1999, pp. 249–56.

Perrow, L. A., *Finding Time: How Corporations, Individuals, and Families Can Benefit From New Work Practices* (Ithaca, NY: Cornell University Press, 1997).

Roemer, T. R., R. Ahmadi, and R. Wang, "Time-Cost Trade-offs in Overlapped Product Development," *Operations Research,* 48 (6) 2000, pp. 858–65.

Smith, P. G., and D.G. Reinersten, *Developing Products in Half the Time* (New York: Van Nostrand Reinhold, 1995).

Verzuh, E., *The Fast Forward MBA in Project Management* (New York: John Wiley, 1999).

Vroom, V. H., *Work and Motivation* (New York: John Wiley & Sons, 1964).

CASE 9.1

International Capital, Inc.—Part B

Given the project network derived in Part A of the case from Chapter 7, Brown also wants to be prepared to answer any questions concerning compressing the project duration. This question will almost always be entertained by the accounting department, review committee, and the client. To be ready for the compression question, Brown has prepared the following data in case it is necessary to crash the project. (Use your weighted average times (t_e) computed in Part A of the International Capital case found in Chapter 7.)

Activity	Normal Cost	Maximum Crash Time	Crash Cost/Day
A	$ 3,000	3	$ 500
B	5,000	2	1000
C	6,000	0	—
D	20,000	3	3,000
E	10,000	2	1,000
F	7,000	1	1,000
G	20,000	2	3,000
H	8,000	1	2,000
I	5,000	1	2,000
J	7,000	1	1,000
K	12,000	6	1,000
Total normal costs = $103,000			

Using the data provided, determine the activity crashing decisions and best-time cost project duration. Given the information you have developed, what suggestions would you give Brown to ensure she is well prepared for the project review committee? Assume the overhead costs for this project are $700 per workday. Will this alter your suggestions?

CASE 9.2

Whitbread World Sailboat Race

Each year countries enter their sailing vessels in the nine-month Round the World Whitbread Sailboat Race. In recent years, about 14 countries entered sailboats in the race. Each year's sailboat entries represent the latest technologies and human skills each country can muster.

Bjorn Ericksen has been selected as a project manager because of his past experience as a master helmsman and because of his recent fame as the "best designer of racing sailboats in the world." Bjorn is pleased and proud to have the opportunity to design, build, test, and train the crew for next year's Whitbread entry for his country. Bjorn has picked Karin Knutsen (as chief design engineer) and Trygve Wallvik (as master helmsman) to be team leaders responsible for getting next year's entry ready for the traditional parade of all entries on the Thames River in the United Kingdom, which signals the start of the race.

As Bjorn begins to think of a project plan, he sees two parallel paths running through the project—design and construction and crew training. Last year's boat will be used for training until the new entry can have the crew on board to learn maintenance tasks. Bjorn calls Karin and Trygve together to develop a project plan. All three agree the major goal is to have a winning boat and crew ready to compete in next year's competition at a cost of $3.2 million. A check of Bjorn's calendar indicates he has 45 weeks before next year's vessel must leave port for the United Kingdom to start the race.

The Kickoff Meeting

Bjorn asks Karin to begin by describing the major activities and the sequence required to design, construct, and test the boat. Karin starts by noting that design of the hull, deck, mast, and accessories should only take six weeks—given the design prints from past race entries and a few prints from other countries' entries. After the design is complete, the hull can be constructed, the mast ordered, sails ordered, and accessories ordered. The hull will require 12 weeks to complete. The mast can be ordered and will require a lead time of eight weeks; the seven sails can be ordered and will take six weeks to get; accessories can be ordered and will take 15 weeks to receive. As soon as the hull is finished, the ballast tanks can be installed, requiring two weeks. Then the deck can be built, which will require five weeks. Concurrently, the hull can be treated with special sealant and friction-resistance coating, taking three weeks. When the deck is completed and mast and accessories received, the mast and sails can be installed, requiring two weeks; the accessories can be installed, which will take six weeks. When all of these activities have been completed, the ship can be sea-tested, which should take five weeks. Karin believes she can have firm cost estimates for the boat in about two weeks.

Trygve believes he can start selecting the 12-man or woman crew and securing their housing immediately. He believes it will take six weeks to get a committed crew on-site and three weeks to secure housing for the crew members. Trygve reminds Bjorn that last year's vessel must be ready to use for training the moment the crew is on-site until the new vessel is ready for testing. Keeping the old vessel operating will cost $4,000 per week as long as it is used. Once the crew is on-site and housed, they can develop and implement a routine sailing and maintenance training program, which will take 15 weeks (using the old vessel). Also, once the crew is selected and on-site, crew equipment can be selected, taking only two weeks. Then crew equipment can be ordered; it will take five weeks to arrive. When the crew equipment and maintenance training program are complete, crew maintenance on the new vessel can begin; this should take 10 weeks. But crew maintenance on the new vessel cannot begin until the deck is complete and the mast, sails, and accessories have arrived. Once crew maintenance on the new vessel begins, the new vessel will cost $6,000 per week until sea training is complete. After the new ship maintenance is complete and while the boat is being tested, initial sailing training can be implemented; training should take seven weeks. Finally, after the boat is tested and initial training is complete, regular sea training can be implemented—weather permitting; regular sea training requires eight weeks. Trygve believes he can put the cost estimates together in a week, given last year's expenses.

Bjorn is pleased with the expertise displayed by his team leaders. But he believes they need to have someone develop one of those critical path networks to see if they can safely meet the start deadline for the race. Karin and Trygve agree. Karin suggests the cost estimates should also include crash costs for any activities that can be compressed and the resultant costs for crashing. Karin also suggests the team complete the following priority matrix for project decision making:

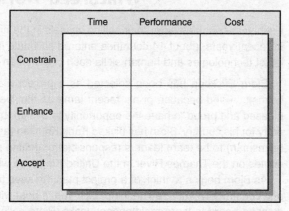

	Time	Performance	Cost
Constrain			
Enhance			
Accept			

FIGURE C9.1   Project Priority Matrix: Whitbread Project

Two Weeks Later

Karin and Trygve submit the following cost estimates for each activity and corresponding crash costs to Bjorn (costs are in thousands of dollars):

Activity		Normal Time	Normal Cost	Crash Time	Crash Cost
A	Design	6	$ 40	4	$ 160
B	Build hull	12	1,000	10	1,400
C	Install ballast tanks	2	100	2	100
D	Order mast	8	100	7	140
E	Order sails	6	40	6	40
F	Order accessories	15	600	13	800
G	Build deck	5	200	5	200
H	Coat hull	3	40	3	40
I	Install accessories	6	300	5	400
J	Install mast and sails	2	40	1	80
K	Test	5	60	4	100
L	Sea trials	8	200	7	450
M	Select crew	6	10	5	20
N	Secure housing	3	30	3	30
O	Select crew equipment	2	10	2	10
P	Order crew equipment	5	30	5	30
Q	Routine sail and maintenance	15	40	12	130
R	Crew maintenance training	10	100	9	340
S	Initial sail training	7	50	5	350

Bjorn reviews the materials and wonders if the project will come in within the budget of $3.2 million and in 45 weeks. Advise the Whitbread team of their situation.

CASE 9.3

Nightingale Project—A

You are the assistant project manager to Rassy Brown, who is in charge of the Nightingale project. Nightingale was the code name given to the development of a handheld electronic medical reference guide. Nightingale would be designed for emergency medical technicians and paramedics who need a quick reference guide to use in emergency situations.

Rassy and her project team were developing a project plan aimed at producing 30 working models in time for MedCON, the biggest medical equipment trade show each year. Meeting the MedCON October 25 deadline was critical to success. All the major medical equipment manufacturers demonstrated and took orders for new products at MedCON. Rassy had also heard rumors that competitors were considering developing a similar product, and she knew that being first to market would have a significant sales advantage. Besides, top management made funding contingent upon developing a workable plan for meeting the MedCON deadline.

The project team spent the morning working on the schedule for Nightingale. They started with the WBS and developed the information for a network, adding activities when needed. Then the team added the time estimates they had collected for each activity. Following is the preliminary information for activities with duration time and predecessors:

Activity	Description	Duration	Predecessor
1	Architectural decisions	10	None
2	Internal specifications	20	1
3	External specifications	18	1
4	Feature specifications	15	1
5	Voice recognition	15	2,3
6	Case	4	2,3
7	Screen	2	2,3
8	Speaker output jacks	2	2,3
9	Tape mechanism	2	2,3
10	Database	40	4
11	Microphone/soundcard	5	4
12	Pager	4	4
13	Barcode reader	3	4
14	Alarm clock	4	4
15	Computer I/O	5	4
16	Review design	10	5,6,7,8,9,10,11,12,13,14,15
17	Price components	5	5,6,7,8,9,10,11,12,13,14,15
18	Integration	15	16,17
19	Document design	35	16
20	Procure prototype components	20	18
21	Assemble prototypes	10	20
22	Lab test prototypes	20	21
23	Field test prototypes	20	19,22
24	Adjust design	20	23
25	Order stock parts	15	24
26	Order custom parts	2	24
27	Assemble first production unit	10	25, FS—8 time units 26, FS—13 time units
28	Test unit	10	27
29	Produce 30 units	15	28
30	Train sales representatives	10	29

Use any project network computer program available to you to develop the schedule for activities (see Case Appendix for further instructions)—noting late and early times, the critical path, and estimated completion for the project.

Prepare a short memo that addresses the following questions:

1. Will the project as planned meet the October 25th deadline?
2. What activities lie on the critical path?
3. How sensitive is this network?

CASE 9.4

Nightingale Project—B

Rassy and the team were concerned with the results of your analysis. They spent the afternoon brainstorming alternative ways for shortening the project duration. They rejected outsourcing activities because most of the work was developmental in nature and could only be done in-house. They considered altering the scope of the project by eliminating some of the proposed product features. After much debate, they felt they could not compromise any of the core features and be successful in the marketplace. They then turned their attention to accelerating the completion of activities through overtime and adding additional technical manpower. Rassy had built into her proposal a discretionary fund of $200,000. She was willing to invest up to half of this fund to accelerate the project, but wanted to hold onto at least $100,000 to deal with unexpected problems. After a lengthy discussion, her team concluded that the following activities could be reduced at the specified cost:

- Development of voice recognition system could be reduced from 15 days to 10 days at a cost of $15,000.
- Creation of database could be reduced from 40 days to 35 days at a cost of $35,000.
- Document design could be reduced from 35 days to 30 days at a cost of $25,000.
- External specifications could be reduced from 18 days to 12 days at a cost of $20,000.
- Procure prototype components could be reduced from 20 days to 15 days at a cost of $30,000.
- Order stock parts could be reduced from 15 days to 10 days at a cost of $20,000.

Ken Clark, a development engineer, pointed out that the network contained only finish-to-start relationships and that it might be possible to reduce project duration by creating start-to-start lags. For example, he said that his people would not have to wait for all of the field tests to be completed to begin making final adjustments in the design. They could start making adjustments after the first 15 days of testing. The project team spent the remainder of the day analyzing how they could introduce lags into the network to hopefully shorten the project. They concluded that the following finish-to-start relationships could be converted into lags:

- Document design could begin 5 days after the start of the review design.
- Adjust design could begin 15 days after the start of field test prototypes.
- Order stock parts could begin 5 days after the start of adjust design.
- Order custom parts could begin 5 days after the start of adjust design.
- Training sales representatives could begin 5 days after the start of test unit and completed 5 days after the production of 30 units.

As the meeting adjourns, Rassy turns to you and tells you to assess the options presented and try to develop a schedule that will meet the October 25th deadline. You are to prepare a report to be presented to the project team that answers the following questions:

1. Is it possible to meet the deadline?
2. If so, how would you recommend changing the original schedule (Part A) and why? Assess the relative impact of crashing activities versus introducing lags to shorten project duration.
3. What would the new schedule look like?
4. What other factors should be considered before finalizing the schedule?

Case Appendix: Technical Details

Create your project schedule and assess your options based on the following information:

1. The project will begin the first working day in January.
2. The following holidays are observed: January 1, Memorial Day (last Monday in May), July 4, Labor Day (first Monday in September), Thanksgiving Day (fourth Thursday in November), December 25 and 26.
3. If a holiday falls on a Saturday, then Friday will be given as an extra day off; if it falls on a Sunday, then Monday will be given as a day off.
4. The project team works Monday through Friday.
5. If you choose to reduce the duration of any one of the activities mentioned, then it must be for the specified time and cost (i.e., you cannot choose to reduce database to 37 days at a reduced cost; you can only reduce it to 35 days at a cost of $35,000).
6. You can only spend up to $100,000 to reduce project activities; lags do not contain any additional costs.

CASE 9.5

The "Now" Wedding—Part A

On December 31 of last year, Lauren burst into the family living room and announced that she and Connor (her college boyfriend) were going to be married. After recovering from the shock, her mother hugged her and asked, "When?" The following conversation resulted:

Lauren: January 21.

Mom: What?

Dad: The Now Wedding will be the social hit of the year. Wait a minute. Why so soon?

Lauren: Because on January 30 Connor, who is in the National Guard, will be shipping out overseas. We want a week for a honeymoon.

Mom: But Honey, we can't possibly finish all the things that need to be done by then. Remember all the details that were involved in your sister's wedding? Even if we start tomorrow, it takes a day to reserve the church and reception hall, and they need at least 14 days' notice. That has to be done before we can start decorating, which takes 3 days. An extra $200 on Sunday would probably cut that 14 day notice to 7 days, though.

Dad: Oh, boy!

Lauren: I want Jane Summers to be my maid of honor.

Dad: But she's in the Peace Corps in Guatemala, isn't she? It would take her 10 days to get ready and drive up here.

Lauren: But we could fly her up in 2 days and it would only cost $1,000.

Dad: Oh, boy!

Mom: And catering! It takes 2 days to choose the cake and decorations, and Jack's Catering wants at least 5 days' notice. Besides, we'd have to have those things before we could start decorating.

Lauren: Can I wear your wedding dress, Mom?

Mother: Well, we'd have to replace some lace, but you could wear it, yes. We could order the lace from New York when we order the material for the bridesmaids' dresses. It takes 8 days to order and receive the material. The pattern needs to be chosen first, and that would take 3 days.

Dad: We could get the material here in 5 days if we paid an extra $20 to airfreight it. Oh, boy!

Lauren: I want Mrs. Jacks to work on the dresses.

Mom: But she charges $48 a day.

Dad: Oh, boy!

Mom: If we did all the sewing we could finish the dresses in 11 days. If Mrs. Jacks helped we could cut that down to 6 days at a cost of $48 for each day less than 11 days. She is very good too.

Lauren: I don't want anyone but her.

Mom: It would take another 2 days to do the final fitting and 2 more days to clean and press the dresses. They would have to be ready by rehearsal night. We must have rehearsal the night before the wedding.

Dad: Everything should be ready rehearsal night.

Mom: We've forgotten something. The invitations!

Dad: We should order the invitations from Bob's Printing shop, and that usually takes 7 days. I'll bet he would do it in 6 days if we slipped him an extra $20!

Mom: It would take us 2 days to choose the invitation style before we could order them and we want the envelopes printed with our return address.

Lauren: Oh! That will be elegant.

Mom: The invitations should go out at least 10 days before the wedding. If we let them go any later, some of the relatives would get theirs too late to come and that would make them mad. I'll bet that if we didn't get them out until 8 days before the wedding, Aunt Ethel couldn't make it and she would reduce her wedding gift by $200.

Dad: Oh, boy!!

Mom: We'll have to take them to the Post Office to mail them and that takes a day. Addressing would take 3 days unless we hired some part-time girls and we can't start until the printer is finished. If we hired the girls we could probably save 2 days by spending $40 for each day saved.

Lauren: We need to get gifts for the bridesmaids. I could spend a day and do that.

Mom: Before we can even start to write out those invitations we need a guest list. Heavens, that will take 4 days to get in order and only I can understand our address file.

Lauren: Oh, Mom, I'm so excited. We can start each of the relatives on a different job.

Mom: Honey, I don't see how we can do it. Why, I've got to choose the invitations and patterns and reserve the church and . . .

Dad: Why don't you just take $3,000 and elope. Your sister's wedding cost me $2,400 and she didn't have to fly people up from Guatemala, hire extra girls and Mrs. Jacks, use airfreight, or anything like that.

---

* This case was adapted from a case originally written by Professor D. Clay Whybark, University of North Carolina, Chapel Hill, N.C.

1. Using a yellow sticky approach (see p. 153), develop a project network for the "Now" Wedding.
2. Create a schedule for the wedding using MS Project. Can you reach the deadline of January 21 for the Now Wedding? If you cannot, what would it cost to make the January 21 deadline and which activities would you change?

CASE 9.6

The "Now" Wedding—Part B

Several complications arose during the course of trying to meet the deadline of January 20 for the Now Wedding rehearsal. Since Lauren was adamant on having the wedding on January 21 (as was Connor for obvious reasons), the implications of each of these complications had to be assessed.

1. On January 1 the chairman of the Vestry Committee of the church was left unimpressed by the added donation and said he wouldn't reduce the notice period from 14 to 7 days.
2. Mother comes down with the three-day flu as she starts work on the guest list January 2.
3. Bob's Printing Service's press was down for one day on January 5th in order to replace faulty brushes in the electric motor.
4. The lace and dress material are lost in transit. Notice of the loss is received on January 10.

CHAPTER 10

Leadership: Being an Effective Project Manager

I couldn't wait to be the manager of my own project and run the project the way I thought it should be done. Boy, did I have a lot to learn!

—*first-time project manager*

This chapter is based on the premise that one of the keys to being an effective project manager is building cooperative relationships among different groups of people to complete projects. Project success does not just depend on the performance of the project team. Success or failure often depends on the contributions of top management, functional managers, customers, suppliers, contractors, and others.

The chapter begins with a brief discussion of the differences between leading and managing a project. The importance of managing project stakeholders is then introduced. Managers require a broad influence base to be effective in this area. Different sources of influence are discussed and are used to describe how project managers build social capital. This management style necessitates constant interacting with different groups of people whom project managers depend on. Special attention is devoted to managing the critical relationship with top management and the importance of leading by example. The importance of gaining cooperation in ways that build and sustain the trust of others is emphasized. The chapter concludes by identifying personal attributes associated with being an effective project manager. Subsequent chapters will expand on these ideas in a discussion of managing the project team and working with people outside the organization.

Managing versus Leading a Project

In a perfect world, the project manager would simply implement the project plan and the project would be completed. The project manager would work with others to formulate a schedule, organize a project team, keep track of progress, and announce what needs to be done next, and then everyone would charge along. Of course no one lives in a perfect world, and rarely does everything go according to plan. Project participants get testy; they fail to complement each other; other departments are unable to fulfill their commitments; technical glitches arise; work takes longer than expected. The project manager's job is to get the project back on track. A manager expedites certain activities; figures out ways to solve technical problems; serves as peacemaker when tensions rise; and makes appropriate trade-offs among time, cost, and scope of the project.

However, project managers do more than put out fires and keep the project on track. They also innovate and adapt to ever-changing circumstances. They often have to deviate from what was planned and introduce significant changes in the project scope and schedule to respond to unforeseen threats or opportunities. For example, customers' needs may change, requiring significant design changes midway through the project. Competitors may release new products that dictate crashing project deadlines. Working relationships among project participants may break down, requiring a reformulation of the project team. Ultimately, what was planned or expected in the beginning may be very different from what was accomplished by the end of the project.

Project managers are responsible for integrating assigned resources to complete the project according to plan. At the same time they need to initiate changes in plans and schedules as persistent problems make plans unworkable. In other words, managers want to keep the project going while making necessary adjustments along the way. According to Kotter these two different activities represent the distinction between management and leadership. Management is about coping with complexity, while leadership is about coping with change.

Good management brings about order and stability by formulating plans and objectives, designing structures and procedures, monitoring results against plans, and taking corrective action when necessary. Leadership involves recognizing and articulating the need to significantly alter the direction and operation of the project, aligning people to the new direction, and motivating them to work together to overcome hurdles produced by the change and to realize new objectives.

Strong leadership, while usually desirable, is not always necessary to successfully complete a project. Well-defined projects that encounter no significant surprises require little leadership, as might be the case in constructing a conventional apartment building in which the project manager simply administrates the project plan. Conversely, the higher the degree of uncertainty encountered on a project—whether in terms of changes in project scope, technological stalemates, breakdowns in coordination between people, and so forth—the more leadership is required. For example, strong leadership would be needed for a software development project in which the parameters are always changing to meet developments in the industry.

It takes a special person to perform both roles well. Some individuals are great visionaries who are good at exciting people about change. Too often though, these same people lack the discipline or patience to deal with the day-to-day drudgeries of managing. Likewise, there are other individuals who are very well organized and methodical but lack the ability to inspire others.

Strong leaders can compensate for their managerial weaknesses by having trusted assistants who oversee and manage the details of the project. Conversely, a weak leader can complement his or her strengths by having assistants who are good at sensing the need to change and rallying project participants. Still, one of the things that makes good project managers so valuable to an organization is that they have the ability to both manage and lead a project. In doing so they recognize the need to manage project interfaces and build a social network that allows them to find out what needs to be done and obtain the cooperation necessary to achieve it.

Managing Project Stakeholders

First-time project managers are eager to implement their own ideas and manage their people to successfully complete their project. What they soon find out is that project success depends on the cooperation of a wide range of individuals, many of whom do not directly report to them. For example, during the course of a system integration project, a project manager was surprised by how much time she was spending negotiating and working with vendors, consultants, technical specialists, and other functional managers:

> Instead of working with my people to complete the project, I found myself being constantly pulled and tugged by demands of different groups of people who were not directly involved in the project but had a vested interest in the outcome.

Too often when new project managers do find time to work directly on the project, they adopt a hands-on approach to managing the project. They choose this style not because they are power-hungry egomaniacs but because they are eager to achieve results. They become quickly frustrated by how slowly things operate, the number of people that have to be brought on board, and the difficulty of gaining cooperation. Unfortunately, as this frustration builds, the natural temptation is to exert more pressure and get more heavily involved in the project. These project managers quickly earn the reputation of "micro managing" and begin to lose sight of the real role they play on guiding a project.

Some new managers never break out of this vicious cycle. Others soon realize that authority does not equal influence and that being an effective project manager involves managing a much more complex and expansive set of interfaces than they had previously anticipated. They encounter a web of relationships that requires a much broader spectrum of influence than they felt was necessary or even possible.

For example, a significant project, whether it involves renovating a bridge, creating a new product, or installing a new information system, will likely involve in one way or another working with a number of different groups of stakeholders. First, there is the core group of specialists assigned to complete the project. This group is likely to be supplemented at different times by professionals who work on specific segments of the project. Second, there are the groups of people within the performing organization who are either directly or indirectly involved with the project. The most notable is top management, to whom the project manager is accountable. There are also other managers who provide resources and/or may be responsible for specific segments of the project, and administrative support services such as human resources, finance, etc. Depending on the nature of the project, there are a number of different groups outside the organization that influence the success of the project; the most important is the customer for which the project is designed (see Figure 10.1).

Each of these groups of individuals brings different expertise, standards, priorities, and agendas to the project. The sheer breadth and complexity of the relationships that need to be managed distinguishes project management from regular management. To be effective, a project manager must understand how these groups can affect the project and develop methods for managing the dependency. The nature of these dependencies is identified here:

- The **project team** manages and completes project work. Most participants want to do a good job, but they are also concerned with their other obligations and how their involvement on the project will contribute to their personal goals and aspirations.
- **Project managers** naturally compete with each other for resources and the support of top management. At the same time they often have to share resources and exchange information.
- **Administrative support** groups, such as human resources, information systems, purchasing agents, and maintenance, provide valuable support services. At the same time they impose constraints and requirements on the project such as the documentation of expenditures and the timely and accurate delivery of information.
- **Functional managers,** depending on how the project is organized, can play a minor or major role toward project success. In matrix arrangements, they may be responsible for assigning project personnel, resolving technical dilemmas, and overseeing the completion of significant segments of the project work. Even in dedicated project teams, the technical input from functional managers may be useful, and acceptance of completed project work may be critical to in-house projects. Functional managers want to cooperate up to a point, but only up to a certain point. They are also concerned with preserving their status within the organization and minimizing the disruptions the project may have on their own operations.

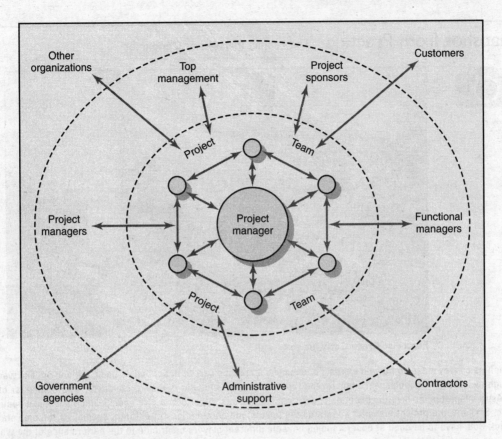

FIGURE 10.1   Network of Stakeholders

- **Top management** approves funding of the project and establishes priorities within the organization. They define success and adjudicate rewards for accomplishments. Significant adjustments in budget, scope, and schedule typically need their approval. They have a natural vested interest in the success of the project, but at the same time have to be responsive to what is best for the entire organization.

- **Project sponsors** champion the project and use their influence to gain approval of the project. Their reputation is tied to the success of the project, and they need to be kept informed of any major developments. They defend the project when it comes under attack and are a key project ally.

- **Contractors** may do all the actual work, in some cases, with the project team merely coordinating their contributions. In other cases, they are responsible for ancillary segments of the project scope. Poor work and schedule slips can affect work of the core project team. While contractors' reputations rest with doing good work, they must balance their contributions with their own profit margins and their commitments to other clients.

- **Government agencies** place constraints on project work. Permits need to be secured. Construction work has to be built to code. New drugs have to pass a rigorous battery of U.S. Food and Drug Administration tests. Other products have to meet safety standards, for example, Occupational Safety and Health Administration standards.

Snapshot from Practice The Project Manager as Conductor

Photodisc Green/Getty Images.

Metaphors convey meaning beyond words. For example, a meeting can be described as being difficult or "like wading through molasses." A popular metaphor for the role of a project manager is that of *conductor*. The conductor of an orchestra integrates the divergent sounds of different instruments to perform a given composition and make beautiful music. Similarly, the project manager integrates the talents and contributions of different specialists to complete the project. Both have to be good at understanding how the different players contribute to the performance of the whole. Both are almost entirely dependent upon the expertise and know-how of the players. The conductor does not have command of all the musical instruments. Likewise, the project manager usually possesses only a small proportion of the technical knowledge to make decisions. As such, the conductor and project manager both facilitate the performance of others rather than actually perform.

Conductors use their arms, baton, and other nonverbal gestures to influence the pace, intensity, and involvement of different musicians. Likewise, project managers orchestrate the completion of the project by managing the involvement and attention of project members. Project managers balance time and process and induce participants to make the right decisions at the right time just as the conductor induces the wind instruments to perform at the right moment in a movement. Each controls the rhythm and intensity of work by managing the tempo and involvement of the players. Finally, each has a vision that transcends the music score or project plan. To be successful they must both earn the confidence, respect, and trust of their players.

- **Other organizations,** depending on the nature of the project, may directly or indirectly affect the project. For example, suppliers provide necessary resources for completion of the project work. Delays, shortages, and poor quality can bring a project to a standstill. Public interest groups may apply pressure on government agencies. Customers often hire consultants and auditors to protect their interests on a project.
- **Customers** define the scope of the project, and ultimate project success rests in their satisfaction. Project managers need to be responsive to changing customer needs and requirements and to meeting their expectations. Customers are primarily concerned with getting a *good deal* and, as will be elaborated in Chapter 11, this naturally breeds tension with the project team.

These relationships are interdependent in that a project manager's ability to work effectively with one group will affect her ability to manage other groups. For example, functional managers are likely to be less cooperative if they perceive that top management's commitment to the project is waning. Conversely, the ability of the project manager to buffer the team from excessive interference from a client is likely to increase her standing with the project team.

The project management structure being used will influence the number and degree of external dependencies that will need to be managed. One advantage of creating a dedicated project team is that it reduces dependencies, especially within the organization, because most of the resources are assigned to the project. Conversely, a functional matrix structure increases dependencies, with the result that the project manager is much more reliant upon functional colleagues for work and staff.

The old-fashioned view of managing projects emphasized directing and controlling subordinates; the new perspective emphasizes managing project stakeholders and anticipating change as the most important jobs. Project managers need to be able to assuage concerns of customers, sustain support for the project at higher levels of the organization, quickly identify problems that threaten project work, while at the same time defend the integrity of the project and the interests of the project participants.

Within this web of relationships, the project manager must find out what needs to be done to achieve the goals of the project and build a cooperative network to accomplish it. Project managers must do so without the requisite authority to expect or demand cooperation. Doing so requires sound communication skills, political savvy, and a broad influence base. See the Snapshot from Practice: The Project Manager as Conductor for more on what makes project managers special.

Influence as Exchange

To successfully manage a project, a manager must adroitly build a cooperative network among divergent allies. Networks are mutually beneficial alliances that are generally governed by the law of reciprocity. The basic principle is that "one good deed deserves another, and likewise, one bad deed deserves another." The primary way to gain cooperation is to provide resources and services for others in exchange for future resources and services. This is the age-old maxim: "Quid pro quo (something for something)." Or in today's vernacular: "You scratch my back, I'll scratch yours."

Cohen and Bradford described the exchange view of influence as "currencies." If you want to do business in a given country, you have to be prepared to use the appropriate currency, and the exchange rates can change over time as conditions change. In the same way, what is valued by a marketing manager may be different from what is valued by a veteran project engineer, and you are likely to need to use different influence currency to obtain the cooperation of each individual. Although this analogy is a bit of an oversimplification, the key premise holds true that in the long run, "debit" and "credit" accounts must be balanced for cooperative relationships to work. Table 10.1 presents the commonly traded organizational currencies identified by Cohen and Bradford; they are then discussed in more detail in the following sections.

Task-Related Currencies

This form of influence comes directly from the project manager's ability to contribute to others' accomplishing their work. Probably the most significant form of this currency is the ability to respond to subordinates' requests for additional manpower, money, or time to complete a segment of a project. This kind of currency is also evident in sharing resources with another project manager who is in need. At a more personal level, it may simply mean providing direct assistance to a colleague in solving a technical problem.

TABLE 10.1   Commonly Traded Organizational Currencies

Source: Adapted from A. R. Cohen and David L. Bradford, *Influence without Authority* (New York: John Wiley & Sons, 1990). Reprinted by permission of John Wiley & Sons, Inc.

Task-related currencies	
Resources	Lending or giving money, budget increases, personnel, etc.
Assistance	Helping with existing projects or undertaking unwanted tasks.
Cooperation	Giving task support, providing quicker response time, or aiding implementation.
Information	Providing organizational as well as technical knowledge.
Position-related currencies	
Advancement	Giving a task or assignment that can result in promotion.
Recognition	Acknowledging effort, accomplishments, or abilities.
Visibility	Providing a chance to be known by higher-ups or significant others in the organization.
Network/contacts	Providing opportunities for linking with others.
Inspiration-related currencies	
Vision	Being involved in a task that has larger significance for the unit, organization, customer, or society.
Excellence	Having a chance to do important things really well.
Ethical correctness	Doing what is "right" by a higher standard than efficiency.
Relationship-related currencies	
Acceptance	Providing closeness and friendship.
Personal support	Giving personal and emotional backing.
Understanding	Listening to others' concerns and issues.
Personal-related currencies	
Challenge/learning	Sharing tasks that increase skills and abilities.
Ownership/involvement	Letting others have ownership and influence.
Gratitude	Expressing appreciation.

Providing a good word for a colleague's proposal or recommendation is another form of this currency. Because most work of significance is likely to generate some form of opposition, the person who is trying to gain approval for a plan or proposal can be greatly aided by having a "friend in court."

Another form of this currency includes extraordinary effort. For example, fulfilling an emergency request to complete a design document in two days instead of the normal four days is likely to engender gratitude. Finally, sharing valuable information that would be useful to other managers is another form of this currency.

Position-Related Currencies

This form of influence stems from the manager's ability to enhance others' positions within their organization. A project manager can do this by giving someone a challenging assignment that can aid their advancement by developing their skills and abilities. Being given a chance to prove yourself naturally generates a strong sense of gratitude. Sharing the glory and bringing to the attention of higher-ups the efforts and accomplishments of others generate goodwill.

Project managers confide that a key strategy useful for gaining the cooperation of professionals in other departments and organizations is figuring out how to make these people look good to their bosses. For example, a project manager worked with a subcontractor whose organization was heavily committed to total quality management (TQM). The project manager made it a point in top-level briefing meetings to point out how quality improvement processes initiated by the contractor contributed to cost control and problem prevention.

Another variation of recognition is enhancing the reputation of others within the firm. "Good press" can pave the way for lots of opportunities, while "bad press" can quickly shut a person off and make it difficult to perform. This currency is also evident in helping to preserve someone's reputation by coming to the defense of someone unjustly blamed for project setbacks.

Finally, one of the strongest forms of this currency is sharing contacts with other people. Helping individuals expand their own networks by introducing them to key people naturally engenders gratitude. For example, suggesting to a functional manager that he should contact Sally X if he wants to find out what is really going on in that department or to get a request expedited is likely to engender a sense of indebtedness.

Inspiration-Related Currencies

Perhaps the most powerful form of influence is based on inspiration. Most sources of inspiration derive from people's burning desire to make a difference and add meaning to their lives. Creating an exciting, bold vision for a project can elicit extraordinary commitment. For example, many of the technological breakthroughs associated with the introduction of the original Macintosh computer were attributed to the feeling that the project members had a chance to change the way people approached computers. A variant form of vision is providing an opportunity to do something really well. Being able to take pride in your work often drives many people.

Often the very nature of the project provides a source of inspiration. Discovering a cure for a devastating disease, introducing a new social program that will help those in need, or simply building a bridge that will reduce a major traffic bottleneck can provide opportunities for people to feel good about what they are doing and that they are making a difference. Inspiration operates as a magnet—pulling people as opposed to pushing people toward doing something.

Relationship-Related Currencies

These currencies have more to do with strengthening the relationship with someone than directly accomplishing the project tasks. The essence of this form of influence is forming a relationship that transcends normal professional boundaries and extends into the realm of friendship. Such relationships develop by giving personal and emotional backing. Picking people up when they are feeling down, boosting their confidence, and providing encouragement naturally breed goodwill. Sharing a sense of humor and making difficult times fun is another form of this currency. Similarly, engaging in non-work-related activities such as sports and family outings is another way relationships are naturally enhanced.

Perhaps the most basic form of this currency is simply listening to other people. Psychologists suggest that most people have a strong desire to be understood and that relationships break down because the parties stop listening to each other. Sharing personal secrets/ambitions and being a wise confidant also creates a special bond between individuals.

Personal-Related Currencies

This last form of currency deals with individual needs and an overriding sense of self-esteem. Some argue that self-esteem is a primary psychological need; the extent to which we can help others feel a sense of importance and personal worth will naturally generate goodwill. A project manager can enhance a colleague's sense of worth by sharing tasks that increase skills and abilities, delegating authority over work so that others experience ownership, and allowing individuals to feel comfortable stretching their abilities. This form of currency can also be seen in sincere expressions of gratitude for the contributions of others. Care, though, must be exercised in expressing gratitude since it is easily devalued when overused. That is, the first *thank you* is likely to be more valued than the twentieth.

The bottom line is that a project manager will be influential only insofar as she can offer something that others value. Furthermore, given the diverse cast of people a project manager depends on, it is important that she be able to acquire and exercise different influence currencies. The ability to do so will be constrained in part by the nature of the project and how it is organized. For example, a project manager who is in charge of a dedicated team has considerably more to offer team members than a manager who is given the responsibility of coordinating the activities of different professionals across different departments and organizations. In such cases, that manager will probably have to rely more heavily on personal and relational bases of influence to gain the cooperation of others.

Social Network Building

Mapping Dependencies

The first step to building a social network is identifying those on whom the project depends for success. The project manager and his or her key assistants need to ask the following questions:

- Whose cooperation will we need?
- Whose agreement or approval will we need?
- Whose opposition would keep us from accomplishing the project?

Many project managers find it helpful to draw a map of these dependencies. For example, Figure 10.2 contains the dependencies identified by a project manager responsible for installing a new financial software system in her company.

It is always better to overestimate rather than underestimate dependencies. All too often, otherwise talented and successful project managers have been derailed because they were blindsided by someone whose position or power they had not anticipated. After identifying whom you will depend on, you are ready to "step into their shoes" and see the project from their perspective:

- What differences exist between myself and the people on whom I depend (goals, values, pressures, working styles, risks)?
- How do these different people view the project (supporters, indifferents, antagonists)?
- What is the current status of the relationship I have with the people I depend on?
- What sources of influence do I have relative to those on whom I depend?

Once you start this analysis you can begin to appreciate what others value and what currencies you might have to offer as a basis on which to build a working relationship. You begin to realize where potential problems lie—relationships in which you have a current debit or no convertible currency. Furthermore, diagnosing another's point of view as well as the basis for their positions will help you anticipate their reactions and feelings about your decisions and actions. This information is vital for selecting the appropriate influence strategy and tactics and conducting win/win negotiations.

For example, after mapping her dependency network, the project manager who was in charge of installing the software system realized that she was likely to have serious problems with the manager of the receipts

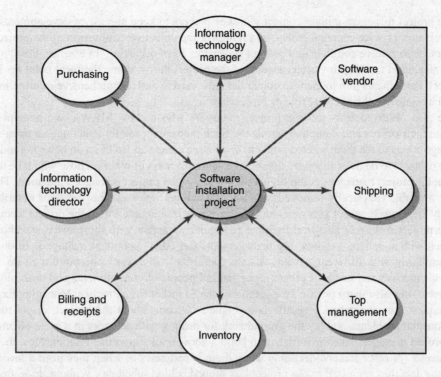

FIGURE 10.2 Dependencies for Financial Software Installation Project

department, who would be one of the primary users of the software. She had no previous history of working with this individual but had heard through the grapevine that the manager was upset with the choice of software and that he considered this project to be another unnecessary disruption of his department's operation. Prior to project initiation the project manager arranged to have lunch with the manager, where she sat patiently and listened to his concerns. She invested additional time and attention to educate him and his staff about the benefits of the new software. She tried to minimize the disruptions the transition would cause in his department. She altered the implementation schedule to accommodate his preferences as to when the actual software would be installed and the subsequent training would occur. In turn, the receipts manager and his people were much more accepting of the change, and the transition to the new software went more smoothly than anticipated.

Management by Wandering Around (MBWA)

The preceding example illustrates the next step in building a supportive social network. Once you have established who the key players are that will determine success, then you initiate contact and begin to build a relationship with those players. Building this relationship requires a management style employees at Hewlett-Packard refer to as "management by wandering around" (MBWA) to reflect that managers spend the majority of their time outside their offices. MBWA is somewhat of a misnomer in that there is a purpose/pattern behind the "wandering." Through face-to-face interactions, project managers are able to stay in touch with what is really going on in the project and build cooperation essential to project success.

Effective project managers initiate contact with key players to keep abreast of developments, anticipate potential problems, provide encouragement, and reinforce the objectives and vision of the project. They are able to intervene to resolve conflicts and prevent stalemates from occurring. In essence, they "manage" the project. By staying in touch with various aspects of the project they become the focal point for information on the project. Participants turn to them to obtain the most current and comprehensive information about the project which reinforces their central role as project manager.

We have also observed less-effective project managers who eschew MBWA and attempt to manage projects from their offices and computer terminals. Such managers proudly announce an open-door policy and encourage others to see them when a problem or an issue comes up. To them no news is good news. This allows their contacts to be determined by the relative aggressiveness of others. Those who take the initiative and seek out the project manager get too high a proportion of the project manager's attention. Those people less readily available (physically removed) or more passive get ignored. This behavior contributes to the adage, "Only the squeaky wheel gets greased," which breeds resentment within the project team.

Effective project managers also find the time to regularly interact with more distal stakeholders. They keep in touch with suppliers, vendors, top management, and other functional managers. In doing so they maintain familiarity with different parties, sustain friendships, discover opportunities to do favors, and understand the motives and needs of others. They remind people of commitments and champion the cause of their project. They also shape people's expectations (see Snapshot from Practice: Managing Expectations). Through frequent communication they alleviate people's concerns about the project, dispel rumors, warn people of potential problems, and lay the groundwork for dealing with setbacks in a more effective manner.

Unless project managers take the initiative to build a network of supportive relationships, they are likely to see a manager (or other stakeholder) only when there is bad news or when they need a favor (e.g., they don't have the data they promised or the project has slipped behind schedule). Without prior, frequent, easy give-and-take interactions around nondecisive issues, the encounter prompted by the problem is likely to provoke excess tension. The parties are more likely to act defensively, interrupt each other, and lose sight of the common problem.

Experienced project managers recognize the need to build relationships before they need them. They initiate contact with the key stakeholders at times when there are no outstanding issues or problems and therefore no anxieties and suspicions. On these social occasions, they engage in small talk and responsive banter. They respond to others' requests for aid, provide supportive counsel, and exchange information. In doing so they establish credit in that relationship, which will allow them to deal with more serious problems down the road. When one person views another as pleasant, credible, and helpful based on past contact, he or she is much more likely to be responsive to requests for help and less confrontational when problems arise.

Managing Upward Relations

Research consistently points out that project success is strongly affected by the degree to which a project has the support of top management. Such support is reflected in an appropriate budget, responsiveness to unexpected needs, and a clear signal to others in the organization of the importance of cooperation.

Visible top management support is not only critical for securing the support of other managers within an organization, but it also is a key factor in the project manager's ability to motivate the project team. Nothing establishes a manager's right to lead more than her ability to defend. To win the loyalty of team members, project managers have to be effective advocates for their projects. They have to be able to get top management to rescind unreasonable demands, provide additional resources, and recognize the accomplishments of team members. This is more easily said than done.

Snapshot from Practice   Managing Expectations*

Dorothy Kirk, a project management consultant and program manager with Financial Solutions Group of Mynd, offers several keen insights about the art of managing stakeholder expectations:

. . . expectations are hardy. All they need to take root is the absence of evidence to the contrary. Once rooted, the unspoken word encourages growth. They can develop and thrive without being grounded in reality. For this reason, project managers do daily battle with unrealistic expectations.

She goes on to offer several tips for managing expectations:

- The way you present information can either clarify or muddy expectations. For example, if you estimate that a task will take 317 hours, you are setting high expectations by your precision. The stakeholder is likely to be unhappy if it takes 323 hours. The stakeholder will not be unhappy with 323 hours if you quoted an estimate of 300–325 hours.
- Recognize that it is only human nature to interpret a situation in one's best interest. For example, if you tell someone it will be done by January, you are inclined to interpret it to your advantage and assume you have to the end of January, while the other person believes it will be done January 1st.
- Seize every opportunity to realign expectations with reality. Too often we avoid opportunities to adjust expectations because we hold onto a false hope that things will somehow work out.
- Do not ask for stakeholder suggestions for improvement if you do not intend to do something with their input. Asking for their input raises expectations.
- State the obvious. What is obvious to you may be obscure to others.
- Don't avoid delivering bad news. Communicate openly and in person. Expect some anger and frustration. Do not get defensive in return. Be prepared to explain the impact of the problems. For example, never say the project is going to be late without being able to give a new date. Explain what you are doing to see that this does not continue to happen.

All stakeholders have expectations about the schedule, cost, and project benefits. Project managers need to listen for, understand, and manage these expectations.

* D. Kirk, "Managing Expectations," *PM Network*, August 2000, pp. 59–62.

Working relationships with upper management is a common source of consternation. Laments like the following are often made by project managers about upper management:

> They don't know how much it sets us back losing Neil to another project.
> I would like to see them get this project done with the budget they gave us.
> I just wish they would make up their minds as to what is really important.

While it may seem counterintuitive for a subordinate to "manage" a superior, smart project managers devote considerable time and attention to influencing and garnering the support of top management. Project managers have to accept profound differences in perspective and become skilled at the art of persuading superiors.

Many of the tensions that arise between upper management and project managers are a result of differences in perspective. Project managers become naturally absorbed with what is best for their project. To them the most important thing in the world is their project. Top management should have a different set of priorities. They are concerned with what is best for the entire organization. It is only natural for these two interests to conflict at times. For example, a project manager may lobby intensively for additional personnel only to be turned down because top management believes that the other departments cannot afford a reduction in staff. Although frequent communication can minimize differences, the project manager has to accept the fact that top management is inevitably going to see the world differently.

Research Highlight — Improving the Performance of New-Product Teams*

Ancona and Caldwell studied the performance of 45 new-product teams in five high-technology companies and produced some startling results. The most significant was that internal team dynamics were not related to performance. That is, high-performance teams were not distinguished by clearer goals, smoother workflow among members, or greater ability to satisfy the individual goals of team members. What related to team performance were level and intensity of external interactions between the project team and the rest of the organization. Ancona and Caldwell identified four key patterns of activity which contribute to creating a high-performance team:

1. *Ambassador* activities are aimed at representing the team to others and protecting the team from interference. The project manager typically takes on this responsibility, which involves buffering the team from political pressures and building support for the project within the hierarchy of the company.

2. *Task coordinator* activities are aimed at coordinating the team's efforts with other units and organizations. Unlike the ambassador role, which is focused upward, these are more lateral activities and involve negotiating and interacting with interested parties within the organization.

3. *Scouts* act as a scout on an expedition; that is, they go out from the team to bring back information about what is going on elsewhere in the organization. This is a much less focused task than task coordinator.

4. *Guard* activities differ from the other activities in that they are intended to keep information and resources inside the team, preventing drainage out of the group. A key guard activity is keeping necessary information secret until it is appropriate to share it.

Ancona and Caldwell found that the importance of these activities varies during the product development life cycle if the project team is to be successful. For example, scouting activities are more critical during the creation phase, when the product idea is being formulated and the team is being developed. Ambassador activities are especially critical during the development phase, when product specifications have been agreed upon and the major task is developing a prototype.

Ancona and Caldwell caution that their findings do not mean that teamwork and the internal operations of a project team are not important to project success. Effective team dynamics are necessary to successfully integrate information from outside sources and coordinate activities across groups. Their research supports the adage that problems and opportunities often lie at the borders of projects, and that one of the primary jobs of a project manager is to manage the interface between his or her team and the rest of the organization.

* D. G. Ancona and D. Caldwell, "Improving the Performance of New-Product Teams," *Research Technology Management,* Vol. 33, No. 2 (March–April 1990), pp. 25–29.

Once project managers accept that disagreements with superiors are more a question of perspective than substance, they can focus more of their energy on the art of persuading upper management. But before they can persuade superiors, they must first prove loyalty. Loyalty in this context simply means that most of the time project managers have to show that they consistently follow through on requests and adhere to the parameters established by top management without a great deal of grumbling or fuss. Once managers have proven loyalty to upper management, senior management is much more receptive to their challenges and requests.

Project managers have to cultivate strong ties with upper managers who are sponsoring the project. As noted earlier, these are high-ranking officials who championed approval and funding of the project; as such, their reputations are aligned with the project. Sponsors are also the ones who defend the project when it is under attack in upper circles of management. They shelter the project from excessive interference (see Figure 10.3). Project managers should *always* keep such people informed of any problems that may cause

Snapshot from Practice   Leading at the Edge*

In 1914, the intrepid explorer Ernest Shackleton embarked on the *Endurance* with his team of seamen and scientists, intent upon crossing the unexplored Antarctic continent. What happened in the two years between their departure and their ultimate incredible rescue has rarely been matched in the annals of survival: a ship crushed by expanding ice pack . . . a crew stranded on the floes of the frozen Weddell Sea . . . two perilous treks in open boats across a raging Southern Ocean . . . a team marooned on the wild, forlorn Elephant Island, stretched to the limits of human endurance.

This adventure provided the basis for the book *Leading at the Edge: Leadership Lessons from the Extraordinary Saga of Shackleton's Antarctic Expedition* written by Dennis Perkins. Perkins provides numerous incidents of how Shackleton's personal example influenced the behavior of his beleaguered crew. For example, from the beginning of the Trans-Atlantic expedition to its end Shackleton consistently encouraged behavior that emphasized caring and respect:

> After the destruction of the *Endurance* Shackleton heated hot milk for the crew and went from tent to tent with the "life giving" drink. After the sail to the island of South Georgia, when the exhausted crew had landed, Shackleton took the first watch, which he kept for three hours instead of the usual one.

Topham/The Image Works.

Crewmembers emulated the caring behaviors that Shackle-ton modeled. A good example of this occurred during one of the most dramatic moments in the *Endurance* saga. The food supply had dwindled to perilously low levels. Less than a week's supply remained, and the tiny ration of seal steak usually served at breakfast was eliminated. The waste meat generally used to feed the dogs was inspected for edible scraps.

Under these wretched conditions, and after a wet sleepless night, an argument broke out among some of the team members. Caught in the middle, one crew member (Greenstreet) spilled his tiny ration of powdered milk and shouted at the biologist (Clark). Alfred Lansing described what happened next:

> Greenstreet paused to get his breath, and in that instant his anger was spent and he suddenly fell silent. Everyone else in the tent became quiet, too, and looked at Greenstreet, shaggy-haired, bearded, and filthy with blubber soot, holding his empty mug in his hand and looking helplessly down into the snow that had thirstily soaked up his precious milk. The loss was so tragic he seemed almost on the point of weeping. Without speaking, Clark reached out and poured some milk into Greenstreet's mug. Then Worsely, then Macklin, and Rickerson and Kerr, Orde-Lees, and finally Blackborrow. They finished in silence.

* Adapted from Dennis N. T. Perkins, *Leading at the Edge: Leadership Lessons from the Extraordinary Saga of Shackleton's Antarctica Expedition* (New York: AMACOM Press, 2000), pp. 94–95; and Alfred Lansing, *Endurance: Shackleton's Incredible Voyage* (New York: Carroll & Graf, 1998), p. 127.

embarrassment or disappointment. For example, if costs are beginning to outrun the budget or a technical glitch is threatening to delay the completion of the project, managers make sure that the sponsors are the first to know.

Timing is everything. Asking for additional budget the day after disappointing third-quarter earnings are reported is going to be much more difficult than making a similar request four weeks later. Good project managers pick the optimum time to appeal to top management. They enlist their project sponsors to lobby their cause. They also realize there are limits to top management's accommodations. Here, the Lone Ranger analogy is appropriate—you have only so many silver bullets, so use them wisely.

Project managers need to adapt their communication pattern to that of the senior group. For example, one project manager recognized that top management had a tendency to use sports metaphors to describe business situations, so she framed a recent slip in schedule by admitting that "we lost five yards, but we still have two plays to make a first down." Smart project managers learn the language of top management and use it to their advantage.

Finally, a few project managers admit ignoring chains of command. If they are confident that top management will reject an important request and that what they want to do will benefit the project, they do it without asking permission. While acknowledging that this is very risky, they claim that bosses typically won't argue with success.

FIGURE 10.3
The Significance of a Project Sponsor

Leading by Example

A highly visible, interactive management style is not only essential to building and sustaining cooperative relationships, it also allows project managers to utilize their most powerful leadership tool—their own behavior. Often, when faced with uncertainty, people look to others for cues as to how to respond and demonstrate a propensity to mimic the behavior of superiors. A project manager's behavior symbolizes how other people should work on the project. Through her behavior a project manager can influence how others act and respond to a variety of issues related to the project. (See Snapshot from Practice: Leading at the Edge for a dramatic example of this.)

To be effective, project managers must "walk the talk" (see Figure 10.4). Six aspects of leading by example are discussed next.

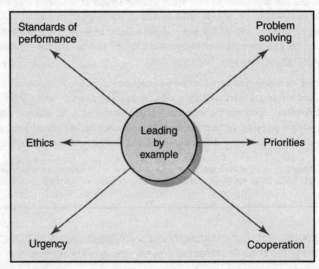

FIGURE 10.4   Leading by Example

Priorities

Actions speak louder than words. Subordinates and others discern project managers' priorities by how they spend their time. If a project manager claims that this project is critical and then is perceived as devoting more time to other projects, then all his verbal reassurances are likely to fall on deaf ears. Conversely, a project manager who takes the time to observe a critical test instead of simply waiting for a report affirms the importance of the testers and their work. Likewise, the types of questions project managers pose communicate priorities. By repeatedly asking how specific issues relate to satisfying the customer, a project manager can reinforce the importance of customer satisfaction.

Urgency

Through their actions project managers can convey a sense of urgency, which can permeate project activities. This urgency in part can be conveyed through stringent deadlines, frequent status report meetings, and aggressive solutions for expediting the project. The project manager uses these tools like a metronome to pick up the beat of the project. At the same time, such devices will be ineffective if there is not also a corresponding change in the project manager's behavior. If they want others to work faster and solve problems quicker, then they need to work faster. They need to hasten the pace of their own behavior. They should accelerate the frequency of their interactions, talk and walk more quickly, get to work sooner, and leave work later. By simply increasing the pace of their daily interaction patterns, project managers can reinforce a sense of urgency in others.

Problem Solving

How project managers respond to problems sets the tone for how others tackle problems. If bad news is greeted by verbal attacks, then others will be reluctant to be forthcoming. If the project manager is more concerned with finding out who is to blame instead of how to prevent problems from happening again, then others will tend to cover their tracks and cast the blame elsewhere. If, on the other hand, project managers focus more on how they can turn a problem into an opportunity or what can be learned from a mistake, then others are more likely to adopt a more proactive approach to problem solving.

Cooperation

How project managers act toward outsiders influences how team members interact with outsiders. If a project manager makes disparaging remarks about the "idiots" in the marketing department, then this oftentimes becomes the shared view of the entire team. If project managers set the norm of treating outsiders with respect and being responsive to their needs, then others will more likely follow suit.

Standards of Performance

Veteran project managers recognize that if they want participants to exceed project expectations then they have to exceed others' expectations of a good project manager. They establish a high standard for project performance through the quality of their daily interactions. They respond quickly to the needs of others, carefully prepare and run crisp meetings, stay on top of all the critical issues, facilitate effective problem solving, and stand firm on important matters.

Ethics

How others respond to ethical dilemmas that arise in the course of a project will be influenced by how the project manager has responded to similar dilemmas. In many cases, team members base their actions on how they think the project manager would respond. If project managers deliberately distort or withhold vital information from customers or top management, then they are signaling to others that this kind of behavior is acceptable. Project management invariably creates a variety of ethical dilemmas; this would be an appropriate time to delve into this topic in more detail.

Ethics and Project Management

Questions of ethics have already arisen in previous chapters that discussed padding of cost and time estimations, exaggerating pay-offs of project proposals, and so forth. Ethical dilemmas involve situations where it is difficult to determine whether conduct is right or wrong. Is it acceptable to falsely assure customers that everything is on track when, in reality, you are only doing so to prevent them from panicking and making matters worse?

In a survey of project managers, 81 percent reported that they encounter ethical issues in their work. These dilemmas range from being pressured to alter status reports, backdate signatures, or shade documentation to mask the reality of project progress to falsifying cost accounts, compromising safety standards to accelerate progress, and approving shoddy work.

Project management is complicated work, and, as such, ethics invariably involve gray areas of judgment and interpretation. For example, it is difficult to distinguish deliberate falsification of estimates from genuine mistakes or the willful exaggeration of project payoffs from genuine optimism. It becomes problematic to determine whether unfulfilled promises were deliberate deception or an appropriate response to changing circumstances.

To provide greater clarity to business ethics, many companies and professional groups publish a code of conduct. Cynics see these documents as simply window dressing, while advocates argue that they are important, albeit limited, first steps. In practice, personal ethics do not lie in formal statutes but at the intersection of one's work, family, education, profession, religious beliefs, and daily interactions. Most project managers report that they rely on their own private sense of right and wrong—what one project manager called his "internal compass." One common rule of thumb for testing whether a response is ethical is to ask, "Imagine that whatever you did was going to be reported on the front page of your local newspaper. How would you like that? Would you be comfortable?"

Unfortunately, scandals at Enron, Worldcom, and Arthur Andersen have demonstrated the willingness of highly trained professionals to abdicate personal responsibility for illegal actions and to obey the directives of superiors (see Snapshot from Practice: The Collapse of Arthur Andersen). Top management and the culture of an organization play a decisive role in shaping members' beliefs of what is right and wrong. Many organizations encourage ethical transgressions by creating a "win at all cost" mentality. The pressures to succeed obscure consideration of whether the ends justify the means. Other organizations place a premium on "fair play" and command a market position by virtue of being trustworthy and reliable.

Many project managers claim that ethical behavior is its own reward. By following your own internal compass your behavior expresses your personal values. Others suggest that ethical behavior is doubly rewarding. You not only are able to fall asleep at night but you also develop a sound and admirable reputation. As will be explored in the next section, such a reputation is essential to establishing the trust necessary to exercise influence effectively.

Building Trust: The Key to Exercising Influence

We all know people who have influence but whom we do not trust; these individuals are often referred to as "political animals" or "jungle fighters." While these individuals are often very successful in the short run, the

---

Snapshot from Practice   The Collapse of Arthur Andersen*

"Think straight and talk straight" was the principle on which Arthur E. Andersen built his accounting firm in the early 1900s. It was a phrase his mother taught him and became the firm's motto. The commitment to integrity and a systematic, planned approach to work were instrumental in Arthur Andersen becoming one of the largest and best-known accounting firms in the world.

Working for Arthur Andersen was not for everyone. It could be a tough culture. It was much too hierarchical and top down for the more free spirited. Many people left after less than two years, believing the rewards did not warrant the demands that were made on them. Others learned to play by the rules and some even thrived. To remain in the firm, staff members were expected to work hard, respect authority of rank, and maintain a high level of conformity. In return they were rewarded with support, promotion, and the possibility of making partner. Those individuals who made a career with the firm grew old together, professionally and personally, and most had never worked anywhere else. To these survivors, Andersen was their second family, and they developed strong loyalties to the firm and its culture. (p. 133)

On October 23, 2001, David Duncan told his Enron project team that they needed to start complying with Andersen's new policy on handling audit documents. The policy had been instituted to make sure that the firm's extraneous paperwork could not be used in court cases. Although the document retention policy required that papers supporting the firm's opinions and audit be retained, it allowed a broad category of secondary documents to be destroyed. The team reacted with stunned silence to Duncan's directive. Then everyone got up and began racing to do what they had been told to do. No one asked Duncan to explain further. None asked whether what they were doing was wrong. No one questioned whether what he or she were doing might be illegal. Andersen's Houston staff just reacted, following orders without question.

On November 9, 2001, the day after the Securities Exchange Commission (SEC) issued a subpoena to Andersen, the shredding stopped. More than one ton of documents had been destroyed and 30,000 e-mails and Enron-related computer files erased. According to Andersen's legal defense team, the shredding was business as usual. The lawyers claimed that the shredding was standard practice for eliminating unnecessary files. To the SEC, it appeared to be the start of a deep cover-up operation. Subsequently one of the most respected accounting firms in the world closed its doors.

* Susan E. Squires, Cynthia J. Smith, Lorna McDougall, and William R. Yeak, *Inside Arthur Andersen: Shifting Values, Unexpected Consequences* (Upper Saddle, NJ: Prentice Hall, 2004).

---

prevalent sense of mistrust prohibits long-term efficacy. Successful project managers not only need to be influential, they also need to exercise influence in a manner that builds and sustains the trust of others.

The significance of trust can be discerned by its absence. Imagine how different a working relationship is when you distrust the other party as opposed to trusting them. When people distrust each other, they often spend inordinate amounts of time and energy attempting to discern hidden agendas and the true meaning of communications and then securing guarantees to promises. They are much more cautious with each other and hesitant to cooperate. Here is what one line manager had to say about how he reacted to a project manager he did not trust:

> Whenever Jim approached me about something, I found myself trying to read between the lines to figure what was really going on. When he made a request, my initial reaction was "no" until he proved it.

Conversely, trust is the "lubricant" that maintains smooth and efficient interactions. When you trust, people are more likely to take your actions and intentions at face value when circumstances are ambiguous. For example, here is what a functional manager had to say about how he dealt with a project manager he trusted:

> If Sally said she needed something, no questions were asked. I knew it was important or she wouldn't have asked.

Trust is an elusive concept. It is hard to nail down in precise terms why some project managers are trusted and others are not. One popular way to understand trust is to see it as a function of character and competence. Character focuses on personal motives (i.e., does he or she want to do the right thing?), while competence focuses on skills necessary to realize motives (i.e., does he or she know the right things to do?).

Stephen Covey resurrected the significance of character in leadership literature in his best selling *Seven Habits of Highly Effective People*. Covey criticized popular management literature as focusing too much on shallow human relations skills and manipulative techniques, which he labeled the personality ethic. He argues that at the core of highly effective people is a character ethic that is deeply rooted in personal values and principles such as dignity, service, fairness, the pursuit of truth, and respect.

One of the distinguishing traits of character is consistency. When people are guided by a core set of principles, they are naturally more predictable because their actions are consistent with these principles. Another feature of character is openness. When people have a clear sense of who they are and what they value, they are more receptive to others. This trait provides them with the capacity to empathize and the talent to build consensus among divergent people. Finally, another quality of character is a sense of purpose. Managers with character are driven not only by personal ambitions but also for the common good. Their primary concern is what is best for their organization and the project, not what is best for themselves. This willingness to subordinate personal interests to a higher purpose garners the respect, loyalty, and trust of others.

The significance of character is summarized by the comments made by two team members about two very different project managers.

At first everyone liked Joe and was excited about the project. But after a while, people became suspicious of his motives. He had a tendency to say different things to different people. People began to feel manipulated. He spent too much time with top management. People began to believe that he was only looking out for himself. It was HIS project. When the project began to slip he jumped ship and left someone else holding the bag. I'll never work for that guy again.

My first impression of Jack was nothing special. He had a quiet, unassuming management style. Over time I learned to respect his judgment and his ability to get people to work together. When you went to him with a problem or a request, he always listened carefully. If he couldn't do what you wanted him to do, he would take the time to explain why. When disagreements arose he always thought of what was best for the project. He treated everyone by the same rules; no one got special treatment. I'd jump at the opportunity to work on a project with him again.

Character alone will not engender trust. We must also have confidence in the competency of individuals before we really trust them. We all know well-intended managers whom we like but do not trust because they have a history of coming up short on their promises. Although we may befriend these managers, we don't like to work with or for them.

Competence is reflected at a number of different levels. First, there is task-related knowledge and skills reflected in the ability to answer questions, solve technical problems, and excel in certain kinds of work. Second, there is competence at an interpersonal level demonstrated in being able to listen effectively, communicate clearly, resolve arguments, provide encouragement, and so forth. Finally, there is organizational competence. This includes being able to run effective meetings, set meaningful objectives, reduce inefficiencies, and build a social network. Too often there is a tendency for young engineers and other professionals to place too much value on task or technical competence. They underestimate the significance of organizational skills. Veteran professionals, on the other hand, recognize the importance of management and place a greater value on organizational and interpersonal skills.

One problem new project managers experience is that it takes time to establish a sense of character and competency. Character and competency are often demonstrated when they are tested, such as when a tough call has to be made or when difficult problems have to be solved. Veteran project managers have the advantage of reputation and an established track record of success. Although endorsements from credible sponsors can help a young project manager create a favorable first impression, ultimately he or she will have to demonstrate character and competence during the course of dealings with others in order to gain their trust.

So far this chapter has addressed the importance of building a network of relationships to complete the project based on trust and reciprocity. The next section examines the nature of project management work and the personal qualities needed to excel at it.

Qualities of an Effective Project Manager

Project management is, at first glance, a misleading discipline in that there is an inherent logic in the progression from formulating a project scope statement, creating a WBS, developing a network, adding resources, finalizing a plan, and reaching milestones. However, when it comes to actually implementing and completing projects, this logic quickly disappears, and project managers encounter a much messier world, filled with inconsistencies and paradoxes. Effective project managers have to be able to deal with the contradictory nature of their work. Some of those contradictions are listed here:

- **Innovate and maintain stability.** Project managers have to put out fires, restore order, and get the project back on track. At the same time they need to be innovative and develop new, better ways of doing things. Innovations unravel stable routines and spark new disturbances that have to be dealt with.
- **See the big picture while getting your hands dirty.** Project managers have to see the big picture and how their project fits within the larger strategy of their firm. There are also times when they must get deeply involved in project work and technology. If they don't worry about the details, who will?
- **Encourage individuals but stress the team.** Project managers have to motivate, cajole, and entice individual performers while at the same time maintaining teamwork. They have to be careful that they are considered fair and consistent in their treatment of team members while at the same time treating each member as a special individual.
- **Hands-off/Hands-on.** Project managers have to intervene, resolve stalemates, solve technical problems, and insist on different approaches. At the same time they have to recognize when it is appropriate to sit on the sidelines and let other people figure out what to do.
- **Flexible but firm.** Project managers have to be adaptable and responsive to events and outcomes that occur on the project. At the same time they have to hold the line at times and tough it out when everyone else wants to give up.
- **Team versus organizational loyalties.** Project managers need to forge a unified project team whose members stimulate one another to extraordinary performance. But at the same time they have to counter the excesses of cohesion and the team's resistance to outside ideas. They have to cultivate loyalties to both the team and the parent organization.

Managing these and other contradictions requires finesse and balance. Finesse involves the skillful movement back and forth between opposing behavioral patterns. For example, most of the time project managers actively involve others, move by increment, and seek consensus. There are other times when project managers must act as autocrats and take decisive, unilateral action. Balance involves recognizing the danger of extremes and that too much of a good thing invariably becomes harmful. For example, many managers have a tendency to always delegate the most stressful, difficult assignments to their best team members. This habit often breeds resentment among those chosen ("why am I always the one who gets the tough work?") and never allows the weaker members to develop their talents further.

There is no one management style or formula for being an effective project manager. The world of project management is too complicated for formulas. Successful project managers have a knack for adapting styles to specific circumstances of the situation.

Research Highlight

Emotional intelligence (EQ) describes the ability or skill to perceive, assess, and manage the emotions of one's self and others. Although the notion of EQ emerged in the 1920s, it was not until Daniel Goleman published his book *Emotional Intelligence* that the concept captured the attention of business people and public alike.

Goleman divided EQ into the following five emotional competences:

- **Self-awareness**—knowing your emotions, recognizing feelings as they occur, and understanding the link between your emotions and your behavior. Self-awareness is reflected in confidence, realistic assessment of personal strengths/weaknesses, and ability to make fun of oneself.
- **Self-regulation**—being able to control disruptive impulses and moods and respond appropriately to situations. Self-regulation is reflected in trustworthiness and openness to change.
- **Self-motivation**— being able to gather up your feelings and pursue goals with energy, passion, and persistence. The hallmarks of self-motivation include a strong desire to achieve and internal optimism.
- **Empathy**—being able to recognize the feelings of others and tuning into their verbal and nonverbal cues. Empathy is reflected in the ability to sustain relationships and in cross-cultural sensitivity.
- **Social skills**—being able to build social networks and rapport with different kinds of people. Social skills include being able to lead change, resolve conflicts, and build effective teams.

Not much imagination is needed to see how EQ would contribute to being an effective project manager.

In Goleman's view, these competences build on each other in a hierarchy. At the bottom of his hierarchy is selfawareness. Some level of self-awareness is needed to move to self-regulation. Ultimately, social skills requires all four of the other competences in order to begin to be proficient at leading others. Experts believe that most people can learn to significantly increase their EQ. Numerous training programs and materials have emerged to help individuals realize their EQ potential.

* T. Bradberry, and J. Graves, *The Emotional Intelligence Quick Book: How to Put Your EQ to Work* (New York: Simon & Schuster, 2005); J. Cabanis-Brewin, "The Human Task of a Project Leader: Daniel Goleman on the Value of High EQ," *PM Network*, November 1999, pp. 38–42.

So, what should one look for in an effective project manager? Many authors have addressed this question and have generated list after list of skills and attributes associated with being an effective manager. When reviewing these lists, one sometimes gets the impression that to be a successful project manager requires someone with superhuman powers. While we agree that not everyone has the right stuff to be an effective project manager, there are some core traits and skills that can be developed to successfully perform the job. Eight of these traits are noted below.

1. **Systems thinker.** Project managers must be able to take a holistic rather than a reductionist approach to projects. Instead of breaking up a project into individual pieces (planning, budget) and managing it by understanding each part, a systems perspective focuses on trying to understand how relevant project factors collectively interact to produce project outcomes. The key to success then becomes managing the interaction between different parts and not the parts themselves.

2. **Personal integrity.** Before you can lead and manage others, you have to be able to lead and manage yourself. Begin by establishing a firm sense of who you are, what you stand for, and how you should behave. This inner strength provides the buoyancy to endure the ups and downs of the project life cycle and the credibility essential to sustaining the trust of others.

3. **Proactive.** Good project managers take action before it is needed to prevent small concerns from escalating into major problems. They spend the majority of their time working within their sphere of influence to solve problems and not dwelling on things they have little control over. Project managers can't be whiners.

4. **High emotional intelligence (EQ).** Project management is not for the meek. Project managers have to have command of their emotions and be able to respond constructively to others when things get a bit out of control. See the Research Highlight: Emotional Intelligence to read more about this concept.

5. **General business perspective.** Because the primary role of a project manager is to integrate the contributions of different business and technical disciplines, it is important that a manager have a general grasp of business fundamentals and how the different functional disciplines interact to contribute to a successful business.

6. **Effective time management.** Time is a manager's scarcest resource. Project managers have to be able to budget their time wisely and quickly adjust their priorities. They need to balance their interactions so no one feels ignored.

7. **Skillful politician.** Project managers have to be able to deal effectively with a wide range of people and win their support and endorsement of their project. They need to be able to sell the virtues of their project without compromising the truth.

8. **Optimist.** Project managers have to display a can-do attitude. They have to be able to find rays of sunlight in a dismal day and keep people's attention positive. A good sense of humor and a playful attitude are often a project manager's greatest strength.

So how does one develop these traits? Workshops, self-study, and courses can upgrade one's general business perspective and capacity for systems thinking. Training programs can improve emotional intelligence and political skills. People can also be taught stress and time management techniques. However, we know of no workshop or magic potion that can transform a pessimist into an optimist or provide a sense of purpose when there is not one. These qualities get at the very soul or being of a person. Optimism, integrity, and even being proactive are not easily developed if there is not already a predisposition to display them.

Summary

To be successful, project managers must build a cooperative network among a diverse set of allies. They begin by identifying who the key stakeholders on a project are, followed by a diagnosis of the nature of the relationships, and the basis for exercising influence. Effective project managers are skilled at acquiring and exercising a wide range of influence. They use this influence and a highly interactive management style to monitor project performance and initiate appropriate changes in project plans and direction. They do so in a manner that generates trust, which is ultimately based on others' perceptions of their character and competence.

Project managers are encouraged to keep in mind the following suggestions:

- *Build relationships before you need them.* Identify key players and what you can do to help them before you need their assistance. It is always easier to receive a favor after you have granted one. This requires the project manager to see the project in systems terms and to appreciate how it affects other activities and agendas inside and outside the organization. From this perspective they can identify opportunities to do good deeds and garner the support of others.

- *Trust is sustained through frequent face-to-face contact.* Trust withers through neglect. This is particularly true under conditions of rapid change and uncertainty that naturally engender doubt, suspicion, and even momentary bouts of paranoia. Project managers must maintain frequent contact with key stakeholders to keep abreast of developments, assuage concerns, engage in reality testing, and focus attention on the project. Frequent face-to-face interactions affirm mutual respect and trust in each other.

Ultimately, exercising influence in an effective and ethical manner begins and ends with how you view the other parties. Do you view them as potential partners or obstacles to your goals? If obstacles, then you wield your influence to manipulate and gain compliance and cooperation. If partners, you exercise influence to gain their commitment and support. People who view social network building as building partnerships see every interaction with two goals: resolving the immediate problem/concern and improving the working relationship so that next time it will be even more effective. Experienced project managers realize that "what goes around comes around" and try at all cost to avoid antagonizing players for quick success.

Key Terms

Emotional intelligence
 (EQ)
Law of reciprocity
Leading by example

Management by wandering
 around (MBWA)
Organizational currencies
Proactive

Project sponsor
Social network building
Stakeholder
Systems thinking

Review Questions

1. What is the difference between leading and managing a project?

2. Why is a conductor of an orchestra an appropriate metaphor for being a project manager? What aspects of project managing are not reflected by this metaphor? Can you think of other metaphors that would be appropriate?

3. What does the exchange model of influence suggest you do to build cooperative relationships to complete a project?

4. What differences would you expect to see between the kinds of influence currencies that a project manager in a functional matrix would use and the influence a project manager of a dedicated project team would use?

5. Why is it important to build a relationship before you need it?

6. Why is it critical to keep the project sponsor informed?

7. Why is trust a function of both character and competence?

8. Which of the eight traits/skills associated with being an effective project manager is the most important? The least important? Why?

Exercises

1. Do an Internet search for the Keirsey Temperament Sorter Questionnaire and find a site that appears to have a reputable self-assessment questionnaire. Respond to the questionnaire to identify your temperament type. Read supportive documents associated with your type. What does this material suggest are the kinds of projects that would best suit you? What does it suggest your strengths and weaknesses are as a project manager? How can you compensate for your weaknesses?

2. Access the Project Management Institute Web site and review the standards contained in PMI Member Ethical Standards section. How useful is the information for helping someone decide what behavior is appropriate and inappropriate?

3. You are organizing an AIDS benefit concert in your hometown that will feature local heavy metal rock groups and guest speakers. Draw a dependency map identifying the major groups of people

that are likely to affect the success of this project. Who do you think will be most cooperative? Who do you think will be the least cooperative? Why?

4. You are the project manager responsible for the overall construction of a new international airport. Draw a dependency map identifying the major groups of people that are likely to affect the success of this project. Who do you think will be most cooperative? Who do you think will be the least cooperative? Why?

5. Identify an important relationship (co-worker, boss, friend) in which you are having trouble gaining cooperation. Assess this relationship in terms of the influence currency model. What kinds of influence currency have you been exchanging in this relationship? Is the "bank account" for this relationship in the "red" or the "black"? What kinds of influence would be appropriate for building a stronger relationship with that person?

6. Each of the following six mini-case scenarios involve ethical dilemmas associated with project management. How would you respond to each situation, and why?

Jack Nietzche

You returned from a project staffing meeting in which future project assignments were finalized. Despite your best efforts, you were unable to persuade the director of project management to promote one of your best assistants, Jack Nietzche, to a project manager position. You feel a bit guilty because you dangled the prospect of this promotion to motivate Jack. Jack responded by putting in extra hours to ensure that his segments of the project were completed on time. You wonder how Jack will react to this disappointment. More importantly, you wonder how his reaction might affect your project. You have five days remaining to meet a critical deadline for a very important customer. While it won't be easy, you believed you would be able to complete the project on time. Now you're not so sure. Jack is halfway through completing the documentation phase, which is the last critical activity. Jack can be pretty emotional at times, and you are worried that he will blow up once he finds he didn't get the promotion. As you return to your office, you wonder what you should do. Should you tell Jack that he isn't going to be promoted? What should you say if he asks about whether the new assignments were made?

Seaburst Construction Project

You are the project manager for the Seaburst construction project. So far the project is progressing ahead of schedule and below budget. You attribute this in part to the good working relationship you have with the carpenters, plumbers, electricians, and machine operators who work for your organization. More than once you have asked them to give 110 percent, and they have responded.

One Sunday afternoon you decide to drive by the site and show it to your son. As you point out various parts of the project to your son, you discover that several pieces of valuable equipment are missing from the storage shed. When you start work again on Monday you are about to discuss this matter with a supervisor when you realize that all the missing equipment is back in the shed. What should you do? Why?

The Project Status Report Meeting

You are driving to a project status report meeting with your client. You encountered a significant technical problem on the project that has put your project behind schedule. This is not good news because completion time is the number one priority for the project. You are confident that your team can solve the problem if they are free to give their undivided attention to it and that with hard work you can get back on schedule. You also believe if you tell the client about the problem, she will demand a meeting with your team to discuss the implications of the problem. You can also expect her to send some of her personnel to oversee the solution to the problem. These interruptions will likely further delay the project. What should you tell your client about the current status of the project?

Gold Star LAN project

You work for a large consulting firm and were assigned to the Gold Star LAN project. Work on the project is nearly completed and your clients at Gold Star appear to be pleased with your performance. During the course of the project, changes in the original scope had to be made to accommodate specific needs of managers at Gold Star. The costs of these changes were documented as well as overhead and submitted to the centralized accounting department. They processed the information and submitted a change order bill for your signature. You are surprised to see the bill is 10 percent higher than what you submitted. You contact Jim Messina in the accounting office and ask if a mistake has been made. He curtly replies that no mistake was made and that management adjusted the bill. He recommends that you sign the document. You talk to another project manager about this and she tells you off the record that overcharging clients on change orders is common practice in your firm. Would you sign the document? Why? Why not?

Cape Town Bio-Tech

You are responsible for installing the new Double E production line. Your team has collected estimates and used the WBS to generate a project schedule. You have confidence in the schedule and the work your team has done. You report to top management that you believe that the project will take 110 days and be completed by March 5. The news is greeted positively. In fact, the project sponsor confides that orders do not have to be shipped until April 1. You leave the meeting wondering whether you should share this information with the project team or not.

Ryman Pharmaceuticals

You are a test engineer on the Bridge project at Ryman Pharmaceuticals in Nashville, Tennessee. You have just completed conductivity tests of a new electrochemical compound. The results exceeded expectations. This new compound should revolutionize the industry. You are wondering whether to call your stockbroker and ask her to buy $20,000 worth of Ryman stock before everyone else finds out about the results. What would you do and why?

References

Ancona, D. G., and D. Caldwell, "Improving the Performance of New-Product Teams," *Research Technology Management,* 33 (2) March-April 1990, pp. 25–29.

Anand, V., B. E. Ashforth, and M. Joshi, "Business as Usual: The Acceptance and Perpetuation of Corruption in Organizations," *Academy of Management Executive,* 19 (4) 2005, pp. 9–23.

Badaracco, J. L. Jr., and A. P. Webb, "Business Ethics: A View from the Trenches," *California Management Review,* 37 (2) Winter 1995, pp. 8–28.

Baker, B., "Leadership and the Project Manager," *PM Network,* December 2002, p. 20.

Baker, W. E., *Network Smart: How to Build Relationships for Personal and Organizational Success* (New York: McGraw-Hill, 1994).

Bennis, W., *On Becoming a Leader* (Reading, MA: Addison-Wesley, 1989).

Bradberry, T., and J. Graves, *The Emotional Intelligence Quick Book: How to Put Your EQ to Work* (New York: Simon & Schuster, 2005).

Cabanis, J., "A Question of Ethics: The Issues Project Managers Face and How They Resolve Them," *PM Network,* December 1996, pp. 19–24.

Cabanis-Brewin, J., "The Human Task of a Project Leader: Daniel Goleman on the Value of High EQ," *PM Network,* November 1999, pp. 38–42.

Cohen, A. R., and D. L. Bradford, *Influence Without Authority* (New York: John Wiley & Sons, 1990).

Covey, S. R., *The Seven Habits of Highly Effective People* (New York: Simon & Schuster, 1989).

Dinsmore, P. C., "Will the Real Stakeholders Please Stand Up?" *PM Network,* December 1995, pp. 9–10.

Gabarro, S. J., *The Dynamics of Taking Charge* (Boston: Harvard Business School Press, 1987).

Hill, L. A., *Becoming A Manager: Mastery of a New Identity* (Boston: Harvard Business School Press, 1992).

Kaplan, R. E., "Trade Routes: The Manager's Network of Relationships," *Organizational Dynamics,* 12 (4) Spring 1984, pp. 37–52.

Kirk, D., "Managing Expectations," *PM Network,* August 2000, pp. 59–62.

Kotter, J. P., "What Leaders Really Do," *Harvard Business Review,* 68 (3) May–June 1990, pp. 103–11.

Kouzes, J. M., and B. Z. Posner, *The Leadership Challenge* (San Francisco: Jossey-Bass, 1987).

Kouzes, J. M., and B. Z. Posner, *Credibility: How Leaders Gain and Lose It. Why People Demand It* (San Francisco: Jossey-Bass, 1993).

Larson, E. W., and J. B. King, "The Systemic Distortion of Information: An Ongoing Management Challenge," *Organizational Dynamics,* 24 (3) Winter 1996, pp. 49–62.

Lewis, M. W., M. A. Welsh, G. E. Dehler, and S.G. Green, "Product Development Tensions: Exploring Contrasting Styles of Project Management," *Academy of Management Journal,* 45 (3) 2002, pp. 546–64.

Peters, L. H., "A Good Man in a Storm: An Interview with Tom West," *Academy of Management Executive,* 16 (4) 2002, pp. 53–63.

Peters, L. H., "Soulful Ramblings: An Interview with Tracy Kidder," *Academy of Management Executive,* 16 (4) 2002, pp. 45–52.

Peters, T., *Thriving on Chaos: Handbook For a Management Revolution* (New York: Alfred A. Knopf, 1988).

Pinto, J. K., and S. K. Mantel, "The Causes of Project Failure," *IEEE Transactions in Engineering Management,* 37 (4) 1990, pp. 269–76.

Pinto, J. K., and D. P. Sleven, "Critical Success Factors in Successful Project Implementation," *IEEE Transactions in Engineering Management,* 34 (1) 1987, pp. 22–27.

Posner, B. Z., "What It Takes to Be an Effective Project Manager," *Project Management Journal,* March 1987, pp. 51–55.

Project Management Institute, *Leadership in Project Management Annual* (Newton Square, PA: PMI Publishing, 2006).

Robb, D. J., "Ethics in Project Management: Issues, Practice, and Motive," *PM Network,* December 1996, pp. 13–18.

Sayles, L. R., *Leadership: Managing in Real Organizations* (New York: McGraw-Hill, 1989), pp. 70–78.

Sayles, L. R., *The Working Leader* (New York: Free Press, 1993).

Senge, P. M., *The Fifth Discipline* (New York: Doubleday, 1990).

Shenhar, A. J., and B. Nofziner, "A New Model for Training Project Managers," *Proceedings of the 28th Annual Project Management Institute Symposium,* 1997, pp. 301–6.

Shtub, A., J. F. Bard, and S. Globerson, *Project Management: Engineering, Technology, and Implementation* (Englewood Cliffs, NJ: Prentice Hall, 1994).

CASE 10.1

Western Oceanography Institute

It was already 72 degrees when Astrid Young pulled into the parking lot at the Western Oceanography Institute (WOI). The radio announcer was reminding listeners to leave out extra water for their pets because the temperature was going to be in the high 90s for the third straight day. Young made a mental note to call her husband, Jon, when she got to her office and make sure that he left plenty of water outside for their cat, Figaro. Young was three-quarters of the way through the Microsoft NT conversion project. Yesterday had been a disaster, and she was determined to get back on top of things.

Astrid Young

Astrid Young was a 27-year-old graduate of Western State University (WSU) with a B.S. degree in management information systems. After graduation she worked for five years at Evergreen Systems in Seattle, Washington. While at WSU she worked part time for an oceanography professor, Ahmet Green, creating a customized database for a research project he was conducting. Green was recently appointed director of WOI, and Young was confident that this prior experience was instrumental in her getting the job as information services (IS) director at the Institute. Although she took a significant pay cut, she jumped at the opportunity to return to her alma mater. Her job at Evergreen Systems had been very demanding. The long hours and extensive traveling had created tension in her marriage. She was looking forward to a normal job with reasonable hours. Besides, Jon would be busy pursuing his MBA at Western State. While at Evergreen, Young worked on Y2000 projects and installed NT servers. She was confident that she had the requisite technical expertise to excel at her new job.

Western Oceanography Institute was an independently funded research facility aligned with Western State University. Approximately 60 full- and part-time staff worked at the Institute. They worked on research grants funded by the National Science Foundation (NSF) and the United Nations (UN), as well as research financed by private industry. There were typically 7 to 8 major research projects under way at any one time as well as 20 to 25 smaller projects. One-third of the Institute's scientists had part-time teaching assignments at WSU and used the Institute to conduct their own basic research.

First Four Months at WOI

Young worked at the Institute for four months prior to initiating the NT conversion project. She made a point of introducing herself to the various groups of people upon her arrival at the Institute. Still, her contact with the staff had been limited. She spent most of her time becoming familiar with WOI's information system, training her staff, responding to unexpected problems, and planning the conversion project. Young suffered from food allergies and refrained from informal staff lunches at nearby restaurants. She stopped regularly attending the biweekly staff meetings in order to devote more time to her work. She now only attended the meetings when there was a specific agenda item regarding her operation.

Last month the system was corrupted by a virus introduced over the Internet. She devoted an entire weekend to restoring the system to operation. A recurring headache was one of the servers code named "Poncho" that would occasionally shut down for no apparent reason. Instead of replacing it, she decided to nurse Poncho along until it was replaced by the new NT system. Her work was frequently interrupted by frantic calls from staff researchers who needed immediate help on a variety of computer-related problems. She was shocked at how computer illiterate some of the researchers were and how she had to guide them through some of the basics of e-mail management and database configuration. She did find time to help Assistant Professor Amanda Johnson on a project. Johnson was the only researcher to respond to Young's e-mail announcing that the IS staff was available to help on projects. Young created a virtual project office on the Internet so that Johnson could collaborate with colleagues from institutes in Italy and Thailand on a UN research grant. She looked forward to the day when she could spend more time on fun projects like that.

Young had a part-time team of five student assistants from the computer science department. At first she was not sure how freely she could delegate work to the students, and she closely supervised their work. She quickly realized that they were all very bright, competent workers who were anxious to leverage this work experience into a lucrative career upon graduation. She admitted that she sometimes had a hard time relating to students who were preoccupied with fraternity bashes and X-games. She lost her temper only once, and that was at Samantha Eggerts for failing to set up an adequate virus screening system that would have prevented the Internet corruption that occurred. She kept a close eye on Eggerts's work after that, but in time, Eggert proved her worth. Young saw a lot of herself in Eggerts's work habits.

The Microsoft NT Conversion Project

Young laid the groundwork for the NT conversion project in her recruitment interview with the director by arguing that conversion was a critical skill she would bring to the position. Once hired she was able to sell the director and his immediate staff on the project, but not without some resistance. Some associate directors questioned whether it was necessary to go through another conversion so soon after the Windows 95 conversion 16 months ago. Some of the researchers lobbied that the money would be better spent on installing a centralized air-conditioning system at WOI. Ultimately, the director signed off on the project after Young assured him that the conversion would be relatively painless and the Institute would then have a state-of-the-art information system.

The conversion was scheduled to take eight weeks to complete and consisted of four major phases: server setup, network installation, data migration, and workstation conversion. The project would be completed during the summer so that the student assistants could work full time on the project. Young and her student team would first need to purchase and set up seven new NT servers. They would then create a new local area network (LAN). Next they would migrate data to the new Oracle NT database. Finally, they would convert the existing 65 client computers into NT workstations capable of functioning on the new system. Young had been actively involved in four similar conversions when working at Evergreen Systems and was confident that she and her team could complete the project with a minimum of technical problems. She also believed that this conversion would not be traumatic to the staff at the Institute because the NT interface was very similar to the Windows 95 interface.

Young knew that in order for the project to be considered successful, there needed to be minimum disruption of daily staff functions. She held a staff briefing meeting to outline the scope of the project and the impact it would have on the Institute's operations. She was disappointed by the light attendance at the meeting. One problem was the irregular hours staff worked at WOI. Several of the researchers were night owls who preferred to work late into the night. Other staff traveled frequently. She ended up holding two other briefing meetings, including one in the evening. Still the attendance was less than desired.

The staff's major concerns were the amount of downtime that would occur and whether the software and databases they were currently using would work on the new system. Young assured them that most of the downtime would occur on the weekends and would be posted well in advance. The only disruption would be two hours necessary to convert their existing computer into a workstation. Young invested extra energy in researching the compatibility issue and sent an e-mail to everyone listing the software that was known to not work in the NT system. The only software problems involved specially written DOS v2.1 or older programs that would not function in the new NT operating environment. In one case, she assigned a student to rewrite and enhance the present program for a researcher. In the other case, she was able to persuade the staff member to use a newer, better program.

Young sent a second e-mail asking staff members to clean up their hard drives and get rid of old, obsolete files because the new NT software would take up considerably more space than the Windows 95 operating system. In some cases, she replaced existing hard drives with bigger drives so that this would not be a problem. She circulated a workstation conversion schedule by e-mail so that staff could pick a preferred time for when their computer would be down and when her assistants could upgrade the computer into a workstation. Seventy percent of the staff responded to the e-mail request, and she and her staff contacted the remaining staff by telephone to schedule the conversion.

The first six weeks of the project went relatively smoothly. The NT servers arrived on time and were installed and configured on schedule. The completion of the network was delayed three days when the fire marshal showed up earlier than planned to inspect the electrical wiring. Young had never met the marshal before and was surprised at how nit-picking he was. They failed the inspection, and it took three days to reschedule and pass inspection. Word about failing the fire inspection circulated the hallways at the Institute. One joker put a Smokey the Bear sign on the IS office door. Young later found out that as a result of a recent fire in town, the fire marshals had been instructed to be extra vigilant in their inspections.

Data migration to the new Oracle database took a little longer than planned because the new version was not as compatible with the old version as advertised. Still, this only added three days to the project. The project was entering the fourth and final phase—conversion of client computers into NT workstations. This phase involved her staff deleting the old operating system and installing new operating software in each computer at the Institute. Young had scheduled two hours per machine and had organized a daily workload of 10 computers so that adequate backup could be made just in case something went wrong.

Young chose to convert the director's office first and told Green that everything was going according to plan. Soon the project began to experience nagging problems. First, some of the staff forgot when they were scheduled to be converted. The team had to wait for them to abandon what they were doing so they could convert the computer. Second, the drivers on some of the computers were not compatible, and the team had to devote extra time downloading new drivers off the Internet. Third, a few of the staff failed to create adequate hard drive space to accommodate the new NT software. In most cases, the team worked with the staff member to delete or compress unnecessary files. One time the staff member could not be found, and Young had to decide which files to delete. This wasn't a problem since the hard drive contained computer games and ancient Word Perfect files. To compound matters, midway through the third day, one of the student assistants, Steve Stills, was diagnosed with a moderate case of carpal tunnel and was told to take two weeks off from computer work.

After three days only 22 computers had been converted to NT stations. Young ended the day by sending an e-mail to the remaining users apologizing for the delays and posting a revised schedule for their system configuration.

The Call

Young and her staff were working diligently on converting computers into NT workstations when she received an urgent call from the director's secretary requesting that she drop everything and come downstairs to the staff meeting. The secretary's voice appeared tense, and Young wondered what was up. As she gathered her things, the student assistant, Eggerts, cleared her throat and confided that there may be problems with some of the Institute's Web sites. She discovered yesterday that some of the links in the Web pages created using Netscape weren't working in the Microsoft environment. Young demanded to know why she wasn't told about this sooner. Eggerts confessed that she thought she had fixed the problem last night. Young told her that they would talk about this when she got back and left.

Young entered the meeting room and immediately recognized that there were more than the usual faces in attendance. The director welcomed her by saying, "We're glad you could find the time to visit with us. My staff meeting has just erupted into a series of complaints about your NT conversion project. As it turns out Dr. Phillips over here can't access his documents because his Word Perfect file mysteriously disappeared. Dr. Simon's geothermal assessment program, which he has used for the past seven years, doesn't seem to work anymore. Now it appears that the Web site we use to coordinate our research with the Oslo Institute is a mess. Everyone is complaining about how the revised installation schedule is going to disrupt work. I want to know why I wasn't informed about these problems. These guys want to lynch me for approving your project!"

1. How would you respond to the director?
2. What mistakes did Young make that contributed to the problems at the end of the case?
3. How could she have managed the conversion project better?

CASE 10.2

Tom Bray

Tom Bray was mulling over today's work schedule as he looked across the bay at the storm that was rolling in. It was the second official day of the Pegasus project and now the real work was about to begin.

Pegasus was a two-month renovation project for AtlantiCorp, a major financial institution headquartered in Boston, Massachusetts. Tom's group was responsible for installing the furniture and equipment in the newly renovated accounts receivable department on the third floor. The Pegasus project was a dedicated project team formed out of AtlantiCorp facilities department with Tom as the project lead.

Tom was excited because this was his first *major league* project and he was looking forward to practicing a new management style—MBWA, aka management by wandering around. He had been exposed to MBWA in a business class in college, but it wasn't until he attended an AtlantiCorp leadership training seminar that he decided to change how he managed people. The trainer was devout MBWA champion ("You can't manage people from a computer!"). Furthermore, the testimonies from his peers reinforced the difference that MBWA can make when it comes to working on projects.

Tom had joined the facilities group at AtlantiCorp five years earlier after working for EDS for six years. He quickly demonstrated technical competences and good work habits. He was encouraged to take all the internal project management workshops offered by AtlantiCorp. On his last two projects he served as assistant project manager responsible for procurement and contract management.

He had read books about the soft side of project management and MBWA made sense—after all, people not tools get projects done. His boss had told him he needed to refine his people skills and work on developing rapport with team members. MBWA seemed like a perfect solution.

Tom reviewed the list of team member names; some of the foreign names were real tongue twisters. For example, one of his better workers was from Thailand and her name was Pinyarat Sirisomboonsuk. He practiced saying "Pin-ya-råt See-rē-som-boon-sook." He got up, tucked in his shirt, and walked out of his office and down to the floor where his team was busy unloading equipment.

Tom said "Hi" to the first few workers he met until he encountered Jack and three other workers. Jack was busy pulling hardware out of a box while his teammates were standing around talking. Tom blurted, "Come on guys, we've got work to do." They quickly separated and began unloading boxes.

The rest of the visit seemed to go well. He helped Shari unload a heavy box and managed to get an appreciative grin from Pinyarat when he almost correctly pronounced her name. Satisfied, Tom went back up to his office thinking that MBWA wouldn't be that tough to do.

After responding to e-mail and calling some vendors, Tom ventured back out to see how things were going downstairs. When he got there, the floor was weirdly quiet. People were busy doing their work and his attempts at generating conversation elicited stiff responses. He left thinking that maybe MBWA is going to be tougher than he thought.

---

1. What do you think is going on at the end of this case?
2. What should Tom do next and why?
3. What can be learned from this case?

CASE 10.3

Cerberus Corporation*

Cerberus is a successful producer of specialty chemicals. It operates nine large campus sites in the United States, with a number of different business units on each site. These business units operate independently, with direct reporting to corporate headquarters. Site functions such as safety, environmental, and facilities management report to a host organization—typically the business unit that is the largest user of their services.

Susan Steele

Susan Steele has worked in the Facilities group at the Cerberus Richmond site for the last two years. The Facilities manager, Tom Stern, reports to the General Manager of the largest business unit on site, the highly profitable Adhesives and Sealants Division. Susan started with Cerberus when she graduated with her business degree from Awsum University. She was excited about her new assignment—leading a project for the first time. She remembered Tom saying, "We've got office furniture dating back to the 80s. There are those ugly green-top desks that look like they came from military surplus! I'm especially concerned about computer workstation ergonomics—it's a major issue that we absolutely must fix! I want you to lead a project to transition our office furniture to the new corporate standard."

Susan assembled her project team: Jeff, the site safety/ergonomics engineer; Gretchen, the space planner; Cindy, the move coordinator; and Kari, the accounting liaison for Facilities. At their first meeting, everyone agreed that ergonomics was the most urgent concern. All five business units responded to a workstation survey that identified injury-causing ergonomics. The team was developing a plan to replace old desks with new, ergo-adjustable furniture by the end of the year. Susan asked Kari about the budget, and Kari responded, "Facilities should not pay for this. We want the individual business units to pay so that the costs will show where they are incurred."

---

* Courtesy of John Sloan, Oregon State University.

Gretchen spoke up: "You know, we've got lots of department moves going on constantly. Everybody is always jockeying for space and location as their business needs change. Besides the ergonomics, could we say that only corporate standard furniture gets moved? That would force changing some of the stuff that's just plain ugly." Everyone agreed that this was a great idea.

Susan presented the project plan to Tom and got a green light to proceed.

Jon Wood

Jon Wood is a planning manager, with 22 years experience at Cerberus. His business unit, Photographic Chemicals Division (PCD), is losing money. Digital photography is continuing to reduce the size of the market, and PCD is having trouble matching the competition's relentless price-cutting. Jon recently transferred to Richmond from corporate headquarters, where he ran the economic forecasting group. He is considered a new broom, and he is determined to sweep clean.

One of Jon's early actions was to negotiate with his general manager for a department move. Money was tight, and the site facilities function charged an arm and a leg for moves (covering all their fixed overhead, the operations people groused). However, Jon felt it was important to move from Building 4, where they were next to Production, to Building 6, where they could be close to Marketing, Forecasting, and Accounting. His General Manager agreed, and there was lots of excitement in his team about their upcoming move. Jon assigned one of his planners, Richard, to work with the Facilities team on the layout and move plan for the group. Things seemed to be going fine—Jon saw Richard sitting down with the move coordinator, and they seemed to be on track.

The day before the move, Jon hung up the phone from a particularly tense teleconference with a Canadian subcontractor. Production was not going well, and product availability would be tight for the rest of the quarter. Clustered around his desk were Richard, Cindy, and a person he hadn't met yet, Susan. After hurried introductions, Susan told Jon that his filing cabinets could not be moved. The cabinets are large lateral files, five feet wide and two feet deep, a combination of both filing cabinets and bookshelves. Jon brought them with him from Corporate because he thought they looked nice with their dark grey steel sides and wood veneer tops. Susan told him that he would have to replace them with new corporate standard cabinets, virtually the same size. Jon said, "You mean you want me to throw away perfectly good filing cabinets and spend another $2,000 on new ones, just so they match? I won't do it!"

Susan replied, "Then I won't authorize the movement of the old cabinets."

Jon said, "You're joking—these cabinets are grey, the new ones are grey—the only difference is the wood top! You'd throw away $2,000 for nothing?"

Susan replied stiffly, "I'm sorry, that's the policy."

Jon said, "I don't care what the policy is. If I have to move them myself, those cabinets are not going to the dump. My division is losing money and I'm not going to throw money away. If you don't like it, you're going to have to get your general manager to convince my general manager to make me do it. Now would you please leave so I can get some work done."

---

1. If you were Steele, what would you do?
2. What, if anything, could Steele have done differently to avoid this problem?
3. What could the management of Cerberus do to more effectively manage situations like this?

CHAPTER 11

Managing Project Teams

The difference in productivity between an average team and a turned-on, high-performing team is not 10 percent, 20 percent, or 30 percent, but 100 percent, 200 percent, even 500 percent!

—Tom Peters, management consultant and writer

The magic and power of teams is captured in the term "synergy," which is derived from the Greek word *sunergos:* "working together." There is positive and negative synergy. The essence of positive synergy can be found in the phrase "The whole is greater than the sum of the parts." Conversely, negative synergy occurs when the whole is less than the sum of the parts. Mathematically, these two states can be symbolized by the following equations:

$$\text{Positive Synergy } 1 + 1 + 1 + 1 + 1 = 10$$
$$\text{Negative Synergy } 1 + 1 + 1 + 1 + 1 = 2 \text{ (or even } -2)$$

Synergy perhaps can best be seen on a basketball court, a soccer pitch, or a baseball diamond. For example, in 2006 the Oregon State University (OSU) baseball team became the first team outside the sun belt in over 45 years to win the College World Series. The OSU Beaver baseball team, comprised mostly of local, small-town talent, with no top major league prospects, won a record six consecutive elimination games to be crowned champions. Positive synergy could be seen in how the Beavers executed sacrifice bunts, recorded stellar double plays, scratched out timely hits, and overcame adversity. "We played as one," first baseman Bill Rowe said, "When someone went down, somebody picked someone up." The newspaper headline perhaps captured the essence: "The Best Team Won."

Although less visible than in team sports, positive and negative synergy can also be observed and felt in the daily operations of project teams. Here is a description from one team member we interviewed:

> Instead of operating as one big team we fractionalized into a series of subgroups. The marketing people stuck together as well as the systems guys. A lot of time was wasted gossiping and complaining about each other. When the project started slipping behind schedule, everyone started covering their tracks and trying to pass the blame on to others. After a while we avoided direct conversation and resorted to e-mail. Management finally pulled the plug and brought in another team to salvage the project. It was one of the worst project management experiences in my life.

This same individual fortunately was also able to recount a more positive experience:

> There was a contagious excitement within the team. Sure we had our share of problems and setbacks, but we dealt with them straight on and, at times, were able to do the impossible. We all cared about the project and looked out for each other. At the same time we challenged each other to do better. It was one of the most exciting times in my life.

The following is a set of characteristics commonly associated with high-performing teams that exhibit positive synergy:

1. The team shares a sense of common purpose, and each member is willing to work toward achieving project objectives.
2. The team identifies individual talents and expertise and uses them, depending on the project's needs at any given time. At these times, the team willingly accepts the influence and leadership of the members whose skills are relevant to the immediate task.
3. Roles are balanced and shared to facilitate both the accomplishment of tasks and feelings of group cohesion and morale.
4. The team exerts energy toward problem solving rather than allowing itself to be drained by interpersonal issues or competitive struggles.
5. Differences of opinion are encouraged and freely expressed.
6. To encourage risk taking and creativity, mistakes are treated as opportunities for learning rather than reasons for punishment.
7. Members set high personal standards of performance and encourage each other to realize the objectives of the project.
8. Members identify with the team and consider it an important source of both professional and personal growth.

High-performing teams become champions, create breakthrough products, exceed customer expectations, and get projects done ahead of schedule and under budget. They are bonded together by mutual interdependency and a common goal or vision. They trust each other and exhibit a high level of collaboration.

The Five-Stage Team Development Model

Just as infants develop in certain ways during their first months of life, many experts argue that groups develop in a predictable manner. One of the most popular models identifies five stages (see Figure 11.1) through which groups develop into effective teams:

1. **Forming.** During this initial stage the members get acquainted with each other and understand the scope of the project. They begin to establish ground rules by trying to find out what behaviors are acceptable with respect to both the project (what role they will play, what performance expectations are) and interpersonal relations (who's really in charge). This stage is completed once members begin to think of themselves as part of a group.
2. **Storming.** As the name suggests, this stage is marked by a high degree of internal conflict. Members accept that they are part of a project group but resist the constraints that the project and group put on their individuality. There is conflict over who will control the group and how decisions will be made. As these conflicts are resolved, the project manager's leadership becomes accepted, and the group moves to the next stage.
3. **Norming.** The third stage is one in which close relationships develop and the group demonstrates cohesiveness. Feelings of camaraderie and shared responsibility for the project are heightened. The norming phase is complete when the group structure solidifies and the group establishes a common set of expectations about how members should work together.
4. **Performing.** The team operating structure at this point is fully functional and accepted. Group energy has moved from getting to know each other and how the group will work together to accomplishing the project goals.

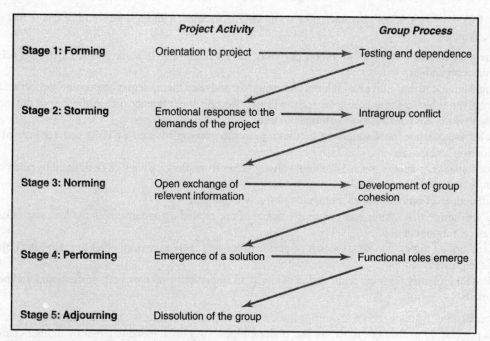

FIGURE 11.1   The Five-Stage Team Development Model

5. **Adjourning.** For conventional work groups, performing is the last stage of their development. However, for project teams, there is a completion phase. During this stage, the team prepares for its own disbandment. High performance is no longer a top priority. Instead attention is devoted to wrapping up the project. Responses of members vary in this stage. Some members are upbeat, basking in the project team's accomplishments. Others may be depressed over loss of camaraderie and friendships gained during the project's life.

This model has several implications for those working on project teams. The first is that the model provides a framework for the group to understand its own development. Project managers have found it useful to share the model with their teams. It helps members accept the tensions of the storming phase, and it directs their focus to moving toward the more productive phases. Another implication is that it stresses the importance of the norming phase, which contributes significantly to the level of productivity experienced during the performing phase. Project managers, as we shall see, have to take an active role in shaping group norms that will contribute to ultimate project success. For an alternative model of group development see the Punctuated Equilibrium Research Highlight.

Situational Factors Affecting Team Development

Experience and research indicate that high-performance project teams are much more likely to develop under the following conditions:

- There are 10 or fewer members per team.
- Members volunteer to serve on the project team.
- Members serve on the project from beginning to end.

Research Highlight	The Punctuated Equilibrium Model of Group Development*

Gersick's research suggests that groups don't develop in a universal sequence of stages as suggested by the five-phase model. Her research, which is based on the systems concept of *punctuated equilibrium,* found that the *timing* of when groups form and actually change the way they work is highly consistent. What makes this research appealing is that it is based on studies of more than a dozen field and laboratory task forces assigned to complete a specific project. This research reveals that each group begins with a unique approach to accomplishing its project that is set in its first meeting and includes the behavior and roles that dominate phase I. Phase I continues until one-half of the allotted time for project completion has expired (regardless of actual amount of time). At this midpoint, a major transition occurs that includes the dropping of the group's old norms and behavior patterns and the emergence of new behavior and working relationships that contribute to increased progress toward completing the project. The last meeting is marked by accelerated activity to complete the project. These findings are summarized in Figure 11.2.

The remarkable discovery in these studies was that each group experienced its transition at the same point in its calendar—precisely halfway between the first meeting and the completion deadline—despite the fact that some groups spent as little as an hour on their project while others spent six months. It was as if the groups universally experienced a midlife crisis at this point. The midpoint appeared to work like an alarm clock, heightening members' awareness that time was limited and they needed to get moving. Within the context of the five-stage model, it suggests that groups begin by combining the forming and norming stages, then go through a period of low performing, followed by storming, then a period of high performing, and finally adjourning.

Gersick's findings suggest that there are natural transition points during the life of teams in which the group is receptive to change and that such a moment naturally occurs at the scheduled midpoint of a project. However, a manager does not want to have to wait 6 months on a complicated 12-month project for a team to get its act together! Here it is important to note that Gersick's groups were working on relatively small-scale projects, i.e., a 4-person bank task force in charge of designing a new bank account in one month and a 12-person medical task force in charge of reorganizing two units of a treatment facility. In most cases no formal project plan was established. If anything, the results point to the importance of good project management and the need to establish deadlines and milestones. By imposing a series of deadlines associated with important milestones, it is possible to create multiple transition points for natural group development. For example, a 12-month construction project can be broken down into six to eight significant milestones with the challenge of meeting each deadline producing the prerequisite tension for elevating team performance.

* Connie J. Gersick, "Time and Transition in Work Teams: Toward a New Model of Group Development," *Academy of Management Journal,* Vol. 31, No. 1 (March 1988), pp. 9–41; and Connie J. Gersick, "Making Time Predictable Transitions in Task Groups," *Academy of Management Journal,* Vol. 32, No. 2 (June 1989), pp. 274–309.

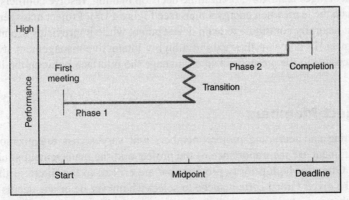

FIGURE 11.2   The Punctuated Equilibrium Model of Group Development

- Members are assigned to the project full time.
- Members are part of an organization culture that fosters cooperation and trust.
- Members report solely to the project manager.
- All relevant functional areas are represented on the team.
- The project involves a compelling objective.
- Members are located within conversational distance of each other.

In reality, it is rare that a project manager is assigned a project that meets all of these conditions. For example, many projects' requirements dictate the active involvement of more than 10 members and may consist of a complex set of interlocking teams comprising more than 100 professionals. In many organizations, functional managers or central manpower offices assign project members with little input from the project manager. To optimize resource utilization, team member involvement may be part time, and/or participants may move in and out of the project team on an as-needed basis. In the case of ad hoc task forces, no member of the team works full time on the project. In many corporations an NIH (not invented here) culture exists that discourages collaboration across functional boundaries.

Team members often report to different managers, and, in some cases, the project manager will have no direct input over performance appraisals and advancement opportunities of team members. Key functional areas may not be represented during the entire duration of the project but may only be involved in a sequential manner. Not all projects have a compelling objective. It can be hard to get members excited about mundane projects such as a simple product extension or a conventional apartment complex. Finally, team members are often scattered across different corporate offices and buildings or, in the case of a virtual project, across the entire globe.

It is important for project managers and team members to recognize the situational constraints they are operating under and do the best they can. It would be naive to believe that every project team has the same potential to evolve into a high-performance team. Under less-than-ideal conditions, it may be a struggle just to meet project objectives. Ingenuity, discipline, and sensitivity to team dynamics are essential to maximizing the performance of a project team.

Building High-Performance Project Teams

Project managers play a key role in developing high-performance project teams. They recruit members, conduct meetings, establish a team identity, create a common sense of purpose or a shared vision, manage a reward system that encourages teamwork, orchestrate decision making, resolve conflicts that emerge within the team, and rejuvenate the team when energy wanes (see Figure 11.3). Project managers take advantage of situational factors that naturally contribute to team development while improvising around those factors that inhibit team development. In doing so they exhibit a highly interactive management style that exemplifies teamwork and, as discussed in the previous chapter, manage the interface between the team and the rest of the organization.

Recruiting Project Members

The process of selecting and recruiting project members will vary across organizations. Two important factors affecting recruitment are the importance of the project and the management structure being used to complete the project. Often for high-priority projects that are critical to the future of the organization, the project manager will be given virtual carte blanche to select whomever he or she deems necessary. For less significant projects, the project manager will have to persuade personnel from other areas within the organization to join the team.

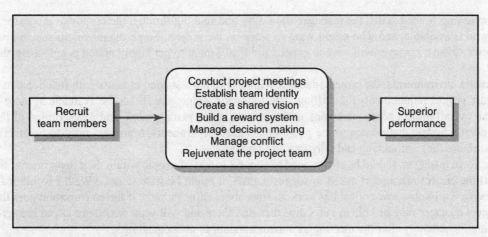

FIGURE 11.3   Creating a High-Performance Project Team

In many matrix structures, the functional manager controls who is assigned to the project; the project manager will have to work with the functional manager to obtain necessary personnel. Even in a project team where members are selected and assigned full time to the project, the project manager has to be sensitive to the needs of others. There is no better way to create enemies within an organization than to be perceived as unnecessarily robbing other departments of essential personnel.

Experienced project managers stress the importance of asking for volunteers. However, this desirable step oftentimes is outside the manager's control. Still, the value of having team members volunteer for the project as opposed to being assigned cannot be overlooked. Agreeing to work on the project is the first step toward building personal commitment to the project. Such commitment will be essential to maintain motivation when the project hits hard times and extra effort is required.

When selecting and recruiting team members, project managers naturally look for individuals with the necessary experience and knowledge/technical skills critical for project completion. At the same time, there are less obvious considerations that need to be factored into the recruitment process:

- *Problem-solving ability.* If the project is complex and fuzzy, then a manager wants people who are good at working under uncertainty and have strong problem identification and solving skills. These same people are likely to be bored and less productive working on straightforward projects that go by the book.
- *Availability.* Sometimes the people who are most available are not the ones wanted for the team. Conversely, if members recruited are already overcommitted, they may not be able to offer much.
- *Technological expertise.* Managers should be wary of people who know too much about a specific technology. They may be technology buffs who like to study but have a hard time settling down and doing the work.
- *Credibility.* The credibility of the project is enhanced by the reputation of the people involved in the project. Recruiting a sufficient number of "winners" lends confidence to the project.
- *Political connections.* Managers are wise to recruit individuals who already have a good working relationship with key stakeholders. This is particularly true for projects operating in a matrix environment in which a significant portion of the work will be under the domain of a specific functional department and not the core project team.
- *Ambition, initiative, and energy.* These qualities can make up for a lot of shortcomings in other areas and should not be underestimated.

After reviewing needed skills, the manager should try and find out through the corporate grapevine who is good, who is available, and who might want to work on the project. Some organizations may allow direct interviews. Often a manager will have to expend political capital to get highly prized people assigned to the project.

In matrix environments, the project manager will have to request appointments with functional managers to discuss project requirements for staffing. The following documents should be available at these discussions: an overall project scope statement, endorsements of top management, and a description of the tasks and general schedule that pertain to the people from their departments. Managers need to be precise as to what attributes they are seeking and why they are important.

Functional managers should be encouraged to suggest names of people within their departments as candidates. If the project manager is asked to suggest names, it might be wise to say, "Well, I would really like Pegi Young, but I know how critical her work is. How about Billy Talbot?" If the conversation goes this way, the project manager may be able to cut a deal then and there and will want to be sure to put the agreement in writing immediately after the meeting as a memorandum of understanding.

If, on the other hand, the functional manager balks at the suggestions and the meeting is not progressing, the project manager should adroitly terminate the conversation with an understanding that the matter will be discussed again in a few days. This technique demonstrates persistence and a desire to do what it takes to resolve the issue. Ultimately, of course, the project manager will have to settle on the best offer. Managers should exercise care not to reveal how different members of the team were selected. The project might be crippled at the start if reluctantly assigned members are identified and the team perceives differences in attitude and commitment.

Conducting Project Meetings

The First Project Team Meeting

Research on team development confirms what we have heard from project managers: The first project kick-off meeting is critical to the early functioning of the project team. According to one veteran project manager:

> The first team meeting sets the tone for how the team will work together. If it is disorganized, or becomes bogged down with little sense of closure, then this can often become a self-fulfilling prophecy for subsequent group work. On the other hand, if it is crisply run, focusing on real issues and concerns in an honest and straightforward manner, members come away excited about being part of the project team.

There are typically three objectives project managers try to achieve during the first meeting of the project team. The first is to provide an overview of the project, including the scope and objectives, the general schedule, method, and procedures. The second is to begin to address some of the interpersonal concerns captured in the team development model: Who are the other team members? How will I fit in? Will I be able to work with these people? The third and most important objective is to begin to model how the team is going to work together to complete the project. The project manager must recognize that first impressions are important; her behavior will be carefully monitored and interpreted by team members. This meeting should serve as an exemplary role model for subsequent meetings and reflect the leader's style.

The meeting itself comes in a variety of shapes and forms. It is not uncommon in major projects for the kick-off meeting to involve one or two days, often at a remote site away from interruptions. This retreat provides sufficient time for preliminary introduction, to begin to establish ground rules, and to define the structure of the project. One advantage of off-site kick-off meetings is that they provide ample opportunity for informal interaction among members during breaks, meals, and evening activities; such informal interactions are critical to forming relationships.

However, many organizations do not have the luxury of holding elaborate retreats. In other cases the scope of project and level of involvement of different participants does not warrant such an investment of time. In these cases, the key operating principle should be KISS (keep it simple stupid!) Too often when constrained by time, project managers try to accomplish too much during the first meeting; in doing so, issues do not get fully resolved, and members come away with an information headache.

The primary goal is to run a productive meeting, and objectives should be realistic given the time available. If the meeting is only one hour, then the project manager should simply review the scope of the project, discuss how the team was formed, and provide an opportunity for members to introduce themselves to the team.

Establishing Ground Rules

Whether as part of an elaborate first meeting or during follow-up meetings, the project manager must quickly begin to establish operational ground rules for how the team will work together. These ground rules involve not only organizational and procedural issues but also normative issues on how the team will interact with each other. Although specific procedures will vary across organizations and projects, some of the major issues that need to be addressed include the following:

Planning Decisions

- How will the project plan be developed?
- What tools will be used to support the project?
- Will a specific project management software package be used? If so, which one?
- Who will enter the planning information?
- What are the specific roles and responsibilities of all the participants?
- Who needs to be informed of decisions? How will they be kept informed?
- What are the relative importance of cost, time, and performance?
- What are the deliverables of the project planning process?
- What format is appropriate for each deliverable?
- Who will approve and sign off at the completion of each deliverable?
- Who receives each deliverable?

Tracking Decisions

- How will progress be assessed?
- At what level of detail will the project be tracked?
- How will team members get data from each other?
- How often will they get this data?
- Who will generate and distribute reports?
- Who needs to be kept informed about project progress, and how will they be informed?
- What content/format is appropriate for each audience?
- Meetings
  - Where will meetings be located?
  - What kind of meetings will be held?
  - Who will "run" these meetings?
  - How will agendas be produced?
  - How will information be recorded?

Snapshot from Practice   Managing Martians*

Courtesy of NASA.

Donna Shirley's 35-year career as aerospace engineer reached a pinnacle in July 1997 when Sojourner—the solar-powered, self-guided, microwave-oven-sized rover—was seen exploring the Martian landscape in Pathfinder's spectacular images from the surface of the red planet. The event marked a milestone in space exploration: No vehicle had ever before roamed the surface of another planet. Shirley, a manager at the Jet Propulsion Laboratory's Mars Exploration Program, headed the mostly male team that designed and built Sojourner. In her insightful memoir, *Managing Martians*, written with Danelle Morton, she makes the following observation about managing creative teams:

> When you are managing really brilliant, creative people, at some point you find it's impossible to command or control them because you can't understand what they are doing. Once they have gone beyond your ability to understand them, you have a choice to make as a manager. You can limit them and the project by your intelligence, which I think is the wrong way to do it. Or you can trust them and use your management skills to keep them focused on the goal.

> A lot of bad managers get threatened when their "subordinates" know more than they do. They either hire people who are inferior to them so they can always feel in control or they bottleneck people who know something they don't so they can maintain control. The whole project suffers from the manager's insecurities.

* Donna Shirley and Danelle Morton, *Managing Martians* (New York: Broadway Books, 1998), pp. 88–89.

Managing Change Decisions

- How will changes be instituted?
- Who will have change approval authority?
- How will plan changes be documented and evaluated?

Relationship Decisions

- What department or organizations will the team need to interact with during the project?
- What are the roles and responsibilities of each organization (reviewer, approver, creator, user)?
- How will all involved parties be kept informed of deliverables, schedule dates, expectations, etc.?
- How will the team members communicate among themselves?
- What information will and won't be exchanged?

Checklists like these are only a guide; items should be added or deleted as needed. Many of these procedures will have already been established by precedent and will only have to be briefly reviewed. For example, *Microsoft Project* or *Primavera* may be the standard software tool for planning and tracking. Likewise, a specific firm is likely to have an established format for reporting status information. How to deal with other issues will have to be determined by the project team. When appropriate, the project manager should actively solicit input from the project team members and draw upon their experience and preferred work habits. This process also contributes to their buying into the operational decisions. Decisions should be recorded and circulated to all members.

During the course of establishing these operational procedures, the project manager, through word and deed, should begin working with members to establish the norms for team interaction. Below are examples of some of the norms researchers have found associated with high-performance teams.

- Confidentiality is maintained; no information is shared outside the team unless all agree to it.
- It is acceptable to be in trouble, but it is not acceptable to surprise others. Tell others immediately when deadlines or milestones will not be reached.
- There is zero tolerance for bulling a way through a problem or an issue.
- Agree to disagree, but when a decision has been made, regardless of personal feelings, move forward.
- Respect outsiders, and do not flaunt one's position on the project team.
- Hard work does not get in the way of having fun.

One way of making these norms more tangible is by creating a project team charter that goes beyond the scope statement of the project and states in explicit terms the norms and values of the team. This charter should be a collaborative effort on the part of the core team. Project managers can lead by proposing certain tenets, but they need to be open to suggestions from the team. Once there is general agreement to the rules of conduct, each member signs the final document to symbolize commitment to the principles it contains.

Unfortunately, in some cases charters become a meaningless ritual because the charter is signed and filed away, never to be discussed again. To have a lasting effect, the charter has to be a legitimate part of the project monitoring system. Just as the team reviews progress toward project objectives, the team assesses the extent to which members are adhering to the principles in the charter.

Project managers play a major role in establishing team norms through personal example. If they freely admit mistakes and share what they have learned from them, other team members will begin to do the same. At the same time, project managers need to intervene when they believe such norms are being violated. They should talk to offenders privately and clearly state their expectations. The amazing thing about groups is that once a group is cohesive, with well-established norms, the members will police themselves so that the manager doesn't have to be the heavy. For example, one project manager confided that his team had a practice of having a small bean bag present at every meeting. If any one member felt that a colleague was shooting hot air or shading the truth, he or she was obligated to toss the bean bag at the speaker.

Managing Subsequent Project Meetings

The project kick-off meeting is one of several kinds of meetings required to complete a project. Other meetings include status report meetings, problem-solving meetings, and audit meetings. Issues unique to these meetings will be discussed in subsequent chapters. For now, here are some general guidelines for running effective meetings. They speak directly to the person chairing the meeting:

- Start meetings on time regardless of whether everyone is present.
- Prepare and distribute an agenda prior to the meeting.
- Identify an adjournment time.

Snapshot from Practice   Mattel's Project Platypus*

AP/Wide World.

Mattel is the largest toy manufacturing company in the world with product lines that include Barbie dolls, Fisher-Price toys, and Hot Wheels. Mattel stumbled when it missed out on the girl empowerment trend in the late 1990s. Vowing never to have this happen again, Mattel re-engineered its product development processes by instituting Project Platypus.

Project Platypus consists of people from a variety of functional areas who leave their regular jobs for three months and move out of Mattel headquarters to a separate location where they work collaboratively on new product ideas. Team members in Mattel's Project Platypus sometimes spend their days dropping eggs from a 14-foot ladder or throwing stuffed animals at each other. It is all part of team-building activities designed to get people to think differently and come up with creative ideas for new toys.

According to Ivy Ross, head of Mattel's girl design division, exercises such as devising a method to prevent an egg from breaking when dropped from 14 feet or throwing stuffed bunnies at a teammate to release inhibitions are ways to get people to think outside the box and discover consumer trends and marketplace changes. "Other companies have skunk works," Ross says, "we have platypus. I looked up the definition and it said, 'an uncommon mix of different species.'"

The strength of the Platypus lies in its members' ability to build on one another's creative ideas. A key group norm is no one owns an idea. Everything belongs to the group, which helps eliminate competitiveness.

Project Platypus is also designed to encourage team bonding, so that people will continue to share ideas and collaborate once the creative ideas move further into product development and production. Previously, product development at Mattel involved a lot of "baton passing," as Ross puts it. Mattel now wants everyone to collaborate in a design and development process where there's a shared sense of ownership and achievement. Participants in the project work in a huge open space with no walls or cubicles. Desks are on wheels to encourage spontaneous sharing and collaboration. Project members can post their sketched ideas on the walls and invite others for suggestions.

The first Project Platypus effort is a new toy called Ello, a hybrid between a construction set and activity kit. Ello sets consist of interconnected pieces that allow children to explore their imagination to build anything from jewelry to buildings. Platypus project teams are continuing to work to develop two to three new product ideas a year.

* Chuck Salter, "Ivy Ross Is Not Playing Around," *Fast Company,* Issue 64, November 2002, p. 104.

- Periodically take time to review how effective previous meetings have been.
- Solicit recommendations and implement changes.
- Assign good recordkeeping.
- Review the agenda before beginning, and tentatively allocate time for each item.
- Prioritize issues so that adjustments can be made given time constraints.
- Encourage active participation of all members by asking questions instead of making statements.
- Summarize decisions, and review assignments for the next meeting.
- Prepare and distribute a summary of the meeting to appropriate people.
- Recognize accomplishments and positive behavior.

Meetings are often considered an anathema to productivity, but this does not have to be the case. The most common complaint is that meetings last too long. Establishing an agenda and adjournment time helps participants budget discussion time and provides a basis for expediting the proceedings. Recordkeeping can be an unwelcome, tedious task. Utilizing laptop computers to record decisions and information in real time can facilitate the communication process. Careful preparation and consistent application of these guidelines can make meetings a vital part of projects.

Establishing a Team Identity

One of the challenges project managers often face in building a team is the lack of full-time involvement of team members. Specialists work on different phases of the project and spend the majority of their time and energy elsewhere. They are often members of multiple teams, each competing for their time and allegiance. Project expert David Frame points out that for many of these specialists a specific project is an abstraction; as a consequence their level of motivation suffers. Project managers need to try to make the project team as tangible as possible to the participants by developing a unique team identity to which participants can become emotionally attached. Team meetings, co-location of team members, team names, and team rituals are common vehicles for doing so.

- *Effective use of meetings.* Periodic project team meetings provide an important forum for communicating project information. A less obvious function of project meetings is to help establish a concrete team identity. During project meetings, members see that they are not working alone. They are part of a larger project team, and project success depends on the collective efforts of all the team members. Timely gatherings of all the project participants help define team membership and reinforce a collective identity.
- *Co-location of team members.* The most obvious way to make the project team tangible is to have members work together in a common space. This is not always possible in matrix environments where involvement is part time and members are working on other projects and activities. A worthwhile substitute for co-location is the creation of a project office, sometimes referred to as the project war room or clubhouse. Such rooms are the common meeting place and contain the most significant project documentation. Frequently, their walls are covered with Gantt charts, cost graphs, and other output associated with project planning and control. These rooms serve as a tangible sign of project effort.
- *Creation of project team name.* The development of a team name such as the "A-Team" or "Casey's Crusaders" is a common device for making a team more tangible. Frequently an associated team logo is also created. Again the project manager should rely on the collective ingenuity of the team to come up with the appropriate name and logo. Such symbols then can be affixed to stationery, T-shirts, coffee mugs, etc., to help signify team membership.

Snapshot from Practice "Rat Fax" Galvanizes ELITE Team at Newspaper*

Knight-Ridder's *Tallahassee Democrat,* like many American newspapers in the late 1980s, was struggling to survive in the face of declining revenues. Fred Mott, the general manager of the *Democrat,* was convinced that the key to the newspaper's future was becoming more customer-focused. Despite his best efforts, little progress was being made toward becoming a customer-driven newspaper. One area that was particularly problematic was advertising, where lost revenues due to errors could be as high as $10,000 a month.

Fred Mott decided to create a team of 12 of his best workers from all parts of the newspaper. They became known as the ELITE team because their mission was to "ELIminate The Errors." At first the team spent a lot of time pointing fingers at each other rather than coming to grips with the error problems at the newspaper. A key turning point came when one member produced what became known as "the rat tracks fax" and told the story behind it. It turns out a sloppily prepared ad arrived through a fax machine looking like "a rat had run across the page." Yet the ad passed through the hands of seven employees and probably would have been printed if it had not been totally unreadable. The introduction of this fax broke the ice, and the team started to admit that everyone—not everyone else—was at fault. Then, recalls one member, "We had some pretty hard discussions. And there were tears at those meetings."

The emotional responses galvanized the group to the task at hand and bonded them to one another. The ELITE team looked carefully at the entire process by which an ad was sold, created, printed, and billed. When the process was examined, the team discovered patterns of errors, most of which could be attributed to bad communication, time pressures, and poor attitude. They made a series of recommendations that completely transformed the ad process at the *Democrat.* Under ELITE's leadership, advertising accuracy rose sharply and stayed above 99 percent. Lost revenues from errors dropped to near zero. Surveys showed a huge positive swing in advertiser satisfaction.

The impact of ELITE, however, went beyond numbers. The ELITE team's own brand of responsiveness to customer satisfaction spread to other parts of the newspaper. In effect this team of mostly frontline workers spearheaded a cultural transformation at the newspaper that emphasized a premium on customer service.

* Jon R. Katzenbach and Douglas K. Smith, *The Wisdom of Teams* (Boston: Harvard Business School Press, 1993), pp. 67–72. Copyright McKinsey & Co., Inc.

- *Get the team to build or do something together early on.* Nothing reinforces a sense of a team more than working on something together. In the case of one international project, the manager simply hosted a potluck dinner where each member brought a dish his or her country was famous for.
- *Team rituals.* Just as corporate rituals help establish the unique identity of a firm, similar symbolic actions at the project level can contribute to a unique team subculture. For example, on one project members were given ties with stripes that corresponded to the number of milestones on the project. After reaching each milestone, members would gather and cut the next stripe off their ties to signify progress. Ralph Katz reports it was common practice for Digital Equipment's alpha chip design team to recognize people who found a bug in the design by giving them a phosphorescent toy roach. The bigger the bug that was discovered, the bigger the toy roach received. Such rituals help set project work apart from mainstream operations and reinforce a special status.

Creating a Shared Vision

Unlike project scope statements, which include specific cost, completion dates, and performance requirements, a *vision* involves the less tangible aspects of project performance. It refers to an image a project team holds in common about how the project will look upon completion, how they will work together, and/or how customers will accept the project. At its simplest level, a shared vision is the answer to the question, "What do we want to create?" Not everyone will have the same vision, but the images should be similar. Visions come in a variety of shapes and forms; they can be captured in a slogan or a symbol or can be written as a formal vision statement.

What a vision is, is not as important as what it does. A vision inspires members to give their best effort. (See A Good Man in a Storm Snapshot.) Moreover, a shared vision unites professionals with different backgrounds and agendas to a common aspiration. It helps motivate members to subordinate their individual agendas and do what is best for the project. As psychologist Robert Fritz puts it, "In the presence of greatness, pettiness disappears." Visions also provide focus and help communicate less tangible priorities, helping members make appropriate judgment calls. Finally, a shared vision for a project fosters commitment to the long term and discourages expedient responses that collectively dilute the quality of the project.

Visions can be surprisingly simple. For example, the vision for a new car could be expressed as a "pocket rocket." Compare this vision with the more traditional product description—"a sports car in the midprice range." The "pocket rocket" vision provides a much clearer picture of what the final product should be. Design engineers would immediately understand that the car will be both small and fast and that the car should be quick at the getaway, nimble in the turns, and very fast in the straightaways. Obviously, many details would have to be worked out, but the vision would help establish a common framework for making decisions.

There appear to be four essential qualities of an effective vision (see Figure 11.4): First, its essential qualities must be able to be communicated. A vision is worthless if it only resides in someone's head. Second, visions have to be challenging but also realistic. For example, a task force directed at overhauling the curriculum at the college of business at a state university is likely to roll its eyes if the dean announces that their vision is to compete against the Harvard Business School. Conversely, developing the best undergraduate business program in that state may be a realistic vision for that task force. Third, the project manager has to believe in the vision. Passion for the vision is an essential element of an effective vision. Finally, it should be a source of inspiration to others.

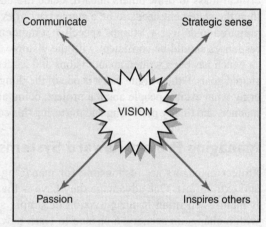

FIGURE 11.4   Requirements for an Effective Project Vision

Once a project manager accepts the importance of building a shared vision, the next question is how to get a vision for a particular project. First, project managers don't get visions. They act as catalysts and midwives for the formation of a shared vision of a project team. In many cases visions are inherent in the scope and objectives of the project. People get naturally excited about being the first ones to bring a new technology to the market or solving a problem that is threatening their organization. Even with mundane projects, there are often ample opportunities for establishing a compelling vision. One way is to talk to various people involved in the project and find out early on what gets them excited about the project. For some it may be doing a better job than on the last project or the satisfaction in the eyes of the customers when the project is over. Many visions evolve reactively in response to competition. For example, the Kodak team responsible for developing the single-use FunSaver camera was driven by the vision of beating a similar effort by Fuji to the market.

Some experts advocate engaging in formal vision-building meetings. These meetings generally involve several steps, beginning with members identifying different aspects of the project and generating ideal scenarios for each aspect. For example, on a construction project the scenarios may include "no accidents," "no lawsuits," "winning a prize," or "how we are going to spend our bonus for completing the project ahead of schedule." The group reviews and chooses the scenarios that are most appealing and translates them into vision statements for the project. The next step is to identify strategies for achieving the vision statements. For example, if one of the vision statements is that there will be no lawsuits, members will identify how they will have to work with the owner and subcontractors to avoid litigation. Next, members volunteer to be the keeper of the flame for each statement. The vision, strategies, and the name of the responsible team member are published and distributed to relevant stakeholders.

In more cases than not, shared visions emerge informally. Project managers collect information about what excites participants about the project. They test bits of their working vision in their conversations with team members to gauge the level of excitement the early ideas elicit in others. To some extent they engage in basic market research. They seize opportunities to galvanize the team, such as a disparaging remark by an executive that the project will never get done on time or the threat of a competing firm launching a similar project. Consensus in the beginning is not essential. What is essential is a core group of at least one-third of the project team that is genuinely committed to the vision. They will provide the critical mass to draw others aboard. Once the language has been formulated to communicate the vision, then the statement needs to be a staple part of every working agenda, and the project manager should be prepared to deliver a "stump" speech at a moment's notice. When problems or disagreements emerge, all responses should be consistent with the vision.

Much has been written about visions and leadership. Critics argue that vision is a glorified substitute for shared goals. Others argue that it is one of the things that separates leaders from managers. The key is discovering what excites people about a project, being able to articulate this source of excitement in an appealing manner, and finally protecting and nurturing this source of excitement throughout the duration of the project.

Managing Project Reward Systems

Project managers are responsible for managing the reward system that encourages team performance and extra effort. One advantage they have is that often project work is inherently satisfying, whether it is manifested in an inspiring vision or simple sense of accomplishment. Projects provide participants with a change in scenery, a chance to learn new skills, and an opportunity to break out of their departmental cocoon. Another inherent reward is what was referred to in *The Soul of the New Machine* as "pinball"—project success typically gives team members an option to play another exciting game.

Still, many projects are underappreciated, boring, interfere with other more significant priorities, and are considered an extra burden. In some of these cases, the biggest reward is finishing the project so that team members can go back to what they really enjoy doing and what will yield the biggest personal payoffs. Unfortunately, when this attitude is the primary incentive, project quality is likely to suffer. In these circumstances, external rewards play a more important role in motivating team performance.

Most project managers we talk to advocate the use of group rewards. Because most project work is a collaborative effort, it only makes sense that the reward system would encourage teamwork. Recognizing individual members regardless of their accomplishments can distract from team unity. Project work is highly interdependent, so it can become problematic to distinguish who truly deserves additional credit. Cash bonuses and incentives need to be linked to project priorities. It makes no sense to reward a team for completing their work early if controlling cost was the number one priority.

One of the limitations of lump-sum cash bonuses is that all too often they are consumed by the household budget to pay the dentist or mechanic. To have more value, rewards need to have lasting significance. Many companies convert cash into vacation rewards, sometimes with corresponding time off. For example, there is one firm that rewarded a project team for getting the job done ahead of schedule with a four-day, all-expenses-paid trip to Walt Disney World for the members' entire families. That vacation not only will be remembered for years, but it also recognizes spouses and children who, in a sense, also contributed to the

Snapshot from Practice   A Good Man in a Storm*

Once upon a time, back in 1976, Data General Corporation needed to come up quickly with a fast, reasonably priced 32-bit mini-computer to compete with Digital Equipment Corporation's VAX. Data General CEO Edson de Castro launched the Fountainhead Project and gave it the best people and ample resources to complete the 32-bit initiative. As a back-up to the Fountainhead project, Data General created the Eagle project within the Eclipse group under the leadership of Tom West. Work on both projects began in 1978.

In 1980 Data General announced its new computer, featuring simplicity, power, and low cost. This computer was not the Fountainhead from the well funded "best" DG group but the Eagle from Tom West's under-funded Eclipse team. Tracy Kidder saw all this happen and told the story in *The Soul of a New Machine,* which won a Pulitzer Prize in 1982. This book, which Kidder thought might be of interest to a handful of computer scientists, has become a project management classic.

In the beginning of his book, Kidder introduces the readers to the book's protagonist Tom West by telling the story of him sailing a yacht across rough seas off the coast of New England. Kidder's title for the prologue was "A Good Man in a Storm."

Twenty years after the Kidder's book was published Tom West was interviewed by Lawrence Peters for the *Academy of Management Executive.* Below are some excerpts that capture Tom's views on managing innovative projects:

On selecting team members:

> You explain to a guy what the challenge was, and then see if his eyes light up.

On motivating team members:

> . . . Challenge was everything. People, especially creative technical people who really want to make a difference, will do whatever is possible or whatever is necessary. I've done this more than once, and I've repeated it over and over. It seems to work.

On the importance of having a vision:

> . . . you've got to find a rallying cry. You need to have something that can be described very simply and has that sort of ring of truth to an engineer that says "yes that's the thing to be doing right now." Otherwise you're going to be rolling rocks up hill all the time.

On the role of being a project manager:

> You have to act as a cheerleader. You have to act as the instructor. You have to constantly bring to mind what the purpose is and what's moving the ball towards the goal post, and what's running sideways, and you have to take up a lot of battles for them. I mean you really don't want your design engineer arguing with the guy in the drafting shop about why he ought to do it the designer's way. I can do that, and I can pull rank too, and sometimes I did just that.

* Tracy Kidder, *The Soul of a New Machine* (New York: Avon Books, 1981); Lawrence H. Peters, "'A Good Man in a Storm': An Interview with Tom West," *Academy of Management Executive,* Vol. 16, No. 4, 2002, pp. 53–60.

project's success. Similarly, other firms have been known to give members home computers and entertainment centers. Wise project managers negotiate a discretionary budget so that they can reward teams surpassing milestones with gift certificates to popular restaurants or tickets to sporting events. Impromptu pizza parties and barbecues are also used to celebrate key accomplishments.

Sometimes project managers have to use negative reinforcement to motivate project performance. For example, Ritti recounts the story of one project manager who was in charge of the construction of a new, state-of-the-art manufacturing plant. His project team was working with a number of different contracting firms. The project was slipping behind schedule, mostly because of a lack of cooperation among the different players. The project manager did not have direct authority over many key people, especially the contractors from the other companies. He did, however, have the freedom to convene meetings at his convenience. So the project manager instituted daily "coordination meetings," which were required of all the principals involved, at 6:30 A.M. The meetings continued for about two weeks until the project got back on schedule. At that time the project manager announced that the next meeting was canceled, and no further sunrise meetings were ever scheduled.

While project managers tend to focus on group rewards, there are times when they need to reward individual performance. This is done not only to compensate extraordinary effort but also to signal to the others what exemplary behavior is. More specifically, among the rewards they use to motivate and recognize individual contributions are the following:

- **Letters of commendation.** While project managers may not have responsibility for their team members' performance appraisals, they can write letters commending their project performance. These letters can be sent to the workers' supervisors to be placed in their personnel files.
- **Public recognition for outstanding work.** Superlative workers should be publicly recognized for their efforts. Some project managers begin each status review meeting with a brief mention of project workers who have exceeded their project goals.
- **Job assignments.** Good project managers recognize that, while they may not have much budgetary authority, they do have substantial control over who does what, with whom, when, and where. Good work should be rewarded with desirable job assignments. Managers should be aware of member preferences and, when appropriate, accommodate them.
- **Flexibility.** Being willing to make exceptions to rules, if done judiciously, can be a powerful reward. Allowing members to work at home when a child is sick or excusing a minor discretion can engender long-lasting loyalty.

We reiterate that individual rewards should be used judiciously, and the primary emphasis should be on group incentives. Nothing can undermine the cohesiveness of a team more than members beginning to feel that others are getting special treatment or that they are being treated unfairly. Camaraderie and collaboration can quickly vanish only to be replaced by bickering and obsessive preoccupation with group politics. Such distractions can absorb a tremendous amount of energy that otherwise would be directed toward completing the project. Individual rewards typically should be used only when everyone in the team recognizes that a member is deserving of special recognition.

Orchestrating the Decision-Making Process

Most decisions on a project do not require a formal meeting to discuss alternatives and determine solutions. Instead decisions are made in real time as part of the daily interaction patterns between project managers, stakeholders, and team members. For example, as a result of routine "how's it going?" question, a project manager discovers that a mechanical engineer is stuck trying to meet the performance criteria for a prototype he is responsible for building. The project manager and engineer go down the hallway to talk to the designers, explain the problem, and ask what, if anything, can be done. The designers distinguish which criteria are essential and which ones they think can be compromised. The project manager then checks with the marketing group to make sure the modifications are acceptable. They agree with all but two of the modifications. The project manager goes back to the mechanical engineer and asks whether the proposed changes would help solve the problem. The engineer agrees. Before authorizing the changes he calls the project sponsor, reviews the events, and gets the sponsor to sign off on the changes. This is an example of how, by practicing MBWA (management by wandering around), project managers consult team members, solicit ideas, determine optimum solutions, and create a sense of involvement that builds trust and commitment to decisions.

Still, projects encounter problems and decisions that require the collective wisdom of team members as well as relevant stakeholders. Group decision making should be used when it will improve the quality of important decisions. This is often the case with complex problems that require the input of a variety of different specialists. Group decision making should also be used when strong commitment to the decision is needed and there is a low probability of acceptance if only one person makes the decision. Participation is used to reduce resistance and secure support for the decision. Group decision making would be called for with controversial problems which have a major impact on project activities or when trust is low within the project team. Guidelines for managing group decision making are provided below.

Facilitating Group Decision Making

Project managers play a pivotal role in guiding the group decision-making process. They must remind themselves that their job is not to make a decision but to facilitate the discussion within the group so that the team reaches a consensus on the best possible solution. Consensus within this context does not mean that everyone supports the decision 100 percent, but that they all agree what the best solution is under the circumstances. Facilitating group decision making essentially involves four major steps. Each step is briefly described next with suggestions for how to manage the process.

1. **Problem identification.** The project manager needs to be careful not to state the problem in terms of choices (e.g., should we do X or Y?). Rather the project manager should identify the underlying problem to which these alternatives and probably others are potential solutions. This allows group members to generate alternatives, not just choose among them. One useful way of defining problems is to consider the gap between where a project is (i.e., the present state) and where it should be (desired state). For example, the project may be four days behind schedule or the prototype weighs two pounds more than the specifications. Whether the gap is small or large, the purpose is to eliminate it. The group must find one or more courses of action that will change the existing state into the desired one.

   If one detects defensive posturing during the problem identification discussion, then it may be wise to postpone the problem-solving step if possible. This allows for emotions to subside and members to gain a fresh perspective on the issues involved.

2. **Generating alternatives.** Once there is general agreement as to the nature of the problem(s), then the next step is to generate alternative solutions. If the problem requires creativity, then brainstorming is commonly recommended. Here the team generates a list of possible solutions on a flipchart or blackboard. During that time the project manager establishes a moratorium on criticizing or evaluating ideas. Members are encouraged to "piggyback" on other's ideas by extending them or combining ideas into a new idea. The object is to create as many alternatives as possible no matter how outlandish they may appear to be. Some project managers report that for really tough problems they have found it beneficial to conduct such sessions away from the normal work environment; the change in scenery stimulates creativity.

3. **Reaching a decision.** The next step is to evaluate and assess the merits of alternative solutions. During this phase it is useful to have a set of criteria for evaluating the merits of different solutions. In many cases the project manager can draw upon the priorities for the project and have the group assess each alternative in terms of its impact on cost, schedule, and performance as well as reducing the problem gap. For example, if time is critical, then the solution that solves the problem as quickly as possible would be chosen.

   During the course of the discussion the project manager attempts to build consensus among the group. This can be a complicated process. Project managers need to provide periodic summaries to help the group keep track of its progress. They must protect those members who represent the minority view

Snapshot from Practice Managing Low-Priority Projects

So far the discussion of team building has been directed primarily to significant projects that command the attention and involvement of assigned members. But what about projects that have low priority for team members: The perfunctory task forces that members begrudgingly join? The committee work people get assigned to do? The part-time projects that pull members away from the critical work they would rather be doing? Projects that cause members to privately question why they are doing this?

There is no magic wand available that transforms mildly interested, part-time project teams into high-performance teams. We interviewed several project managers about such project scenarios. They all agreed that these can be very difficult and frustrating assignments and that there are limits to what is possible. Still, they offered tips and advice for making the best of the situation. Most of these tips focus on building commitment to the project when it does not naturally exist.

One project manager advocated orchestrating a large "time" investment upfront on such projects—either in the form of a lengthy meeting or a significant early assignment. He viewed this as a form of down payment that members would forfeit if they didn't carry the project to completion.

Others emphasize interjecting as much fun into activities as possible. Here rituals discussed under building team identity come into play. People become committed because they enjoy working together on the project. One project manager even confided that the perfect attendance at her project meetings was due primarily to the quality of the doughnuts she provided.

Another strategy is to make the benefits of the project as real to the team members as possible. One project manager escalated commitment to a mandated accidents prevention task force by bringing accident victims to a project meeting. Another project manager brought the high-ranking project sponsor to recharge the team by reinforcing the importance of the project to the company.

Most project managers emphasized the importance of building a strong personal relationship with each of the team members. When this connection occurs, members work hard not so much because they really care about the project but because they don't want to let the project manager down. Although not couched in influence currency terms, these managers talked about getting to know each member, sharing contacts, offering encouragement, and extending a helping hand when needed.

Finally, all project managers cautioned that nothing should be taken for granted on low-priority projects. They recommend reminding people about meetings and bringing extra copies of materials to meetings for those who have forgotten them or can't find them. Project managers should remain in frequent contact with team members and remind them of their assignments. One manager summed it up best when he said, "Sometimes it all boils down to just being a good nag."

and ensure that such views get a fair hearing. They need to guarantee that everyone has an opportunity to share opinions and no one individual or group dominates the conversation. It may be useful to bring a two-minute timer to regulate the use of air time. When conflicts occur, managers need to apply some of the ideas and techniques discussed in the next section.

Project managers need to engage in consensus testing to determine what points the group agrees on and what are still sources of contention. They are careful not to interpret silence as agreement; they confirm agreement by asking questions. Ultimately, through thoughtful interaction, the team reaches a "meeting of the minds" as to what solution is best for the project.

4. **Follow-up.** Once the decision has been made and implemented, it is important for the team to find the time to evaluate the effectiveness of the decision. If the decision failed to provide the anticipated solution, then the reasons should be explored and the lessons learned added to the collective memory bank of the project team.

Managing Conflict within the Project

Disagreements and conflicts naturally emerge within a project team during the life of the project. Participants will disagree over priorities, allocation of resources, the quality of specific work, solutions to discovered problems, and so forth. Some conflicts support the goals of the group and improve project performance. For example, two members may be locked in a debate over a design trade-off decision involving different features of a product. They argue that their preferred feature is what the primary customer truly wants. This disagreement may force them to talk to or get more information from the customer, with the result that they realize neither feature is highly valued, but instead the customer wants something else. On the other hand, conflicts can also hinder group performance. Initial disagreements can escalate into heated arguments with both parties storming out of the room and refusing to work together.

Thamhain and Wilemon's research revealed that the sources of conflict change as projects progress along the project life cycle. Figure 11.5 summarizes the major sources of conflict in each phase.

During project definition, the most significant sources of conflict are priorities, administrative procedures, schedule, and workforce. Disputes occur over the relative importance of the project compared with other activities, which project management structure to use (especially how much control the project manager should have), the personnel to be assigned, and the scheduling of the project into existing workloads.

During the planning phase, the chief source of conflict remains priorities, followed by schedules, procedures, and technical requirements. This is the phase where the project moves from a general concept to a detailed set of plans. Disagreements often emerge over the final schedule, the availability of resources, communication and decision making procedures, and technical requirements for the project.

During the execution phase, friction arises over schedule slippage, technical problems, and staff issues. Milestones become more difficult to meet because of accumulating schedule slippages. This leads to tension within the team as delays prevent others from starting or completing their work. Managing the trade-offs between time, cost, and performance becomes paramount. Project managers must decide between letting the schedule slip, investing additional funds to get back on track, or scaling back the scope of the project in order to save time. Technical problems involve finding solutions to unexpected problems and integrating the contributions of different people. The strain of the project may be expressed in interpersonal conflicts as well as pressures to use resources more effectively.

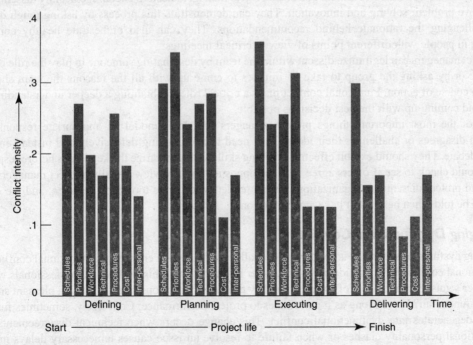

FIGURE 11.5   Conflict Intensity over the Project Life Cycle

During the delivery phase, schedules continue as the biggest source of conflict as schedule slippages make it more difficult to meet target completion dates. Pressures to meet objectives coupled with growing anxiety over future assignments increases interpersonal tensions. Technical problems are rare since most of them have been worked out during the earlier phases.

Encouraging Functional Conflict

The demarcation between functional and dysfunctional conflict is neither clear nor precise. In one team, members may exchange a diatribe of four-letter expletives and eventually resolve their differences. Yet in another project team, such behavior would create irreconcilable divisions and would prohibit the parties from ever working together productively again. The distinguishing criterion is how the conflict affects project performance, not how individuals feel. Members can be upset and dissatisfied with the interchange, but as long as the disagreement furthers the objectives of the project, then the conflict is functional. Project managers should recognize that conflict is an inevitable and even a desirable part of project work; the key is to encourage functional conflict and manage dysfunctional conflict.

A shared vision can transcend the incongruities of a project and establish a common purpose to channel debate in a constructive manner. Without shared goals there is no common ground for working out differences. In the previous example involving the design trade-off decision, when both parties agreed that the primary goal was to satisfy the customer, there was a basis for more objectively resolving the dispute. Therefore, agreeing in advance which priority is most important—cost, schedule, or scope—can help a project team decide what response is most appropriate.

Sometimes it's not the presence of conflict, but the absence of conflict that is the problem. Oftentimes as a result of compressed time pressures, self-doubt, and the desire to preserve team harmony, members are reluctant to voice objections. This hesitation robs the team of useful information that might lead to better solutions and the avoidance of critical mistakes. Project managers need to encourage healthy dissent in order to improve problem solving and innovation. They can demonstrate this process by asking tough questions and challenging the rationale behind recommendations. They can also orchestrate healthy conflict by bringing in people with different points of view to critical meetings.

Project managers can legitimize dissent within the team by designating someone to play the role of devil's advocate or by asking the group to take 15 minutes to come up with all the reasons the team should not pursue a course of action. Functional conflict plays a critical role in obtaining a deeper understanding of the issues and coming up with the best decisions possible.

One of the most important things project managers can do is model an appropriate response when someone disagrees or challenges their ideas. They need to avoid acting defensively and instead encourage critical debate. They should exhibit effective listening skills and summarize the key issues before responding. They should check to see if others agree with the opposing point of view. Finally, project managers should value and protect dissenters. Organizations have a tendency to create too many yes-men, and the emperor needs to be told when he doesn't have any clothes on.

Managing Dysfunctional Conflict

Managing dysfunctional conflict is a much more challenging task than encouraging functional conflict. First, dysfunctional conflict is hard to identify. A manager might have two highly talented professionals who hate each other's guts, but in the heat of competition they produce meritorious results. Is this a pleasant situation? No. Is it functional? Yes, as long as it contributes to project performance. Conversely, sometimes functional conflict degenerates into dysfunctional conflict. This change occurs when technical disagreements evolve into irrational personality clashes or when failure to resolve an issue causes unnecessary delays in critical project work.

The second major difficulty managers face is that there is often no easy solution to dysfunctional conflict. Project managers have to decide among a number of different strategies to manage it; here are five possibilities:

1. **Mediate the conflict.** The manager intervenes and tries to negotiate a resolution by using reasoning and persuasion, suggesting alternatives and the like. One of the keys is trying to find common ground. In some cases the project manager can make the argument that the win/lose interchange has escalated to the point that it has become lose/lose for everyone and now is the time to make concessions.

2. **Arbitrate the conflict.** The manager imposes a solution to the conflict after listening to each party. The goal is not to decide who wins but to have the project win. In doing so, it is important to seek a solution that allows each party to save face; otherwise the decision may provide only momentary relief. One project manager admits that she has had great success using a King Solomon approach to resolving conflict. She confided she announces a solution that neither party will like and gives the opponents two hours to come up with a better solution they can both agree on.

3. **Control the conflict.** Reducing the intensity of the conflict by smoothing over differences or interjecting humor is an effective strategy. If feelings are escalating, the manager can adjourn the interaction and hope cooler heads prevail the next day. If the conflict continues to escalate, project assignments may need to be rearranged if possible so that two parties don't have to work together.

4. **Accept it.** In some cases the conflict will outlive the life of the project and, though a distraction, it is one the manager has to live with.

5. **Eliminate the conflict.** Sometimes the conflict has escalated to the point that it is no longer tolerable. In this case the manager removes the members involved from the project. If there is a clear villain then only he or she should be removed. If, as is often the case, both parties are at fault, then it would be wise if possible to eliminate both individuals. Their removal would give a clear signal to the others on the team that this kind of behavior is unacceptable.

In summary, project managers establish the foundation for functional conflict by establishing clear roles and responsibilities, developing common goals or a shared vision, and using group incentives that reward collaboration. Project managers have to be adroit at reading body language to identify unspoken disagreement. They also have to keep in touch with what is going on in a project to identify small problems that might escalate into big conflicts. Well-timed humor and redirecting the focus to what is best for the project can alleviate the interpersonal tensions that are likely to flare up on a project team.

Rejuvenating the Project Team

Over the course of a long project, a team sometimes drifts off course and loses momentum. The project manager needs to swing into action to realign the team with the project objectives and step on the pedal. There are both formal and informal ways of doing this. Informally, the project manager can institute new rituals like the "toy roaches" to reenergize a team. On one project that was experiencing rough going, the project manager stopped work and took the team bowling to relieve frustrations. On another project, a manager showed her team the movie *The Shawshank Redemption* to rekindle hope and commitment to success.

Another option is to have the project sponsor give a pep talk to the "troops." In other cases, a friendly challenge can reinvigorate a team. For example, one project sponsor offered to cook a five-course meal if the project got back on track and hit the next milestone.

Sometimes more formal action needs to be taken. The project manager may recognize the need for a team-building session devoted to improving the work processes of the team. This meeting is particularly appropriate if she senses that the team is approaching a transition point in its development. The goal of such a session is to improve the project team's effectiveness through better management of project demands and group processes. It is an inward look by the team at its own performance, behavior, and culture for the purpose of eliminating dysfunctional behaviors and strengthening functional ones. The project team critiques its performance, analyzes its way of doing things, and attempts to develop strategies to improve its operation.

Oftentimes an external consultant is hired, or an internal staff specialist is assigned to facilitate the session. This process brings a more objective, outside perspective to the table, frees the project manager to be part of the process, and provides a specialist trained in group dynamics. Furthermore, if preliminary information is to be collected, team members may be more candid and open to an outsider.

One caveat about using outside consultants is that too often managers resort to this as a method for dealing with a problem that they have been unable or unwilling to deal with. The marching order to the consultant is "fix my team for me." What the managers fail to recognize is that one of the keys to fixing the team is improving the working relationship between themselves and the remainder of the team. For such sessions to be effective, project managers have to be willing to have their own role scrutinized and be receptive to changing their own behavior and work habits based on the comments and suggestions of the project team.

Consultants use a wide variety of team-building techniques to elevate team performance. Here is a brief description of one of the more common approaches. The first step is to gather information and make a preliminary diagnosis of team performance. Whether through individual interviews or in a group forum, the consultant asks general questions about the project team performance, that is, what obstacles are getting in the way of the team being able to perform better? This information is summarized in terms of themes. When everyone has understood the themes, the group ranks them in terms of both their importance and the extent the team has ownership over them. This last dimension is critical. *Ownership* refers to whether the team has direct influence over the issue. For example, a team probably has little influence over delivery of contracted supplies, but team members do control how quickly they inform each other of sudden changes in plans.

If the group becomes preoccupied with issues outside its control, the meeting can quickly evolve into a demoralizing gripe session. Therefore, the most important issues they have direct control over become the subjects of the agenda. During the course of the meeting, much interpersonal and group process information will be generated, and that is examined too. Thus, the group works on two sets of items: the agenda items and the items that emerge from the interaction of the participants. This is where the expertise of the external facilitator becomes critical for identifying interaction patterns and their implications for team performance.

As important problems are discussed, alternatives for action are developed. The team-building session concludes by deciding on specific action steps for remedying problems and setting target dates for who will do what, when. These assignments can be reviewed at project status meetings or at a special follow-up session.

It has become fashionable to link team-building activities with outdoor experiences. The outdoor experience—whether it is whitewater rafting down the Rogue River in Oregon or rock climbing in Colorado—places group members in a variety of physically challenging situations that must be mastered through teamwork, not individual effort. By having to work together to overcome difficult obstacles, team members are supposed to experience increased self-confidence, more respect for another's capabilities, and a greater commitment to teamwork. No empirical data are available to support such exotic endeavors other than the enthusiastic support of the participants. Such activities are likely to provide an intense common experience that may accelerate the social development of the team. Such an investment of time and money communicates the importance of teamwork and is considered by some a perk for being on the project. At the same time, unless the lessons from these experiences can be immediately transferred to actual project work, their significance is likely to vanish.

Managing Virtual Project Teams

Building a high-performance project team among a mixture of part-time and full-time members is a challenging task. Consider how much more challenging it is to build a team when members cannot engage in face-to-face interactions. Such would be the case for a virtual project team in which the team members are geographically situated so that they may seldom, if ever, meet face-to-face as a team. For example, Hewlett-Packard's integrated circuit business headquarters and a portion of the R&D facilities are located in Palo Alto, California; the two wafer fabrication operations are located in Corvallis, Oregon, and Fort Collins, Colorado; and the packaging assembly process is primarily in Singapore and Korea. It is not uncommon for professionals at each of these locations to be involved in the same project. When team members are spread across different time zones and continents, the opportunity for direct communication is severely limited. Electronic communication such as the Internet, e-mail, and teleconferencing takes on much more importance in virtual projects because this is the primary means of communication. See Snapshot from Practice: Managing Virtual Global Teams for an example of how this works.

Snapshot from Practice   Managing Virtual Global Teams*

Carl A. Singer, a senior program manager at IBM Global Services, described how global time zones were used to complete a time intensive project. The project required subject matter experts (SMEs) to document existing best practices in maintenance domain and to port these into a knowledge management tool. The most proficient SMEs available were on opposite sides of the globe—Australia and Scotland. Review and control of the project was from the United States.

Management realized that just working harder and smarter was not going to meet the time and quality targets. For this project they used the dimension of time to their benefit. Applying sound management principles as well as taking advantage of electronic communication systems, the team was able to create a virtual 24-hour workday for quick responses and accelerated reviews.

Each team consisted of veteran professionals familiar with the rigors of time-pressured consulting projects. A local point person was identified for each team and mutually agreed-upon targets, terminology, and processes were established.

An all-hands kick-off meeting was organized in which participants were able to socialize, understand local and projectwide constraints, and finalize an agreed-upon plan. The meeting was held at a corporate hotel with dining accommodations. The facility was considered an "assisted living community for IBM consultants." This hastened recovery from jet lag and provided an interruption-free work environment.

Upon returning to their home bases, each team created the majority of their deliverables independently with periodic three-way conference calls to maintain coordination. A project control book was established electronically so that all participants had access to the latest project documents.

The final phase of the project required intense interfacing and reviews between the teams. These reviews necessitated changes to deal with concerns, differences among subprojects, and other issues. It was here that the worldwide nature of the project was leveraged. Using a "dry cleaning approach" (in by 5 P.M. out by 9 A.M.) team members in Australia and Scotland were able to address issues generated during the U.S.-based external reviews and provide concrete responses by the beginning of the next business day. Conference calls at 6:00 A.M. (U.S. EST) were used to coordinate responses and resolve issues. Conference calls at the end of the U.S. workday were used to finalize issues and assignments. Figure 11.6 depicts the 24-hour clock used to align communication schedules.

Telephone conferencing was used instead of videoconferencing due to the setup lead time and because it would force participants to leave their offices. E-mail was used extensively for general communication. An electronic repository of project work was used to coordinate global involvement. In practice, a participant could draft a document and deposit it electronically only to wake up the next day to find the document annotated with suggested revisions. Likewise, one could start the day by checking an in-basket populated with documents to review and issues to address. Over time, "G'day" and "Cheers" crept into the U.S. speech—a clear indicator of team cohesion.

Singer identified a number of lessons learned from the project. These included:

- The all-hands kick-off meeting was critical for establishing goals and procedures as well as "rules of courtesy."
- Loosen the reins—establish clear deliverables and then step out of the way and let the professionals do their work.
- Establish and enforce agreed-upon quality standards and deliverable templates.
- Maintain a regular schedule of conference calls, even if only to say "Hello, we have nothing to talk about today." Conference calls should be guided by pre-established agendas, note-taking procedures, and reviews.

* Carl A. Singer, "Leveraging a Worldwide Project Team," *PM Network*, April 2001, pp. 36–40.

United States (East Coast)	Australia	Scotland	Comments
12 midnight	2 PM	5 AM	
1 AM	3 PM	6 AM	
2 AM	4 PM	7 AM	
3 AM	5 PM	8 AM	
4 AM	6 PM	9 AM	Australia handoff for off-shift review
5 AM	7 PM	10 AM	
6 AM	8 PM	11 AM	3-way conferencing window (primary)
7 AM	9 PM	12 noon	3-way conferencing window (primary)
8 AM	10 PM	1 PM	3-way conferencing window (primary)
9 AM	11 PM	2 PM	
10 AM	12 midnight	3 PM	
11AM	1 AM	4 PM	
12 noon	2 AM	5 PM	Scotland handoff for off-shift review
1 PM	3 AM	6 PM	
2 PM	4 AM	7 PM	
3 PM	5 AM	8 PM	
4 PM	6 AM	9 PM	3-way conferencing window (secondary)
5 PM	7 AM	10 PM	3-way conferencing window (secondary)
6 PM	8 AM	11 PM	U.S. handoff for off-shift review
7 PM	9 AM	12 midnight	
8 PM	10 AM	1 AM	
9 PM	11 AM	2 AM	
10 PM	12 noon	3 AM	
11 PM	1 PM	4 AM	
12 midnight	2PM	5 AM	

☐ Prime time   ☐ Secondary time   ▨ Downtime

FIGURE 11.6   24-Hour Global Clock

Two of the biggest challenges involved in managing a virtual project team are developing trust and effective patterns of communication. Trust is difficult to establish in virtual project management. Unlike working as a traditional team, where members can see whether someone has done what they say they have done, virtual team members depend on the word of distant members. At the same time, it can be difficult to trust someone whom you may have met only one or two times or not at all. Geographical separation also prohibits the informal social interactions that are often essential to building camaraderie among team members. As one virtual team member put it, "You can't have a beer together over the Internet."

So how can a project manager facilitate the development of trust within a virtual team? First, if it is impossible to hold a face-to-face meeting in the beginning, managers need to orchestrate the exchange of social information—who everyone is and some personal background information during the initial electronic interchange. Second, they need to set clear roles for each team member. Ideally, specific tasks should be assigned to each member so that they can make an immediate contribution to the project. Trust in virtual projects grows through team member reliability, consistency, and responsiveness. Finally, the project manager must consistently display enthusiasm and an action orientation in all messages; this spirit will hopefully spread to other team members.

The second major challenge for managing a virtual project team is to establish effective patterns of communication. E-mail and faxes are great for communicating facts—but not the feelings behind the facts; nor do they allow for real-time communication. Conference calls and project chat rooms can help, but they also have their limitations. Videoconferencing is a significant improvement over nonvisual electronic forms of communication. Still, it is a very expensive medium, and real-time interaction is available on only the most advanced and expensive systems. The maxim is match technology to the communication need. Here are some guidelines developed by 3M for use on their distributed projects:

- *When to e-mail.* To distribute important information and news in a one-to-one or one-to-many frame of reference.
- *When to use electronic bulletin boards.* To encourage discussion and flush out diversity of opinion on issues.
- *When to videoconference.* Videoconference when you need to see each other's face and expressions. This is important during the early phases of a project, when you are building relationships and developing a common understanding of what needs to be done. Use, again, when working on critical decisions and/or contentious issues.
- *When to use conference calls.* When people in different locations are working with common documents, presentations, sketches, and models. Use for status report meetings and to sustain social camaraderie.
- *When to fly.* Fly to build or repair trust. Use travel budget to get all key players together early on to instill commitment to the goals of the project and engage in team-building activities.

Even with the best communication system, managers have to overcome the problem of time zone differences, cultural nuances, and finding a convenient time for people to conference.

Below are some additional tips for alleviating communication problems and enhancing the performance of virtual teams:

1. **Keep team members informed on how the overall project is going.** Use shareware or develop a central access point such as either a Web site or LAN account to provide members with updated project schedules. Team members need to know where they fit in the big picture.
2. **Don't let team members vanish.** Virtual teams often experience problems getting in touch with each other. Use an Internet scheduling software to store members' calendars.

3. **Establish a code of conduct to avoid delays.** Team members need to agree not only on what, when, and how information will be shared but also on how and when they will respond to it. Develop a priority system to distinguish messages that require immediate response from those with longer time frames.

4. **Establish clear norms and protocols for surfacing assumptions and conflicts.** Because most communication is nonvisual, project managers cannot watch body language and facial expressions to develop a sense of what is going on. They need to probe deeper when communicating to force members to explain their viewpoints, actions, and concerns more clearly; they must double-check comprehension.

5. **Share the pain.** Do not require everyone to conform to your time zone and preferences. Rotate meeting times so that all team members have a turn working according to their clock.

To some extent managing a virtual project team is no different from managing a regular project team. The key is working within the constraints of the situation to develop effective ways for team members to interact and combine their talents to complete the project.

Project Team Pitfalls

High-performance project teams can produce dramatic results. However, like any good thing, there is a dark side to project teams that managers need to be aware of. We referred to this phenomenon as *projectitis* in Chapter 3. In this section we examine in more detail some of the pathologies that high-performance project teams can succumb to and highlight what project managers can do to reduce the likelihood of these problems occurring.

Groupthink

Janis first identified *groupthink* as a factor that influenced the misguided 1961 Bay of Pigs invasion of Cuba. His term refers to the tendency of members in highly cohesive groups to lose their critical evaluative capabilities. This malady appears when pressures for conformity are combined with an illusion of invincibility to suspend critical discussion of decisions. As a result decisions are made quickly with little consideration of alternatives; often the practice leads to fiascoes that, after the fact, appear totally improbable. Some of the symptoms of groupthink include the following:

- *Illusion of invulnerability.* The team feels invincible. It is marked by a high degree of esprit de corps, an implicit faith in its own wisdom, and an inordinate optimism that allows group members to feel complacent about the quality of their decisions.
- *Whitewash of critical thinking.* The group members discuss only a few solutions, ignoring alternatives; they fail to examine the adverse consequences that could follow their preferred course of action; and they too quickly dismiss any alternatives that, on the surface, appear to be unsatisfactory.
- *Negative stereotypes of outsiders.* "Good guy/bad guy" stereotypes emerge in which the group considers any outsiders who oppose their decisions as the bad guys, who are perceived as incompetent and malicious and whose points are unworthy of serious consideration.
- *Direct pressure.* When a team member does speak out or question the direction in which the team is headed, direct pressure is applied to the dissenter. He or she is reminded that speed is important and that the aim is agreement, not argument.

Bureaucratic Bypass Syndrome

Project teams are often licensed to get things done without having to go through normal protocols of the parent organization. Bypassing bureaucratic channels is appealing and invigorating. However, if bypassing becomes a way of life, it results in the rejection of bureaucratic policies and procedures, which provide the glue for the overall organization. A team that operates outside the organization may alienate other workers who are constrained by the norms and procedures of the organization; eventually, these outside bureaucrats will find ways to put up roadblocks and thwart the project team.

Team Spirit Becomes Team Infatuation

High-performance project teams can be a tremendous source of personal satisfaction. The excitement, chaos, and joy generated by working on a challenging project can be an invigorating experience. Leavitt and Lipman-Blumen even go so far as to say that team members behave like people in love. They become infatuated with the challenge of the project and the talent around them. This total preoccupation with the project and the project team, while contributing greatly to the remarkable success of the project, can leave in its wake a string of broken professional and personal relationships that contribute to burnout and disorientation upon completion of the project.

Going Native

Going native is a phrase first used by the British Foreign Service during colonial times to describe agents who assumed the customs, values, and prerogatives of their foreign country assignment. They did so to the point that they were no longer representing the best interests of the British government but rather those of the natives. This same phenomenon can occur within project teams working abroad or in those who become closely identified with their customers. In essence, the customer's interests take precedence over the parent organization's interests. This change in viewpoint can lead to excessive scope creep and open defiance of corporate policy and interests.

Dealing with these maladies is problematic because, in most cases, they are a distortion of a good thing, rather than a simple evil. Awareness is the first step for prevention. The next step is to take preemptive action to reduce the likelihood of these pitfalls occurring. For example, managers can reduce the isolation of the project team by creating work-related connections outside the project team. These interactions naturally occur in a matrix environment where members work on multiple projects and maintain ties to their home

---

Snapshot from Practice   Nominal Group Technique*

GE Appliances, U.S. West, Marriott Corp., and Hewlett-Packard are among the many firms that use nominal group technique (NGT) to guide decisions on projects. The NGT begins by gathering project team members and/or stakeholders around a table and identifying the project problem at hand. Each member then writes his or her solutions. Next, each member presents his or her solution to the group, and the leader writes these solutions on a chart. No criticism is allowed. This process continues until all of the ideas have been expressed. Each solution then is discussed and clarified by the group. After all the ideas have been discussed, the group members privately rank-order their preferred solutions. The balloting is tallied to create a rank-ordering of each solution. These steps are repeated if necessary to refine the list further in order to get the most preferred solution.

NGT provides an orderly process for dealing with potentially inflammatory problems. It also prevents groupthink from occurring. NGT discourages any pressure to conform to the wishes of a high-status, powerful group member since all ideas are discussed and all preferences are expressed privately. Creativity should be enhanced since members are able to offer a solution based on their expertise and viewpoint. Finally, important decisions can be made in a relatively timely manner. NGT works best when there is a well-defined problem.

* Andrew Delbeeq, Andrew H. Van de Ven, and D. H. Gustafson, *Group Techniques for Program Planning* (Glenview, II: Scott Foresman, 1975).

department. Likewise, the isolation of dedicated project teams can be reduced by the timely involvement of external specialists. In either case, the active involvement of relevant members of the parent organization at project status meetings can help maintain the link between the project and the rest of the organization. If the team appears to be suffering from groupthink, then the project manager can encourage functional conflict by playing a devil's advocate role to encourage dissent or using a structured problem-solving approach like the nominal group technique (see Snapshot). Finally, formal team-building sessions may reveal dysfunctional norms and refocus the attention of the team on project objectives.

Summary

Project managers must often work under less-than-ideal conditions to develop a cohesive team committed to working together and completing the project to the best of their abilities. They have to recruit personnel from other departments and manage the temporary involvement of team members. They have to bring strangers together and quickly establish a set of operational procedures that unite their efforts and contributions. They have to be skilled at managing meetings so that they do not become a burden but rather a vehicle for progress. Project managers need to forge a team identity and a shared vision, which command the attention and allegiance of participants. They need to use group incentives to encourage teamwork while recognizing when it is appropriate to single out individuals for special recognition. Project managers have to encourage functional conflict that contributes to superior solutions while being on guard against dysfunctional conflict that can break a team apart. In doing these things, they have to be careful not to do too good a job and avoid the pitfalls of excessive group cohesion.

While agendas, charters, visions, rewards, and so forth, are important tools and techniques, it has been emphasized both in this chapter and in Chapter 10 that the most important tool a project manager has to build an effective project team is his or her own behavior. Just as the founding members of an organization shape the culture of the organization, the project manager shapes and influences the internal culture of the project team. A positive example can define how team members respond to changes, how they handle new tasks, and how they relate to one another and the rest of the organization. There is no easy way to lead by example. It requires personal conviction, discipline, sensitivity to team dynamics, and a constant awareness of how personal actions are perceived by others.

Key Terms

Brainstorming	Nominal group technique	Project vision
Dysfunctional conflict	(NGT)	Team building
Functional conflict	Positive synergy	Team rituals
Groupthink	Project kick-off meeting	Virtual project team

Review Questions

1. What are the differences between the five stage model of team development and the punctuated equilibrium model?
2. What are the elements of an effective project vision? Why are they important?
3. Why should a project manager emphasize group rewards over individual rewards?
4. What is the difference between functional and dysfunctional conflict on a project?

5. When would it be appropriate to hold a formal team-building session on a project?

6. What are the unique challenges to managing a virtual project team?

7. What can a project manager do to avoid some of the pitfalls of a highly cohesive project team?

Exercises

1. The following activities are based on a recently completed group project that you have been involved in. This project may have been a student project, a work project, or an extracurricular project.

   a. Analyze the development of the team in terms of the five-phase model and the punctuated equilibrium model. Which model does the best job of describing how the team evolved?

   b. Analyze the group in terms of the nine situational factors that influence team development. What factors positively contributed to group performance? What factors negatively contributed to group performance? How did the group try to overcome the negative factors? What could you have done differently to overcome these negative factors?

   c. Analyze how effectively the group managed meetings. What did the group do well? What didn't the group do well? If the group were formed again, what specific recommendations would you make about how the group should manage meetings?

2. Assume that you have the following decision-making options: (1) make the decision on your own with available information, (2) consult others before making a decision, and (3) call a meeting and reach a consensus, seeking to arrive at a final decision everyone can agree on. Which approach would you use to make each of the following decisions and why?

   a. You are the project leader for Casino Night on campus, a charitable event organized by your group to raise money for the homeless. The event was a big success, garnering a net profit of $3,500. Before the event your team researched nearby organizations that support the homeless and to whom the money could be given. You narrowed the choices to the "Chunk of Coal House" and "St. Mary's Soup Kitchen." Eventually your group decided that the funds be given to Chunk of Coal. You are about to write a check to its director when you read in the local newspaper that the Chunk of Coal House has terminated operations. What should you do with the money?

   b. You are a golf course designer hired by Trysting Tree Golf Club to renovate their golf course. You have worked closely with the board of directors of the club to develop a new layout that is both challenging and aesthetically pleasing. Everyone is excited about the changes. The project is nearly 75 percent complete when you encounter problems on the 13th hole. The 13th hole at Trysting Tree is a 125-yard par three in which golfers have to hit their tee shots over a lake to a modulated green. During the construction of the new tee box, workers discovered that an underground spring runs beneath the box to the lake. You inspected the site and agreed with the construction supervisor that this could create serious problems, especially during the rainy winter months. After surveying the area, you believe the only viable option would be to extend the hole to 170 yards and create elevated tees on the adjacent hillside.

   c. You are the leader of a new product development project. Your team has worked hard on developing a third-generation product that incorporates new technology and meets customer demands. The project is roughly 50 percent complete. You have just received a report from the marketing department detailing a similar product that is about to be released by a competitor. The product appears to utilize radical new design principles that expand the functionality of the product. This poses a serious threat to the success of your project. Top management is considering canceling your project and starting over again. They want you to make a recommendation.

3. The following activities are based on a current or recently completed group project that you have been involved in. This project may be a student project, a work project, or an extracurricular project.

   a. How strong is the team identity on this project and why?

   b. What could participants do to strengthen team identity?

   c. What kind of informal activities could be used to rejuvenate the team? Why would these activities work?

References

Cleland, D. I., "Team Building: The New Strategic Weapon," *PM Network,* Vol. 11 (1) 1997.

Coutu, D. L., "Organization Trust in Virtual Teams," *Harvard Business Review,* Vol. 76 (3) 1998, pp. 20–21.

DeMarco, T., and T. Lister, *Peopleware: Productive Projects and Teams,* 2nd ed. (New York: Dorsett House, 1999).

Foti, R., "The Virtual Handshake," *PM Network,* March 2004, pp. 28–37.

Frame, J. D., *Managing Projects in Organizations* (San Francisco: Jossey-Bass, 1995).

Janis, I. L., *Groupthink* (Boston: Houghton Mifflin, 1982).

Katz, R., "How a Team at Digital Equipment Designed the 'Alpha' Chip," *The Human Side of Managing Technological Innovation,* 2nd ed. Ed. Ralph Katz (New York: Oxford University Press, 2004), pp. 121–33.

Katzenbach, J. R., and D. K. Smith, *The Wisdom of Teams* (Boston: Harvard Business School Press, 1993).

Kidder, T., *The Soul of a New Machine* (New York: Avon Books, 1981).

Kirkman, B. L., B. Rosen, C. B. Gibson, P. E. Tesluk, and S. O. McPherson, "Five Challenges to Virtual Team Success: Lessons From Sabre, INC.," *Academy of Management Executive,* 16 (2) 2002, pp. 67–79.

Leavitt, H. J., and J. Lipman-Blumen, "Hot Groups," *Harvard Business Review,* Vol. 73 1995, pp. 109–16.

Linetz, B. P., and K. P. Rea, *Project Management for the 21st Century* (San Diego: Academic Press, 2001).

Maier, N. R. F., *Problem Solving and Creativity in Individuals and Groups* (Belmont, CA: Brooks-Cole, 1970).

Maznevski, M. L., and K. M. Chudoba, "Bridging Space over Time: Global Virtual Team Dynamics and Effectiveness," *Organization Science*, Vol. 11 (5), September–October 2000, pp. 473–92.

Peters, T., *Thriving on Chaos: Handbook for a Management Revolution* (New York: Knopf, 1988).

Ritti, R. R., *The Ropes to Skip and the Ropes to Know: Studies in Organizational Behavior* (New York: Wiley, 1982).

Senge, P. M., *The Fifth Discipline* (New York: Doubleday, 1990).

Thamhain, H. J., and D. L. Wilemon, "Conflict Management in Project Life Cycle," *Sloan Management Review,* Vol. 16 (3) 1975, pp. 31–41.

Thoms, P., "Creating a Shared Vision With a Project Team," *PM Network,* January 1997, pp. 33–35.

3M, "Leading a Distributed Team," *www.3m.com/meetingnetwork/readingroom/meetingguide_distribteam. html.* Accessed June 6, 2006.

Townsend, A. M., S. DeMarie, and A. R. Hendrickson, "Virtual Teams: Technology and the Workplace of the Future," *Academy of Management Executive,* Vol. 12 (3) 1998, pp. 17–29.

Tuchman, B. W., and M. C. Jensen, "Stages of Small Group Development Revisited," *Group and Organizational Studies,* Vol. 2 1997, pp. 419–27.

Vroom, V. H., and A. G. Jago, *The New Leadership* (Englewood Cliffs, NJ: Prentice Hall, 1988).

APPENDIX 11.1

Project Human Resource Management

Introduction

In the final analysis, some aspects of human association are inevitable in any set of activities whether they are primarily industrial, economic, political, social or cultural in nature. Project management is no exception. Understandably, proficiency in understanding the human behavior and making skillful use of the knowledge and techniques for managing the group of human resources is an extremely important contributor to success in project management.

Human behavior is very complex in nature and no simple theories for understanding human behavior or techniques for successfully managing them for achieving specific objectives have been established so far. There are some general principles for setting up and maintaining effective relationships in an industrial or commercial organization, but there is probably more art than science to it. It is with this backdrop, that the discussion on human relation aspect in project management should be approached.

The approach of PMBOK® Guide for project human resources management is focused specifically on four aspects:

1. *Different types of organizational structures* for project management and the impact of the organization structure on effectiveness in managing project and efficient use of human resources
2. *Professional and ethical behavior* of the project manager and project team
3. *Project manager's leadership qualities in building and managing high performance project teams* with judicious use of ways
   - to motivate the team
   - to influence the behavior of team members through forms of sources for power as well as leading by setting an example
   - to negotiate effectively and manage the conflict within the team
4. *Four processes for project human relations management*, which embody generally recognized good practices for successful project management

1. Different Forms of Organizational Structures

All organization structures serve two purposes:

- Division of labour of the tasks required to be performed for effective functioning of organization as a unit, and
- Formal structuring of the roles, responsibilities, and reporting relationships necessary for coordinating the activities of all members of the organization.

Projects are performed within the ambits of the organization and the nature of the organization structure as a whole and particularly, the organization of the project management team within the organization play a very important part in how the projects are managed. Depending on the power or position of the project manager and his reporting relationship to the higher management on one hand and the roles and reporting relationships of the project team members with the project manager on the other, the project organizations can be classified into three distinct types:

- *Functional Organization*
- *Projectized Organization (Organizing Projects as Dedicated Teams) and*
- *Matrix Organizations (Weak, Balanced and Strong Matrix Organizations)*

In Chapter 3, 'Organization: Structure and Culture'), the above different project management structures are described and the advantages and disadvantages associated with each structure have been discussed in detail. The interested readers should revisit that part at this point for a comprehensive view on project organization structures and their relevance to effective and efficient project management.

The other three topics will be presented in what follows.

2. Code of Ethics for the Project Management Profession

PMI ® has all along laid heavy stress on this aspect of the project management profession. A code of ethics for the project management profession was created at PMI 1982 symposium on Project Management, updated and approved in 1989 and again in 1995.

As stated in the Appendix B of the new PMI Code of Ethics and Professional Conduct, "Since the 1998 Code was adopted, many dramatic changes have occurred within PMI and the business world. PMI membership has grown significantly. A great deal of growth has also occurred in regions outside North America. In the business world, ethics scandals have caused the downfall of global corporations and non-profits organization, causing public outrage and sparking increased government regulations. Globalization has brought economies closer together but has caused a realization that our practice of ethics may differ from culture to culture. The rapid, continuing pace of technological change has provided new opportunities, but has also introduced new challenges, including new ethical dilemmas." For these reasons, in 2003, the PMI Board of Directors called for the re-examination of our codes of ethics. In 2004, the PMI Board commissioned the Ethics Standards Review Committee (ESRC) to review the codes of ethics and develop a process for revising the codes. In 2005, the Board commissioned the Ethics Standards Development Committee to deliver the reviewed code by the end of 2006. This Code of Ethics and Professional Development was approved by the PMI Board of Directors in October 2006.

The result of this effort is a Code of Ethics and Professional Conduct that not only describes the ethical values to which the global project management community aspires, but also addresses the specific conduct that is mandatory for every individual bound by this Code. This code affirms four values as its foundation, which the global project management community defined as most important: responsibility, respect, fairness and honesty.

The code text provided on PMI®'s website is reproduced below here; interested persons can go to the original PMI®'s site and also see other details about the organization.

Project Management Institute
Code of Ethics and Professional Conduct
Chapter 1. Vision and Applicability

1.1 Vision and Purpose

As practitioners of project management, we are committed to doing what is right and honorable. We set high standards for ourselves and we aspire to meet these standards in all aspects of our lives at work, at home, and in service to our profession.

This Code of Ethics and Professional Conduct describes the expectations that we have of ourselves and our fellow practitioners in the global project management community. It articulates the ideals to which we aspire as well as the behaviors that are mandatory in our professional and volunteer roles.

The purpose of this Code is to instill confidence in the project management profession and to help an individual become a better practitioner. We do this by establishing a profession-wide understanding of appropriate behavior. We believe that the credibility and reputation of the project management profession is shaped by the collective conduct of individual practitioners.

We believe that we can advance our profession, both individually and collectively, by embracing this Code of Ethics and Professional Conduct. We also believe that this code will assist us in making wise decisions, particularly when faced with difficult situations where we may be asked to compromise our integrity or our values.

Our hope that this Code of Ethics and Professional Conduct will serve as a catalyst for others to study, deliberate, and write about ethics and values. Further, we hope that it will ultimately be used to build upon and evolve our profession.

1.2 Persons to Whom the Code Applies

The Code of Ethics and Professional Conduct applies to:

1.2.1 All PMI members

1.2.2 Individuals who are not members of PMI but meet one or more of the following criteria:

1 Non-members who hold a PMI certification
2 Non-members who apply to commence a PMI certification process
3 Non-members who serve PMI in a volunteer capacity.

Comment: *Those holding a Project Management Institute (PMI®) credential (whether members or not) were previously held accountable to the Project Management Professional (PMP®) or Certified Associate in Project Management (CAPM®) Code of Professional Conduct and continue to be held accountable to the PMI Code of Ethics and Professional Conduct. In the past, PMI also had separate ethics standards for members and for credentialed individuals. Stakeholders who contributed input to develop this Code concluded that having multiple codes was undesirable and that everyone should be held to one high standard. Therefore, this Code is applicable to both PMI members and individuals who have applied for or received a credential from PMI, regardless of their membership in PMI.*

1.3 Structure of the Code

The Code of Ethics and Professional Conduct is divided into sections that contain standards of conduct which are aligned with the four values that were identified as most important to the project management community. Some sections of this Code include comments. Comments are not mandatory parts of the Code, but provide examples and other clarification. Finally, a glossary can be found at the end of the standard. The glossary defines words and phrases used in the Code. For convenience, those terms defined in the glossary are underlined in the text of the Code.

1.4 Values that Support this Code

Practitioners from the global project management community were asked to identify the values that formed the basis of their decision making and guided their actions. The values that the global project management community defined as most important were: responsibility, respect, fairness and honesty. This Code affirms these four values as its foundation.

1.5 Aspirational and Mandatory Conduct

Each section of the Code of Ethics and Professional Conduct includes both aspirational standards and mandatory standards. The aspirational standards describe the conduct that we strive to uphold as practitioners. Although adherence to the aspirational standards is not easily measured, conducting ourselves in accordance with these is an expectation that we have of ourselves as professionals as it is not optional.

The mandatory standards establish firm requirements and in some cases, limit or prohibit practitioner behavior. Practitioners who do not conduct themselves in accordance with these standards will be subject to disciplinary procedures before PMI's Ethics Review Committee.

Comment: *The conduct covered under the aspirational standards and conduct covered under the mandatory standards are not mutually exclusive; that is, one specific act or omission could violate both aspirational and mandatory standards.*

Chapter 2. Responsibility

2.1 Description of Responsibility

Responsibility is our duty to take ownership for the decisions we make or fail to make, the actions we take or fail to take, and the consequences that result.

2.2 Responsibility: Aspirational Standards

As practitioners in the global project management community:

2.2.1 We make decisions and take actions based on the best interests of society, public safety and the environment.

2.2.2 We accept only those assignments that are consistent with our background, experience, skills and qualifications.

Comment: *Where developmental or stretch assignments are being considered, we ensure that key stakeholders receive timely and complete information regarding the gaps in our qualifications so that they may make informed decisions regarding our suitability for a particular assignment.*

In the case of a contracting arrangement, we only bid on work that our organization is qualified to perform and we assign only qualified individuals to perform the work.

2.2.3 We fulfill the commitments that we undertake, so we do what we say we will do.

2.2.4 When we make errors or omissions, we take ownership and make corrections promptly. When we discover errors or omissions caused by others, we communicate them to the appropriate body as soon they are discovered. We accept accountability for any issues resulting from our errors or omissions and any resulting consequences.

2.2.5 We protect proprietary or confidential information that has been entrusted to us.

2.2.6 We uphold this Code and hold each other accountable to it.

2.3 Responsibility: Mandatory Standards

As practitioners in the global project management community, we require the following of ourselves and our fellow practitioners:

Regulations and Legal Requirements

2.3.1 We inform ourselves and uphold the policies, rules, regulations and laws that govern our work, professional, and volunteer activities.

2.3.2 We report unethical or illegal conduct to appropriate management and, if necessary, to those affected by the conduct.

Comment: *These provisions have several implications. Specifically, we do not engage in any illegal behavior, including but not limited to theft, fraud, corruption, embezzlement or bribery. Further, we do not take or abuse the property of others, including intellectual property, nor do we engage in slander or libel. In focus groups conducted with practitioners around the globe, these types of illegal behaviors were mentioned as being problematic.*

As practitioners and representatives of our profession, we do not condone or assist others in engaging in illegal behavior. We report any illegal or unethical conduct. Reporting is not easy and we recognize that it may have negative consequences. Since recent corporate scandals, many organizations have adopted policies to protect employees who reveal the truth about illegal or unethical activities. Some governments have also adopted legislation to protect employees who come forward with the truth.

Ethics Complaints
2.3.3 We bring violations of this Code to the attention of the appropriate body for resolution.
2.3.4 We only file ethics complaints when they are substantiated by facts.

Comment: *These provisions have several implications. We cooperate with PMI concerning ethics violations and the collection of related information whether we are a complainant or a respondent. We also abstain from accusing others of ethical misconduct when we do not have all the facts. Further, we pursue disciplinary action against individuals who knowingly make false allegations against others.*
2.3.5 Disciplinary action against an individual who retaliates against a person raising ethics concerns.

Chapter 3. Respect

3.1 Description of Respect

Respect is our duty to show a high regard for ourselves, others, and the resources entrusted to us. Resources entrusted to us may include people, money, reputation, the safety of others and natural or environmental resources.

An environment of respect engenders trust, confidence and performance excellence by fostering mutual cooperation, that is, an environment where diverse perspectives and views are encouraged and valued.

3.2 Respect: Aspirational Standards

As practitioners in the global project management community:
3.2.1 We inform ourselves about the norms and customs of others and avoid engaging in behaviors they might consider disrespectful.
3.2.2 We listen to others' points of view, seeking to understand them.
3.2.3 We approach directly those persons with whom we have a conflict or disagreement. 3.2.4 We conduct ourselves in a professional manner, even when it is not reciprocated.

Comment: *An implication of these provisions is that we avoid engaging in gossip and avoid making negative remarks to undermine another person's reputation. We also have a duty under this Code to confront others who engage in these types of behaviors.*

3.3 Respect: Mandatory Standards

As practitioners in the global project management community, we require the following of ourselves and our fellow practitioners:

3.3.1 We negotiate in good faith.

3.3.2 We do not exercise the power of our expertise or position to influence the decisions or actions of others in order to benefit personally at their expense.

3.3.3 We do not act in an abusive manner toward others.

3.3.4 We respect the property rights of others.

Chapter 4. Fairness

4.1 Description of Fairness

Fairness is our duty to make decisions and act impartially and objectively. Our conduct must be free from competing self interest, prejudice, and favoritism.

4.2 Fairness: Aspirational Standards

As practitioners in the global project management community:

4.2.1 We demonstrate transparency in our decision-making process.

4.2.2 We constantly reexamine our impartiality and objectivity, taking corrective action as appropriate.

Comment: *Research with practitioners indicated that the subject of conflicts of interest is one of the most challenging faced by our profession. One of the biggest problems practitioners report is not recognizing when we have conflicted loyalties and recognizing when we are inadvertently placing ourselves or others in a situation where there is conflict of interest situation. We as practitioners must proactively search for potential conflicts and help each other by highlighting each other's potential conflicts of interest and insisting that they be resolved.*

4.2.3 We provide equal access to information to those who are authorized to have that information.

4.2.4 We make opportunities equally available to qualified candidates.

Comment: *An implication of these provisions is that in the case of a contracting arrangement, we provide equal access to information during the bidding process.*

4.3 Fairness: Mandatory Standards

As practitioners in the global project management community, we require the following of ourselves and our fellow practitioners:

Conflict of Interest Situations

4.3.1 We proactively and fully disclose any real or potential conflicts of interest to the appropriate stakeholders.

4.3.2 When we realize that we have a real or potential *conflict of interest*, we refrain from engaging in the decision-making process or otherwise attempting to influence outcomes, unless or until, we have made full disclosure to the affected stakeholders; we have an approved mitigation plan; and we have obtained the consent of the stakeholders to proceed.

Comment: *A conflict of interest occurs when we are in a position to influence decisions or other outcomes on behalf of one party when such decisions or outcomes could affect one or more other parties with which we have competing loyalties. For example, when we are acting as an employee, we have a duty of loyalty to our employer. When we are acting as a PMI volunteer, we have a duty of loyalty to the Project Management Institute. We must recognize these divergent interests and refrain from influencing decisions when we have a conflict of interest.*

Further, even if we believe that we can set aside our divided loyalties and make decisions impartially, we treat the appearance of a conflict of interest as a conflict of interest and follow the provisions described in the Code.

Favoritism and Discrimination

4.3.3 We do not hire, fire, reward, punish, award or deny contracts based on personal considerations, including but not limited to, favoritism, nepotism or bribery.

4.3.4 We do not discriminate against others based on, but not limited to, gender, race, age, religion, disability, nationality or sexual orientation.

4.3.5 We apply the rules of the organization (employer, Project Management Institute, or other group) without favoritism or prejudice.

Chapter 5. Honesty

5.1 Description of Honesty

Honesty is our duty to understand the truth and act in a truthful manner both in our communications and in our conduct.

5.2 Honesty: Aspirational Standards

As practitioners in the global project management community:

5.2.1 We earnestly seek to understand the truth.

5.2.2 We are truthful in our communications and in our conduct.

5.2.3 We provide accurate information in a timely manner.

Comment: *An implication of these provisions is that we take appropriate steps to ensure that the information we are basing our decisions upon or providing to others is accurate, reliable, and timely. This includes having the courage to share bad news even when it may be poorly received. Also, when outcomes are negative, we avoid burying information or shifting blame to others. When outcomes are positive, we avoid taking credit for the achievements of others. These provisions reinforce our commitment to be both honest and responsible.*

5.2.4 We make commitments and promises, implied or explicit, in good faith.

5.2.5 We strive to create an environment in which others feel safe to tell the truth.

5.3 Honesty: Mandatory Standards

As practitioners in the global project management community, we require the following of ourselves and our fellow practitioners:

5.3.1 We do not engage in or condone behavior that is designed to deceive others, including but not limited to, making misleading or false statements, stating half-truths, providing information out of context or withholding information that, if known, would render our statements as misleading or incomplete.

5.3.2 We do not engage in dishonest behavior with the intention of personal gain or at the expense of another.

Comment: *The aspirational standards exhort us to be truthful. Half-truths and non-disclosures intended to mislead stakeholders are as unprofessional as affirmatively making misrepresentations. We develop credibility by providing complete and accurate information.*

APPENDIX A

A.1 History of This Standard

PMI's vision of project management as an independent profession drove our early work in ethics. In 1981, the PMI Board of Directors formed an Ethics, Standards and Accreditation Group. One task required the group to deliberate on the need for a code of ethics for the profession. The team's report contained the first documented PMI discussion of ethics for the project management profession. This report was submitted to the PMI Board of Directors in August 1982 and published as a supplement to the August 1983 *Project Management Quarterly*.

In the late 1980's, this standard evolved to become the Ethics Standard for the Project Management Professional [PMP®]. In 1997, the PMI Board determined the need for a member code of ethics. The PMI Board formed the Ethics Policy Documentation Committee to draft and publish an ethics standard for PMI's membership. The Board approved the new Member Code of Ethics in October 1998. This was followed by Board approval of the Member Case Procedures in January 1999, which provided a process for the submission of an ethics complaint and a determination as to whether a violation had occurred.

Since the 1998 Code was adopted, many dramatic changes have occurred within PMI and the business world. PMI membership has grown significantly. A great deal of growth has also occurred in regions outside North America. In the business world, ethics scandals have caused the downfall of global corporations and non-profit organizations, causing public outrage and sparking increased government regulations. Globalization has brought economies closer together but has caused a realization that our practice of ethics may differ from culture to culture. The rapid, continuing pace of technological change has provided new opportunities, but has also introduced new challenges, including new ethical dilemmas.

For these reasons, in 2003 the PMI Board of Directors called for the reexamination of our codes of ethics. In 2004, the PMI Board commissioned the Ethics Standards Review Committee [ESRC] to review the codes of ethics and develop a process for revising the codes. The ESRC developed processes that would encourage active participation by the global project management community. In 2005, the PMI Board approved the processes for revising the code, agreeing that global participation by the project management community was paramount. In 2005, the Board also commissioned the Ethics Standards Development Committee to carry out the Board-approved process and deliver the revised code by the end of 2006. This Code of Ethics and Professional Development was approved by the PMI Board of Directors in October 2006.

A.2 Process Used to Create This Standard

The first step by the Ethics Standards Development Committee [ESDC] in the development of this Code was to understand the ethical issues facing the project management community and to understand the values and viewpoints of practitioners from all regions of the globe. This was accomplished by a variety of mechanisms including focus group discussions and two internet surveys involving practitioners, members, volunteers, and people holding a PMI certification. Additionally, the team analyzed the ethics codes of 24 non-profit associations from various regions of the world, researched best practices in the development of ethics standards, and explored the ethics-related tenets of PMI's strategic plan.

This extensive research conducted by the ESDC provided the backdrop for developing the exposure draft of the PMI Code of Ethics and Professional Conduct. The exposure draft was circulated to the global project management community for comment. The rigorous, standards development processes established by the American National Standards Institute were followed during the development of the Code because these processes were used for PMI technical standard development projects and were deemed to represent the best practices for obtaining and adjudicating stakeholder feedback to the exposure draft.

The result of this effort is a Code of Ethics and Professional Conduct that not only describes the ethical values to which the global project management community aspires, but also addresses the specific conduct that is mandatory for every individual bound by this Code. Violations of the PMI Code of Ethics and Professional Conduct may result in sanctions by PMI under the ethics Case Procedures.

The ESDC learned that as practitioners of project management, our community takes its commitment to ethics very seriously and we hold ourselves and our peers in the global project management community accountable to conduct ourselves in accordance with the provisions of this Code.

APPENDIX B

B.1 Glossary

Abusive Manner. Conduct that results in physical harm or creates intense feelings of fear, humiliation, manipulation, or exploitation in another person.

Conflict of Interest. A situation that arises when a practitioner of project management is faced with making a decision or doing some act that will benefit the practitioner or another person or organization to which the practitioner owes a duty of loyalty and at the same time will harm another person or organization to which the practitioner owes a similar duty of loyalty. The only way practitioners can resolve conflicting duties is to disclose the conflict to those affected and allow them to make the decision about how the practitioner should proceed.

Duty of Loyalty. A person's responsibility, legal or moral, to promote the best interest of an organization or other person with whom they are affiliated.

Project Management Institute [PMI]. The totality of the Project Management Institute, including its committees, groups and chartered components such as chapters, colleges and specific interest groups.

PMI Member. A person who has joined the Project Management Institute as a member.

PMI-Sponsored Activities. Activities that include, but are not limited to, participation on a PMI Member Advisory Group, PMI standard development team, or another PMI working group or committee. This also includes activities engaged in under the auspices of a chartered PMI component organization, whether it is in a leadership role in the component or another type of component educational activity or event.

Practitioner. A person engaged in an activity that contributes to the management of a project, portfolio, or program, as part of the project management profession.

PMI Volunteer. A person who participates in PMI-sponsored activities, whether a member of the Project Management Institute or not.

3. Project Manager's Leadership Qualities

Building and Managing High Performance Project Teams.

3.1 Project Manager's Role

Organization appoints a project manager for looking after or managing the project and achieving the objectives for which the project is authorized. Therefore the first and foremost task for a project manager is to discharge this duty. His role is different from other managers in the functional area which look after some specific areas of the organization's operation (like a specific production, maintenance or quality control department in a manufacturing plant, accounts or finance function, marketing, sales, human relations management, etc.). Just as the project is a 'temporary endeavor for creating a unique product or service', the project manager is a manager assigned for managing just that specific task which is "the project". So, what is a project manager expected to bring to the table to discharge his duty satisfactorily? The chances for a project manager to succeed in this role and successfully completing the project would depend on to what extent or degree his background includes the following three:

(i) Project management knowledge and skills

The project manager should be familiar with generally accepted good project management practices, knowledge, skills, tools & techniques for planning and managing a project.

He should, therefore, have knowledge of the project management process groups for initiating, planning, executing, controlling and closing the project. He should also be conversant with the project management processes in different knowledge areas such as managing project's scope, time, cost, quality, communication, human relations, risk and procurement. More importantly, he should be able to take a holistic view of these different component plans and requirements and unify and integrate them into a whole cohesive project plan. This would require him to balance the conflicting requirements of different stakeholders and project objectives, make suitable trade-offs and proactively manage the project risk.

(ii) Domain expertise

The next importance, in the project manager's background, would be his domain expertise. The project manager for a chemical manufacture plant should know chemical engineering and preferably also the specific chemical; project manger for a marketing campaign should be a seasoned professional in the marketing; project manger for a banking project should know about the general nature of banking operations. A strong domain expertise is very helpful in empowering the project manager to take the decision of coordinating or trade-off nature about some crucial issue in project management.

(iii) General management experience

Finally, as explained at the start of this appendix, the project manager has to proactively manage relationship with a large number of different interest groups include the sponsors and stakeholders, members of project team, client, vendors and contractors, officials of statutory regulation agencies and special public interest groups. The project manager for a major project should be a mature individual, having years of experience in working with people and organizations. He should have developed during this working experience skills for communication, negotiation and conflict resolution capabilities and ability to handle unexpected situations coming up during project planning and execution.

3.2 Leadership, Management Style and Professional Ethics

The personal leadership style and ability to build and manage a motivated high performance project team would greatly improve the chance for project success. The project manager would need to employ the leadership style in the situational context of the nature of the industry, the project and the project phase. For execution phase of very traditional industrial projects, a directive and controlling style might suit better, while for initiating or planning phases of new product or research and development projects, a collaborative and consultative approach would be more helpful. A judicious mixture of both basic management styles (described by McGregor in his famous theory as 'Theory X' and 'Theory Y') is very necessary for all project management situations. Above all, his personal conduct should provide a role model for the team members to follow and at all times it should be above board and fully complying with the professional ethics for project management profession.

Chapter 10, 'Leadership: Being an Effective Project Manager', offers discussion on the issues related to project leadership, management style and professional ethics in somewhat more details:

- Managing versus leading a project
- Managing project stakeholders
- Exercising power and use of influence as an exchange
- Building trust: the key to exercising influence
- Social network building
- Ethics and project management, and

- Qualities of an effective project manager

The interested readers should refer to it for further discussion of this topic.

4. Project Human Resource Management Processes

Project human resource management involves preparing a plan for the human resources for the project and building and managing a high performance project management team. This in turn would involve acquiring the project team, training and developing the team members and managing the team to be able to function at desired high performance level to ensure project success. This aspect of building and managing a team would require influencing the project team (motivation, conflict resolution and negotiation) and ensuring ethical and professional behavior of all project team members.

PMBOK® GUIDE, 4th Edition, includes 4 processes in the project human resource management knowledge area:

- Develop Human Resource Plan (Planning Process Group)
- Acquire Project Team (Executing Process Group)
- Develop Project Team (Executing Process Group), and
- Manage Project Team (Executing Process Group)

We will briefly overview the processes and the inputs, tools and techniques and outputs associated with them.

4.1 Develop Human Resource Plan

The basic idea underlying the process is to make sure that a plan is developed for assigning a person or a group of persons (or a vendor in case of outsourced product service) to each and every task or activity of the project. The process involves identifying and documenting the project roles, responsibilities and reporting relationships and creating a plan for project staffing. In some cases, when the available personnel in the organization require some specific supplementary training, identifying the need and planning for such training is also a part of this process.

Inputs

- How many persons and with what skill level are required for all project activities is the starting point input. The output of the activity resource requirement process would provide these details.
- The availability of the required people within the organization and the organization's recruitment or training policies and procedures is the next input for this process; it is classified as one of the enterprise environmental factor.
- The experience of creating the project teams and organization structures for similar earlier projects and the historical information and templates available for use in the organization's archives is the third input; it is classified as organizational process assets.

Tools and Techniques

Organization Chart—The technique to be used for the process is construction of organization charts which would show roles, responsibilities and reporting relationships. The organization charts can be hierarchical (in case of pure projectized or pure functional form of project organization structure) or matrix-based charts. The usual way to show the matrix-based organization chart is to prepare a *Responsibility Assignment Matrix* showing the role or responsibility of the person for any specific project activity.

Outputs

The output of the process is a comprehensive *Human Resource Plan*.

Contents of Human Resource Plan
Human Resource Plan should contain:

■ *The roles and responsibilities of the project team*—The role would be like a job description, identifying the main activity for which a person would be accountable. The responsibility would describe the specific work he would be responsible to complete for the project. Along with this, the person's authority for normal working and the competence or skill required to do the job are also included to make the plan comprehensive.

■ *Project organization chart*—This would include the inter-relationship between the different members of the project organization showing the reporting relationship and extended responsibility and accountability of the function.

■ *Staffing Management Plan*—Need for people is different during the different phases and activities of the project. The exact staffing requirement, resource calendar and expected requirement and release dates for staff and general staff management policies for recruitment, remuneration, training, leave, recognition and reward, etc. are also a part of staffing management plan.

4.2 Acquire Project Team

The planning to ensure that the required team member or resource would be available at the time scheduled for project activity is essentially the part of this process. The emphasis is usually on claiming and reserving rare resources from the organization's pool. The project manager's detailed planning and communicating & negotiating skills play an important role in effectiveness in this process.

Inputs

Human Resource Plan—the output of the earlier process, is the main input for this process. In effect, the human resources, which you planned for carrying out the project activities, are acquired either as fulltime team members or according to the resource calendar for activities.

Tools and Techniques

Pre-assignment—The easiest and surest way to acquire project team would be to get the key team members pre-assigned. The importance of the project in the organization's strategic plan and the project manager's negotiating skills play a part.

Negotiation—Project manager's negotiating skills and power or influencing play a major role in securing the scarce resources for project team.

Outputs

Project Staff Assignments are the full-time project team members and the project team organization chart.

Resource Calendars cover the persons who are going to work for specific time for specific activities. The above two complement each other and complete the required project team composition.

4.3 Develop Project Team

The process involves improving the technical competence of the team members and facilitating the administrative processes to permit closer interaction and building a cohesive team.

Inputs

Completion of the project team (through staff assignments, pre-assignments or resource calendars) is the starting point for the team development process.

Tools and Techniques

In this process, tools and techniques assume much more importance than the inputs.

- *Training*—For removing the specific technical deficiencies related to project tasks is the simpler and explicit form of team development.
- *Team Building Activities*—This is the more difficult part and it puts to test the leadership and general management skills of the project manager. The general principles of good team building are unambiguous task assignments, clear description of authority and reporting relationships, fairness in treatment of rewards and recognitions (without favoritism) and transparent communication on project status. All this is easier said than done and the great project managers and average ones have distinctly different levels of performance in this area.

The organization behavior (OB) theories have identified five stages for building high performance teams and dismantling them painlessly and fairly after the task completion.

1. *Forming*—In this phase, the induction of project team members and their becoming familiar with the project tasks, project team organization and other team members takes place.
2. *Storming*—The interaction between the members (and sometimes conflicts between the members) takes place in this phase. Project manager's communication, negotiation and conflict resolution skills are called for here for effective team building.
3. *Norming*—The conflicts having been resolved and rough edges honed for collaborative work, the team members work for the project goals.
4. *Performing*—The team members strive to attain project goals; the project manager's influencing skills, inspiring the team members with his vision and leading by personal example would be the norms here.
5. *Adjourning*—The team completes the work and the team members are reassigned other tasks in the organization. It is project manager's professional responsibility to facilitate the rehabilitation of the members.

A major part of this Chapter 11: 'Managing Project Teams' is devoted to discussion on developing and managing the project team:

- The five-stage team development model
- Situational factors affecting team development
- Building high performance teams
  - Recruiting suitable project members
  - Conducting project meetings
  - Establishing a team identity
  - Creating a shared vision
  - Managing project reward system
  - Orchestrating decision making process, and
  - Managing conflicts within the project
- Managing Virtual teams (effect of spread of organization across the country and globalization)
- Dysfunctional teams—diagnosis and recommendations for revitalization

The interested readers should revisit that part at this point.

Co-location: In cross functional teams far flung over different geographical areas or seated in distant unconnected places, the development of close bond between the team members is inhibited. Co-location, when possible, is considered an effective way in building high performance teams.

Output

Effectively and cohesively working high performance team is the output.

4.4 Manage Project Team

This process is for monitoring the performance of the project team, providing feedback, resolving conflicts and issues and fostering the team spirit to enable the team to perform as a cohesive unit and make the project a success.

Inputs

Like all performance review processes, this process also requires on one hand the work planned for each team member and compare it with the actual performance carried out to measure the performance. Accordingly *project staff assignments* (output of process Acquire Project Team and *Organization Charts or Responsibility Assignment matrix* (output of Develop Human Resource Plan) are inputs for planned work. *Team Performance Assessment* is an input providing a measure of actual performance. *Performance Reports* is one more metric for the results achieved. The comparison of planned versus actual performance gives basis for assessment and feedback for individual team member's performance.

Tools & Techniques

The techniques called for managing the project team effectively are for empowering the team to give high performance requires:

- Creation of a culture for cooperation and collaboration between the team members and
- Influencing the team members with the shared vision for project objectives.

These techniques are:

Managing the conflict between the team members (to improve collaboration and cooperation between the team members)

Performance appraisals (to provide feedback and guidance for improved performance)

Leadership and influencing skills (to share the project vision and strive for higher performance level)

Delegating tasks and democratic decision making process (to allow sense of accomplishment and ownership of tasks)

As mentioned earlier, these techniques are discussed in detail in the main body of this chapter and, therefore, not repeated here.

Outputs

The monitoring and *feedback of the performance to the team members* on one hand and sending the record for *organizational performance appraisal* system are two main outputs. Staffing changes may be found from the performance reviews and they in turn could require *change requests for project team.*

CASE 11.1

Kerzner Office Equipment

Amber Briggs looked nervously at her watch as she sat at the front of a large table in the cafeteria at Kerzner Office Equipment. It was now 10 minutes after 3:00 and only 10 of the 14 members had arrived for the first meeting of the Kerzner anniversary task force. Just then two more members hurriedly sat down and mumbled apologies for being late. Briggs cleared her throat and started the meeting.

Kerzner Office Equipment

Kerzner Office Equipment is located in Charleston, South Carolina. It specializes in the manufacture and sales of high-end office furniture and equipment. Kerzner enjoyed steady growth during its first five years of existence with a high-water employment mark of more than 1,400 workers. Then a national recession struck, forcing Kerzner to lay off 25 percent of its employees. This was a traumatic period for the company. Justin Tubbs was brought in as the new CEO, and things began to slowly turn around. Tubbs was committed to employee participation and redesigned operations around the concept of self-managing teams. The company soon introduced an innovative line of ergonomic furniture designed to reduce back strain and carpal tunnel. This line of equipment proved to be a resounding success, and Kerzner became known as a leader in the industry. The company currently employs 1,100 workers and has just been selected for the second straight time by the *Charleston Post and Courier* as one of the 10 best local firms to work for in South Carolina.

Amber Briggs

Amber Briggs is a 42-year-old human resource specialist who has worked for Kerzner for the past five years. During this time she has performed a variety of activities involving recruitment, training, compensation, and team building. David Brown, vice president of human resources, assigned Briggs the responsibility for organizing Kerzner's 10th anniversary celebration. She was excited about the project because she would report directly to top management.

CEO Tubbs briefed her as to the purpose and objectives of the celebration. Tubbs stressed that this should be a memorable event and that it was important to celebrate Kerzner's success since the dark days of the layoffs. Moreover, he confided that he had just read a book on corporate cultures and believed that such events were important for conveying the values at Kerzner. He went on to say that he wanted this to be an employee celebration—not a celebration conjured up by top management. As such, she would be assigned a task force of 14 employees from each of the major departments to organize and plan the event. Her team was to present a preliminary plan and budget for the event to top management within three months. When discussing budgets, Tubbs revealed that he felt the total cost should be somewhere in the $150,000 range. He concluded the meeting by offering to help Briggs in any way he could to make the event a success.

Soon thereafter Briggs received the list of the names of the task force members, and she contacted them either by phone or e-mail to arrange today's meeting. She had to scramble to find a meeting place. Her cubicle in human resources was too small to accommodate such a group, and all the meeting rooms at Kerzner were booked or being refurbished. She settled on the cafeteria because it was usually deserted in the late afternoon. Prior to the meeting she posted the agenda on a flipchart (see Figure C11.1) adjacent to the table. Given everyone's busy schedules, the meeting was limited to just one hour.

The First Meeting

Briggs began the meeting by saying, "Greetings. For those who don't know me, I'm Amber Briggs from human resources and I've been assigned to manage the 10th anniversary celebration at Kerzner. Top management wants this to be special event—at the same time they want it to be our event. This is why you are here. Each of you represents one of the major departments, and together our job is to plan and organize the celebration." She then reviewed the agenda and asked each member to introduce him/herself. The tall, red-haired woman to the right of Briggs broke the momentary silence by saying, "Hi, I'm Cara Miller from Plastics. I guess my boss picked me for this task force because I have a reputation for throwing great parties."

In turn each member followed suit. Below is a sampling of their introductions:

Agenda	
3:00	Introductions
3:15	Project overview
3:30	Ground rules
3:45	Meeting times
4:00	Adjourn

FIGURE C11.1
Celebration Task Force

"Hi, I'm Mike Wales from maintenance. I'm not sure why I'm here. Things have been a little slow in our department, so my boss told me to come to this meeting."

"I'm Megan Plinski from domestic sales. I actually volunteered for this assignment. I think it will be a lot of fun to plan a big party."

"Yo, my name is Nick Psias from accounting. My boss said one of us had to join this task force, and I guess it was my turn."

"Hi, I'm Rick Fennah. I'm the only one from purchasing who has been here since the beginning. We've been through some rough times, and I think it is important to take time and celebrate what we've accomplished."

"Hi, I'm Ingrid Hedstrom from international sales. I think this is a great idea, but I should warn you that I will be out of the country for most of the next month."

"I'm Abby Bell from engineering. Sorry for being late, but things are a bit crazy in my department."

Briggs circled the names of the two people who were absent and circulated a roster so that everyone could check to see if their phone numbers and e-mail addresses were correct. She then summarized her meeting with Tubbs and told the group that he expected them to make a formal presentation to top management within 10 weeks. She acknowledged that they were all busy people and that it was her job to manage the project as efficiently as possible. At the same time, she reiterated the importance of the project and that this would be a very public event: "If we screw up, everyone will know about it."

Briggs went over the ground rules and emphasized that from now on meetings would start on time and that she expected to be notified in advance if someone was going to be absent. She summarized the first part of the project as centering on five key questions: when, where, what, who, and how much? She created a stir in the group when she responded to a question about cost by informing them that top management was willing to pay up to $150,000 for the event. Megan quipped, "This is going to be one hell of a party."

Briggs then turned the group's attention to identifying a common meeting time. After jousting for 15 minutes, she terminated the discussion by requesting that each member submit a schedule of free time over the next month by Friday. She would use this information and a new planning software to identify optimal times. She ended the meeting by thanking the members for coming and asking them to begin soliciting ideas from co-workers about how this event should be celebrated. She announced that she would meet individually with each of them to discuss their role on the project. The meeting was adjourned at 4:00 P.M.

1. Critique Briggs's management of the first meeting. What, if anything, should she have done differently?
2. What barriers is she likely to encounter in completing this project?
3. What can she do to overcome these barriers?
4. What should she do between now and the next meeting?

CASE 11.2

Ajax Project

Tran was taking his dog Callie on her evening walk as the sun began to set over the coastal range. He looked forward to this time of the day. It was an opportunity to enjoy some peace and quiet. It was also a time to review events on the Ajax project and plot his next moves.

Ajax is the code name given by CEBEX for a high-tech security system project funded by the U.S. Department of Defense (DOD). Tran is the project manager and his core team consisted of 30 full-time hardware and software engineers.

Tran and his family fled Cambodia when he was four years old. He joined the U.S. Air Force when he was 18 and used the education stipend to attend Washington State University. He joined CEBEX upon graduating with a dual degree in mechanical and electrical engineering. After working on a variety of projects for 10 years Tran decided he wanted to enter management. He went to night school at the University of Washington to earn an MBA.

Tran became a project manager for the money. He also thought he was good at it. He enjoyed working with people and making the right things happen. This was his fifth project and up to now he was batting .500, with half of his projects coming ahead of schedule. Tran was proud that he could now afford to send his oldest to Stanford University.

Ajax was one of many defense projects the CEBEX Corporation had under contract with DOD. CEBEX is a huge defense company with annual sales in excess of $30 billion and more than 120,000 employees worldwide. CEBEX's five major business areas are Aeronautics, Electronic Systems, Information & Technology Services, Integrated Systems & Solutions, and Space Systems. Ajax was one of several new projects sponsored by the Integrated Systems & Solutions division aimed at the homeland security business. CEBEX was confident that it could leverage its technical expertise and political connections to become a major player in this growing market. Ajax was one of several projects directed at designing, developing, and installing a security system at an important government installation.

Tran had two major concerns when he started the Ajax project. The first was the technical risks inherent in the project. In theory the design principles made sense and the project used proven technology. Still the technology had never been applied in the field in this matter. From past experience, Tran knew there was a big difference between the laboratory and the real world. He also knew that integrating the audio, optical, tactile, and laser subsystems would test the patience and ingenuity of his team.

The second concern involved his team. The team was pretty much split down the middle between hardware and electrical engineers. Not only did these engineers have different skill sets and tend to look at problems differently, but generational differences between the two groups were evident as well. The hardware engineers were almost all former military, family men with conservative attire and beliefs. The electrical engineers were a much motlier crew. They tended to be young, single, and at times very cocky. While the hardware engineers talked about the Seattle Mariners, raising teenagers, and going to Palm Desert to play golf, the software engineers talked about Vapor, the latest concert at the Gorge amphitheater, and going mountain biking in Peru.

To make matters worse, tension between these two groups within CEBEX festered around salary issues. Electrical engineers were at a premium, and the hardware engineers resented the new hires' salary packages, which were comparable to what they were earning after 20 years of working for CEBEX. Still the real money was to be made from the incentives associated with project performance. These were all contingent on meeting project milestones and the final completion date.

Before actual work started on the project, Tran arranged a two-day team-building retreat at a lodge on the Olympic peninsula for his entire team as well as key staff from the government installation. He used this time to go over the major objectives of the project and unveil the basic project plan. An internal consultant facilitated several team-building activities that made light of cross-generational issues. Tran felt a real sense of camaraderie within the team.

The good feelings generated from the retreat carried over to the beginning of the project. The entire team bought into the mission of the project and technical challenges it represented. Hardware and electrical engineers worked side by side to solve problems and build subsystems.

The project plan was built around a series of five tests, with each test being a more rigorous verification of total system performance. Passing each test represented a key milestone for the project. The team was excited about conducting the first alpha test one week early—only to be disappointed by a series of minor technical glitches that took two weeks of problem solving to resolve. The team worked extra hard to make up for the lost time. Tran was proud of the team and how hard members had worked together.

The Alpha II test was conducted on schedule, but once again the system failed to perform. This time three weeks of debugging was needed before the team received the green light to move to the next phase of the project. By this time, team goodwill had been tested, and emotions were a bit frayed. A cloud of disappointment descended over the team as hopes of bonuses disappeared with the project falling further behind schedule. This was augmented by cynics who felt that the original schedule was unfair and the deadlines were impossible to begin with.

Tran responded by starting each day with a status meeting where the team reviewed what they accomplished the previous day and set new objectives for that day. He believed these meetings were helpful in establishing positive momentum and reinforcing a team identity among the engineers. He also went out of his way to spend more time with the "troops," helping them solve problems, offering encouragement, and a sincere pat on the back when one was deserved.

He was cautiously optimistic when the time came to conduct the Alpha III test. It was the end of the day when the switch was turned on, but nothing happened. Within minutes the entire team heard the news. Screams could be heard down the hallway. Perhaps the most telling moment was when Tran looked down at the company's parking lot and saw most of his project team walking by themselves to their cars.

As Callie chased some wild bunnies, Tran pondered what he should do next.

1. How effective has Tran been as a project manager? Explain.
2. What problem(s) does Tran face?
3. How would you go about solving them? Why?

CASE 11.3

Franklin Equipment, Ltd.*

Franklin Equipment, Ltd. (FEL), with headquarters and main fabrication facilities in Saint John, New Brunswick, was founded 75 years ago to fabricate custom-designed large machines for construction businesses in the Maritime Provinces. Over the years its product lines became strategically focused on creating rock-crushing equipment for dam and highway construction and for a few other markets that require the processing of aggregate. FEL now designs, fabricates, and assembles stationary and portable rock-crushing plants and services its own products and those of its competitors.

* Courtesy of John A. Drexler Jr., Oregon State University.

In the 1970s, FEL began to expand its market from the Maritime Provinces to the rest of Canada. FEL currently has several offices and fabrication facilities throughout the country. More recently, FEL has made a concerted effort to market its products internationally.

Last month, FEL signed a contract to design and fabricate a rock-crushing plant for a Middle East construction project, called Project Abu Dhabi. Charles Gatenby secured this contract and has been assigned as project manager. This project is viewed as a coup because FEL has wanted to open up markets in this area for a long time and has had difficulty getting prospective customers to realize that FEL is a Canadian firm and not from the United States. Somehow these customers view all North American vendors as the same and are reluctant to employ any of them because of international political considerations.

A project of this scope typically starts with the selection of a team of managers responsible for various aspects of the design, fabrication, delivery, and installation of the product. Manager selection is important because the product design and fabrication vary with the unique needs of each customer. For example, the terrain, rock characteristics, weather conditions, and logistical concerns create special problems for all phases of plant design and operations. In addition, environmental concerns and labor conditions vary from customer to customer and from region to region.

In addition to the project manager, all projects include a design engineer; an operations manager, who oversees fabrication and on-site assembly; and a cost accountant, who oversees all project financial and cost reporting matters. Each of these people must work closely together if a well-running plant is to be delivered on time and within cost constraints. Because international contracts often require FEL to employ host nationals for plant assembly and to train them for operations, a human resource manager is also assigned to the project team. In such cases, the human resource manager needs to understand the particulars of the plant specifications and then use this knowledge to design selection procedures and assess particular training needs. The human resource manager also needs to learn the relevant labor laws of the customer's country.

FEL assigns managers to project teams based on their expertise and their availability to work on a particular project given their other commitments. This typically means that managers without heavy current project commitments will be assigned to new projects. For instance, a manager finishing one project will likely be assigned a management position on a new project team. The project manager typically has little to say about who is assigned to his or her team.

Because he secured Project Abu Dhabi and has established positive working relationships with the Abu Dhabi customer, Gatenby was assigned to be project manager. Gatenby has successfully managed similar projects. The other managers assigned to Project Abu Dhabi are Bill Rankins, a brilliant design engineer, Rob Perry, operations manager with responsibility for fabrication and installation, Elaine Bruder, finance and cost accounting manager, and Sam Stonebreaker, human resource manager. Each of these managers has worked together on numerous past projects.

A few years ago, FEL began contracting for team facilitator services from several consulting firms to help new project teams operate effectively. Last month, FEL recruited Carl Jobe from one of these consulting firms to be a full-time internal consultant. A number of managers, including Gatenby, were so impressed with Jobe's skills that they convinced FEL top management of the need to hire a permanent internal facilitator; Jobe was the obvious choice.

Because Gatenby was instrumental in hiring Jobe at FEL, he was excited at the prospect of using Jobe to facilitate team building among Project Abu Dhabi team members. Gatenby was very proud of having secured this project and had expected to be appointed project manager. He knew that this project's success would be instrumental in advancing his own career.

Gatenby told Jobe, "This project is really important to FEL and to me personally. I really need for you to help us develop into a team that works well together to achieve the project's goals within budget. I've observed your success in developing teams on other projects, and I expect you'll do the same for Project Abu Dhabi. I'll take care of you if you help me make this work."

Jobe outlined for Gatenby how he would proceed. Jobe would begin by interviewing team members individually to learn their perceptions of each other and of the promises and pitfalls of being involved in this project. Meetings of the entire team would follow these interviews using the information he collected to help establish a team identity and a shared vision.

Jobe interviewed Bruder first. She expressed skepticism about whether the project could succeed. During the interview, Bruder appeared to be distant, and Jobe could not figure out why he had not established good rapport with her. Bruder intimated that she expected a lot of cost overruns and a lot of missed production deadlines. But not knowing Jobe well, Bruder was reluctant to identify any specific barriers to the project's success. While she would not directly say so, it was clear to Jobe that Bruder did not want to be a part of Project Abu Dhabi. Jobe left this interview confused and wondering what was going on.

Jobe's next interview was with Perry, the operations manager. Perry has worked at FEL for 15 years, and he immediately came to the point: "This project is not going to work. I cannot understand why upper management keeps assigning me to work on projects with Rankins. We simply cannot work together, and we don't get along. I've disliked him from day one. He keeps dropping the fact that he has earned all these advanced degrees from Purdue. And he keeps telling us how things are done there. I know he's better educated than I am, and he's really smart. But I'm smart too and am good at what I do. There's no need for Rankins to make me feel like an idiot because I don't have a degree. Jobe, I'll be honest with you. Rankins has only been here for five years, but I hold him personally responsible for my problem with alcohol, and for its resulting effect on my marriage. I got divorced last year, and it's Rankins's fault."

Jobe next talked with Rankins, who said, "I don't care what you do. Perry and I simply can't work closely together for the nine months it will take to get it done. One of us will kill the other. Ever since I arrived at FEL, Perry has hated my guts and does everything he can to sabotage my designs. We usually worry about customers creating change orders; here it's the fabrication and operations manager who is responsible for them. Perry second-guesses everything I do and makes design changes on his own, and these are always bad decisions. He is out of control. I swear he stays awake at nights thinking up ways to ruin my designs. I don't have this problem with any other manager."

Jobe left these interviews thoroughly discouraged and could not imagine what would come up in his interview with Stonebreaker. But Stonebreaker was quite positive: "I enjoy these international projects where I get to travel abroad and learn about different cultures. I can't wait to get started on this."

Jobe asked Stonebreaker about the ability of various team members to work together. Stonebreaker replied, "No problem! We've all worked together before and have had no problems. Sure, there have been ruffled feathers and hurt feelings between Rankins and Perry. Rankins can be arrogant and Perry stubborn, but it's never been anything that we can't work around. Besides, both of them are good at what they do—both professionals. They'll keep their heads on straight."

Jobe was even more bewildered. Gatenby says this project's success rides on Jobe's facilitation skills. The finance manager appears to want off this project team. The design engineer and operations manager admit they detest each other and cannot work together. And the human resources manager, having worked on projects with Perry and Rankins before, expects a rosy working relationship and anticipates no problems.

Jobe had a second meeting with Gatenby. Before discussing the design of the teambuilding sessions, he asked questions to learn what Gatenby thought about the ability of team members to work together. Gatenby admitted that there has been very bad blood between Perry and Rankins, but added, "That's why we hired you. It's your job to make sure that the history between those two doesn't interfere with Project Abu Dhabi's success. It's your job to get them to work well together. Get it done."

Their dialogue toward the end of this meeting progressed as follows:

Jobe: "Why do you expect Rankins and Perry to work well together, given their history? What incentives do they have to do so?"

Gatenby: "As you should know, FEL requires formal goal setting between project managers and functional managers at the beginning of each project. I've already done this with Bruder, Stonebreaker, Perry, and Rankins. Perry and Rankins have explicit goals stating they must work well together and cooperate with each other."

Jobe: "What happens if they do not meet these goals?"

Gatenby: "I've already discussed this with top management. If it appears to me after two months that things are not working out between Perry and Rankins, FEL will fire Rankins."

Jobe: "Does Perry know this?"

Gatenby: "Yes."

---

1. Evaluate the criteria FEL uses to assign managers to project teams. What efficiencies do these criteria create? What are the resulting problems?
2. Why is it even more important that project team members work well together on international projects such as Project Abu Dhabi?
3. Discuss the dilemma that Jobe now faces.
4. What should Jobe recommend to Gatenby?

Case 11.4

Kalpataru Team

Introduction

As a leader of the project team, the role of a project manager is to ensure that the entire project team works effectively and efficiently as a coherent unit for project success. Therefore, it is as much important for him to pay attention to managing human relation aspects of the team as focusing on the project related specific major issues. The project manager has to pay close attention to selection of key team members with complimentary skills and mutual compatibility in day-to-day working, excellent communication- listening and persuading, developing empathetic relationship with the team members, and inspiring them with the project vision which would lead them to subordinate personal agenda in favour of project objectives. Above all, he should be able to lead by his own example and project himself as a true leader of his team. The case study describes the formation and working of a project team in an engineering consultancy organization and in the process highlights the relevance of these issues to the project success.

The Task

The heat and sultry atmosphere in the late October in a non-air conditioned office in Mumbai was sufficient to make most people uncomfortable and uneasy, but Hitesh Mehta had some more reasons to feel depressed. He had returned from USA after a stint of 12 years after his post-graduate study in mechanical engineering and working there in the prestigious Flour Corporation office as a senior design team leader. He had returned at a very short notice about 4 months back learning about his father's heart attack and hospitalization. His father was now back home and recuperating and he could feel the sense of relief seen on his mother's and father's faces seeing him around. Being a bachelor, Hitesh had no problems of adjustment of other family members about his stay in India. At first, he had thought of his stay in India as just temporary to tide over the emergency of his father's sickness. He thought that once his father had stable good health, he would be able to persuade his parents to join with him in USA on his return there. On an afterthought, he decided to stay over in India for about a year or so. It was in that context, that he took up the offer of Synergy Engineering Consultants (Synergy) to head their special projects section. Synergy had hoped that while handling some special projects, Hitesh would be able to incorporate into the group some improved practices in handling the engineering design assignments. Five weeks on the job, and Hitesh had started having serious doubts about the wisdom of his decision to stay back longer and particularly his decision to take up a temporary job with Synergy in the meantime.

The ringing of his intercom woke him up from his deep thoughts. It was a call from the Chairman Ramesh Lal calling him for a discussion in his office. When Hitesh reached Mr. Lal's office, Arun Desai, HR Director and B.K. Sarkar, Director Finance, were already there. As soon as Raman Patel, Director Engineering, joined the group, Mr. Lal opened the discussion on the special agenda for which this meeting was called.

"We have finally won the tender for preparing the detailed mechanical engineering drawings for the Nuclear Power Corporation, for which we had bid two months back. This is the kind of breakthrough I was looking for. Once we perform creditably on two or three such prestigious assignments, we can move ahead as a leading premium quality engineering consultant", Mr. Lal introduced the agenda for discussion.

"The entire utilities and off sites piping?" inquired Raman Patel.

"No, they have split the order into the cooling water, process water and DM water piping. The total work is not large at all – may be around 6,000 man-hours of eighteen or twenty piping lay-outs and sections, about 400 piping isometrics, some piping supports drawings, and bill of materials summary. We have done many much much larger and more complex jobs, I know. It is not the size or complexity of the job, and let me confide that the way we had bid aggressively to beat the competition and get this order, we will probably not make any money on the job either. The reason I want all of us to treat it as an important assignment is only for our strategy to be able to add the name of Nuclear Power Corporation (NPC) to our clients' list. The name adds prestige; so we must do it well and definitely strive to secure from the client a letter of appreciation for a work well done. That's the crux of the situation. After all, who would know what actual detailed engineering we did for them?"

There was a brief silence, while the group digested the information. Then Raman Patel broke the silence and asked, "When are we expected to start and what is the deadline for final completion?"

"By the end of the next week, we should get formal delivery of the relevant details of the basic engineering package to start our work that would include the equipment layout plans and sections, utility requirements of the process equipment, the equipment drawings and the piping specifications which they want us to follow for the cooling water, process water and DM water services. But it is the usual stuff from the prime engineering contractor, United Engineers India and I have here with me a set of the draft on which the final version is based. We would have about 3 months to complete our job. Say, we would need to organize a group of about 8-10 engineers & draftsmen to work on the job and, of course, a lot of overtime." Ramesh Lal summed up the situation.

There was a pregnant silence for a few seconds.

"The timing . .... . The timing is a bit problematical," whispered Raman Patel. "Our contract with the union is up for renewal in the next month and the union workers have already started to put pressure on all members to work to rules, refuse overtime, sort of slow down. The design engineers, though they are not a part of the union, look the other way when these things go on; after all they would have to work with these draftsmen on an hour-to-hour basis once this struggle for the contract renewal is over. So, the job, which could have been done with no sweat at all, is likely to test our managerial ability"

"So, what do you suggest? It would be indeed very difficult to back out at this stage, but bad as it would be, it would be much preferable to our attempting and failing on the job" Ramesh Lal concluded.

"No.... ", Raman hesitated and then continued, "Not back out, but, I think we should handle it differently from our regular jobs. May be as a special project? "and then he looked around the table and smiled at Hitesh.

That is how, after some further discussion, Hitesh got his special project assignment for Nuclear Power Corporation piping detailed engineering.

Kalpataru Team

As heading the Special Projects Cell, Hitesh was not a line manager and the only staffs directly reporting to him was a management trainee engineer Pushpakant and the secretary Geeta. He was to coordinate with the other functional line managers including the heads of different engineering departments, procurement head and three site construction managers and get services of the engineers, draftsmen, site supervisors and other technical personnel to get his special projects planned and executed.

Returning to his office, Hitesh called Pushpakant and briefed him on the meeting's proceedings and the new special project assigned to him. Pushpakant was a mechanical engineering graduate, not too bright academically but quite skillful in interpersonal relations. He had joined as a management trainee about a year back only, but in that relatively short time, he had built up friendly working relationships with most people in the office. So, he was quite up-to-date with the undercurrents of corporate politics and could feel the pulse of the middle managers and lower level workers.

On learning about the next special project assignment, he sensed the problems lurking ahead. "Is it the Kalpakam Nuclear Power plant, which is so much in the news every day? It would be a very prestigious assignment, Sir; something we would be able to talk with our friends with pride", Pushpakant started with enthusiasm and then slipped in the caveat, "But, we will have a very difficult time, Sir. In this project, the emphasis will be mostly on detailed engineering drafting of layouts, sections and isometric drawings, and not on engineering designs or calculations. The draftsmen and junior engineers' union is just getting ready to intensify their struggle for negotiating the next 3-years agreement. They would like to put pressure on the management by putting as many roadblocks in operations as possible for forcing the management to accept the terms in the union's demands. And what better target they would want than this type of prestigious project?"

Hitesh considered this and the realities of the situation started gradually to sink in. Then in a measured tone, he went ahead explaining the plan he had in mind. "I had not thought about this union situation to be so serious. I had just thought that we would form a small team of about 10 or 12 piping draftsmen and two group leaders. The group leaders would help in preparing the master plans, feeding the junior draftsmen with the details necessary to prepare the piping isometrics and keep an eye on the overall accuracy of the work. One good piping engineer can spot-check the layouts and isometrics for improving the accuracy and keeping tab on the total work flow. Now, I see that we will indeed have difficult times because mostly we would have to get the drawings out from draftsmen. Any way, the jobs is in our lap and let's try to do the best we can. I am personally determined to make it a success. Building a nuclear plant of this capacity is a work of national importance. I would feel deeply hurt if our group would fail in making our small personal contributions to this national cause. So let us start. Who would you suggest to take in our team as group leaders for the drafting team?"

"We want the top talent on this, right? My personal choice would be Sudhakar Joshi. He is the person you should take as a group leader for this job. He has over 10 years of experience in piping and some earlier work also in mechanical equipment drawings. He is very meticulous and thorough. The only problem is, I am afraid, that he will not agree to work as a group leader for this job. You see, he is one of the three union leaders and you don't expect that he would cooperate to make things easy for the management at the time of intensified struggle."

"From what you say, he appears to be the right person to work as group leader for this job. Then, let me ask you, do you feel that he will not take up this assignment willingly or that he might sabotage the work if we make him accept it?"

"No, he would never sabotage. That way he is a straight forward and principled man. But he will just not accept", Pushpakant responded.

"In that case I would at least want to try to persuade him to take this job. I hope to win him over and build the team around him", Hitesh mused.

"Well, in Hindu mythology, there is a concept of a tree, Kalpataru. If a person would be sitting under such a tree, all wishes of the person would be answered. Sir, if you succeed in winning him over, you would have a winning team – let me call it the 'Kalpataru Team' .The name Kalpataru is also suggestive of Kalpakam Project." Pushpakant chuckled.

"OK, let us try to build the 'Kalpataru Team'. I will talk with Sudhakar tomorrow morning. In the meanwhile, take a look at this draft specifications to check if there are no surprises."

Inducting the Key Team Member

The next morning, Hitesh invited Sudhakar in his cabin for a talk. Hitesh had met Sudhakar earlier, but had noticed nothing particularly remarkable about him. Now Hitesh started observing closely and making notes in his mind. He noticed that Sudhakar was a medium height, lean man, neatly dressed and wearing glasses. He spoke rather slowly and with a typical Maharashtrian accent, but talked in a focused manner and he could articulate well what he wanted to convey.

Hitesh explained to him the background of the project, the engineering design and drafting work involved. He stressed on the prestigious nature of the assignment, national importance of the Kalpakam Project and the prominent position of National Nuclear Power Corporation in the Indian scene. He explained the urgency in completing the assignment in 3 months time, even if meeting that schedule required doing a lot of overtime. Finally, Hitesh told him that he wanted to take him as the group leader for this project.

Hitesh found Sudhakar quite quick on grasping the nature of the work. His eyes sparkled with interest while grasping the technical details of the work. Then he appeared to be deeply engrossed in thinking out his response. Finally he slowly started to reply, "Sir, this is indeed a very nice project and I feel good that you want to take me up as a group leader for this job. But, in the interest of this important work, I should suggest that you take some one else as a group leader this time".

"But why another person? I am told *you are just the right person* in our company to work as a group leader for this job."

"Well, I am happy if you have heard good reports about me. But there is a special reason that I should not work as a group leader for this job now. Since you joined the company only a few weeks back, you may not be aware, but I am one of the three leaders of the junior engineers and draftsmen's union. We have formulated a plan as a part of our strategy to intensify struggle to force management to accept our demands. And they are very fair demands, Sir, I assure you: we are going to ask all draftsmen to work by rules. Not to take any initiatives themselves and make design sketches or drawings strictly according to instructions only. If any major changes are required, insist on written instructions from design engineers or supervisors. If a minor detail is missing, just wait at the board until the supervisor comes around and clears that up before drawing the next line. No volunteering of information for improvement. *Strictly no overtime*. I have been working as a piping draftsman for over 10 years and I know, if any one should know, that no group of ten or twelve draftsmen would complete this job in 3 months, unless they take initiatives in preparing drawings and actively cooperate. And the kind of deadline for completion you mention will require full cooperation and very heavy overtime. Almost the entire group to be working on the job for 3-4 hours overtime each day. Now, on one hand, how do I go about my work as a conscientious group leader without asking people to do overtime? And on the other hand how should I ask them to disregard the policy of our union, which I advocate to them as a union leader? Some other time, I would have been happy and proud to accept the assignment. But, not now. I cannot refuse to accept the assignment, if you decide to give it to me; but I must make my position clear that in that case, you would not have an effective group leader in your team; like everybody else, I would have to work to rules. Please consider farming this out to some other smaller drafting agency."

There was a silence for a moment, till Hitesh recovered from the impact. Then he stared," Sudhakar, I am so glad that you put the position so transparently. In fact, your approach makes me more sure of project success now with you as the group leader than I had earlier thought. But, I would respect your feeling and position and not force you to accept the assignment. I too wish that the job had not come at such a time to our company. But then, we have to take things as they come. You know our company and the jobs we got so far. Do you recall any past jobs, which were so prestigious or important? The western world is bent on making the progress of our nuclear development as tough as possible. Waiving aside the tempting rewards and recognition in overseas job offers, some dedicated scientists, who have chosen to work for our atomic energy program, are trying to build the peaceful nuclear power plant in face of such express hostility of the western world. Kalpakam Power Project is a challenge for the Indian scientists and engineers to meet self-reliance of engineering in nuclear energy field. It is the duty of every Indian, who would be in a position to work on and actively contribute towards success of this effort, to do his best. I will share with you my personal feelings and views on this. May be I might not continue working in India, or for that matter, for Synergy Consultants, and I might return to my Flour Corporation job in USA in the next few months. But I imagine, whatever course I might happen to choose a few months from now, if this job is done well, then when I would look back on my professional career years later, I would surely remember with pride my own contribution to this national project—though a very small one." Hitesh stopped to reflect and then added, "Sudhakar, I understand your feelings and position. If you do not want to take up the Group Leader's position now, then I would not pressurize or force you. But, I have one suggestion. Think coolly on what we discussed and come back and tell me about your decision the first thing next week Monday morning."

Sudhakar knocked on Hitesh's cabin door late Monday afternoon—almost just before quitting time. Hitesh waved him in. "Sir, I had a hard thinking to do for the last two days and finally I have decided to accept your suggestion and join as a group leader of the Kalpakam Project Team", Sudhakar said without any preface taking his seat on a chair, "I have talked about it with our other union brothers. Sir, we all also understand the overall bigger picture and we have decided that our union struggle would not to come in the way of this national effort. I have resigned as the joint secretary of the union, so that there is no personal conflict of interest. As a special exception, the union would not object to our taking up in our team 3-4 senior and competent draftsmen and their doing overtime if necessary, but we would have to make-do for the rest of help from the trainee draftsmen's pool only. The union's struggle would remain as intense as ever as far as other projects are concerned; in fact, it may turn more intense."

Hitesh just offered his hand for hand-shake and added, "I am happy about your decision and feel proud of the commitment you have shown. We will make this project like a show-piece work. I have just one question. Do you think the trainee draftsmen would be able to give the right quality of work?"

"Sir, don't worry on that score. Since major part of the work is preparing piping isometrics, all that is required for preparing those drawings is for the draftsmen to properly sketch out and enter the details prepared by senior draftsmen. There is no problem with the draftsmanship quality as such with these trainee draftsmen; they just cannot be depended to work out the details independently. We will make sure that they get all details and we will check the drawings prepared by them rather more thoroughly".

Forming the Project Team and Project Launch

Hitesh asked Pushpakant the next day morning to sit down with Sudhakar and finalize the list of the project team members. "If Sudhakar has agreed to take up this assignment as a group leader, we have succeeded in making a right start." Pushpakant was enthusiastic. "Well, then Sudhakar, you and I shall meet today afternoon and review the list".

That afternoon, after the list was reviewed Hitesh suggested, "OK, I will take this list and clear it with Raman Patel to check if any of the proposed team members are working on some other urgent projects, so that they can be immediately released for our work. Once our list is final, then tomorrow afternoon, we will have our first project team meeting."

"Meeting?" Sudhakar was a bit taken back, but he quickly checked himself and said, "Sure, we will be ready."

Raman Patel cleared the list except for one senior draftsman, who was working on another urgent assignment and could not be spared. Sudhakar replaced him with another comparable experience draftsman.

Hitesh took Ramesh Lal's appointment and explained to him the developments so far. He explained that some special arrangements might be necessary to facilitate the group to work during regular hours and especially for overtime work. Hitesh told him, that for a start, he envisaged the need for the draftsmen in his group for special transport arrangement in the evening and availability of canteen facilities after office hours. He added that as and when he ran into a wall, he might want to come back to Mr. Lal to get his support. Mr. Lal assured Hitesh full support of the management on all reasonable issues.

In the meeting held in the canteen, Hitesh explained the nature of the project work, the types of drawings to be prepared and the tight schedule for completing the drawings. He stressed the importance of the project in context of national development and the prestige it would bring to the company, if the job was well done. "Two things are very important for this project, each of our drawings must be entirely free from errors or slips. So if you have any doubts, check, recheck or ask Sudhakar, Pushpakant or me. Secondly, we have to complete this job on a very tight dead line and so, not only would we have to work sincerely during the regular time, we would also have to be ready to put in overtime of up to 2-3 hours every working day, if necessary. You would not be able to avail the regular staff bus ride back, when you work overtime; we would make special arrangement for all people who stay back to reach the nearest suburban railway station. Our canteen does not serve tea or snacks after regular office hours. I would talk to the canteen contractor and ask him to make arrangements for serving tea and snacks after office hours. I believe, our good work will bring satisfaction and prestige to all of us and the company. Any questions?" Hitesh posed, but there were no questions. Then Hitesh continued, "So, all of you are ready to start from tomorrow for next 3 months of hard work?" There rose from the group a quiet hum indicating the group's acceptance.

The Kalptaru Team Camp

The list of drawings and the plan for completing them was prepared in the next two days and the selected senior draftsmen started working on he piping plans and sections assigned to them. It was easy to spot who worked on the Kalpataru team in this rather large spread out hall: the drafting tables, over which the lights were on after the office hours till late evening!

After a week, Pushpakant suggested, "Sir, rather than having these draftsmen working on Kalpataru Team scattered all over the hall, why don't we get them together in a small group in a small hall?"

"A good idea, but where is that 'small hall'?"

"In the back side of the records room, there is a space to accommodate 10-12 drafting tables. It will be little cramped, but close working of the group would be helpful".

Hitesh liked the idea and got it done in the next 2 days. Now at the back of the records room was the camp of Kalpataru Team—a group of about 12 draftsmen closely working together for the whole day and doing overtime till about 9:00 PM practically every day. At 5 PM, as all regular workforces closed the shop and left, snacks and tea were ordered and served and the Kalpataru Team camp would turn into a mini-canteen!

After two weeks, the group started working with firm commitment to their tasks. Every one knew the overall plan of work and their own share in the group efforts. There was a strong peer pressure if some one appeared to be not up to the task. If someone had a difficulty, his peers would help him out. The identity of the team became so strong that it was felt even by other engineers and draftsmen in the company, who started referring to the group by the name christened by Pushpakant—the "Kalpataru Team". The overtime became such a common practice that if some table was unoccupied after the office hours, it became conspicuous. Hitesh and Pushpakant also started doing overtime and working out some engineering details, re-checking the finished drawings or planning the next week's work. More than anything else, Hitesh wanted the team members to know and feel that as a team leader he was also ready to work as hard as other team members and subordinate his own personal agenda for the group's greater objectives. Not that there was no friction whatsoever. The differences of opinion and spirited arguments did take place now and then. Under intense work pressure, all people become more edgy. But they never allowed this small friction to come in the way of overall group's work plan.

The team members started knowing other members more closely—not just the names, where they lived and what other family members were. But also some special details like whose children were studying what, if there was any major sickness in the family, who likes hockey and who played cricket in the school team.

So Hitesh was surprised to see Kumaram working after regular office hours that day. "Isn't today your two-year old son's birth day party? I thought you would leave today on regular time" Hitesh observed. "Yes, it is Viren's birthday, and I would have left on regular time if I had completed this piping section, as I thought I would, before the stipulated time. But I need some more time. The isometrics of three draftsmen will be held up till I complete it. So I decided to complete it and go. I called my wife and explained that I would be an hour and a half late".

When Kumaram was finally ready to leave for the day, Hitesh came over to his table and slipped in a small package. "A toy car set for your son: I appreciate your staying back on your own. Have good celebrations and don't forget to bring a piece of cake for your group! ". Kumaram could not say much except muttering a sincere "Thank you, Sir".

Mid-term Review

Mid-term project review was scheduled after 5 weeks in the conference room. The senior managers of the company attended such review meetings.

Two days before the meeting, Hitesh discussed with Sudhakar and Pushpakant, the type of data and information, which should be available for the mid-term review and asked them to prepare it. The next day, he reviewed it with them, polished it a bit, and finally told them, "O.K., this is fine. Now be ready to present it to the review meeting tomorrow afternoon." This took Pushpakant and Sudhakar by surprise; they did not expect to attend the high level project review meeting. Hitesh understood the expression on their face and responded, "Well, you are far more familiar with the fine details, so you may as well present them and answer any queries our senior managers might have".

For Pushpakant and Sudhakar, it was a new experience to meet the top managers of the company in such a review meeting. They prepared well for the presentation—the drawings, which were completed; the drawings, which were scheduled and the time they would take, the technical queries pending clarification from the client, and so on. At the meeting, Hitesh gave a brief overview of the project indicating that the project was going so far well and that further details would be presented by his assistants. He introduced Pushpakant and Sudhakar to the group, and they gave the detailed presentation.

After the meeting, when they were alone, Raman Patel remarked to Mr. Lal, "The project is doing fine. Hitesh is really fortunate to get hold of good assistants and draftsmen to work on this job". Mr. Lal did not miss the subtle undertone in Raman Patel's remark of belittling of Hitesh's own personal contribution to the project success. Ordinarily, he might have ignored such petty rivalry. This time, though, he was so impressed by exemplary work done by a new man on his managerial team that he felt necessary to go to his rescue with a smiling repartee, " Yes, Raman, but they have been here all this time!"

Eleven weeks passed and the just two days before the set deadline, all drawings were completed. The whole day was spent in preparing the sets and arranging them in the proper order for packing and couriering. The entire team assembled at the end of the day—but this time just for celebration of a job well done and sharing a few snacks and cold drinks. The success of the Kalpataru Team had by this time become a common talk in the company and every one associated with it started feeling the pride of belonging to this team.

Ramesh Lal called Hitesh to his office and said, "I want to talk to your Kalpataru Team before you disband it. Just remind me to drop in by the day end".

"I am very happy with the way you have worked together to make this project a success. In fact, you have shown all of us in this company a new pathway", Ramesh Lal told the team, "Let me share with you that the negotiations with the union are almost in the final stage. We have agreed on certain increases in basic wages, overtime compensation and amenities. I was not sure in the beginning if we could afford this higher burden, but now I am convinced that we would be able to do well with the good name and marketing push this success might give. Though technically, the union agreement would be signed and come into force from the first of the next month, I have decided to make the new agreement overtime payment rates applicable retroactively to the overtime work you did for this project". This announcement was greeted by the team with spontaneous enthusiasm.

"And something else, which I am sure you all would be happy to hear", Ramesh Lal continued, "We have decided to promote Hitesh to be the Deputy Director—Engineering". Ramesh Lal's announcement caught everyone, including Hitesh, by surprise. The announcement started to draw great applause, when Hitesh intervened and said, "I feel so deeply satisfied that we all made a success of this project. All of you in the project team deserve credit particularly Pushpakant and Sudhakar. At the same time, the visibility of the project in the organization and the support of the top management, from Mr. Lal and all other top managers, also played a major role in the project success. So, it is a combination of all these that has culminated in success. I feel happy and proud that the company has considered rewarding me with a promotion. However, I must now share with you all, and you Mr. Lal, particularly, a closely guarded personal secret. My ex-boss at Flour Corporation had asked me four weeks back to return to USA and join back there. He gave me an offer that was like the proverbial 'offer you cannot refuse'. I told him that I needed a month more to honour my current commitments and wind up if he could wait that long. He has graciously extended my joining time and in the long term interest of my professional career, I have decided to accept that offer. My parents will join me there as soon as visa formalities are taken care of. I was just waiting to bring this common effort to a winning close before I left the company".

In the silence that fell, even scratching of a 2-B pencil on a drawing paper would have been audible!

Questions and Points for Discussions

1. In this chapter, 'Five-Stage Team Development Model' and 'Situational Factors Affecting Team Development' are described. Explain how the description in that model and the identified factors conform or otherwise with the case details.

2. The chapter highlights a few hints on 'Building High-Performance Project Teams':
   - Recruiting Project Members
   - Conducting Project Meetings
   - Establishing a Team Identity
   - Creating a Shared Vision
   - Managing Project Rewards System,
   - Orchestrating the Decision-Making Process,
   - Managing Conflict within the Project', and
   - Rejuvenating the Project Team

   In the light of the details given in the case, discuss how relevant these techniques or hints appear for building a high-performance team.

3. The earlier chapter, 'Leadership: Being an Effective Project Manager', focused on the role played by the leadership qualities of the project manager in building successful project teams. Discuss the background, general managerial approach and personal character (professional ethics and empathy with the team members) of Hitesh in his role as a project manager in context of that chapter.

4. Notice the professional ethics observed by the principal characters of this project team: Sudhakar Joshi and Hitesh Mehta.

CHAPTER 12

Outsourcing: Managing Interorganizational Relations

. . . being a good partner has become a key corporate asset. I call it a company's collaborative advantage. In the global economy, a well-developed ability to create and sustain fruitful collaborations gives companies a significant competitive leg up.

—Rosabeth Moss Kanter, *Harvard Business School professor*

It is rare in today's flat world to find important projects that are being completed totally in-house. Outsourcing or contracting significant segments of project work to other companies is commonplace. For example, nine states attempting to unify the accounting of all their state agencies did not have the internal resources to implement such a large project. Hence, project teams were formed consisting of personnel from software, hardware, and accounting firms to implement the projects. Small high-tech firms outsource research to determine what features customers value in new products they are developing. Even industry giants such as Microsoft and Intel commonly hire independent firms to test new products they are developing.

Contracting project work has long been the norm in the construction industry, where firms hire general contractors who, in turn, hire and manage cadres of subcontractors to create new buildings and structures. For example, the Chunnel project, which created a transportation tunnel between France and England, involved more than 250 organizations. Contracting is not limited to large projects. For example, an insurance company worked with an outside contractor to develop an answering service that directs customers to specific departments and employees. The trend for the future suggests that more and more projects will involve working with people from different organizations.

This chapter extends the previous two chapters' discussion of building and managing relations by focusing specifically on issues surrounding working with people from other organizations to complete a project. First, the advantages and disadvantages of outsourcing project work are introduced. This is followed by a discussion of *best practices* used by firms to outsource and collaborate with each other on projects. The focus then shifts to the art of negotiating, which is at the heart of effective collaboration. Negotiating skills and techniques for resolving disagreements and reaching optimal solutions are then presented. The chapter closes with a brief note on managing customer relations. In addition, an appendix on contract management is included to augment our discussion of how organizations work together on projects.

Outsourcing Project Work

The term outsourcing has traditionally been applied to the transferring of business functions or processes (e.g., customer support, IT, accounting) to other, often foreign companies. For example, when you call your Internet provider to solve a technical problem you are likely to talk to a technician in Bangalore, India, or Bucharest, Romania. Outsourcing is now being applied to contracting significant chunks of project work. For example, HP and Dell work closely with hard drive manufacturers to develop next-generation laptops. Toyota and DaimlerChrysler collaborate with suppliers to develop new automobile platforms.

The shift toward outsourcing is readily apparent in the film industry. During the golden era of Hollywood, huge, vertically integrated corporations made movies. Studios such as MGM, Warner Brothers, and 20th Century–Fox owned large movie lots and employed thousands of full-time specialists—set designers, camera people, film editors, and directors. Star actors like Humphrey Bogart and Marilyn Monroe were signed to exclusive studio contracts for a set number of films (e.g., six films over three years). Today, most movies are made by a collection of individuals and small companies who come together to make films project-by-project. This structure allows each project to be staffed with the talent most suited to its demands rather than choosing from only those people the studio employs. This same approach is being applied to the creation of new products and services. For example, see Figure 12.1.

Figure 12.1 depicts a situation in which a zero-gravity reclining chair is being developed. The genesis for the chair comes from a mechanical engineer who developed the idea in her garage. The inventor negotiates a contract with a catalog firm to develop and manufacture the chair. The catalog company in turn creates a project team of manufacturers, suppliers, and marketing firms to create the new chair. Each participant adds requisite expertise to the project. The catalog firm brings its brand name and distribution channels to the project. Tool and die firms provide customized parts which are delivered to a manufacturing firm that will

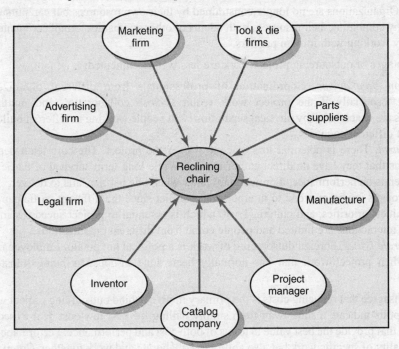

FIGURE 12.1   Reclining Chair Project

produce the chair. Marketing firms refine the design, develop packaging, and test market potential names. A project manager is assigned by the catalog firm to work with the inventor and the other parties to complete the project.

Many outsourced projects operate in a virtual environment in which people are linked by computers, faxes, computer-aided design systems, and video teleconferencing. They rarely, if ever, see one another face-to-face. On other projects, participants from different organizations work closely together, for example, at a construction site or in shared office space. In either case, people come and go as services are needed, much as in a matrix structure, but they are not formal members of one organization, just technical experts who form a temporary alliance with an organization, fulfill their contractual obligations, and then move on to the next project.

The advantages of outsourcing project work are many:

1. *Cost reduction*. Companies can secure competitive prices for contracted services, especially if the work can be outsourced offshore. Furthermore, overhead costs are dramatically cut since the company no longer has to internally maintain the contracted services.
2. *Faster project completion*. Not only can work be done more cheaply, but it can also be done faster. Competitive pricing means more resources for the dollar. For example, you can hire three Indian software engineers for the price of one American software engineer. Furthermore, outsourcing can provide access to equipment that can accelerate completion of project tasks. For example, by contracting a backhoe operater you are able to accomplish in four hours what it would take landscaping crew four days to complete.
3. *High level of expertise*. A high level of expertise and technology can be brought to bear on the project. A company no longer has to keep up with technological advances. Instead, it can focus on developing its core competencies and hire firms with the know-how to work on relevant segments of the project.
4. *Flexibility*. Organizations are no longer constrained by their own resources but can pursue a wide range of projects by combining their resources with talents of other companies. Small companies can instantly go global by working with foreign partners.

The disadvantages of outsourcing project work are less well documented:

1. *Coordination breakdowns*. Coordination of professionals from different organizations can be challenging, especially if the project work requires close collaboration and mutual adjustment. Breakdowns are exacerbated by physical separation with people working in different buildings, different cities, if not different countries.
2. *Loss of control*. There is potential loss of control over the project. The core team depends on other organizations that they have no direct authority over. While long-term survival of participating organizations depends on performance, a project may falter when one partner fails to deliver.
3. *Conflict*. Projects are more prone to interpersonal conflict since the different participants do not share the same values, priorities, and culture. Trust, which is essential to project success, can be difficult to forge when interactions are limited and people come from different organizations.
4. *Internal morale issues*. Foreign outsourcing of work is a political hot potato. Employee morale is likely to suffer when project work that has normally been done in-house is being transferred to other companies.

Few people disagree that reducing costs is the primary motive behind outsourcing project work. However, recent industry polls indicate a shift away from simply nailing the best low-cost deal to securing services from companies that provide the best value in terms of both cost and performance. Performance is not limited to simply the quality of specific work but also ability to collaborate and work together. Companies are doing their homework to determine "Can we work with these people?"

Snapshot from Practice   Competing Against the Giants*

SATT Control (SC) is a Swedish electronics firm that sells electronic products and control systems worldwide. It has 550 employees in Sweden and about the same number abroad. So how does SC successfully bid against such electronic giants as ABB, Siemens, and Hewlett-Packard on major contracts for equipment that the company has never sold before? In the words of Hedberg and his coauthors, SC does so by acting as system integrator. In this role SC recruits a contracting syndicate by preparing a system description and dividing the system into various subsystems with each potential partner bidding for a part of the system. SC's ability to describe the system and divide it into subsystems that can be outsourced are two of its core competencies.

Another core competence at SC is project management. After the company has received an order for a project, one of the first actions taken is to work with the customer to develop clear specification of functions. While time consuming, this process is critical to be successful. The first step is to specify what the system is supposed to do, before deciding how it is to be done. This is commonly referred to as designing system architecture. It is crucial that the specifications are correct at the outset otherwise errors reappear all down the line. SC works hard at developing a common agreement among all the partners as to what the basic concept of the project is.

SC is also adroit at establishing a collaborative atmosphere among all the partners. The key is instilling a sense of "what is good for you is good for me." This comes from a history of treating each other with mutual respect and drafting contracts that share risks not isolate risks.

* B. Hedberg, G. Dahlgren, J. Hansson, and N-G. Olve, *Virtual Organi-zations and Beyond* (New York: Wiley, 1997), pp. 82–84.

Best Practices in Outsourcing Project Work

This section describes some of the best practices we have observed being used by firms that excel in project management (see Figure 12.2). Although the list is by no means comprehensive, it reflects strategies used by organizations with extensive outsourcing experience. These practices reveal an underlying theme in how firms approach contracted work on projects. Instead of the traditional master–slave relationship between owner and provider or buyer and seller, all parties work together as partners sharing the ultimate goal of a successful project. See the Snapshot from Practice: Competing against Giants for an example of how a small firm leverages this approach to succeed in a very competitive industry.

Differences between the traditional approach and the partnering approach to managing contracted relationships are summarized in Table 12.1. Partnering requires more than a simple hand-shake. It typically entails a significant commitment of time and energy to forge and sustain collaborative relations among all parties. This commitment is reflected in the seven best practices which will be discussed next.

- Well-defined requirements and procedures.
- Extensive training and team-building activities.
- Well-established conflict management processes in place.
- Frequent review and status updates.
- Co-location when needed.
- Fair and incentive-laden contracts.
- Long-term outsourcing relationships.

FIGURE 12.2   Best Practices in Outsourcing Project Work

TABLE 12.1   Key Differences Between Partnering and Traditional Approaches to Managing Contracted Relationships

Partnering Approach	Traditional Approach
Mutual trust forms the basis for strong working relationships.	Suspicion and distrust; each party is wary of the motives for actions by the other.
Shared goals and objectives ensure common direction.	Each party's goals and objectives, while similar, are geared to what is best for them.
Joint project team exists with high level of interaction.	Independent project teams; teams are spatially separated with managed interactions.
Open communications avoid misdirection and bolster effective working relationships.	Communications are structured and guarded.
Long-term commitment provides the opportunity to attain continuous improvement.	Single project contracting is normal.
Objective critique is geared to candid assessment of performance.	Objectivity is limited due to fear of reprisal and lack of continuous improvement opportunity.
Access to each other's organization resources is available.	Access is limited with structured procedures and self-preservation taking priority over total optimization.
Total company involvement requires commitment from CEO to team members.	Involvement is normally limited to project-level personnel.
Integration of administrative systems equipment takes place.	Duplication and/or translation takes place with attendant costs and delays.
Risk is shared jointly among the partners, which encourages innovation and continuous improvement.	Risk is transferred to the other party.

Well-Defined Requirements and Procedures

Convincing people from different professions, organizations, and cultures to work together is difficult. If expectations and requirements are fuzzy or open to debate, this is even harder. Successful firms are very careful in selecting the work to be outsourced. They often chose to contract only work with clearly defined deliverables with measurable outcomes. For example, contractors hire electric firms to install heating and air-conditioning systems, electronic firms use design firms to fabricate enclosures for their products, and software development teams outsource the testing of versions of their programs. In all of these cases, the technical requirements are spelled out in detail. Even so, communicating requirements can be troublesome, especially with foreign providers (see the Snapshot From Practice: Four Strategies for Communicating with Outsourcers) and extra care has to be taken to ensure that expectations are understood.

Not only do requirements have to be spelled out, but the different firms' project management systems need to be integrated. Common procedures and terminology need to be established so that different parties can work together. This can be problematic when you have firms with more advanced project management systems working with less developed organizations. Surprisingly, this often is the case when U.S. firms outsource software work to India. We have heard reports that Indian providers are shocked at how unsystematic their U.S. counterparts are in their approach to managing software projects.

Snapshot from Practice   Four Strategies for Communicating with Outsourcers*

Dr. Adam Kolawa offers four strategies for overcoming poor communication with offshore project partners.

Strategy 1: Recognize Cultural Differences

Realize that not everyone you communicate with shares your assumptions. What is obvious to you is not necessarily obvious to your partner. This is especially true with foreign outsourcers. As an American, you likely assume that laws are generally obeyed. Believe it or not, that's generally not true in most of the world, where laws are guidelines that are not necessarily followed. This can lead to major communication problems! You think if you write a contract, everybody is going to adhere to it. For many people, a contract is merely a suggestion.

Strategy 2: Choose the Right Words

When you explain your requirements to an outsourcer, word choice is critical. For many outsourcers, English is still a foreign language—even in India, where both outsourcing and the English language are common. No matter how prevalent English has become, your outsourcer might have a basic understanding of each word you utter yet be not completely clear on the exact meaning of the message you're trying to convey. This is why you should speak in a direct manner using short sentences made of basic, simple words.

Strategy 3: Confirm Your Requirements

You should take the following steps to confirm that the outsourcer thoroughly understands your requirements:

1. *Document your requirements.* Follow up your conversations in writing. Commit your requirements to paper for the outsourcer. Many people understand written language better than spoken language, probably because they have more time to process the message.

2. *Insist your outsourcer re-document your requirements.* Leave nothing to chance. Require outsourcers to write the requirements in their own words. If outsourcers cannot relay to you what you explained to them, then they didn't understand.

3. *Request a prototype.* After the requirements are written, ask the outsourcer to create a prototype for you. This is a safety net to ensure that your wants and needs are positively understood. Ask the provider to sketch what you want your final product to look like or build—a quick, simple program that reflects how the final product will look.

Strategy 4: Set Deadlines

Another important cultural difference relates to schedules and deadlines. To most Americans, a deadline is a set completion date. In many other cultures, a deadline is a suggestion that maybe something will be finished by that indicated date. To ensure that outsourced work is completed on time it is imperative to add a penalty clause to your contract or enforce late fees.

Although these strategies were directed toward working with foreign outsourcers, you would be surprised to find how many project managers use them when working with their American counterparts!

* Adam Kolawa, "Four Strategies for Communicating with Outsourcers," *Enterprise Systems Journal* at www.esj.com, accessed September 13, 2005.

The best companies address this issue up front instead of waiting for problems to emerge. First they assess "fit" between providers' project management methods and their own project management system. This is a prime consideration in choosing vendors. Work requirements and deliverables are spelled out in detail in the procurement process. They invest significant time and energy to establishing project communication systems to support effective collaboration.

Finally, whenever you work with other organizations on projects, security is an important issue. Security extends beyond competitive secrets and technology to include access to information systems. Firms have to establish robust safeguards to prevent information access and the introduction of viruses due to less secure provider systems. Information technology security is an additional cost and risk that needs to be addressed up front before outsourcing project work.

Extensive Training and Team-Building Activities

Too often managers become preoccupied with the plans and technical challenges of the project and assume that people issues will work themselves out over time. Smart firms recognize that people issues are as important, if not more important than technical issues. They train their personnel to work effectively with people from other organizations and countries. This training is pervasive. It is not limited to management but involves all the people, at all levels, who interact with and are dependent upon outsourcers. Whether in a general class on negotiation or a specific one on working with Chinese programmers, team members are provided with a theoretical understanding of the barriers to collaboration as well as the skills and procedures to be successful.

The training is augmented by interorganizational team-building sessions designed to forge healthy relationships before the project begins. Team-building workshops involve the key players from the different firms, for example, engineers, architects, lawyers, specialists, and other staff. In many cases, firms find it useful to hire an outside consultant to design and facilitate the sessions. Such a consultant is typically well-versed in interorganizational team building and can provide an impartial perspective to the workshop.

The length and design of the team-building sessions will depend on the experience, commitment, and skill level of the participants. For example, one project, in which the owner and the contractors were relatively inexperienced at working together, utilized a three-day workshop. The first day was devoted to ice-breaking activities and establishing the rationale behind partnering. The conceptual foundation was supported by exercises and minilectures on teamwork, synergy, win/win, and constructive feedback. The second day began by examining the problems and barriers that prevented collaboration in the past. Representatives from the different organizations were separated and each asked the following:

- What actions do the other groups engage in that create problems for us?
- What actions do we engage in that we think create problems for them?
- What recommendations would we make to improve the situation?

The groups shared their responses and asked questions on points needing clarification. Agreements and disparities in the lists were noted and specific problems were identified. Once problem areas were noted, each group was assigned the task of identifying its specific interests and goals for the project. Goals were shared across groups, and special attention was devoted to establishing what goals they had in common. Recognition of shared goals is critical for transforming the different groups into a cohesive team.

The team-building sessions often culminate with the creation of a project charter signed by all of the participants. This charter states their common goals for the project as well as the procedures that will be used to achieve these goals (see Figure 12.3 for an example of the first page of a project charter).

Well-Established Conflict Management Processes in Place

Conflict is inevitable on a project and, as pointed out in the previous chapter, disagreements handled effectively can elevate performance. Dysfunctional conflict, however, can catch fire and severely undermine project success. Outsourced projects are susceptible to conflicts since people are unaccustomed to working together and have different values and perspectives. Successful firms invest significant time and energy up front in establishing the "rules of engagement" so that disagreements are handled constructively.

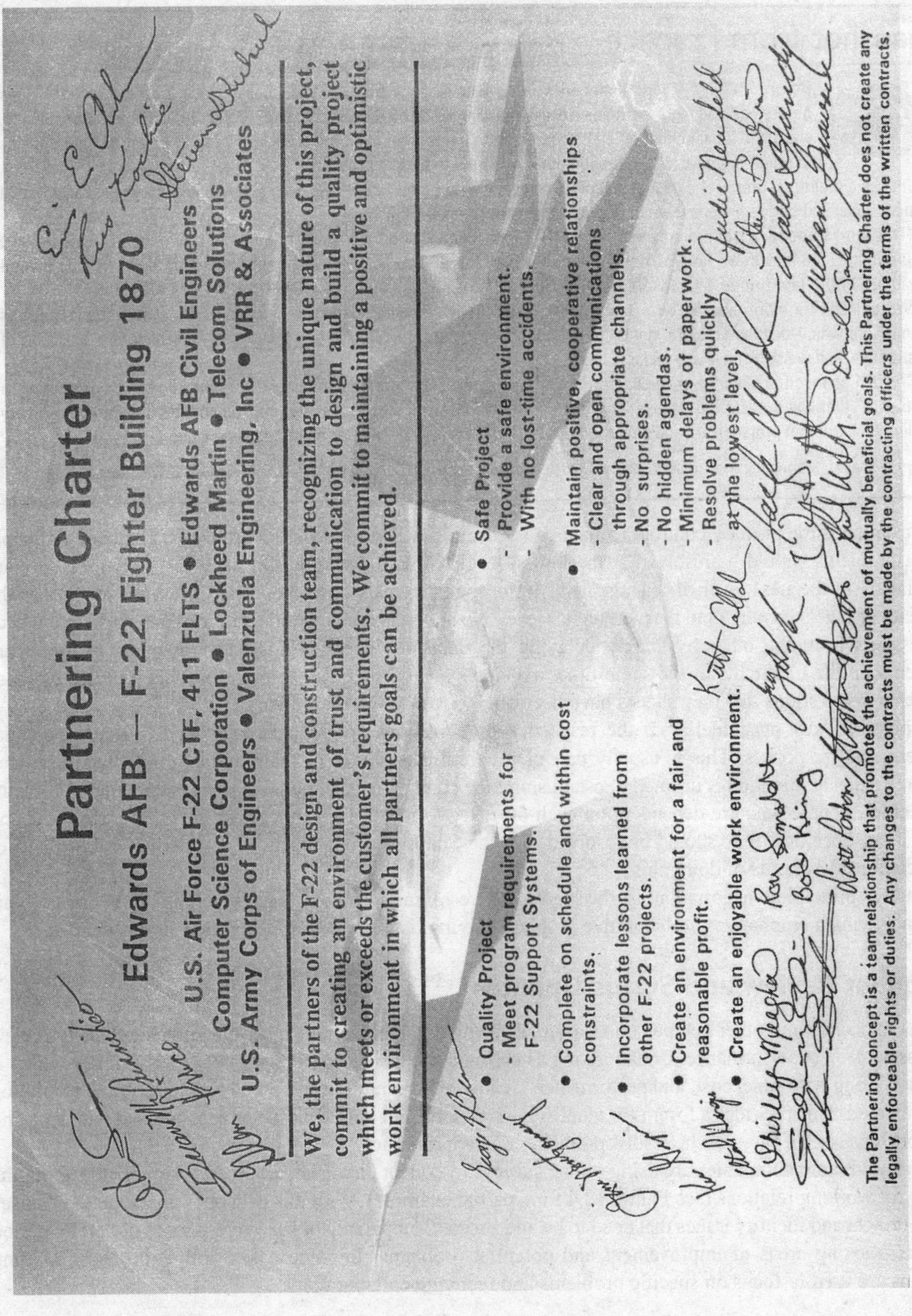

Partnering Charter

Edwards AFB – F-22 Fighter Building 1870

U.S. Air Force F-22 CTF, 411 FLTS • Edwards AFB Civil Engineers
Computer Science Corporation • Lockheed Martin • Telecom Solutions
U.S. Army Corps of Engineers • Valenzuela Engineering, Inc • VRR & Associates

We, the partners of the F-22 design and construction team, recognizing the unique nature of this project, commit to creating an environment of trust and communication to design and build a quality project which meets or exceeds the customer's requirements. We commit to maintaining a positive and optimistic work environment in which all partners goals can be achieved.

- **Quality Project**
  - Meet program requirements for F-22 Support Systems.
- Complete on schedule and within cost constraints.
- Incorporate lessons learned from other F-22 projects.
- Create an environment for a fair and reasonable profit.
- Create an enjoyable work environment.

- **Safe Project**
  - Provide a safe environment.
  - With no lost-time accidents.
- Maintain positive, cooperative relationships
  - Clear and open communications through appropriate channels.
  - No surprises.
  - No hidden agendas.
  - Minimum delays of paperwork.
  - Resolve problems quickly at the lowest level.

The Partnering concept is a team relationship that promotes the achievement of mutually beneficial goals. This Partnering Charter does not create any legally enforceable rights or duties. Any changes to the contracts must be made by the contracting officers under the terms of the written contracts.

FIGURE 12.3 Project Partnering Charter

Snapshot from Practice   "Partnering" a Flu Shot for Projects*

Before starting a bond-financed school construction project, Ohio does what a theater company does before opening night—it holds a dress rehearsal. Led by Cleveland-based Project Management Consultants, state and local school officials, construction managers, and architects get together before building begins to figure out how to talk to each other and how to handle problems.

Just as a theatrical dress rehearsal can allow a company to find and fix glitches before they ruin a show, preconstruction partnering can find early solutions to problems before they become lawsuits.

"This works because traditionally everyone does their own work on a project, behind their own walls," said Jeffrey Applebaum, a construction lawyer and managing director of Project Management Consultants, a wholly owned subsidiary of the law firm of Thompson, Hine, & Flory. "We're taking down the walls. This is more efficient."

"We couldn't be more pleased with this process," said Randy Fischer, executive director of the Ohio School Facilities Commission, which distributes state money to school construction projects. "We are currently administering $3 billion of construction, and we don't have any major disputes."

Crystal Canan, chief of contract administration for the commission, offered a medical metaphor, comparing partnering to a "flu shot" that will prevent the debilitating effects of litigation, work stoppages, and communication breakdowns. "Every building construction project is a candidate for the flu," Canan said. "We see partnering as a vaccination."

* Mary Wisneiski, "Partnering Used to Curb Costs in Ohio School Construction," *Bond Buyer*, 11/22/2000, 334 (31023) 3/4p, 2bw.

Escalation is the primary control mechanism for dealing with and resolving problems. The basic principle is that problems should be resolved at the lowest level within a set time limit (say, 24 hours), or they are "escalated" to the next level of management. If so, the principals have the same time limit to resolve the problem, or it gets passed on to the next higher level. No action is not an option. Nor can one participant force concessions from the other by simply delaying the decision. There is no shame in pushing significant problems up the hierarchy; at the same time, managers should be quick to point out to subordinates those problems or questions that they should have been able to resolve on their own.

If possible, key personnel from the respective organizations are brought together to discuss potential problems and responses. This is usually part of a coordinated series of team-building activities discussed earlier. Particular attention is devoted to establishing the change management control system where problems often erupt. People who are dependent on each other try to identify potential problems that may occur and agree in advance how they should be resolved. See the Snapshot from Practice: "Partnering" a Flu Shot for Projects for the benefits of doing this.

Finally, principled negotiation is the norm for resolving problems and reaching agreements. This approach, which emphasizes collaborative problem solving, is discussed in detail later in this chapter.

Frequent Review and Status Updates

Project managers and other key personnel from all involved organizations meet on a regular basis to review and assess project performance. Collaborating as partners is considered a legitimate project priority which is assessed along with time, cost, and performance. Teamwork, communication, and timely problem resolution are evaluated. This provides a forum for identifying problems not only with the project but also with working relationships so that they can be resolved quickly and appropriately.

More and more companies are using online surveys to collect data from all project participants about the quality of working relations (see Figure 12.4 for a partial example). With this data one can gauge the "pulse" of the project and identify issues that need to be addressed. Comparison of survey responses period by period permits tracking areas of improvement and potential problems. In some cases, follow-up team-building sessions are used to focus on specific problems and recharge collaboration.

Evaluation of partnering process: attitudes, teamwork, process.
(Collected separately from owner and contractor participants, compared, and
aggregated.)

1. Communications between the owner/contractor personnel are

1	2	3	4	5

| Difficult, guarded | | | | Easy, open, up front |

2. Top management support of partnering process is

1	2	3	4	5

| Not evident or inconsistent | | | | Obvious and consistent |

3. Problems, issues, or concerns are

1	2	3	4	5

| Ignored | | | | Attacked promptly |

4. Cooperation between owner and contractor personnel is

1	2	3	4	5

| Cool, detached, unresponsive, removed | | | | Genuine, unreserved, complete |

5. Responses to problems, issues, or concerns frequently become

1	2	3	4	5

| Personal issues | | | | Treated as project problems |

FIGURE 12.4   Sample Online Survey

Finally, when the time to celebrate a significant milestone arrives, no matter who is responsible, all parties gather if possible to celebrate the success. This reinforces a common purpose and project identity. It also establishes positive momentum going into the next phase of the project.

Co-Location When Needed

One of the best ways to overcome interorganizational friction is to have people from each organization working side by side on the project. Smart companies rent or make available the necessary accommodations so that all key project personnel can work collectively together. This allows the high degree of face-to-face interaction needed to coordinate activities, solve difficult problems, and form a common bond. This is especially relevant for complex projects in which close collaboration from different parties is required to be successful. For example, the U.S government provides housing and common office space for all key contractors responsible for developing disaster response plans.

Our experience tells us that co-location is critical and well worth the added expense and inconvenience. When creating this is not practically possible, the travel budget for the project should contain ample funds to support timely travel to different organizations.

Co-location is less relevant for independent work that does not require ongoing coordination between professionals from different organizations. This would be the case if you are outsourcing discrete, independent deliverables like beta testing or a marketing campaign. Here normal channels of communication can handle the coordination issues.

Fair and Incentive-Laden Contracts

When negotiating contracts the goal is to reach a fair deal for all involved. Managers recognize that cohesion and cooperation is undermined if one party feels he or she is being unfairly treated by others. They also realize that negotiating the best deal in terms of price can come back to haunt them with shoddy work and change order gouging.

Performance-based contracts, in which significant incentives are established based on priorities of the project, are becoming increasingly popular. For example, if time is critical, then contractors accrue payoffs for beating deadlines; if scope is critical, then bonuses are issued for exceeding performance expectations. At the same time contractors are held accountable with penalty clauses for failure to perform up to standard, meet deadlines, and/or control costs. More specific information about different types of contracts is presented in this chapter's appendix on contract management.

Companies recognize that contracts can discourage continuous improvement and innovation. Instead of trying some new, promising technique that may reduce costs, contractors will avoid the risks and apply tried and true methods to meet contracted requirements. Companies that treat contractors as partners consider continuous improvement as a joint effort to eliminate waste and pursue opportunities for cost savings. Risks as well as benefits are typically shared 50/50 between the principals, with the owner adhering to a fast-track review of proposed changes.

How the U.S. Department of Defense reaps the benefits of continuous improvement through value engineering is highlighted in the Snapshot from Practice: Value Engineering Awards.

Long-Term Outsourcing Relationships

Many companies recognize that major benefits can be enjoyed when outsourcing arrangements extend across multiple projects and are long term. For example, Corning and Toyota are among the many firms that have forged a network of long-term strategic partnerships with their suppliers. A recent study indicates that the average large corporation is involved in around 30 alliances today versus fewer than 3 in the early 1990s. Among the many advantages for establishing a long-term partnership are the following:

- **Reduced administrative costs**—The costs associated with bidding and selecting a contractor are eliminated. Contract administration costs are reduced as partners become knowledgeable of their counterpart's legal concerns.
- **More efficient utilization of resources**—Contractors have a known forecast of work while owners are able to concentrate their workforce on core businesses and avoid the demanding swings of project support.
- **Improved communication**—As partners gain experience with each other, they develop a common language and perspective, which reduces misunderstanding and enhances collaboration.
- **Improved innovation**—The partners are able to discuss innovation and associated risks in a more open manner and share risks and rewards fairly.
- **Improved performance**—Over time partners become more familiar with each other's standards and expectations and are able to apply lessons learned from previous projects to current projects.

Snapshot from Practice   U.S. Department of Defense's Value Engineering Awards*

Photo by Sgt. Ken Hammond, U.S. Air Force.

As part of an effort to cut costs the United States Department of Defense (DoD) issues annual Value Engineering Awards. Value engineering is a systematic process to analyze functions to identify actions to reduce cost, increase quality, and improve mission capabilities across the entire spectrum of DoD systems, processes, and organizations. The Value Engineering Awards Program is an acknowledgment of outstanding achievements and encourages additional projects to improve in-house and contractor productivity.

In 2002 HBA Architecture, Engineering, and Interior Design, a Virginia Beach–based firm, was selected as the Outstanding Navy Contractor. HBA's work on three projects was cited in the award:

- Design Maintenance and Operations Facility for the 2nd Marine Division Reconnaissance Battalion in Camp Lejeune, NC. Unique to the project was a curved glass wall designed to prevent infiltration by conventional listening devices and an 80 foot tall parachute drying tower that will double as a reppeling platform for training.
- Renovation of an aircraft maintenance hangar originally constructed in 1954 at Cherry Point, NC. A major portion of the work was devoted to the Under-Floor Aqueous Fire Fighting Foam (AFFF) Fire Suppression System throughout the hangar bays.
- Aircraft stripping facility addition at Naval Aviation Dept. in Cherry Point, NC. Designed a new PMB (Plastic Media Blasting) Hangar enclosure and training spaces to allow the Navy to strip aircraft as large as the V-22 (Ospry). PMB is a dry abrasive blasting process, designed to replace chemical stripping operations and conventional sand blasting.

HBA was recognized for using state-of-the-art electronic technologies to produce functional design alternatives and communicate project value improvement that could be evaluated efficiently by the client. These efforts saved $20 million in design costs and $1.6 million in life-cycle costs.

During fiscal 2001, more than 2,100 in-house value engineer proposals and contractor-initiated value engineering change proposals were accepted by the Department of Defense with projected savings in excess of $768 million.

* http://www.defenselink.mil/news/Nov2002/b11222002_bt596-02.html

Working as partners is a conscious effort on the part of management to form collaborative relationships with personnel from different organizations to complete a project. For outsourcing to work, the individuals involved need to be effective negotiators capable of merging interests and discovering solutions to problems that contribute to the project. The next section addresses some of the key skills and techniques associated with effective negotiation.

The Art of Negotiating

Effective negotiating is critical to successful collaboration. All it takes is one key problem to explode to convert a sense of "we" into "us versus them." At the same time, negotiating is pervasive through all aspects of project management work. Project managers must negotiate support and funding from top management. They must negotiate staff and technical input from functional managers. They must coordinate with other project managers and negotiate project priorities and commitments. They must negotiate within their project team to determine assignments, deadlines, standards, and priorities. Project managers must negotiate prices and standards with vendors and suppliers. A firm understanding of the negotiating process, skills, and tactics is essential to project success.

Many people approach negotiating as if it is a competitive contest. Each negotiator is out to win as much as he or she can for his or her side. Success is measured by how much is gained compared with the other party. While this may be applicable when negotiating the sale of a house, it is not true for project management. *Project management is not a contest!* First, the people working on the project, whether they represent different companies or departments within the same organization, are not enemies or competitors but rather allies or partners. They have formed a temporary alliance to complete a project. For this alliance to work requires a certain degree of trust, cooperation, and honesty. Second, although the parties within this alliance may have different priorities and standards, they are bound by the success of the project. If conflicts escalate to the point where negotiations break down and the project comes to a halt, then everyone loses. Third, unlike bartering with a street vendor, the people involved on project work have to continue to work together. Therefore, it behooves them to resolve disagreements in a way that contributes to the long-term effectiveness of their working relationship. Finally, as pointed out in the previous chapter, conflict on a project can be good. When dealt with effectively it can lead to innovation, better decisions, and more creative problem solving.

Project managers accept this noncompetitive view of negotiation and realize that negotiation is essentially a two-part process: The first part deals with reaching an agreement; the second part is the implementation of that agreement. It is the implementation phase, not the agreement itself, that determines the success of negotiations. All too often, managers reach an agreement with someone only to find out later that they failed to do what they agreed to do or that their actual response fell far short of expectations. Experienced project managers recognize that implementation is based on satisfaction not only with the outcome but also with the process by which the agreement was reached. If someone feels bullied or tricked into doing something, this feeling will invariably be reflected by halfhearted compliance and passive resistance.

Veteran project managers do the best they can to merge individual interests with what is best for the project and come up with effective solutions to problems. Fisher and Ury from the Harvard Negotiation Project champion an approach to negotiating that embodies these goals. It emphasizes developing win/win solutions while protecting yourself against those who would take advantage of your forthrightness. Their approach is called *principled negotiation* and is based on four key points listed in Table 12.2 and discussed in the following sections.

TABLE 12.2 Principled Negotiation

1. Separate the people from the problem
2. Focus on interests, not positions
3. Invent options for mutual gain
4. When possible, use objective criteria

Separate the People from the Problem

Too often personal relations become entangled with the substantive issues under consideration. Instead of attacking the problem(s), people attack each other. Once people feel attacked or threatened their energy naturally goes to defending themselves, and not to solving the problem. The key, then, is to focus on the problem—not the other person—during the negotiation. Avoid personalizing the negotiation and framing the negotiation as a contest. Instead, try to keep the focus on the problem to be resolved. In Fisher and Ury's words: *Be hard on the problem, soft on the people.*

By keeping the focus on the issues and not the personalities, negotiators are better able to let the other person blow off steam. On important problems it is not uncommon for people to become upset, frustrated, and angry. However, one angry attack produces an angry counterattack, and the discussion quickly escalates into a heated argument, an emotional chain reaction.

In some cases people use anger as a means of intimidating and forcing concessions because the other person wishes to preserve the relationship. When people become emotional, negotiators should keep a cool head and remember the old German proverb, "Let anger fly out the window." In other words, in the face of an emotional outburst, imagine opening a window and letting the heat of the anger out the window. Avoid taking things personally, and redirect personal attacks back to the question at hand. Don't react to the emotional outburst, but try to find the issues that triggered it. Skilled negotiators keep their cool under stressful times and, at the same time, build a bond with others by empathizing and acknowledging common sources of frustration and anger.

While it is important to separate the people from the problem during actual negotiations, it is beneficial to have a friendly rapport with the other person prior to negotiating. Friendly rapport is consistent with the social network tenet introduced in Chapter 10 of building a relationship before you need it. Reduce the likelihood of misunderstandings and getting off on the wrong foot by having a history of interacting in a friendly, responsive manner with the other person. If, in the past, the relationship has been marked by healthy give-and-take, in which both parties have demonstrated a willingness to accommodate the interests of the other, then neither individual is likely to adopt an immediate win/lose perspective. Furthermore, a positive relationship adds a common interest beyond the specific points of contention. Not only do both parties want to reach an agreement that suits their individual interests, but they also want to do so in a manner that preserves their relationship. Each is therefore more likely to seek solutions that are mutually beneficial.

Focus on Interests, Not Positions

Negotiations often stall when people focus on positions:

I'm willing to pay $10,000. No, it will cost $15,000.
I need it done by Monday. That's impossible, we can't have it ready until Wednesday.

While such interchanges are common during preliminary discussions, managers must prevent this initial posturing from becoming polarized. When such positions are stated, attacked, and then defended, each party figuratively begins to draw a line he or she will not cross. This line creates a win/lose scenario in which someone has to lose by crossing the line in order to reach an agreement. As such, the negotiations can become a war of wills, with concessions being seen as a loss of face.

The key is to focus on the interests behind your positions (what you are trying to achieve) and separate these goals from your ego as best you can. Not only should you be driven by your interests, but you should try to identify the interests of the other party. Ask why it will cost so much or why it can't be done by Monday. At the same time, make your own interests come alive. Don't just say that it is critical that it be done by Monday; explain what will happen if it isn't done by Monday.

Sometimes when the true interests of both parties are revealed, there is no basis for conflict. Take, for example, the Monday versus Wednesday argument. This argument could apply to a scenario involving a project manager and the production manager of a small, local firm that was contracted to produce prototypes of a new generation of computer mouse. The project manager needs the prototypes on Monday to demonstrate to a users' focus group. The production manager said it would be impossible. The project manager said this would be embarrassing because marketing had spent a lot of time and effort setting up this demonstration. The production manager again denied the request and added that he already had to schedule overtime to meet the Wednesday delivery date. However, when the project manager revealed that the purpose of the focus group was to gauge consumers' reactions to the color and shape of the new devices, not the finished product, the conflict disappeared. The production manager told the project manager that she could pick up the samples today if she wanted because production had an excess supply of shells.

When focusing on interests, it is important to practice the communication habit: *Seek first to understand, then to be understood*. This involves what Stephen Covey calls empathetic listening, which allows a person to fully understand another person's frame of reference—not only what that person is saying but also how he or she feels. Covey asserts that people have an inherent need to be understood. He goes on to observe that satisfied needs do not motivate human behavior, only unsatisfied needs do. People try to go to sleep when they are tired, not when they are rested. The key point is that until people believe they are being understood, they will repeat their points and reformulate their arguments. If, on the other hand, you satisfy this need by seeking first to understand, then the other party is free to understand your interests and focus directly on the issues at hand. Seeking to understand requires discipline and compassion. Instead of responding to the other person by asserting your agenda, respond by summarizing both the facts and feelings behind what the other person has said and checking the accuracy of comprehension.

Invent Options for Mutual Gain

Once the individuals involved have identified their interests, then they can explore options for mutual gain. This is not easy. Stressful negotiations inhibit creativity and free exchange. What is required is collaborative brainstorming in which people work together to solve the problem in a way that will lead to a win/win scenario. The key to brainstorming is separating the inventing from the deciding. Begin by taking 15 minutes to generate as many options as possible. No matter how outlandish any option is, it should not be subject to criticism or immediate rejection. People should feed off the ideas of others to generate new ideas. When all the possible options are exhausted, then sort through the ideas that were generated to focus on those with the greatest possibilities.

Clarifying interests and exploring mutual options create the opportunity for dovetailing interests. Dovetailing means one person identifies options that are of low cost to them but of high interest to the other party. This is only possible if each party knows what the other's needs are. For example, in negotiating price with a parts supplier, a project manager learned from the discussion that the supplier was in a cash flow squeeze after purchasing a very expensive fabrication machine. Needed cash was the primary reason the supplier had taken such a rigid position on price. During the brainstorming session, one of the options presented was to prepay for the order instead of the usual payment on delivery arrangement. Both parties seized on this option and reached an amicable agreement in which the project manager would pay the supplier for the entire job in advance in exchange for a faster turnaround time and a significant price reduction. Such opportunities for win/win agreements are often overlooked because the negotiators become fixated on solving their problems and not on opportunities to solve the other person's problems.

When Possible, Use Objective Criteria

Most established industries and professions have developed standards and rules to help deal with common areas of dispute. Both buyers and sellers rely on the blue book to establish price parameters for a used car. The construction industry has building codes and fair practice policies to resolve proof of quality and safe work procedures. The legal profession uses precedents to adjudicate claims of wrongdoing.

Whenever possible, you should insist on using external, objective criteria to settle disagreements. For example, a disagreement arose between a regional airlines firm and the independent accounting team entrusted with preparing the annual financial statement. The airline firm had made a significant investment by leasing several used airplanes from a larger airline. The dispute involved whether this lease should be classified as an operating or capital lease. This was important to the airline because if the purchase was classified as an operating lease, then the associated debt would not have to be recorded in the financial statement. However, if the purchase was classified as a capital lease, then the debt would be factored into the financial statement and the debt/equity ratio would be much less attractive to stockholders and would-be investors. The two parties resolved this dispute by deferring to formulas established by the Financial Accounting Standards Board. As it turns out the accounting team was correct, but, by deferring to objective standards, they were able to deflect the disappointment of the airline managers away from the accounting team and preserve a professional relationship with that firm.

Dealing with Unreasonable People

Most people working on projects realize that in the long run it is beneficial to work toward mutually satisfying solutions. Still, occasionally you encounter someone who has a dominant win/lose attitude about life and will be difficult to deal with. Fisher and Ury recommend that you use negotiation jujitsu when dealing with such a person. That is, when the other person begins to push, don't push back. As in the martial arts, avoid pitting your strengths against another's directly; instead use your skill to step aside and turn that person's strength to your ends. When someone adamantly sets forth a position, neither reject it nor accept it. Treat it as a possible option and then look for the interests behind it. Instead of defending your ideas, invite criticism and advice. Ask why it's a bad idea and discover the other's underlying interest.

Those who use negotiation jujitsu rely on two primary weapons. They ask questions instead of making statements. Questions allow for interests to surface and do not provide the opponent with something to attack. The second weapon is silence. If the other person makes an unreasonable proposal or attacks you personally, just sit there and don't say a word. Wait for the other party to break the stalemate by answering your question or coming up with a new suggestion.

The best defense against unreasonable, win/lose negotiators is having what Fisher and Ury call a strong BATNA (best alternative to a negotiated agreement). They point out that people try to reach an agreement to produce something better than the result of not negotiating with that person. What those results would be (BATNA) is the true benchmark for determining whether you should accept an agreement. A strong BATNA gives you the power to walk away and say, "No deal unless we work toward a win/win scenario."

Your BATNA reflects how dependent you are on the other party. If you are negotiating price and delivery dates and can choose from a number of reputable suppliers, then you have a strong BATNA. If on the other hand there is only one vendor who can supply you with specific, critical material on time, then you have a weak BATNA. Under these circumstances you may be forced to concede to the vendor's demands. At the same time, you should begin to explore ways of increasing your BATNA for future negotiations. This can be done by reducing your dependency on that supplier. Begin to find substitutable material or negotiate better lead times with other vendors.

Negotiating is an art. There are many intangibles involved. This section has reviewed some time-tested principles of effective negotiating based on the groundbreaking work of Fisher and Ury. Given the significance of negotiating, you are encouraged to read their book as well as others on negotiating. In addition, attending training workshops can provide an opportunity to practice these skills. You should also take advantage of day-to-day interactions to sharpen negotiating acumen.

A Note on Managing Customer Relations

In Chapter 4 it was emphasized that ultimate success is not determined by whether the project was completed on time, within budget, or according to specifications, but whether the customer is satisfied with what has been accomplished. Customer satisfaction is the bottom line. Bad news travels faster and farther than good news. For every happy customer who shares his satisfaction regarding a particular product or service with another person, a dissatisfied customer is likely to share her dissatisfaction with eight other people. Project managers need to cultivate positive working relations with clients to ensure success and preserve their reputations.

Customer satisfaction is a complex phenomenon. One simple but useful way of viewing customer satisfaction is in terms of met expectations. According to this model, customer satisfaction is a function of the extent to which perceived performance (or outcome) exceeds expectations. Mathematically, this relationship can be represented as the ratio between perceived performance and expected performance (see Figure 12.5). When performance falls short of expectations (ratio < 1), the customer is dissatisfied. If the performance matches expectations (ratio = 1), the customer is satisfied. If the performance exceeds expectations (ratio > 1), the customer is very satisfied or even delighted.

$$\underset{\text{Dissatisfied}}{0.90} = \frac{\text{Perceived performance}}{\text{Expected performance}} = \underset{\text{Very satisfied}}{1.10}$$

FIGURE 12.5   The Met-Expectations Model of Customer Satisfaction

High customer satisfaction is the goal of most projects. However, profitability is another major concern. Exceeding expectations typically entails additional costs. For example, completing a construction project two weeks ahead of schedule may involve significant overtime expenses. Similarly, exceeding reliability requirements for a new electronic component may involve considerably more design and debugging effort. Under most circumstances, the most profitable arrangement occurs when the customer's expectations are only slightly exceeded. Returning to the mathematical model, with all other things being equal, one should strive for a satisfaction ratio of 1.05, not 1.5!

The met-expectations model of customer satisfaction highlights the point that whether a client is dissatisfied or delighted with a project is not based on hard facts and objective data but on perceptions and expectations. For example, a customer may be dissatisfied with a project that was completed ahead of schedule and under budget if he thought the work was poor quality and that his fears and concerns were not adequately addressed. Conversely, a customer may be very satisfied with a project that was over budget and behind schedule if she felt the project team protected her interests and did the best job possible under adverse circumstances.

Project managers must be skilled at managing customer expectations and perceptions. Too often they deal with these expectations after the fact when they try to alleviate a client's dissatisfaction by carefully explaining why the project cost more or took longer than planned. A more proactive approach is to begin to shape the proper expectations up front and accept that this is an ongoing process throughout the life of a

Research Highlight

IT Project Managers Doubling as Client Account Executives*

Webber and Torti studied the multiple roles project managers play on IT projects. Based on a comprehensive set of interviews with project managers and clients in three different information-technology service organizations, they identified five key roles critical to successfully implement IT projects in client organizations: entrepreneur, politician, friend, marketer, and coach. They are described in part in Table 12.3.

Webber and Torti observed that instead of maintaining a clearly defined relationship with the client, project managers become part of the client organization. They report that project managers attempt to "dress like the client, act like the client, and participate in the client organization's activities (i.e., social gatherings, blood drives, etc.)." They become such an integral part of their existence that many client employees, over the course of time, forget that the project manager is not an employee of the client organization. This helps establish a degree of trust essential to effective collaboration.

*S. S. Webber, and M. T. Torti, "Project Managers Doubling as Client Account Executives," *Academy of Management Executive*, Vol. 18, No. 1, pp. 60–71, 2004.

TABLE 12.3   Project Roles, Challenges, and Strategies

Project Manager Roles	Challenges	Strategies
Entrepreneur	Navigate unfamiliar surroundings	Use persuasion to influence others
Politician	Understand two diverse cultures (parent and client organization)	Align with the powerful individuals
Friend	Determine the important relationships to build and sustain outside the team itself	Identify common interests and experiences to bridge a friendship with the client
Marketer	Understand the strategic objectives of the client organization	Align new ideas/proposals with the strategic objectives of the client organization
Coach	Motivate client team members without formal authority	Provide challenging tasks to build the skills of the team members

project. Project managers need to direct their attention both to the customer's base expectations, the standard by which perceived performance will be evaluated, and to the customer's perceptions of actual performance. The ultimate goal is to educate clients so that they can make a valid judgment as to project performance.

Managing customer expectations begins during the preliminary project approval phase of negotiations. It is important to avoid the temptation to oversell the virtues of a project to win approval because this may create unrealistic expectations that may be too difficult, if not impossible, to achieve. At the same time, project proponents have been known to lower customer expectations by underselling projects. If the estimated completion time is 10 to 12 weeks, they will promise to have the project completed within 12 to 14 weeks, therefore increasing the chances of exceeding customer expectations by getting the project completed early.

Once the project is authorized, the project manager and team need to work closely with the client organization to develop a well-defined project scope statement that clearly states the objectives, parameters, and limits of the project work. The project scope statement is essential to establishing customer expectations regarding the project. It is critical that all parties are in agreement as to what is to be accomplished and that people are reading as best they can from the same page. It is also important to share significant risks that might disrupt project execution. Customers do not like surprises, and if they are aware in advance of potential problems they are much more likely to be accepting of the consequences.

Once the project is initiated it is important to keep customers abreast of project progress. The days when you would simply take orders from customers and tell them to return when the project is done are over. More and more organizations and their project managers are treating their customers as de facto members of the project team and are actively involving them in key aspects of project work. In the case of consulting assignments project managers sometimes *morph* into a member of the client organization (see Research Highlight: IT Project Managers).

Project managers need to keep customers informed of project developments so that customers can make adjustments in their own plans. When circumstances dictate changing the scope or priorities of the project, project managers need to be quick to spell out as best they can the implications of these changes to the customers so that they can make an informed choice. Active customer involvement allows customers to naturally adjust their expectations in accordance with the decisions and events that transpire on a project, while at the same time, the customer's presence keeps the project team focused on the customer's objectives for the project.

Active customer involvement also provides a firmer basis for assessing project performance. The customer not only sees the results of the project but also acquires glimpses of the effort and actions that produced those results. Naturally project managers want to make sure these glimpses reflect favorably on their project teams, so they exercise extra care that customer interactions are handled in a competent and professional manner. In some respects, customer perceptions of performance are shaped more by how well the project team deals with adversity than by actual performance. Project managers can impress customers with how diligently they deal with unexpected problems and setbacks. Likewise, industry analysts have noted that customer dissatisfaction can be transformed into customer satisfaction by quickly correcting mistakes and being extremely responsive to customer concerns.

Managing customer relations on a project is a broad topic; we have only highlighted some of the central issues involved. This brief segment concludes with two words of advice passed on by veteran project managers:

Speak with one voice. Nothing erodes confidence in a project more than for a customer to receive conflicting messages from different project members. The project manager should remind team members of this fact and work with them to ensure that appropriate information is shared with customers.

Speak the language of the customer. Too often project members respond to customer inquiries with technical jargon that exceeds the customer's vocabulary. Project managers and members need to describe problems, trade-offs, and solutions in ways that the customer can understand.

Summary

Outsourcing has become an integral part of project management. More and more companies are collaborating with each other on projects to compete in today's business world. The advantages of outsourcing include cost reduction, quicker completion times, greater flexibility, and higher level of expertise. Disadvantages include coordination problems, loss of control, conflicts, and declining morale.

A number of proactive best practices have emerged among firms that have mastered the outsourcing process. These practices include establishing well-defined requirements and procedures and utilizing fair and incentive-laden contracts. Team-building sessions are held before the project begins to forge relationships between personnel from different organi-zations. Escalation guidelines for resolving conflicts are established, as are provisions for process improvement and risk sharing. On highly critical work, arrangements are made so that key personnel work together, face to face. Joint assessments of how well people are collaborating is the norm during status report briefings. Finally, many companies are realizing the benefits of forming long-term alliances with each other on projects. The ultimate goal is to work together as partners.

Effective negotiating skills are essential to working on projects as partners. People need to resolve differ-ences at the lowest level possible in order to keep the project on track. Veteran project managers realize that negotiating is not a competitive game and work toward collaborative solutions to problems. They accomplish this by separating people from the problem, focusing on interests and not positions, inventing options for mutual gain, and relying on objective criteria whenever possible to resolve disagreements. They also recognize the importance of developing a strong BATNA, which provides them with the leverage necessary to seek collaborative solutions.

Customer satisfaction is the litmus test for project success. Project managers need to take a proactive approach to managing customer expectations and perceptions. They need to actively involve customers in key decisions and keep them abreast of important developments. Active customer involvement keeps the project team focused on the objectives of the project and reduces misunderstandings and dissatisfaction.

Key Terms

Best alternative to a negotiated agreement (BATNA)	Co-location Escalation Met-expectations model	Outsourcing Partnering charter Principled negotiation

Review Questions

1. Why do firms outsource project work?
2. What are the best practices used by firms to outsource project work?
3. What does the term "escalate" refer to, and why is it essential to project success?
4. Why is the principled negotiation approach recommended for negotiating agreements on projects?
5. What does the acronym BATNA refer to, and why is it important to being a successful negotiator?
6. How can a project manager influence customer expectations and perceptions?

Exercises

1. Break into groups of four to five students. Assign half of the groups the role of Owner and the other half the role of Contractor.

   Owners: After saving for many years you are about to hire a contractor to build your "dream home." What are your objectives for this project? What concerns or issues do you have about working with a general contractor to build your home?

   Contractors: You specialize in building customized homes. You are about to meet with prospective owners to begin to negotiate a contract for building their "dream home." What are your objectives for this project? What concerns or issues do you have about working with the owners to build their home?

Each Owner group meets with another Contractor group and shares their objectives, concerns, and issues.

Identify what objectives, issues, and concerns you have in common and which ones are unique. Discuss how you could work together to realize your objectives. What would be the keys to working as partners on this project?

2. Enter "outsourcing" in an Internet search engine and browse different Web sites. Who appears to be interested in outsourcing? What are the advantages of outsourcing? What are the disadvantages? Does outsourcing mean the same thing to different people? What are future trends in outsourcing?

References

Cowan, C., C. F. Gray, and E. W. Larson, "Project Partnering," *Project Management Journal,* Vol. 12, No. 4, December 1992, pp. 5–15.

Covey, S. R., *The Seven Habits of Highly Effective People* (New York: Simon and Schuster, 1990).

DiDonato, L. S., "Contract Disputes: Alternatives for Dispute Resolution (Part 1)," *PM Network,* May 1993, pp. 19–23.

Drexler, J. A. and E. W. Larson, "Partnering: Why Project Owner-Contractor Relationships Change," *Journal of Construction Engineering and Management,* Vol. 126, No. 4, July/August 2000, pp. 293–397.

Dyer, S., *Partner Your Project* (Warwickshire, UK: Pendulum Pub., 1997).

Economy, P., *Business Negotiating Basics* (Burr Ridge, IL: Irwin Professional Publishing, 1994).

Fisher, R. and W. Ury, *Getting to Yes: Negotiating Agreement without Giving In,* 2nd ed. (New York: Penguin Books, 1991).

Hedberg, B., G. Dahlgren, J. Hansson, and N. Olve, *Virtual Organizations and Beyond* (New York: Wiley, 1997).

Hoang, H. and F. T. Rothaermel, "The Effect of General and Partner-Specific Alliance Experience on Joint R&D Project Performance," *Academy of Management Journal,* Vol. 48, No. 2, 2005, pp. 332–45.

Kanter, R. M., "Collaborative Advantage: The Art of Alliances," *Harvard Business Review,* July–August 1994, pp. 92–113.

Kezsbom, D. S., D. L. Schilling, and K. A. Edward, *Dynamic Project Management* (New York: Wiley, 1989).

Larson, E. W., "Project Partnering: Results of a Study of 280 Construction Projects," *Journal of Management Engineering,* Vol. 11, No. 2, March/April 1995, pp. 30–35.

Larson, E. W., "Partnering on Construction Projects: A Study of the Relationship between Partnering Activities and Project Success," *IEEE Transactions in Engineering Management,* Vol. 44, No. 2, May 1997, pp. 188–95.

Larson, E. W. and J. A. Drexler, "Barriers to Project Partnering: Report from the Firing Line," *Project Management Journal,* Vol. 28, No. 1, March 1997, pp. 46–52.

Magenau, J. M. and J. K. Pinto, "Power, Influence, and Negotiation in Project Management," in *The Wiley Guide to Managing Projects,* P. W. G. Morris and J. K. Pinto (Eds.), (New York: Wiley, 2004), pp. 1033–60.

Nambisan, S., "Designing Virtual Customer Environments for New Product Development: Toward a Theory," *Academy of Management Review,* Vol. 27, No. 3, 2002, pp. 392–413.

Nissen, M. E., "Procurement: Process Overview and Emerging Project Management Techniques," in *The Wiley Guide to Managing Projects*, P. W. G. Morris and J. K. Pinto (Eds.), (New York: Wiley, 2004), pp. 643–54.

Quinn, R. E., S. R. Faerman, M. P. Thompson, and M. R. McGrath, *Becoming a Master Manager: A Competency Framework* (New York: Wiley, 1990).

Schultzel, H. J. and V. P. Unruh, *Successful Partnering: Fundamentals for Project Owners and Contractors* (New York: Wiley, 1996).

Shell, G. R., *Bargaining for Advantage: Negotiation Strategies for Reasonable People* (New York: Penguin, 2000).

APPENDIX 12.1

Contract Management

Since most outsourced work on projects is contractual in nature, this appendix discusses the different kinds of contracts that are used, their strengths and weaknesses, and how contracts shape the motives and expectations of different participants. Contract management is a key element of any project procurement management system. It is beyond the scope of this book to describe this system. However, the basic processes are listed here to put contract management and related topics like RFP (see Appendix 2.1) in perspective. Six main steps comprise procurement management:

- **Planning purchases and acquisitions** involves determining what to procure, when, and how. This entails the classic build-versus-buy analysis as well as determination of the type of contract to use.
- **Planning contracting** involves describing the requirements for products or services desired from outsourcing and identifying potential suppliers or sellers. Outputs include procurement documents such as a Request for Proposal (RFP) as well as selection criteria.
- **Requesting seller responses** involves obtaining information, quotes, bids, or proposals from sellers and providers. The main outputs of this process include a qualified sellers list and specific proposals.
- **Selecting sellers** involves choosing from potential suppliers through a process of evaluating potential providers and negotiating a contract.
- **Administering the contract** involves managing the relationship with the selected seller or provider.
- **Closing the contract** involves completion and settlement of the contract.

Most companies have purchasing departments that specialize in procurement. Often purchasing agents will be assigned to project teams and they work with other team members to come up with optimum solutions for the project. Even if project teams are not directly involved in contract negotiations and the decision to outsource project work, it is important that the team understand the procurement process and the nature of different kinds of contracts.

Contracts

A contract is a formal agreement between two parties wherein one party (the contractor) obligates itself to perform a service and the other party (the client) obligates itself to do something in return, usually in the form of a payment to the contractor. For example, an insurance firm contracted with a consulting firm to reprogram segments of their information system to conform to MS Vista.

A contract is more than just an agreement between parties. A contract is a codification of the private law, which governs the relationship between the parties to it. It defines the responsibilities, spells out the conditions of its operations, defines the rights of the parties in relationship to each other, and grants remedies to a party if the other party breaches its obligations. A contract attempts to spell out in specific terms the transactional obligations of the parties involved as well as contingencies associated with the execution of the contract. An ambiguous or inconsistent contract is difficult to understand and enforce.

There are essentially two different kinds of contracts. The first is the "fixed-price" contract in which a price is agreed upon in advance and remains fixed as long as there are no changes to scope or provisions of the agreement. The second is a "cost-plus" contract in which the contractor is reimbursed for all or some of the expenses incurred during the performance of the contract. Unlike the fixed-price contract, the final price is not known until the project is completed. Within these two types of contracts, several variations exist.

Fixed-Price Contracts

Under a fixed-price (FP) or lump-sum agreement, the contractor agrees to perform all work specified in the contract at a fixed price. Clients are able to get a minimum price by putting out the contract to competitive bid. Advertising an invitation for bid (IFB) that lists customer requirements usually results in low bids. Prospective contractors can obtain IFB notices through various channels. In the case of large business organizations and government agencies, potential contractors can request to be included on the bidder's list in the area of interest. In other cases, IFBs can be found by scanning appropriate industry media such as newspapers, trade journals, and Web sites. In many cases, the owner can put restrictions on potential bidders, such as requiring that they be ISO 9000 certified.

With fixed-price contract bids, the contractor has to be very careful in estimating target cost and completion schedule because once agreed upon, the price cannot be adjusted. If contractors overestimate the target cost in the bidding stage, they may lose the contract to a lower-priced competitor; if the estimate is too low, they may win the job but make little or no profit.

Fixed-price contracts are preferred by both owners and contractors when the scope of the project is well defined with predictable costs and low implementation risks. Such might be the case for producing parts or components to specifications, executing training programs, or orchestrating a banquet. With fixed-price contracts, clients do not have to be concerned with project costs and can focus on monitoring work progress and performance specifications. Likewise, contractors prefer fixed-price contracts because the client is less likely to request changes or additions to the contract. Fewer potential changes reduce project uncertainty and allow the contractors to more efficiently manage their resources across multiple projects.

The disadvantage of a fixed-price contract for owners is that it is more difficult and more costly to prepare. To be effective, design specifications need to be spelled out in sufficient detail to leave little doubt as to what is to be achieved. Because the contractor's profit is determined by the difference between the bid and the actual costs, there is some incentive for contractors to use cheaper quality materials, perform marginal workmanship, or extend the completion date to reduce costs. The client can counteract these by stipulating rigid end-item specifications and completion date and by supervising work. In many cases, the client will hire a consultant who is an expert in the field to oversee the contractor's work and protect the client's interest.

The primary disadvantage of a fixed-price contract for contractors is that they run the risk of underestimating. If the project gets into serious trouble, cost overruns may make the project unprofitable, and, in some cases, may lead to bankruptcy. To avoid this, contractors have to invest significant time and money to ensure that their estimates are accurate.

Contracts with long lead times such as construction and production projects may include escalation provisions that protect the contractor against external cost increases in materials, labor rates, or overhead expenses. For example, the price may be tied to an inflation index, so it can be adjusted to sudden increases in labor and material prices, or it may be redetermined as costs become known. A variety of redetermination contracts are used. Some establish a ceiling price for a contract and permit only downward adjustments, others permit upward and downward adjustments; some establish one readjustment period at the end of the project, others use more than one period. Redetermination contracts are appropriate where engineering and design efforts are difficult to estimate or when final price cannot be estimated for lack of accurate cost data.

While, in principle, redetermination contracts are used to make appropriate adjustments in cost uncertainties, they are prone to abuse. A contractor may win an initial low bid contract, initiate the contracted work, and then "discover" that the costs are much higher than expected. The contractor can take advantage of redetermination provisions and a client's ignorance to justify increasing the actual cost of the contract. The contract evolves into a cost-plus contract.

To alleviate some of the disadvantages of a fixed-price contract while maintaining some certainty as to final cost, many fixed-price contracts contain incentive clauses designed to motivate contractors to reduce costs and improve efficiency. For example, a contractor negotiates to perform the work for a target price based on target cost and a target profit. A maximum price and maximum profit are also established. If the total cost ends up being less than the target cost, the contractor makes a higher profit up to the profit maximum. If there is a cost overrun, the contractor absorbs some of the overrun until a profit floor is reached.

Profit is determined according to a formula based on a cost-sharing ratio (CSR). A CSR of 75/25, for example, indicates that for every dollar spent above target costs, the client pays 75 cents and the contractor pays 25 cents. This provision motivates contractors to keep costs low since they pay 25 cents on every dollar spent above the expected cost and earn 25 cents more on every dollar saved below the expected cost. Fixed-price incentive contracts tend to be used for long-duration projects with fairly predictable cost estimates. The key is being able to negotiate a reasonable target cost estimate. Unscrupulous contractors have been known to take advantage of the ignorance of the client to negotiate an unrealistically high target cost and use performance incentives to achieve excessive profits.

Cost-Plus Contracts

Under a cost-plus contract the contractor is reimbursed for all direct allowable costs (materials, labor, travel) plus an additional fee to cover overhead and profit. This fee is negotiated in advance and usually involves percentage of the total costs. On small projects this kind of contract comes under the rubric "time and materials contract" in which the client agrees to reimburse the contractor for labor cost and materials. Labor costs are based on an hourly or daily rate, which includes direct and indirect costs as well as profit. The contractor is responsible for documenting labor and materials costs.

Unlike fixed contracts, cost-plus contracts put the burden of risk on the client. The contract does not indicate what the project is going to cost until the end of the project. Contractors are supposed to make the best effort to fulfill the specific technical requirements of the contract but cannot be held liable, in spite of their best efforts, if the work is not produced within the estimated cost and time frame. These contracts are often criticized because there is little formal incentive for the contractors to control costs or finish on time because they get paid regardless of the final cost. The major factor motivating contractors to control costs and schedule is the effect overruns have on their reputation and their ability to secure future business.

The inherent weakness of cost-plus contracts has been compensated for by a variety of incentive clauses directed at providing incentives to contractors to control costs, maintain performance, and avoid schedule overruns. Contractors are reimbursed for costs, but instead of the fee being fixed, it is based on an incentive formula and subject to additional provisions. This is very similar to fixed-price incentive contracts, but instead of being based on a target cost, the fee is based on actual cost, using a cost-sharing formula.

Most contracts are concerned with the negotiated cost of the project. However, given the importance of speed and timing in today's business world, more and more contracts involve clauses concerning completion dates. To some extent schedule incentives provide some cost-control measures because schedule slippage typically but not always involves cost overruns. Schedule incentives/penalties are stipulated depending on the significance of time to completion for the owner. For example, the contract involving the construction of a new baseball stadium is likely to contain stiff penalties if the stadium is not ready for opening day of the season. Conversely, time-constrained projects in which the number one priority is getting the project completed as soon as possible are likely to include attractive incentives for completing the project early.

A good example of this can be seen in the Northridge Earthquake Snapshot from Practice (Chapter 9) in which the construction firm pulled out all the stops to restore the damaged highway system 74 days ahead of schedule. The firm received a $14.8 million bonus for these efforts!

Figure A12.1 summarizes the spectrum of risk to the buyer and supplier for different kinds of contracts. Buyers have the lowest risk with firm fixed-price contracts because they know exactly what they will need to pay the supplier. Buyers have the most risk with cost-plus percentage of cost contracts because they do not know in advance what the suppliers' costs will be and suppliers may be motivated to increase costs. From the suppliers' perspective, the cost-plus contract offers the least risk and the firm fixed-price contract entails the most risk.

Contract Change Control System

A contract change control system defines the process by which the contract may be modified. It includes the paperwork, tracking systems, dispute resolution procedures, and approval levels necessary for authorizing changes. There are a number of reasons a contract may need to be changed. Clients may wish to alter the original design or scope of the project once the project is initiated. This is quite common as the project moves from concept to reality. For example, an owner may wish to add windows after inspecting the partially completed homesite. Market changes may dictate adding new features or increasing the performance requirements of equipment. Declining financial resources may dictate that the owner cut back on the scope of the project. The contractor may initiate changes in the contract in response to unforeseen legitimate problems. A

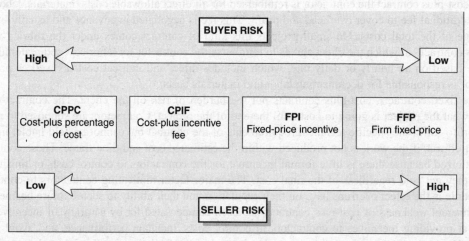

FIGURE A12.1   **Contract Type versus Risk**

building contractor may need to renegotiate the contract in the face of excessive groundwater or the lack of availability of specified materials. In some cases, external forces may dictate contract changes, such as a need to comply with new safety standards mandated by the federal government.

There need to be formal, agreed-upon procedures for initiating changes in the original contract. Contract change orders are subject to abuse. Contractors sometimes take advantage of owners' ignorance to inflate the costs of changes to recoup profit lost from a low bid. Conversely, owners have been known to "get back" at contractors by delaying approval of contract changes, thus delaying project work and increasing the costs to the contractor. All parties need to agree upon the rules and procedures for initiating and making changes in the original terms of the contract in advance.

Contract Management in Perspective

Contract management is not an exact science. For decades, the federal government has been trying to develop a more effective contract administration system. Despite their best efforts, abuses are repeatedly exposed in the news media. The situation is similar to trying to take a wrinkle out of an Oriental rug. Efforts to eliminate a wrinkle in one part of the rug invariably create a wrinkle in another part. Likewise, each new revision in government procurement procedures appears to generate a new loophole that can be exploited. There is no perfect contract management system. Given the inherent uncertainty involved in most project work, no contract can handle all the issues that emerge. Formal contracts cannot replace or eliminate the need to develop effective working relationships between the parties involved that are based on mutual goals, trust, and cooperation. For this reason, the earlier discussion of best practices, in outsourcing and effective negotiating is very important.

Appendix Review Questions

1. What are the fundamental differences between fixed-price and cost-plus contracts?
2. For what kinds of projects would you recommend that a fixed-price contract be used? For what kinds of projects would you recommend that a cost-plus contract be used?

Appendix References

Angus, R. B., N. A. Gundersen, and T. P. Cullinane, *Planning, Performing, and Controlling Projects* (Upper Saddle River, NJ: Prentice Hall, 2003).

Cavendish, J. and M. Martin, *Negotiating and Contracting for Project Management* (Upper Darby, PA: Project Management Institute, 1982).

Fleming, Q. W., *Project Procurement Management: Contracting, Subcontracting, Teaming* (Tustin, CA: FMC Press, 2003).

Fraser, J., *Professional Project Proposals* (Aldershot, U.K.: Gower/Ashgate, 1995).

Lowe, D., "Contract Management" in *The Wiley Guide to Managing Projects,* P. W. G. Morris and J. K. Pinto (Eds.), (New York: Wiley, 2004), pp. 678–707.

Schwalbe, K., *Information Technology Project Management,* 4th ed. (Boston: Thomson Course Technology, 2006).

Worthington, M. M. and L. P. Goldsman, *Contracting with the Federal Government,* 4th ed. (New York: Wiley, 1998).

APPENDIX 12.2

Project Procurement Management

1. An Overview of Project Procurement Function

In the modern global context and major projects, most organizations need to outsource some part of the project work to an external agency 'to provide a product, service or result', which would form a part of the project in hand. In major construction projects, it is a well accepted tradition to parcel out the contracts for special construction work to the specialist agencies (agencies or contractors for civil construction, electrical installation, piping mechanical erection and even further specialization in each of them for specialty in piping or mechanical installation). But such outsourcing is necessary also for several high technology or essentially knowledge-based work.

In this introductory part, we shall take up discussion of

 (i) Necessity for outsourcing and the benefits of procurement
 (ii) Difference between the project procurement and procurement for routine operations
(iii) Good practices for project procurement
(iv) Different types of project contracts, their special advantages and limitations, selecting the type of contract most suitable for different types of project

In the later part of this appendix, we shall discuss the approach to procurement management outlined in the PMBOK® Guide, 4th Edition, 2008, and how it relates to the good procurement practices.

1.1 Necessity for Outsourcing—Benefits and Limitations of Project Procurement

As mentioned earlier, most organizations may need the necessity for outsourcing project work. When an organization does not have the capability to complete a part of the project work, it has to outsource that particular work to an external agency. Even when the organization may have the basic capability to execute a particular task, make versus buy analysis might indicate the outsourcing to be a better option.

An organization may need to procure products or project services from external agencies for any of the following reasons:

- Supplementing its own capacity for the outsourced work for faster project schedule
- Contracting out the work to a specialized agency, which can offer lower cost product or services than what the organization can manage
- Ensuring higher quality of workmanship or product features from a specialized agency
- Availing technology or expertise, which the organization does not have
- Transferring the overall risk for delivering the product or service of acceptable quality standard as per project schedule to the supplier at some cost premium
- Increasing the capability for accepting project of larger scope by outsourcing the work for which the organization does not have capability. For bidding on mega projects, it is a very common practice to form a consortium of several organizations, which combine to offer the project delivery.

Of course, farming out project work to external agencies is not an unmixed blessing. The organization has to be vigilant about the issues of reduced control during execution, necessity of close coordination, arranging for stage-wise inspection of work to ensure quality workmanship and delivery, sharing the business or technology data with outsiders and related confidentiality issues, and assuming the risk of the contracting agency's lapses on project outcomes, among others. The project manager has to weigh these factors and decide on the basis of costs versus benefits analysis, what and how much of the project product or services should be procured from outside.

1.2 Difference Between Project Procurement and Procurement for Operation

The main differences between the project and operation procurements are rooted in the transient and temporary nature of project work compared to operation and the necessity of delivering the project objectives under cost and schedule constraints. In case of operating purchases, the suppliers are established over a period and the cost, quality and delivery issues have been sorted out over a period. For project work, the organization may not have sufficient experience of dealing with the suppliers and awareness of the pitfalls to be avoided in contracting the specialized work. Ordinarily, the organization's procurement departments can help out the project procurement by providing the data on suppliers, the price levels and availabilities of the products and services in the market, the standard procurement terms or contracts, and the expertise in the process of technical and commercial negotiations. All the same, it would be worthwhile to keep in mind the following points for efficient project procurement:

(i) *Precision in formulating technical & performance specifications:* Technical and performance specifications should be unambiguous and applicable quality standards to meet quality requirements should be included. The contract should include a clause for stage-wise inspection if necessary for ensuring quality conformance and delivery schedule.

(ii) *Precision in negotiating the scope of supply:* The scope of supply should be unambiguous and the inclusions and exclusions from the contracted product should be clearly mentioned to effectively manage the interface of the contracted work with other project work or work in scope of other contractors.

(iii) *Selection of the type of contract:* The project contracts can be of different type and each type has some benefits and some limitations. Choice of the type of contract to suit the nature of project work to be contracted should be based on careful analysis of the technical and performance requirements of the product or service and the project need for minimizing cost or ensuring quality and timely delivery.

(iv) *Selection of the vendor:* The processes of vendor qualification and evaluation of technical bids should precede the short-listed contractors for commercial negotiations.

(v) *Contract drafting:* The contract should very clearly spell out the critical issues related to supply, whether it is the quality of the product or services or delivery at a specific time. The contract should include clauses for proper emphasis on the critical issues (delivery penalty clause and stage-wise inspection and release of payment for ensuring promised delivery and stage-wise inspection of raw materials, production process validation say, welding and inspection routines for ensuring quality of delivered product or service).

(vi) *Contract Administration:* The project manager should always pay attention to the following three important aspects for contract administration:

- *Close follow-up on quality of work and whether the pace of working is adequate for meeting the desired delivery:* Project meetings and periodic reviews for site contract work and visits to the supplier's plant to check progress in case of delivery of a complete product or system would ensure conformance to contracted quality and delivery.

- *Payment Terms:* The contractor should be paid no more than the completed contract work. At the same time, the certification of completed contracted work should be prompt.

- *Maintaining relationship:* It should be borne in mind that the maintaining a pleasant and efficient working relationship with a vendor and his key personnel is as much in project interest as the vendor's interest. Sometimes, the project organization's team members assume overbearing and somewhat unreasonable posture towards contractors and their employees. This would often give rise to problems at critical project stage.

1.3 Good Procurement Management Practices

(i) *Review all major work packages and decide which products or services should be considered for outsourcing.* The criteria for this preliminary screening should be
- Whether the organization has captive spare capability for delivering the product or service
- Whether the outsourcing agency can provide desired quality of the product on desired delivery schedule
- Whether the outsourcing would cede control over delivery of a critical item
- Whether outsourcing would make it necessary to share some closely guarded business or technical secrets
- Whether the cost of outsourced product or service would equal or exceed the cost if organization delivered the service departmentally (essentially 'Make versus Buy' analysis)

(ii) *Prepare for outsourcing the products or services to be procured*
   (a) Prepare Statement of Work (SOW) for the contract. It should include
   - Detailed performance requirements and technical specifications
   - Drawings for size, layouts or termination points for battery limits
   - Applicable quality standards or tests
   - Unambiguous scope of supply—specifying clearly the boundaries of scope of supply (inclusions and exclusions)
   - Delivery requirements
   (b) Prepare a list of pre-qualified suppliers (or review the list of qualified vendors from organization's procurement group and select).
   (c) Decide on the type of contract most suitable from scope of supply, quality, delivery, and cost or the product or service required and draft the contract terms (or select the suitable template and modify it by including the special contract terms for inclusion).
   (d) Review the nature of work under contract and try to envisage the changes likely in the quantity of required items, quality standards, unspecified new items, etc. Include the clauses for change management. Decide the terms of payment and specify the milestones to be reached for specific payments. Include clauses for termination of contract and arbitration.
   (e) Prepare independent estimate of the cost of supply of the product or service, which would serve as a benchmark for preliminary screening the vendor offers and price negotiations with the short-listed suppliers.

(iii) *Select vendor for product or service and place order*
   (a) Invite bids for quotations, requests for proposals or tenders for contracts
   (b) Offer explanations where necessary and get all bids, offers, or tender offers on equal technical footing.
   (c) Prepare technical bid analysis and short-list the vendors whose offers are acceptable.
   (d) Prepare commercial evaluations and short-list vendors for final negotiations
   (e) Negotiate with the prospective vendors for the supply and place order with the successful bidder.

(iv) *Administer contract*
   (a) Periodic performance review for quality and work progress
   (b) Certification of contracted work against agreed milestones in the contract payment terms and facilitating the payment for certified work.

(c) Administer change control clauses of the contract certifying the changes as they occur and certifying the corresponding incremental payments for the certified changes

(d) Maintain records of technical work (quantity measurements, any change in specifications of supply or as-built drawings) for project archives.

The section 'Best Practices in Outsourcing Project Work' in the chapter gives an elaborate account of this topic. The recap of the subject above is merely for providing the continuity and connection in the discussion of the good procurement practices and how the procurement processes described in PMBOK® Guide ensures those practices.

1.4 Different Types of Contracts

Appendix 12.1 describes the different types of contracts, their suitability for specific types of project works and their advantage and limitations. So it is not repeated here.

2. Project Procurement Processes

With the above overview of the key issues in project procurement, we shall proceed to how PMBOK® Guide, 4th Edition, 2008 proceeds to address these issues and ensure good project procurement practices.

PMBOK® Guide lists four processes managing project procurement—one each in the planning, executing, monitoring & controlling and closing process groups as follows:

2.1 Plan Procurements (Planning Process Group)
2.2 Conduct Procurements (Executing Process Group)
2.3 Administer Procurements (Monitoring & Controlling Process Group), and
2.4 Close Procurements (Closing Process Group)

We shall briefly review the inputs, tools and techniques and outputs of these processes.

2.1 Plan Procurements (Planning Process Group)

This process involves reviewing the products and services required for completing the work packages for all project deliverables and deciding which products or services should be outsourced and how.

The process would have to come up with all decisions, procedures and policies for project procurement. It would include:

- Review of all project work and list make versus buy decisions for all project purchases
- Prepare detailed Statement of Works (SOW) for the work decided to be outsourced (narrative description of work to be performed accompanied by technical specifications, overall assembly or layout drawings, performance specifications and acceptance testing)
- Prepare procurement documents
  - The nature of procurement process [whether procurement should be based on request for Information (RFI), invitation for bids(Bids), request for proposals (RFP) or notice and floating of tenders (Tender)]
  - The type of contract [some form of firm fixed price contract (FFP), cost reimbursable contact (CR), or time and material contract (T & M)]
  - Templates for purchase orders or tenders
  - Applicable quality standards and technical and performance specifications to ensure quality
  - Payment terms and their linkage to milestones in supply of contracted work (advance with orders, raw materials acquisition, stage-wise processing and reaching milestones in work completion stages, etc.)
  - Criteria for selecting the vendors and their prequalification if necessary
  - Change and risk management procedures

Inputs

Understandably, procurement planning needs review of the work packages for deliverables of the entire project and assessment of the impact of the outsourcing on project scope, quality, cost and schedule. The list of inputs is, therefore, quite exhaustive. PMBOK® Guide lists the following inputs, most of which follow from common sense and logic. Some special inputs are treated at the end of the list.

- *Scope Baseline* (scope statement, WBS and WBS Dictionary)
- *Requirements Documentation* (Focusing on special legal, IPR or contractual and operational safety and health requirements)
- *Risk Register*
- *Risk Related Contract Decisions* (specially concerned with what risks for quality, cost or schedule the organization wants to transfer to the outsourcing agency and at what cost premium if any)
- *Project Schedule*
- *Activity Cost Estimates* and *Cost Baseline*
- *Enterprise Environmental Factors* (price and availability of products and services in the market, typical terms and conditions for contracted work in the industry and within the organization)
- *Organizational Process Assets* (all assistance which the project procurement can get from organization's group for routine procurement operation and the information on procurements for earlier similar projects)
- *Teaming or Collaboration Agreements:* This input requires special mention and discussion. When the project is organized as a consortium or when the outsourced work content is a very large part of the total project in terms of scope and cost, the relationship between the collaborators is based on some common collaboration agreement and all terms included in the agreement. The technical collaboration, licensing of specific technologies, technical and financial collaboration agreement for project work are relationships that fall in this category. For such outsourcing work the project manger has to take extra care in observing the terms of the collaboration and maintain pleasant and efficient working relationship with the partnering organization and their key managers.

Tools & Techniques

Tools and techniques essentially involve what to buy, how to buy and from whom to buy. PMBOK® lists the following tools and techniques:

- *Make-or-Buy Decisions* (Decision of what to outsource and what to produce departmentally)
- *Contract Types* (How to buy once the decision to outsource is made) Project manager and project team key members must have good conceptual background, working knowledge of contract work practices, and pitfalls and advantages of different types of contracts. The types of contracts have been described in details in the Appendix 12.1: 'Contract Management' and a brief summary is given in the table elsewhere in this appendix. So they are not repeated here.
- *Expert Judgment* (Special inputs from consultants on technology related issues, legal advice for collaboration agreements or major contractual work, procurement practices and procurement negotiations for some product or services, etc.)

Outputs

The process outputs are *Procurement Management Plan, Procurement Statement of Works (SOW), Procurement Documents, Make versus Buy Decisions* and *Source Selection Criteria*. In this process discussion, we have already referred elsewhere to outputs other than procurement management plan, which is briefly described below.

Procurement Management Plan: It summarizes the decisions reached from the use of tools and techniques on the overall project management on all inputs for planning project procurement. It outlines how the procurement management will be carried out throughout the procurement step or cycle for all outsourced products or services. With this omnibus scope for contents, it could include:

- The types of contracts to be used
- Risk management issues
- Managing interface between operating procurement set up and project procurement set up
- Standard purchase order or tender templates to be used
- Whether independent estimates for cost will be made and how they will be made
- How the prospective sellers' bids will be evaluated and negotiated
- Procedures for pre-qualification of suppliers, and so on

Procurement Management Plan essentially deals with the methods and procedures to be used for the rest of the project procurement processes. When an organization has several projects going on for over a period, the methodology for procurement processes is likely to be well set. In such a situation, there may be no need for a formal procurement management plan and some important points jotted down informally for reference might serve the purpose of a procurement management plan.

2.2 Conduct Procurements (Executing Process Group)

This process, belonging to execution process group, is concerned with actually managing the outsourcing of products and services according to the planning for procurement set down in the earlier process. It would, therefore, include all activities necessary for completing the procurement processes till the orders are placed for all items planned to be outsourced:

- Floating Bids, Requests for Proposals (RFPs) or Tenders, preferably to the pre-qualified vendors list, availing the Statement of Works (SOW) and type of contract decided in procurement planning
- Evaluating the bids, proposals or tenders received from technical and commercial aspects
- Requesting and availing special guidance for technology related, legal or other contractual issues from consultants or experts
- Negotiating with the short-listed vendors and placing the order or contract on the selected vendor

Once the purchase orders or tender contracts are issued, the monitoring and controlling process, 'Administer Procurement', takes over.

Inputs

Essentially, the inputs for conducting procurements are the project management plan and all documents prepared for procurement planning in the earlier process. Most of the inputs, based on the common sense and understanding the basic outsourcing process, do not require elaborate explanation. PMBOK® Guide mentions these inputs to come up with a following comprehensive list:

Project Management Plan: The requirements and impacts of the component plans of the overall project plan (scope baseline, cost management plan, project schedule, risk register, communication management plan and so forth) need to be taken into account while conducting procurements.

Procurement Documents, Source Selection Criteria, Qualified Sellers List, Make versus Buy Decisions, Organizational Process Assets (List of pre-qualified sellers or current sellers for some products to the operating group), *Teaming or Collaboration Agreements* (all of these being outputs of Plan Procurements Process or data collected as input for that process) are other inputs in the list.

Tools and Techniques

PMBOK ® Guide lists the following tools and techniques that also more or less self-evident once the basic nature of the process and what it aims to accomplish is grasped.

- *List of Qualified Sellers:*
  Placing Advertisements for the Requirements, Reviewing Industry Magazines for Identifying Leading Suppliers, Internet Information and *Organizational Process Assets* (vendors known to the organization for earlier projects) could be useful for preparing a list of qualified sellers
- *Bidder's Conferences:* They involve the meetings with individual parties or a common conference with all prospective suppliers to ensure that all suppliers are brought to a common base of understanding the total scope of supply—technical specifications and contractual requirements for applicable quality standards and delivery schedule. This is a very important part of conducting the procurements.
- *Techniques for evaluation of proposal* from technical and commercial aspects
- *Negotiations with Short-listed Vendors*
- *Expert Judgment* (availing advice from technology or industry experts within the organization or external consultants, legal and contractual issues and other experts)

Outputs

The list of selected sellers for outsourcing and *the award of purchase orders or specific contracts* for product services are the primary outputs. Secondary outputs include *Updates of Project Management Plans* (updates of scope, cost, and schedule baselines and procurement management plan), *Updates of Project Documents* (updates in Risk Register, Requirements Documentation, etc.), and *Resource Calendars* (taking into account the schedule negotiated with the suppliers while placing contracts).

Appendix 12.1 and some parts of this appendix include brief discussions and references to issues involved in drafting, negotiating and awarding contracts. Effective and efficient contracting is at the heart of the procurement management. To describe the intricacies of the subject is beyond the scope of this appendix, which is meant only as reference for mapping the procurement management processes described in PMBOK® Guide with the overall project procurement activities. The interested readers could read some special books, which provide elaborate discussion only on this subject, and get a perspective of the issues and intricacies.

2.3 Administer Procurements (Monitoring and Controlling Process Group)

Administering the contract is the process of monitoring and controlling the contract during its execution and managing the changes along the course as necessary, so that the product or service is delivered according to contracted scope, specified quality standard, agreed schedule and agreed cost budget. Over and above the supply of contracted product or service by the seller and the payment for it according to agreed payment schedule by the buyer, the legal aspect of the contract must always remain in the view-scope of the project manager and his team.

Administering the contract requires the project manager and his team to maintain as close as necessary contact with the supplier and interact effectively for mutually satisfactory results. This would involve:

- Developing a common understanding and acceptance of the contract for discharging the duties for mutual satisfaction
- Seller's preparation of drawings and detailed specifications for tailoring the product or service to precise contracted requirements and their review and approval by the buyer
- Periodic review of the progress of the work to meet the delivery schedule and prompt certification of the agreed milestones for release of payments to the seller

- Inspection, testing and quality audits during the contract period—stage-wise inspection when necessary
- Managing the change during contract execution—record of the change and the mutually agreed impacts on the cost or schedule revision
- Acceptance tests before closing the contract—performance tests and verifying technical specifications
- Hand-over of technical documentation for project archives (design drawings, as-built drawings, operation and maintenance manuals, technical specifications and other details of bought out components incorporated into his product by the seller, recommended spare parts lists, etc.)

Inputs

One set of inputs specify what the contract should deliver. They include:

- *Project Management Plan* (its Procurement Management Plan part)
- *Procurement Documents* (SOW and other technical and contractual documents) and
- *Contract*

The other set of inputs include the report of exact work performance and corrective actions taken

- *Performance Reports* (the status reports of work completed and milestones achieved)
- *Work Performance Information* (quality audit or other inspection and testing results records, cost and payment records, etc.)
- *Records of Approved Change Requests* (Record of agreed change in the contracted work scope and agreed impacts in the project quality, schedule and cost)

Tools and Techniques

Administering the procurements would require a close liaison with the supplier for assuring the performance of the contract on mutually beneficial terms. The tools and techniques to accomplish this aim include:

- *Performance Reviews:* This would include a comprehensive review of the seller's performance for work progress for completing the deliverables in the contract scope to agreed quality standards, at budgeted cost, and agreed schedule. The performance reviews of major contracts would be an important part of project status review report.
- *Inspection and Audit Reports:* The audits and inspection by the buyer of the seller's work in progress would be helpful for assessing the compliance to quality standards as well as the work progress to meet the agreed schedule. Suitable corrective action can be taken based on these inspection reports.
- *Contract Change Control System:* This is a very important tool for administering procurements. The system should include:
  - Procedures and authorities for initiating changes
  - Procedures and authority levels for assessment of impacts of proposed changes on the cost, quality and schedule
  - The authority levels and procedures for approval of changes, and
  - Incorporation of approved changes in the project work and updating the project plans and project documents

  The procurement change control system should be apart of the integrated change control procedures for the entire project.
- *Payments Schedule:* The project team should promptly certify the work as soon as seller reports its completion and submits the request for authorization of payment.
- *Contract Administration Records:* The project team should maintain a proper record of all important details of the contract. This would include a copy of the original contract, periodic performance review and inspection reports, change requests and their evaluation reports, payment records, correspondence and technical details useful for operating the product of the project.

- *Dispute Settlement and Claims Administration:* One sticky issue in administering contracts is settling the disputes, more often about the changes and their effects on contract work and resolving the claim. Mutually accommodating negotiations would be a preferred method for resolving such issues but in rare cases it might be necessary to take recourse to provision in the contract for settling the disputes by third part arbitration.

Outputs

- *Procurement Documentation:* The procurement documentation should include a proper record of the important contract stages. The original contract, the record of requested and approved changes, the inspection and testing reports, status reports submitted by seller, correspondence, the periodically submitted bills and accompanying data, certification papers and actual payment records, issue log, material technical changes, final technical and performance testing reports before acceptance and other useful technical and contractual details.
- *Change Requests:* Though change requests form a part of the overall procurement documentation, this special mention is to emphasize its importance in procurement administration. The record of change requests by the seller (or buyer), assessment of the change impact on cost and schedule, rejected change requests and approved requests should be documented.
- *Updates of Project Management Plan:* Procurement Management Plan, Schedule Baseline, and Cost Baselines should be updated based on the actual contract performance data.

2.4 Close Procurements (Closing Process Group)

This is the last of the procurement management processes and involves bringing to an orderly and formal close all project procurements.

A large part of the activities in this phase of procurements is administrative in nature. The activities in closing procurements might be:

- Carrying out final check of all deliverables and preparing a check list of inadequately completed or defective items and getting them executed or repaired by the seller
- Carrying out final performance testing of the product for acceptance and closing the contract
- Final certification of all contract work and authorizing payments
- Collecting technical details for maintenance and operation
- Settling unresolved disputes and claims

In some instances, it may be necessary to terminate the contract before its normal completion. In such case, the contract's termination clause comes into operation and the additional work of buyer and seller's representatives making joint records of work executed till the termination and authorization of payment also becomes necessary.

Inputs

Procurement Management Plan, (component of Project Management Plan) and *Procurement Documentation* for individual contract are the inputs for the process.

Tools and Techniques

Inspection and Testing for final acceptance, Negotiated for Settlements and *Procurement Records System* are the tools and techniques for the process.

Outputs

The main output of the process is essentially a *Closed Contract or Procurement.*

Update of Organizational Process: The secondary outputs from the process are the project records, which serve as project archives and are useful for the operation and maintenance of the contract's product or service and addition to the knowledge-base of the organization for similar projects in future.

CASE 12.1

The Accounting Software Installation Project

Sitting in her office, Karin Chung is reviewing the past four months of the large corporate accounting software installation project she has been managing. Everything seemed so well planned before the project started. Each company division had a task force that provided input into the proposed installation along with potential problems. All the different divisions had been trained and briefed on exactly how their division would interface and use the forthcoming accounting software. All six contractors, which included one of the Big Five consulting companies, assisted in developing the work breakdown structure—costs, specifications, time.

Karin hired a consultant to conduct a one-day "partnering" workshop attended by the major accounting heads, a member of each task force group, and key representatives from each of the contractors. During the workshop, several different team-building exercises were used to illustrate the importance of collaboration and effective communication. Everyone laughed when Karin fell into an imaginary acid pit during a human bridge-building exercise. The workshop ended on an upbeat note with everyone signing a partnering charter that expressed their commitment to working together as partners to complete the project.

Two Months Later

One task force member came to Karin to complain that the contractor dealing with billing would not listen to his concerns about problems that could occur in the Virginia division when billings are consolidated. The contractor had told him, the task force member, he had bigger problems than consolidation of billing in the Virginia division. Karin replied, "You can settle the problem with the contractor. Go to her and explain how serious your problem is and that it will have to be settled before the project is completed."

Later in the week in the lunchroom she overheard one consulting contractor badmouthing the work of another—"never on time, interface coding not tested." In the hallway the same day an accounting department supervisor told her that tests showed the new software will never be compatible with the Georgia division's accounting practices.

While concerned, Karin considered these problems typical of the kind she had encountered on other smaller software projects.

Four Months Later

The project seemed to be falling apart. What happened to the positive attitude fostered at the team-building workshop? One contractor wrote a formal letter complaining that another contractor was sitting on a coding decision that was delaying their work. The letter went on: "We cannot be held responsible or liable for delays caused by others." The project was already two months behind, so problems were becoming very real and serious. Karin finally decided to call a meeting of all parties to the project and partnering agreement.

She began by asking for problems people were encountering while working on the project. Although participants were reluctant to be first for fear of being perceived as a complainer, it was not long before accusations and tempers flared out of control. It was always some group complaining about another group. Several participants complained that others were sitting on decisions that resulted in their work being held up. One consultant said, "It is impossible to tell who's in charge of what." Another participant complained that although the group met separately on small problems, it never met as a total group to assess new risk situations that developed.

Karin felt the meeting had degenerated into an unrecoverable situation. Commitment to the project and partnering appeared to be waning. She quickly decided to stop the meeting and cool things down. She spoke to the project stakeholders: "It is clear that we have some serious problems, and the project is in jeopardy. The project must get back on track, and the backbiting must stop. I want each of us to come to a meeting Friday morning with concrete suggestions of what it will take to get the project back on track and specific actions of how we can make it happen. We need to recognize our mutual interdependence and bring our relationships with each other back to a win/win environment. When we do get things back on track, we need to figure out how to stay on track."

1. Why does this attempt at project partnering appear to be failing?
2. If you were Karin, what would you do to get this project back on track?
3. What action would you take to keep the project on track?

CASE 12.2

Goldrush Electronics Negotiation Exercise

Objective

The purpose of this case is to provide you with an opportunity to practice negotiations.

Procedure

Step 1

The class is divided into four groups, each comprising the project management group for one of four projects at Goldrush Electronics.

Step 2

Read the Goldrush Electronics "Background Information" section given below. Then read the instructions for the project you represent. Soon you will meet with the management of the other projects to exchange personnel. Plan how you want to conduct those meetings.

Background Information

Goldrush Electronics (GE) produces a range of electronic products. GE has a strong commitment to project management. GE operates as a projectized organization with each project organized as a fully dedicated team. The compensation system is based on a 40 1 30 1 30 formula. Forty percent is based on your base salary, 30 percent on your project performance, and 30 percent on overall performance of the firm.

Four new product development projects have been authorized. They are code named: Alpha, Beta, Theta, and Zeta. The preliminary assignment of personnel is listed below. You are assigned to represent the management of one of these projects.

The policy at GE is that once preliminary assignments are made project managers are free to exchange personnel as long as both parties agree to the transaction. You will have the opportunity to adjust your team by negotiating with other project managers.

Alpha Project		
Software Engineer	**Hardware Engineer**	**Design Engineer**
Jill	Cameron	Mitch
John	Chandra	Marsha
Beta Project		
Software Engineer	**Hardware Engineer**	**Design Engineer**
Jake	Casey	Mike
Jennifer	Craig	Maria
Theta Project		
Software Engineer	**Hardware Engineer**	**Design Engineer**
Jack	Chuck	Monika
Johan	Cheryl	Mark
Zeta Project		
Software Engineer	**Hardware Engineer**	**Design Engineer**
Jeff	Carlos	Max
Juwoo	Chad	Maile

Personnel may be traded for one or more other personnel.

Step 3

Meet and negotiate with the other project managers.

Step 4

Individual project scores are totaled and posted.

Step 5

Discussion Questions

1. What was your initial strategy before starting the actual negotiations? How did you view the other groups?
2. Did your initial strategy change once negotiations began? If so how and why?
3. What could top management at GE have done to make it easier to reach agreement with the other groups?

CHAPTER 13

Progress and Performance Measurement and Evaluation

How does a project get one year late?
... One day at a time.

—*Frederick P. Brooks, The Mythical Man Month, p. 153*

Evaluation and control are part of every project manager's job. Control by "wandering around" and/or "involvement" can overcome most problems in small projects. But large projects need some form of formal control. Control holds people accountable, prevents small problems from mushrooming into large problems, and keeps focus. Except for accounting controls, project control is not performed well in most organizations. Control is one of the most neglected areas of project management. Unfortunately, it is not uncommon to find resistance to control processes. In essence, those who minimize the importance of control are passing up a great opportunity to be effective managers and, perhaps, allow the organization to gain a competitive edge. Neglecting control in organizations with multiple projects is even more serious. For effective control, the project manager needs a single information system to collect data and report progress on cost, schedule, and specifications. The general structure of such a system is discussed next.

Structure of a Project Monitoring Information System

A project monitoring system involves *determining what* data to collect; *how, when,* and *who* will collect the data; *analysis* of the data; and *reporting* current progress.

What Data Are Collected?   Data collected are determined by *which* metrics will be used for project control. Typical key data collected are actual activity duration times, resource usage and rates, and actual costs, which are compared against planned times, resources, and budgets. Since a major portion of the monitoring system focuses on cost/schedule concerns, it is crucial to provide the project manager and stakeholders with data to answer questions such as:

- What is the current status of the project in terms of schedule and cost?

- How much will it cost to complete the project?
- When will the project be completed?
- Are there potential problems that need to be addressed now?
- What, who, and where are the causes for cost or schedule overruns?
- What did we get for the dollars spent?
- If there is a cost overrun midway in the project, can we forecast the overrun at completion?

The performance metrics you need to collect should support answering these questions. Examples of specific metrics and tools for collecting data will be discussed in detail later in this chapter.

Collecting Data and Analysis   With the determination of what data are collected, the next step is to establish who, when, and how the data will be assembled. Will the data be collected by the project team, contractor, independent cost engineers, project manager? Or will the data be derived electronically from some form of surrogate data such as cash flow, machine hours, labor hours, or materials in place? Should the reporting period be one hour, one day, one week, or what? Is there a central repository for the data collected and is someone responsible for its dissemination?

   Electronic means of collecting data have vastly improved data assembly, analysis, and dissemination. Numerous software vendors have programs and tools to analyze your customized collected data and present it in a form that facilitates monitoring the project, identifying sources of problems, and updating your plan.

Reports and Reporting   First, who gets the progress reports? We have already suggested that different stakeholders and levels of management need different kinds of project information. Senior management's major interest is usually, "Are we on time and within budget? If not what corrective action is taking place?" Likewise, an IT manager working on the project is concerned primarily about her deliverable and specific work packages. The reports should be designed for the right audience.

   Typically, project progress reports are designed and communicated in written or oral form. A common topic format for progress reports follows:

- Progress since last report
- Current status of project
  1. Schedule
  2. Cost
  3. Scope
- Cumulative trends
- Problems and issues since last report
  1. Actions and resolution of earlier problems
  2. New variances and problems identified
- Corrective action planned

Given the structure of your information system and the nature of its outputs, we can use the system to interface and facilitate the project control process. These interfaces need to be relevant and seamless if control is to be effective.

The Project Control Process

Control is the process of comparing actual performance against plan to identify deviations, evaluate possible alternative courses of actions, and take appropriate corrective action. The project control steps for measuring and evaluating project performance are presented below.

1. Setting a baseline plan.
2. Measuring progress and performance.
3. Comparing plan against actual.
4. Taking action.

Each of the control steps is described in the following paragraphs.

Step 1: Setting a Baseline Plan

The baseline plan provides us with the elements for measuring performance. The baseline is derived from the cost and duration information found in the work breakdown structure (WBS) database and time-sequence data from the network and resource scheduling decisions. From the WBS the project resource schedule is used to time-phase all work, resources, and budgets into a baseline plan. See Chapter 8.

Step 2: Measuring Progress and Performance

Time and budgets are quantitative measures of performance that readily fit into the integrated information system. Qualitative measures such as meeting customer technical specifications and product function are most frequently determined by on-site inspection or actual use. This chapter is limited to quantitative measures of time and budget. Measurement of time performance is relatively easy and obvious. That is, is the critical path early, on schedule, or late; is the slack of near-critical paths decreasing to cause new critical activities? Measuring performance against budget (e.g., money, units in place, labor hours) is more difficult and is *not* simply a case of comparing actual versus budget. Earned value is necessary to provide a realistic estimate of performance against a time-phased budget. Earned value (EV) is defined as the budgeted cost of the work performed.

Step 3: Comparing Plan against Actual

Because plans seldom materialize as expected, it becomes imperative to measure deviations from plan to determine if action is necessary. Periodic monitoring and measuring the status of the project allow for comparisons of actual versus expected plans. It is crucial that the timing of status reports be frequent enough to allow for early detection of variations from plan and early correction of causes. Usually status reports should take place every one to four weeks to be useful and allow for proactive correction.

Step 4: Taking Action

If deviations from plans are significant, corrective action will be needed to bring the project back in line with the original or revised plan. In some cases, conditions or scope can change, which, in turn, will require a change in the baseline plan to recognize new information.

The remainder of this chapter describes and illustrates monitoring systems, tools, and components to support managing and controlling projects. Several of the tools you developed in the planning and scheduling chapters now serve as input to your information system for monitoring performance. Monitoring time performance is discussed first, followed by cost performance.

Monitoring Time Performance

A major goal of progress reporting is to catch any negative variances from plan as early as possible to determine if corrective action is necessary. Fortunately, monitoring schedule performance is relatively easy. The project network schedule, derived from the WBS/OBS, serves as the baseline to compare against actual performance.

Gantt charts (bar charts) and control charts are the typical tools used for communicating project schedule status. As suggested in Chapter 6, the Gantt chart is the most favored, used, and understandable. This kind of chart is commonly referred to as a tracking Gantt chart. Gantt and control charts serve well as a means for tracking and trending schedule performance. Their easy-to-understand visual formats make them favorite tools for communicating project schedule status—especially to top management, who do not usually have time for details. Adding actual and revised time estimates to the Gantt chart gives a quick overview of project status on the report date.

Tracking Gantt Chart

Figure 13.1 presents a baseline Gantt chart and a tracking Gantt chart for a project at the end of period 6. The solid bar below the original schedule bar represents the actual start and finish times for completed activities or any portion of an activity completed (see activities A, B, C, D, and E). For example, the actual start time for activity C is period 2; the actual finish time is period 5; the actual duration is three time units, rather than four scheduled time periods. Activities in process show the actual start time until the present; the extended bar represents the remaining scheduled duration (see activities D and E). The remaining expected duration for activities D and E are shown with the hatched bar. Activity F, which has not started, shows a revised estimated actual start (9) and finish time (13).

Note how activities can have durations that differ from the original schedule, as in activities C, D, and E. Either the activity is complete and the actual is known, or new information suggests the estimate of time be revised and reflected in the status report. In activity D the revised duration is expected to be four time units,

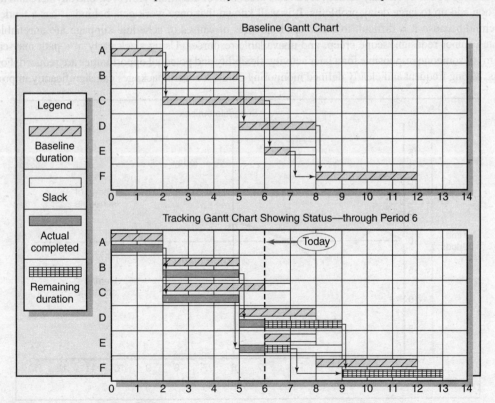

FIGURE 13.1   Baseline Gantt Chart

which is one time period longer than the original schedule. Although sometimes the Gantt chart does not show dependencies, when it is used with a network, the dependencies are easily identified if tracing is needed.

Control Chart

This chart is another tool used to monitor past project schedule performance and current performance and to estimate future schedule trends. Figure 13.2 depicts a project control chart. The chart is used to plot the difference between the scheduled time on the critical path at the report date with the actual point on the critical path. Although Figure 13.2 shows the project was behind early in the project, the plot suggests corrective action brought the project back on track. If the trend is sustained, the project will come in ahead of schedule. Because the activity scheduled times represent average durations, four observations trending in one direction indicate there is a very high probability that there is an identifiable cause. The cause should be located and action taken if necessary. Control chart trends are very useful for giving warning of potential problems so appropriate action can be taken if necessary.

Control charts are also frequently used to monitor progress toward milestones, which mark events and as such have zero duration. Milestones are significant project events that mark major accomplishments. To be effective, milestones need to be concrete, specific, measurable events. Milestones must be easily identifiable by all project stakeholders—for example, product testing complete. Critical merge activities are good candidates for milestones. Control charts very similar to the example shown in Figure 13.2 are often used to record and communicate project progress toward a milestone.

Schedule slippage of one day seldom receives a great deal of attention. However, one day here and another there soon add up to large delay problems. It is well known that once work gets behind, it has a tendency to stay behind because it is difficult to make up. Examples of causes of schedule slippage are unreliable time estimates, minor redesign, scope creep, and unavailable resources. Using slack early in a path may create a problem for someone responsible for a later activity; flexibility and potential opportunities are reduced. For these reasons, having frequent and clearly defined monitoring points for work packages can significantly improve the

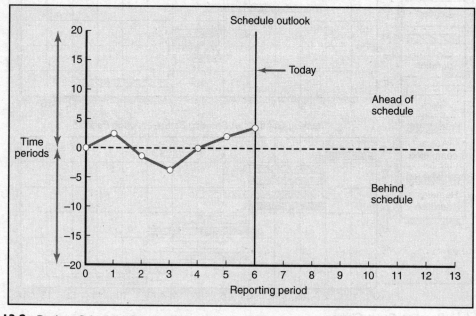

FIGURE 13.2   Project Schedule Control Chart

Snapshot from Practice   Status Reports at Microsoft*

At Microsoft each software product has a corresponding project status report. Project teams send these reports each month to Bill Gates and other top executives as well as to the managers of all related projects. The status reports are brief and have a standard format. Gates can read most of them quickly and still spot potential project delays or changes he does not want. He especially looks for schedule slips, cutting too many product features, or the need to change a specification. Gates usually responds to the relevant managers or developers directly by electronic mail. Status reports are an important mechanism for communicating between top management and projects. As Gates explains:

"I get all the status reports. Right now there might be a hundred active projects. . . . [The status reports] contain the schedule, including milestones dates, and any change in spec, and any comments about 'Hey, we can't hire enough people,' or 'Jeez, if this OLE (Object Linking and Embedding) 2 Mac release isn't done, we're just going to have to totally slip.'. . . They know [their report] goes up to all the people who manage all the other groups that they have dependencies with. So if they don't raise it in the status report and then two months later they say something, that's a breakdown in communication. . . . The internal group is totally copied on those things, so it's sort of the consensus of the group."

* From *Microsoft Secrets: The World's Most Powerful Software Company Creates Technology*. Copyright © 1995 by Michael A. Cusumano and Richard W. Selby.

chances of catching schedule slippage early. Early detection reduces the chance of small delays growing to large ones and thereby reducing opportunities for corrective action to get back on schedule. See Snapshot from Practice: Status Reports at Microsoft.

Development of An Earned Value Cost/Schedule System

Earned value is not new; although its initial use was in military contracts, in recent years the private sector has come to depend on the system for managing multiple and large projects.

The original earned value cost/schedule system was pioneered by the U.S. Department of Defense (DOD) in the 1960s. It is probably safe to say project managers in every major country are using some form of the system. The system is being used on internal projects in the manufacturing, pharmaceutical, and high-tech industries. For example, organizations such as EDS, NCR, Levi Strauss, Tektronics, and Disney have used earned value systems to track projects. The basic framework of the earned value system is withstanding the test of time. Most project management software includes the original framework; many systems have added industry-specific variations to more precisely track progress and costs. This chapter presents the "generic" core of an integrated cost/schedule information system.

The earned value system starts with the time-phased costs that provide the project budget *baseline,* which is called the planned budgeted value of the work scheduled (PV). Given this time-phased baseline, comparisons are made with actual and planned schedule and costs using earned value. The earned value approach provides the missing links not found in conventional cost-budget systems. At any point in time, a status report can be developed for the project.

The earned value cost/schedule system uses several acronyms and equations for analysis. Table 13.1 presents a glossary of these acronyms. You will need this glossary as a reference. In recent years acronyms have been shortened to be more phonetically friendly. This movement is reflected in material from the Project Management Institute, in project management software, and by most practitioners. This text edition follows the recent trend. The acronyms found in brackets represent the older acronyms, which are often found in software programs. To the uninitiated, the terms used in practice appear horrendous and intimidating. However, once a few basic terms are understood, the intimidation index will evaporate.

TABLE 13.1 Glossary of Terms

EV	Earned value for a task is simply the percent complete times its original budget. Stated differently, EV is the percent of the original budget that has been earned by actual work completed. [The older acronym for this value was BCWP—budgeted cost of the work performed.]
PV	The planned time-phased baseline of the value of the work scheduled. An approved cost estimate of the resources scheduled in a time-phased cumulative baseline [BCWS—budgeted cost of the work scheduled].
AC	Actual cost of the work completed. The sum of the costs incurred in accomplishing work. [ACWP—actual cost of the work performed].
CV	Cost variance is the difference between the earned value and the actual costs for the work completed to date where $CV = EV - AC$.
SV	Schedule variance is the difference between the earned value and the baseline line to date where $SV = EV - PV$.
BAC	Budgeted cost at completion. The total budgeted cost of the baseline or project cost accounts.
EAC	Estimated cost at completion.
ETC	Estimated cost to complete remaining work.
VAC	Cost variance at completion. VAC indicates expected actual over- or underrun cost at completion.

Following five careful steps ensures that the cost/schedule system is integrated. These steps are outlined here. Steps 1, 2, and 3 are accomplished in the planning stage. Steps 4 and 5 are sequentially accomplished during the execution stage of the project.

1. Define the work using a WBS. This step involves developing documents that include the following information (see Chapters 4 and 5):
   a. Scope.
   b. Work packages.
   c. Deliverables.
   d. Organization units.
   e. Resources.
   f. Budgets for each work package.
2. Develop work and resource schedule.
   a. Schedule resources to activities (see Chapter 8).
   b. Time-phase work packages into a network.
3. Develop a time-phase budget using work packages included in an activity. The cumulative values of these budgets will become the baseline and will be called the planned budgeted cost of the work scheduled (PV). The sum should equal the budgeted amounts for all the work packages in the cost accounts (See Chapter 8).
4. At the work package level, collect the actual costs for the work performed. These costs will be called the actual cost of the work completed (AC). Collect percent complete and multiply this times the original budget amount for the value of the work actually completed. These values will be called earned value (EV).
5. Compute the schedule variance ($SV = EV - PV$) and cost variance ($CV = EV - AC$). Prepare hierarchical status reports for each level of management—from work package manager to customer or project manager. The reports should also include project rollups by organization unit and deliverables. In addition, actual time performance should be checked against the project network schedule.

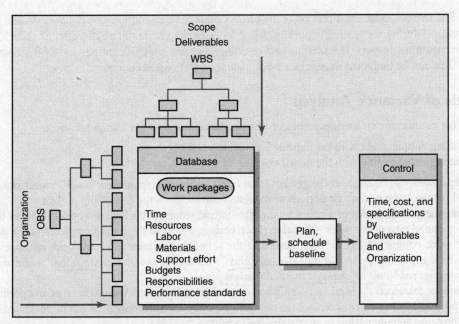

FIGURE 13.3 Project Management Information System Overview

Figure 13.3 presents a schematic overview of the integrated information system, which includes the techniques and systems presented in earlier chapters. Those who have tenaciously labored through the early chapters can smile! Steps 1 and 2 are already carefully developed. Observe that control data can be traced backward to specific deliverables and organization unit responsible.

The major reasons for creating a baseline are to monitor and report progress and to estimate cash flow. Therefore, it is crucial to integrate the baseline with the performance measurement system. Costs are placed (time-phased) in the baseline exactly as managers expect them to be "earned." This approach facilitates tracking costs to their point of origin. In practice, the integration is accomplished by using the same rules in assigning costs to the baseline as those used to measure progress using earned value. You may find several rules in practice, but percent complete is the workhorse most commonly used. Someone familiar with each task estimates what percent of the task has been completed or how much of the task remains.

Percent Complete Rule

This rule is the heart of any earned value system. The best method for assigning costs to the baseline under this rule is to establish frequent checkpoints over the duration of the work package and assign completion percentages in dollar terms. For example, units completed could be used to assign baseline costs and later to measure progress. Units might be lines of code, hours, drawings completed, cubic yards of concrete in place, workdays, prototypes complete, etc. This approach to percent complete adds "objectivity" to the subjective observation approaches often used. When measuring percent complete in the monitoring phase of the project, it is common to limit the amount earned to 80 or 90 percent until the work package is 100 percent complete.

What Costs Are Included in Baselines?

The baseline (PV) is the sum of the cost accounts, and each cost account is the sum of the work packages in the cost account. Three direct costs are typically included in baselines—labor, equipment, and materials. The reason: these are direct costs the project manager can control. Overhead costs and profit are typically added later by accounting processes. Most work packages should be discrete, of short time span, and have measurable outputs. If materials and/or equipment are a significant portion of the cost of work packages, they can be budgeted in separate work packages and cost accounts.

Methods of Variance Analysis

Generally the method for measuring accomplishments centers on two key computations:

1. Comparing earned value with the expected schedule value.
2. Comparing earned value with the actual costs.

These comparisons can be made at the project level or down to the cost account level. Project status can be determined for the latest period, all periods to date, and estimated to the end of the project.

Assessing the current status of a project using the earned value cost/schedule system requires three data elements—planned cost of the work scheduled (PV), budgeted cost of the work completed (EV), and actual cost of the work completed (AC). From these data the schedule variance (SV) and cost variance (CV) are computed each reporting period. *A positive variance indicates a desirable condition, while a negative variance suggests problems or changes that have taken place.*

Cost variance tells us if the work accomplished costs more or less than was planned at any point over the life of the project. If labor and materials have not been separated, cost variance should be reviewed carefully to isolate the cause to either labor or materials—or to both.

Schedule variance presents an overall assessment of *all* work packages in the project scheduled to date. It is important to note schedule variance contains *no* critical path information. Schedule variance measures progress in dollars rather than time units. Therefore, it is unlikely that any translation of dollars to time will yield accurate information telling if any milestone or critical path is early, on time, or late (even if the project occurs exactly as planned). *The only accurate method for determining the true time progress of the project is to compare the project network schedule against the actual network schedule to measure if the project is on time* (refer to Figure 13.1). However, SV is very useful in assessing the direction all the work in the project is taking—after 20 or more percent of the project has been completed.

Figure 13.4 presents a sample cost/schedule graph with variances identified for a project at the current status report date. Note the graph also focuses on what remains to be accomplished and any favorable or unfavorable trends. The "today" label marks the report date (time period 25) of where the project has been and where it is going. Because our system is hierarchical, graphs of the same form can be developed for different levels of management. In Figure 13.4 the top line represents the actual costs (AC) incurred for the project work to date. The middle line is the baseline (PV) and ends at the scheduled project duration (45). The bottom line is the budgeted value of the work actually completed to date (EV) or the earned value. The dotted line extending the actual costs from the report date to the new estimated completion date represents revised estimates of *expected* actual costs; that is, additional information suggests the costs at completion of the project will differ from what was planned. Note that the project duration has been extended and the variance at completion (VAC) is negative (BAC − EAC).

Another interpretation of the graph uses percentages. At the end of period 25, 75 percent of the work was scheduled to be accomplished. At the end of period 25, the value of the work accomplished is 50 percent. The actual cost of the work completed to date is $340, or 85 percent of the total project budget. The graph suggests the project will have about a 18 percent cost overrun and be five time units late. The current status of the project shows the cost variance (CV) to be over budget by $140 (EV − AC = 200 − 340 = −140). The schedule variance (SV) is negative $100 (EV − PV = 200 − 300 = −100), which suggests the project is behind schedule. Before moving to an example, consult Figure 13.5 to practice interpreting the outcomes of cost/schedule graphs. Remember, PV is your baseline and anchor point.

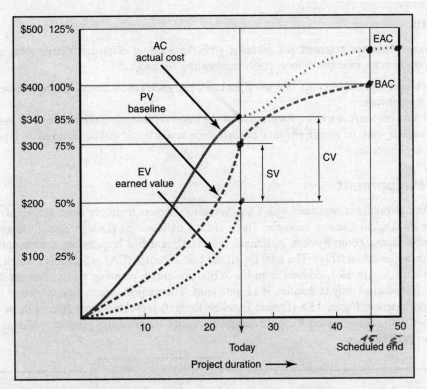

FIGURE 13.4   Cost/Schedule Graph

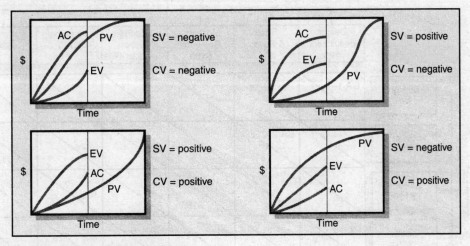

FIGURE 13.5   Earned-Value Review Exercise

Developing a Status Report: A Hypothetical Example

Working through an example demonstrates how the baseline serves as the anchor from which the project can be monitored using earned value techniques.

Assumptions

Because the process becomes geometrically complex with the addition of project detail, some simplifying assumptions are made in the example to more easily demonstrate the process:

1. Assume each cost account has only one work package, and each cost account will be represented as an activity on the network.
2. The project network early start times will serve as the basis for assigning the baseline values.
3. From the moment work on an activity task begins, some actual costs will be incurred each period until the activity is completed.

Baseline Development

Figure 13.6 (Work Breakdown Structure with Cost Accounts) depicts a simple work breakdown structure (WBS/OBS) for the Digital Camera example. There are six deliverables (Design Specifications, Shell & Power, Memory/Software, Zoom System, Assemble, and Test), and five responsible departments (Design, Shell, Storage, Zoom, and Assembly). The total for all the cost accounts (CA) is $320,000, which represents the total project cost. Figure 13.7, derived from the WBS, presents a planning Gantt chart for the Digital Camera project. The planned project duration is 11 time units. This project information is used to time-phase the project budget baseline. Figure 13.8 (Project Baseline Budget) presents a worksheet with an early start baseline developed with costs assigned. They are assigned "exactly" as managers plan to monitor and measure schedule and cost performance.

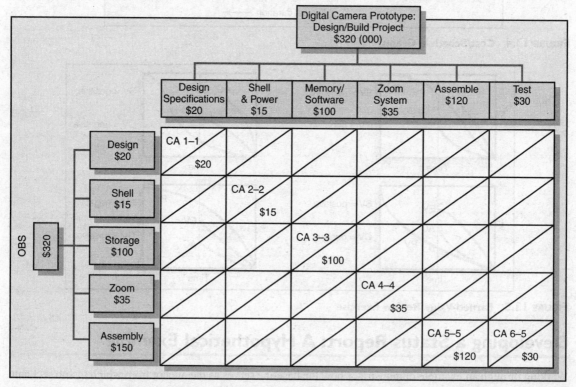

FIGURE 13.6   Work Breakdown Structure with Cost Accounts

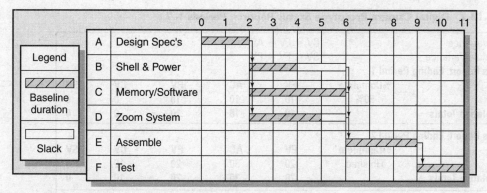

FIGURE 13.7   Digital Camera Prototype Project Baseline Gantt Chart

ACT/WP	DUR	ES	LF	SL	Total PV	0	1	2	3	4	5	6	7	8	9	10	11
A	2	0	2	0	20	10	10										
B	2	2	6	2	15			5	10								
C	4	2	6	0	100			20	30	30	20						
D	3	2	6	1	35			15	10	10							
E	3	6	9	0	120							30	40	50			
F	2	9	11	0	30										10	20	
Total PV by period						10	10	40	50	40	20	30	40	50	10	20	
Cumulative PV by period						10	20	60	110	150	170	200	240	290	300	320	

Schedule information spans DUR, ES, LF, SL, Total PV. *Baseline budget needs* spans the Time period columns 0–11.

FIGURE 13.8   Digital Camera Prototype Project Baseline Budget ($000)

Development of the Status Report

A status report is analogous to a camera snapshot of a project at a specific point in time. The status report uses earned value to measure schedule and cost performance. Measuring earned value begins at the work package level. Work packages are in one of three conditions on a report date:

1. Not yet started.
2. Finished.
3. In-process or partially complete.

Earned values for the first two conditions present no difficulties. Work packages that are not yet started earn zero percent of the PV (budget). Packages that are completed earn 100 percent of their PV. In-process packages apply the percent complete rule to the PV baseline to measure earned value (EV). In our camera example we will only use the percent complete rule to measure progress.

Table 13.2 presents the completed, separate status reports of the Digital Camera Prototype project for periods 1 through 7. Each period percent complete and actual cost were gathered for each task from staff in the field. The schedule and cost variance are computed for each task and the project to date. For example, the status in period 1 shows only Task A (Design Specifications) is in process and it is 50 percent complete

TABLE 13.2 Digital Camera Prototype Status Reports: Periods 1–7

| Cost Variance | | CV = EV − AC | | | | |
| Schedule Variance | | SV = EV − PV | | | | |

Status Report: Ending Period 1

Task	%Complete	EV	AC	PV	CV	SV
A	50%	10	10	10	0	0
Cumulative Totals		**10**	**10**	**10**	**0**	**0**

Status Report: Ending Period 2

Task	%Complete	EV	AC	PV	CV	SV
A	Finished	20	30	20	−10	0
Cumulative Totals		**20**	**30**	**20**	**−10**	**0**

Status Report: Ending Period 3

Task	%Complete	EV	AC	PV	CV	SV
A	Finished	20	30	20	−10	0
B	33%	5	10	5	−5	0
C	20%	20	30	20	−10	0
D	60%	21	20	15	+1	+6
Cumulative Totals		**66**	**90**	**60**	**−24**	**+6**

Status Report: Ending Period 4

Task	%Complete	EV	AC	PV	CV	SV
A	Finished	20	30	20	−10	0
B	Finished	15	20	15	−5	0
C	50%	50	70	50	−20	0
D	80%	28	30	25	−2	+3
Cumulative Totals		**113**	**150**	**110**	**−37**	**+3**

Status Report: Ending Period 5

Task	%Complete	EV	AC	PV	CV	SV
A	Finished	20	30	20	−10	0
B	Finished	15	20	15	−5	0
C	60%	60	100	80	−40	−20
D	80%	28	50	35	−22	−7
Cumulative Totals		**123**	**200**	**150**	**−77**	**−27**

Status Report: Ending Period 6

Task	%Complete	EV	AC	PV	CV	SV
A	Finished	20	30	20	−10	0
B	Finished	15	20	15	−5	0
C	80%	80	110	100	−30	−20
D	Finished	35	60	35	−25	0
Cumulative Totals		**150**	**220**	**170**	**−70**	**−20**

Status Report: Ending Period 7

Task	%Complete	EV	AC	PV	CV	SV
A	Finished	20	30	20	−10	0
B	Finished	15	20	15	−5	0
C	90%	90	120	100	−30	−10
D	Finished	35	60	35	−25	0
E	0%	0	0	30	0	−30
F	0%	0	0	0	0	0
Cumulative Totals		**160**	**230**	**200**	**−70**	**−40**

and actual cost for the task is 10. The planned value at the end of period 1 for Task A is 10 (See Figure 13.8). The cost and schedule variance are both zero, which indicates the project is on budget and schedule. By the end of period 3, Task A is finished. Task B (Shell & Power) is 33 percent complete and AC is 10; Task C is 20 percent complete and AC is 30; and D is 60 percent complete and AC is 20. Again, from Figure 13.8 *at the end of period 3,* we can see that the PV for Task A is 20 (10 + 10 = 20), for task B is 5, for Task C is 20, and for Task D is 15. At the end of period 3 it is becoming clear the actual cost (AC) is exceeding the value of the work completed (EV). The cost variance (see Table 13.2) for the project at the end of period 3 is negative 24. Schedule variance is positive 6, which suggests the project may be ahead of schedule.

It is important to note that since earned values are computed from costs (or sometimes labor hours or other metrics), the relationship of costs to time is not one-for-one. For example, it is possible to have a negative SV variance when the project is actually ahead on the critical path. Therefore, it is important to remember, SV is in dollars and is not an accurate measure of time; however, it is a fairly good indicator of the status of the whole project in terms of being ahead or behind schedule after the project is over 20 percent complete. Only the project network, or Tracking Gantt chart, and actual work completed can give an accurate assessment of schedule performance down to the work package level.

By studying the separate status reports for periods 5 through 7, you can see the project will be over budget and behind schedule. By period 7 tasks A, B, and D are finished, but all are over budget—negative 10, 5, and 25. Task C (Memory/Software) is 90 percent complete. Task E is late and hasn't started because Task C is not yet completed. The result is that, at the end of period 7, the digital camera project is over budget $70,000, with a schedule budget over $40,000.

Figure 13.9 shows the graphed results of all the status reports through period 7. This graph represents the data from Table 13.2. The cumulative actual costs (AC) to date and the earned value budgeted costs to date (EV) are plotted against the original project baseline (PV). The cumulative AC to date is $230; the cumulative EV to date is $160. Given these cumulative values, the cost variance (CV = EV − AC) is negative $70 (160 − 230 = −70). The schedule variance (SV = EV − PV) is negative $40 (160 − 200 = −40). Again, recall that only the project network or Tracking Gantt chart can give an accurate assessment of schedule performance down to the work package level.

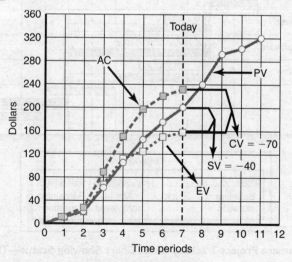

FIGURE 13.9   Digital Camera Prototype Summary Graph ($000)

A Tracking Gantt bar chart for the Digital Camera Prototype is shown in Figure 13.10. From this figure you can see Task C (Memory/Software), which had an original duration of 4 time units, now is expected to require 6 time units. This delay of 2 time units for Task C will also delay Tasks E and F two time units and result in the project being late 2 time periods.

Figure 13.11 shows an oversimplified project rollup at the end of period 7. The rollup is by deliverables and organization units. For example, the Memory/Software deliverable has an SV of $ −10 and a CV of −30. The responsible "Storage" department should have an explanation for these variances. Similarly, the assembly department, which is responsible for the Assemble and Test deliverables, has an SV of $ −30 due to the delay of Task C (see Figure 13.10). Most deliverables look unfavorable on schedule and cost variance.

In more complex projects, the crosstabs of cost accounts by deliverables and organization units can be very revealing and more profound. This example contains the basics for developing a status report, baseline development, and measuring schedule and cost variance. In our example, performance analysis had only one level above the cost account level. Because all data are derived from the detailed database, it is relatively easy to determine progress status at all levels of the work and organization breakdown structures. Fortunately, this same current database can provide additional views of the current status of the project and forecast costs at the completion of the project. Approaches for deriving additional information from the database are presented next.

To the uninitiated, a caveat is in order. In practice budgets may not be expressed in total dollars for an activity. Frequently, budgets are time-phased for materials and labor separately for more effective control over costs. Another common approach used in practice is to use labor hours in place of dollars in the earned value system. Later, labor hours are converted to dollars. The use of labor hours in the earned value system is the *modus operandi* for most construction work. Labor hours are easy to understand and are often the way many time and cost estimates are developed. Most earned value software easily accommodates the use of labor hours for development of cost estimates.

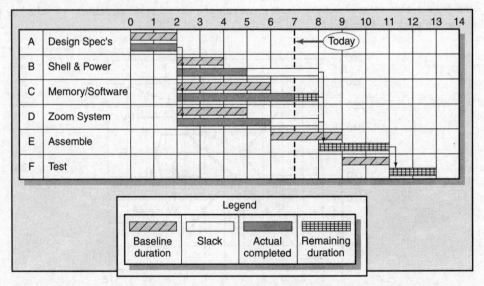

FIGURE 13.10   Digital Camera Project-Tracking Gantt Chart Showing Status—Through Period 7

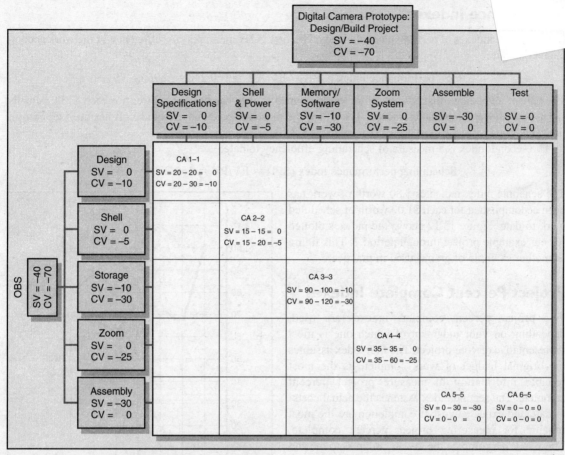

FIGURE 13.11 Project Rollup End Period 7 ($000)

Indexes to Monitor Progress

Practitioners sometimes prefer to use schedule and cost indexes over the absolute values of SV and CV, because indexes can be considered efficiency ratios. Graphed indexes over the project life cycle can be very illuminating and useful. The trends are easily identified for deliverables and the whole project.

Indexes are typically used at the cost account level and above. In practice, the database is also used to develop indexes that allow the project manager and customer to view progress from several angles. An index of 1.00 (100 percent) indicates progress is as planned. An index greater than 1.00 shows progress is better than expected. An index less than 1.00 suggests progress is poorer than planned and deserves attention. Table 13.3 presents the interpretation of the indexes.

TABLE 13.3 Interpretation of Indexes

Index	Cost (CPI)	Schedule (SPI)	
>1.00	Under cost	Ahead of schedule	greater than 1
=1.00	On cost	On schedule	
<1.00	Over cost	Behind schedule	

Performance Indexes

There are two indexes of performance efficiency. The first index measures *cost* efficiency of the work accomplished to date:

$$\text{Cost performance index (CPI)} = EV/AC = 160/230 = .696 \text{ or } .70$$

The CPI of .696 shows that $.70 worth of work planned to date has been completed for each $1.00 actually spent—an unfavorable situation indeed. The CPI is the most accepted and used index. It has been tested over time and found to be the most accurate, reliable, and stable.

The second index is a measure of scheduling efficiency to date:

$$\text{Scheduling performance index (SPI)} = EV/PV = 160/200 = .80$$

The schedule index indicates $.80 worth of work has been accomplished for each $1.00 worth of scheduled work to date. Figure 13.12 shows the indexes plotted for our example project through period 7. This figure is another example of graphs used in practice.

Project Percent Complete Indexes

Two project percent complete indexes are used, depending on your judgment of which one is most representative of your project. The first index assumes the original budget of work complete is the most reliable information to measure project percent complete. The second index assumes the actual costs-to-date and expected cost at completion are the most reliable for measuring project percent complete. These indexes compare the to-date progress to the end of the project. The implications underlying use of these indexes are that conditions will not change, no improvement or action will be taken, and the information in the database is accurate. The first index looks at percent complete in terms of *budget* amounts:

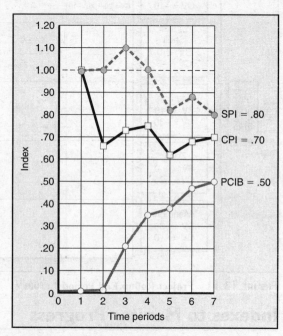

FIGURE 13.12 Indexes Periods 1–7

$$\text{Percent complete index PCIB} = EV/BAC = 160/320 = .50\ (50\%)$$

This PCIB indicates the work accomplished represents 50 percent of the total budgeted (BAC) dollars to date. Observe that this calculation does not include actual costs incurred. Because actual dollars spent do not guarantee project progress, this index is favored by many project managers when there is a high level of confidence in the original budget estimates.

The second index views percent complete in terms of *actual* dollars spent to accomplish the work to date and the actual expected dollars for the completed project (EAC). For example, at the end of period 7 the staff re-estimates that the EAC will be 575 instead of 320. The application of this view is written as

$$\text{Percent complete index PCIC} = AC/EAC = 230/575 = .40\ (40\%)$$

Some managers favor this index because it contains actual and revised estimates that include newer, more complete information.

These two views of percent complete present alternative views of the "real" percent complete. These percents may be quite different as shown above. (Note: The PCIC index was not plotted in Figure 13.12. The new figures for EAC would be derived each period by estimators in the field.)

Technical Performance Measurement

Measuring technical performance is as important as measuring schedule and cost performance. Although technical performance is often assumed, the opposite can be true. The ramifications of poor technical performance frequently are more profound—something works or it doesn't if technical specifications are not adhered to.

Assessing technical performance of a system, facility, or product is often accomplished by examining the documents found in the scope statement and/or work package documentation. These documents should specify criteria and tolerance limits against which performance can be measured. For example, the technical performance of a software project suffered because the feature of "drag and drop" was deleted in the final product. Conversely, the prototype of an experimental car exceeded the miles per gallon technical specification and, thus, its technical performance. Frequently tests are conducted on different performance dimensions. These tests become an integral part of the project schedule.

It is very difficult to specify how to measure technical performance because it depends on the nature of the project. Suffice it to say, measuring technical performance must be done. Technical performance is frequently where quality control processes are needed and used. Project managers must be creative in finding ways to control this very important area.

Software for Project Cost/Schedule Systems

Software developers have created sophisticated schedule/cost systems for projects that track and report budget, actual, earned, committed, and index values. These values can be labor hours, materials, and/or dollars. This information supports cost and schedule progress, performance measurements, and cash flow management. Recall from Chapter 5 that budget, actual, and committed dollars usually run in different time frames (see Figure 5.6). A typical computer-generated status report includes the following information outputs:

1. Schedule variance (EV − PV) by cost account and WBS and OBS.
2. Cost variance (EV − AC) by cost account and WBS and OBS.
3. Indexes—total percent complete and performance index.
4. Cumulative actual total cost to date (AC).
5. Expected costs at completion (EAC).
6. Paid and unpaid commitments.

The variety of software packages, with their features and constant updating, is too extensive for inclusion in this text. Software developers and vendors have done a superb job of providing software to meet the information needs of most project managers. Differences among software in the last decade have centered on improving "friendliness" and output that is clear and easy to understand. Anyone who understands the concepts and tools presented in Chapters 4, 5, 6, 8, and 13 should have little trouble understanding the output of any of the popular project management software packages.

Additional Earned Value Rules

Although the percent complete rule is the most-used method of assigning budgets to baselines and for cost control, there are additional rules that are very useful for reducing the overhead costs of collecting detailed data on percent complete of individual work packages. (An additional advantage of these rules, of course, is that they remove the often subjective judgments of the contractors or estimators as to how much work has actually been completed.) The first two rules are typically used for short-duration activities and/or small-cost activities. The third rule uses gates before the total budgeted value of an activity can be claimed.

- **0/100 rule.** This rule assumes credit is earned for having performed the work once it is completed. Hence, 100 percent of the budget is earned when the work package is completed. This rule is used for work packages having very short durations.
- **50/50 rule.** This approach allows 50 percent of the value of the work package budget to be earned when it is started and 50 percent to be earned when the package is completed. This rule is popular for work packages of short duration and small total costs.
- **Percent complete with weighted monitoring gates.** This more recent rule uses subjective estimated percent complete in combination with hard, tangible monitoring points. This method works well on long-duration activities that can be broken into short, discrete work packages of no more than one or two report periods. These discrete packages limit the subjective estimated values. For example, assume a long-duration activity with a total budget of $500. The activity is cut into three sequentially discrete packages with monitoring gates representing 30, 50, and 100 percent of the total budget. The earned amount at each monitoring gate cannot exceed $150, $250, and $500. These hard monitoring points serve as a check on overly optimistic estimates.

Notice the only information needed for the first two rules is that the work package has started and the package has been completed. For those who wish to explore the application of these two rules, or who are studying for certification, Appendix 13.1 presents two exercises that apply these rules along with the percent complete rule.

The third rule is frequently used to authorize progress payments to contractors. This rule supports careful tracking and control of payments; it discourages payment to contractors for work not yet completed. (See Fleming and Koppelman for an excellent discussion of applying earned value rules.)

Forecasting Final Project Cost

There are basically two methods used to revise estimates of future project costs. In many cases both methods are used on specific segments of the project. The result is confusion of terms in texts, in software, and among practitioners in the field. We have chosen to note the differences between the methods.

The first method allows experts in the field to change original baseline durations and costs because new information tells them the original estimates are not accurate. We have used EAC_{re} to represent revisions made by experts and practitioners associated with the project. The revisions from project experts are almost always used on smaller projects.

The equation for calculating revised estimated cost at completion (EAC_{re}) is as follows:

$$EAC_{re} = AC + ETC_{re}$$

where EAC_{re} = revised estimated cost at completion.
        AC = cumulative actual cost of work completed to date.
        ETC_{re} = revised estimated cost to complete remaining work.

A second method is used in large projects where the original budget is less reliable. This method uses the actual costs to date plus an efficiency index ($CPI = EV/AC$) applied to the remaining project work. When the estimate for completion uses the CPI as the basis for forecasting cost at completion, we use the acronym EAC_f. The equation is presented here.

The equation for this forecasting model (EAC_f) is as follows:

$$EAC_f = ETC + AC$$

$$ETC = \frac{\text{Work remaining}}{CPI} = \frac{BAC - EV}{EV/AC}$$

where EAC_f = estimated total cost at completion.
   ETC = estimated cost to complete remaining work.
   AC = cumulative actual cost of work completed to date.
   CPI = cumulative cost index to date.
   BAC = total budget of the baseline.
   EV = cumulative budgeted cost of work completed to date.

The following information is available from our earlier example; the estimate cost at completion (EAC_f) is computed as follows:

Total baseline budget (BAC) for the project	$320
Cumulative earned value (EV) to date	$160
Cumulative actual cost (AC) to date	$230

$$EAC_f = \frac{320 - 160}{160/230} + 230 = \frac{160}{.7} + 230 = 229 + 230$$

$$EAC_f = 459$$

The final project projected cost forecast is $459,000 versus $320,000 originally planned.

Another popular index is the To Complete Performance Index (TCPI), which is useful as a supplement to the estimate at complete (EAC_f) computation. This ratio measures the amount of value each *remaining* dollar in the budget must earn to stay within the budget. The index is computed for the Digital Camera project at the end of period 7.

$$TCPI = \frac{BAC - EV}{BAC - AC} = \frac{320 - 160}{320 - 230} = \frac{160}{90} = 1.78$$

The index of 1.78 indicates that each remaining dollar in the budget must earn $1.78 in value. There is more work to be done than there is budget left. Clearly, it would be tough to increase productivity that much to make budget. The work to be done will have to be reduced or you will have to accept running over budget. If the TCPI is less than 1.00, you should be able to complete the project without using all of the remaining budget. A ratio of less than 1.00 opens the possibility of other opportunities such as improving quality, increasing profit, or expanding scope.

Research data indicate that on large projects that are more than 15 percent complete, the model performs well with an error of less than 10 percent. This model can also be used for WBS and OBS cost accounts that have been used to forecast remaining and total costs. It is important to note that this model assumes conditions will not change, the cost database is reliable, EV and AC are cumulative, and past project progress is representative of future progress. This objective forecast represents a good starting point or benchmark that management can use to compare other forecasts that include other conditions and subjective judgments.

Exhibit 13.1 presents an abridged monthly status report similar to one used by a project organization. The form is used for all projects in their project portfolio. (Note that the schedule variance of −$22,176 does not translate directly to days. The 25 days were derived from the network schedule.)

EXHIBIT 13.1 Monthly Status Report

Project number: 163   **Project manager:** Connor Gage
Project priority now: 4
Status as of: April 1, 2007
Earned value figures:

PV	EV	AC	SV	CV	BAC
588,240	566,064	596,800	−22,176	−30,736	1,051,200
EAC	**VAC**	**EAC$_f$**	**CPI**	**PCIB**	**PCIC**
1,090,640	−39,440	1,107,469	.95	.538	.547

Project description: A computer-controlled conveyor belt that will move and position items on the belt with accuracy of less than one millimeter.

Status summary: The project is approximately 25 days behind schedule. The project has a cost variance of ($30,736).

Explanations: The schedule variance has moved from noncritical activities to those on the critical path. Integration first phase, scheduled to start 3/26, is now expected to start 4/19, which means it is approximately 25 days behind schedule. This delay is traced to the loss of the second design team which made it impossible to start utilities documentation on 2/27 as planned. This loss illustrates the effect of losing valuable resources on the project. The cost variance to date is largely due to a design change that cost $21,000.

Major changes since last report: The major change was loss of one design team to the project.

Total cost of approved design changes: $21,000. Most of this amount is attributed to the improved design of the serial I/O drivers.

Projected cost at completion: EAC$_f$ is estimated to be $1,107,469. This represents an overrun of −$56,269, given a CPI of .95. The CPI of .95 causes the forecast to be greater than the VAC −$39,440.

Risk watch: Nothing suggests the risk level of any segments has changed.

Another summary report is shown in the Snapshot from Practice: Trojan Decommissioning Project. Compare the differences in format.

Other Control Issues

Scope Creep

Large changes in scope are easily identified. It is the "minor refinements" that eventually build to be major scope changes that can cause problems. These small refinements are known in the field as *scope creep*. For example, the customer of a software developer requested small changes in the development of a custom accounting software package. After several minor refinements, it became apparent the changes represented a significant enlargement of the original project scope. The result was an unhappy customer and a development firm that lost money and reputation.

Although scope changes are usually viewed negatively, there are situations when scope changes result in positive rewards. Scope changes can represent significant opportunities. In product development environments, adding a small feature to a product can result in a huge competitive advantage. A small change in the production process may get the product to market one month early or reduce product cost.

Snapshot from Practice   Trojan Decommissioning Project

Brendan McDermid/EPA/Landov.

Portland General Electric Company has been charged with decommissioning the Trojan Nuclear Plant. This is a long and complex project extending over two decades. The first segment of the project of moving the used reactors to a storage location is complete and was awarded the Project of the Year, 2000, by the Project Management Institute (PMI). The remainder of the project—decontamination of the remaining structures and waste—is ongoing.

The figure on page 442 shows their earned value status report through December 2000. This report measures schedule and cost performance for monitoring the project. The report also serves as a basis for funding for rate filings with the Public Utilities Commission.

The SPI (0.94) suggests the project schedule is falling behind. Resolving issues with a major vendor and solutions for technical problems should solve these delay problems. The CPI (1.14) for the project is positive. Some of this good cost performance is attributed to partnering and incentive arrangements with vendors and labor unions.

Interview with Michael B. Lackey, general manager, Trojan, PGE (September 2001).

Scope creep is common early in projects—especially in new-product development projects. Customer requirements for additional features, new technology, poor design assumptions, etc., all manifest pressures for scope changes. Frequently these changes are small and go unnoticed until time delays or cost overruns are observed. Scope creep affects the organization, project team, and project suppliers. Scope changes alter the organization's cash flow requirements in the form of fewer or additional resources, which may also affect other projects. Frequent changes eventually wear down team motivation and cohesiveness. Clear team goals are altered, become less focused, and cease being the focal point for team action. Starting over again is annoying and demoralizing to the project team because it disrupts project rhythm and lowers productivity. Project suppliers resent frequent changes because they represent higher costs and have the same effect on their team as on the project team.

The key to managing scope creep is change management. One project manager of an architectural firm related that scope creep was the biggest risk his firm faced in projects. The best defense against scope creep is a well-defined scope statement. Poor scope statements are one of the major causes of scope creep.

A second defense against scope creep is stating what the project is not, which can avoid misinterpretations later. (Chapter 7 discusses the process. See Figure 7.9 to review key variables to document in project changes.) First, the original baseline must be well defined and agreed upon with the project customer. Before the project begins, it is imperative that clear procedures be in place for authorizing and documenting scope changes by the customer or project team. If a scope change is necessary, the impact on the baseline should be clearly documented—for example, cost, time, dependencies, specifications, responsibilities, etc. Finally, the scope change must be quickly added to the original baseline to reflect the change in budget and schedule; these changes and their impacts need to be communicated to all project stakeholders.

Baseline Changes

Changes during the life cycle of projects are inevitable and will occur. Some changes can be very beneficial to project outcomes; changes having a negative impact are the ones we wish to avoid. Careful project definition can minimize the need for changes. The price for poor project definition can be changes that result in cost overruns, late schedules, low morale, and loss of control. Change comes from external sources or from within. Externally, for example, the customer may request changes that were not included in the original scope statement and that will require significant changes to the project and thus to the baseline. Or the government may render requirements that were not a part of the original plan and that require a revision of the project scope. Internally, stakeholders may identify unforeseen problems or improvements that change the scope of the project. In rare cases scope changes can come from several sources. For example, the Denver International Airport automatic baggage handling system was an afterthought supported by several project stakeholders that included the Denver city government, consultants, and at least one airline customer. The additional $2 billion in costs were staggering, and the airport opening was delayed 16 months. If this automatic baggage scope change had been in the original plan, costs would have been only a fraction of the overrun costs, and delays would have been reduced significantly. Any changes in scope or the baseline should be recorded by the change control system that was set in place during risk control planning. (See Chapter 7.)

Generally, project managers monitor scope changes very carefully. They should allow scope changes only if it is clear that the project will fail without the change, the project will be improved significantly with the change, or the customer wants it and will pay for it. This statement is an exaggeration, but it sets the tone for approaching baseline changes. The effect of the change on the scope and baseline should be accepted and signed off by the project customer. Figure 13.13 depicts the cost impact of a scope change on the baseline at a point in time—"today." Line A represents a scope change that results in an increase in cost. Line B represents a scope change that decreases cost. Quickly recording scope changes to the baseline keeps the computed earned values valid. Failure to do so results in misleading cost and schedule variances.

Care should be taken to not use baseline changes to disguise poor performance on past or current work. A common signal of this type of baseline change is a constantly revised baseline that seems to match results. Practitioners call this a "rubber baseline" because it stretches to match results. Most changes will not result in serious scope changes and should be absorbed as positive or negative variances. Retroactive changes for work already accomplished should not be allowed. Transfer of money among cost accounts should not be allowed after the work is complete. Unforeseen changes can be handled through the contingency reserve. The project manager typically makes this decision. In some large projects, a partnering "change review team," made up of members of the project and customer teams, makes all decisions on project changes.

Cost/Budget Performance				Decommissioning Cumulative Costs				Nominal Year Dollars		
Portland General Electric Co.-Trojan Nuclear Plant				Report Run: 23-Jan-01 8:13 A.M.		Report Number: DECT005			Page :	1 of 1
	Dec 2000			Year-to-Date			YTD	2000	CPI	SPI
Description	PV	EV	AC	PV	EV	AC	Variance EV-AC	PV	EV/AC	EV/PV
ISFSI	193,014	182,573	162,579	3,655,677	3,586,411	3,263,995	322,416	3,655,677	1.10	0.98
RVAIR	0	0	0	0	0	399	(399)	0	0.00	0.00
Equip removal—AB/FB	79,083	79,649	73,899	497,197	504,975	308,461	196,514	497,197	1.64	1.02
Equip removal—other	0	0	0	0	(36,822)	519	(37,341)	0	0.00	0.00
Embed piping—AB/FB	3,884	0	2,118	532,275	540,232	515,235	24,997	532,275	1.05	1.01
Embed piping—other	0	0	3,439	175,401	210,875	79,235	131,640	175,401	2.66	1.20
Surface decon—AB/FB	29,935	23,274	21,456	1,266,685	1,293,315	1,171,712	121,603	1,266,665	1.10	1.02
Surface decon—other	2,875	2	11,005	308,085	199,853	251,265	(51,412)	308,085	0.80	0.65
Surface decon—containment	680,502	435,657	474,427	5,271,889	4,950,528	4,823,338	127,190	5,271,889	1.03	0.94
Radwaste disposal	884,873	453,032	(28,675)	10,680,118	8,276,616	10,807,916	(2,531,300)	10,880,118	0.77	0.77
Final survey	58,238	57,985	27,091	780,990	780,990	700,942	80,048	780,990	1.11	1.00
Nonradiological areas	92,837	91,956	58,538	2,471,281	2,376,123	834,643	1,541,480	2,471,281	2.85	0.96
Staffing	714,806	714,509	468,858	9,947,775	9,947,775	8,241,383	1,706,392	9,947,775	1.21	1.00
ISFSI—Long-term ops	85,026	85,028	19,173	2,004,398	2,004,398	337,206	1,667,192	2,004,398	5.94	1.00
Labor loadings	258,289	258,289	240,229	3,216,194	3,216,194	2,755,604	460,590	3,216,194	1.17	1.00
Material loadings	17,910	17,910	(95,128)	211,454	211,454	136,973	74,481	211,454	1.54	1.00
Corporate governance	153,689	228,499	228,521	1,814,523	1,814,523	1,814,520	3	1,814,523	1.00	1.00
Undistributable costs	431,840	401,720	242,724	5,541,679	5,575,879	4,007,732	1,567,947	5,541,679	1.39	1.01
Total decommissioning	3,688,081	3,008,081	1,905,084	48,375,399	45,453,119	40,051,079	5,402,040	48,375,399	1.13	0.94
Total (less ISFSI and RVAIR)	3,493,467	2,845,508	1,743,485	44,719,720	41,886,710	36,788,680	5,080,024	44,719,720	1.14	0.94

The Costs and Problems of Data Acquisition

Data acquisition is time consuming and costly. The Snapshot from Practice: A Pseudo-Earned Value Percent Complete Approach captures some of the frequent issues surrounding resistance to data collection of percent complete for earned value systems. Similar pseudo-percent complete systems have been used by others. Such pseudo-percent complete approaches appear to work well in multiproject environments that include several small and medium-sized projects. Assuming a one-week reporting period, care needs to be taken to develop work packages with a duration of about one week long so problems are identified quickly. For large projects, there is no substitute for using a percent complete system that depends on data collected through observation at clearly defined monitoring points.

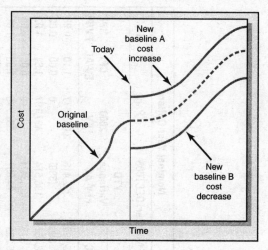

FIGURE 13.13   Scope Changes to a Baseline

In some cases data exist but are not sent to the stakeholders who need information relating to project progress. Clearly, if the information does not reach the right people in a timely manner, you can expect serious problems. Your communication plan developed in the project planning stage can greatly mitigate this problem by mapping out the flow of information and keeping stakeholders informed on all aspects of project progress and issues. See Figure 13.14 for an internal communication plan for a WiFi Project. The information developed in this chapter contributes significant data to support your communication plan and ensures correct dissemination of the data.

What Information	When?	Mode?	Responsible?	Recipient?
Milestone report	Bimonthly	E-mail	Project office	Senior management
Time/cost report	Weekly	E-mail	Project office	Staff and customer
Risk report	Weekly	E-mail	Project office	Staff and customer
Issues	Weekly	E-mail	Anyone	Staff and customer
Team meeting times	Weekly	Meeting	Project manager	Staff and customer
Outsourcing performance	Bimonthly	Meeting	Project manager	Project office, staff, and customer
Change requests	Anytime	Document	Project manager, customer, design	Project office, staff, and customer
Stage gate decisions	Monthly	Meeting	Project office	Senior management

FIGURE 13.14   Conference Center WiFi Project Communication Plan

Snapshot from Practice A Pseudo-Earned Value Percent Complete Approach

A consultant for the U.S. Forest Service suggested the use of earned value to monitor the 50-plus timber sale projects taking place concurrently in the district. As projects were completed, new ones were started. Earned value was tried for approximately nine months. After a nine-month trial, the process was to be reviewed by a task force. The task force concluded the earned value system provided good information for monitoring and forecasting project progress; however, the costs and problems of collecting timely percent complete data were unacceptable because there were no funds available to collect such data.

The level of detail dilemma was discussed, but no suggestions satisfied the problem. The discussion recognized that too little data fail to offer good control, while excessive reporting requires paperwork and people, which are costly. The task force concluded progress and performance could be measured using a pseudo-version of percent complete while not giving up much accuracy for the total project. This modified approach to percent complete required that very large work packages (about 3 to 5 percent of all work packages in a project) be divided into smaller work packages for closer control and identification of problems sooner. It was decided work packages of about a week's duration would be ideal. The pseudo-version required only a telephone call and "yes/no" answers to one of the following questions to assign percent complete:

Has work on the work package started?	No = 0%
Working on the package?	Yes = 50%
Is the work package completed?	Yes = 100%

Data for the pseudo-earned value percent complete system was collected for all 50-plus projects by an intern working fewer than eight hours each week.

Summary

The best information system does not result in good control. Control requires the project manager to *use* information to steer the project through rough waters. Control and Gantt charts are useful vehicles for monitoring time performance. The cost/schedule system allows the manager to have a positive influence on cost and schedule in a timely manner. The ability to influence cost decreases with time; therefore, timely reports identifying adverse cost trends can greatly assist the project manager in getting back on budget and schedule. The integrated cost/schedule model provides the project manager and other stakeholders with a snapshot of the current and future status of the project. The benefits of the cost/schedule model are as follows:

1. Measures accomplishments against plan and deliverables.
2. Provides a method for tracking directly to a problem work package and organization unit responsible.
3. Alerts all stakeholders to early identification of problems, and allows for quick, proactive corrective action.
4. Improves communication because all stakeholders are using the same database.
5. Keeps customer informed of progress, and encourages customer confidence that the money spent is resulting in the expected progress.
6. Provides for accountability over individual portions of the overall budget for each organizational unit.

With your information system in place, you need to use your communication plan to keep stakeholders informed so timely decisions can be made to ensure the project is managed effectively.

Key Terms

Baseline budget

Control chart

Cost performance index (CPI)

Cost variance (CV)

Earned value (EV)

Estimated cost at completion (EAC)

Percent complete index

Schedule performance index (SPI)

Schedule variance (SV)

Scope creep

To complete performace index (TCPI)

Tracking Gantt chart

Variance at completion (VAC)

Review Questions

1. How does a Tracking Gantt chart help communicate project progress?

2. How does earned value give a clearer picture of project schedule and cost status than a simple plan versus actual system?

3. Schedule variance (SV) is in dollars and does not directly represent time. Why is it still useful?

4. How would a project manager use the CPI?

5. What are the differences between BAC and EAC?

6. Why is it important for project managers to resist changes to the project baseline? Under what conditions would a project manager make changes to a baseline? When would a project manager not allow changes to a baseline?

Exercises

1. In month 9 the following project information is available: actual cost is $2,000, earned value is $2,100, and planned cost is $2,400. Compute the SV and CV for the project.

2. On day 51 a project has an earned value of $600, an actual cost of $650, and a planned cost of $560. Compute the SV, CV, and CPI for the project. What is your assessment of the project on day 51?

3. Given the project network and baseline information below, complete the form to develop a status report for the project at the end of period 4 and the end of period 8. From the data you have collected and computed for periods 4 and 8, what information are you prepared to tell the customer about the status of the project at the end of period 8?

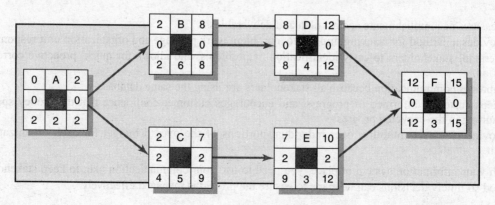

Task	Dur.	ES	LF	Slack	Budget (PV)	0	1	2	3	4	5	6	7	8	9	10	11	12	13	14
A	2	0	2	0	400	200	200													
B	6	2	8	0	2400			200	600	200	600	200	600							
C	5	2	9	2	1500			200	400	500	100	300								
D	4	8	12	0	1600									400	400	400	400			
E	3	7	12	2	900								300	400	200					
F	3	12	15	0	600													200	100	300
Period PV total						200	200	400	1000	700	700	500	900	800	600	400	400	200	100	300
Cumulative PV total						200	400	800	1800	2500	3200	3700	4600	5400	6000	6400	6800	7000	7100	7400

Project baseline (PV) (in $)

End of Peroid 4

Task	Actual % Complete	EV	AC	PV	CV	SV
A	Finished	—	300	400	—	—
B	50%	—	1000	800	—	—
C	33%	—	500	600	—	—
D	0	—	0	—	—	—
E	0	—	0	—	—	—
Cumulative Totals		—	—	—	—	—

End of Peroid 8

Task	Actual % Complete	EV	AC	PV	CV	SV
A	Finished	—	300	400	—	—
B	Finished	—	2200	2400	—	—
C	Finished	—	1500	1500	—	—
D	25%	—	300	0	—	—
E	33%	—	300	—	—	—
F	0	—	0	—	—	—
Cumulative Totals		—	—	—	—	—

4. Given the following project network, baseline, and status information, develop status reports for periods 1–4 and complete the project summary graph (or a similar one). Report the final SV, CV, CPI, and PCIB. Based on your data, what is your assessment of the current status of the project? At completion?

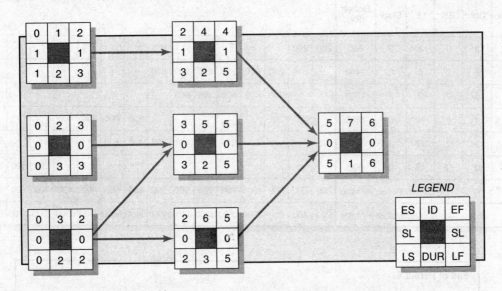

	Schedule information					Baseline budget needs ($ 000)						
ACT/ WP	DUR	ES	LF	SL	Total PV	Time period						
						0	1	2	3	4	5	6
1	2	0	3	1	12	4	8					
2	3	0	3	0	15	3	7	5				
3	2	0	2	0	8	4	4					
4	2	2	5	1	6			3	3			
5	2	3	5	0	10				6	4		
6	3	2	5	0	9			3	3	3		
7	1	5	6	0	5							5
		Total PV by period				11	19	11	12	7	5	
		Cumulative PV by period				11	30	41	53	60	65	

Status Report: Ending Period 1

Task	%Complete	EV	AC	PV	CV	SV
1	50%	——	6	4	——	——
2	40%	——	8	3	——	——
3	25%	——	3	——	——	——
Cumulative Totals		——	17	——	——	——

Status Report: Ending Period 2

Task	%Complete	EV	AC	PV	CV	SV
1	Finished	——	13	——	——	——
2	80%	——	14	——	——	——
3	75%	——	8	——	——	——
Cumulative Totals		——	35	——	——	——

Status Report: Ending Period 3

Task	%Complete	EV	AC	PV	CV	SV
1	Finished	12	13	——	——	——
2	80%	——	15	——	——	——
3	Finished	——	10	——	——	——
4	50%	——	4	——	——	——
5	0%	——	0	——	——	——
6	33.3%	——	4	——	——	——
Cumulative Totals		——	——	——	——	——

Status Report: Ending Period 4

Task	%Complete	EV	AC	PV	CV	SV
1	Finished	12	13	——	——	——
2	Finished	15	18	——	——	——
3	Finished	——	10	——	——	——
4	Finished	——	8	——	——	——
5	30%	——	3	——	——	——
6	66.7%	——	8	——	——	——
7	0%	——	0	——	——	——
Cumulative Totals		——	——	——	——	——

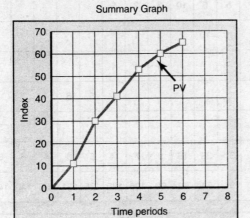

Summary Graph

5. The following labor hours data have been collected for a nanotechnology project for periods 1 through 6. Compute the SV, CV, SPI, and CPI for each period. Plot the EV and the AC on the summary graph provided (or a similar one). Plot the SPI, CPI, and PCIB on the index graph provided (or a similar one). What is your assessment of the project at the end of period 6?

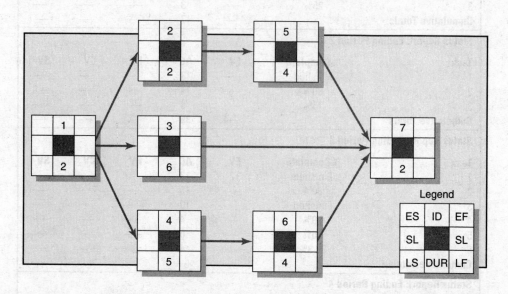

		Schedule information				Baseline budget needs–labor hours (00)														
ACT/ WP	DUR	ES	LF	SL	Total PV	Time period														
						0	1	2	3	4	5	6	7	8	9	10	11	12	13	14
1	2	0	2	0	20	10	10													
2	2	2	7	3	24			16	8											
3	6	2	11	3	30			5	5	10	3	2	5							
4	5	2	7	0	25			10	10	2	2	1								
5	4	4	11	3	16					4	4	4	4							
6	4	7	11	0	20								5	5	6	4				
7	2	11	13	0	10													5	5	
Total PV by period						10	10	31	23	16	9	7	14	5	6	4	5	5		
Cumulative PV by period						10	20	51	74	90	99	106	120	125	131	135	140	145		

Status Report: Ending Period 1

Task	%Complete	EV	AC	PV	CV	SV
1	50%	—	500	1000	—	—
Cumulative Totals		—	**500**	**1000**	—	—

Status Report: Ending Period 2

Task	%Complete	EV	AC	PV	CV	SV
1	Finished	—	1500	2000	—	—
Cumulative totals		—	**1500**	**2000**	—	—

Status Report: Ending Period 3

Task	%Complete	EV	AC	PV	CV	SV
1	Finished	2000	1500	2000	—	—
2	0%	—	0	—	—	—
3	10%	—	200	—	—	—
4	20%	—	500	—	—	—
Cumulative Totals		—	**2200**	—	—	—

Status Report: Ending Period 4

Task	%Complete	EV	AC	PV	CV	SV
1	Finished	2000	1500	2000	—	—
2	50%	—	1000	—	—	—
3	30%	—	800	—	—	—
4	40%	—	1500	—	—	—
Cumulative Totals		—	**4800**	—	—	—

Status Report: Ending Period 5

Task	%Complete	EV	AC	PV	CV	SV
1	Finished	2000	1500	2000	—	—
2	Finished	—	2000	—	—	—
3	50%	—	800	—	—	—
4	60%	—	1500	—	—	—
5	25%	—	400	—	—	—
Cumulative Totals		—	**6200**	—	—	—

Status Report: Ending Period 6

Task	%Complete	EV	AC	PV	CV	SV
1	Finished	2000	1500	2000	—	—
2	Finished	—	2000	—	—	—
3	80%	—	2100	—	—	—
4	80%	—	1800	—	—	—
5	50%	—	600	—	—	—
Cumulative Totals		—	**8000**	—	—	—

Period	SPI	CPI	PCIB
1	—	—	—
2	—	—	—
3	—	—	—
4	—	—	—
5	—	—	—
6	—	—	—

SPI = EV/PV
CPI = EV/AC
PCIB = EV/BAC

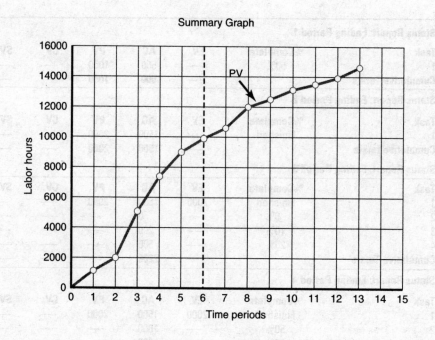

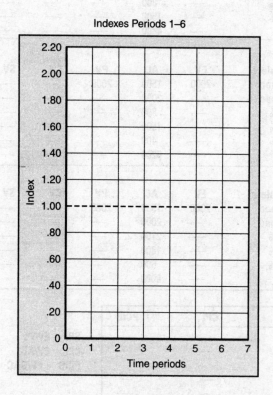

6. The following data have been collected for a British health care IT project for two-week reporting periods 2 through 12. Compute the SV, CV, SPI, and CPI for each period. Plot the EV and the AC on the summary graph provided. Plot the SPI, CPI, and PCIB on the index graph provided. (You may use your own graphs.) What is your assessment of the project at the end of period 12?

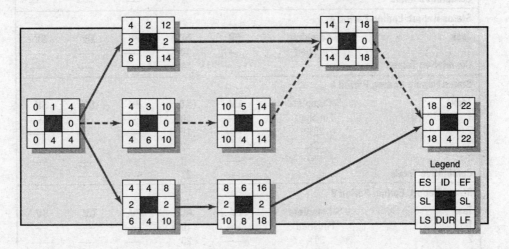

				Baseline (PV) ($00)												
Task	Dur.	ES	LF	Slack	PV ($00)	0	2	4	6	8	10	12	14	16	18	20	22
1	4	0	4	0	8	4	4										
2	8	4	14	2	40			10	10	10	10						
3	6	4	10	0	30			10	15	5							
4	4	4	10	2	20			10	10								
5	4	10	14	0	40							20	20				
6	8	8	18	2	60						20	20	10	10			
7	4	14	18	0	20									10	10		
8	4	18	22	0	30											20	10
			Period PV total			4	4	30	35	35	50	30	20	10	20	10
			Cumulative PV total			4	8	38	73	108	158	188	208	218	238	248

Status Report: Ending Period 2

Task	%Complete	EV	AC	PV	CV	SV
1	50%	—	4	—	—	—
Cumulative totals		—	4	—	—	—

Status Report: Ending Period 4

Task	%Complete	EV	AC	PV	CV	SV
1	Finished	—	10	—	—	—
Cumulative Totals		—	10	—	—	—

Status Report: Ending Period 6

Task	%Complete	EV	AC	PV	CV	SV
1	Finished	—	10	—	—	—
2	25%	—	15	—	—	—
3	33%	—	12	—	—	—
4	0%	—	0	—	—	—
Cumulative Totals		—	37	—	—	—

Status Report: Ending Period 8

Task	%Complete	EV	AC	PV	CV	SV
1	Finished	—	10	—	—	—
2	30%	—	20	—	—	—
3	60%	—	25	—	—	—
4	0%	—	0	—	—	—
Cumulative Totals		—	55	—	—	—

Status Report: Ending Period 10

Task	%Complete	EV	AC	PV	CV	SV
1	Finished	—	10	—	—	—
2	60%	—	30	—	—	—
3	Finished	—	40	—	—	—
4	50%	—	20	—	—	—
5	0%	—	0	—	—	—
6	30%	—	24	—	—	—
Cumulative Totals		—	124	—	—	—

Status Report: Ending Period 12

Task	%Complete	EV	AC	PV	CV	SV
1	Finished	—	10	—	—	—
2	Finished	—	50	—	—	—
3	Finished	—	40	—	—	—
4	Finished	—	40	—	—	—
5	50%	—	30	—	—	—
6	50%	—	40	—	—	—
Cumulative Totals		—	210	—	—	—

Period	SPI	CPI	PCIB
2	—	—	—
4	—	—	—
6	—	—	—
8	—	—	—
10	—	—	—
12	—	—	—

SPI = EV/PV
CPI = EV/AC
PCIB = EV/BAC

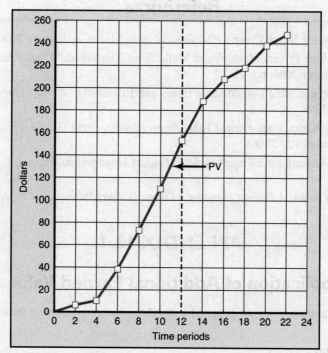

Summary Graph

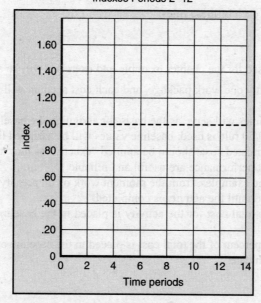

Indexes Periods 2–12

References

Abramovici, A. "Controlling Scope Creep," *PM Network,* Vol. 14, No. 1, January 2000, pp. 44–48.

Anbari, F. T., "Earned Value Project Management Method and Extensions," *Project Management Journal,* Vol. 34, No. 4, December 2003, pp. 12–22.

Brandon, D. M. Jr., "Implementing Earned Value Easily and Effectively," *Project Management Journal,* Vol. 29, No. 3, June 1998, pp. 11–17.

Fleming, Q. and Joel M. Koppelman, *Earned Value Project Management,* 3rd ed. (Project Management Institute, Newton Square, PA, 2006).

Kerzner, H. "Strategic Planning for a Project Office," *Project Management Journal,* Vol. 34, No. 2, June 2003, pp. 13–25.

Webb, A. *Using Earned Value: A Project Manager's Guide,* (Gower Publishing Co., Aldershot, UK, 2003).

APPENDIX 13.1

The Application of Additional Earned Value Rules

The following example and exercises are designed to provide practice in applying the following three earned value rules:

- Percent complete rule
- 0/100 rule
- 50/50 rule

See the chapter for an explanation of each of these rules.

Simplifying Assumptions

The same simplifying assumptions used for the chapter example and exercises will be also used here.

1. Assume each cost account has only one work package, and each cost account will be represented as an activity on the network.
2. The project network early start times will serve as the basis for assigning the baseline values.
3. Except when the 0/100 rule or 50/50 rule is used, baseline values will be assigned linearly, unless stated differently. (Note: In practice estimated costs should be applied "exactly" as they are expected to occur so measures of schedule and cost performance are useful and reliable.)
4. For purposes of demonstrating the examples, from the moment work on an activity begins, some actual costs will be incurred each period until the activity is completed.
5. When the 0/100 rule is used, the total cost for the activity is placed in the baseline on the early finish date.
6. When the 50/50 rule is used, 50 percent of the total cost is placed in the baseline on the early start date and 50 percent on the early finish date.

Appendix Exercises

1. Given the information provided for development of a product warranty project for periods 1 through 7, compute the SV, CV, SPI, and CPI for each period. Plot the EV and the AC on the PV graph provided.

Explain to the owner your assessment of the project at the end of period 7 and the future expected status of the project at completion. Figure A13.1.1A presents the project network. Figure A13.1.1B presents the project baseline noting those activities using the 0/100 (rule 3) and 50/50 (rule 2) rules. For example, activity 1 uses rule 3, the 0/100 rule. Although the early start time is period 0, the budget is not placed in the time-phased baseline until period 2 when the activity is planned to be finished (EF). This same procedure has been used to assign costs for activities 2 and 7. Activities 2 and 7 use the 50/50 rule. Thus, 50 percent of the budget for each activity is assigned on its respective early start date (time period 2 for activity 2 and period 11 for activity 7) and 50 percent for their respective finish dates. Remember, when assigning earned value as the project is being implemented, if an activity actually starts early or late, the earned values must shift with the actual times. For example, if activity 7 actually starts in period 12 rather than 11, the 50 percent is not earned until period 12.

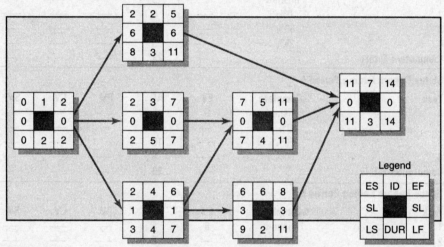

FIGURE A13.1.1A

EV Rule	ACT/ WP	DUR	ES	LF	SL	Total PV	0	1	2	3	4	5	6	7	8	9	10	11	12	13	14
Schedule information							**Baseline budget needs**														
											Time period									
③	1	2	0	2	0	6		6													
②	2	3	2	11	6	20			10		10										
①	3	5	2	7	0	30			9	6	6	6	3								
①	4	4	2	7	1	20			8	2	5	5									
①	5	4	7	11	0	16								4	4	4	4				
①	6	2	6	11	3	18								9	9						
②	7	3	11	14	0	8												4			4
Total PV by period							0	6	27	8	21	11	12	13	4	4	4	4	0		4
Cumulative PV by period							0	6	33	41	62	73	85	98	102	106	110	114	114		118

Rule
1 = %complete
2 = 50/50
3 = 0/100

FIGURE A13.1.1B

Status Report: Ending Period 1

Task	%Complete	EV	AC	PV	CV	SV
1	0%	—	3	0	—	—
Cumulative Totals		—	3	0		

Status Report: Ending Period 2

Task	%Complete	EV	AC	PV	CV	SV
1	Finished	6	5	—	—	—
Cumulative Totals		6	5			

Status Report: Ending Period 3

Task	%Complete	EV	AC	PV	CV	SV
1	Finished	6	5	—	—	—
2	0%	—	5	—	—	—
3	30%	—	7	—	—	—
4	25%	—	5	—	—	—
Cumulative Totals		—	22			

Status Report: Ending Period 4

Task	%Complete	EV	AC	PV	CV	SV
1	Finished	6	5	—	—	—
2	0%	—	7	—	—	—
3	50%	—	10	—	—	—
4	50%	—	8	—	—	—
Cumulative Totals		—	30			

Status Report: Ending Period 5

Task	%Complete	EV	AC	PV	CV	SV
1	Finished	6	5	—	—	—
2	50%	—	8	—	—	—
3	60%	—	12	—	—	—
4	70%	—	10	—	—	—
Cumulative Totals		—	35			

Status Report: Ending Period 6

Task	%Complete	EV	AC	PV	CV	SV
1	Finished	6	5	—	—	—
2	50%	—	10	—	—	—
3	80%	—	16	—	—	—
4	Finished	—	15	—	—	—
Cumulative Totals		—	46			

Status Report: Ending Period 7

Task	%Complete	EV	AC	PV	CV	SV
1	Finished	6	5	—	—	—
2	Finished	—	14	—	—	—
3	Finished	—	20	—	—	—
4	Finished	—	15	—	—	—
5	0%	—	0	—	—	—
6	50%	—	9	—	—	—
Cumulative Totals		—	63			

Period	SPI	CPI	PCIB
1	—	—	—
2	—	—	—
3	—	—	—
4	—	—	—
5	—	—	—
6	—	—	—
7	—	—	—

SPI = EV/PV
CPI = EV/AC
PCIB = EV/BAC

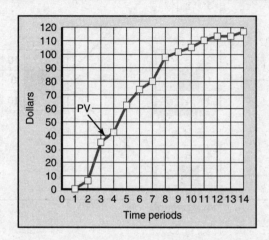

FIGURE A13.1.1C

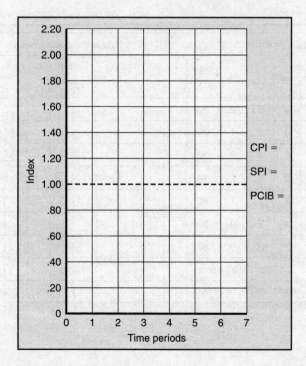

CPI =

SPI =

PCIB =

FIGURE A13.1.1D

2. Given the information provided for development of a catalog product return process for periods 1 through 5, assign the PV values (using the rules) to develop a baseline for the project. Compute the SV, CV, SPI, and CPI for each period. Explain to the owner your assessment of the project at the end of period 5 and the future expected status of the project at the completion.

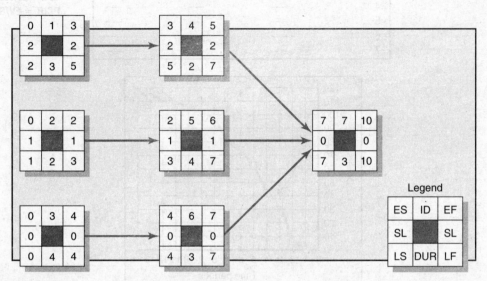

FIGURE A13.1.2A

Schedule information							Baseline budget needs											
EV Rule	ACT/ WP	DUR	ES	LF	SL	Total PV	Time period											
							0	1	2	3	4	5	6	7	8	9	10	
②	1	3	0	5	2	30												
③	2	2	0	3	1	20												
②	3	4	0	4	0	30												
③	4	2	3	7	2	10												
②	5	4	2	7	1	40												
①	6	3	4	7	0	30												
①	7	3	7	10	0	60												
Total PV by period																		
Cumulative PV by period																		

Rule
1 = %complete
2 = 50/50
3 = 0/100

FIGURE A13.1.2B

Status Report: Ending Period 1

Task	%Complete	EV	AC	PV	CV	SV
1	40%	—	8	—	—	—
2	0%	—	12	—	—	—
3	30%	—	10	—	—	—
Cumulative Totals		—	30	—	—	—

Status Report: Ending Period 2

Task	%Complete	EV	AC	PV	CV	SV
1	80%	—	20	—	—	—
2	Finished	—	18	—	—	—
3	50%	—	12	—	—	—
Cumulative Totals		—	50	—	—	—

Status Report: Ending Period 3

Task	%Complete	EV	AC	PV	CV	SV
1	Finished	—	27	—	—	—
2	Finished	—	18	—	—	—
3	70%	—	15	—	—	—
4	0%	—	5	—	—	—
5	30%	—	8	—	—	—
Cumulative Totals		—	73	—	—	—

Status Report: Ending Period 4

Task	%Complete	EV	AC	PV	CV	SV
1	Finished	—	27	—	—	—
2	Finished	—	18	—	—	—
3	Finished	—	22	—	—	—
4	0%	—	7	—	—	—
5	60%	—	22	—	—	—
Cumulative Totals		—	96	—	—	—

Status Report: Ending Period 5

Task	%Complete	EV	AC	PV	CV	SV
1	Finished	—	27	—	—	—
2	Finished	—	18	—	—	—
3	Finished	—	22	—	—	—
4	Finished	—	8	—	—	—
5	70%	—	24	—	—	—
6	30%	—	10	—	—	—
Cumulative Totals		—	109	—	—	—

Period	SPI	CPI	PCIB
1	—	—	—
2	—	—	—
3	—	—	—
4	—	—	—
5	—	—	—

SPI = EV/PV
CPI = EV/AC
PCIB = EV/BAC

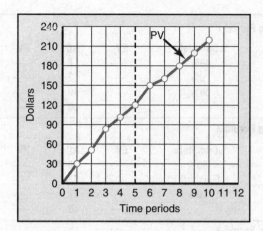

Figure A13.1.2C

APPENDIX 13.2

Obtaining Project Performance Information from MS Project

The objective of this appendix is to illustrate how one can obtain the performance information discussed in Chapter 13 from MS Project. One of the great strengths of MS Project is its flexibility. The software provides numerous options for entering, calculating, and presenting project information. Flexibility is also the software's greatest weakness in that there are so many options that working with the software can be frustrating and confusing. The intent here is to keep it simple and present basic steps for obtaining performance information. Students with more ambitious agendas are advised to work with the software tutorial or consult one of many instructional books on the market.

For purposes of this exercise we will use the Digital Camera project, which was introduced in Chapter 13. In this scenario the project started as planned on March 1 and today's date is March 7. We have received the following information on the work completed to date:

Design Spec.s took 2 days to complete at a total cost of $20.

Shell & Power took 3 days to complete at a total cost of $25.

Memory/Software is in progress with 4 days completed and two days remaining. Cost to date is $100.

Zoom System took 2 days to complete at a cost of $25.

All tasks started on time.

Step 1 Entering Progress Information

We enter this progress information in the TRACKING TABLE from the GANTT CHART VIEW ▶ TABLE:

TABLE A13.2A   Tracking Table

ID	Task Name	Act. Start	Act. Finish	% Comp.	Act. Dur.	Rem. Dur.	Act. Cost	Act. Work
1	**Digital Camera Prototype**	**3/1**	**NA**	**61%**	**6.72 days**	**4.28 days**	**$170.00**	**272 hrs**
2	Design Spec.s	3/1	3/2	100%	2 days	0 days	$20.00	32 hrs
3	Shell & Power	3/3	3/7	100%	3 days	0 days	$25.00	40 hrs
4	Memory/Software	3/3	NA	67%	4 days	2 days	$100.00	160 hrs
5	Zoom System	3/3	3/4	100%	2 days	0 days	$25.00	40 hrs
6	Assemble	NA	NA	0%	0 days	3 days	$0.00	0 hrs
7	Test	NA	NA	0%	0 days	2 days	$0.00	0 hrs

Note that the software automatically calculates the percent complete and actual finish, cost, and work. In some cases you will have to override these calculations if they are inconsistent with what actually happened. **Be sure to check** to make sure the information in this table is displayed the way you want it to be.

The final step is to enter the current status date (March 7). You do so by clicking PROJECT ▶ PROJECT INFORMATION and inserting the date into the status date window.

Step 2 Accessing Progress Information

MS Project provides a number of different options for obtaining progress information. The most basic information can be obtained from VIEW ▶ REPORTS ▶ COSTS ▶ EARNED VALUE.

TABLE A13.2B   Earned Value Table

ID	Task Name	PV	EV	AC	SV	CV	EAC	BAC	VAC
2	Design Spec.s	$20.00	$20.00	$20.00	$0.00	$0.00	$20.00	$20.00	$0.00
3	Shell & Power	$15.00	$15.00	$25.00	$0.00	($10.00)	$25.00	$15.00	($10.00)
4	Memory/Software	$100.00	$70.00	$100.00	($30.00)	($30.00)	$153.85	$100.00	($53.85)
5	Zoom System	$35.00	$35.00	$25.00	$0.00	$10.00	$25.00	$35.00	$10.00
6	Assemble	$0.00	$0.00	$0.00	$0.00	$0.00	$120.00	$120.00	$0.00
7	Test	$0.00	$0.00	$0.00	$0.00	$0.00	$30.00	$30.00	$0.00
		$170.00	$140.00	$170.00	($30.00)	($30.00)	$373.85	$320.00	($53.85)

When you scale this table to 80 percent you can obtain all the basic CV, SV and VAC information on one convenient page.

Note: Older versions of MS Project use the old acronyms:

BCWS = PV

BCWP = EV

ACWP = AC

and the EAC is calculated using the CPI and is what the text refers to as EAC_f.

Step 3 Accessing CPI Information

To obtain additional cost information such as CPI and TCPI click from the GANTT CHART view click TABLE ▶ MORE TABLES ▶ EARNED VALUE COST INDICATORS, which will display the following information:

TABLE A13.2C   Earned Value Cost Indicators Table

ID	Task Name	PV	EV	CV	CV%	CPI	BAC	EAC	VAC	TCPI
1	**Digital Camera Prototype**	$170.00	$140.00	($30.00)	−21%	0.82	$320.00	$373.85	($53.85)	1.2
2	Design Spec.s	$20.00	$20.00	$0.00	0%	1	$20.00	$20.00	$0.00	
3	Shell & Power	$15.00	$15.00	($10.00)	−66%	0.6	$15.00	$25.00	($10.00)	
4	Memory/Software	$100.00	$70.00	($30.00)	−42%	0.7	$100.00	$153.85	($53.85)	
5	Zoom System	$35.00	$35.00	$10.00	28%	1.4	$35.00	$25.00	$10.00	
6	Assemble	$0.00	$0.00	$0.00	0%	0	$120.00	$120.00	$0.00	
7	Test	$0.00	$0.00	$0.00	0%	0	$30.00	$30.00	$0.00	

Step 4 Accessing SPI Information

To obtain additional schedule information such as SPI from the GANTT CHART view, click TABLE ▶ MORE TABLES ▶ EARNED VALUE SCHEDULE INDICATORS, which will display the following information:

TABLE 13.2D   Earned Value Schedule Indicators Table

ID	Task Name	PV	EV	SV	SV%	SPI
1	**Digital Camera Prototype**	$170.00	$140.00	($30.00)	−18%	0.82
2	Design Spec.s	$20.00	$20.00	$0.00	0%	1
3	Shell & Power	$15.00	$15.00	$0.00	0%	1
4	Memory/Software	$100.00	$70.00	($30.00)	−30%	0.7
5	Zoom System	$35.00	$35.00	$0.00	0%	1
6	Assemble	$0.00	$0.00	$0.00	0%	0
7	Test	$0.00	$0.00	$0.00	0%	0

Step 5 Creating a Tracking Gantt Chart

You can create a Tracking Gantt Chart like the one presented on page 465 by simply clicking VIEW ▶ TRACKING GANTT

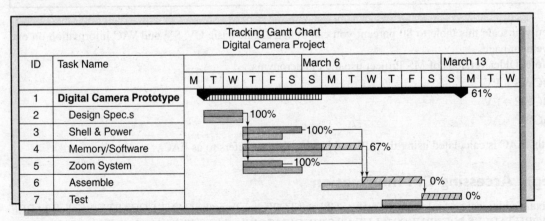

FIGURE 13.2E   Tracking Gantt Chart

CASE 13.1

Scanner Project

You have been serving as Electroscan's project manager and are now well along in the project. Develop a narrative status report for the board of directors of the chain store that discusses the status of the project to date and at completion. Be as specific as you can using numbers given and those you might develop. Remember, your audience is not familiar with the jargon used by project managers and computer software personnel; therefore, some explanation may be necessary. Your report will be evaluated on your detailed use of the data, your total perspective of the current status and future status of the project, and your recommended changes (if any).

Electroscan, Inc.
555 Acorn Street, Suite 5
Boston, Massachusetts

29 In-store Scanner Project
(thousands of dollars)
Actual Progress as of January 1

Name	PV	EV	AC	SV	CV	BAC	EAC$_f$	
Scanner project	420	395	476	−25	−81	915	1103	
H 1.0 Hardware	92	88	72	−4	16	260	213	
H 1.1 Hardware specifications (DS)	20	20	15	0	5	20	15	
H 1.2 Hardware design (DS)	30	30	25	0	5	30	25	
H 1.3 Hardware documentation (DOC)	10	6	5	−4	1	10	8	
H 1.4 Prototypes (PD)	2	2	2	0	0	40	40	
H 1.5 Test prototypes (T)	0	0	0	0	0	30	30	
H 1.6 Order circuit boards (PD)	30	30	25	0	5	30	25	
H 1.7 Preproduction models (PD)	0	0	0	0	0	100	100	
OP 1.0 Operating system	195	150	196	−45	−46	330	431	
OP 1.1 Kernel specifications (DS)	20	20	15	0	5	20	15	
OP 1.2 Drivers	45	55	76	10	−21	70	97	
OP 1.2.1 Disk drivers (DEV)	25	30	45	5	−15	40	60	
OP 1.2.2 I/O drivers (DEV)	20	25	31	5	−6	30	37	
OP 1.3 Code software	130	75	105	−55	−30	240	336	
OP 1.3.1 Code software (C)	30	20	40	−10	−20	100	200	
OP 1.3.2 Document software (DOC)	45	30	25	−15	5	50	42	
OP 1.3.3 Code interfaces (C)	55	25	40	−30	−15	60	96	
OP 1.3.4 Beta test software (T)	0	0	0	0	0	30	30	
U 1.0 Utilities	87	108	148	21	−40	200	274	
U 1.1 Utilities specifications (DS)	20	20	15	0	5	20	15	
U 1.2 Routine utilities (DEV)	20	20	35	0	−15	20	35	
U 1.3 Complex utilities (DEV)	30	60	90	30	−30	100	150	
U 1.4 Utilities documentation (DOC)	17	8	8	−9	0	20	20	
U 1.5 Beta test utilities (T)	0	0	0	0	0	40	40	
S 1.0 System integration	46	49	60	3	−11	125	153	
S 1.1 Architecture decisions (DS)	9	9	7	0	2	10	8	
S 1.2 Integration hard/soft (DEV)	25	30	45	5	−15	50	75	
S 1.3 System hard/software test (T)	0	0	0	0	0	20	20	
S 1.4 Project documentation (DOC)	12	10	8	−2	2	15	12	
S 1.5 Integration acceptance testing (T)	0	0	0	0	0	30	30	

CHAPTER 14

Project Audit and Closure

A project is complete when it starts working for you, rather than you working for it.

— *Scott Allen*

Mistakes are made; the unexpected happens; conditions change. In organizations that have several projects going on concurrently, it is prudent to have periodic reality checks on current and recently completed projects and their role in the organization's future. The project audit includes three major tasks:

1. Evaluate if the project delivered the expected benefits to all stakeholders. Was the project managed well? Was the customer satisfied?
2. Assess what was done wrong and what contributed to successes.
3. Identify changes to improve the delivery of future projects.

The project audit and report are instruments for supporting continuous improvement and quality management. We learn from past mistakes and what we did right.

Unfortunately, it is estimated that about 90 percent of all projects are not seriously reviewed or audited. The most common reason given is "we're too busy to stop and assess how well we manage projects." This is a big mistake. Without reflective assessment, valuable lessons learned are forgotten and mistakes are repeated. Sadly, those projects that are audited tend to be major failures or disasters. This is another big mistake. One tends to learn only what *not* to do from failures, not what to do. By examining both successes and failures, better practices can be incorporated into the project management system of an organization.

We have observed that organizations that seriously audit their projects are leaders in their fields. These organizations are vigorously committed to continuous improvement and organizational learning.

This chapter begins by discussing different kinds of project audits as well as the audit process. The emergence of maturity models to benchmark the evolution of project management practices is addressed next, followed by issues related to project closure. The chapter concludes by discussing the evaluation of team and individual performance on a project.

Project Audits

Project audits are more than the status reports suggested in Chapter 13, which check on project performance. Project audits do use performance measures and forecast data. But project audits are more inclusive. Project audits review why the project was selected. Project audits include a reassessment of the project's role in the organization's priorities. Project audits include a check on the organizational culture to ensure it facilitates the type of project being implemented. Project audits assess if the project team is functioning well and is appropriately staffed. Audits of projects in process should include a check on external factors that might change where the project is heading or its importance—for example, technology, government laws, competitive products. Project audits include a review of all factors relevant to the project and to managing future projects.

Project audits can be performed while a project is in process and after a project is completed. There are only a few minor differences between these audits.

- **In-process project audits.** Project audits early in projects allow for corrective changes, if they are needed, on the audited project or others in progress. In-process project audits concentrate on project progress and performance and check if conditions have changed. For example, have priorities changed? Is the project mission still relevant? In rare cases, the audit report may recommend closure of a project that is in process.
- **Postproject audits.** These audits tend to include more detail and depth than in-process project audits. Project audits of completed projects emphasize improving the management of future projects. These audits are more long-term oriented than in-process audits. Postproject audits do check on project performance, but the audit represents a broader view of the project's role in the organization; for example, were the strategic benefits claimed actually delivered?

The depth and detail of the project audit depend on many factors. Some are listed in Table 14.1. Because audits cost time and money, they should include no more time or resources than are necessary and sufficient. Early in-process project audits tend to be perfunctory unless serious problems or concerns are identified. Then, of course, the audit would be carried out in more detail. Because in-process project audits can be worrisome and destructive to the project team, care needs to be taken to protect project team morale. The audit should be carried out quickly, and the report should be as positive and constructive as possible. Postproject audits are more detailed and inclusive and contain more project team input.

TABLE 14.1
Factors Influencing Audit Depth and Detail

- Organization size
- Project importance
- Project type
- Project risk
- Project size
- Project problems

In summary, plan the audit, and limit the time for the audit. For example, in post-project audits, for all but very large projects, a one-week limit is a good benchmark. Beyond this time, the marginal return of additional information diminishes quickly. Small projects may require only one or two days and one or two people to conduct an audit.

The priority team functions well in selecting projects and monitoring performance—cost and time. However, reviewing and evaluating projects and the process of managing projects is usually delegated to independent audit groups. Each audit group is charged with evaluating and reviewing *all* factors relevant to the project and to managing future projects. The outcome of the project audit is a report.

The Project Audit Process

Below are guidelines that should be noted before you conduct a project audit. The guidelines below will improve your chances for a successful audit.

Guidelines for Conducting a Project Audit

1. First and foremost, the philosophy must be that the project audit is not a witch hunt.
2. Comments about individuals or groups participating in the project are no-nos. Keep to project issues, not what happened or by whom.
3. Audit activities should be intensely sensitive to human emotions and reactions. The inherent threat to those being evaluated should be reduced as much as possible.

4. Accuracy of data should be verifiable or noted as subjective, judgmental, or hearsay.
5. Senior management should announce support for the project audit and see that the audit group has access to all information, project participants, and (in most cases) project customers.
6. The attitude toward a project audit and its aftermath depends on the modus operandi of the audit leadership and group. The objective is not to prosecute. The objective is to learn and conserve valuable organization resources where mistakes have been made. Friendliness, empathy, and objectivity encourage cooperation and reduce anxiety.
7. The audit should be completed as quickly as is reasonable.
8. The audit leader should be given access to senior management above the project manager.

With these guidelines in mind, the process of the project audit is conveniently divided into three steps: initiation and staffing, data collection and analysis, and reporting. Each step is discussed next.

Step 1: Initiating and Staffing

Initiation of the audit process depends primarily on organization size and project size along with other factors. However, every effort should be made to make the project audit a normal process rather than a surprise notice. In small organizations and projects where face-to-face contact at all levels is prevalent, an audit may be informal and only represent another staff meeting. But even in these environments the content of a formal project audit should be examined and covered with notes made of the lessons learned. In medium-sized organizations that have several projects occurring simultaneously, initiation can come from a formal project review group, from the project priority team, or be automatic. For example, in the latter case, all projects are audited at specific stages in the project life cycle—perhaps when a project is 10 to 20 percent complete in time or money, 50 percent complete, and after completion. The automatic process works well because it removes the perceptions that a project has been singled out for evaluation and that someone might be on a witch hunt. In large projects, the audit may be planned for major milestones.

There are rare circumstances that require an unplanned project audit, but they should be few and far between. For example, in a project that involved the development of a very large computer accounting system for multiple locations, one major consulting firm (of many) gave notice of withdrawal from the project, with no apparent reason. The project customer became alarmed that perhaps there was a serious fundamental problem in the project that caused the large consulting firm to drop out. A project audit identified the problem. The problem was one of sexual harassment by members of a small consulting firm toward members of the larger consulting firm. The small consulting firm engagement was terminated and replaced with a firm of similar expertise. The larger firm agreed to remain with the project.

A major tenet of the project audit is that the outcome must represent an independent, outside view of the project. Maintaining independence and an objective view is difficult, given that audits are frequently viewed as negative by project stakeholders. Careers and reputations can be tarnished even in organizations that tolerate mistakes. In less forgiving organizations, mistakes can lead to termination or exile to less significant regions of an organization. Of course, if the result of an audit is favorable, careers and reputations can be enhanced. Given that project audits are susceptible to internal politics, some organizations rely on outside consulting firms to conduct the audits.

Step 2: Data Collection and Analysis

Each organization and project is unique. Therefore, the specific kinds of information that will be collected will depend on the industry, project size, newness of technology, and project experience. These factors can influence the nature of the audit. However, information and data are gathered to answer questions similar to those suggested next.

Organization View

1. Was the organizational culture supportive and correct for this type of project? Why? Why not?
2. Was senior management's support adequate?
3. Did the project accomplish its intended purpose?
   a. Is there a clear link to organizational strategy and objectives?
   b. Does the priority system reflect importance to the future of the organization?
   c. Has the environment (internal or external) changed the need for the project's completion (if project is still in process)?
4. Were the risks for the project appropriately identified and assessed? Were contingency plans used? Were they realistic? Have risk events occurred that have an impact greater than anticipated?
5. Were the right people and talents assigned to this project?
6. If the project was completed, have staff been fairly assigned to new projects?
7. What does evaluation from outside contractors suggest?
8. Were the project start-up and hand-off successful? Why? Was the customer satisfied?

Project Team View

1. Were the project planning and control systems appropriate for this type of project? Should all similar size and type of projects use these systems? Why? Why not?
2. Did the project conform to plan? Was the project over or under budget and schedule? Why?
3. Were interfaces and communications with project stakeholders adequate and effective?
4. If the project is completed, have staff been fairly assigned to new projects?
5. Did the team have adequate access to organizational resources—people, budget, support groups, equipment? Were there resource conflicts with other ongoing projects? Was the team managed well?
6. What does evaluation from outside contractors suggest?

The audit group should not be limited to these questions. The audit group should include other questions related to their organization and project type—e.g., research and development, marketing, information systems, construction, facilities. The generic questions above, although overlapping, represent a good starting point and will go a long way toward identifying project problem and success patterns.

Step 3: Reporting

The major goal of the audit report is to improve the way future projects are managed. Succinctly, the report attempts to capture needed changes and lessons learned from a current or finished project. The report serves as a training instrument for project managers of future projects.

Audit reports need to be tailored to the specific project and organizational environment. Nevertheless, a generic format for all audits facilitates development of an audit database and a common outline for those who prepare audit reports and the managers who read and act on their content. A very general outline common to those found in practice is as follows.

Classification

The classification of projects by characteristics allows prospective readers and project managers to be selective in the use of the report content. Typical classification categories include the following:

- Project type—e.g., development, marketing, systems, construction.
- Size—monetary.
- Number of staff.
- Technology level—low, medium, high, new.
- Strategic or support.

Other classifications relevant to the organization should be included.

Analysis

The analysis section includes succinct, factual review statements of the project. For example,

- Project mission and objectives.
- Procedures and systems used.
- Organization resources used.

Recommendations

Usually audit recommendations represent major corrective actions that should take place. See, for example, Snapshot from Practice: Post Katrina: New Orleans Announces New Evacuation Plan for 2006 Hurricane Season. However, it is equally important to recommend positive successes that should be continued and used in future projects. Postproject audits may be the place to give credit to the project team for an outstanding contribution.

Lessons Learned

These do not have to be in the form of recommendations. Lessons learned serve as reminders of mistakes easily avoided and actions easily taken to ensure success. In practice, new project teams reviewing audits of past projects similar to the one they are about to start have found audit reports very useful. Team members will frequently remark later, "The recommendations were good, but the 'lessons learned' section really helped us avoid many pitfalls and made our project implementation smoother."

Appendix

The appendix may include backup data or details of analysis that would allow others to follow up if they wished. It should not be a dumping ground used for filler; only critical pertinent information should be attached.

Project Closure

Every project comes to an end, eventually. On some projects the end may not be as clear as would be hoped. Although the scope statement may define a clear ending for a project, the actual ending may or may not correspond. Fortunately, a majority of projects are blessed with a well-defined ending. Regular project audits and a priority team will identify those projects that should have endings different from those planned.

Conditions for Project Closure

Normal

The most common circumstance for project closure is simply a completed project. In the case of "turnkey" projects, such as building a new manufacturing facility or creating a customized information system, the

---

Snapshot from Practice   Post Katrina: City of New Orleans Announces New
Evacuation Plan for 2006 Hurricane Season*

On August 29, 2005, Hurricane Katrina, a category 4 hurricane with winds greater than 145 miles per hour, hit the Gulf Coast with devastating effect. The next day two levees in New Orleans broke and water poured in, covering 80 percent of the city and rising to 20 feet in some areas. Many people climbed onto roofs to escape. The storm ended up killing more than 1,300 people in Louisiana and Mississippi.

While investigations into local, state, and federal responses will continue, the City of New Orleans unveiled a new plan based on lessons learned from Katrina for the forthcoming 2006 hurricane season.

"The Superdome and Morial Convention Center became a scene of misery for days after the August 29 hurricane as thousands of evacuees, many of them ill or elderly, languished with shortages in food and water. In the future, [Mayor Ray] Nagin said, the Convention Center will be a staging point not a shelter." The city negotiated a deal with Homeland Security so that AMTRAK trains would be used to supplement buses in mandatory evacuation of citizens.

"The new plan will take effect for any storms stronger than a Category 2, which have sustained winds of 111 miles per hour or higher. . . . ."

The plan also addresses specific problems that arose during Katrina, such as tourists being stranded in hotels and looters raiding stores and damaging property.

"By default, whether we like it or not, we are the most experienced in this [disaster] in the United States," New Orleans homeland security director Terry Ebbert said.

Ebbert said the emergency plan calls for a central hotel guest processing center with the aim of ensuring those with return plane tickets can rebook earlier departures.

People with special medical needs and the elderly would be picked up by city, school, and church buses and taken to the train station or evacuated by bus to shelters farther north.

For security, 3,000 National Guard troops could be stationed with local police throughout the city prior to a storm, and a dusk-to-dawn curfew would be in place once the evacuation was over, Police Superintendent Warren Riley said.

"It will be an overwhelming force." Riley said. "When citizens leave, they will have no doubt their property is protected. Obviously, it is far beyond what we have done in the past."

"The new evacuation plan applies to a city that now has a vastly reduced population, less than half its pre-storm number of about 455,000."

* Bret Martel, Associated Press, "New Orleans Evacuation Plan for 2006 Hurricane Season: More Buses, No Superdome Shelter," *The San Diego Union Tribune*, May 2, 2006.

---

finish is marked by the transfer of ownership to the customer. For many development projects, the end involves handing off the final design to production and the creation of a new product or service line. For other internal projects, such as system upgrades or creation of new inventory control systems, the end occurs when the output is incorporated into ongoing operations. Some modifications in scope, cost, and schedule probably occurred during implementation.

Premature

For a few projects, the project may be completed early with some parts of the project eliminated. For example, in a new-product development project, a marketing manager may insist on production models before testing:

> Give the new product to me now, the way it is. Early entry into the market will mean big profits! I know we can sell a bizzillion of these. If we don't do it now, the opportunity is lost!

The pressure is on to finish the project and send it to production. Before succumbing to this form of pressure, the implications and risks associated with this decision should be carefully reviewed and assessed by senior management and all stakeholders. Too frequently, the benefits are illusory, dangerous, and carry large risks. Why have the original project scope and objectives changed? If early project closure occurs, it should have the support of all project stakeholders. This decision should be left to the audit group, project priority team, or senior management.

Perpetual

Some projects never seem to end. That is, the project appears to develop a life of its own. Although these projects are plagued with delays, they are viewed as desirable when they finally are completed. The major characteristic of this kind of project is constant "add-ons." The owner or others continuously require more small changes that will improve the project outcome—product or service. These changes typically represent "extras" perceived as being part of the original project intent. Examples are adding features to software, to product design, to systems, or to construction projects. Constant add-on changes suggest a poorly conceived project scope. More care in upfront definition of the project scope and limitations will reduce the add-on phenomenon.

At some point the project manager or audit group needs to call the project design locked to bring closure. Although these projects are exhibiting scope, cost, and schedule creep, facing the fact that the project should be brought to an end is not an easy chore. An interesting study by Isabelle Royer chronicles "perpetual" projects of two French companies that lasted well over a decade. Essilor, maker of "progressive" lenses that correct for nearsightedness, and Lafarge, maker of building materials, each had projects that started with much fanfare only to fail to make significant progress. Signs of problems were ignored and allowed the doomed projects to drag on for over 10 years before being killed. Both companies absorbed millions of dollars of lost investment.

Project managers or audit/priority groups have several alternatives available for projects displaying characteristics of being perpetual. They can redefine the project end or scope so that closure is forced. They can limit budget or resources. They can set a time limit. All alternatives should be designed to bring the project to an end as quickly as possible to limit additional costs and still gain the positive benefits of a completed project. The audit group should recommend methods for bringing final closure to this type of project. Failed projects are usually easy to identify and easy for an audit group to close down. However, every effort should be made to communicate the technical reasons for termination of the project; project participants should not be left with an embarrassing stigma of working on a project that failed.

Failed Project

In rare circumstances projects simply fail—for a variety of reasons. For example, developing a prototype of a new technology product may show the original concept to be unworkable. Or in the development of a new pharmaceutical drug, the project may need to be abandoned because side effects of the drug are deemed unacceptable. See Snapshot from Practice: Project Canceled.

Changed Priority

The priority team continuously revises project selection priorities to reflect changes in organizational direction. Normally these changes are small over a period of time, but periodically major shifts in organization require dramatic shifts in priorities. In this transition period, projects in process may need to be altered or canceled. Thus, a project may start with a high priority but see its rank erode or crash during its project life cycle as conditions change. For example, a computer game company found their major competitor placed a 64-bit, 3-D game on the market while their product development projects still centered

Snapshot from Practice   Project Canceled*

Germany is the major crossroad for Europe's international commercial trucks. The German government felt the need to have international trucks (over 12 tons) using their road infrastructure assist in paying for the road maintenance and additional new infrastructure. The project objectives were clear—a new electronic truck toll-collection system that ensures accurate charges and easy fee collection across German, Swiss, and Austrian highways by August 31, 2003. The technology relied on global positioning systems (GPS), telecommunications, and software to record miles and charges, without using toll booths along the highways.

Several problems sabotaged the project. Time-to-market deadlines were impossible to meet. Delayed launch dates were caused by technical problems with truck tracking units and software that failed to function as expected. Interface communication with public and private stakeholders failed. As a result, the August 2003 deadline was never met. The revised November 2003 deadline was not met. Finally, in March 2004 the German government pulled the plug and canceled the project.

The cancellation of the project had serious impacts on other governmental programs. The shortfall of not receiving the revenue from the new toll system is estimated at $1.6 billion. Some of those revenues were destined for a high-speed maglev train in Munich and other infrastructure projects.

Lessons learned reveal that lack of project management knowledge was evident. More importantly, failure to identify and assess the impact of schedule and complex technology risks resulted in the death of the project. Perhaps a simpler, cheaper microwave system recommended by the Swiss and Austrians to be operational by 2005 would have sufficed.

* "Case Analysis: Taking a Toll," *PM Network,* Vol. 18, No. 3, March, 2004, p. 1.

on 32-bit games. From that moment on, 32-bit game projects were considered obsolete and met sudden deaths. The priority team of this company revised organization priorities. Audit groups found it easy to recommend closure for many projects, but those on the margin or in "gray areas" still presented formidable analysis and difficult decisions.

In some cases the original importance of the project was misjudged; in some the needs have changed. In other situations implementation of the project is impractical or impossible. Because the audit group and priority team are periodically reviewing a project, the changed perception of the project's role (priority) in the total scheme of things becomes apparent quickly. If the project no longer contributes significantly to organization strategy, the audit group or priority team needs to recommend the project be terminated. In many termination situations, these projects are integrated into related projects or routine daily operations.

Termination of "changed priority" projects is no easy task. The project team's perception may be that the project priority is still high in relation to other projects. Egos and, in some cases perhaps, jobs are on the line. Individuals or teams feel success is just over the horizon. Giving up is tantamount to failure. Normally, rewards are given for staying with a project when the chips are down, not giving up. Such emotional issues make project termination difficult.

There is little advantage to placing blame on individuals. Other modes should be used to "justify" early project closure or to identify a project problem—for example, customer needs or tastes have changed, technology is ahead of this project, or competition has a better, more advanced product or service. These examples are external to the organization and perceived as beyond anyone's control. Another approach that weakens close team loyalty is changing team members or the project manager. This approach tends to minimize team commitment and makes closing the project easier, but it should only be used as a last resort. Minimizing embarrassment should be a primary goal for a project review group closing down an unfinished project.

Signals for Continuing or Early Project Closure

Persons who are preparing to join a project audit group for the first time would find it rewarding to read a few studies that identify barriers to project success and the antithesis, factors that contribute to success. Knowledge of these factors will suggest areas to review in an audit. These factors signal where problems or success patterns might exist. In rare cases their existence may signal problems and the need for an in-process project to be terminated early.

A number of studies have examined this area. There is surprising conformity among these studies. For example, all of these studies (and others) rank poor project definition (scope) as a major barrier to project success. There is no evidence these factors have changed over the years, although some differences in relative importance have been noted in different industries. See Research Highlight—Chaos: Software Projects. Table 14.2 presents the barriers identified by 1,654 participating project managers in a survey by Gobeli and Larson. The signals noted in Table 14.2 can be useful to audit groups in their preliminary review of in-process projects or even in postproject audits.

TABLE 14.2   Barriers to Project Success

Activity*	Barrier	Incidence(%)
Planning	Unclear definition	16%
32%	Poor decision making	9
	Bad information	3
	Changes	4
Scheduling	Tight schedule	4
12%	Not meeting schedule	5
	Not managing schedule	3
Organizing	Lack of responsibility or accountability	5
11%	Weak project manager	5
	Top management interference	1
Staffing	Inadequate personnel	5
12%	Incompetent project manager	4
	Project member turnover	2
	Poor staffing process	1
Directing	Poor coordination	9
26%	Poor communication	6
	Poor leadership	5
	Low commitment	6
Controlling	Poor follow-up	3
7%	Poor monitoring	2
	No control system	1
	No recognition of problems	1

* To interpret the table, note that 32 percent of the 1,654 participants reported the barriers under "Planning," 12 percent reported the barriers under "Scheduling," and so on.

The Closure Decision

For an incomplete project, the decision to continue or close down the project is fundamentally an organizational resource allocation decision. Should the organization commit additional resources to complete the project and realize the project objectives? This is a complex decision. The rationale for closing or proceeding is often based on many cost factors that are primarily subjective and judgmental. Thus, care needs to be taken to avoid inferences concerning groups or individuals. The audit report needs to focus on organizational goals, changing conditions, and changing priorities requiring reallocation of scarce organizational resources.

Research Highlight

The Standish Group International is a market research and advisory firm specializing in mission- critical software and electronic commerce. They have conducted and published extensive research on the success and failure of software development/application projects. Their research, code name "Chaos," shows that a staggering 31 percent of software projects will be canceled before they are ever completed. In addition, 53 percent of projects will cost 189 percent of their original estimates. In terms of success, on the average only 16 percent of software projects are completed on time and within budget. In larger companies, the success rate is much worse—9 percent. The Standish Group estimated that in 1995 American companies and government agencies spent $81 billion for canceled software projects.

The Chaos research is based on "key findings" from research surveys and personal interviews. The respondents were information technology (IT) executive managers. The sample included large, medium, and small companies across major industry segments, for example, banking; securities; manufacturing; retail; wholesale; health care; insurance service; and local, state, and federal organizations. The total sample size was 365 respondents and represented 8,380 projects.

Based on an in-depth comparison of successful versus unsuccessful software projects, the Standish Group created a success potential chart that identifies key factors associated with project success. The success criteria were weighted based on the input from the surveyed IT managers. The most important criterion, "user involvement," was given 19 success points, while the least important, "hard-working, focused staff," was given 3 success points. The following chart lists the criteria in order of importance:

* Used by permission of the Standish Group International, Inc., 196 Old Town House Rd., West Yarmouth, MA 02673. The CHAOS report was updated in 2001. Although improvement was noted (e.g., cost overruns were reduced to 145 percent), the magnitude of the core problems remains the same.

Success Criteria	Points
1. User involvement	19
2. Executive management support	16
3. Clear statement of requirements	15
4. Proper planning	11
5. Realistic expectations	10
6. Smaller project milestones	9
7. Competent staff	8
8. Project team ownership	6
9. Clear vision and objectives	3
10. Hard-working, focused staff	3
Total	100

When the audit group or priority team suggests closure, the announcement may need to come from a CEO position if the effect is large or if key egos are involved. But, in most cases, the closure decision is left to the audit group or priority team. Prior to announcement of closure, a plan for future assignment of the project team members should be in place.

Project Closure Process

As the project nears the end of its life cycle, people and equipment are directed to other activities or projects. Carefully managing the closure phase is as important as any other phase of the project. The major challenges for the project manager and team members are over. Getting the project manager and team members to wrap up the odds and ends of closing down the project is sometimes difficult. For example, accounting for equipment and completing final reports are perceived as boring by project professionals who are action-oriented individuals. They are looking forward to new opportunities and challenges. The major activities found in project terminations are developing a plan, staffing, communicating the plan, and implementing the plan.

The typical close-out plan includes answers to questions similar to these:

- What tasks are required to close the project?
- Who will be responsible for these tasks?
- When will closure begin and end?
- How will the project be delivered?

Staffing is usually not a significant issue if the termination is not a sudden hatchet job. If the project is suddenly canceled early, before completion, it may be judicious to seek someone other than the project manager to close out the project. In successful, completed projects, the project manager is the likely choice for closing down the project. In this case it is best to have the project manager's next assignment known; this will serve as an inducement to terminate the project as quickly as possible and move on to new challenges.

Communicating the termination plan and schedule early allows the project team to (1) accept the psychological fact the project will end and (2) prepare to move on. The ideal scenario is to have the team member's next assignment ready when the termination is announced. Conversely, a major dilemma in the termination phase is that project participants are looking forward to future projects or other opportunities. The project manager's challenge is to keep the project team focused on the project activities and delivery to the customer until the project is complete. Project managers need to be careful to maintain their enthusiasm for completing the project and hold people accountable to deadlines, which are prone to slip during the waning stages of the project.

Implementing the closedown plan includes several wrap-up activities. Many organizations develop lengthy lists for closing projects as they gain experience. These are very helpful and ensure nothing is overlooked. Implementing closedown includes the following five major activities:

1. Getting delivery acceptance from the customer.
2. Shutting down resources and releasing to new uses.
3. Reassigning project team members.
4. Closing accounts and seeing all bills are paid.
5. Evaluating the project team, project team members, and the project manager.

Figure 14.1 depicts a partial closedown checklist for the Euro Conversion Project for a space company. See Appendix 14.1 for another example used by the state of Virginia.

Orchestrating the closure of a project can be a difficult task. Implementing closure usually takes place in an emotionally charged web of happiness from successful completion of the project and sadness that newly forged friendships are now being severed as individuals go their separate ways. It is customary in organizations to arrange a celebration of the completion of the project; this could range from an informal pizza party after work to a more formal banquet including speeches and awards or certificates of recognition for participants. Such a festivity provides a sense of closure and emotional release for the participants as they bid farewell to each other. For less successful projects, this ending can take the form of a ceremonial wake; even though the atmosphere may be less than festive, such an event can also provide a sense of closure and help people move on with their lives.

It is important to remember that dragging out the project closure process can also drag out costs that continue for the life of the project. If the project is not completed and earning the benefits promised, the interest costs of the money spent for the project continue, along with other continuing costs. Not only that, but for contracted projects final payment is not received until after the closeout.

Project	Euro Conversion	Customer	Finance Department
Project manager	Hans Kramer	Completion date	12 December XX

	Due date	Person responsible	Notes
1. Document finance department acceptance	16/12	Hans	
2. Customer training in Euro software	28/12	Joan	Train all departments before conversion
3. Archive all			
Schedules/actuals	31/12	Maeyke	
Budgets/actual costs	31/12	Maeyke	
Changes	31/12	Maeyke	
4. Close out all accounts with vendors	31/12	Guido	
5. Close out all work orders	31/12	Mayo	
6. Close out partner accounts	31/12	Guido	
7. Reassign project staff	16/12	Sophie	
8. Evaluation of			
Vendors	31/12	Mayo	Use standard questionnaire for vendors
Staff members	31/12	Sophie	Have HR department develop and administer
9. Final report and lessons learned meeting	4/1	Hans	Send notice to all stakeholders
10. Lessons learned archive to database	10/1	Maeyke	Contact IS department
tribute awards		Sophie	Notify all stakeholders

FIGURE 14.1   Euro Conversion—Project Closure Checklist

Team, Team Members, and Project Manager Evaluations

Auditing includes performance evaluations of the project team, individual team members, and the project manager. See Research Highlight: Measures of Team Performance. Evaluation of performance is essential to encourage changes in behavior and to support individual career development and continuous improvement through organization learning. Evaluation implies measurement against specific criteria. Experience corroborates that before commencement of the project the stage must be set so all expectations, standards, supportive organization culture, and constraints are in place; if not, the effectiveness of the evaluation process will suffer.

Research Highlight

Measures of Team Performance*

If team evaluation is not done well in practice, how bad is it? Joseph Fusco surveyed 1,667 project managers representing 134 different projects. Fifty-two percent of the respondents indicated their team received no collective evaluation of their team performance. Of the 22 percent who indicated their team was evaluated, further probing found their evaluation was informal, lasting little more than 20 minutes. This apparent lack of team evaluation practices may be sending the wrong signal. Individual team members can slough off poor team performance by relying on the old saying, "I did my job." Strong team evaluation practices need to emphasize team members are "in this together," while minimizing individual performance. Nearly every company in Fusco's survey lacked an effective project management reward system.

*Joseph Fusco, "Better Policies Provide the Key to Implementing Project Management," *Project Management Journal*, Vol. 28, No. 3, September 1997, p. 38.

In a macro sense, the evidence today suggests that performance evaluation in each of these realms is not done well. The major reasons cited by practitioners are twofold:

1. Evaluations of individuals are still left to supervisors of the team member's home department.
2. Typical measures of team performance center on time, cost, and specifications.

Most organizations do not go beyond these measures, although they are important and critical. Organizations should consider evaluating the team-building process, effectiveness of group decision and problem-solving processes, group cohesion, trust among team members, and quality of information exchanged. Addressing evaluation of teams, team members, and project managers is extremely complex and project dependent. The discussion that follows touches on some of the major issues and approaches found in practice.

Team Evaluation

Before an auditing of the project team can be effective and useful, a minimum core of conditions needs to be in place before the project begins (see Chapter 11). Some conditions are listed here in the form of questions:

1. Do standards for measuring performance exist? (You can't manage what you can't measure.) Are the goals clear for the team and individuals? Challenging? Attainable? Lead to positive consequences?
2. Are individual and team responsibilities and performance standards known by all team members?
3. Are team rewards adequate? Do they send a clear signal that senior management believes the synergy of teams is important?
4. Is a clear career path for successful project managers in place?
5. Does the team have discretionary authority to manage short-term difficulties?
6. Is there a relatively high level of trust emanating from the organization culture?
7. Team evaluation should go beyond time, cost, and specifications. Are there criteria beyond these triple threat criteria? The "characteristics of highly effective teams" from Chapter 11 can easily be adapted as measurements of team effectiveness.

These "in-place conditions" will support any evaluation approach for teams and their members.

In practice, the actual team evaluation process takes many forms—especially when evaluation goes beyond time, budget, and specifications. The typical mechanism for evaluation of teams is a survey administered by a consultant, a staff member from the human resources department, or through computer e-mail. The survey is normally restricted to team members, but, in some cases, other project stakeholders interacting with the team may be included in the survey. When the results are tabulated, the team meets with senior management, and the results are reviewed. An example of a partial survey is found in Table 14.3.

TABLE 14.3   Sample Team Evaluation and Feedback Survey

	Disagree				Agree
Using the scale below, assess each statement.					
1. The team shared a sense of common purpose, and each member was willing to work toward achieving project objectives.	1	2	3	4	5
2. Respect was shown for other points of view. Differences of opinion were encouraged and freely expressed.	1	2	3	4	5
3. All interaction among team members occurred in a comfortable, supportive atmosphere.	1	2	3	4	5

This session is comparable to the team-building sessions described in Chapter 11 except that the focus is on using the survey results to assess the development of the team, its strengths and weaknesses, and the lessons that can be applied to future project work. The results of team evaluation surveys are helpful in changing behavior, stressing the importance of supporting the team approach, and continuous improvement.

Individual Team Member and Project Manager Evaluation

Team evaluation is crucial, but at some point a project manager is likely to be asked to evaluate the performance of individual members. Such an evaluation will typically be required as part of the closure process and will then be incorporated in the annual performance appraisal system of the organization. These evaluations constitute a major element of an individual's personnel file and often form the basis for making decisions about promotions, future job assignments, merit pay increases, and other rewards.

Organizations vary in the extent to which project managers are actively involved in performing the appraisal process. In organizations where projects are managed within a functional organization or functional matrix, the individual's area manager, not the project manager, is responsible for assessing performance. The area manager may solicit the project manager's opinion of the individual's performance on a specific project; this will be factored into the individual's overall performance. In a balanced matrix, the project manager and the area manager jointly evaluate an individual's performance. In project matrix and project organizations in which the lion's share of the individual's work is project related, the project manager is responsible for appraising individual performance. One new process, which appears to be gaining wider acceptance, is the multirater appraisal or "360-degree feedback," which involves soliciting feedback concerning team members' performance from all the people their work affects. This would include not only project and area managers, but also peers, subordinates, and even customers. See Snapshot from Practice: The 360-Degree Feedback.

Performance appraisals generally fulfill two important functions. The first is developmental in nature; the focus is on identifying individual strengths and weaknesses and developing action plans for improving performance. The second is evaluative and involves assessing how well the person has performed in order to determine salary or merit adjustments. These two functions are not compatible. Employees, in their eagerness to find out how much pay they will receive, tend to tune out constructive feedback on how they can improve their performance. Likewise, managers tend to be more concerned with justifying their decision than engaging in a meaningful discussion on how the employee can improve his or her performance. It is difficult to be both a coach and a judge. As a result, several experts on performance appraisal systems recommend that organizations separate performance reviews, which focus on individual improvement, and pay reviews, which allocate the distribution of rewards.

Snapshot from Practice   The 360-Degree Feedback*

More and more companies are discarding the traditional superior-subordinate performance feedback process and replacing it with 360-degree feedback systems. The 360-degree feedback approach gathers behavioral observations from many sources within the organization and includes employee self-assessment. The individual completes the same structured evaluation process that superiors, project team members, peers and, in many cases, external customers use to evaluate a performance. Survey questionnaires, augmented by a few open-ended questions, are typically used to gather information.

Summary results are compared against organizational strategies, values, and business objectives. The feedback is communicated to the individual with the assistance of the company's human resource department or an outside consultant. The technique is used by a growing number of firms including General Electric, AT&T, Mobil Oil, Nabisco, Hewlett-Packard, and Warner-Lambert.

The objective of the 360-degree process is to identify areas for individual improvement. When anonymous feedback solicited from others is compared with the individual's self-evaluations, the individual may form a more realistic picture of her strengths and weaknesses. This may prompt behavioral change if the weaknesses identified were previously unknown to the individual. Such appears to be the case for Jerry Wallace, an up-and-coming manager at General Motors. "The strongest message I got was that I need to delegate more," he says, "I thought I'd been doing it. But I need to do it more and sooner. My people are saying, 'Turn me loose.'"

Many firms obtain feedback from internal and external project customers. For example, a client may evaluate a project manager or member of the project team according to, "How effectively does the individual get things done without creating unnecessary adversarial relationships?" Incorporating customer feedback in the evaluation process underscores collaboration and the importance of client expectations in determining project success.

William J. Miller, a program director at Du Pont, helped install a 360-degree feedback system for 80 scientists and support people. "A high or low score didn't predict a scientist's ability to invent Teflon," says Miller. "But what feedback did was really improve the ability of people to work in teams. Their regard for others and behaviors that were damaging and self-centered are what changed."

* Brian O'Reilly, "360 Feedback Can Change Your Life," *Fortune,* October, 17, 1994, pp. 93–100; Robert Hoffman, "Ten Reasons You Should Be Using 360 Degree Feedback," *HR Magazine,* April 1995, pp. 82–85; Dick Cochran, "Finally, a Way to Completely Measure Project Manager Performance," *PM Network,* September 2000, pp. 75–80.

In some matrix organizations, project managers conduct the performance reviews, while area managers are responsible for pay reviews. In other cases, performance reviews are part of the project closure process, and pay reviews are the primary objective of the annual performance appraisal. Other organizations avoid this dilemma by allocating only group rewards for project work. The remaining discussion is directed at reviews designed to improve performance because pay reviews are often outside the jurisdiction of the project manager.

Performance Review

Organizations employ a wide range of methods to review individual performance on a project. In general, all review methods of individual performance center on the technical and social skills brought to the project and team. Some organizations rely simply on an informal discussion between the project manager and the project member. Other organizations require project managers to submit written essays that describe and assess an individual's performance on a project. Many organizations use rating scales similar to the team evaluation survey in which the project manager rates the individual according to a certain scale (i.e., from 1 to 5) on a number of relevant performance dimensions (i.e., teamwork, customer relations). Some organizations augment these rating schemes with behaviorally anchored descriptions of what constitutes a 1 rating, a 2 rating, and so forth. Each method has its strengths and weaknesses, and, unfortunately, in many organizations the appraisal systems were designed to support mainstream operations and not unique project work. The bottom line is that project managers have to use the performance review system mandated by their organization as best they can.

Regardless of the method, the project manager needs to sit down with each team member and discuss his or her performance. Here are some general tips for conducting performance reviews:

- Always begin the process by asking the individual to evaluate his or her own performance. First, this approach may yield valuable information that you were not aware of. Second, the approach may provide an early warning for situations in which there is disparity in assessments. Finally, this method reduces the judgmental nature of the discussion.
- Avoid, when possible, drawing comparisons with other team members; rather, assess the individual in terms of established standards and expectations. Comparisons tend to undermine cohesion and divert attention away from what the individual needs to do to improve performance.
- When you have to be critical, focus the criticism on specific examples of behavior rather than on the individual personally. Describe in specific terms how the behavior affected the project.
- Be consistent and fair in your treatment of all team members. Nothing breeds resentment more than if, through the grapevine, individuals feel that they are being held to a different standard than are other project members.
- Treat the review as only one point in an ongoing process. Use it to reach an agreement as to how the individual can improve his or her performance.

Both managers and subordinates may dread a formal performance review. Neither side feels comfortable with the evaluative nature of the discussion and the potential for misunderstanding and hurt feelings. Much of this anxiety can be alleviated if the project manager is doing her job well. Project managers should be constantly giving team members feedback throughout the project so that individual team members can have a pretty good idea how well they have performed and how the manager feels before the formal meeting.

While in many cases the same process that is applied to reviewing the performance of team members is applied to evaluating the project manager, many organizations augment this process, given the importance of the position to their organization. This is where conducting the 360-degree review is becoming more popular. In project-driven organizations, directors or vice presidents of project management will be responsible for collecting information on a specific project manager from customers, vendors, team members, peers, and other managers. This approach has tremendous promise for developing more effective project managers.

Summary

Project audits enhance individual and organizational change and improvement. In this chapter processes for conducting project audits and developing the report were examined. Project closures and the importance of conducting team and individual evaluations were also reviewed. Key points of the chapter include the following:

- It is better to have automatic times or points when audits will take place. Surprises should be avoided.
- Audits of projects (especially those in process) need to be conducted carefully and with sensitivity to human reactions. The audit should focus on issues, problems, and successes and avoid references to groups or individuals.
- The audit is best staffed with individuals independent of the project.
- Audit reports need to be used and accessible.

- Audits support an organizational culture that vigorously promotes continuous improvement and organizational learning.
- Project closures should be planned and orderly regardless of the type of closure.
- Certain "core conditions" should be in place to support team and individual evaluation.
- Both individual and team evaluations should be conducted, and performance reviews should be separated from pay or merit reviews.

Competitive conditions appear to be forcing more organizations to adopt continuous improvement and organizational learning. Regular use of project audits has yielded dramatic improvements in the way projects are managed. As more members of these organizations are learning from project mistakes and what is contributing to project successes, the process of managing projects is continuously improving in their respective organizations. The major instrument for implementing this philosophy will be the project audit and report.

Since the purpose of the audit it to improve performance, the project maturity model is a good approach for checking project management performance and improvement for the organization over the long haul. Using the model as a starting benchmark, improvements can easily be tracked to higher levels.

Key Terms

In-process project audit	Project audit report	Team evaluation
Performance review	Project closure	360-degree review
Postproject audit		

Review Questions

1. How does the project audit differ from the performance measurement control system discussed in Chapter 13?
2. What major information would you expect to find in a project audit?
3. Why is it difficult to perform a truly independent, objective audit?
4. What are the five major activities for closing a project?
5. Comment on the following statement: "We cannot afford to terminate the project now. We have already spent more than 50 percent of the project budget."
6. Why should you separate performance reviews from pay reviews? How?

Exercises

1. Consider a course that you recently completed. Perform an audit of the course (the course represents a project and the course syllabus represents the project plan). Summarize the results of the audit as a report organized in accordance with the outline in the section "Step 3: Reporting."
2. Imagine you are conducting an audit of the International Space Station project. Research press coverage and the Internet to collect information on the current status of the project. What are the successes and failures to date? What forecasts would you make about the completion of the project, and why? What recommendations would you make to top management of the program, and why?
3. Interview a project manager who works for an organization that implements multiple projects. Ask the manager what kind of closeout procedures are used to complete a project and whether projects are audited.

References

Cochran, D., "Finally, a Way to Completely Measure Project Manager Performance," *PM Network,* September 2000, pp. 75–80.

Fincher, A. and G. Levin, "Project Management Maturity Model," *Proceedings of the 28th Annual PMI Symposium* (Newtown Square, PA: PMI, 1997), pp. 1028–35.

Fretty, P., "Why Do Projects Really Fail?" *PM Network,* March 2006, pp. 45–48.

Gobeli, D. and E. W. Larson, "Barriers Affecting Project Success," in *1986 Proceedings Project Management Institute: Measuring Success* (Upper Darby, PA: Project Management Institute, 1986), pp. 22–29.

Hoffman, R., "Ten Reasons You Should Be Using 360 Degree Feedback," *HRMagazine,* April 1995, pp. 82–85.

Ibbs, W. C. and Y. H. Kwak, "Assessing Project Maturity," *Project Management Journal,* Vol. 31, No. 1, March 2000, pp. 32–43.

Kwak, Y. H. and C. W. Ibbs, "Calculating Project Management's Return on Investment," *Project Management Journal,* Vol. 31, No. 2, March 2000, pp. 38–47.

Pippett, D. D. and J. F. Peters, "Team Building and Project Management: How Are We Doing?" *Project Management Journal,* Vol. 26, No. 4, December 1995, pp. 29–37.

Royer, I., "Why Bad Projects Are So Hard to Kill," *Harvard Business Review,* February 2003, pp. 49–56.

Software Engineering Institute (SEI). (See website at http://www.sei.cmu/edu/activities/sema/profile.html.)

Stewart, W. E., "Balanced Scorecard for Projects" (2000 International Student Paper Award Winner), *Project Management Journal,* Vol. 32, No. 1, March 2001, pp. 38–47.

Wheatly, M., "Over the Bar," *PM Network,* Vol. 17, No. 1, January, 2003, pp. 40–45.

Yates, J. K. and S. Aniftos, "ISO 9000 Series of Quality Standards and the E/C Industry," *Project Management Journal,* Vol. 28, No. 2, June 1997, pp. 21–31.

APPENDIX 14.1

Project Closeout Checklist

Section 5: Project Closeout

Project Closeout Transition Checklist

Provide basic information about the project including: Project Title—The proper name used to identify this project; Project Working Title—The working name or acronym that will be used for the project; Proponent Secretary—The Secretary to whom the proponent agency is assigned or the Secretary that is sponsoring an enterprise project; Proponent Agency—The agency that will be responsible for the management of the project; Prepared by—The person(s) preparing this document; Date/Control Number—The date the checklist is finalized and the change or configuration item control number assigned.

Project Title: _____ **Project Working Title:** _____
Proponent Secretary: _____ **Proponent Agency:** _____
Prepared by: _____ **Date/Control Number:** _____

Complete the Status and Comments columns. In the Status column indicate: Yes, if the item has been addressed and completed; No, if the item has not been addressed, or is incomplete; N/A, if the item is not applicable to this project. Provide comments or describe the plan to resolve the item in the last column.

	Item	Status	Comments/Plan to Resolve
1	Have all the product or service deliverables been accepted by the customer?		
1.1	Are there contingencies or conditions related to the acceptance? If so, describe in the Comments.		
2	Has the project been evaluated against each performance goal established in the project performance plan?		
3	Has the actual cost of the project been tallied and compared to the approved cost baseline?		
3.1	Have all approved changes to the cost baseline been identified and their impact on the project documented?		
4	Have the actual milestone completion dates been compared to the approved schedule?		
4.1	Have all approved changes to the schedule baseline been identified and their impact on the project documented?		
5	Have all approved changes to the project scope been identified and their impact on the performance, cost, and schedule baselines documented?		
6	Has operations management formally accepted responsibility for operating and maintaining the product(s) or service(s) delivered by the project?		
6.1	Has the documentation relating to operation and maintenance of the product(s) or service(s) been delivered to, and accepted by, operations management?		

6.2	Has training and knowledge transfer of the operations organization been completed?		
6.3	Does the projected annual cost to operate and maintain the product(s) or service(s) differ from the estimate provided in the project proposal? If so, note and explain the difference in the Comments column.		
7	Have the resources used by the project been transferred to other units within the organization?		
8	Has the project documentation been archived or otherwise disposed as described in the project plan?		
9	Have the lessons learned been documented in accordance with the Commonwealth Project Management guideline?		
10	Has the date for the post implementation review been set?		
10.1	Has the person or unit responsible for conducting the post implementation review been identified?		

Signatures

The Signatures of the people below relay an understanding that the key elements within the Closeout Phase section are complete and the project has been formally closed.

Position/Title	Name	Date	Phone Number

Source: http://www.vita.virginia.gov/projects/cpm/cpmDocs/CPMG-SEC5-Final.pdf

APPENDIX 14.2

Project Quality Management

Definitions of Quality

Quality is a word in very common usage in day-to-day language and, therefore, everybody has formed some very personal concept of what quality should mean. More over, in the past few decades, considerable thought and work have been invested in working out systems which should address the issue of improving and sustaining the quality of activities of the commercial enterprises and industrial organizations. The specific definitions of quality provided in these systems introduce another element of ambiguity in the meaning of the word. Therefore, for a start, we would review the essence of definitions provided in some of the better known quality management systems and how they relate to the definition and approach used in PMBOK® Guide.

Juran's definition emphasizes 'Fitness (of product) for use'.

Phillip Crosby's emphasis is on 'conformance to requirements'.

Edward Deming sees three cornerstones for quality: the characteristics of the product itself, how the users interact and use the product and instructions for use.

ISO 9000 (published by ISO, International Organization for Standardization) defines quality as 'the degree to which a set of inherent characteristics fulfills requirements'.

The approach to project quality management presented in the PMBOK® Guide is generally compatible with the ISO definition of quality: "the totality of characteristics of an entity that bear on its ability to satisfy the client's stated or implied needs" (ISO 8400, 1994). In the context of project management, the project stakeholders are the clients and, hence, satisfactory project quality management should meet the project objectives set down by all stakeholders of the project.

Definitions of Project Quality Management

One school of thought regards project quality, 'the inherent characteristics which fulfill requirements', to be an integral part and parcel of the basic project objectives and the project deliverables based on them. This approach holds that the project work to be completed is invariably stipulated to be performed to meet certain quality standards or performance criteria and hence, managing quality of the product of the project is often not treated as a separate issue, but only as a part of the project scope management. This is the approach taken in Chapter 4, 'Defining the Project'.

PMI offers a different approach and discusses quality management as a separate knowledge area for project management. According to this departure in approach, project quality management includes the processes and the activities of the performing organization that determine quality policies, objectives and responsibilities so that the project will satisfy the needs for which it was undertaken.

We describe below the framework presented by PMBOK® GUIDE, which treats project quality management as a separate knowledge area.

Approach to Project Quality Management

Since PMI's definition of quality is aligned with ISO, the project quality is judged according to its ability to satisfy the needs of the project stakeholders. The project stakeholders can be visualized to be of two distinct categories:

- *The project sponsors:* These stakeholders are involved in financing the project or with the management of the project performing organization committed to delivering the project results. Their focus is on the *effectiveness and efficiency of how the project is managed* with emphasis on whether the project is completed within budget and on time, how project communication or procurement was managed and so on.
- *The actual users of the product of the project:* These stakeholders are interested in *the long-term quality aspects during the product's lifetime.* Their focus would be on how the product of the project meets the technical specifications or performance requirements.

For example, for a project for a large scale development of a residential area, the project sponsor would be the project construction or development organization and its management. From the sponsor's point of view, expectation from the project management is that all construction envisaged for the project is completed on schedule and within the budgeted cost. The actual users of the residential complex would be the people who buy and live in these homes. Their expectations concern certain functional and aesthetic aspects of the building like the building layout plans, architectural features, quality of construction for long life, quality of materials and finishes used in construction, maintainability and low maintenance costs, etc.

The first category of stakeholders is concerned with the quality of project management, while the second category of the stakeholders is concerned with the product resulting from the project. The project quality management, therefore, must address the issues of both the management of the project as well as the product of the project. In other words, project quality management should ensure.

- *Efficient and effective project management in terms of meeting the scope, cost and schedule objectives, and*
- *Incorporating into the product of the project the quality desired by the end users during the product's life time*

PMBOK® Guide's Alignment with Paradigms of Modern Quality Management Systems

In the recent years, quality management for operations has come into limelight in management literature. New insights in the subject have been attained and several quality management systems and quality improvement movements incorporating these insights have been proposed. PMBOK® GUIDE recognizes the importance of these approaches and supports the concepts advocated by eminent quality movement leaders summarized below:

1. *Customer Satisfaction:* Quality of the product of the project must meet the customer's requirement ("Fitness for Use" as enunciated by Joseph Juran).This would involve understanding the customer's requirements, defining and evaluating them and managing them by formulating a proper quality plan and delivering accordingly.
2. *Prevention over Inspection:* "The quality is planned, designed and built into the product and not inspected in".

3. *Continuous Improvement:* Initiatives are undertaken for continuous improvement of the product quality. Adopt "Plan-Do-Check-Act cycle (recommended by Schewhart and Deming).

4. *Management Responsibility:* The final responsibility for building the quality into a product rests with the management. Without strong support of the management, the project team would not be able to muster the resources necessary for building in the product quality (recommended by Edward Deming).

5. *Ishikawa's seven and techniques for quality control based on statistical analysis:* Cause-and-effects diagrams (Fishbone diagrams), control charts, Flowcharting, Histograms, Pareto Charts, Run Charts and Scatter Diagrams (for regression analysis).

6. *The Subtle Distinction in the Connotations of the Commonly Used Other Quality Terms:*

   ▪ <u>Quality and Grade</u>   Grades refer to the categories assigned to products for same general functional service but different technical specifications or characteristics. So the product with different features and technical characteristics would have different grades. A car may be available in a basic model just for serving transportation function or it may have a number of additional features. The grade has nothing to do with the quality. A high grade product with many technical attributes and features may have poor quality (frequent failures, high maintenance cost, etc.). On the other hand, a low grade product, with few basic functional features, may have high quality (high reliability, accuracy in basic service, etc.)

   ▪ <u>Precision and Accuracy</u>   Accuracy refers to how far the measured value may be from the true value. Precision concerns the repeatability of the performance that is reflected by the size of scatter or spread between different measurements of the same true value. A product can have high accuracy and low precision; for a product giving readings 103,100 and 97 for a true value of 100, the accuracy is high (- the mean of three readings is exactly the true value), but the individual readings have high spread +/- 3%, i.e. the precision is low. On the other hand, a low accuracy and high precision product might give the values 102,103, and 104; here the spread is just +/- 1 %, but the mean of three readings is 3 % far from the true value that reflects a fairly inaccurate performance.

   ▪ <u>Standards & Regulations</u>   The standards are meant to convey general good practice; they have no legal or compulsion associated with it. On the other hand, the regulations are formal legal instruments and it is mandatory to follow them.

Key Issues in Project Quality Management

In the light of above background, PMBOK® GUIDE essentially focuses on building into the product the quality, which will meet the satisfaction criteria for the deliverables of the project. Accordingly, its approach recognizes processes for planning the quality, testing and inspection as an on-going process for quality assurance and quality control activities involving analyzing and improving the project activities for continuous improvement.

As discussed earlier, the key issues in project quality management revolve around a balanced trade-off between:

▪ *Effectiveness and efficiency of how the project is managed*—reflecting the viewpoints of project sponsors and project performing organization's management, and

▪ *Long-term quality aspects during the product's lifetime*—reflecting the viewpoint of the actual users of the product of the project

Project Quality Management Processes

PMBOK® GUIDE identifies 3 processes to address the key issues of project quality management:

- Plan Quality (a process in the project planning group)
- Perform Quality Assurance (a process in the project executing group)
- Perform Quality Control (a process in the project monitoring and controlling group)

Let us look at these three processes of focusing on the inputs, tools & techniques and the outputs from the processes in more detail.

1. Plan Quality (A process in the project planning group)

Plan Quality is the process of identifying quality requirements and/or standards for the project and product and documenting how the project will demonstrate compliance.

Major Outputs

This process is meant to provide the blue print for comprehensive planning for project quality, which would include the following outputs:

- *Quality Management Plan*: This would form a component of the comprehensive project plan and provide overarching description of how the organization's quality management policy will be implemented, what quality standards and quality related operating procedures will be enforced and how the rest of quality management planning, executing and controlling processes will be carried out.
- *Quality Metrics:* Quality metrics are specific measurable attributes of the project's product and how the quality control process will measure them and the applicable standards for acceptance in terms of precise tolerances.
- *Quality Checklists:* These tools, based on lessons learnt from earlier projects, systematically summarize the attributes or characteristics of a particular component or work package result, which the project team should check to ensure the desired quality level.
- *Process Improvement Plan:* This would provide the road map for how the current processes used in project execution can be improved by analysis of their existing status and tools for process improvement.

Major Inputs

The major inputs for this process are basically

- *The nature and quantum of work to be carried out* (from project scope baseline—i.e. scope statement, WBS and WBS Dictionary- outputs from "create WBS" process in scope management)
- *The stakeholders' criteria for satisfaction from the project deliverables* (from stakeholders' register—an output of "collect requirement "process in project scope management)
- *Organization's quality policies, procedures and guidelines and lessons learned on earlier similar projects* (from the organization's project records and written as well as unwritten traditions for quality management—often referred to as "organizational process assets")
- *Government rules and regulations and industry standards and practices for product quality* (often referred to as "enterprise environmental factors")
- *Other relevant parts of project plan components:* The relevant information from project plan for time, cost and risk management (cost performance baseline, schedule baseline and risk register)

Major Tools and Techniques

Quality management has developed into a major management attention area and quality planning process could use a number of the tools and techniques borrowing from the organization's quality management practices as well as techniques described in the literature. General familiarity with these techniques and their application in the plan quality process are expected from the PMP certification aspirants. Hence, these tools and techniques are listed below and described very briefly; their detailed description would have to be obtained from specific quality management literature for those interested in details.

Cost-Benefit Analysis

It is an economic analysis of cost of achieving a particular quality level and the benefit of cost savings from avoiding rework due to quality achievement.

Cost of Quality

This tool aims to analyze the cost of providing a particular quality level. This concept requires some elaboration. The cost of quality is the total of the cost for achieving the conformance of the product to the desired quality and the penalty costs on account of the non-performance of the product to desired quality standards.

- *The cost of conformance* consists of cost for building a quality product (Prevention Costs—costs for training, documentation, and specific equipment) and the cost to inspect and assess the quality (Appraisal Costs—Testing and Inspection costs, Destructive testing, etc.)
- *The cost of non-conformance* consists of internal failure costs (failures found in the project, which require reworking and scrap) and external failure costs (costs related to product liability, warranties and lost business opportunities)

Control Charts

The process control charts are tools for control of quality from repetitive processes used during project activities. They are based on the statistical analysis of the process performance to determine whether a project activity is based on a process which is stable and has a predictable performance or not. Ordinarily, 3 standard deviation limits about the mean are stipulated as upper and lower process limits. When the inspection and testing reveal the performance of the process to lie beyond the upper or lower limit or if 7 consecutive points lie on the same side of the process mean, the process is assessed to be out of control and suitable adjustments are made to bring it back under control. Generally, the upper and lower control limits, which represent the natural limits for a stable process in control, are taken into account while setting the tolerance for acceptance for quality plan.

Benchmarking

Benchmarking involves comparing the planned or actual performance of the project on hand with the similar characteristics from another project (another company or competitor or another department of the same organization) in order to set an improved standard and method of measuring it. The idea is based on the reference levels used in civil engineering surveys. It can be used as a tool for setting the quality standard during preparation of Quality Plan.

Design of Experiments

It is a statistical method for developing an optimized design for how the experiments should be planned for identifying which factors would influence the desired characteristic to what extent. Ordinarily, an optimized combination of factors could be obtained from this experimental analysis, which would permit much greater variation or tolerance in the input factors without sacrificing the impact on the desired characteristic. Tagucci's *Robust Design* technique is based on this and the statistical analysis is known as 'Analysis of Variance' ('ANOVA'). The technique has wider application in routine operations and manufacture than for project work, but it could be helpful in some large number of repetitive project tasks, like welding for structural components, RCC work, etc.

Statistical Sampling

Statistical sampling can be used to minimize the cost of inspection and testing in case of project activities requiring a large number of repetitive works. The published sampling tables provide the size of the sample for a population from which it is drawn; this could provide the basis for the quantum of testing or inspection to be carried out for a project and permit to estimate the cost of quality.

Flowcharting

Flowcharts present in a sequential nature project activities. From a critical analysis of this chart, the sources for quality problems can be anticipated and accordingly decision points based on suitable testing could be included. Quality Plan would include such testing at critical points decided by flowchart analysis.

2. Perform Quality Assurance (A process in the project executing group)

This process involves carrying out all work related to achieving the quality planned in the earlier process during project execution. Essentially it would involve carrying out physical inspection, testing, and performance evaluation of the deliverables. If any deficiencies are spotted during inspection and testing, corrective actions are recommended and taken. If any change in the planning or execution would contribute towards higher quality, such changes are also recommended.

Distinction between Perform Quality Assurance and Perform Quality Control processes

There is a close similarity between the Perform Quality Assurance and Perform Quality Control processes. Both use similar or common procedures used for inspection and testing; however reporting and analysis in case of quality assurance is just to be sure that the right procedures are used in operation and convince the stakeholders about the quality built into the product of the project. The analysis and reporting in case of quality control is to determine the cause and effect relationship and measure and control the project activity to make it conform to quality plan standards. Quality Assurance is concerned with process being stable and defects being prevented, while Quality Control is concerned with detecting the defects and repair of defective project work.

Inputs

The nature of the process being to assure that project work under execution conforms to Quality Plan, most of the outputs of the Plan Quality process are inputs for this process. These inputs are: Quality Management Plan, Quality Checklists, and Quality Metrics. The work performance information, from test and inspection results and cost and schedule status reports, provides the actual performance data. The comparison of the work performance with the quality plan and quality metrics gives the quality assurance data.

Tools and Techniques

Most of the tools and techniques used for Plan Quality and Perform Quality Control process are applicable.

Quality Audits

The only special technique for this process is Quality Audits. Quality Audit is a systematic independent and documented process for obtaining evidence and evaluating it to determine to what extent the project activities comply with the policies, procedures and process steps followed in the organization. The degree of independence depends on the real purpose of the Quality Audit; it could be an outside independent agency or an independent authority unit from the same organization.

Outputs

Reports confirming that proper policies and procedures have been used for building in the quality are the main output.

Change requests to prevent defects or request for rework or repair of defective work are other outputs. Quality Audit Reports have more credibility and are better relied as instruments for quality assurance. Together, these reports update the project documentation.

3. Perform Quality Control (A process in the monitoring & controlling group)

Quality Control process includes activities in monitoring specific project performance and comparing it with quality standard, laid down to check if the work complies with it. While the nature of quality assurance process is merely collecting the information concerning the quality, quality control is more actively involved in carrying out controlled actions for achieving quality—viz. monitoring and recording the results of quality activities for assessing the performance and recommending necessary changes.

The project team involved with quality control activities should be able to distinguish between

- *Prevention and Inspection* (Building the quality in by doing the right thing the first time is prevention and preferred mode of quality control. Removing the defectives from reaching the customer by inspection is less preferred mode of quality control)
- *Attribute sampling and variables sampling* (Samples are assessed for either meeting or not meeting the standard—like 'Go-Not-Go' Gauge for attribute sampling. A continuous scale for the degree of conformance to standard is used for variable sampling), and
- *Tolerance and Control Limits* (Tolerance is based on acceptability of the work result and is independent of the natural process variations; if the tolerance is stricter than the natural process variation limits, the inspection is used to weed out unacceptable specimens. Control Limits indicate the limits based on the variations which would occur in the process naturally. In a statistical process control, the standard deviation calculated from the measurements of the randomly occurring variations is used for setting the control limits—Upper Control Limit (UCL) is set at mean plus 3 standard deviations and Lower Control Limit is set at mean minus 3 standard deviations. When the process is stable and in control, 99.73 % of the population is expected to fall within the UCL and LCL.)

Inputs

The Quality Management Plan, Quality Metrics and Quality Checklists from the Plan Quality process are one set of inputs and serve to provide the quality standards to be compared with. Work performance measurement, obtained by inspection and testing and comparing the planned versus actual performance for technical, schedule and cost and metrics provides another set of inputs.

Tools and Techniques

Tools and techniques for quality control are based on *seven basic tools of quality recommended by Ishikawa:*

(i) *Cause-Effect or Fishbone Diagrams:* They give diagrammatic representation between various potential sources of defective work and defects. The analysis based on this presentation (asking "Why?-Why? Or How?-How?) can be helpful in getting at the root causes of the quality problems and improving the quality by addressing the issues involved.

(ii) *Control Charts:* These charts are based on statistical process control and described above and as one of the tools and techniques of Plan Quality process.

(iii) *Flowcharting:* This technique is also described earlier as one of the tools and techniques of Plan Quality process.

(iv) *Histogram:* This technique involves creating a bar chart with the causes of poor quality plotted on X-axis and the frequency of the occurrence of that condition on Y-axis. Histogram gives a graphical presentation and provides a focus on the most important of quality issues immediately.

(v) *Pareto Chart:* This is a specific histogram, where the bars of the chart are ordered according to the frequency of occurrence, which immediately brings attention to the most serious of the quality issues. This type of presentation, used first by Pareto, show that typically a very small number of causes account for a major portion of the quality issues or defects—say, only 20 % of all causes account for 80 % of the defects. Hence it is also referred to as 80/20 principle.

(vi) *Run Chart:* This chart is just like Control Chart, but without the accompanying analysis and the Upper Control Limit and Lower Control Limit shown on it.

(vii) *Scatter Diagram:* This is merely a plot of the points corresponding to two specific variables for a particular observation point. The points might show a scatter, but might also show a trend line, which presents the general nature of relationship between the two variables. This relationship is called the regression line and if it is a straight line, it is called linear regression.

Seven techniques described above based on Ishikawa's statistical analysis are useful in analyzing and focusing on the relationship between various cause and the corresponding quality issues or defects. They are useful in preventing defects or building in the quality in the product of the project.

Two more techniques for improving quality rely not on building the quality but preventing the defective project work to reach the customer. They are inspection and statistical sampling technique for inspection.

Outputs

The outputs of this process are *quality control measurements* (documented data of test results), *validated deliverables* (from documented tests and accompanying analysis), and *organizational process assets* (Up-dated checklists, improved quality metrics and improved processes with preventive and defects corrective procedures).

CASE 14.1

Maximum Megahertz Project

Olaf Gundersen, the CEO of Wireless Telecom Company, is in a quandary. Last year he accepted the Maximum Megahertz Project suggested by six up-and-coming young R&D corporate stars. Although Olaf did not truly understand the technical importance of the project, the creators of the project needed only $600,000, so it seemed like a good risk. Now the group is asking for $800,000 more and a six-month extension on a project that is already four months behind. However, the team feels confident they can turn things around. The project manager and project team feel that if they hang in there a little longer they will be able to overcome the roadblocks they are encountering—especially those that reduce power, increase speed, and use a new technology battery. Other managers familiar with the project hint that the power pack problem might be solved, but "the battery problem will never be solved." Olaf believes he is locked into this project; his gut feeling tells him the project will never materialize, and he should get out. John, his human resource manager, suggested bringing in a consultant to axe the project. Olaf is thinking maybe he should do that on this project if it needs to be terminated.

Olaf decided to call his friend Dawn O'Connor, the CEO of an accounting software company. He asked her, "What do you do when project costs and deadlines escalate drastically? How do you handle doubtful projects?" Her response was, "Let another project manager look at the project. Ask: 'If you took over this project tomorrow, could you bring the project in on time and within budget with the extended time and additional money?' If the answer is no, I call my top management team together and have them review the doubtful project in relation to other projects in our project portfolio." Olaf feels this is good advice.

Unfortunately, the Maximum Megahertz Project is not an isolated example. Over the last five years there have been three projects that were never completed. "We just seemed to pour more money into them, even though we had a pretty good idea the projects were dying. The cost of those projects was high; those resources could have been better used on other projects." Olaf wonders, "Do we ever learn from our mistakes? How can we develop a process that catches errant projects early? More importantly, how do we ease a project manager and team off an errant project without embarrassment?" Olaf certainly does not want to lose the six bright stars on the Maximum Megahertz Project.

Olaf is contemplating how his growing telecommunications company should deal with the problem of identifying projects that should be terminated early, how to allow good managers to make mistakes without public embarrassment, and how they all can learn from their mistakes.

Give Olaf a plan of action for the future that attacks the problem. Be specific and provide examples that relate to Wireless Telecom Company.

CASE 14.2

Project Quality: A Dialogue with the Zen Master

Introduction

The case presents the basic concepts on project quality management generally following the guidelines and processes suggested by Project Management Institute (PMI), U.S.A. At the same time, the main thrust of teachings of Quality Gurus like Joseph Juran, Philip Crosby and Edward Deming are also included in the passing. To make the presentation interesting and easy to follow, the case is written as an imaginary scenario of a dialogue on this subject between a Zen Master and his disciples.

The Zen master sat under the banyan tree in a lotus seating pause with the eyes closed. He had a very lean body and shaved head and he wore a saffron robe. Written all over his face was peace—the kind of all-encompassing peace, which could be expected to be found only on the face of a Zen master. The disciples started flowing in and quietly taking their seats without a word.

After a while, the master opened his eyes. The silence continued to rule the place for another 10 minutes. Then one of the disciples slowly spoke in a hushed voice, 'Master, we want to learn today something about quality and how to improve the quality of construction projects we are managing". The question was not incorrectly aimed. This Zen master was a modern Guru; he had read a lot, understood and experienced life in many facets and was capable of counseling about many things including project quality.

After a pregnant silence of a few seconds, the master slowly spoke, "And, what is quality?"

"Fitness for use", one disciple offered.

"Yes, which is how Joseph Juran put it", replied the master, "Can you elaborate?"

"Well, it means that customers' or stakeholders' expectations are fully met or even exceeded. The product or service fully conforms to the specifications via the spoken or unspoken needs of the clients. Meaning the product or service provides all that the customer expected it to do at the time of acquiring it and meets the real needs ..."

Another interrupted, "The totality of characteristics of an entity that bear on its ability to satisfy (customer's) stated or implied needs; that's the way ISO 8400, 1994: Quality management & Quality Assurance defines it".

"There should be 'zero defect', as we heard Quality Guru Philip Crosby recommend it" offered the third one.

"All of that's true." said the master, "So you all know what quality means in general and how quality gurus define it. Now, how do you perceive the quality management defined in the context of your construction projects?"

One of the groups offered, "I look at the quality of project management as meeting two distinct criteria:

- First, the quality of the project construction should be up to the planned level and meeting the requirements set down by the organization, and
- Secondly, the project management must ensure that the thresholds set down on the cost, time and resource values for the project are achieved."

"Very well said." said the master encouragingly, "The distinction you made is very important. Project quality management touches both these aspects—the quality of the product of the project as well as the quality of how the project is managed; and not many keep this distinction in mind. Now, let us leave out for a while the aspect of quality of managing the project—that is, managing the project within approved budget and on time; you all are getting training for this at a business school. Let's focus for the moment on the first aspect of quality you mentioned. How would you proceed to go about systematically for meeting the objectives for the quality of construction, that is, the quality of the product created by the project?"

"First we must go through the quality planning process," said one.

"And how would you go about doing that?" the master asked.

Several disciples started replying.

"We need to have the rules, standards and guidelines set down by the government, industry associations or common industry practice, the so called environmental factors for the enterprise enveloping the organization as well as the project"

"We need to have the policies, procedure and the guidelines for quality management in the organization's operations and other projects".

"The project scope statement should provide the key inputs. It should document the overall project objectives, the project deliverables and what standards they should meet. It should state the measurable objective criteria for stakeholders' satisfaction—the criteria for acceptance of the product by the clients or stakeholders for accepting the project deliverables."

"All of you are correct", the master encouraged, "All successful journeys start with the clear idea of the destination to reach. We must first know the destination we want to reach in our quality journey and that is what a quality management plan would serve as. Now, how will you translate this planning into concrete actionable documents?"

Again, there was a cacophony of voices.

"The quality plan should describe how the project management team would implement the organization's quality policy. It should ensure that the concepts, designs and the vision included in the project brief are actually incorporated into the detailed project planning and followed during the project construction by quality assurance and closely monitored and controlled by quality control"

"The plan should state the quality metrics that would clearly specify the specific characteristic of the product or deliverable and how precisely it would be measured and evaluated."

"I have found the quality check lists very useful for this purpose. They are helpful in a systematic and comprehensive review of all important characteristics, which we might otherwise miss out in the midst of project rush"

"Great", the master responded. "Those documents would surely help to serve as the basic tools for quality management plan, which is the first step in the project quality management. Now that the first process for project quality management would be properly in place, what would you need to ensure during the execution that the quality plan is implemented and all those quality metrics, check-lists and standards are satisfied? In other words, how would you carry out quality assurance during actual project execution phase?"

"We will have to start with the overall plan, metrics and the check lists for quality, we talked about. Then, of course, we need the feedback on how exactly the work is being carried out: we would need to carry out inspection of the construction at the site during the process of construction and the site inspection reports with their records. If the inspection reports show that construction methods or the outcome of construction activities is not up to the standards set in the plan, we have to willy-nilly order corrective action to enforce the quality edict. That's how we assure quality", one disciple offered. "Include with the general inspection, the quality control measurements—like the sand analysis, the bricks strength, the quality of cement, the strengths of the cast test cubes, the size and spacing of reinforcing bars and all that stuff. Quite routine quality control tests, nothing glamorous about them, but they form the backbone of quality assurance for construction."

"Very true", the master supported,"The great Michael Angelo once said, 'Attention to trifles make perfection, but perfection is no trifle'. Though it would be too much to expect any one to strive for the kind of perfection Michael Angelo tried to achieved in his master sculpture Pieta, attention to details is indeed the key to high quality."

"For large projects, you can also have periodic quality audits. Some one, preferably outside the project team, should carry out quality audit at some pre-determined time frames or project phase end. Such quality audits by outsiders from the project team ensure objectivity and blind spots of the members of the project team are compensated." a lean man in a corner added.

"Your father was a chartered accountant?" the Zen master asked smilingly and the whole group burst out laughing.

After a pause for laughter to subside, another disciple ventured, "If the problem appears to be generic, then it would be wise to carry out the root-cause analysis of the construction problem linking the underlying cause to the quality problem persisting- what they call Ishikawa Diagrams." "That's very important," another supported." Quality must be built in and not inspected into, that is the basic premise of modern effective quality management. Root-cause analysis would point a direction for consistently carrying out high quality work."

"And let me mention another Japanese buzz word in quality management discussions—what the Japanese call the Kaizen Approach. Continuous efforts for improvement for quality—a people centered approach with getting not only the entire project team but even the contractors workers committed to quality improvement".

"Good ... Good", approved the master, "And when you mentioned quality control process, did you have in mind any techniques or tools specifically to monitor and improve the quality?"

"There are many tools and techniques", responded one, "statistical process control (with the control charts and the mean value and upper and lower control limits). This could be systematically applied to all RCC or structural steel construction ..."

"Acceptance sampling based on acceptable quality level (AQL), if we need to inspect far too many samples for a given activity ... " added another.

"Flow-charting to improve the work process flow and understand how successive steps are linked to quality. This is similar to Ishikawa diagram except that chronological relationship is taken into account here", a third disciple ventured.

"For concentrating on the most acute problem first, we can use Pareto Diagrams - a sort of frequency distribution diagram linking the type or category of identified cause with the number of defects or quality deficiency it generated. It is a sort of 80/20 rule: A few important causes account for a vast majority of effects; identify and take corrective action on them and your majority of defect problems will be taken care of."

One disciple, who had not uttered a word so far, intervened somewhat authoritatively "Let's not talk theory. We all know it or can learn from the books. Let us learn from the master, how we can apply in practice these quality management aspects in our green field construction projects."

"Well, what are your views?" the master turned to him and asked. The Zen master hardly ever preached directly. He was adept at the Socratic method of asking the questions and leading the discussion to bring out the learning.

"Well the first thing which comes to my mind is that though every project team member should be vigilant about the quality aspect and insist on the work performance to meet the quality standards, it is the management, which bears a major responsibility in delivering quality. If the infrastructure or resources provided, the materials and worker skills made available are not up to what the quality output would need, there is hardly anything that the project team member can accomplish".

"You are echoing Edwards Deming", the master responded, "Indeed, no organization can turn out a high quality product unless the top management is committed to provide the resources needed to achieve quality. But I know your organization. It is in the forefront of executing the prestigious mega projects. I presume that they would provide you with the necessary infrastructure, men, materials and technology. So the question is only how you should go about it systematically. Tell me what thoughts occur to you".

"I have several thoughts rushing in my mind and I will blurt them out as they occur without trying to evaluate them. Like brainstorming", the disciple replied, and then in almost a single breath, he continued:

- Firstly we do not have detailed technical specifications of the deliverables for the project. We any way do not make a formal work breakdown structure; the work contents or work packages are just listed. I believe we should have those specs set down for all critical or important work packages, in effect, quality metrics should be clearly set.
- Second, quality check-lists should be continually up-dated in light of quality audits and made available to all project teams in the organization
- Third, many of our clients may be familiar with and accustomed to international levels of infrastructure; we should constantly keep on benchmarking our infrastructure facilities with such international standards and attempt to upgrade our facilities. This is particularly important for our organization, which is one of the national leaders in construction projects.
- Fourth, the quality function deployment techniques should be employed to translate vague observations by site visitors into concrete actionable specifications.

And one very important necessary condition for all this to happen is the strong management support for the project team in whatever reasonable time or cost is necessary to achieve quality. Yes! I realize that I keep coming back to the Edward Deming point of view I started with. But it is very important. In the rush of finishing the project and the inevitable over-runs likely, the project team is under great pressure to take short cuts on quality to meet cost and schedule objectives. Project team would need the top management's support...." here he stopped for catching his breath.

The master intervened before he could start again, "Well, well; that is enough. So you know practically all that you need to know about quality in project management. There is really nothing much more on this in the whole project management book of knowledge. You have made a very good start in thinking through what you need to do to achieve the highest quality standards in construction. But remember, it is just a start. Contemplate... contemplate more. All that you need to know will reveal itself to you. Just contemplate what you need to do and then ... just do it"

After a brief silence, he added, "And I would go back to do what I need to do, that is, meditation".s

So saying the master closed his eyes and started breathing deeply and peacefully. The silence reigned supreme for a while and then one by one all disciples left.

Questions for Discussion

Compare the formal description of the quality management processes given in PMBOK® Guide with the informal descriptions given here.

Similarly identify and compare informal presentation of the inputs and tools and techniques given in this with the corresponding formal presentation.

CHAPTER 15

International Projects

The principal benefit of living abroad is that it enables us to get glimpses of ourselves as others see us and to realize that others' views are more accurate than ours. Progress begins with grasping the truth about ourselves, however unpleasant it may be.

—*Russel Ackoff, The Wharton School, University of Pennsylvania*

Projects are frequently classified as domestic, overseas, foreign, or global. A domestic project is one performed in its native country for a resident firm (a construction firm building a bridge in its state). An overseas project is one executed in a foreign country for a native firm (a Swedish company building a truck factory in the United States for their native company). A foreign project is executed in a foreign country for a foreign firm (a U.S. firm developing an information system in Malaysia for Malaysian banks). A global project consists of teams formed from professionals spanning multiple countries, continents, and cultures with their work integrated for the entire enterprise (e.g., multinational enterprise developing a global distribution system). Global teams are a crisscross of functions, work locale, markets, culture, and products. Today, these distinctions become blurred as the world economy and organizations become more integrated.

This chapter targets the international project manager who must resettle in a foreign environment to manage the project. The chapter also includes useful information for project professionals working overseas as well as those working on virtual projects involving colleagues from different countries.

There is no generally accepted framework or road map for project managers given international assignments. These project managers typically face a difficult set of problems—for example, absence from home, friends, and sometimes family; personal risks; missed career opportunities; foreign language, culture, and laws; adverse conditions. Of course there are positives—for example, increased income, increased responsibilities, career opportunities, foreign travel, new lifetime friends. How the international project manager adapts and approaches problems encountered in the host country often determines the success or failure of a project.

This chapter focuses on four major issues surrounding the management of international projects. First, major environmental factors that impact project selection and implementation are briefly highlighted. Second, an example of how organizations decide where to expand globally is provided. Third, the challenge of working in a strange and foreign culture is addressed. Finally, how companies select and train professionals for international projects is discussed. Although by no means comprehensive, this chapter attempts to provide a solid understanding of the major issues and challenges confronting the international project manager.

Environmental Factors

The major challenge international project managers face is the reality that what works at home may not work in a foreign environment. Too often project managers impose practices, assumed to be superior, from their home country on host-country nationals without questioning applicability to the new environment. Although there are similarities between domestic and international projects, it is a fact that good management practices vary across nations and cultures. It is these differences that can turn an international project into a nightmare. If potential international project managers have a keen awareness of differences in the host country's environment from their own domestic environment, dangers and obstacles of the global project can be reduced or avoided. There are several basic factors in the host country's environment that may alter how projects will be implemented: legal/political, security, geographical, economic, infrastructure, and culture (see Figure 15.1).

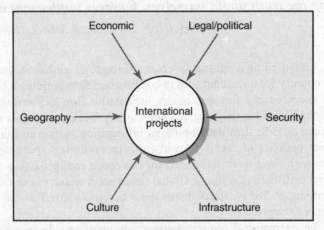

FIGURE 15.1   Environmental Factors Affecting International Projects

Legal/Political

Expatriate project managers should operate within the laws and regulations of the host country. Political stability and local laws strongly influence how projects will be implemented. Typically, these laws favor protection of local workers, suppliers, and environment. For example, how much control will be imposed from government agencies? What is the attitude of federal and state bureaucracies toward regulations and approval policies that can cause project delays? How much government interference or support can one expect? For example, an expatriate project manager based in Ho Chi Minh City observed:

> There is a common saying among the barflies about doing business in Vietnam: "The government interprets the law for its friends, and applies the law to strangers." Vietnam is no place for strangers to do business. The foreign investment law is tailored to approve investments based on the government's view of how a company and its project will further certain economic and social objectives.

The constraints imposed by national and local laws need to be identified and adhered to. Are local ecological laws restrictive? Will manufacturing a new product in a computer chip plant require exporting toxic waste materials? What are the pollution standards? How will labor laws affect the use of indigenous workers to complete the project? Given laws that affect business vary widely across countries, qualified legal assistance is essential.

Government corruption is a very real part of international business. In China various forms of obligatory "profit sharing" with city officials in the Hainan province have been reported. Employment of relatives, donations, and other "favors" are an expected cost of doing business in that region. The *Wall Street Journal* reports that Russia has become a nation in which corruption is both pervasive and arbitrary: "Without the structure the Communist Party provided, people did not know whom to pay and many anarchistic bribe collectors stepped up with their hands out."

Political stability is another key factor in deciding to implement a project in a foreign country. What are the chances that there will be a change in the party in power during the project? Are the tax provisions and government regulations stable or subject to change with the winds of political change? How are laws made, and what is the past record of fairness? How are labor unions treated in the political realm? Does labor unrest exist? Is there a chance for a coup d'état? Contingency plans need to be established to respond to emergencies.

Security

International terrorism is a fact of life in today's world. Tim Daniel, chief operating officer of International SOS Assistance, Inc., reported that the number of his firm's clients doubled after September 11th. SOS is a security firm that specializes in evacuating expatriates from dangerous situations around the world. The company cites PricewaterhouseCoopers, Nortel Networks Corp., and Citigroup among its clients.

While the 9/11 attacks magnified the fact that Americans are vulnerable to terrorism at home, they also heightened security concerns for working abroad. For example, after September 11th, several American firms canceled or scaled back projects in potential hotspots such as Pakistan and the Philippines. Others reported increased pressures from expatriates who wanted to return home with their families. On June 3, 2004, the Nobel Peace Prize-winning relief agency *Médecins Sans Frontières* (Doctors Without Borders) suspended all Afghan projects after five of its aid workers were killed in an ambush claimed by the former Taliban regime.

Crime is another factor. The growing presence of the Russian Mafia has discouraged many foreign firms from setting up operations in the former Soviet Union. Kidnapping of American professionals is also a very real threat in many parts of the world.

Security nationally involves the capacity of a country's military and police forces to prevent and respond to attacks. In many foreign countries, American firms will have to augment the countries' security system. For example, it is common practice to hire tribal bodyguards in such places as Angola and Uzbekistan.

Another real cost associated with international terrorism is the ease of commerce across borders. Heightened security measures have created border congestions that have expanded the time and cost of moving personnel, materials, and equipment across countries. These constraints need to be factored into the budget and schedule of projects.

Risk management is always a vital part of project management. It plays an even bigger role in managing projects overseas. For example, Strohl Systems Group, a global leader in recovery-planning software and services, includes the following among the questions it uses to evaluate vulnerability to terrorism: Have you included possible terrorist targets (facilities and personnel) in your hazard and vulnerability analysis? Have you conducted a counterterrorism exercise complete with law enforcement, fire, medical, and emergency management participation? What should your organization's policy be on negotiating with a person threatening a terrorist act?

Managing projects in a dangerous world is a tough assignment. Security precautions are major cost considerations not only in dollars and cents, but also in the psychological well-being of personnel sent abroad. Effective risk management is critical to success.

Geography

One factor that is often underestimated until project personnel actually arrive at a foreign destination is the geography of the country. Imagine what it is like to deplane from a modern aircraft and encounter the 105-degree heat and 90 percent humidity of Jakarta, Indonesia, or three feet of fresh snow and 225-degree temperatures in Kokkla, Finland. Whether it is the wind, the rain, the heat, the jungle, or the desert, more than one project manager has asserted that their greatest challenge was overcoming the "elements." Mother Nature cannot be ignored.

The planning and implementation of a project must take into account the impact the country's geography will have on the project. For example, a salvage operation off the coast of Greenland can only be scheduled one month out of the year because the waterway is frozen over during the remainder of the year. Construction projects in Southeast Asia have to accommodate the monsoon season when rainfall can be as high as 50 inches per month. Geography does not just affect outdoor projects. It can have an indirect effect on "indoor" projects. For example, one information systems specialist reported that his performance on a project in northern Sweden declined due to sleep deprivation. He attributed his problems to the 20 hours of daylight this part of the world experiences during summer months. Finally, extreme weather conditions can make extraordinary demands on equipment. Projects can grind to a halt because of equipment breakdown under the brunt of the elements. Working under extreme conditions typically requires special equipment, which increases the costs and complexity of the project.

Before beginning a project in a foreign land, project planners and managers need to study carefully the unique characteristics of the geography of that country. They need to factor into project plans and schedules such items as climate, seasons, altitude, and natural geographical obstacles. See the Snapshot from Practice: The Filming of *Apocalypse Now* for an example of a poorly planned endeavor in the Phillipines.

Economic

How business is conducted in the host country can influence project success. Basic economic factors in foreign countries and regions influence choices of site selection and how business will be conducted for potential projects. The gross domestic product (GDP) of a country suggests the level of development of a country. A faltering economy may indicate fewer sources of capital funding. For example, changes in protectionist strategies of a host country, such as import quotas and tariffs, can quickly alter the viability of projects. Other factors such as balance of payments, currency fluctuations, hyperinflation, population growth, education level of workforce, and market size can influence project choices and operations. For example, the economic downturn in Southeast Asia during the late 1990s saw local economies in Thailand, Malaysia, and Indonesia being devastated by inflation rates in excess of 60 percent. A company can protect against currency fluctuations by hedging or tying costs to a strong currency such as the U.S. dollar, British pound, or Euro. Still, the social upheaval caused by such dramatic economic events cannot be underestimated.

Bartering is a form of compensation that is still used by some countries and organizations. For example, one project in Africa was paid in goat skins. The goat skins were eventually sold to an Italian manufacturer of gloves. Another project along the Caspian Sea was paid for in oil. There is a small group of firms that specialize in bartering for project contractors. These intermediaries charge a commission to sell the bartered goods (e.g., oil) for the contractor. However, dealing with commodities can be a risky enterprise.

Skills, educational level, and labor supply prevalent in a host country can determine the choice of a project site. Is project selection driven by low wage levels or availability of technically skilled talent? For example, you can hire three computer programmers in India for the price of one programmer in the United States. Conversely, many high-tech companies are willing to endure the additional expense of setting up joint projects in Switzerland and Germany to take advantage of their engineering prowess.

Snapshot from Practice   The Filming of *Apocalypse Now**

In February 1976, Francis Ford Coppola took his Hollywood film crew to the Philippines to shoot *Apocalypse Now,* a film adaptation of Joseph Conrad's *Heart of Darkness* within the context of the Vietnam conflict. The Philippines was chosen because the terrain was similar to Vietnam's, and the government was willing to rent its helicopter force for the movie. At the time, the U.S. military was unwilling to cooperate on a film about Vietnam. An additional advantage was cheap labor. Coppola was able to hire more than 300 laborers at $1 to $3 per day to construct elaborate production sets, including an impressive Cambodian temple. *Apocalypse Now* was scheduled for 16 weeks of shooting at a budget of $12 to $14 million.

Months earlier, George Lucas, of *Star Wars* fame, warned Coppola against filming the movie in the Philippines. He said, "It's one thing to go over there for three weeks with five people and scrounge some footage with the Filipino Army, but if you go over there with a big Hollywood production, the longer you stay the more in danger you are of getting sucked into the swamp." His words turned out to be prophetic.

A civil war was going on between government forces and communist rebels. Shooting was repeatedly interrupted because the Philippine military ordered their helicopter pilots to leave the set and fly to the mountains to fight the rebels.

In May 1976, a typhoon struck the Philippine Islands, destroying most of the movie sets. The film team was forced to shut down production and returned to the United States for two months.

The lead character was played by Martin Sheen, who suffered a serious heart attack under the stress and heat of the filming and had to return to the United States. Coppola scrambled to film the scenes that did not require Sheen, but eventually production came to a standstill until Sheen's return nine weeks later.

The entire project proved to be a traumatic experience for Coppola, who had enjoyed Academy Award success with his previous *Godfather* movies, "There were times when I thought I was going to die, literally, from the inability to move the problems I had. I would go to bed at four in the morning in a cold sweat."

Film production ended in May 1977 after more than 200 days of shooting. The final cost was about $30 million. To date, *Apocalypse Now* has earned more than $150 million throughout the world.

* *Hearts of Darkness: A Filmmaker's Apocalypse* (Paramount Pictures, 1991).

Infrastructure

Infrastructure refers to a country or community's ability to provide the services required for a project. Infrastructure needs for a project could be communication, transportation, power, technology, and education systems. For example, developing an electric steel plant to be near a major market requires a reliable supply of electric power. If reliable power is not sufficient, other alternatives need to be considered. Software projects across borders are common today; however, they depend on reliable telecommunication networks. These networks simplify and facilitate project coordination and management among project stakeholders in different locations. If the project depends on a high ratio of vendor suppliers, good roads, and other transportation modes such as air and seaports, a good infrastructure will be imperative.

An example of a project that failed to take into account the needs and infrastructure of the host nation involved a U.S. company that was awarded the contract for building a hospital in an African nation. The local African officials wanted a "low-tech" health care facility that would take local traditions into consideration. Because their relatives generally accompanied patients, space had to be provided for them, too. Electricity was not reliably supplied, and it was doubtful whether well-educated doctors would want to spend careers away from the city. Therefore, the locals wanted a hospital for basic care with minimum technology. The construction company doing the building, on the other hand, had a preconceived notion of what a hospital should be and was not going to be accused of building a second-rate facility. It built a modern hospital that could have stood in any U.S. city. The building was completed; however, even after several years it was not used because the electricity was not sufficient, the air-conditioning could not be used, and doctors refused to live in the rural area.

Organizations need to consider the needs of the families of personnel they send overseas. Will the facilities and living conditions for the expatriate families place an undue hardship on families? Will schooling for children be available? The welfare and comfort of expatriate families play an important role in retaining good project managers and promoting their peak performance.

Culture

Visiting project managers must accept and respect the customs, values, philosophies, and social standards of their host country. Global managers recognize that if the customs and social cultural dimensions of the host country are not accommodated, projects will not succeed. Too many project audits and final reports of international projects reflect challenges and problems linked to cultural differences.

For most project managers, the biggest difference in managing an international project is operating in a national culture where things are done differently. For example, most developed nations use the same project management techniques (CPM, risk analysis, trade-off analysis). However, how activity work is performed can be very different in the host country.

Will English be the operating language, or will the project manager need to be fluent in the foreign language? Will translation services be available and sufficient? Communication problems—because of language differences—often become a major problem in carrying out even simple tasks. Although the use of translators can help tremendously, their use does not solve the communication problem completely because something is lost in translation. For example, consider the disastrous consequences of differences in interpretations and expectations between the Brazilians and Americans highlighted in the Snapshot from Practice: River of Doubt.

Will religious factors influence the project? For example, religious factors touched the spouse of a Scandinavian project manager responsible for building a water desalination plant from sea water in a Middle East country. She was restricted to the living compound for families of foreign guest workers. Going outside the compound to a nearby city meant covering her head, arms, and legs and being accompanied by another woman or, preferably, a man. A physical altercation in the city concerning her clothing was traumatic for her. She left the country and returned home. Her husband requested a transfer back home three months later. The loss of the original project manager from the project required the assigned project manager to establish relationships with the project team and host country's nationals to get the project moving smoothly again.

Not only do project managers have to adapt to the culture of the host country, but oftentimes overseas projects require working with people from different countries. For example, on a light rail project in the Philippines, an American firm was hired to oversee the interests of local real estate companies who were funding the project. The American project manager had to work with Czech representatives who were providing the rail equipment, Japanese engineers responsible for building the rail, Australian bankers who were providing additional financing, an Indian firm that were the principal architects, as well as the native Filipinos.

Of all the factors, working within a multicultural environment is most often the greatest challenge for project managers. It will be dealt with in detail later in this chapter.

Project Site Selection

As the project manager studies the factors contributing to site selection, he will see that inherent in all of these factors is the risk level senior management and directors are willing to accept for the potential rewards of a successful international project. One approach for the project manager to digest, clarify, and understand

Snapshot from Practice   River of Doubt*

After his crushing election defeat in 1912 as a third-party candidate, former president Theodore ("Teddy") Roosevelt set his sights on a grand adventure, the first descent of an unmapped rapids-choked tributary of the Amazon aptly titled the "River of Doubt." Together with Brazil's most famous explorer, Candido Mariano da Silva Rondon, Roosevelt accomplished a feat that belongs in the annals of great expeditions.

Along the way, Roosevelt and his men faced an unbelievable series of hardships, losing their canoes and supplies to crushing whitewater rapids, and enduring starvation, Indian attacks, disease, drowning, and even murder within their ranks. Candice Millard brings alive these extraordinary events in her nonfiction thriller *The River of Doubt*. While her account details the ill-fated journey it also reveals insights into international project management as it describes the collaboration between the American and Brazilian cohorts. While each party ultimately earned the respect and admiration of the other, friction between the two parties simmered from the outset.

One source of consternation was the amount of supplies and luggage that the Americans required for the journey. Warned that the luggage requirements of the former president and his party would be extensive, the Brazilian commodore Rondon ordered 110 mules and 17 pack oxen to be used for the expedition's overland journey across the Brazilian highland to the great river. Surely, he felt, this would be more than necessary for such a trip.

The Brazilians were astounded by the sheer volume of baggage that was unloaded from Roosevelt's ship, the *Vandycks*. There were mountains of crates: guns and ammunition, chairs and tables, tents and cots, equipment for collecting preserving specimens, surveying the river, and cooking meals. An exhausted stevedore elicited a roar of laughter from the onlooking crowd when he announced, "Nothing lacking but the piano!"

Rather than risk embarrassment by telling Roosevelt that they were not prepared to take so much luggage, Rondon scrambled to find additional animals. Extra oxen and mules were located, but they were far from tame. Loaded with supplies, the oxen would buck and throw off the packs. The expedition was delayed as gauchos (South American cowboys) endeavored to "break" the animals as quickly as possible.

Within days of finally setting off across the vast highlands, Roosevelt and his men began to experience the harsh realities that were to plague the expedition. After crossing a bone-strewn graveyard of oxen and mules that had starved to death or been eaten during previous expeditions, they were stunned by the sight of unopened supply crates, all clearly marked "Roosevelt South American Expedition." The pack animals, still making their weary away across the plateau ahead of the them, had begun bucking off their heavy loads!

As the officers rode slowly past the boxes, they wondered what they were leaving behind and how precious it might become in the months ahead. Little did they know how true those fears would be.

* Candice Millard, *The River of Doubt* (New York: Doubleday), 2005.

the factors leading to the selection of a specific project is to use a risk matrix similar to those found in Chapter 7. The major difference lies in the selection of the risk factors for different project sites.

Figure 15.2 presents a truncated matrix for project site selection of the construction of a laser printer factory in Singapore, India, or Ireland. In this example, political stability, worker skill and supply, culture compatibility, infrastructure, government support, and product-to-market advantage were the major assessment factors. Each project site is compared against each factor. Figure 15.3 depicts a further breakdown of the infrastructure evaluation factor. In this example, transportation, educated workforce, utilities, telecommunications, and vendor suppliers are considered important to evaluating the infrastructure for each site. The scores given in Figure 15.3 are used to assign values to the infrastructure factor of the assessment matrix, Figure 15.2. In this project, Ireland was the choice. Clearly, Singapore and Ireland were very close in terms of infrastructure and several other factors. However, the major assessment factor of using Ireland to access the EEC (product-to-market advantage) turned the decision.

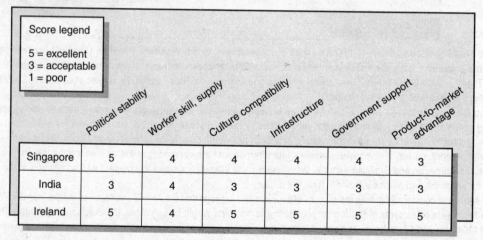

	Political stability	Worker skill, supply	Culture compatibility	Infrastructure	Government support	Product-to-market advantage
Singapore	5	4	4	4	4	3
India	3	4	3	3	3	3
Ireland	5	4	5	5	5	5

Score legend
5 = excellent
3 = acceptable
1 = poor

FIGURE 15.2   Assessment Matrix Project Site Selection

Given the macro economic factors, the firm's strategic posture toward global projects, and the major considerations for selecting this project, it is imperative the project manager quickly become sensitized to the foreign cultural factors that can spell project success or failure.

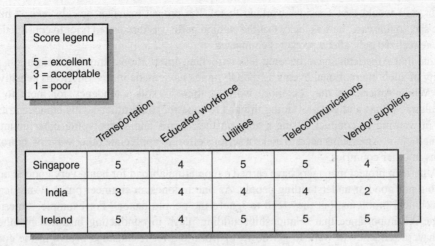

Score legend 5 = excellent 3 = acceptable 1 = poor	Transportation	Educated workforce	Utilities	Telecommunications	Vendor suppliers
Singapore	5	4	5	5	4
India	3	4	4	4	2
Ireland	5	4	5	5	5

FIGURE 15.3   Evaluation Matrix Breakdown for Infrastructure

Cross-Cultural Considerations: A Closer Look

The concept of culture was introduced in Chapter 3 as referring to the unique personality of a particular firm. More specifically, culture was defined as a system of shared norms, beliefs, values, and customs that bind people together, creating shared meaning and a unique identity. *Culture* is a concept created for descriptive purposes and depends on the group that is the focus of attention. For example, within a global context culture can refer to certain regions (i.e., Europeans, Arabs), to specific nations (i.e., French, Thai), or to certain ethnic or religious groups (i.e., Kurds, African-Americans). This chapter looks at national cultures; we freely recognize that many cultural characteristics are borderless and that there is considerable variation within any one country. Still, national cultures provide a useful anchor for understanding different habits, customs, and values around the world.

Right or wrong, Americans have a reputation for not being able to work effectively in foreign cultures. (When we use the term "American," we are referring to people from the United States; we apologize to our friends in Canada and Central and South America.) In the 1960s, the term "Ugly American" encapsulated the apparent indifference of Americans to native cultures when working or traveling abroad. Americans are often criticized for being parochial; that is, they view the world solely through their own eyes and perspectives. People with a parochial perspective do not recognize that other people have different ways of living and working effectively. American parochial attitudes probably reflect the huge domestic market of the United States, the geographic isolation of the United States, and the reality that English is becoming the international business language in many parts of the world.

It is important that Americans working on international projects anticipate cultural differences. Take, for example, a project manager from a large North American construction company who was given responsibility to select a site for the design and construction of a large fish-processing plant in a West African country. The manager assessed potential sites according to the availability of reliable power, closeness to transportation, nearness to the river for access of fishing boats from the Atlantic Ocean, proximity to main markets, and availability of housing and people for employment. After evaluating alternative sites, the project manager chose the optimum location. Just prior to requesting bids from local contractors for some of the site preparation, the manager discovered, in talking to the contractors, that the site was located on ground considered sacred by the local people, who believed this site was the place where their gods resided. None of the local people upon whom the project manager was depending for staff would ever consider working there! The project manager quickly revised his choice and relocated the site. In this case, he was lucky that the cultural gaffe was discovered prior to construction. Too often these errors are realized only after a project is completed.

Some argue that Americans have become less parochial. International travel, immigration, movies, and the popularity of such international events as the Olympics have made more Americans sensitive to cultural differences. While Americans may be more worldly, there is still a tendency for them to believe that American cultural values and ways of doing things are superior to all others. This ethnocentric perspective is reflected in wanting to conduct business only on their terms and stereotyping other countries as lazy, corrupt, or inefficient. Americans need to make a serious effort to appreciate other ways of approaching work and problems in other countries.

Finally, American project managers have earned a reputation abroad for being very good at understanding technology but not good at understanding people. As one Indonesian engineer put it, "Americans are great at solving technical problems, but they tend to ignore the people factor." For example, Americans tend to underestimate the importance that relationship building plays in conducting business in other countries. Americans have a tendency to want to get down to work and let friendships evolve in the course of their work. In most other cultures just the opposite is true. Before a foreigner works with you, he wants to get to know you as a person. Trust is not established by credentials but rather evolves from personal interaction. Business deals often require a lengthy and elaborate courtship. For example, it may take five to eight meetings before Arab managers are even willing to discuss business details.

Adjustments

Two of the biggest adjustments Americans typically have to make in working abroad are adapting to the general pace of life and the punctuality of people. In America "time is money," and a premium is placed on working quickly. Other cultures do not share Americans' sense of urgency and are accustomed to a much slower pace of life. They can't understand why Americans are always in such a hurry. Punctuality varies across cultures. For example, Americans will generally tolerate someone being 5 to 10 minutes late. In contrast, among Peruvians, the period before an apology or explanation for being late is expected might be 45 minutes to an hour!

While working on multicultural projects, managers sometimes encounter ethical dilemmas that are culturally bound. For example, the 1999 Olympic site selection scandal featured the sordid details of committee members peddling their votes for a wide range of gifts (i.e., university scholarships for their children, extravagant trips). In many societies such "bribes" or "tributes" are expected and the only way to conduct meaningful business. Moreover, many cultures will not grant a female project manager the same respect they will a male project manager. Should U.S. management increase project risk or violate its own sex-discrimination policy?

These cultural differences are just the tip of the iceberg. There are numerous "How to Do Business in . . ." books written by people who have traveled and worked abroad. Although these books may lack rigor, they typically do a good job of identifying local customs and common mistakes made by outsiders. On the other hand, anthropologists have made significant contributions to our understanding of why and how the cultures of societies are different (see the accompanying Research Highlights). Students of international project management are encouraged to study these works to gain a deeper understanding of the root causes of cultural diversity.

So what can be said to prepare people to work on international projects? The world is too diverse to do justice in one chapter to all the cultural variations managers are likely to encounter when working on international projects. Instead, a sample of some of these differences will be highlighted by discussing working

Research Highlight

Cross-Cultural Orientations*

Anthropologists Kluckhohn and Strodtbeck assert that cultural variations reflect how different societies have responded to common issues or problems throughout time (see Figure 15.4). Five of the issues featured in their comparative framework are discussed here.

- *Relation to nature*—This issue reflects how people relate to the natural world around them and to the supernatural. Should people dominate their environment, live in harmony with it, or be subjugated to it? North Americans generally strive to harness nature's forces and change them as they need. Other societies, as in India, strive to live in harmony with nature. Still other societies see themselves at the mercy of physical forces and/or subject to the will of a supreme being. Life in this context is viewed as predetermined, preordained, or an exercise in chance.

- *Time orientation*—Does the culture focus on the past, present, or future? For example, many European countries focus on the past and emphasize maintaining tradition. North Americans, on the other hand, are less concerned with tradition and tend to focus on the present and near future. Paradoxically, Japanese society, while rich with tradition, has a much longer time horizon.

- *Activity orientation*—This issue refers to a desirable focus of behavior. Some cultures emphasize "being" or living in the moment. This orientation stresses experiencing life and seeking immediate gratification. Other cultures emphasize "doing" and emphasize postponing immediate gratification for greater accomplishment. A third alternative is the "control" orientation, where people restrain their desires by detaching themselves from objects. The activity dimension affects how people approach work and leisure and the extent to which work-related concerns pervade their lives. It is reflected in the age-old question, "Do we live to work or work to live?"

- *Basic nature of people*—Does a culture view people as good, evil, or some mix of these two? In many Third World countries, people see themselves as basically honest and trustworthy. Conversely, some Mediterranean cultures have been characterized as taking a rather evil view of human nature. North Americans are somewhere in between. They see people as basically good but stay on guard so as not to be taken advantage of.

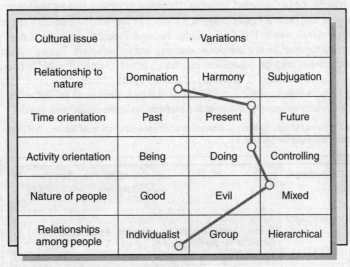

FIGURE 15.4   Kluckhohn-Strodtbeck's Cross-Cultural Framework

Note: The line indicates where the United States tends to fall along these issues.

- *Relationships among people*—This issue concerns the responsibility one has for others. Americans, for instance, tend to be highly individualistic and believe everyone should take care of him- or herself. In contrast, many Asian societies emphasize concern for the group or community he or she is a member of. A third variation is hierarchical, which is similar to the group except that in these societies groups are hierarchically ranked, and membership is essentially stable over time. This is a characteristic of aristocratic societies and caste systems.

The Kluckhohn and Strodtbeck framework provides a basis for a deeper understanding of cultural differences. At the same time, they warn that not all members of a culture practice the same behavior all the time, and, as in the United States, there is likely to be considerable variation within a given culture.

* F. Kluckhohn and F. L. Strodtbeck, *Variations in Value Orientations* (Evanston, IL: Row, Peterson, 1961).

Research Highlight   Hofstede Framework*

The Hofstede framework grew from a study of 88,000 people working in IBM subsidiaries in 50 countries and 3 multicountry regions. Based on responses to a 32-item questionnaire, Dutch social scientist Geert Hofstede developed different dimensions for examining cultures:

1. Individualism versus collectivism. Identifies whether a culture holds individuals or the group responsible for each member's welfare.
2. Power distance. Describes the degree to which a culture accepts status and power differences among its members.
3. Uncertainty avoidance. Identifies a culture's willingness to accept uncertainty and ambiguity about the future.
4. Masculinity-femininity. Describes the degree to which the culture emphasizes competitive and achievement-oriented behavior or displays concerns for relationships.

Figure 15.5 shows how he ranked selected countries according to collectivism-individualism and power distance. Wealth appears to influence both factors. Power distance is correlated with income inequality in a country while individualism is correlated with national wealth (Per Capita Gross National Product). As a result high power distance and collectivism are often found together, as are low power distance and individualism. This can affect decision making on project teams. For example, while the high collectivism may lead a project team in Thailand to operate consensually, the high power distance may cause decisions to be heavily influenced by the desires of the project manager. Conversely, a similar team operating in more individualistic and low power distance such as Great Britain or America might make decisions with more open debate including challenging the preferences of the project manager.

* *Culture's Consequences: Comparing Values, Behaviors, Institutions and Organizations Across Nations,* 2nd Edition. (Thousand Oaks, CA: Sage Publications, 2001). http://www.geerthofstede.nl

Collectivism		Columbia, Peru, Thailand, Singapore, Mexico, Turkey, Indonesia
Individualism	Israel, Finland, Germany, Ireland, New Zealand, Canada, Great Britain, United States	Spain, South Africa, France, Italy, Belgium
	Low power distance	High power distance

FIGURE 15.5   Sample Country Clusters on Hofstede's Dimensions of Individualism-Collectivism and Power Distance

on projects in four different countries: Mexico, France, Saudi Arabia, and China. We apologize to our readers outside the United States because briefings are presented from the viewpoint of a U.S. project manager working in these countries. Still, in an effort not to be too ethnocentric, we present a fifth scenario for foreign project managers assigned to working in the United States. Although by no means exhaustive, these briefings provide a taste of what it is like to work in and with people from these countries.

Working in Mexico

America developed historically in an environment where it was important for strangers to be able to get along, interact, and do business. On the American frontier almost everyone was a stranger, and people had to both cooperate and keep their distance. The New England Yankee sentiment that "Good fences make good neighbors" expresses this American cultural value well. Conversely, Mexico developed historically in an environment where the only people to trust were family and close friends—and by extension, people who were known to those whom you knew well. As a consequence, personal relationships dominate all aspects of Mexican business. While Americans are generally taught not to do business with friends, Mexicans and other Latin Americans are taught to do business with no one but friends.

The significance of personal relationships has created a *compadre* system in which Mexicans are obligated to give preference to relatives and friends when hiring, contracting, procuring, and sharing business opportunities. North Americans often complain that such practices contribute to inefficiency in Mexican firms. While this may or may not be the case, efficiency is prized by Americans, while Mexicans place a higher value on friendship.

Mexicans tend to perceive Americans as being "cold." They also believe that most Americans look down on them. Among the most effective things an American can do to prevent being seen as a typical *Gringo* is to take the time and effort in the beginning of a working relationship to really get to know Mexican counterparts. Because family is all-important to Mexicans, a good way for developing a personal relationship is exchanging information about each other's family. Mexicans will often gauge people's trustworthiness by the loyalty and attention they devote to their family.

The *mañana* syndrome reflects another cultural difference between Americans and Mexicans. Mexicans have a different concept of time than Americans do. Mexicans feel confined and pressured when given deadlines; they prefer open-ended schedules. They generally consider individuals to be more important than sticking to a schedule. If a friend drops in at work, most Mexicans will stop and talk, regardless of how long it takes, and even if chatting makes their work late. This sometimes contributes to the erroneous perception that Mexicans lack a work ethic. Quite the contrary; given a minimal incentive, Mexicans can be quite industrious and ambitious.

Finally, as in many other cultures, Mexicans do not share Americans' confidence that they control their own destiny. While Americans are taught, "When the going gets tough, the tough get going," Mexicans are taught, "Taking action without knowing what is expected or wanted can have dangerous consequences." Mexicans tend to be more cautious and want to spend more time discussing risks and potential problems that Americans might dismiss as improbable or irrelevant.

Other useful guidelines for working with Mexicans on projects include the following:

1. Americans tend to be impersonal and practical when making arguments; Mexicans can be very passionate and emotional when arguing. They enjoy a lively debate.
2. Where Americans tend to use meetings as the place to work things out publicly, Mexicans tend to see meetings as the place where persons with authority ratify what has been decided during informal private discussions.
3. While Mexicans can be emotional, they tend to shy away from any sort of direct confrontation or criticism. A long silence often indicates displeasure or disagreement.

4. Speech in Mexico is often indirect. People rarely say no directly but are more likely to respond by saying maybe *(quizas),* or by saying "I will think about it" or changing the subject. Yes *(si)* is more likely to mean "I understand you" than "yes."

5. Titles are extremely important in Mexico and are always used when a person is introducing him- or herself or being introduced. Pay as much attention to remembering a person's title as to remembering his or her name.

Today, with NAFTA and increased international business activity in Mexico, old traditions are disappearing. American managers report that cultural differences are less evident in northern Mexico where many multinational firms operate. Here *hora americana* (American time) rather than *hora mexicana* tends to be used when dealing with foreigners. Project managers should devote up-front effort to understanding how much older mores of Mexican culture apply to their project.

Working in France

Some Americans consider the French the most difficult to work with among Europeans. This feeling probably stems from a reflection of the French culture, which is quite different from that in the United States.

In France, one's social class is very important. Social interactions are constrained by class standing, and during their lifetimes most French people do not encounter much change in social status. Unlike an American, who through hard work and success can move from the lowest economic stratum to the highest, a successful French person might, at best, climb one or two rungs up the social ladder. Additionally, the French are very status conscious and like to provide signs of this status, such as knowledge of literature and arts; a well-designed, tastefully decorated house; and a high level of education.

The French tend to admire or be fascinated with people who disagree with them; in contrast, Americans are more attracted to those who agree with them. As a result, the French are accustomed to conflict and, during negotiations, accept the fact that some positions are irreconcilable and must be accepted as such. Americans, on the other hand, tend to believe that conflicts can be resolved if both parties make an extra effort and are willing to compromise. Also, the French often determine a person's trustworthiness based on their firsthand, personal evaluation of the individual's character. Americans, in contrast, tend to evaluate a person's trustworthiness on the basis of past achievements and other people's evaluations.

The French are often accused of lacking an intense work ethic. For example, many French workers frown on overtime and on average they have one of the longest vacations in the world (four to five weeks annually). On the other hand, the French enjoy a reputation for productive work, a result of the French tradition of craftsmanship. This tradition places a greater premium on quality rather than on getting things accomplished quickly.

Most French organizations tend to be highly centralized with rigid structures. As a result, it usually takes longer to carry out decisions. Because this arrangement is quite different from the more decentralized organizations in the United States, many U.S. project managers find the bureaucratic red tape a source of considerable frustration.

In countries like the United States, a great deal of motivation is derived from professional accomplishments. The French do not tend to share this same view of work. While they admire American industriousness, they believe that quality of life is what really matters. As a result they attach much greater importance to leisure time, and many are unwilling to sacrifice the enjoyment of life for a dedication to project work.

Cautions to remember with the French include these:

1. The French value punctuality. It is very important to be on time for meetings and social occasions.

2. Great importance is placed on neatness and taste. When interacting with French businesspeople, pay close attention to your own professional appearance and appear cultured and sophisticated.

3. The French can be very difficult to negotiate with. Often, they ignore facts, no matter how convincing they may be. They can be quite secretive about their position. It is difficult to obtain information from them, even in support for their position. Patience is essential for negotiating with them.

4. French managers tend to see their work as an intellectual exercise. They do not share the American view of management as an interpersonally demanding exercise, where plans have to be constantly "sold" upward and downward using personal skills.

5. The French generally consider managers to be experts. They expect managers to give precise answers to work-related questions. To preserve their reputation, some French managers act as if they know the answers to questions even when they don't.

Working in Saudi Arabia

Project management has a long tradition in Saudi Arabia and other Arab countries. Financed by oil money, European and American firms have contributed greatly to the modernization of Arab countries. Despite this tradition, foreigners often find it very hard to work on projects in Saudi Arabia. A number of cultural differences can be cited for this difficulty.

One is the Arabian view of time. In North America, it is common to use the cliché, "The early bird gets the worm." In Saudi Arabia, a favorite expression is, "Bukra insha Allah," which means, "Tomorrow if God wills," an expression that reflects the Saudis' approach to time. Unlike Westerners, who believe they control their own time, Arabs believe that Allah controls time. As a result, when Saudis commit themselves to a date in the future and fail to show up, there is no guilt or concern on their part because they have no control over time in the first place. In planning future events with Arabs, it pays to hold lead time to a week or less, because other factors may intervene or take precedence.

An associated cultural belief is that destiny depends more on the will of a supreme being than on the behavior of individuals. A higher power dictates the outcome of important events, so individual action is of little consequence. As a result, progress or the lack of progress on a project is considered more a question of fate than effort. This leads Saudis to rely less on detailed plans and schedules to complete projects than Americans do.

Another important cultural contrast between Saudi Arabians and Americans is emotion and logic. Saudis often act on the basis of emotion; in contrast, those in an Anglo culture are taught to act on logic. During negotiations, it is important not only to share the facts but also to make emotional appeals that demonstrate your suggestion is the right thing to do.

Saudis also make use of elaborate and ritualized forms of greetings and leave-takings. A businessperson may wait far past the assigned meeting time before being admitted to a Saudi office. Once there, the individual may find a host of others present; one-on-one meetings are rare. Moreover, during the meeting there may be continuous interruptions. Visitors arrive and begin talking to the host, and messengers may come in and go out on a regular basis. The businessperson is expected to take all this activity as perfectly normal and to remain composed and ready to continue discussions as soon as the host is prepared to do so.

Initial meetings are typically used to get to know the other party. Business-related discussions may not occur until the third or fourth meeting. Business meetings typically conclude with an offer of coffee or tea. This is a sign that the meeting is over and that future meetings, if there are to be any, should now be arranged.

Saudis attach a great deal of importance to status and rank. When meeting with them, defer to the senior person. It is also important never to criticize or berate anyone publicly. This causes the individual to lose face; the same is true for the person who makes these comments. Mutual respect is expected at all times.

Other useful guidelines for working in an Arab culture such as Saudi Arabia include the following:

1. It is important never to display feelings of superiority because this makes the other party feel inferior. No matter how well someone does something, the individual should let the action speak for itself and not brag or draw attention to himself.
2. A lot of what gets done is a result of going through administrative channels in the country. It is often difficult to sidestep a lot of this red tape, and efforts to do so can be regarded as disrespect for legal and governmental institutions.
3. Connections are extremely important in conducting business. More important people get fast service from less important people. Close relatives take absolute priority; nonrelatives are kept waiting.
4. Patience is critical to the success of business negotiations. Time for deliberations should be built into all negotiations to prevent a person from giving away too much in an effort to reach a quick settlement.
5. Important decisions are usually made in person and not by correspondence or telephone. While Saudis seek counsel from many people, the ultimate power to make a decision rests with the person at the top, and this individual relies heavily on personal impressions, trust, and rapport.

Working in China

In recent years the People's Republic of China (PRC, or China, for short) has moved away from isolation to encourage more business with the rest of the world. While China holds tremendous promise, many Western firms have found working on projects in China to be a long, grueling process that often results in failure. One of the primary reasons for problems is the failure to appreciate Chinese culture.

Chinese society, like those of Japan and Korea, is influenced by the teachings of Confucius (551–478 B.C.). Unlike America, which relies on legal institutions to regulate behavior, in Confucian societies the primary deterrent against improper or illegal behavior is shame or loss of face. Face is more than simply reputation. There is a Chinese saying that, "Face is like the bark of a tree; without its bark, the tree dies." Loss of face not only brings shame to individuals but also to family members. A member's actions can cause shame for the entire family, hampering that family from working effectively in Chinese society.

In China, "whom you know is more important than what you know." The term *guanxi* refers to personal connections with appropriate authorities or individuals. China observers argue that *guanxi* is critical for working with the Chinese. Chinese are raised to distrust strangers, especially foreigners. Trust is transmitted via *guanxi*. That is, a trusted business associate of yours must pass you along to his trusted business associates. Many outsiders criticize *guanxi,* considering it to be like nepotism where decisions are made regarding contracts or problems based on family ties or connections instead of an objective assessment of ability.

Many believe that the quickest way to build *guanxi* relationships is through tendering favors. Gift-giving, entertainment at lavish banquets, questionable payments, and overseas trips are common. While Westerners see this as nothing short of bribery, the Chinese consider it essential for good business. Another common method for outsiders to acquire *guanxi* is by hiring local intermediaries, who use their connections to create contacts with Chinese officials and businesspeople.

In dealing with the Chinese, you must realize they are a collective society in which people pride themselves on being a member of a group. For this reason, you should never single out a Chinese for specific praise because this is likely to embarrass the individual in front of his peers. At the same time, you should avoid the use of "I" because it conveys that the speaker is drawing attention to himself or herself.

Chinese do not appreciate loud, boisterous behavior, and when speaking to each other they maintain a greater physical distance than is typical in America. Other cautions include the following:

1. Once the Chinese decide who and what is best, they tend to stick to their decisions. So while they may be slow in formulating a plan, once they get started they make good progress.

Snapshot from Practice   Project Management X-Files

Americans tend to discount the significance of luck and believe that good fortune is generally a result of hard work. In other cultures, luck takes on greater significance and has supernatural ramifications. For example, in many Asian cultures certain numbers are considered lucky, while others are unlucky. In Hong Kong the numbers 7, 3, and especially 8 (which sounds like the word for prosperity) are considered lucky, while the number 4 is considered unlucky (because it is pronounced like the word "death"). Hong Kong businesspeople go to great lengths to avoid the number 4. For example, there is no fourth floor in office and hotel buildings. Business executives have been known to reject ideal sites in heavily congested Hong Kong because the address would contain the number 4. They pay premium prices for suitable sites containing addresses with the lucky numbers. Likewise, Hong Kong business managers avoid scheduling important events on the fourth day of each month and prefer to arrange critical meetings on the eighth day.

Hong Kong is also a place where the ancient art of *Feng shui* (literally "wind water") is practiced. This involves making sure a site and buildings are aligned in harmony with the earth's energy forces so that the location will be propitious. Feng shui practitioners are often called in on construction projects to make sure that the building is aligned correctly on the site. In some cases, the technical design of the

Rob Brimson/Taxi/Getty Images.

building is changed to conform to the recommendations of such experts. Similarly, Feng shui experts have been known to be called in when projects are experiencing problems. Their recommendations may include repositioning the project manager's desk or hanging up mirrors to deflect the flow of unharmonious influences away from the building or site of the project.

In cultures where luck is believed to play a role in business, people who discount luck may not only insult the luck seekers, they may risk being thought negligent in not paying enough attention to what is viewed as a legitimate business concern.

2. Reciprocity is important in negotiations. If Chinese give concessions, they expect some in return.
3. The Chinese tend to be less animated than Americans. They avoid open displays of affection and physical contact; they are more reticent and reserved than Americans.
4. The Chinese place less value on the significance of time and often get Americans to concede concessions by stalling.
5. In Confucian societies those in position of power and authority are obligated to assist the disadvantaged. In return they gain face and a good reputation.

For more insights on Chinese culture see the Snapshot from Practice: Project Management X-Files.

Working in the United States

In the world of international projects, professionals from other countries will come to the United States to manage projects. To them, the United States is a foreign assignment. They will have to adapt their management style to the new environment they find in the States.

Immigration has made the United States a melting pot of diverse cultures. While many are quick to point out the differences between North and South, Silicon Valley and Wall Street, social anthropologists have identified certain cultural characteristics that shape how many Americans conduct business and manage projects.

Mainstream Americans are motivated by achievement and accomplishment. Their identity and, to a certain extent, their self-worth are measured by what they have achieved. Foreigners are often astounded by the material wealth accumulated by Americans and the modern conveniences most Americans enjoy. They are also quick to point out that Americans appear too busy to truly enjoy what they have achieved.

Americans tend to idolize the self-made person who rises from poverty and adversity to become rich and successful. Most Americans have a strong belief that they can influence and create their future, that with hard work and initiative, they can achieve whatever they set out to do. Self-determination and pragmatism dominate their approach to business.

Although Americans like to set precise objectives, they view planning as a means and not an end. They value flexibility and are willing to deviate from plans and improvise if they believe change will lead to accomplishment. Obstacles on a project are to be overcome, not worked around. Americans think they can accomplish just about anything, given time, money, and technology.

Americans fought a revolution and subsequent wars to preserve their concept of democracy, so they resent too much control or interference, especially by governments. While more an ideal than practice, there is deep-rooted belief in American management philosophy that those people who will be affected by decisions should be involved in making decisions. Many foreign businesspeople are surprised at the amount of autonomy and decision-making authority granted to subordinates. Foreign personnel have to learn to interact with American professionals below their rank in their own organizations.

Businesspeople from different African, Asian, and Latin American countries are amazed and often somewhat distressed at the rapid pace of America. "Getting things done" is an American characteristic. Americans are very time-conscious and efficient. They expect meetings to start on time. They tinker with gadgets and technological systems, always searching for easier, better, more efficient ways of accomplishing things. American professionals are often relentless in pursuing project objectives and expect that behavior of others also.

Americans in play or business generally are quite competitive, reflecting their desire to achieve and succeed. Although the American culture contains contradictory messages about the importance of success (i.e., "It's not whether you win or lose but how you play the game" versus "nice guys finish last"), winning and being number one are clearly valued in American society. Foreigners are often surprised at how aggressively Americans approach business with adversarial attitudes toward competitors and a desire to not just meet but to exceed project goals and objectives.

Other guidelines and cautions for working with Americans on projects include:

1. More than half of U.S. women work outside the home; females have considerable opportunity for personal and professional growth, guaranteed by law. It is not uncommon to find women in key project positions. Female professionals expect to be treated as equals. Behavior tolerated in other countries would be subject to harassment laws in the States.

2. In the United States, gifts are rarely brought by visitors in a business situation.

3. Americans tend to be quite friendly and open when first meeting someone. Foreigners often mistake this strong "come-on" for the beginning of a strong reciprocal friendship. This is in contrast to many other cultures where there is more initial reserve in interpersonal relations, especially with strangers. For many foreigners, the American comes on too strong, too soon, and then fails to follow up with the implicitly promised friendship.

4. Although in comparison to the rest of the world Americans tend to be informal in greeting and dress, they are a noncontact culture (e.g., they avoid embracing in public usually) and Americans maintain certain physical/psychological distance with others (e.g., about two feet) in conversations.

5. American decision making is results oriented. Decisions tend to be based on facts and expected outcomes, not social impact.

Summary Comments about Working in Different Cultures

These briefings underscore the complexity of working on international projects. It is common practice to rely on intermediaries—often natives who are foreign educated—to bridge the gap between cultures. These intermediaries perform a variety of functions. They act as translators. They use their social connections to expedite transactions and protect the project against undue interference. They are used to sidestep the touchy bribery/gift dilemma (see the accompanying Snapshot from Practice). They serve as cultural guides, helping outsiders understand and interpret the foreign culture. In today's world, there are a growing number of consulting firms that perform these functions by helping foreign clients work on projects in their country.

The international briefings also highlight the importance of project managers doing their homework and becoming familiar with the customs and habits of the host country they are going to be working in. As far as possible, the project should be managed in such a way that local-country norms and customs are honored. However, there are limits to the extent to which you should accommodate foreign cultures. *Going native* is generally not an alternative. After all, it took a Russian his entire life to learn how to be a Russian. It would be foolish to think an outsider could learn to be one in six months, two years, or perhaps ever.

The remainder of this chapter focuses on the selection and training of project personnel for international projects. But before these issues are discussed, this section concludes with a discussion of the phenomenon of culture shock, which can have a profound effect on a foreigner's performance on a project in a strange culture.

Culture Shock

My first few weeks in Chiang Mai [Thailand] were filled with excitement. I was excited about the challenge of building a waste treatment plant in a foreign country. I was fascinated with Thai customs and traditions, the smells and sights of the night market. Soon I noticed a distinct change in my attitude and behavior. I started having

---

Snapshot from Practice   Dealing with Customs

Will corruption influence the project? Bribes are illegal in the United States, but in some countries they are the usual way to do business. For example, one American project manager in a foreign country requested that a shipment of critical project equipment be sent "overnight rush." Two days later, inquiries to the sender confirmed the materials had been delivered to the nearby airport. Further inquiries to the port found the shipment "waiting to pass customs." Locals quickly informed the American that money paid to the chief customs inspector would expedite clearance. The American project manager's response was, "I will not be held hostage. Bribes are illegal!" Two more days of calling government officials did not move the shipment from customs. The manager related his problem to a friendly businessman of the host nation at a social affair. The local businessman said he would see if he could help. The shipment arrived the next morning at 10:00 A.M. The American called his local business friend and thanked him profusely. "I owe you one." "No," replied the local. "You owe me a $50 dinner when I visit you in the States." The use of an intermediary in such situations may be the only avenue available to a manager to reduce the stress and personal conflict with the U.S. value system.

problems sleeping and lacked energy. I became irritable at work, frustrated by how long things took to accomplish, and how I couldn't seem to get anything accomplished. I started staying up late at night watching CNN in my hotel room.

This engineer is experiencing what many would call "culture shock." *Culture shock* is a natural psychological disorientation that most people suffer when they move into a culture different from their own. The culture shock cycle has four stages (see Figure 15.6):

1. *Honeymoon*—You start your overseas assignment with a sense of excitement. The new and the unusual ~~ welcomed. At first it is amusing not to understand or be understood. Soon a sense of frustration begins to set in.
2. *Irritability and hostility*—Your initial enthusiasm is exhausted, and you begin to notice that differences are greater than you first imagined. You become frustrated by your inability to get things done as you are accustomed to. You begin to lose confidence in your abilities to communicate and work effectively in the different culture.
3. *Gradual adjustment*—You begin to overcome your sense of isolation and figure out how to get things done in the new culture. You acquire a new perspective of what is possible and regain confidence in your ability to work in the culture.
4. *Adaptation*—You recover from your sense of psychological disorientation and begin to function and communicate in the new culture.

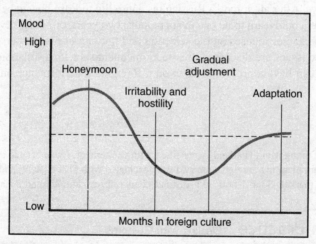

FIGURE 15.6   Culture Shock Cycle

Culture shock is not a disease but a natural response to immersing yourself in a new environment. Culture shock results from a breakdown in your selective perception and effective interpretation system. At a subliminal level, your senses are being bombarded by a wide variety of strange sounds, sights, and smells. At the same time, the normal assumptions you are accustomed to using in your home culture to interpret perceptions and to communicate intentions no longer apply. When this happens, whether in a business context or in normal attempts to socialize, confusion and frustration set in. The natives' behavior does not seem to make sense, and, even more importantly, your behavior does not produce expected results. Frustration occurs because you are used to being competent in such situations and now find you are unable to operate effectively.

Culture shock is generally considered a positive sign that the professional is becoming involved in the new culture instead of remaining isolated in an expatriate ghetto. The significant question is how best to manage culture shock, not how to avoid it. The key appears to be managing the stress associated with culture shock.

Stress-related culture shock takes many forms: disappointment, frustration, withdrawal, anxiety, and physiological responses such as fatigue, sleeplessness, and headaches. Stress is induced by the senses being overwhelmed by foreign stimuli and the inability to function effectively in a strange land. Stress is exacerbated when one encounters disturbing situations that, as a foreigner, are neither understood nor condoned. For example, many North Americans are appalled by the poverty and hunger in many underdeveloped countries.

Coping with Culture Shock

There are a wide range of stress management techniques for coping with culture shock. One method does not necessarily work any better than another; success depends on the particular individual and situation involved. Some people engage in regular physical exercise programs, some practice meditation and relaxation exercises, and others find it healthy to keep a journal.

Many effective international managers create "stability zones." They spend most of their time immersed in the foreign culture but then briefly retreat into an environment—a stability zone—that closely recreates home. For example, when one of the authors was living in Kraków, Poland, with his family, they would routinely go to the Polish movie houses to see American movies with Polish subtitles. The two hours spent hearing English and seeing a familiar environment on the screen had a soothing effect on everyone.

On the project, managers can reduce the stress caused by culture shock by recognizing it and modifying their expectations and behavior accordingly. They can redefine priorities and develop more realistic expectations as to what is possible. They can focus their limited energy on only the most important tasks and relish small accomplishments.

After three to six months, depending on the individual and assignment, most people come up from their culture shock "low" and begin living a more normal life in the foreign country. They talk to acquaintances from the host country and experienced outsiders from their own culture to find out how to behave and what to expect. Little by little they learn how to make sense of the new environment. They figure out when "yes" means "yes" and when it means "maybe" and when it means "no." They begin to master the language so that they can make themselves understood in day-to-day conversations.

The vast majority of people eventually make the adjustment, although for some people it can take much longer than three to six months. A smaller number never recover, and their international experience turns into a nightmare. Some exhibit severe stress symptoms (e.g., alcoholism, drug abuse, nervous breakdown) and must return home before finishing their assignment.

Professionals can use project work as a bridge until they adjust to their new environment. Unfortunately, spouses who do not work do not have this advantage. When spouses are left to cope with the strange environment on their own, they often have a much more difficult time overcoming culture shock. The effect on spouses cannot be underestimated. The number one reason expatriate managers return home is that their spouses failed to adjust to the new environment.

Project professionals working overseas accept that they are in a difficult situation and that they will not act as effectively as they did at home, especially in the initial stages. They recognize the need for good stress management techniques, including stability zones. They also recognize that it is not an individual problem and invest extra time and energy to help their spouses and families manage the transition. At the same time, they appreciate that their colleagues are experiencing similar problems and are sensitive to their needs. They work together to manage the stress and pull out of a culture shock low as quickly as possible.

It is somewhat ironic, but people who work on projects overseas experience culture shock twice. Many professionals experience the same kind of disorientation and stress when they return home, although it is usually less severe. For some, their current job has less responsibility and is boring compared with the challenge of their overseas assignment. For others, they have problems adjusting to changes made in the home organization while they were gone. This can be compounded by financial shock when the salary and fringe benefits they became accustomed to in the foreign assignment are now lost, and adjusting to a lower standard of living is difficult. It typically takes six months to a year before managers operate again at full effectiveness after a lengthy foreign assignment.

Selection and Training for International Projects

When professionals are selected for overseas projects and they do not work out, the overall costs can be staggering. Not only does the project experience a serious setback, but the reputation of the firm is damaged in the region. This is why many firms have developed formal screening procedures to help ensure the careful selection of personnel for international projects. Organizations examine a number of characteristics to determine whether an individual is suitable for overseas work. They may look for work experience with cultures other than one's own, previous overseas travel, good physical and emotional health, a knowledge of a host nation's language, and even recent immigration background or heritage. Prospective candidates and their family members are often interviewed by trained psychologists, who assess their ability to adapt and function in the new culture.

While there is growing appreciation for screening people for foreign assignments, the number one reason for selection is that the personnel assigned are the best people available for the technical challenges of the project. Technical know-how takes precedence over cross-cultural sensitivity or experience. As a consequence, training is critical to fill in the cultural gaps and prepare individuals to work in a foreign land.

Training varies widely, depending on the individual, company, nature of the project, and cultures to work with. Project professionals assigned to foreign countries should have a minimal understanding of the following areas:

- Religion.
- Dress codes.
- Education system.
- Holidays—national and religious.
- Daily eating patterns.
- Family life.
- Business protocols.
- Social etiquette.
- Equal opportunity.

An example of a short-term training program is the one developed by Underwriter Laboratories, Inc., to train staff who travel to Japan to work with clients on projects. The program is designed around a series of mini-lectures that cover topics ranging from how to handle introductions to the proper way to exchange gifts to the correct way of interpreting Japanese social and business behavior. The two-day program consists of lectures, case studies, role plays, language practice, and a short test on cultural terminology; it concludes with a 90-minute question-and-answer period. At the end of the program, participants have a fundamental understanding of how to communicate with the Japanese. More importantly, they know the types of information they lack and how to go about learning more to become effective intercultural communicators.

Other training programs are more extensive. For example, Peace Corps volunteers undergo an intense two- to four-month training program in their country of service. The training includes classes on the history and traditions of the country, intensive language instruction, and cross-cultural training as well as home-stays with local families. Many companies outsource training to one of the many firms specializing in overseas and intercultural training.

Figure 15.7 attempts to link the length and type of training with the cultural fluency required to successfully complete the project. Three different learning approaches are highlighted:

1. The "information-giving" approach—the learning of information or skills from a lecture-type orientation.
2. The "affective" approach—the learning of information/skills that raise the affective responses on the part of the trainee and result in cultural insights.
3. The "behavioral/experiential" approach—variant of the affective approach technique that provides the trainee with realistic simulations or scenarios.

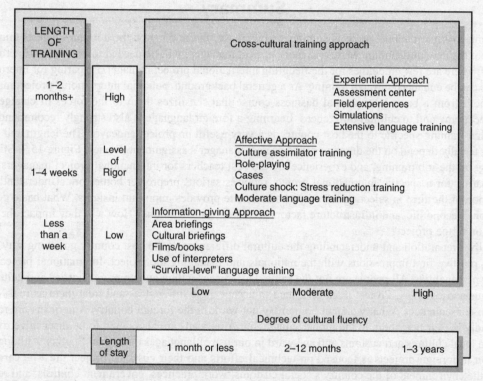

FIGURE 15.7   Relationship between Length and Rigor of Training and Cultural Fluency Required

According to this framework, the length and level of training would depend on the degree of cultural fluency required to be successful. In general, the longer the person is expected to work in the foreign country, the more intensive the training should be. Length of stay should not be the only consideration; high levels of cultural fluency, and therefore more extensive training, may be required to perform short-term, intense projects. In addition, location is important. Working in Australia will likely require less cultural fluency than working on a project in Pakistan.

While English is rapidly becoming the international language for business in many parts of the world, you should not underestimate the value of being able to speak the language of the host country. At a minimum you should be able to exchange basic pleasantries in the native tongue. Most foreigners consider this a sign of respect, and even if you stumble they appreciate the effort.

In many situations translators are used to facilitate communication. While time-consuming, this is the only way to communicate with non-English-speaking personnel. Be careful in the selection of translators, and do not just assume they are competent. For example, one of the authors enlisted the help of a Polish translator to conduct a meeting with some Polish managers. After the meeting the translator, who taught English at a local university, asked if the author "had good time." I responded that I felt things went well. The translator repeated her question. Puzzled, I reaffirmed that I felt things went well. After the interchange was repeated several times, the translator finally grabbed my wrist, pointed at my watch, and asked again if I "had good time?" Doubts arose concerning the accuracy of the meeting translation!

Summary

The number of international projects continues to increase, and nothing on the horizon suggests things will change in the new millennium. More and more project managers will be needed to implement international projects. There are few guidelines for the fledgling international project manager. Preparing for international projects can be enhanced through training. As a general background, potential international project managers can benefit from a basic international business course that sensitizes them to the forces of change in the global economy and to cultural differences. Learning a foreign language is also strongly recommended.

Further training specific to the host country is a very useful preproject endeavor. The length and type of training usually depend on the duration of the project manager's assignment. Review Figure 15.7. Still, self-learning, on-the-job training, and experience are the best teachers for international project managers.

Preparing for a specific international project requires serious preproject homework. Understanding the motivation of the firm in selecting the project and its site provides important insights. What basic political, geographic, economic, and infrastructure factors were key considerations? How will they impact the implementation of the project?

Finally, preparation and understanding the cultural differences of the host country go a long way toward making positive first impressions with the nationals and managing the project. International projects have distinct personalities. All people are not the same. Differences within and among countries and cultures are numerous and complex. Project managers need to accept these differences and treat them as real—or live with the consequences. What works at home may not work in the foreign country. Americans are regarded as friendly by our neighbors in the global village, but Americans are also noted to be insensitive to differences in local cultures and customs and awkward in our use of languages other than English. Although most attention in foreign projects is focused on technical efforts and their cost, the project must be carried out within the environment of the country's social customs, work practices, government controls, and religious beliefs. In most cultures, sincerity and flexibility will pay off.

Key Terms

Cross-cultural orientations	Culture shock	International projects
Culture	Infrastructure	

Review Questions

1. How do environmental factors affect project implementation?
2. What role do local intermediaries play in helping an outsider complete a project?
3. Why is it important to honor the customs and traditions of a country when working on an international project?
4. What is culture shock? What can you do to reduce the negative effects of culture shock?
5. How should you go about preparing yourself for an international project?

Exercises

1. Interview someone who has worked or lived in a foreign country for more than six months.
   a. What was his experience with culture shock?
   b. What did he learn about the culture of the country he lived in?
   c. What advice would he give to someone who would be working on a project in that country?
2. Try as best you can to apply the Kluckhohn-Strodtbeck cross-cultural framework to the four countries discussed in this chapter: Mexico, France, Saudi Arabia, and China. Where do you think these countries lie on each of the cultural issues?
3. Place in order the following countries in terms of what you would think would be the least to most corrupt:

   United States, Finland, Saudi Arabia, Russia, Australia, Hong Kong, Brazil, China, Kenya, Indonesia, Germany, Chile.

   Use an Internet search engine to find the most recent International Corruptions Perceptions Index (CPI) released by the Berlin-based organization Transparency International.
   a. Check your predictions with the Index.
   b. How well did you do? What countries surprised you? Why?

References

Ackoff, R. L., *Ackoff's Fables: Irreverent Reflections on Business and Bureaucracy* (New York: Wiley, 1991), p. 221.

Alder, N., *International Dimensions of Organizational Behavior,* 2nd ed. (Boston: PWS-Kent Publishing, 1991).

Borsuk, R., "In Indonesia, a Twist on Spreading the Wealth: Decentralization of Power Multiplies Opportunities for Bribery, Corruption," *The Wall Street Journal,* January 29, 2003, p. A16.

Contingency Planning and Management.com, "Strohl Systems Offers Terrorism Readiness Questionnaire," September 24, 2001.

Deneire, M. and M. Segalla, "Mr. Christian Pierret, Secretary of State for Industry (1997–2002), on French Perspectives on Organizational Leadership and Management," *Academy of Management Executive,* 16 (4), November 2002, pp. 25–30.

Doh, J. P., P. Rodriguez, K. Uhlenbruck, J. Collins, and L. Eden, "Coping with Corruption in Foreign Markets," *Academy of Management Executive,* 17 (3) August 2003, pp. 114–127.

Graham, J. L. and N. M. Lam, "The Chinese Negotiation," *Harvard Business Review,* October 1, 2003, pp. 82–91.

Graham, S., "Relief Agency Suspends Afghan Operations," *www.guardian.co.uk,* June 3, 2004.

Hallowell, R., D. Bowen, and C-I. Knoop, "Four Seasons Goes to Paris," *Academy of Management Executive,* 16 (4), November 2002, pp. 7–24.

Henry, W. L. and J. J. DiStefano, *International Project Management,* 2nd ed. (Boston: PWS-Kent Publishing, 1992).

Hodgetts, R. M. and F. Luthans, *International Management: Culture, Strategy, and Behavior,* 5th ed. (Boston: McGraw-Hill/Irwin, 2003).

Hofstede, G., *Cultures Consequences: International Difference in Work-Related Values* (Beverly Hills, CA: Sage Publishing, 1980).

Hooker, J., *Working across Cultures* (Stanford, CA: Stanford Business Books, 2003).

Kluckhohn, F. and F. L. Strodtbeck, *Variations in Value Orientations* (Evanston, IL: Row, Peterson, 1961).

Krane, J., "Intelligence Companies Help Overseas Business Travelers," *The Cincinnati Enquirer,* April 2, 2002, website.

Kras, E., *Management in Two Cultures: Bridging the Gap between U.S. and Mexican Managers,* rev. ed. (Yarmouth, ME: Intercultural Press, 1995).

Lieberthal, K. and G. Lieberthal, "The Great Transition," *Harvard Business Review,* October 1, 2003, pp. 71–81.

Mendenhall, M. E., E. Dunbar, and G. R. Oddou, "Expatriate Selection, Training, and Career-Pathing: A Review and Critique," *Human Resource Management,* 26 (3), Fall 1987, pp. 331–45.

Milosevic, D. Z., "Echoes of the Silent Language of Project Management," *Project Management Journal,* 30 (1), March 1999, pp. 27–39.

Ricks, D. A., *Blunders in International Business* (London: Blackwell, 2000).

Saunders, C., C. Van Slyke, and D. R. Vogel "My Time or Yours? Managing Time Visions in Global Virtual Teams," *Academy of Management Executive,* 18 (1), 2004, pp. 19–31.

Scown, M. J., "Managers Journal: Barstool Advice for the Vietnam Investor," *Asian Wall Street Journal,* July 15, 1993.

Tung, R. L., "Expatriate Assignments: Enhancing Success and Minimizing Failure," *Academy of Management Executive,* 1 (2) 1987, pp. 117–26.

Yeung I. and R. L. Tung, "Achieving Business Success in Confucian Societies: The Importance of Guanxi (Connections)," *Organizational Dynamics,* 25 (2), Autumn 1996, pp. 54–65.

CASE 15.1

AMEX, Hungary

Michael Thomas shouted, "Sasha, Tor-Tor, we've got to go! Our driver is waiting for us." Thomas's two daughters were fighting over who would get the last orange for lunch that day. Victoria ("Tor-Tor") prevailed as she grabbed the orange and ran out the door to the Mercedes Benz waiting for them. The fighting continued in the back seat as they drove toward the city of Budapest, Hungary. Thomas finally turned around and grabbed the orange and proclaimed that he would have it for lunch. The back seat became deadly silent as they made their way to the American International School of Budapest.

After dropping the girls off at the school, Thomas was driven to his office in the Belvéros area of Budapest. Thomas worked for AMEX Petroleum and had been sent to Budapest four months earlier to set up business operations in central Hungary. His job was to establish 10 to 14 gas stations in the region by purchasing existing stations, building new ones, or negotiating franchise arrangements with existing owners of stations. Thomas jumped at this project. He realized that his career at AMEX was going nowhere in the United States, and if he were going to realize his ambitions, it would be in the "wild, wild east" of the former Soviet empire. Besides, Thomas's mother was Hungarian, and he could speak the language. At least he thought he could until he arrived in Budapest and realized that he had greatly exaggerated his competence.

As he entered the partially refurbished offices of AMEX, he noticed that only three of his staff were present. No one knew where Miklos was, while Margit reported that she would not be at work today because she had to stay at home to take care of her sick mother. Thomas asked Béla why the workmen weren't present to work on finishing the office. Béla informed him that the work had to be halted until they received approval from the city historian. Budapest, anxious to preserve its historical heritage, required that all building renovations be approved by the city historian. When Thomas asked Béla how long it would take, Béla responded, "Who knows—days, weeks, maybe even months." Thomas muttered "great" to himself and turned his attention to the morning business. He was scheduled to interview prospective employees who would act as station managers and staff personnel.

The interview with Ferenc Erkel was typical of the many interviews he held that morning. Erkel was a neatly dressed, 42-year-old, unemployed professional who could speak limited English. He had a masters degree in international economics and had worked for 12 years in the state-owned Institute for Foreign Trade. Since being laid off two years ago, he has been working as a taxicab driver. When asked about his work at the Institute, Erkel smiled sheepishly and said that he pushed paper and spent most of the time playing cards with his colleagues.

To date Thomas had hired 16 employees. Four quit within three days on the job, and six were let go after a trial period for being absent from work, failing to perform duties, or showing a lack of initiative. Thomas thought that at this rate it would take him over a year just to hire his staff.

Thomas took a break from the interview schedule to scan the *Budapest Business Journal,* an English newspaper that covered business news in Hungary. Two items caught his eye. One article was on the growing threat of the Ukrainian Mafia in Hungary, which detailed extortion attempts in Budapest. The second story was that inflation had risen to 32 percent. This last item disturbed Thomas because at the time only one out of every five Hungarian families owned a car. AMEX's strategy in Hungary depended on a boom in first-time car owners.

Thomas collected his things and popped a few aspirin for the headache he was developing. He walked several blocks to the Kispipa restaurant where he had a supper meeting with Hungarian businessman Zoltán Kodaly. He had met Kodaly briefly at a reception sponsored by the U.S. consulate for American and Hungarian businesspeople. Kodaly reportedly owned three gas stations that Thomas was interested in.

Thomas waited, sipping bottled water for 25 minutes. Kodaly appeared with a young lady who could not have been older than 19. As it turned out Kodaly had brought his daughter Annia, who was a university student, to act as translator. While Thomas made an attempt to speak in Hungarian at first, Kodaly insisted that they use Annia to translate.

After ordering the house specialty, *szekelygulas,* Thomas immediately got down to business. He told Kodaly that AMEX was willing to make two offers to him. They would like to either purchase two of his stations at a price of $150,000 each, or they could work out a franchise agreement. Thomas said AMEX was not interested in the third station located near Klinikak because it would be too expensive to modernize the equipment.

Annia translated, and as far as Thomas could tell she was doing a pretty good job. At first Kodaly did not respond and simply engaged in side conversations with Annia and exchanged pleasantries with people who came by. Thomas became frustrated and reiterated his offer. Eventually Kodaly asked what he meant by franchising, and Thomas tried to use the local McDonald's as an example of how it worked. He mentioned that Kodaly would still own the stations, but he would have to pay a franchisee fee, share profits with AMEX, and adhere to AMEX procedures and practices. In exchange, AMEX would provide petroleum and funds to renovate the stations to meet AMEX standards.

Toward the end of the meal Kodaly asked what would happen to the people who worked at the stations. Thomas asserted that according to his calculation the stations were overstaffed by 70 percent and that to make a profit, at least 15 workers would have to be let go. This statement was greeted with silence. Kodaly then turned the conversation to soccer and asked Thomas if it was true that in America girls play "football." Thomas said that both of his daughters played AYSO soccer in America and hoped to play in Hungary. Kodaly said girls don't play football in Hungary and that Annia was an accomplished volleyball player. Thomas pressed Kodaly for a response to his offer, but Kodaly rose and thanked Thomas for the meal. He said he would think about his offer and get back in touch with him.

Thomas left the Kispipa wondering if he would ever see Kodaly again. He returned to his office where an urgent message was waiting from Tibor. Tibor was responsible for retrofitting the first station Thomas had purchased for AMEX. The new tanks had not arrived from Vienna, and the construction crew had spent the day doing nothing. After several phone calls he found out that the tanks were being held at the border by customs. This irritated him because he had been assured by local officials that everything had been taken care of. He asked his secretary to schedule an appointment with the Hungarian trade office as soon as possible.

At the end of the day he checked his e-mail from the States. There was a message from headquarters asking about the status of the project. By this time he had hoped to have his office staffed and up and running and at least three stations secured. So far he had only one-third of his staff, his office was in shambles, and only one station was being retrofitted. Thomas decided to wait until tomorrow to respond to the e-mail.

Before returning home Thomas stopped off at the English Pub, a favorite hangout for expats in Budapest. There he met Jan Krovert, who worked for a Dutch company that was building a large discount retail store on the outskirts of Badapest. Thomas and Krovert often talked about being "strangers in a strange land" at the pub. Thomas talked about the interviews and how he could just see in their eyes that they didn't have the drive or initiative to be successful. Krovert responded that Hungary has high unemployment but a shortage of motivated workers. Krovert confided that he no longer interviewed anyone over the age of 30, claiming that what fire they had in their bellies was burned out after years of working in state-run companies.

---

1. What are the issues confronting Thomas in this case?
2. How well is Thomas dealing with these issues?
3. What suggestions would you have for Thomas in managing this project?

CASE 15.2

Ghost Stories

On December 26, 2004, an earthquake reaching 9.1 on the Richter scale triggered a series of devastating tsunamis off the coast of Indonesia. They spread throughout the Indian Ocean, killing large numbers of people and inundating coastal communities across South and Southeast Asia, including parts of Indonesia, Sri Lanka, India, and Thailand. The 2004 Asian tsunami was one of the deadliest catastrophes in modern history, with more than 220,000 lives lost.

Nils Lofgrin, who had managed several construction projects in Australia and New Guinea, was sent by his construction firm to restore a five-star resort along the Andaman coast in southern Thailand that had been ravaged by this tsunami. Casualties at the resort included 12 staff and 37 guests. This was Nils's first assignment in Thailand.

Nils flew down and toured the site. His assessment of the damage was that it was not as severe as feared. The basic infrastructure was intact but debris needed to be cleared and the resort refurbished. He reported back to headquarters that with a bit of luck he should have the resort up and running in matter of months. Little did he realize how soon he would regret making such a promise.

The problems began immediately when he was unable to recruit workers to help clean up the mess at the resort. The Burmese migrant workers who comprised a significant portion of the workforce in this region had fled into the hills out of growing fears of being arrested and deported. Even when he offered double wages he was not able to recruit many Thais. At first he attributed their reluctance to the shock caused by the devastation of the tsunami. Everyone he met seemed to know someone who had died or even worse had just disappeared. But he soon realized there was more going on than just shock.

Nils was at a restaurant having a lunch with a Thai friend when an animated discussion broke out among some Thai patrons nearby. He asked his friend what was going on. The friend said someone was telling the story of a local taxi driver who had picked up three foreign tourists and was driving them to Kata Beach when he looked around and found his cab empty. Another told the story of a local family whose telephone rings constantly through the day and night. When answered, the voices of missing friends and relatives cry out for help.

Nils sank in his chair when he began to realize that no one wanted to work for him because prospective workers believed that the region and his resort are haunted by ghosts.

---

1. What options are available to Nils?
2. What would you do and why?

CHAPTER 16

Oversight

Without continual growth and progress, such words as achievement and success have no meaning.

—Benjamin Franklin

Up to now this text has primarily been devoted to tools and techniques for successfully managing specific projects. It is important now to stop and look at the big picture to see how these methodologies fit within an organization's ability to manage projects to achieve strategic objectives. *Oversight* is the term that has emerged to reflect how organizations oversee their project management systems.

This chapter identifies some current oversight practices and efforts to improve the management of projects over the long haul. Unresolved issues confronting the field are also identified and discussed. Because the premise is that project management has a bright future, the chapter appropriately concludes with suggestions on how to pursue a career in project management.

Project Oversight

In the last few years the paradigm shift to project oversight/governance has been profound. Project oversight can be defined as *a set of principles and processes to guide and improve the management of projects*. The intent is to ensure projects meet the needs of the *organization* through standards, procedures, accountability, efficient allocation of resources, and continuous improvement in the management of projects. A second purpose is to support the project manager. We estimate over 95 percent of project-driven organizations have been implementing some form of oversight for several years. Progress has been rapid and steady. The typical activities of project oversight cover two dimensions: organization and project. Here are some of the major oversight activities used in practice:

At the Organization Level

- Project selection.
- Portfolio management.
- Improving the way all projects are managed over time.
- Assessing and elevating the maturity level of the organization's project management system.
- Using the balanced scorecard approach to review progress on strategic priorities.

At the Project Level

- Review projects' objectives.
- Decide on issues raised by the project manager such as resource needs and escalation.

- Track and assist the project to resolve bottlenecks.
- Review status reports from the project manager.
- Audit and review lessons learned.
- Authorize any major deviations from the original scope.
- Cancel the project.

All of these activities are designed to bring consistency, structure, accountability, and improvement to the management of projects. Today, project oversight, through an executive committee, oversight group, or a project office, covers every aspect of managing projects in the organization.

Importance of Oversight to the Project Manager

What does this solid paradigm shift mean to a project manager who is normally in charge of only one or two projects? Four things. First, in almost all cases oversight is interested in supporting and helping the project manager where needed. This is an improvement over the past. Second, the oversight function determines the environment in which the project manager will implement his or her project. This can affect the management of a project in a positive or negative manner. Third, depending on the size and complexity of the project, methods used to hold the project manager responsible and accountable will influence how performance is measured. Finally, the project manager, who is responsible for day-to-day management, will probably be reporting to this oversight group at predetermined phases in the project. In short, project oversight supports project management at the organization and project levels.

As a project manager you need to be aware of how these oversight activities can and will influence management of your projects. A short description of each of these oversight activities follows.

Portfolio Project Management

When project effort moves from tactical to strategic, project selection, project processes, and resources are brought under one system known as portfolio project management. Remember from Chapter 2 that portfolio management integrates projects with current priorities, strategic thrust, and overall allocation of scarce organization resources. Here is a typical definition:

Portfolio project management is the centralized management of projects to ensure that the allocation of resources to projects is directed toward projects that contribute the greatest value to organization goals.

Project portfolio management supports management of multiple projects in a coordinated way to obtain the benefits not available from managing them individually. The development of portfolio project management is complemented by the movement to use project management offices.

Project Office

Most project-driven organizations have set up project offices. The appearance of a project office frequently follows the implementation of project portfolio management efforts. The project office is now used as the vehicle to support and manage oversight activities. Here is one definition:

The *project office (PO)* is the unit responsible for the continued support of consistent application of selection criteria, standards, and processes; training of and general assistance to project managers; and continued improvement and use of best practices.

The project office frequently includes project portfolio management. Project portfolios and project offices both result in an integration function for planning and control. The PO also supports the integration of the processes of managing projects within the social/ cultural environment of the organization. High-tech firms

Snapshot from Practice   The Project Office*

As more and more companies embrace project management as a critical vehicle for realizing corporate objectives, they are creating centralized project offices (POs) to oversee and improve the management of projects. PO functions vary widely by organization and need. In some cases, they serve as a simple clearinghouse for project management information. In other cases, they recruit, train, and assign managers to specific projects. As POs mature and evolve over time, they become full-service providers of project management expertise within a firm. The different services POs may provide include the following:

- Creating and maintaining the internal project management information system.
- Recruiting and selecting project managers both within and outside the organization.
- Establishing standardized project planning and reporting methodologies.
- Training personnel in project management techniques and tools.
- Auditing ongoing and recently completed projects.
- Developing comprehensive risk management programs.
- Providing in-house project management consulting and mentoring services.
- Maintaining an internal project management library containing critical documents, including project plans, funding papers, test plans, audit reports, and so forth.
- Establishing and benchmarking best practices in project management.
- Maintaining and tracking the portfolio of projects within an organization.

A good example of how project offices evolve is the global project office (GPO) at Citibank's Global Corporate Bank. GPO originated at the grassroots level within the small world of Operations and Technology for Global Cash Management. Committed to bringing order to the chaos of managing projects, GPO instituted training programs and professional project management practices on a very small scale. Soon the success of GPO-supported projects caught the eye of upper management. Within three years the department was expanded to offer a full range of PO services across Citibank's entire banking operation. GPO's mission is to establish project management as a core competency throughout the entire Citibank organization.

* T. R. Block, and J. D. Frame, "Today's Project Office: Gauging Attitudes," *PM Network,* August, 2001; W. Gradante, and D. Gardner, "Managing Projects from the Future, Not from the Past," *Proceedings of the 29th Annual Project Management Institute 1998 Seminars and Symposium* (Newtown Square, PA: Project Management Institute, 1998), pp. 289–94.

such as Hewlett-Packard (HP), International Business Machines (IBM), and Dell all use project offices to coordinate projects and to ensure best practices are being used to manage projects. For example, HP has project offices in Europe/Middle East, Americas, Asia Pacific, and Japan with several others planned. Because projects are used to implement strategy, HP has created a new position—vice president of project offices. Project offices ensure a consistent approach to all projects in all locations. See Snapshot from Practice: The Project Office.

Figures 16.1 and 16.2 provide an example of a report the project office provides senior management of an international organization. Note that such a report requires a standard format for all projects. Figure 16.1 depicts a project portfolio cost summary report developed for top management. Figure 16.2 presents the same summary for project schedules. Additional detailed information for any specific highlighted project—such as the project schedule, cost status report, project team—is only a double click away. For example, the Smart Card project in the European Economic Community (EEC) appears to be behind schedule. The cause can be identified by "drilling down" to the project schedule, WBS, resources, or issues. Standard project formats such as these provide a wealth of information in multiproject organizations.

Project offices are known to result in positive benefits such as the following:

- They serve as a bridge between senior management and project managers.
- They support integration of all project management processes from selection through project closure and lessons learned.

Net Services, Inc.	View Cost ▼	Project Portfolio Cost Summary ($ 000)							Date:		
Location	Project ID	Description	PV	EV	AC	CPI	SPI	PCIB	BAC	EAC	VAC
Summary	All	Portfolio							$18,120		
United States									$10,500		
○	01-003	Digitize Fingerprints-FBI	3,000	3,500	3,230	1.08	1.17	97.2%	3,600	3,322	278
○	01-011	Encryption	270	250	250	1.00	0.93	71.4%	350	350	0
○	01-002	Internet Protocol--CIA						0.0%	950		
○	01-009	Supply Chain Partners	90	90	90	1.00	1.00	16.7%	540	540	0
	01-012	Bonus Mileage Awards						0.0%	630		
●	01-005	E-sales Claims	150	140	150	0.93	0.93	35.0%	400	429	-29
●	01-011	Procurement Net	400	340	380	0.89	0.85	27.6%	1,230	1,375	-145
○	01-008	Smart Tag Tracking	850	900	900	1.00	1.06	32.1%	2,800	2,800	0
Asia/Pacific									$2,800		
○	02-007	Currency Conversion	125	120	120	1.00	0.96	80.0%	150	150	0
○	02-002	Billing System	280	280	280	1.00	1.00	70.0%	400	400	0
○	02-005	Web-Based Cash Flow	210	220	200	1.10	1.05	73.3%	300	273	27
	02-004	Olympic Simulation						0.0%	1,950		
EEC									$4,820		
●	03-008	Smart Card	145	110	140	0.79	0.76	18.3%	600	764	-164
	03-003	Warranty						0.0%	70		
	03-004	Simulation--ESA						0.0%	800		
●	03-005	Air Reservation Net	510	490	520	0.94	0.96	35.0%	1,400	1,486	-86
●	03-007	Pilot Internet Log Syst.	540	490	550	0.89	0.91	57.6%	850	954	-104
○	03-006	Internet Telephone Syst.	850	850	860	0.99	1.00	77.3%	1,100	1,113	-13

Side icons: Gantt, Network, Resource, Status, WBS, Sponsor, Team, Priority, Issues

LEGEND
○ Under Budget
◐ On Budget
● Over Budget

FIGURE 16.1 Project Portfolio Cost Summary Report for Top Management

Location	Project ID	Description	Project Manager	Start Date	Finish Date	SPI
Summary	All	Portfolio				
United States						
01-003	Digitize Fingerprints-FBI	Beth Gage	11/15	8/15	1.17
01-011	Encryption	Alfonso Buco	1/1	9/25	0.93
01-002	Internet Protocol--CIA		10/1	6/1	
01-009	Supply chain partners	Mike Chow	6/5	11/16	1.00
01-012	Bonus Mileage Awards	Sally Peters	8/1	2/12	
01-005	E-sales Claims	Kevin Lee	2/4	11/15	0.93
01-011	Procurement Net	Tzvi Jafarri	5/5	12/30	0.85
01-008	Smart Tag Tracking	Jan Snyder	3/1	12/4	1.06
Asia/Pacific						
02-007	Currency Conversion	Jeff Bush	2/1	7/10	0.96
02-002	Billing System	Kia Wong	10/7	10/5	1.00
02-005	Web-Based Cash Flow	Naoki Oshima	2/15	9/15	1.05
02-004	Olympic Simulation		7/12	2/10	
EEC						
03-008	Smart Card	Ido Alons	4/16	9/15	0.76
03-003	Warranty	Connor Gage	8/11	12/12	
03-004	Simulation--ESA	Ib Ericson	9/15	2/13	
03-005	Air Reservation Net	Dragan Milosovik	3/22	1/12	0.96
03-007	Pilot Internet Log Syst.	Ken Thompson	3/1	10/3	0.91
03-006	Internet Telephone Syst.	Ann McGraddy	8/10	9/29	1.00

FIGURE 16.2   Project Portfolio Schedule Summary Report for Project Schedules

- Through training they support the movement of the organization to a higher level of project management maturity.

The growth in the application of portfolio project management and project offices will continue. Portfolio management and project offices strongly influence how a project manager will manage his or her respective project. A more recent oversight activity has been the quick implementation of phase gate reviews.

Phase Gate Methodology

Following the emergence of the project office and project portfolios came the use of phase gate methodology. It provides an in-depth review of individual projects at *specific phases* in the project life cycle. These reviews cover assessments to continue or kill the project, reassess resource allocation, reassess prioritization, and evaluate execution progress, as well as strategic alignment decisions. The phase review process serves the organization by having gatekeepers (usually selected from several areas of the firm) perform the review. The phase gate process is also designed to support the project manager on decisions and other issues such as escalation and resource needs. The idea of phase gate methodology fits effortlessly into the oversight function of the project office. Phase gate methodology was originally developed for product development, but the application of the methodology has grown beyond new-product development to include all projects in the portfolio. One study by Morris and Jamieson showed 85 percent of those surveyed use phase review gates, while 85 percent who did not thought they should.

The original *Stage-Gate™* model was pioneered by Robert G. Cooper several decades ago to improve management of new-product development. The original model incorporates five stages: preliminary investigation, detailed investigation, development, testing and validation, and full production and market launch. Stages precede gates and represent information developed to enable gatekeepers to make the right decision at the next gate. These decision points at each gate are known as go, kill, hold, or recycle decisions. Given the information developed for each stage, the gatekeepers (the oversight team) can decide to continue with the project, abort the project, or revise/recycle.

Today, variations of the original model are being used across all industries to help manage project portfolios. These variations are not limited to new-product development. The number of stages and gates varies. But the idea of oversight review several times throughout the project life cycle appears in all models. Each gate check will always, at a minimum, check the project against alignment with current strategic goals.

Phase gate methodology has appeal because it provides a clean-cut, structured process that can be consistently applied across all projects in the portfolio. Distinct review stages and go/kill gates comprise this oversight function. The major goals for phase gating are to ensure oversight and support for the project manager and the project team, to direct organization resources toward strategic goals, and to reduce the number of projects that do not support the forward direction of the organization. A multiproject organization having employees spread across many time zones that does not use some form of phase review methodology is rare. For example, companies such as 3M, General Motors, Northern Telecom, DuPont, Intel, Hewlett-Packard, and Dell all use some form of phase gating to manage projects.

The phase gate review process can be defined as a *structured process to review, evaluate, and document outcomes in each project phase and to provide management with information to guide resource deployment toward strategic goals.* This oversight activity begins with project selection and tracking the project life cycle through closure and lessons learned. Phase gates need to occur at consistent points in the project life cycle so each project encounters similar gates at predefined authorization points.

The phase review process may appear similar to the project audit discussed in an earlier chapter. Some overlap does occur, but the focus here is more integrated and holistic. Individual projects are reviewed as part of a total portfolio. For example, have strategic priorities changed the importance of the project? If the priorities of the organization have changed, a project that is executing on time, on budget, and meeting the project goals may have to be "killed." Phase review takes place at each phase from project selection through lessons learned as opposed to the audit, which often takes place at the end of the project. Phase gating provides a larger perspective to managing multiple projects in a project portfolio. Gatekeepers first focus on organization needs, with individual project needs second.

Figure 16.3 is a flow diagram of an abridged, generic variation of phase gate methodology that has application across all types of projects.

The decision gates focus on go/kill decisions based on major questions such as those shown in Gates 1 and 2 below (see the "Pull the Plug" reference). At a minimum each gate should include three components:

1. Required deliverables (e.g., project goals, progress, variances).
2. Gate criteria and specific outputs (e.g., adjusting project scope, schedule).
3. A clear yes/no decision on whether to go ahead.

The criteria for all of the gates during the project are selected *before* the start of the project.

The value of phase gating methods rests firmly on having enough information to support the gate decision. Significant amounts of support data must be gathered to answer critical gate questions. Fortunately, you can readily discern that following the best practices shown in earlier chapters will prepare you to easily answer critical gate questions. Frequent questions from practice for each gate are presented here.

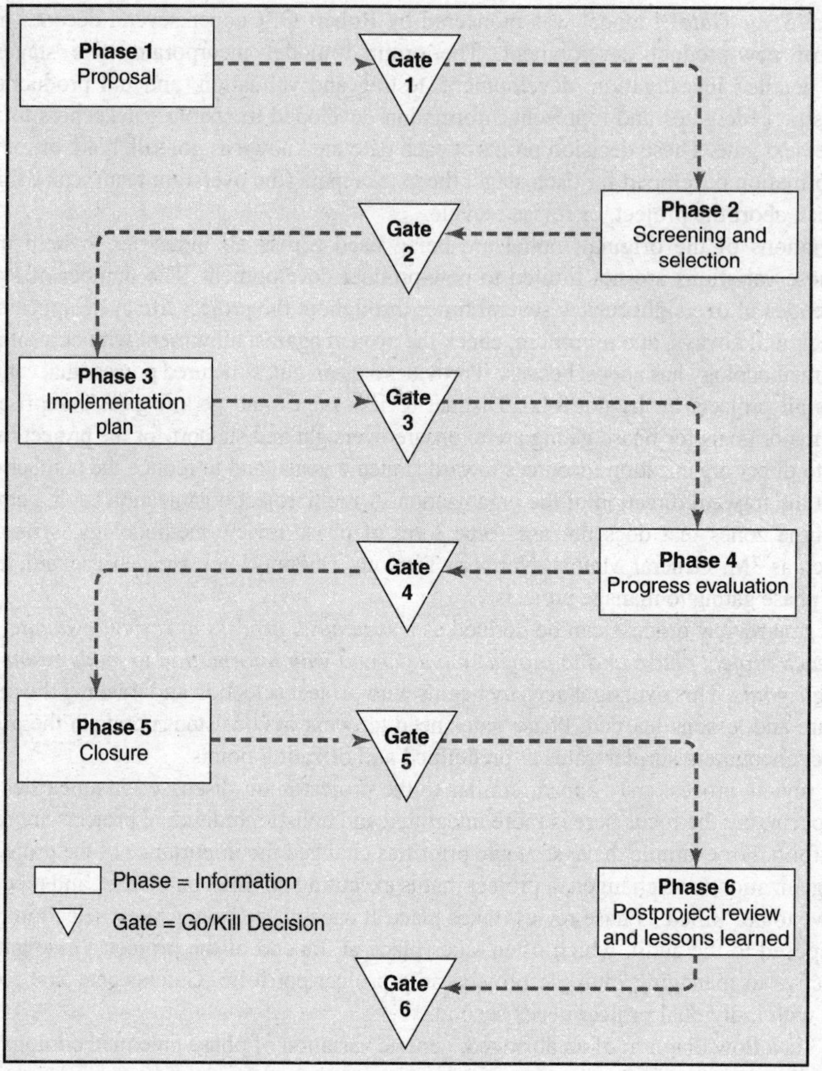

FIGURE 16.3   Abridged Generic Phase Gate Process Diagram

Gate 1: Proposal Decision

- What business problem does the proposed project solve?
- Does this project align with our strategic direction?
- What type of project is this? Strategic, organization maintenance, "must," etc.?
- Should the project be considered?

This *proposal* phase answers a fundamental question: Is the project a good idea and does it solve a business problem or issue? Basically, anyone can propose a project. However, the proposal should provide enough key information to allow an oversight team to decide if the proposal should be considered further. For example, the information might include the business problem the proposed project will solve, the urgency of the project, and clear, relevant project objectives. Gate 1 provides information at a minimal expenditure of cost and resources and in a short time, so the project can be reevaluated more thoroughly if it is perceived to have merits.

Gate 2: Selection Decision

- Is the sponsor identified and supportive?
- Should this project be selected and implemented?
- How does the project support the organization strategy and goals?
- Is it important to implement this project now? Why?
- What is the impact or risk of not doing this project?
- What are the project's ROI and/or nonfinancial benefits?
- How does the project fit our skills and culture?
- What metrics will be used to measure progress? Success?
- What are the major risks for this project?
- Will this project be implemented internally or outsourced?
- Will our business culture support this project?
- How long and how large is this project?

The *selection* review includes a thorough analysis based on selection criteria. The gating group uses weighted scoring model criteria, which typically include project risks, costs, resource needs, urgency, financial analysis, benefits, identified sponsor, and other criteria found in selection models. Many information requirements for Gate 2 are discussed in detail in Chapter 2 (see project selection section) and should answer most of the decision criteria for this phase review.

Gate 3: Implementation Plan Decision

- Are the project scope, tasks, milestones and deliverables, and gates established and acceptable?
- Are the resources needed identified and available?
- Are tasks sequenced and is a time-phased budget established?
- Are appropriate performance metrics in place for tracking the project?
- Are project risks identified and is how they will be managed clearly stated?
- Are all stakeholders identified?
- Is the stakeholder communication plan complete and appropriate?
- Is a formal change management system in place?
- Are accountability metrics in place and is responsibility assigned?

The *implementation plan* review information should include the planning document developed in earlier chapters. For example, what are the specific goals for the project and what are the major deliverables (scope)? What tasks will be performed to complete the deliverables (WBS)? How are tasks sequenced (network)? When will the tasks be performed (schedule)? What resources are needed to complete the tasks (resource schedule)? What are the estimated costs for the tasks (time-phased budget)? What and how will performance be measured (variance metrics)? How will information be collected and distributed (communication plan)? What and how will project risks be identified and handled (risk plan)? What vendors will be used for procurement?

Gate 4: Progress Evaluation Decision

- Is the project still aligned with business requirements?
- Are activities completed according to the project plan?

- Are the technical requirements of the project being met?
- Are contractors meeting defined performance requirements?
- Are there urgent corrective actions that must be done quickly?
- Are time, costs, and scope performances within acceptable limits?
- Have the project objectives changed?
- What risks can be retired?

Your *progress evaluation* review covers the control activities of tracking progress, identifying variances from your plan, and taking corrective action. A major chunk of the data requirements for the phase review are simply measures against the project plan. Tracking progress and identifying variances against scope, time, budget, and control of changes and identified risks are easily accomplished using available software (see Chapters 7 and 13). For example, if the project is not going according to plan, your risk assessment plan may help you decide an action to be taken. Beyond these quantitative measures, there are always "issues" that deserve attention. Moreover, project priority must be checked against strategy to determine whether this measure is still valid. If not, a change in scope or killing the project may be necessary. Don Kingsberry, director of HP's Global Program Management Office, describes HP's progress phase review succinctly: We have "42 health checks on current projects. We look at risks, issues, critical path analysis, resource analysis, sponsorship, alignment with strategy, earned value metrics, dependency, and other factors impacting the triple constraints of project management: time, cost, and scope." (See Boyer for more on HP's efforts.)

Gate 5: Closure

- Did the project deliver the business outcomes? Were the metrics and benefits used to justify the project met?
- Were project scope objectives met?
- Were project cost and schedule met?
- Are contracts closed out?
- Are the end users satisfied?
- Have staff been recognized and reassigned?
- Was the organization culture right for this type of project?
- Was senior management support adequate?
- Were the right people assigned to the project?
- Were project risks identified and assessed realistically?
- Did technology overextend our competencies?
- How will the project be delivered?

The *closure* and lessons learned activities closely follow the closure activities found in the audit chapter. Some organizations have wrapped phases 5 and 6—closure and lessons learned—into a single gate.

Gate 6: Lessons Learned

- Have we identified what went wrong and what contributed to success?
- Have changes to improve delivery of future projects been communicated and archived?
- What hindered or contributed to delivering the expected ROI or business outcomes?
- Can others learn from this experience?
- What changes in scope or quality were made?
- Who will be responsible for archiving the lessons learned?

The questions shown above for each phase only touch the surface of those found in practice. Some are formalized, others very porous and less structured, but all phase review models are designed to check management of a project from selection to lessons learned. Key benefits of using phase gating are:

- Provides excellent training for functional staff who serve on oversight review groups.
- Encourages a larger perspective and role of projects within the organization.
- Is a clear-cut process, easily understood, and applicable to all projects in a portfolio.
- Provides a structured process for a project office to follow on all projects.
- Eliminates poor value projects.
- Supports faster decision making with predefined deliverables for each gate.

See Snapshot from Practice: Phase Gate Side Benefits for a project manager's opinion on the benefits of phase gating.

Another key oversight function is benchmarking your project management maturity against others in your industry.

Organization Project Management Maturity

Individual audits and phase gate reviews can yield valuable lessons that team members can apply to future project work. A more encompassing look, from an organizationwide point of view, uses a project maturity model that strives for a never-ending goal to continuously improve the management of projects. It is well established that project-driven companies with higher maturity levels are more successful in managing projects than those lacking project maturity programs. Project maturity has become a competitive edge. Companies are increasingly using outsourcing or external contractors and RFPs (Request for proposals) to look for contractors that have reached high maturity levels. Harold Kerzner, a project management consultant and professor, eloquently states why a company should pursue maturity:

> Given the fact that many executives today view their company as a stream of projects, project management permeates the entire organization, mandating that maturity is necessary. So only those companies that want to stay in business and remain competitive should pursue maturity. The alternative is rather unpleasant. (Quoted in Mueller.)

The purposes of all maturity models, and many are available, are to enable organizations to assess their progress in implementing the best practices in their industry and continuously move to improvement. It is important to understand that the model does not ensure success; it serves only as a measuring stick and an indicator of progress.

The term *maturity model* was coined in the late 1980s from a research study by the United States government and the Software Engineering Institute (SEI) at Carnegie Mellon University. The government wanted a tool to predict successful software development by contractors. The outcome of this research was the Capability Maturity Model (CMM). The model focuses on guiding and assessing organizations in implementing concrete best practices of managing software development projects. Since its development, the model is used across all industries.

One newer model has received a great deal of publicity. In January 2004, after eight years of development, the Project Management Institute (PMI) rolled out its second version of the Organizational Project Maturity Model. The latest version is called OPM3 (See *www.pmi.org/opm3*). Typically, these models are divided into a continuum of growth levels: initial, repeatable, defined, managed, and optimized. Figure 16.4 presents our version, which borrows liberally from other models.

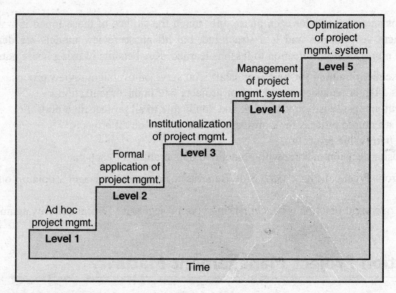

FIGURE 16.4   Project Management Maturity Model

Level 1: Ad Hoc Project Management   No consistent project management process is in place. How a project is managed depends upon the individuals involved. Characteristics of this level include

- No formal project selection system exists—projects are done because people decide to use them or because a high-ranking manager orders them done.
- How any one project is managed varies by individual and thus is unpredictable.
- No investment is made in project management training.
- Working on projects is a struggle because it goes against the grain of established policies and procedures.

Level 2: Formal Application of Project Management   The organization applies established project management procedures and techniques. This level is often marked by tension between project managers and line managers who need to redefine their roles. Features of this level include

- Standard approaches to managing projects, including scope statements, WBS, and activity lists, are used.
- Quality emphasis is on the product or outcome of the project and is inspected instead of built in.
- The organization is moving in the direction of a stronger matrix with project managers and line managers working out their respective roles.
- Recognition of the need for cost control, not just scope and time management, is growing.
- No formal project priority selection system is established.
- Limited training in project management is provided.

Level 3: Institutionalization of Project Management   An organizationwide project management system, tailored to specific needs of the organization with the flexibility to adapt the process to unique characteristics of the project, is established. Characteristics of this level include

- An established process for managing projects is evident by planning templates, status report systems, and checklists for each stage of the project life cycle.
- Formal criteria are used to select projects.
- Project management is integrated with quality management and concurrent engineering.
- Project teams try to build in quality, not simply inspect it.
- The organization is moving toward a team-based reward system to recognize project execution.
- Risk assessment derived from WBS and technical analyses and customer input is in place.
- The organization offers expanded training in project management.
- Time-phased budgets are used to measure and monitor performance based on earned value analysis.
- A specific change control system for requirements, cost, and schedule is developed for each project, and a work authorization system is in place.
- Project audits tend to be performed only when a project fails.

Level 4: Management of Project Management System   The organization develops a system for managing multiple projects that are aligned with strategic goals of the organization. Characteristics of this level include

- Portfolio project management is practiced; projects are selected based on resource capacity and contribution to strategic goals.
- A project priority system is established.
- Project work is integrated with ongoing operations.
- Quality improvement initiatives are designed to improve both the quality of the project management process and the quality of specific products and services.
- Benchmarking is used to identify opportunities for improvement.
- The organization has established a Project Management Office or Center for Excellence.
- Project audits are performed on all significant projects and lessons learned are recorded and used on subsequent projects.
- An integrative information system is established for tracking resource usage and performance of all significant projects. See Snapshot from Practice: Acer Attacks Costly Delays.

Snapshot from Practice   Acer Attacks Costly Delays*

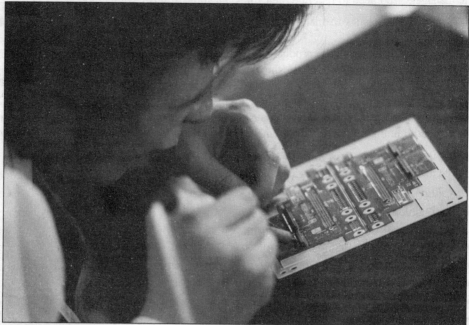

Tom Wagner/Corbis.

In today's rapidly changing world, the risk of failing to develop new products for the market on time is the difference between success and failure. The Mobile Systems Unit (MSU) of Taiwan computer maker Acer, which produces computer notebooks, operates under extreme time-to-market pressures. By 1998 MSU development cycles had shrunk to eight months. Still, missing the market introduction window by only one month on any given model eliminated the unit's profit potential for that model.

MSU did a companywide analysis into the causes of costly delays in their projects. They discovered that schedule variance was a function of multiple causes. Vendors would occasionally not deliver sufficient volumes of a promised new component on time. Major customers such as IBM would change their requirements. Design problems with the motherboard would cause additional design loops. Negotiations among multiple parties might change internal specifications. Administrative pressure on engineers and insufficiently documented procedures led to shortcuts in testing, causing major rework at a more costly stage.

Acer attacked the multiple causes on multiple fronts. First, MSU management created resource buffers in the form of slack capacity by canceling two projects that were already delayed. This wasn't easy, because one was to be a showpiece, top-of-the-line model, and the decision to kill it was hotly contested. MSU then concentrated on improving documentation of operating procedures in order to increase testing coverage and facilitate the training of young engineers. Those steps reduced the number of correction loops during product development and improved the quality of the company's manufacturing ramp-up. Acer also concentrated the responsibility of product specifications in one group, thereby reducing negotiation loops and internally caused specification changes. Over the next two years, MSU more than doubled its sales and gained significant market share.

* B. Einhorn, "Acer's About Face," *BusinessWeek (International Edition)*, April 23, 2000.

Level 5: Optimization of Project Management System   The focus is on continuous improvement through incremental advancements of existing practices and by innovations using new technologies and methods. Features include

- A project management information system is fine-tuned: specific and aggregate information is provided to different stakeholders.
- An informal culture that values improvement drives the organization, not policies and procedures.
- There is greater flexibility in adapting the project management process to demands of a specific project.

Progress from one level to the next will not occur overnight. The Software Engineering Institute estimates the following median times for movement:

- Maturity level 1 to 2 is 22 months.
- Maturity level 2 to 3 is 29 months.
- Maturity level 3 to 4 is 25 months.
- Maturity level 4 to 5 is 13 months.

Why does it take so long? One reason is simply organizational inertia. It is difficult for social organizations to institute significant changes while at the same time maintaining business efficacy. "How do we find time to change when we are so busy just keeping our heads above water?"

A second significant reason is that one cannot leapfrog past any one level. Just as a child cannot avoid the trials and tribulations of being a teenager, people within an organization have to work through the unique challenges and problems of each level to get to the next level. Learning of this magnitude naturally takes time and cannot be avoided by using quick fixes or simple remedies.

Our best-guess estimates are that most companies are in the throes of moving from level 2 to level 3 and that fewer than 10 percent of those firms that actively practice project management are at either level 4 or 5. Remember, project maturity is not an end; project maturity is a never-ending process of continuous improvement. An additional view of the success of the projects you have selected over time is discussed next.

Assessing the Effectiveness of the Project Selection over the Long Haul: The Balanced Scorecard Model

Project priority selection models select which actions (projects) best support organizational strategy. The balanced scorecard model differs from selection models by reviewing projects over a longer horizon—5 to 10 years after the project is implemented. It is more "macro" in perspective than project selection models. This model measures the results of major activities taken to support the overall vision, mission, and goals of the organization. It helps answer two questions: Did we select the right projects? Did the projects contribute to long-range strategic direction of the firm? American Express, the U.S. Department of Transportation, ExxonMobil, Kaiser Permanente, National Semiconductor, and others are known to be using their own customized models of the balanced scorecard. (See Kaplan and Norton.)

The scorecard model limits measures of performance to goals in four main areas: *customer, internal, innovation and learning, and financial measures.* For example, a performance measure for a customer might be industry ranking for sales, quality, or on-time projects. Internal measures that influence employees' actions could mean time to market or reduction of design time to final product. Innovation and learning measures frequently deal with process and product innovation and improvement. For example, the percentage of sales or profit from new products is often used as a performance goal and measure. Project improvement savings from partnering agreements are another example of an innovation and learning measure. Finally, financial measures such as ROI, cash flow, and projects on budget reflect improvement and actions that contribute value to the bottom line.

These four perspectives and performance measures keep vision and strategy at the forefront of employees' actions. The basic assumption underlying the balanced scorecard model is that people will take the necessary actions to improve the performance of the organization on the given measures and goals. The balanced scorecard model and priority selection models should never conflict with each other. If a conflict exists, both models should be reviewed and conflicts eliminated. When both models are used in project-driven organizations, focus on vision, strategy, and implementation are reinforced. Both models encourage employees to determine the actions needed to improve performance.

In summary, all oversight practices are directed to improving the way the organization manages all projects. How projects are managed in your organization will depend heavily on the level of project oversight and maturity. As oversight continues to evolve, you will need to view your job as a project manager from a broader, top-down view of project management in your organization and even in the total field of project management.

Unresolved Issues

While we are fairly confident in our observations and resulting inferences, there are still some unresolved issues confronting project management. Two of these are virtual project management and the management of projects under high levels of uncertainty:

- How far can virtual project management evolve?

In Chapter 11 we introduced the subject of virtual project teams in which members primarily interact electronically. Today, most project communication is limited to e-mail, teleconferencing, faxes, and, in some cases, videoconferencing. As telecommunication systems become more reliable worldwide and videoconferencing with high-definition resolution becomes readily available, project teams will be able to hold meetings in which geographically separated members visually interact with each other; e-mail will be augmented by video messages. Similarly, telephone conversations will be replaced by direct video interaction using PCs.

Some companies with access to the latest technology are experimenting with 24-hour product design teams. These teams have members scattered across the time zones so that work on a project is nonstop. For example, team members work on the project during normal hours in New York and then electronically pass their work to members in Hawaii, who are beginning their workday when the New York team is about to go home. The Hawaiian team passes their work to a team in Bangkok, Thailand, which, in turn, passes their work to a team situated in Copenhagen, Denmark. The Danish team passes their work to the New York team, and the cycle is repeated. Although it is too early to say how successful this tag-team approach to project management will be, it exemplifies the potential that exists given the information technology that is available today.

Clearly in the world of the future, project professionals will have access to technology to reduce the barriers of distance and time and improve their ability to interact in a virtual domain. The question is, what are the limits to virtual project management? What kinds of projects and under what circumstances will virtual project management best work? Or not work? Will different skill sets and personal characteristics be required to work in a virtual environment? What protocols, habits, and procedures need to be developed to successfully manage a virtual project team? Will visual, video interaction enhance the development of trust among physically separated team members? Conversely, new technology often produces unintended side effects (smog in the case of the gasoline engine; carpal tunnel in the case of PCs). What are the potential negative physical and psychological side effects of working in a virtual environment? How will workers respond if their sleep is periodically interrupted by urgent calls from Krakow, Poland, or if they have to make sure they are home from the movies at 11:00 P.M. so they can participate in a video project meeting?

Answers to these questions and others will emerge as organizations experiment with virtual project management.

- How do we manage projects under high levels of uncertainty?

Research on project success and failure consistently points to poor planning as a major reason behind project failures. The general recommendation is that more time and attention should be devoted to clearly defining the scope of the project and developing the project plan. However, poor planning may not simply be a result of a lack of effort but rather due to the inherent difficulty of planning a project under conditions of high uncertainty. For example, software development projects are notorious for being completed significantly over budget and behind schedule. Is this a result of poor planning? Or an innate characteristic of project work that involves tightly coupled activities, trial-and-error problem solving, and shifting design parameters?

Modern project management planning tools and techniques are well suited to accomplish projects in which the scope is well defined. They are less well suited to manage projects with vaguely defined or unstable scope. Purists would argue that this is a moot point because, by definition, project management involves only endeavors with well-defined objectives. While this is a neat "academic" solution to the problem, it does not mirror the reality of project management today. More and more people are engaged in projects in which, by intent, the initial scope is broadly defined or subject to significant change. Customers' needs change. Top management strategies and priorities change. Innovations create the impossible. Competitors change the playing field. In today's business world, certainty is a luxury, and a premium is placed on flexibility.

The key question is how to effectively manage projects with loosely defined or *unstable scope* accompanied by high levels of *uncertainty*. How do managers plan a project for which they are not sure what the final outcome will be? How do they develop a project control system that is both flexible and responsive yet, at the same time, ensures accountability and yields reliable projections? How do they avoid paralysis through overanalysis yet, at the same time, engage in prudent risk management? How do they know when it is appropriate to freeze the scope or design of the project and begin formal implementation? Conversely, using uncertainty as an excuse for not planning and flying into the wind by the seat of the pants is an invitation for disaster.

The next decade should see a whirlwind of attention to the problem of managing projects with ill-defined project scopes and project uncertainties. Answers to the problem are not obvious. Some of the ideas and techniques will be short-term fads. Others will withstand the test of time and make significant contributions to the project management body of knowledge.

Career Issues and Paths

Career Paths

There is no set career path for becoming a project manager. Career avenues vary from industry to industry, organization to organization, and from profession to profession. What can be said is that advancement occurs incrementally. You don't simply graduate and become a project manager. As in other careers you have to work your way up to the position. For example, in project-based organizations such as construction firms, you may begin by working on several projects as an assistant engineer, then take an assignment as a project analyst. From there you are promoted to principal engineer, advance to assistant project manager, assume the role of project manager over a small project, and then continue to bigger, riskier projects. In other organizations, project management careers run parallel with functional advancement with many crossovers. For example, at Intel a management information systems (MIS) specialist might start his career as a designer, then take an assignment as a project specialist, later work as a project manager, and then return to a functional position as head of a department or as a product manager.

Other people find that their project management responsibilities expand as they move up the organization's hierarchy. For example, a former marketing student began her career as an assistant buyer for a large retail company. She then became area sales manager at a specific store and became involved on a part-time basis in a series of projects acting as a facilitator of focus groups. She was promoted to buyer and eventually became a store manager. In her current position she coordinates a variety of projects ranging from improving the sales acumen of her salesforce to altering the physical layout of the store. Although the title of project manager does not appear in her job description, more than 50 percent of her work involves managing projects.

Temporary Assignments

One aspect of project managing that is unique is the temporary nature of assignments. With line appointments, promotions are for the most part permanent and there is a natural, hierarchical progression to positions with greater authority and responsibility. In the example of the former marketing student, she progressed from assistant buyer to sales manager to buyer to store manager. Only under very unusual circumstances would she regress to being a buyer. Conversely, tenure is rarely granted to project managers. Once the project is completed, the manager may return to his previous department, even to a lesser position. Or, depending on the projects available, he may be assigned to manage a more or less significant project. Future work depends on what projects are available at the time the individual is available and how well the last project went. A promising career can be derailed by one unsuccessful project.

Pursuing a Career

If you are considering pursuing a career in project management, you should first find out what specific project job opportunities exist in your company. You should talk to people in project management positions and find out how they got to where they are and what advice they can give you. Because career paths, as noted earlier, vary from organization to organization, you need to be attuned to the unique pathways within your company. For example, retail companies naturally assign marketing managers to projects.

Once you have concluded that you wish to pursue a career in project management, or see project management as an avenue for advancement, you need to share your aspirations with your immediate superior. Your superior can champion your ambitions, sanction additional training in project management, and assign immediate work that will contribute to your project skill base.

Professional Training and Certification

Most project managers have never received formal training in project management. They mastered the job through on-the-job training, buttressed by occasional workshops on specific project topics such as project scheduling or negotiating contracts. It wasn't until recently that universities started offering courses on project management outside of schools of engineering; to date there are only a handful of degree programs in project management. Regardless of your level of training you will likely need to supplement your education. Many large companies have in-house training programs on project management. For example, Hewlett-Packard has more than 32 training modules in its project management curriculum, which is organized around five levels of experience: project team, new project manager, project manager, experienced project manager, and manager of project managers. Take advantage of professional workshops, which can cover a range of specific project management tools and topics. Continued education should not be restricted to project management. Many technical professionals return to universities to complete an MBA or take night classes in management to expand their general business background.

Many professionals find it beneficial to join the Project Management Institute (PMI). Membership entitles you to subscriptions to PMI publications including the academic *Project Management Journal* and the *PM Network,* a trade magazine. PMI sponsors workshops and national forums on project management. When you join PMI you also become a member of one of the more than 200 local chapters across North America. These chapters meet on a monthly basis and provide project managers with opportunities to network and learn from each other. In addition, PMI, as part of its effort to advance the profession, certifies mastery of project manager competency through a formal examination that covers the entire body of knowledge of project management. Passing the exam and being certified as a project management professional (PMP) or certified associate in project management (CAPM) is a clearly visible way to signal your competence and interest.

Gaining Visibility

As you accumulate knowledge and techniques, you need to apply them to your immediate job situation. Most people's jobs entail some form of project, whether realizing a mandated objective or simply figuring out ways to improve the quality of performance. Gantt charts, responsibility matrixes, CPM networks, and other project management tools can be used to plan and implement these endeavors. It may also be wise to look outside the workplace for opportunities to develop project management skills. Active involvement in your local community can provide numerous opportunities to manage projects. Organizing a local soccer tournament, managing a charitable fund-raising event, or coordinating the renovation of the neighborhood park can allow you to practice project management. Furthermore, given the volunteer nature of most of these projects, they can provide you with an excellent training ground to sharpen your ability to exercise influence without formal authority.

Regardless of how competent and worthy you are, your project management skills must be visible to others for them to be recognized. Many project managers' careers began by volunteering for task forces and small projects. Ideally you should select task forces and projects that allow you access to higher-ups and other departments within your organization, providing you with opportunities to develop contacts.

This was certainly true for a former student of ours named Bob who escaped the trenches of a large corporation by volunteering to lead the organization's annual United Way campaign. While an important cause, directing the United Way campaign was generally given to someone who was expendable. This was true for Bob, whose career had bottomed out. Bob took advantage of the United Way task force to show off his project management skills. Through recruiting key participants, establishing a shared vision, managing milestones, and contagious enthusiasm the campaign was a resounding success, shattering previous records. Bob's efforts caught the attention of top management and he was rewarded with more project work.

Mentors

In pursuing your ambition you should continually be on the lookout for a mentor. Most fast-track managers acknowledge that mentors played a significant role in their advancement. Mentors are typically superiors who take a special interest in you and your career. They use their clout to champion your ambitions and act as a personal coach, teaching you "the ropes to skip and the ropes to know." This special treatment does not come without a price. Mentors typically require fervent loyalty and superior performance; after all, the mentor's reputation rests on your performance. How do you find a mentor? Most people say it just happens. But it doesn't happen to everyone. Mentors typically seek A+ workers, not C workers, and you must make your abilities known to others.

Many organizations have instituted formal mentoring programs in which experienced project managers are assigned to promising young managers. Although the relationship may not evolve to the personal level experienced with an informal mentor, designated mentors play a very similar role in coaching and championing one's professional progress. You should take advantage of this opportunity to learn as much as you can from these seasoned veterans.

Since much project work is temporary and contractual in nature, it is important to develop professional contacts that may lead to future work. Attending conferences, trade fairs, and workshops provides good opportunities to "network" and develop social connections that might precipitate project assignments. These social/professional networks can provide a safety net for project work during times of downsizing and layoffs.

Success in Key Projects

Ultimately your goal is to accumulate a portfolio of project management experiences that broaden your skill base and reputation. Early on you should choose, when possible, projects with the greatest learning opportunities. Pick projects more for the quality of the people working on them than for the scope of the projects. There is no better way to learn how to be an effective project manager than by watching one at work. Keep a diary of your observations and review and refine lessons learned. Later, as your confidence and competency grow, you should try to get involved in projects that will enhance your reputation within the firm. Remember the comments about customer satisfaction. You want to exceed your superior's expectations. Avoid run-of-the-mill projects or assignments. Seek high-profile projects that have some risks and tangible payoffs. At the same time, be careful to be involved in projects commensurate with your abilities.

Finally, despite your efforts you may find that you are not making satisfactory progress toward your career goals. If this is your appraisal, you may wish to seriously consider moving to a different company or even a different industry that might provide more project management opportunities. Hopefully you have managed to accumulate sufficient project management experience to aid in your job search. One advantage of project work over general management is that it is typically easier to highlight and "sell" your accomplishments. A second advantage is that project management is a portable skill set, applicable to a wide range of industries and situations.

Summary

The twenty-first century should be the Golden Age for project management. Not only will there be an increased demand for project management skills and know-how, but organizations will continue to evolve and change to support more effective project management. Project oversight will be a driving force behind these changes. Instead of trying to get projects done despite everything else, the organization's culture, structure, reward system, and administrative systems will be reengineered to support successful project management. Organization mastery of the process of managing projects will be critical to business growth and survival.

The project manager of the new millennium will be a businessperson with responsibilities that encompass the total organization. The past 30 years have seen the transition from a technically oriented project manager to one skilled in all aspects of business. Worldwide competition will direct projects toward technology transfer, infrastructure, consumer goods, environment/ecological recovery, defense, and fundamental needs. The future project manager will be comfortable in foreign or domestic settings and will understand the needs of people in all social settings. The project-driven organization will recognize the project manager as an agent of change and, from their ranks, select the senior managers of tomorrow.

Twenty years from now career paths in project management should be more clearly defined. Until then, people wishing to pursue a career in project management should take advantage of the transition and improvise within the constraints of their situation to develop their project management skills. They should volunteer to work on task forces, take advantage of training opportunities, and apply project management tools and techniques to their work. They should signal to their superiors their interest in project management and garner project assignments. Over time they should accumulate a portfolio of project management experiences that establishes their skill base and reputation as someone who gets things done quickly and done right.

Conclusions

By studying this text you have been exposed to the major elements of the process of managing projects. When you apply these ideas and techniques to real project situations, we offer two suggestions.

1. Maintain a sense of the big picture. Engage regularly in what some have called "helicopter management," which means expand your perspective beyond immediate concerns and assess how the project fits in the larger scheme of things. Project managers need to constantly assess how the project fulfills the mission and strategy of the firm, how the project is affecting the rest of the organization, whether the expectations of stakeholders are changing, and what key project interfaces have to be managed.

2. Remember that successful project management is essentially a balancing act. Project managers need to balance the soft (people) side of project management with the hard (technical) side, the demands of top management with the needs of team members, short-term gain with long-term need, and so forth.

Key Terms

Balanced scorecard	Phase gating	Project management maturity
Mentor	Portfolio management	Project office (PO)
Oversight		

Review Questions

1. What are the major economic forces that serve as an impetus for using oversight/governance tools and processes?
2. The Super Web Design president asked you to justify present and future oversight activities. Answer her request.
3. What are the three major advantages to an organization using a maturity model?
4. "We aren't big enough to have a project office, but we need the discipline of project management methods and standards." What advice would you give the CEO of this organization? Justify.
5. How can a mentor advance someone's career in project management?
6. Experts predict that most people will undergo at least three major career changes in their working life. If so, then why is project management an important skill set to master?

Exercises

1. Reread the "Day in a Life" case in Chapter 1. How would you assess her effectiveness now that you have studied project management? What part of Rachel's experience contributes to her success?
2. Access the Project Management Institute's home page at *www.pmi.org*. Review the qualifications necessary to earn certification as a project management professional and certified associate in project management. If possible, take the practice exam. How well did you do?

References

Baker, B., "The Nominees Are . . . ," *PM Network,* Vol. 18, No. 6, June 2004, p. 23.

Boyer, C., "Make Profit Your Priority," *PM Network,* Vol. 17, No. 10, October, 2003, p. 40.

Cochran, D., "Finally, A Way to Completely Measure Project Manager Performance," *PM Network,* Vol. 14, No. 9, September 2000, pp. 75–80.

Cooper, R. G., *Winning at New Products: Accelerating the Idea from Idea to Launch* (Cambridge, MA: Perseus Publishing, 2001).

Cooper, R. G., *Product Leadership: Creating and Launching Superior New Products* (Cambridge, MA: Perseus Publishing, 2000).

Cooper, R. G., S.J. Edgett, and E. J. Kleinschmidt, *Portfolio Management for New Products* (Reading, MA: Addison-Wesley, 1998).

Dinsmore, P. C., "Toward a Corporate Project Management Culture: Fast Tracking into the Future," *Proceedings of the Project Management Institute 28th Annual Seminars and Symposium* (Newton Square, PA: Project Management Institute, 1997).

Ibbs, C. W. and Y. H. Kwak, "Assessing Project Maturity," *Project Management Journal,* Vol. 31, No. 1, March 2000, pp. 32–43.

Kaplan, R. S. and D. Norton, "The Balanced Scorecard—Measures that Drive Performance," *Harvard Business Review,* January–February 1992, pp. 73–79. Note: A CD simulation is available from Harvard Customer Service, Product 8387. This interactive simulation provides hands-on experience for learning more about the method.

Lientz, B. P. and K. P. Rea, *Project Management for the 21st Century* (San Diego: Academic Press, 1995).

Mackay, H., *Dig Your Well before You're Thirsty* (New York: Doubleday, 1997).

Martin, P. and K. Tate, *Getting Started in Project Management* (New York: Wiley, 2004).

Morris, P. W. and A. Jamieson, "Moving from Corporate Strategy to Project Strategy," *Project Management Journal,* Vol. 36, No. 4. December 2005, pp. 5–18.

Mueller, E., "Maturity, Do or Die?" *PM Network,* Vol. 20, No. 2, February 2006, p. 32.

Norrie, J. and D. H. T. Walker, "A Balanced Scorecard Approach to Project Management Leadership," *Project Management Journal,* Vol. 35, No. 4, December 2004, pp. 47–56.

"Pull the Plug," *PM Network,* Vol. 20, No. 6, June 2006, pp. 39–42.

Rover, I., "Why Bad Projects Are So Hard to Kill," *Harvard Business Review,* February 2003, pp. 49–56.

Stewart, W. E., "Balanced Scorecard for Projects," *Project Management Journal,* Vol. 32, No. 1, March 2001, pp. 38–47. (2000 International Student Paper Award Winner.)

CASE 16.1

Don't Tell Me What You Have Done. Tell Me What You Are Going to Do

The firm has been merged with a larger firm carrying a similar product line of information technology consumer and industry products. One major goal of the merger was to save costs by eliminating duplication and improving management. Weeks before the merger, Lauren (not her real name) had just been promoted to project office director of the smaller firm. She assumed her position would be absorbed into the project office of the large firm. Mentally, Lauren was prepared to start job hunting. Maybe she should change careers and go back to a job that used her bachelor's degree in political science. Two weeks after the merger was finalized, others, including herself, received a letter to report for an interview with the new company senior management "conversion" vice president. Lauren spent three days gathering materials to substantiate all of her past accomplishments, to demonstrate her management skills, and to show her potential value to the new firm. When the big day came, Lauren entered the office of the interviewer with approximately nine inches of substantiating material. She was prepared!

The first few minutes were spent explaining her past roles in the firm, the new project office, and other niceties. She explained to the VP she had all of the materials with her to back up her statements and he could take them if he wished. He replied, "I am not as interested in your past accomplishments as I am in your possible future accomplishments. Here is the need. Projects eat up about 40 percent of our yearly expenses. We need to cut 10 million off those expenses. In five minutes tell me how you will do it and how it will be verified."

Her last statement at the end of four minutes was: "I can give you five million within the next year. Ten million is too big a stretch."

His retort was, "Lauren, can you get five in six months?"

(Gulp.) "I'm pretty sure I can."

"Congratulations, Lauren, you are now the new project office director of this continental division."

In 500 words or less, write what you believe Lauren could have used as key points to get the position.

Lientz, B. P. and K. P. Rea, *Project Management for the 21st Century* (San Diego: Academic Press, 1998).

Mackey, H., *Dig Your Well before You're Thirsty* (New York: Doubleday, 1997).

Martin, P. and K. Tate, *Getting Started in Project Management* (New York: Wiley, 2001).

Morris, P. W. and A. Jamieson, "Moving from Corporate Strategy to Project Strategy," *Project Management Journal*, ...

Mueller, E., "Maturity Do or Die," *PM Network*, Vol. 20, No. 2, February 2006, pp. 32.

Norrie, J. and D. H. T. Walker, "A Balanced Scorecard Approach to Project Management Leadership," *Project Management Journal*, Vol. 35, No. 4, December 2004, pp. 47-56.

Royer, I., "Why Bad Projects Are So Hard to Kill," *Harvard Business Review*, February 2003, pp. 19-36.

Stewart, W. E., "Balancing Scorecard for Projects," ...

Computer Project Exercises

In developing the exercises, trade-offs had to be made to enrich the learning experience. One of the major problems students initially encounter is data and detail overload. This reduces their ability to identify project and data problems and to compare alternatives. Although the project found in the exercises is real, it has been reduced and detail has been eliminated many times to concentrate on applying project management principles and understanding linkages. In addition, other simplifying assumptions have been made so that students and instructors can trace problems and discuss outcomes. These assumptions detract from reality, but they keep the focus on the objectives of the exercises and reduce student frustration with software intricacies. Moving from these exercises to real projects is primarily one of increasing detail. The simplifying assumptions are given below (make sure they are included in "default," "preferences," and/or "options" sections of the software used):

Blue Zuma Project

The ARC Company specializes in developing and selling a wide range of high-quality scooters. Sales representatives report that there is a growing demand for racing scooters. ARC's president, Robin Lane, is excited about the possibilities and predicts that one day these kinds of razor scooters will be featured in X-Game events. ARC is a small company and uses a strong matrix to optimally utilize limited manpower.

The Project Priority Matrix for the Blue Zuma Project is:

	Time	Scope	Cost
Constrain		X	
Enhance	X		
Accept			X

Part I

You are a member of a project team assigned to develop the new razor scooter code named "Blue Zuma." Table A1.1 contains the information necessary to create a project schedule. For the purpose of this case assume the following:

1. The project begins January 2, 2008.
2. The following holidays are observed: January 1, Memorial Day (last Monday in May), July 4th, Labor Day (first Monday in September), Thanksgiving Day (4th Thursday in November), December 25 and 26.

TABLE A1.1   Blue Zuma Project

ID	Task Name	Duration	Predecessors	Resources
1	Product development project			
2	Market analysis	25 days		Marketing (4)
3	Product design	40 days	2	Marketing (1) Design (4) Development (2) Industrial (1) Purchasing (1)
4	Manufacturing study	20 days	2	Industrial (4) Development (2)
5	Product design selection	10 days	3,4	Marketing (2) Design (3) Development (2) Industrial (2) Purchasing (.25)
6	Detailed marketing plan	15 days	5	Marketing (4)
7	Manufacturing process	30 days	5	Design (1) Development (2) Industrial (4)
8	Detailed product design	50 days	5	Marketing (2) Design (4) Development (2) Industrial (2) Purchasing (.25)
9	Test prototype	10 days	8	Design (3) Development (2)
10	Finalized product design	25 days	7,9	Marketing (2) Design (3) Development (3) Industrial (2)
11	Order components	7 days	10	Purchasing (1)
12	Order production equipment	14 days	10	Purchasing (1)
13	Install production equipment	35 days	11F-S + 20 days, 12F-S + 40 days	Development (3) Industrial (4) Design (1)
14	Celebrate	1 day	6,13	Development (4) Industrial (4) Design (4) Marketing (4) Purchasing (1)

3. If a holiday falls on a Saturday, then Friday will be given as an extra day off, and if it falls on a Sunday, then Monday will be given as a day off.

4. The project team works eight-hour days, Monday through Friday.

Construct a network schedule for this project and prepare a memo that answers the following questions:

1. When is the project estimated to be completed? How long will the project take?
2. What is the critical path for the project?
3. Which activity has the greatest amount of slack?
4. How sensitive is this network?
5. Identify two sensible milestones and explain your choices.
6. Compare the advantages/disadvantages of displaying the schedule as a network versus a Gantt chart.

Include the following printouts:

- A Gantt chart.
- A network diagram highlighting the critical path.
- A schedule table reporting ES, LS, EF, LF, and slack for each activity.

Part 2

The following personnel have been assigned to the Blue Zuma project team:

- 4 marketing specialists

- 4 design engineers
- 4 development engineers
- 4 industrial engineers
- 1 purchasing agent

Use the file from Part 1 and the information contained in Tables A1.1 and A1.2 to assign resources to the project schedule.

TABLE A1.2 Blue Zuma Project Resources

Resource	$/hour	Number Available
Marketing specialist	$60	4
Design engineer	$90	4
Development engineer	$80	4
Industrial engineer	$70	4
Purchasing agent	$50	1

Part A

Prepare a memo that addresses the following questions:

1. Which if any of the resources are overallocated?
2. Which activities involve overallocated resources?
3. Assume that the project is time constrained and try to resolve any overallocation problems by leveling within slack. What happens?
4. What is the impact of leveling within slack on the sensitivity of the network?

Include a Gantt chart with the schedule table after leveling within slack.

Part B

Prepare a memo that addresses the following questions:

1. Assume that the project is resource constrained and no additional personnel are available. How long will the project take given the resources assigned? (Hint: Undo leveling performed in Part A before answering this question.)

Note: No splitting of activities is allowed.

2. How does the new duration compare with the estimated completion date generated from Part 1? What does this tell you about the impact resources can have on a schedule?

Include a Gantt chart with a schedule table depicting the resource-constrained schedule.

Part 3

Top management is not happy with the resource-constrained schedule generated at the end of Part 2. Robin Lane, the president, has promised retailers that production of the new scooters would start on February 1, 2009.

1. What options are available to meet this new deadline if the project is not resource constrained?
2. What options are available to meet this deadline if the project is resource constrained?

Dewey Martin, director of product development, has managed to make the following personnel available to work on specific activities on the project. Since there is an acute shortage of personnel at ARC he requests that you only use additional manpower that will help meet the new deadline. Your objective is to develop a schedule which will satisfy the deadline with minimum additional resource usage. The available personnel and impact on activity duration are presented in Table A1.3.

TABLE A1.3   Blue Zuma Project Crashing Options

Activity	Additional Resources	Revised Duration Estimates
Detailed marketing plan	Marketing (2)	10 days
Detailed product design	Design (1) Development (1)	42 days
Install production equipment	Industrial (1) Development (1)	27 days

Pay rates for additional personnel: Marketing, $70/hour; Design, $100/hour; Development, $90/hour; and Industrial, $80/hour.

Prepare a memo that addresses the following questions:

1. Which additional personnel assignments would you choose to complete the project within the original deadline? Explain your choices as well as the reasons for not choosing other options.
2. How have these changes affected the sensitivity of the network?

Include a Gantt chart with a schedule table presenting the new schedule.

Note: You cannot go back and relevel resources. These new resources are only available for the stated specific tasks according to the schedule created at the end of Part 2.

Part 4

Robin Lane and top management have approved the schedule generated at the end of Part 3. Save the file containing this schedule as a baseline schedule.

Prepare a memo that addresses the following questions:

1. How much is the project estimated to cost?
2. What activity is estimated to cost the most to complete?
3. What resource commands the greatest total cost?
4. During which month of the project are the highest and lowest costs expected to occur? What are those costs?
5. What likely costs are not contained in this budget?

Include a table containing the estimated costs for each activity and a cash flow schedule for each month of the project.

Part 5

Today's date is August 16, 2008. Table A1.4 summarizes the information regarding activities accomplished to date.

Robin Lane has requested a written status report for the Blue Zuma project.

1. Your status report should include a table containing the PV, EV, AC, BAC, EAC, SV, CV, and CPI for each activity and the whole project. The report should also address the following questions:
   a. How is the project progressing in terms of cost and schedule?

TABLE A1.4   Blue Zuma Project Update

Activity	Start Date	Finish Date	Actual Duration	Remaining Duration
Market analysis	1/2/08	2/1/08	23	
Product design	2/4/08	3/20/08	34	
Manufacturing study	3/21/08	4/22/08	23	
Product design selection	4/23/08	5/13/08	15	
Manufacturing process	8/1/08		11	25
Detailed product design	5/14/08	7/31/08	55	
Test prototype	8/1/08	8/15/08	11	

b. What activities have gone well? What activities have not gone well?

c. What do the PCIB and PCIC indicate in terms of how much of the project has been accomplished to date?

d. What is the forecasted cost at completion (EAC_F)? What is the predicted VAC_f?

e. Report and interpret the TCPI for the project at this point in time.

f. What is the estimated date of completion?

g. How well is the project doing in terms of its priorities?

Try to present the above information in a form worthy of consideration by top management.

Include a tracking Gantt chart with your report.

Note: Enter August 15 as the status report date since you are preparing your report on the 16th.

2. While preparing your report you receive a phone call from Jim Keltner, a fellow project manager. He is calling to see if one of the industrial engineers assigned to your project would be available to work on his project from August 22 to 27, 2008. What would you tell him?

Part 6

Robin Lane has authorized using Management Reserves to expedite the shipping of components at an additional cost of $50,000. She has asked you to update completion and cost estimates for the Blue Zuma project. Table A1.5 presents the revised estimates generated by the Zuma project team.

TABLE A1.5   Blue Zuma Project Revised Estimates to Completion

Activity	Start Date	Finish Date	Actual Duration
Market analysis	1/2/08	2/1/08	23
Product design	2/4/08	3/20/08	34
Manufacturing study	3/21/08	4/22/08	23
Product design selection	4/23/08	5/13/08	15
Detailed marketing plan	10/28/08	11/24/08	20
Manufacturing process	8/1/08	9/18/06	34
Detailed product design	5/14/08	7/31/08	55
Test prototype	8/1/08	8/15/08	11
Finalized product design	9/19/08	10/16/08	20
Order components	10/31/08	11/6/08	5
Order production equipment *	10/17/08	11/3/08	12
Install production equipment	12/9/08	1/22/09	30
Celebrate	1/23/09	1/23/09	1

* Add $50,000 expediting costs.

Based on this new information prepare a memo that answers the following questions:

1. When will the project be completed? How does this compare with the baseline completion date?
2. What is the new estimated cost at completion (EAC)? What is the new VAC? How does this compare with VAC based on the EAC_F generated in Part 5? Which of the two VACs would you have the greatest confidence in and why?
3. How do you think Robin will react given the priorities for this project?

Include a tracking Gantt with a cost table for the estimated completion schedule.

Conveyor Belt Project

Part 1

Project Description

The new computer-controlled conveyor belt is an exciting project that moves and positions items on the conveyor belt within <1 millimeter. The project will produce a new system for future installations, and for replacement of those in the field, at a low cost. The computer-controlled conveyor belt has the potential to be a critical unit in 30 percent of the systems installed in factories. The new system is also easier to update with future technologies.

The Project Priority Matrix for the Conveyor Belt Project (CBP) is:

	Time	Scope	Cost
Constrain	X		
Enhance		X	
Accept			X

Table A1.6 has been developed for you to use in completing the project exercises.

Assignment

Develop the WBS outline using the software available to you.

Question

Does this information (WBS) allow you to define any milestones of the project? Why or why not? What are they?

Remember: Save your file for future exercises!

Part 2

Use your file from Part 1 and the information provided below to complete this exercise. (See Table A1.7.)

1. Each work package will represent an activity.
2. The project begins January 4, 2010.
3. The following holidays are observed: January 1, Memorial Day (last Monday in May), July 4th, Labor Day (first Monday in September), Thanksgiving Day (4th Thursday in November), December 25 and 26.

TABLE A1.6 Conveyor Belt Project; WBS

Conveyor Belt Project	
Hardware	Hardware specifications
	Hardware design
	Hardware documentation
	Prototypes
	Order circuit boards
	Assemble preproduction models
Operating system	Kernel specifications
	Drivers
	Disk drivers
	Serial I/O drivers
	Memory management
	Operating system documentation
	Network interface
Utilities	Utilities specifications
	Routine utilities
	Complex utilities
	Utilities documentation
	Shell
System integration	Architectural decisions
	Integration first phase
	System hard/software test
	Project documentation
	Integration acceptance testing

TABLE A1.7 Conveyor Belt Project; Schedule

Activity	Description	Resource	Duration (days)	Preceding Activity
1	Architectural decisions	Design	25	—
2	Hardware specifications	Development, design	50	1
3	Kernel specifications	Design	20	1
4	Utilities specifications	Development, design	15	1
5	Hardware design	Design, development	70	2
6	Disk drivers	Assembly, development	100	3
7	Memory management	Development	90	3
8	Operating system documentation	Design, documentation	25	3
9	Routine utilities	Development	60	4
10	Complex utilities	Development	80	4
11	Utilities documentation	Documentation, design	20	4
12	Hardware documentation	Documentation, design	30	5
13	Integration first phase	Assembly, development	50	6,7,8,9,10,11,12
14	Prototypes	Assembly, development	80	13
15	Serial I/O drivers	Development	130	13
16	System hard/software test	Assembly	25	14,15
17	Order circuit boards	Purchasing	5	16
18	Network interface	Development	90	16
19	Shell	Development	60	16
20	Project documentation	Documentation, development	50	16
21	Assemble preproduction models	Assembly, development	30	17F-S, lag 50 days
22	Integrated acceptance testing	Assembly, development	60	18,19,20,21

4. If a holiday falls on a Saturday then Friday will be given as an extra day off, and if it falls on a Sunday, then Monday will be given as a day off.
5. The project team work eight-hour days, Monday through Friday.

Warning: Experience has taught students to frequently make separate backup files for each exercise. The software is never as friendly as users expect!

Construct a network schedule for the conveyor belt project and prepare a memo that addresses the following questions:

1. When is the project estimated to be completed? How long will the project take?
2. What is the critical path(s) for the project?
3. Which activity has the greatest amount of slack?
4. How sensitive is this network?
5. Identify two sensible milestones and explain your choices.
6. Compare the advantages/disadvantages of displaying the schedule as a network versus a Gantt chart.

Include the following printouts:

- A Gantt chart.
- A network diagram highlighting the critical path.
- A schedule table reporting. ES, LS, EF, LF, and slack for each activity.

Hint: the project should be completed in 530 days.
Remember: Save your file for future exercises!

Part 3

Remember the old saying, "A project plan is not a schedule until resources are committed." This exercise illustrates this subtle, but very important, difference.

Part A

Using your files from Part 2 input resources and their costs if you have not already done so. All information is found in Tables A1.7 and A1.8.

TABLE A1.8 Organization Resources

Name	Group	Cost ($/hr)
Design	R&D (2 teams)	$100
Development	R&D (2 teams)	70
Documentation	R&D (1 team)	60
Assembly/test	R&D (1 team)	70
Purchasing	Procurement (1 team)	40

Prepare a memo that addresses the following questions:

1. Which if any of the resources are overallocated?
2. Assume that the project is time constrained and try to resolve any overallocation problems by leveling within slack. What happens?
3. What is the impact of leveling within slack on the sensitivity of the network?

Include a Gantt chart with the schedule table after leveling within slack.

4. Assume the project is resource constrained and resolve any overallocation problems by leveling outside of slack. What happens? What are the managerial implications?
5. What options are available at this point in time?

Include a Gantt chart with the schedule table after leveling outside of slack.

Note: No splitting of activities is allowed.
Note: No partial assignments (i.e., 50 percent). All resources must be assigned 100 percent.

Part B

When you show the resource-constrained network to top management, they are visibly shaken. After some explanation and negotiation they make the following compromise with you:

- The project must be completed no later than February 2, 2012 (530 days).
- You may assign two additional development teams.
- If this does not suffice, you may hire other development teams from the outside. Hire as few external teams as possible because they cost $50 more per hour than your inside development people.

Internal Development

Add as many development units (teams) as needed to stay within the 530 days. If you need more than the two units, examine all possibilities. Select the cheapest possibilities! Change as few activities as possible. It is recommended you keep work packages which require cooperation of several organizational units inside your company. You decide how best to do this.

Hint: Undo leveling prior to adding new resources.

Once you have obtained a schedule that meets the time and resource constraints, prepare a memo that addresses the following questions:

1. What changes did you make and why?
2. How long will the project take?
3. How did these changes affect the sensitivity of the network?

Include a Gantt chart with a schedule table presenting the new schedule.

Part 4

Based on the file created at the end of Part 3, prepare a memo that addresses the following questions:

1. How much will the project cost?
2. What does the cash flow statement tell you about how costs are distributed over the lifespan of the project?

Include a monthly cash flow and a cost table for the project.

Once you are confident that you have the final schedule, save the file as a baseline. **Hint:** Save a backup file just in case without baseline!

Part 5

Prepare status reports for each of the first four quarters of the project given the information provided here. This requires saving your resource schedule as a baseline and inserting the appropriate status report date in the program. Assume that no work has been completed on the day of the status report.

Your status report should include a table containing the PV, EV, AC, BAC, EAC, SV, CV, and CPI for each activity and the whole project. The report should also address the following questions:

1. How is the project progressing in terms of cost and schedule?
2. What activities have gone well? What activities have not gone well?
3. What do the PCIB and PCIC indicate in terms of how much of the project has been accomplished to date?
4. What is the forecasted cost at completion (EAC$_f$)? What is the predicted VAC$_f$?
5. Report and interpret the TCPI for the project at this point in time.
6. What is the estimated date of completion?
7. How well is the project doing in terms of its priorities?

Try to present the above information in a form worthy of consideration by top management.
   Include a Tracking Gantt chart with each report.

First Quarter, April 1, 2010

Table A1.9 summarizes the information regarding activities accomplished to date.
   Be sure to save your file after each quarterly report and use it to build the next report!

TABLE A1.9   April 1, 2010

Activity	Start Date	Finish Date	Actual Duration	Remaining Duration
Hardware specifications	2/9/10		37	8
Kernel specifications	2/8/10	3/12/10	25	0
Disk drivers	3/15/10		13	87
Memory management	3/15/10		13	77
Op. systems documentation	3/15/10		13	7
Utilities specifications	3/8/10	3/29/10	16	0
Complex utilities	3/30/10		2	85
Architectural decisions	1/4/10	2/5/10	25	0

Second Quarter, July 1, 2010

Table A1.10 summarizes the information regarding activities accomplished since the last report.

Third Quarter, October 1, 2010

Table A1.11 summarizes the information regarding activities accomplished since the last report.

Fourth Quarter, January 1, 2011

Table A1.12 summarizes the information regarding activities accomplished since the last report.

TABLE AI.10   July 1, 2010

Activity	Start Date	Finish Date	Actual Duration	Remaining Duration
Hardware specifications	2/9/10	4/12/10	45	0
Hardware design	4/13/10		56	11
Kernel specifications	2/8/10	3/12/10	25	0
Disk drivers	3/15/10		77	33
Memory management	3/15/10		77	19
Op. systems documentation	3/15/10	4/16/10	25	0
Utilities specifications	3/8/10	3/29/10	16	0
Routine utilities*	4/26/10		47	18
Complex utilities	3/30/10		66	25
Utilities documentation	5/3/10	6/2/10	22	0
Architectural decisions	1/4/10	2/5/10	25	0

* The project manager for the external development team that was hired to perform routine utilities reported that due to commitments to other clients they would be able to start on that activity 4/26/10.

TABLE AI.11   October 1, 2010

Activity	Start Date	Finish Date	Actual Duration	Remaining Duration
Hardware specifications	2/9/10	4/12/10	45	0
Hardware design	4/13/10	7/16/10	67	0
Hardware documentation	7/19/10	8/24/10	27	0
Kernel specifications	2/8/10	3/12/10	25	0
Disk drivers	3/15/10	8/17/10	110	0
Memory management	3/15/10	7/30/10	98	0
Op. systems documentation	3/15/10	4/16/10	25	0
Utilities specifications	3/8/10	3/29/10	16	0
Routine utilities	4/26/10	7/27/10	65	0
Complex utilities	3/30/10	8/11/10	95	0
Utilities documentation	5/3/10	6/2/10	22	0
Architectural decisions	1/4/10	2/5/10	25	0
Integration 1st phase	8/25/10		26	24

Part 6

You have received revised estimates for the remaining activities at the end of the fourth quarter:

- Prototypes will be completed on 3/8/11.
- Serial I/O drivers will be completed on 6/30/11.
- System hardware/software test will start on 7/1/11 and take 25 days.
- Order circuit boards will start on 8/8/11 and take 5 days.
- Assemble preproduction model will begin on 10/14/11 and take 18 days.
- Project documentation is expected to start on 8/8/11 and will take 55 days.
- Network interface is expected to start on 8/8/11 and will take 99 days.
- Shell is expected to start on 8/8/11 and will take 55 days.
- Integrated acceptance testing is expected to start on 12/29/11 and will take 54 days.

TABLE A1.12 January 1, 2011

Activity	Start Date	Finish Date	Actual Duration	Remaining Duration
Hardware specifications	2/9/10	4/12/10	45	0
Hardware design	4/13/10	7/16/10	67	0
Hardware documentation	7/19/10	8/24/10	27	0
Prototypes	11/11/10		34	44
Kernel specifications	2/8/10	3/12/10	25	0
Disk drivers	3/15/10	8/17/10	110	0
Serial I/O drivers	11/11/10		34	119
Memory management	3/15/10	7/30/10	98	0
Op. systems documentation	3/15/10	4/16/10	25	0
Utilities specifications	3/8/10	3/29/10	16	0
Routine utilities	4/26/10	7/27/10	65	0
Complex utilities	3/30/10	8/11/10	95	0
Utilities documentation	5/3/10	6/2/10	22	0
Architectural decisions	1/4/10	2/5/10	25	0
Integration 1st phase	8/25/10	11/10/10	55	0

Prepare a memo that addresses the following questions:

1. What is the new EAC for the project? How long should the project take given these revised estimates?
2. How happy will top management be with these forecasts given the priorities of the project?
3. What recommendations would you make?

Include a revised schedule, a Tracking Gantt chart, and cost table with your memo.

Glossary

A

activity   Task(s) of the project that consumes time while people/equipment either work or wait.

activity duration   Estimate of time (hours, days, weeks, months, etc.) necessary to complete a project task.

actual cost of the work completed (AC)   The sum of the cost incurred in accomplishing work. Previously this was called the actual cost of the work performed (ACWP).

actual cost of the work performed (ACWP)   Actual cost of the work performed in a given time period. The sum of the costs incurred in accomplishing work.

AOA   Activity-on-arrow method for drawing project networks. The activity is shown as an arrow.

AON   Activity-on-node method for drawing project networks. The activity is on the node (rectangle).

apportionment method   Costs allocated to a specific segment of a project by using a percentage of planned total cost—for example, framing a house might use 25 percent of the total cost, or coding a teaching module 40 percent of total cost.

avoiding risk   Elimination of the risk cause before the project begins.

B

backward pass   The method used to compute the late start and finish times for each activity in the project network.

balanced matrix   A matrix structure in which the project manager and functional managers share roughly equal authority over the project. The project manager decides what needs to be done; functional managers are concerned with how it will be accomplished.

balanced scorecard method   Model that measures the long-run results of major program activities in four areas—customer, internal, innovation and learning, and financial.

bar chart   A graphic presentation of project activities depicted as a time-scaled bar line (also called a Gantt chart).

baseline   A concrete document and commitment; it represents the first real plan with cost, schedule, and resource allocation. The planned cost and schedule performance are used to measure actual cost and schedule performance. Serves as an anchor point for measuring performance.

BATNA   Best alternative to a negotiated agreement. Strong or weak BATNA indicates your power to negotiate with the other party.

bottom-up estimates   Detailed estimates of work packages usually made by those who are most familiar with the the task (also called micro estimates).

brainstorming   Generating as many ideas/solutions as possible without critical judgment.

budget at completion (BAC)   Budgeted cost at completion. The total budgeted cost of the baseline or project cost accounts.

budget reserve   Reserve setup to cover identified risks that may occur and influence baseline tasks or costs. These reserves are typically controlled by the project manager and the project team. See management reserve.

budgeted cost of the work performed (BCWP)   The value for completed work measured in terms of the planned budget for the work. The earned value or original budgeted cost for work actually completed.

build-own-operate-transfer (BOOT)   A risk management provision in which the prime contractor not only builds the facility, but also takes over ownership until its operation capacity has been proven before final transfer of ownership to the client.

burst activity   An activity that has more than one activity immediately following it.

C

capability maturity model (CMM)   A framework which describes the evolutionary stages of project management systems.

change control   The process of documenting, reviewing, accepting or rejecting change, and documenting any change to the project baseline.

change management system   A defined process for authorizing and documenting changes in the scope of a project.

chart of accounts   A hierarchical numbering system used to identify tasks, deliverables, and organizational responsibility in the work breakdown structure.

co-location   A situation in which project members including those from different organizations work together in the same location.

communication plan   A plan that defines information to be collected and distributed to stakeholders based on their requirements.

concurrent engineering or simultaneous engineering   Cross-functional teamwork in new-product development projects that provides product design, quality engineering, and manufacturing process engineering all at the same time.

consensus decision making   Reaching a decision that all involved parties basically agree with and support.

contingency fund   See contingency reserve.

contingency plan   A plan that covers possible identified project risks that may materialize over the life of the project.

contingency reserve   Usually an amount of money or time set aside to cover identified and unforeseen project risks.

contract   A formal agreement between two parties wherein one party (the contractor) obligates itself to perform a service and the other party (the client) obligates itself to do something in return, usually in the form of a payment to the contractor.

cost account   A control point of one or more work packages used to plan, schedule, and control the project. The sum of all the project cost accounts represents the total cost of the project.

cost performance index (CPI)   The ratio of work performed to actual costs (EV/AC).

cost-plus contract   A contract in which the contractor is reimbursed for all direct allowable costs (materials, labor, travel) plus an additional fee to cover overhead and profit.

cost variance (CV)   The difference between EV and AC ($CV = EV - AC$). Tells if the work accomplished cost more or less than was planned at any point over the life of the project.

crash point   The most a project activity time can realistically be compressed with the resources available to the organization.

crash time   The shortest time an activity can be completed (assuming a reasonable level of resources).

critical path   The longest activity path(s) through the network. The critical path can be distinguished by identifying the collection of activities that all have the same minimum slack.

critical path method (CPM)   A scheduling method based on the estimates of time required to complete activities on the critical path. The method computes early, late, and slack times for each activity in the network. It establishes a planned project duration, if one is not imposed on the project.

culture   The totality of socially transmitted behavior patterns, beliefs, institutions, and all other products of human work and thought characteristic of a community or country.

culture shock   A natural psychological disorientation that most people suffer when they move to a culture different from their own.

D

dedicated project team   An organizational structure in which all of the resources needed to accomplish a project are assigned full time to the project.

deliverable   A major product or result that must be finished to complete the project.

Delphi Technique   A group method to predict future events—e.g., time, cost.

direct costs   Costs that are clearly charged to a specific work package—usually labor, materials, or equipment.

dummy activity   An activity that does not consume time; it is represented on the AOA network as a dashed line. A dummy activity is used to ensure a unique identification number for parallel activities and used to maintain dependencies among activities on the project network.

duration (DUR)   The time needed to complete an activity, a path, or a project.

dysfunctional conflict   Disagreement that does not improve project performance.

E

early finish (EF)   The earliest an activity can finish if all its preceding activities are finished by their early finish times (EF = ES + DUR).

early start (ES)   The earliest an activity can start. It is the largest early finish of all its immediate predecessors (ES = EF − DUR).

earned value (EV)   The physical work accomplished plus the authorized budget for this work. Previously this was called the budgeted cost of work performed (BCWP).

emotional intelligence (EQ)   The ability or skill to perceive, assess, and manage the emotions of one's self and others.

escalation   A control mechanism for resolving problems in which people at the lowest appropriate level attempt to resolve a problem within a set time limit or the problem is "escalated" to the next level of management.

estimated cost at completion (EAC)   The sum of actual costs to date plus revised estimated costs for the work remaining in the WBS. The text uses EAC_{re} to represent revisions made by experts and practitioners associated with the project. A second method is used in large projects where the original budget is less reliable. This method uses the actual costs to date plus an efficiency index (CPI = EV/AC) applied to the remaining project work. When the estimate for completion uses the CPI as the basis for forecasting cost at completion, we use the acronym EAC$_f$, where **EAC$_f$** = estimated costs at completion. Includes costs to date plus revised estimated costs for the work remaining. (Uses formula to complute EAC.)

ETC$_f$ Estimated cost to complete (uses formula to compute estimates).

ETC$_{re}$ Estimated cost to complete (uses expert estimates).

event   A point in time when an activity(s) is started or completed. It does not consume time.

F

failure mode and effects analysis (FMEA)   Each potential risk is assessed in terms of severity of impact, probability of the event occurring, and ease of detection.

fast-tracking   Accelerating project completion typically by rearranging the network schedule and using start-to-start lags.

fixed-price or "lump sum" contract   A contract in which the contractor agrees to perform all the work specified in the contract at a predetermined, fixed price.

float   See slack.

forecast at completion (FAC)   The forecasted cost at completion—using forecast equation.

forward pass   The method for determining the early start and finish times for each activity in the project network.

free slack   The maximum amount of time an activity can be delayed from its early start (ES) without affecting the early start (ES) of any activity immediately following it.

function points   Points derived from past software projects to estimate project time and cost, given specific features of the project.

functional conflict   Disagreement that contributes to the objectives of the project.

functional manager   A manager responsible for activities in a specialized department or function (e.g., engineering, marketing, finance).

functional organization   A hierarchical organizational structure in which departments represent individual disciplines such as engineering, marketing, purchasing.

G

Gantt chart   See bar chart.

going native   Adopting the customs, values, and prerogatives of a foreign culture.

Golden Rule   Do unto others as you would wish them to do unto you.

groupthink   A tendency of members in highly cohesive groups to lose their critical evaluative capabilities.

H

hammock activity   A special-purpose, aggregate activity that identifies the use of fixed resources or costs over a segment of the project—e.g., a consultant. Derives its duration from the time span between other activities.

heuristic   A rule of thumb used to make decisions. Frequently found in scheduling projects. For example, schedule critical activities first, then schedule activities with the shortest duration.

I

implementation gap   The lack of consensus between the goals set by top management and those independently set by lower levels of management. This lack of consensus leads to confusion and poor allocation of organization resources.

indirect costs   Costs that cannot be traced to a particular project or work package.

infrastructure   Basic services (i.e., communication, transportation, power) needed to support project completion.

in-process project audit   Project audits early in projects that allow for corrective changes if they are needed on the audited project or others in progress.

insensitive network   A network in which the critical path is likely to remain stable during the life of the project.

international project   A project that includes tasks that will be completed in different countries.

ISO 9000   A set of standards governing the requirements for documentation of a quality program.

J

joint evaluation   A process in which different parties involved in a project evaluate how well they work together.

L

lag   The amount of time between the end of one activity and the start of another. A duration assigned to the activity dependency. The minimum amount of time a dependent activity must be delayed to begin or end.

lag relationship   The relationship between the start and/or finish of a project activity and the start and/or finish of another activity. The most common lag relationships are (1) finish-to-start, (2) finish-to-finish, (3) start-to-start, and (4) start-to-finish.

late finish (LF)   The latest an activity can finish and not delay a following activity (LF = LS + DUR).

late start (LS)   The latest an activity can start and not delay a following activity. It is the largest late finish (LF) of all activities immediately preceding it (LS = LF − DUR).

law of reciprocity   People are obligated to grant a favor comparable to the one they received.

leading by example   Exhibiting the behaviors you want to see in others.

learning curves   A mathematical curve used to predict a pattern of time reduction as a task is performed over and over.

leveling (smoothing)   A technique used to lower the maximum demand for a resource by using slack to realign resource.

M

management by wandering around (MBWA)   A management style in which managers spend the majority of their time outside their offices interacting with key people.

management reserve   A percentage of the total project budget reserved for contingencies. The fund exists to cover unforeseen, new problems—not unnecessary overruns. The reserve is designed to reduce the risk of project delays. Management reserves are typically controlled by the project owner or project manager. See budget reserve.

matrix   Any organizational structure in which the project manager shares responsibility with the functional managers for assigning priorities and for directing the work of individuals assigned to the project.

maturity model   A model used to assess project management practices against others in the same industry and to guide and continuously strive to improve the management of projects. Most maturity models recognize levels of maturity so organizations can gauge their relative maturity against others in their industry.

mentor   Typically a more experienced manager who acts as a personal coach and champions a person's ambitions.

merge activity   An activity that has more than one activity immediately preceding it.

met-expectations model   Customer satisfaction is a function of the extent to which perceived performance exceeds expectations.

milestone   An event that represents significant, identifiable accomplishment toward the project's completion.

mitigating risk   Action taken to either reduce the likelihood that a risk will occur and/or the impact the risk will have on the project.

Monte Carlo simulation   A method of simulating project activity durations using probabilities. The method identifies the percentage of times, activities, and paths that are critical over thousands of simulations.

N

negative reinforcement   A motivational technique in which negative stimuli are removed once desired behavior is exhibited.

net present value (NPV)   A minimum desired rate of return discount (e.g., 15 percent) is used to compute present value of all future cash inflows and outflows.

network   A logic diagram arranged in a prescribed format (e.g., AOA or AON) consisting of activities, sequences, interrelationships, and dependencies.

network organization   An alliance of several organizations created for the purpose of creating products and services for customers.

network sensitivity   The likelihood that the critical path will change on a project.

nominal group technique (NGT)   A structured problem-solving process in which members privately rank-order preferred solutions.

O

objective   An end you seek to create or acquire. Should be specific, measurable, realistic, assignable, and include a time frame for accomplishment.

organization breakdown structure (OBS)   A structure used to assign responsibility for work packages.

organizational culture   A system of shared norms, beliefs, values, and assumptions held by an organization's members.

organizational currencies   A set of currencies used as a medium of exchange within organizations to influence behavior.

organizational politics   Actions by individuals or groups of individuals to acquire, develop, and use power and other resources to obtain preferred outcomes when there is uncertainty or disagreement over choices.

outsourcing   Contracting for the use of external sources (skills) to assist in implementing a project.

overhead costs   Typically organization costs that are not directly linked to a specific project. These costs cover general expenses such as upper management, legal, market promotion, and accounting. Overhead costs are usually charged per unit of time or as a percentage of labor or material costs.

oversight   A set of principles and processes to guide and improve the management of projects. The intent is to ensure projects meet the needs of the organization through standards, procedures, accountability, efficient allocation of resources, and continuous improvement in the management of projects.

P

padding estimates   Adding a safety factor to a time or cost estimate to ensure the estimate is met when the project is executed.

parallel activity   One or more activities that can be carried on concurrently or simultaneously.

partnering   See project partnering.

partnering charter   A formal document that states common goals as well as cooperative procedures used to achieved these goals which is signed by all parties working on a project.

path   A sequence of connected activities.

payback method   The time it takes to pay back the project investment (investment/net annual savings). The method does not consider the time value of money or the life of the investment.

performance review   In general, all review methods of individual performance center on the technical and social skills brought to the project and team. These reviews stress personal improvement and are frequently used for salary and promotion decisions.

phase estimating   This estimating method begins with a macro estimate for the project and then refines estimates for phases of the project as it is implemented.

phase gating   A structured process to review, evaluate, and document outcomes at each project phase and to provide management with information to guide resource deployment toward strategic goals.

phase project delivery   Delivering useful parts of a project in phases instead of when the project is entirely completed.

planned value (PV)   The planned time-phased baseline of the value of the work scheduled. Previously this was called budgeted cost of work scheduled (BCWS).

plan of record   The current official plan for the project in terms of scope, budget, and schedule.

portfolio management   Centralized selection and management of a portfolio of projects to ensure that allocation of resources is directed and balanced toward the strategic focus of the organization.

positive synergy   A characteristic of high-performance teams in which group performance is greater than the sum of individual contributions.

precedence diagram method   A method used to construct a project network that uses nodes (e.g., a rectangle) to represent activities and connecting arrows to indicate dependencies.

principled negotiation   A process of negotiation that aims to achieve win/win results.

priority matrix   A matrix that is set up before the project begins that establishes which criterion among cost, time, and scope will be enhanced, constrained, or accepted.

priority system   The process used to select projects. The system uses selected criteria for evaluating and selecting projects that are strongly linked to higher-level strategies and objectives.

priority team   The group (sometimes the project office) responsible for selecting, overseeing, and updating project priority selection criteria.

proactive   Working within your sphere of influence to accomplish something.

process breakdown structure (PBS)   A phase-oriented grouping of project activities that defines the total scope of the project. Each descending level represents an increasingly detailed description of project work.

project   A complex, nonroutine, one-time effort to create a product or service limited by time, budget, and specifications.

project audit report   A report that includes classification of the project, analysis of information gathered, recommendations, lessons learned, and an appendix of backup information.

project cost—duration graph   A graph that plots project cost against time; it includes direct, indirect, and total cost for a project over a relevant range of time.

project interfaces   The intersections between a project and other groups of people both within and outside the organization.

projectitis   A social phenomenon in which project members exhibit inappropriately intense loyalty to the project.

project kick off meeting   Typically the first meeting of the project team.

project life cycle   The stages found in all projects—definition, planning, execution, and delivery.

project management   The application of knowledge, skills, tools, and techniques to project activities to meet the project requirements.

Project Management Professional (PMP)   An individual who has met specific education and experience requirements set forth by the Project Management Institute, has agreed to adhere to a code of professional conduct, and has passed an examination designed to objectively assess and measure project management knowledge. In addition, a PMP must satisfy continuing certification requirements or lose the certification.

project office (PO)   A centralized unit within an organization or department that oversees and improves the management of projects.

project oversight   See oversight.

project manager   The individual responsible for managing a project.

project organization   An organizational structure in which core work is accomplished by project teams.

project partnering   A nonbinding method of transforming contractual relationships into a cohesive, cooperative project team with a single set of goals and established procedures for resolving disputes in a timely manner.

project portfolio   Group of projects that have been selected for implementation balanced by project type, risk, and ranking by selected criteria.

project screening matrix   A matrix used to assess and compare the relative value of projects being considered for implementation.

project sponsor   Typically a high-ranking manager who champions and supports a project.

project vision   An image of what the project will accomplish.

R

ratio (parametric) methods   Uses the ratio of past actual costs for similar work to estimate the cost for a potential project. This macro method of forecasting cost does not provide a sound basis for project cost control since it does not recognize differences among projects.

resource   Any person, groups, skill, equipment or material used to accomplish a task, work package, or activity.

resource-constrained project   A project that assumes resources are limited (fixed) and therefore time is variable.

resource profile   A chart showing the usage of a resource in a project over time. It is common to try to reduce the peak of the resource usage by leveling or smoothing, thereby improving the utilization of the resource.

responsibility matrix　A matrix whose intersection point shows the relationship between an activity (work package) and the person/group responsible for its completion.

risk　The chance that an undesirable project event will occur and the consequences of all its possible outcomes.

risk breakdown structure (RBS)　A hierarchical depiction of the identified project risks arranged by risk category and subcategory that identifies the various areas and causes of potential risks.

risk profile　A list of questions that addresses traditional areas of uncertainty on a project.

risk severity matrix　A tool used to assess the impact of risks on a project.

S

"sacred cow"　A project that is a favorite of a powerful management figure who is usually the champion for the project.

scenario analysis　A process in which potential risk events are identified and analyzed.

schedule performance index (SPI)　The ratio of work performed to work scheduled (EV/PV).

schedule variance (SV)　The difference between the planned dollar value of the work actually completed and the value of the work scheduled to be completed at a given point in time ($SV = EV - PV$). Schedule variance contains no critical path information.

scope creep　The tendency for the scope of a project to expand once it has started.

scope statement　A definition of the end result or mission of a project. Scope statements typically include project objectives, deliverables, milestones, specifications, and limits and exclusions.

sensitivity of a network　The likelihood that the critical path(s) will change once the project begins to be implemented.

sharing risk　Allocating proportions of risk to different parties.

slack (SL)　Time an activity can be delayed before it becomes critical.

social network building　The process of identifying and building cooperative relationships with key people.

sociotechnical perspective　A focus on the interaction between tools/methods and people.

splitting　A scheduling technique in which work is interrupted on one activity and the resource is assigned to another activity for a period of time, then reassigned to work on the original activity.

stakeholders　Individuals and organizations that are actively involved in the project, or whose interests may be positively or negatively affected as a result of project execution or completion. They may also exert influence over the project and its results.

strong matrix　A matrix structure in which the project manager has primary control over project activities and functional managers support project work.

systems thinking　A holistic approach to viewing problems that emphasizes understanding the interactions among different problem factors.

T

task　See activity.

team-building　A process designed to improve the performance of a team.

team evaluation   Evaluating the performance of the project team using a minimum core of conditions in place before the project began. Evaluation practices should emphasize the team as a whole, while minimizing individual performance.

team rituals   Ceremonial actions that reinforce team identity and values.

template method   Use of a prepared form to develop project networks, costs, and time estimates.

360-degree feedback   A multirater appraisal system based on performance information that is gathered from multiple sources (superiors, peers, subordinates, customers).

time and cost databases   Collection of actual versus estimated times and costs of work packages over many projects that are used for estimating new project tasks and their expected possible error.

time buffer   A contingency amount of time for an activity to cover uncertainty—for example, availability of a key resource or merge event.

time-constrained project   A project that assumes time is fixed and, if resources are needed, they will be added.

time-phased baseline   A cost baseline that is derived from the WBS and project schedule. The budgeted costs are distributed to mirror the project schedule.

time-phased budgets   Planned costs that are broken down by distinct time periods (e.g., $5,000 per week) for a work package, as opposed to a budget for a whole job/project (6 months for a total of $130,000). Time phasing allows better cost control by measuring the actual rate of expenditure versus the planned expenditure rate over small pieces of the project.

total slack (TS)   The amount of time an activity can be delayed and not affect the project duration (TS = LS − ES or LF − EF).

Tracking Gantt   A Gantt chart that compares planned versus actual schedule information.

transferring risk   Shifting responsibility for a risk to another party.

triple constraint   The competing demands of time, cost, and scope. These constraints frequently represent trade-off decisions to be dealt with by the project manager and/or sponsor.

top-down estimates   Rough estimates that use surrogates to estimate project time and cost (also called macro estimates).

V

variance at completion (VAC)   Indicates expected actual cost over- or underrun at completion (VAC = BAC − EAC).

virtual project team   Spatially separated project team whose members are unable to communicate face to face. Communication is usually by electronic means.

W

weak matrix   A matrix structure in which functional managers have primary control over project activities and the project manager coordinates project work.

work breakdown structure (WBS)   A hierarchical method that successively subdivides the work of the project into smaller detail.

work package   A task at the lowest level of the WBS. Responsibility for the package should be assigned to one person and, if possible, limited to 80 hours of work.

Acronyms

AC	Actual cost of work completed		**IFB**	Invitation for bid
ACWP	Actual cost of work performed		**KISS**	Keep it simple, stupid
AOA	Activity-on-arrow		**LF**	Late finish
AON	Activity-on-node		**LS**	Late start
BAC	Budget at completion		**MBWA**	Management by wandering around
BATNA	Best alternative to a negotiated agreement		**NIH**	Not invented here
BCWP	Budgeted cost of work performed		**NPV**	Net present value
BCWS	Budgeted cost of work scheduled		**OBS**	Organization breakdown structure
BOOT	Build-own-operate-transfer		**PBS**	Process breakdown structure
CAPM	Certified Associate in Project Management		**PCI**	Percent complete index
			PCIB	Percent complete index—budget costs
CCPM	Critical-chain approach to project planning and management		**PCIC**	Percent complete index—actual costs
CPI	Cost performance index		**PDM**	Precedence diagramming method
CPM	Critical path method		**PERT**	Project evaluation review technique
CV	Cost variance		**PO**	Project office
DUR	Duration		**PMP**	Project Management Professional
EAC	Estimate at completion (with revised cost estimates)		**PV**	Planned value of work scheduled
EF	Early finish		**RBS**	Risk breakdown structure
EQ	Emotional intelligence		**RM**	Responsibility matrix
ES	Early start		**SL**	Slack
ETC	Estimate to complete		**SPI**	Schedule performance index
EV	Earned value		**SV**	Schedule variance
FAC	Forecast at completion		**TCPI**	To complete performance index
FF	Free float		**VAC**	Variance at completion
			WBS	Work breakdown structure

Project Management Equations

$$PCIB = \frac{EV}{BAC}$$

$$CV = EV - AC$$

$$CPI = \frac{EV}{AC}$$

➔$$EAC_f = \frac{(BAC - EV)}{\left(\frac{EV}{AC}\right)} + AC$$

$$EAC_{re} = AC + ETC_{re}$$

$$t_e = \frac{a + 4m + b}{6}$$

$$\sigma_{t_e} = \left(\frac{b - a}{6}\right)^2$$

$$ETC = \frac{(BAC - EV)}{\left(\frac{EV}{AC}\right)}$$

AC=How much you have spent so far

$$TCPI = \frac{(BAC - EV)}{(BAC - AC)}$$

$$PCIC = \frac{AC}{EAC}$$

$$SV = EV - PV$$

$$SPI = \frac{EV}{PV}$$

➔$$VAC_f = BAC - EAC_f$$

$$VAC_{re} = BAC - EAC_{re}$$

$$\sigma_{T_E} = \sqrt{\Sigma \sigma_{t_e}^{\ 2}}$$

$$Z = \frac{T_S - T_E}{\sqrt{\Sigma \sigma_{t_e}^{\ 2}}}$$ ← variance values

$$((b-a)/6)^2$$

ARCAUF

$EV = (budgeted\ value \times Percent\ complet) + ...$

$BAC = total\ budget\ of\ baseline$
(eg. 4 sides × 2000$ to do each side)

$PV:$ how much completed so far (use budgeted vales).

Index